William Shakespeare

The Plays and Poems of William Shakspeare in Sixteen Volumes

William Shakespeare

The Plays and Poems of William Shakspeare in Sixteen Volumes

ISBN/EAN: 9783741178122

Manufactured in Europe, USA, Canada, Australia, Japa

Cover: Foto ©Andreas Hilbeck / pixelio.de

Manufactured and distributed by brebook publishing software (www.brebook.com)

William Shakespeare

The Plays and Poems of William Shakspeare in Sixteen Volumes

THE PLAYS AND POEMS

OF

WILLIAM SHAKSPEARE.

VOLUME THE FOURTH.

CONTAINING

COMEDY OF ERRORS.
MUCH ADO ABOUT NOTHING.
LOVE's LABOUR's LOST.
MIDSUMMER-NIGHT's DREAM.

DUBLIN:

Printed by JOHN EXSHAW, No. 98, Grafton-Street.

1794.

COMEDY OF ERRORS.

PERSONS REPRESENTED.

Solinus, *Duke of Ephesus.*
Ægeon, *a Merchant of Syracuse.*

Antipholus of Ephesus*, ⎫ *Twin Brothers, and Sons to*
Antipholus of Syracuse, ⎭ *Ægeon and Æmilia, but unknown to each other.*

Dromio of Ephesus, ⎫ *Twin Brothers, and Attendants on*
Dromio of Syracuse, ⎭ *the two Antipholus's.*
Balthazar, *a Merchant.*
Angelo, *a Goldsmith.*
A Merchant, Friend to Antipholus *of Syracuse.*
Pinch, *a School-master, and a Conjurer.*

Æmilia, *Wife to Ægeon, an Abbess at Ephesus.*
Adriana, *Wife to Antipholus of Ephesus.*
Luciana, *her Sister.*
Luce, *her Servant.*
A Courtezan.

Jailer, Officers, and other Attendants.

SCENE, Ephesus.

" In the old copy, these brothers are occasionally styled, Antipholus *Erotes*, or *Errotis*; and Antipholus *Sereptus*; meaning, perhaps—*erraticus*, and *surreptus*. One of these twins *wandered* in search of his brother, who had been *forced* from Æmilia by fishermen of Corinth. The following acrostic is the argument to the *Menæchmi* of Plautus: Delph. Edit. p. 654.

    Mercator Siculus, cui erant gemini filii,
    Ei, surrepto altero, ipsos obiiget.
    Nomen surreptitii illi indit qui domi est
    Avus paternus, facit Menæchmum Sosiclem.
    Et is germanum, postquam adolevit, quæritat
    Circum omnes oras. Post Epidamnum devenit;
    Hic fuerat auctus ille surreptitius.
    Menæchmum civem credunt omnes advenam:
    Eumque appellant, meretrix, uxor, et socer.
    Ii se cognoscunt fratres postremo invicem.

The *translator*, W. W. calls the brothers, Menæchmus *Sosicles*, and Menæchmus the *traveller*. Whensoever *Shakspeare* adopted *erraticus* and *surreptus* (which either he or his editors have miss-spelt) these distinctions were soon dropt, and throughout the rest of the entries the twins are styled of *Syracuse* or *Ephesus*. STEEVENS.

COMEDY OF ERRORS¹.

ACT I. SCENE I.

A Hall in the Duke's Palace.

Enter DUKE, ÆGEON, *Jailer, Officers, and other Attendants.*

Æge. Proceed, Solinus, to procure my fall,
And, by the doom of death, end woes and all.
Duke. Merchant of Syracusa, plead no more;
I am not partial, to infringe our laws:

---

¹ Shakspeare certainly took the general plan of this comedy from a translation of the *Menæchmi* of Plautus, by W. W. i. e. (according to Wood) William Warner, in 1595, whose version of the acrostical argument already quoted, is as follows:

"Two twinne-borne sonnes a Sicill marchant had,
"Menechmus one, and Sosicles the other;
"The first his father lost, a little lad;
"The grandsire namde the latter like his brother:
"This (growne a man) long travell tooke to seeke
"His brother, and to Epidamnum came,
"Where th' other dwelt inricht, and him so like,
"That citizens there take him for the same;
"Father, wife, neighbours, each mistaking either,
"Much pleasant error, ere they meete togither."

Perhaps the last of these lines suggested to Shakspeare the title for his piece.—See this translation of the *Menæchmi*, among *Six old Plays on which Shakspeare founded*, &c. published by S. Leacroft, Charing-Cross. STEEVENS.

I suspect this and all other plays where much rhime is used, and especially in long hobbling verses, to have been among Shakspeare's more early productions. BLACKSTONE.

This comedy, I believe, was written in 1593. See *An Attempt to ascertain the order of Shakspeare's Plays*, Vol. I. MALONE.

The enmity and discord, which of late
Sprung from the rancorous outrage of your Duke
To merchants, our well-dealing countrymen—
Who, wanting gilders to redeem their lives,
Have seal'd his rigorous statutes with their bloods—
Excludes all pity from our threat'ning looks.
For, since the mortal and intestine jars
'Twixt thy seditious countrymen and us,
It hath in solemn synods been decreed,
Both by the Syracusans and ourselves,
To admit no traffic to our adverse towns:
Nay, more,
If any, born at Ephesus, be seen
At any Syracusan marts and fairs,
Again, If any, Syracusan born,
Come to the bay of Ephesus, he dies,
His goods confiscate to the Duke's dispose;
Unless a thousand marks be levied,
To quit the penalty, and to ransom him.
Thy substance, valued at the highest rate,
Cannot amount unto a hundred marks;
Therefore, by law thou art condemn'd to die.

Æge. Yet this my comfort; when your words are done,
My woes end likewise with the evening sun.

Duke. Well, Syracusan, say, in brief, the cause
Why thou departedst from thy native home;
And for what cause thou cam'st to Ephesus.

Æge. A heavier task could not have been impos'd,
Than I to speak my griefs unspeakable:
Yet that the world may witness, that my end
Was wrought by nature, not by vile offence [2],
I'll utter what my sorrow gives me leave.
In Syracusa was I born; and wed
Unto a woman, happy but for me,
And by me too [3], had not our hap been bad.
With her I liv'd in joy; our wealth increas'd,
By prosperous voyages I often made

---

[2] *— by nature, not by vile offence,*] Not by any criminal act, but by natural affection, which prompted me to seek my son at Ephesus. MALONE.

[3] *And by me too,—*] *Too,* which is not found in the original copy, was added by the editor of the second folio, to complete the metre.
MALONE.

To Epidamnum, till my factor's death;
And he, great care of goods at random left [4],
Drew me from kind embracements of my spouse:
From whom my absence was not six months old,
Before herself (almost at fainting, under
The pleasing punishment that women bear,)
Had made provision for her following me,
And soon, and safe, arrived where I was.
There had she not been long, but she became
A joyful mother of two goodly sons;
And, which was strange, the one so like the other,
As could not be distinguish'd but by names.
That very hour, and in the self-same inn,
A poor mean woman [5] was delivered
Of such a burden, male twins, both alike:
Those, for their parents were exceeding poor,
I bought, and brought up to attend my sons.
My wife, not meanly proud of two such boys,
Made daily motions for our home return:
Unwilling I agreed; alas, too soon.
We came aboard:
A league from Epidamnum had we sail'd,
Before the always-wind-obeying deep
Gave any tragic instance of our harm:
But longer did we not retain much hope:
For what obscured light the heavens did grant
Did but convey unto our fearful minds
A doubtful warrant of immediate death;
Which, though myself would gladly have embrac'd,
Yet the incessant weepings of my wife,
Weeping before for what she saw must come,
And piteous plainings of the pretty babes,
That mourn'd for fashion, ignorant what to fear,
Forc'd me to seek delays for them and me.
And this it was—for other means was none.—

[4] *And he, great care of goods at random left,*] Surely we should read:
  And *the* great care of goods at random left
  Drew me, &c.
The text, as exhibited in the old copy, can scarcely be reconciled to grammar. MALONE.

[5] *A* poor *mean woman*—] Poor is not in the original copy. It was inserted for the sake of the metre by the editor of the second folio.
  MALONE.

The

The sailors fought for safety by our boat,
And left the ship, then sinking-ripe, to us:
My wife, more careful for the latter-born,
Had fasten'd him unto a small spare mast,
Such as sea-faring men provide for storms;
To him one of the other twins was bound,
Whilst I had been like heedful of the other.
The children thus dispos'd, my wife and I,
Fixing our eyes on whom our care was fix'd,
Fasten'd ourselves at either end the mast;
And floating straight, obedient to the stream,
Were carry'd towards Corinth, as we thought.
At length the sun, gazing upon the earth,
Dispers'd those vapours that offended us;
And, by the benefit of his wish'd light,
The seas wax'd calm, and we discovered
Two ships from far making amain to us,
Of Corinth that, of Epidaurus this:
But ere they came,—O, let me say no more!
Gather the sequel by that went before.

Duke. Nay, forward, old man, do not break off so;
For we may pity, though not pardon thee.

Ege. O, had the gods done so, I had not now
Worthily term'd them merciless to us!
For, ere the ships could meet by twice five leagues,
We were encounter'd by a mighty rock;
Which being violently borne upon⁶,
Our helpful ship was splitted in the midst,
So that, in this unjust divorce of us,
Fortune had left to both of us alike
What to delight in, what to sorrow for.
Her part, poor soul! seeming as burdened
With lesser weight, but not with lesser woe,
Was carried with more speed before the wind;
And in our sight they three were taken up
By fishermen of Corinth, as we thought.
At length another ship had seiz'd on us;
And, knowing whom it was their hap to save,
Gave helpful welcome⁷ to their shipwreck'd guests;

⁶ —*borne* upon,] The original copy reads—borne *up.* The additional syllable was supplied by the editor of the second folio. MALONE.

⁷ Gave helpful *welcome*—] Old Copy—*healthful* welcome. Corrected by the editor of the second folio.—So, in *K. Henry IV.* P. i.

" And gave the tongue a *helpful* welcome." MALONE.

Aud

And would have reft the fishers of their prey,
Had not their bark been very flow of fail,
And therefore homeward did they bend their course.—
Thus have you heard me fever'd from my bliss;
That by misfortunes was my life prolong'd,
To tell sad stories of my own mishaps.
  Duke. And, for the fake of them thou sorrowest for,
Do me the favour to dilate at full
What hath befall'n of them, and thee [8], till now.
  Æge. My youngest boy, and yet my eldest care,
At eighteen years became inquisitive
After his brother; and importun'd me,
That his attendant, (for his case was like [9],
Reft of his brother; but retain'd his name,)
Might bear him company in the quest of him:
Whom whilst I labour'd of a love to see,
I hazarded the loss of whom I lov'd.
Five summers have I spent in farthest Greece,
Roaming clean through [1] the bounds of Asia,
And, coasting homeward, came to Ephefus;
Hopeless to find, yet loth to leave unsought,
Or that, or any place that harbours men.
But here must end the story of my life;
And happy were I in my timely death,
Could all my travels warrant me they live.
  Duke. Haplefs Ægeon, whom the fates have mark'd
To bear the extremity of dire mishap!
Now, trust me, were it not against our laws,
Against my crown, my oath, my dignity,
Which princes, would they, may not disannul,
My soul should sue as advocate for thee.
But, though thou art adjudged to the death,
And passed sentence may not be recall'd,
But to our honour's great disparagement,
Yet will I favour thee in what I can:
Therefore, merchant, I'll limit thee this day,

---

  [8] —*and* thee, *till now.*] The first copy erroneously reads—and *they.* The correction was made in the second folio. MALONE.
  [9] —*for his case was like*—] The original copy has—*so* his. The emendation was made by the editor of the second folio. MALONE.
  [1] —*clean through*—] In the northern parts of England this word is still used instead of *quite, fully, perfectly, completely.* STEEVENS.

B 4   To

COMEDY OF ERRORS.

To seek thy help [2] by beneficial help:
Try all the friends thou hast in Ephesus;
Beg thou, or borrow, to make up the sum,
And live; if not [3], then thou art doom'd to die:—
Jailer, take him to thy custody.

   Jail. I will, my Lord.

   Æge. Hopeless, and helpless, doth Ægeon wend [4],
But to procrastinate his lifeless end.   *[Exeunt.*

SCENE II.

A public Place.

Enter ANTIPHOLUS *and* DROMIO *of Syracuse, and a Merchant.*

   Mer. Therefore, give out, you are of Epidamnum,
Lest that your goods too soon be confiscate.
This very day, a Syracusan merchant
Is apprehended for arrival here;
And, not being able to buy out his life,
According to the statute of the town,
Dies ere the weary sun set in the west.
There is your money that I had to keep.

   Ant. S. Go bear it to the Centaur, where we host,
And stay there, Dromio, till I come to thee.
Within this hour it will be dinner time:
Till that, I'll view the manners of the town,
Peruse the traders, gaze upon the buildings,
And then return, and sleep within mine inn;
For with long travel I am stiff and weary.
Get thee away.

   Dro. S. Many a man would take you at your word,
And go indeed, having so good a mean.   *[Exit* DRO. S.

   Ant. S. A trusty villain, Sir; that very oft,
When I am dull with care and melancholy,
Lightens my humour with his merry jests.
What, will you walk with me about the town,
And then go to my inn, and dine with me?

---

[2] *To seek thy help*—] Mr. Pope and some other modern editors read—To seek thy *life*, &c. But the jingle has much of Shakspeare's manner. MALONE.

[3] — *if not*,] Old copy—*as*. Corrected in the second folio. MALONE.

[4] — *wend*,] i. e. go. An obsolete word. STEEVENS.

                                                       Mer.

Mer. I am invited, Sir, to certain merchants,
Of whom I hope to make much benefit;
I crave your pardon. Soon, at five o'clock,
Please you, I'll meet with you upon the mart,
And afterwards consort you till bed-time¹;
My present business calls me from you now.

Ant. S. Farewell till then: I will go lose myself,
And wander up and down to view the city.

Mer. Sir, I commend you to your own content.
                                               [*Exit* Merchant.

Ant. S. He that commends me to mine own content,
Commends me to the thing I cannot get.
I to the world am like a drop of water,
That in the ocean seeks another drop;
Who, falling there to find his fellow forth,
Unseen, inquisitive, confounds himself:
So I, to find a mother, and a brother,
In quest of them, unhappy, lose myself.

Enter Dromio *of Ephesus.*

Here comes the almanac of my true date.—
What now? How chance, thou art return'd so soon?

Dro. E. Return'd so soon! rather approach'd too late:
The capon burns, the pig falls from the spit;
The clock hath strucken twelve upon the bell,
My mistress made it one upon my cheek:
She is so hot, because the meat is cold;
The meat is cold, because you come not home;
You come not home, because you have no stomach;
You have no stomach, having broke your fast;
But we, that know what 'tis to fast and pray,
Are penitent for your default to-day.

Ant. S. Stop in your wind, Sir; tell me this, I pray;
Where have you left the money that I gave you?

Dro. E. O,—sixpence, that I had o'Wednesday last,
To pay the sadler for my mistress' crupper;—
The sadler had it, Sir, I kept it not.

Ant. S. I am not in a sportive humour now:

---

¹ *And afterwards* consort *you till bed-time;*] We should read, I believe,
"And afterwards consort *with* you till bed-time."
So, in *Romeo and Juliet:*
"Mercutio, thou consort'*st with* Romeo." MALONE.

Tell me, and dally not, where is the money?
We being strangers here, how dar'st thou trust
So great a charge from thine own custody?

Dro. E. I pray you, jest, Sir, as you sit at dinner:
I from my mistress come to you in post;
If I return, I shall be post indeed [6];
For she will score your fault upon my pate.
Methinks, your maw, like mine, should be your clock [7],
And strike you home without a messenger.

Ant. S. Come, Dromio, come, these jests are out of season;
Reserve them till a merrier hour than this;
Where is the gold I gave in charge to thee?

Dro. E. To me, Sir? why you gave no gold to me.

Ant. S. Come on, Sir knave, have done your foolishness,
And tell me how thou hast dispos'd thy charge.

Dro. E. My charge was but to fetch you from the mart:
Home to your house, the Phœnix, Sir, to dinner;
My mistress, and her sister, stay for you.

Ant. S. Now, as I am a christian, answer me,
In what safe place you have dispos'd my money;
Or I shall break that merry-sconce [8] of yours,
That stands on tricks when I am undispos'd:
Where is the thousand marks thou had'st of me?

Dro. E. I have some marks of yours upon my pate,
Some of my mistress' marks upon my shoulders,
But not a thousand marks between you both.—
If I should pay your worship those again,
Perchance, you will not bear them patiently.

Ant. S. Thy mistress' marks! what mistress, slave, hast thou?

---

[6] ——— *I shall be post indeed,*
For she will score your fault upon my pate.] Perhaps, before writing was a general accomplishment, a kind of rough reckoning concerning wares issued out of a shop was kept by chalk or notches on a *post*, till it could be entered on the books of a trader. So *Kitely* the merchant making his jealous enquiries concerning the familiarities used to his wife, *Cob* answers:—" if I saw any body to be kiss'd, unless they would have kiss'd the *post* in the middle of the warehouse;. &c." STEEVENS.

So, in *Every Woman in her Humour*, 1609:

" *Just.* Out of my doors, knave, thou entered'st not my doors; I have no *chalk* in my house; my *posts* shall not be guarded with a little sing-song." MALONE.

[7] —— *your clock,*] The old copy reads—*your cook.* Mr. Pope made the change. MALONE.

[8] —— *that merry* sconce—] *Sconce* is *head.* STEEVENS.

Dro. E.

Dro. E. Your worship's wife, my mistress at the Phœnix;
She that doth fast, till you come home to dinner.
And prays, that you will hie you home to dinner.
 Ant. S. What, wilt thou flout me thus unto my face,
Being forbid? There, take you that, Sir knave.
 Dro. E. What mean you, Sir? for God's sake, hold
  your hands;
Nay, an you will not, Sir, I'll take my heels.
                                [*Exit* DROMIO, E.
 Ant. S. Upon my life, by some device or other,
The villain is o'er-raught [9] of all my money.
They say, this town is full of cozenage [1];
As, nimble jugglers, that deceive the eye,
Dark-working sorcerers, that change the mind,
Soul-killing witches, that deform the body [2];
Disguised cheaters, prating mountebanks,
And many such like liberties of sin [3]:

---

[9] *— o'er-raught —*] That is, *over-reached*. JOHNSON.

[1] *They say, this town is full of cozenage*:] This was the character the ancients give of it. Hence Ἐφέσια ἀλεξιφάρμακα was proverbial amongst them. Thus Menander uses it, and Ἐφέσια γράμματα, in the same sense. WARBURTON.

[2] *As, nimble jugglers, that deceive the eye,
 Dark-working sorcerers, that change the mind,
 Soul-killing witches, that deform the body;*] Perhaps the epithets have been misplaced, and the lines should be read thus:
 Soul-killing *sorcerers, that change the mind,*
 Dark-working *witches, that deform the body;*
This change seems to remove all difficulties.—By *soul-killing* I understand destroying the rational faculties by such means as make men fancy themselves beasts. JOHNSON."
 Witches or sorcerers themselves, as well as those who employed them, were supposed to forfeit their souls by making use of a forbidden agency. In that sense, they may be said to destroy the souls of others as well as their own. I believe Dr. Johnson has done as much as was necessary to remove all difficulty from the passage.
 The hint for this enumeration of cheats, &c. Shakspeare received from the old translation of the *Menæchmi*, 1595: " For this assure yourselfe, this towne *Epidamnum* is a place of outrageous expences, exceeding in all ryot and lasciviousnesse; and (I heare) as full of ribaulds, parasites, drunkards, catchpoles, cony-catchers, and sycophants, as it can hold: then for curti-zans, &c." STEEVENS.

[3] *— liberties of sin:*] Sir T. Hanmer reads, *libertines*, which, as the author has been enumerating not acts but persons, seems right.
                                JOHNSON.

If it prove so, I will be gone the sooner.
I'll to the Centaur, to go seek this slave;
I greatly fear my money is not safe. [*Exit.*

ACT II. SCENE I.

A public Place.

Enter ADRIANA *and* LUCIANA.

Adr. Neither my husband, nor the slave return'd,
That in such haste I sent to seek his master!
Sure, Luciana, it is two o'clock.
   Luc. Perhaps, some merchant hath invited him,
And from the mart he's somewhere gone to dinner.
Good sister, let us dine, and never fret:
A man is master of his liberty:
Time is their master; and, when they see time,
They'll go, or come: If so, be patient, sister.
   Adr. Why should their liberty than ours be more?
   Luc. Because their business still lies out o' door.
   Adr. Look, when I serve him so, he takes it ill [4].
   Luc. O, know, he is the bridle of your will.
   Adr. There's none, but asses, will be bridled so.
   Luc. Why head-strong liberty is lash'd with woe [5].
There's nothing, situate under heaven's eye,
But hath his bound, in earth, in sea, in sky:
The beasts, the fishes, and the winged fowls,
Are their males' subject, and at their controls:
Men, more divine, the masters of all these [6],
Lords of the wide world, and wild watry seas,
Indued with intellectual sense and souls,
Of more pre-eminence than fish and fowls,

---

[4] — *ill.*] This word, which the rhime seems to countenance, was furnished by the editor of the second folio. The first has—*thus.* MALONE.

[5] *Adr. There's none, but asses, will be bridled so.*
   Luc. Why head-strong liberty is lash'd with woe.] The meaning of this passage may be, that those who refuse the *bridle* must bear the *lash*, and that woe is the punishment of head-strong liberty. STEEVENS.

[6] *Men—the masters, &c.*] The old copy has *Man—the master*, &c. and in the next line—*Lord.* Corrected by Sir T. Hanmer. MALONE.

Are

Are mafters to their females, and their lords:
Then let your will attend on their accords.

Adr. This fervitude makes you to keep unwed.
Luc. Not this, but troubles of the marriage-bed.
Adr. But, were you wedded, you would bear fome fway.
Luc. Ere I learn love, I'll practife to obey.
Adr. How if your hufband ftart fome other where⁴?
Luc. Till he come home again, I would forbear.
Adr. Patience, unmov'd, no marvel though fhe paufe⁷;
They can be meek, that have no other caufe.
A wretched foul, bruis'd with adverfity,
We bid be quiet, when we hear it cry;
But were we burden'd with like weight of pain,
As much, or more, we fhould ourfelves complain:
So thou, that haft no unkind mate to grieve thee,
With urging helplefs patience⁸ would'ft relieve me:
But, if thou live to fee like right bereft,
This fool-begg'd⁹ patience in thee will be left.

Luc. Well, I will marry one day, but to try:—
Here comes your man, now is your hufband nigh.

Enter Dromio *of Ephefus.*

Adr. Say, is your tardy mafter now at hand?
Dro. E. Nay, he is at two hands with me, and that my two ears can witnefs.
Adr. Say, didft thou fpeak with him? Know'ft thou his mind?
Dro. E. Ay, ay, he told his mind upon mine ear:
Befhrew his hand, I fcarce could underftand it.
Luc. Spake he fo doubtfully, thou couldft not feel his meaning?

---

⁴ —*ftart fome other* where?] I fufpect that *where* has here the power of a noun. So, in *K. Lear:*
   " Thou lofeft *here*, a better *where* to find."
The fenfe is, *How, if your hufband flys off in purfuit of fome other woman?* So again, p. 16: " —his eye doth homage *otherwhere.*"
Otherwife fignifies—*in other places.* STEEVENS.

⁷ —*fhe paufe;*] To *paufe* is to reft, to be in quiet. JOHNSON.

⁸ *With urging helplefs patience*—] By exhorting me to patience, which *affords no help.* So in our author's *Venus and Adonis:*
   " As thofe poor birds that helplefs berries faw." MALONE.

⁹ —*fool-begg'd—*] She feems to mean, by *fool begg'd patience,* that patience which is fo near to idiotical fimplicity, that your next relation would take advantage from it to reprefent you as a *fool,* and *beg* the guardianfhip of your fortune. JOHNSON.

Dro. E.

Dro. E. Nay, he ſtruck ſo plainly, I could too well feel his blows; and withal ſo doubtfully, that I could ſcarce underſtand them [9].

Adr. But ſay, I pr'ythee, is he coming home?
It ſeems, he hath great care to pleaſe his wife.

Dro. E. Why, miſtreſs, ſure my maſter is horn-mad.

Adr. Horn-mad, thou villain?

Dro. E. I mean not cuckold-mad; but, ſure, he's ſtark mad:
When I deſir'd him to come home to dinner,
He aſk'd me for a thouſand marks in gold [1]:
'Tis *dinner-time,* quoth I: *My gold,* quoth he:
Your meat doth burn, quoth I; *My gold,* quoth he:
Will you come home, quoth I [2]? *My gold,* quoth he:
Where is the thouſand marks I gave thee, villain?
The pig, quoth I, *is burn'd*; *My gold,* quoth he:
My miſtreſs, Sir, quoth I; *Hang up thy miſtreſs:*.
I know not thy miſtreſs; out on thy miſtreſs!

Luc. Quoth who?

Dro. L. Quoth my maſter:
I know, quoth he, *no houſe, no wife, no miſtreſs;*—
So that my errand, due unto my tongue,
I thank him, I bare home upon my ſhoulders;
For, in concluſion, he did beat me there.

Adr. Go back again, thou ſlave, and fetch him home.

Dro. E. Go back again, and be new beaten home?
For God's ſake, ſend ſome other meſſenger.

Adr. Back, ſlave, or I will break thy pate acroſs.

Dro. E. And he will bleſs that croſs with other beating:
Between you I ſhall have a holy head.

Adr. Hence, prating peaſant; fetch thy maſter home.

Dro. E. Am I ſo round with you, as you with me [3]?

---

[9] — *that I could ſcarce* underſtand *them.*] i. e. that I could ſcarcely ſtand under them. This quibble, poor as it is, ſeems to have been the favourite of Shakſpeare. It has been already introduced in the *Two Gentlemen of Verona:* " — my ſtaff *underſtands me.*" STEEVENS.

[1] — *a thouſand marks in gold;*] The old copy reads—*a hundred* marks. The correction was made in the ſecond folio. MALONE.

[2] — *will you come* home, *quoth I?*] The word *home,* which the metre requires, but is not in the authentic copy of this play, was ſuggeſted by Mr. Capell. MALONE.

[3] *Am I ſo* round *with you, as you with me,*] He plays upon the word *round,* which ſignified *ſpherical* applied to himſelf, and *unreſtrained,* or *free in ſpeech* or *action,* ſpoken of his miſtreſs. So the king, in *Hamlet,* bids the queen be *round* with Let ſon. JOHNSON.

That

That like a foot-ball you do spurn me thus?
You spurn me hence, and he will spurn me hither:
If I last in this service, you must case me in leather⁴.
[*Exit.*

Luc. Fye, how impatience lowreth in your face!
Adr. His company must do his minions grace,
Whilst I at home starve for a merry look⁵.
Hath homely age the alluring beauty took
From my poor cheek? then he hath wasted it:
Are my discourses dull? barren my wit?
If voluble and sharp discourse be marr'd,
Unkindness blunts it, more than marble hard.
Do their gay vestments his affections bait?
That's not my fault, he's master of my state:
What ruins are in me, that can be found
By him not ruin'd? then is he the ground
Of my defeatures⁵: My decayed fair⁶
A sunny look of his would soon repair:
But, too unruly deer⁷, he breaks the pale,

And

⁴ — *case me in leather.*] Still alluding to a football, the bladder of which is always covered with leather. STEEVENS.

⁵ *While I at home starve for a merry look.*] So, in our poet's 47th Sonnet:
 " When that mine eye is *famish'd for a look.*" MALONE.

⁵ *Of my defeatures:*] By *defeatures* is here meant *alteration of features.* At the end of this play the same word is used with somewhat different signification. STEEVENS.

⁶ — *My decayed fair*] Shakspeare uses the adjective *gilt,* as a substantive, for *what is gilt,* and in this instance *fair* for *fairness.* Τὸ μὲν καλὸν, is a similar expression. In the *Midsummer Night's Dream,* the old quartos read:
 " Demetrius loves your *fair.*"
Again, in Shakspeare's 68th Sonnet:
 " Before these bastard signs of *fair* were born."
Again, in the 83d Sonnet:
 " And therefore to your *fair* no painting set." STEEVENS.

Fair is frequently used *substantively* by the writers of Shakspeare's time. So Marston, in one of his satires:
 " As the greene meads, whose native outward *faire*
 " Breathes sweet perfumes into the neighbour air." FARMER.

⁷ *But, too unruly deer,*] The ambiguity of *deer* and *dear* is borrowed, poor as it is, by Waller, in his poem on a lady's *Girdle:*
 " This was my heaven's extremest sphere,
 " The pale that held my lovely *deer.*" JOHNSON.
Shakspeare has played upon this word in the same manner in his *Venus and Adonis:*
 " Fondling,

And feeds from home; poor I am but his stale⁸.
  Luc. Self-harming jealousy!—fye, beat it hence.
  Adr. Unfeeling fools can with such wrongs dispense.
I know his eye doth homage other-where;
Or else, what lets it but he would be here?
Sister, you know, he promis'd me a chain;—
Would that alone, alone he would detain⁹,
So he would keep fair quarter with his bed!
I see, the jewel, best enamelled,
Will lose his beauty; and though gold 'bides still,
That others touch, yet often touching will
Wear gold: and no man, that hath a name,
But falshood and corruption doth it shame¹.

Since

      " Fondling, faith she, since I have hemm'd thee here,
        " Within the circuit of this ivory *pale*,
        " I'll be thy park, and thou shalt be my *deer*;
        " Feed where thou wilt, on mountain or on dale."
The lines of Waller seem to have been immediately copied from these.
MALONE.

⁸ —*poor I am but his stale.*] "*Stale* to catch these thieves;" in the *Tempest,* undoubtedly means a *fraudulent bait.* Here it seems to imply the same as *stalking-horse, pretence.* I am, says Adriana, but his *pretended wife,* the mask under which he covers his amours. So, in the *Misfortunes of Arthur,* 1587:
      " Was I then chose and wedded for his *stale,*
      " To looke and gape for his retireless fancies
      " Puft back and flittering spread to every winde?"
Again, in the old translation of the *Menæchmi* of Plautus, 1595, from whence Shakspeare borrowed the expression: "He makes me a *stale* and a laughing-stock." STEEVENS.

Perhaps *stale* may have the same meaning as the French word *chaperon.* Poor I am but the *cover* for his infidelity. COLLINS.

⁹ *Would that alone* alone *he would detain,*] The first copy reads:
    Would that alone a *love*, &c.
The correction was made in the second folio. MALONE.

¹ *I see, the jewel, best enamelled,
  Will lose his beauty; and though gold 'bides still,
  That others touch, yet often touching will
  Wear gold: and no man, that hath a name,
  But falshood and corruption doth it shame.*] This passage in the original copy is very corrupt. It reads:
    ———— *yet the* gold 'bides still
    That others touch; *and* often touching will
    Where gold; and no man, that hath a name
    By falshood, &c.
The word *though* was suggested by Mr. Steevens; all the other emendations by Mr. Pope and Dr. Warburton. *Wear* is used as a dis-
syllable,

Since that my beauty cannot please his eye,
I'll weep what's left away, and weeping die.
Luc. How many fond fools serve mad jealousy! [*Exeunt.*

SCENE II.

The same.

Enter ANTIPHOLUS *of* Syracuse.

Ant. S. The gold, I gave to Dromio, is laid up
Safe at the Centaur; and the heedful slave
Is wander'd forth, in care to seek me out,
By computation, and mine host's report.
I could not speak with Dromio, since at first
I sent him from the mart: See, here he comes.

Enter DROMIO *of* Syracuse.

How now, Sir? is your merry humour alter'd?
As you love strokes, so jest with me again.
You know no Centaur? you receiv'd no gold?
Your mistress sent to have me home to dinner?
My house was at the Phœnix? Wast thou mad,
That thus so madly thou didst answer me?
Dro. S. What answer, Sir? when spake I such a word?
Ant. S. Even now, even here, not half an hour since.
Dro. S. I did not see you since you sent me hence,
Home to the Centaur, with the gold you gave me.
Ant. S. Villain, thou didst deny the gold's receipt;
And told'st me of a mistress, and a dinner;
For which, I hope, thou felt'st I was displeas'd.
Dro. S. I am glad to see you in this merry vein:
What means this jest? I pray you, master, tell me.
Ant. S. Yea, dost thou jeer, and flout me in the teeth?
Think'st thou, I jest? Hold, take thou that, and that.
[*beating him.*
Dro. S. Hold, Sir, for God's sake: now your jest is earnest:

---

syllable. The commentator last mentioned, not perceiving this, reads
—and *so* no man, &c. which has been followed, I think improperly, by
the subsequent editors.

The observation concerning gold, is found in one of the early dramatic pieces, *Damon and Pythias*, 1582:

" ———— *gold* in time does *wear* away,

" And other precious things do fade: Friendship does ne'er decay."
MALONE.

Upon

Upon what bargain do you give it me?

Ant. S. Becaufe that I familiarly fometimes
Do ufe you for my fool, and chat with you,
Your fawcinefs will jeft upon my love,
And make a common of my ferious hours[2].
When the fun fhines, let foolifh gnats make fport,
But keep in crannies, when he hides his beams.
If you will jeft with me, know my afpect,
And fafhion your demeanour to my looks,
Or I will beat this method in your fconce.

Dro. S. Sconce, call you it? fo you would leave battering, I had rather have it a head: an you ufe thefe blows long, I muft get a fconce for my head, and infconce it too[3]; or elfe I fhall feek my wit in my fhoulders. But, I pray, Sir, why am I beaten?

Ant. S. Doft thou not know?

Dro. S. Nothing, Sir; but that I am beaten.

Ant. S. Shall I tell you why?

Dro. S. Ay, Sir, and wherefore; for, they fay, every why hath a wherefore.

Ant. S. Why, firft,—for flouting me; and then, wherefore—For urging it the fecond time to me.

Dro. S. Was there ever any man thus beaten out of feafon?
When, in the why, and the wherefore, is neither rhime
   nor reafon?—
Well, Sir, I thank you.

Ant. S. Thank me, Sir? for what?

Dro. S. Marry, Sir, for this fomething that you gave me for nothing.

Ant. S. I'll make you amends next[4], to give you nothing for fomething. But fay, Sir, is it dinner-time?

Dro. S. No, Sir; I think, the meat wants that I have.

Ant. S. In good time, Sir, what's that?

Dro. S. Bafting.

Ant. S. Well, Sir, then 'twill be dry.

Dro. S. If it be, Sir, pray you eat none of it.

Ant. S. Your reafon?

---

[2] *And make a common of my ferious hours.*] i. e. intrude on them when you pleafe. The allufion is to thofe tracts of ground deftined to common ufe, which are thence called commons. STEEVENS.

[3] *and infconce it*] A *fconce* was a petty fortification. STEEVENS.

[4] *— next.*] Our author probably wrote:—neat *time*. MALONE.

Dro. S.

Dro. S. Left it make you choleric [5], and purchase me another dry-basting.

Ant. S. Well, Sir, learn to jest in good time: There's a time for all things.

Dro. S. I durst have deny'd that, before you were so choleric.

Ant. S. By what rule, Sir?

Dro. S. Marry, Sir, by a rule as plain as the plain bald pate of father Time himself.

Ant. S. Let's hear it.

Dro. S. There's no time for a man to recover his hair, that grows bald by nature.

Ant. S. May he not do it by fine and recovery?

Dro. S. Yes, to pay a fine for a peruke, and recover the lost hair of another man.

Ant. S. Why is Time such a niggard of hair, being, as it is, so plentiful an excrement?

Dro. S. Because it is a blessing that he bestows on beasts: and what he hath scanted men in hair [6], he hath given them in wit.

Ant. S. Why, but there's many a man hath more hair than wit.

Dro. S. Not a man of those, but he hath the wit to lose his hair [7].

Ant. S. Why, thou didst conclude hairy men plain dealers without wit.

Dro. S. The plainer dealer, the sooner lost: Yet he loseth it in a kind of jollity.

Ant. S. For what reason?

Dro. S. For two; and found ones too.

Ant. S. Nay, not found, I pray you.

[5] *Left it make you choleric*, &c.] So, in the *Taming of the Shrew*:
"I tell thee Kate, 'twas burnt and dry'd away,
"And I expressly am forbid to touch it,
"For it engenders choler, planteth anger, &c." STEEVENS.

[6] —*and what he hath scanted men in hair*,] The old copy reads— scanted *them*. The emendation is Mr. Theobald's.—The same error is found in the Induction to *K. Henry IV.* P. ii. edit. 1623:
"Stuffing the ears of *them* with false reports." MALONE.

[7] *Not a man of those, but he hath the wit to lose his hair.*] That is, *Those that have more hair than wit,* are easily entrapped by loose women, and suffer the consequences of lewdness, one of which, in the first appearance of the disease in Europe, was the loss of hair.
JOHNSON.

Dro. S.

Dro. S. Sure ones then.
Ant. S. Nay, not sure, in a thing falling⁸.
Dro. S. Certain ones then.
Ant. S. Name them.
Dro. S. The one, to save the money that he spends in tiring⁹; the other, that at dinner they should not drop in his porridge.
Ant. S. You would all this time have proved, there is no time¹ for all things.
Dro. S. Marry, and did, Sir; namely, no time² to recover hair lost by nature.
Ant. S. But your reason was not substantial, why there is no time to recover.
Dro. S Thus I mend it: Time himself is bald, and therefore, to the world's end, will have bald followers.
Ant. S. I knew, 'twould be a bald conclusion: But soft! who waits us yonder?

Enter ADRIANA *and* LUCIANA.

Adr. Ay, ay, Antipholus, look strange, and frown;
Some other mistress hath thy sweet aspects,
I am not Adriana, nor thy wife.
The time was once, when thou unurg'd would'st vow,
That never words were music to thine ear³,
That never object pleasing in thine eye,
That never touch well-welcome to thy hand,
That never meat sweet-savour'd in thy taste,
Unless I spake, or look'd, or touch'd, or carv'd to thee.
How comes it now, my husband, oh, how comes it,

---

⁸ —*falsing.*] This word is now obsolete. Spenser and Chaucer often use the verb to *false*. The author of the *Revisal* would read *falling.* STEEVENS.

⁹ —*that he spends in tiring;*] The old copy reads—*in trying.* The correction was made by Mr. Pope. MALONE.

¹ —*there is no time.*] The old copy reads—*here is,* &c. The editor of the second folio made the correction. MALONE.

² —*no time,* &c.] The first folio has—*in no time,* &c. *In* was rejected by the editor of the second folio. Perhaps the word should rather have been corrected. The author might have written—*e'er no time,* &c. See many instances of this corruption in a note on *All's Well that Ends Well,* Act i. sc. i. MALONE.

³ *That never words were music to thine ear,*] Imitated by Pope in his *Epistle from Sappho to Phaon:*
 "My music then you could for ever hear,
 "And all my words were music to your ear." MALONE.

That

That thou art then estranged from thyself?
Thyself I call it, being strange to me,
That, undividable, incorporate,
Am better than thy dear self's better part.
Ah, do not tear away thyself from me;
For know, my love, as easy may'st thou fall⁴
A drop of water in the breaking gulph,
And take unmingled thence that drop again,
Without addition, or diminishing,
As take from me thyself, and not me too.
How dearly would it touch thee to the quick,
Should'st thou but hear I were licentious?
And that this body, consecrate to thee,
By ruffian lust should be contaminate?
Would'st thou not spit at me, and spurn at me,
And hurl the name of husband in my face,
And tear the stain'd skin off my harlot-brow,
And from my false hand cut the wedding-ring,
And break it with a deep-divorcing vow?
I know thou canst; and therefore, see, thou do it.
I am possess'd with an adulterate blot;
My blood is mingled with the crime of lust⁵:
For, if we two be one, and thou play false,
I do digest the poison of thy flesh,
Being strumpeted⁶ by thy contagion.
Keep then fair league and truce with thy true bed;
I live dis-stain'd⁷, thou undishonoured.

Ant. S. Plead you to me, fair dame? I know you not:
In Ephesus I am but two hours old,
As strange unto your town, as to your talk;
Who, every word by all my wit being scann'd,
Want wit in all one word to understand.

Luc. Fye, brother! how the world is chang'd with you:
When were you wont to use my sister thus?
She sent for you by Dromio home to dinner.

⁴ — *may'st thou fall*—] To *fall* is here a verb active. STEEVENS.
⁵ — *with the crime of lust:*] Dr. Warburton reads—*with the grime*—. So, again in this play; "A man may go over shoes in the *grime* of it." MALONE.
⁶ *Being strumpeted*—] Shakspeare is not singular in his use of this verb. So, in Heywood's *Iron Age*, 1632:
"By this mistress basely *strumpeted*." STEEVENS.
⁷ *I live dis-stain'd*,] i. e. *unstained, undefiled.* THEOBALD.

Ant. S.

Ant. S. By Dromio?

Dro. S. By me?

Adr. By thee; and this thou didst return from him—
That he did buffet thee, and, in his blows
Deny'd my house for his, me for his wife.

Ant. S. Did you converse, Sir, with this gentlewoman?
What is the course and drift of your compact?

Dro. S. I, Sir? I never saw her till this time.

Ant. S. Villain, thou liest; for even her very words
Didst thou deliver to me on the mart.

Dro. S. I never spake with her in all my life.

Ant. S. How can she thus then call us by our names,
Unless it be by inspiration?

Adr. How ill agrees it with your gravity,
To counterfeit thus grossly with your slave,
Abetting him to thwart me in my mood?
Be it my wrong you are from me exempt [8],
But wrong not that wrong with a more contempt.
Come, I will fasten on this sleeve of thine:
Thou art an elm, my husband, I a vine [9];
Whose weakness, marry'd to thy stronger state [1],
Makes me with thy strength to communicate:
If aught possess thee from me, it is dross,
Usurping ivy, briar, or idle moss [2];
Who, all for want of pruning, with intrusion
Infect thy sap and live on thy confusion.

Ant. S. To me she speaks; she moves me for her theme:
What, was I marry'd to her in my dream?

---

[8] *— you are from me exempt.*] Exempt, separated, parted. The sense is, If I am doomed to suffer the wrong of separation, yet injure not with contempt me who am already injured. JOHNSON.

[9] *Thou art an elm, my husband; I a vine;*]
    Lentæ, qui, velut assitas
    Vitis implicat arbores,
    Implicabitur in tuum
    Complexum." *Catul.* 57.
So Milton, Par. Lost. B. V:
    " ——— They led the vine
    " To wed her elm. She spous'd, about him twines
    " Her marriageable arms." MALONE.

[1] *— stronger state.*] The old copy has—*stranger*. Corrected by Mr. Rowe. MALONE.

[2] *— idle moss;*] i. e. moss that produces no fruit, but being unfertile is useless. So, in *Othello:*—" autres vast, and deserts *idle.*"
STEEVENS.

Or sleep I now, and think I hear all this?
What error drives our eyes and ears amiss?
Until I know this sure uncertainty,
I'll entertain the offer'd fallacy ³.

Luc. Dromio, go bid the servants spread for dinner.
Dro. S. O, for my beads! I cross me for a sinner.
This is the fairy land;—O, spight of spights!—
We talk with goblins, owls ⁴, and elvish sprights ⁵;
If we obey them not, this will ensue,
They'll suck our breath, or pinch us black and blue.
Luc. Why prat'st thou to thyself, and answer'st not?
Dromio, thou drone ⁶, thou snail, thou slug, thou sot!
Dro. S. I am transformed, master, am not I * ?

---

³ *the offer'd fallacy.*] The old copy reads—" the *freed* fallacy." The emendation was suggested by an anonymous correspondent of Mr. Steevens. Mr. Pope reads, I think, with less probability,—the *favour'd* fallacy; which has been followed by the subsequent editors. MALONE.

⁴ *We talk with goblins, owls,*—] It was an old popular superstition, that the scrietch-owl sucked out the breath and blood of infants in the cradle. On this account, the Italians called witches, who were supposed to be in like manner mischievously bent against children, *stryga* from *strix*, the *scrietch-owl*. This superstition they derived from their Pagan ancestors. See Ovid. Fast. Lib. vi. WARBURTON.

Ghastly owls accompany *elvish ghosts* in *Spenser's* Shepherd's *Calendar for June.* So, in *Sherringham's* Disceptatio de Anglorum Gentis Origine, p. 333. Lares, Lemures *Stryges*, Lamiæ, Muses (Gastæ dicti) et similes monstrorum Greges, Elvarum Chorea dicebatur." Much the same is said in *Olaus Magnus de Gentibus Septentrionalibus*, p. 112, 113.
TOLLET.

Owls are also mentioned in *Cornucopia, or Pasquil's Night-cap, or Antidote for the Head-ach*, 1623. *p*. 38:
" Dreading no dangers of the dark-some night,
" No *owls*, hobgoblins, ghosts, nor water-spright." STEEVENS.

Owls was changed by Mr. Theobald into *ouphs*: and how, it is objected, should Shakspeare know that *striges* or scrietch-owls were considered by the Romans as witches? The notes of Mr. Tollet and Mr. Steevens, as well as the following passage in the *London Prodigal*, a comedy, 1605, afford the best answer to this question: " 'Soul, I think, I am sure cross'd or *witch'd* with an owl." MALONE.

⁵ —elvish *sprights*;] The epithet *elvish* is not in the first folio, but the second has—*elves* sprights. STEEVENS.

All the emendations made in the second folio having been merely arbitrary, any other suitable epithet of two syllables may have been the poet's word. Mr. Rowe first introduced—*elvish*. MALONE.

⁶ *Dromio, thou drone,*] The old copy reads—Dromio, thou *Dromio*, &c. The emendation was made by Mr. Theobald. MALONE.

* —am not I?] Old copy—am *I not*. Corrected by Mr. Theobald.
MALONE.

⁷ *Ant. S.*

Ant. S. I think, thou art, in mind, and so am I.
Dro. S. Nay, master, both in mind, and in my shape.
Ant. S. Thou hast thine own form.
Dro. S. No, I am an ape.
Luc. If thou art chang'd to aught, 'tis to an ass.
Dro. S. 'Tis true; she rides me, and I long for grass.
'Tis so, I am an ass; else it could never be,
But I should know her as well as she knows me.
Adr. Come, come, no longer will I be a fool,
To put the finger in the eye and weep,
Whilst man, and master, laugh my woes to scorn.—
Come, Sir, to dinner; Dromio, keep the gate:
Husband, I'll dine above with you to-day,
And shrive you [?] of a thousand idle pranks:
Sirrah, if any ask you for your master,
Say, he dines forth, and let no creature enter.—
Come, sister:—Dromio, play the porter well.
Ant. S. Am I in earth, in heaven, or in hell?
Sleeping or waking? mad, or well-advis'd?
Known unto these, and to myself disguis'd!
I'll say as they say, and persever so,
And in this mist at all adventures go.
Dro. S. Master, shall I be porter at the gate?
Adr. Ay, let none enter, lest I break your pate.
Luc. Come, come, Antipholus, we dine too late.

[*Exeunt.*

ACT III. SCENE. I.

The same.

Enter ANTIPHOLUS *of* Ephesus, DROMIO *of* Ephesus,
ANGELO, *and* BALTHAZAR.

Ant. E. Good signior Angelo, you must excuse us all;
My wife is shrewish, when I keep not hours:
Say, that I linger'd with you at your shop,

[?] *And shrive you—*] That is, I will *call you to confession*, and make you tell your tricks. JOHNSON.

To

To see the making of her carkanet [8],
And that to-morrow you will bring it home.
But here's a villain, that would face me down
He met me on the mart; and that I beat him,
And charg'd him with a thousand marks in gold;
And that I did deny my wife and house:—
Thou drunkard, thou, what didst thou mean by this?

Dro. E. Say what you will, Sir, but I know what I know:
That you beat me at the mart, I have your hand to show:
If the skin were parchment, and the blows you gave were ink,
Your own hand-writing would tell you what I think.

Ant. E. I think, thou art an ass.

Dro. E. Marry, so it doth appear
By the wrongs I suffer, and the blows I bear [9],
I should kick, being kick'd; and, being at that pass,
You would keep from my heels, and beware of an ass.

Ant. E. You are sad, Signior Balthazar: Pray God, our cheer
May answer my good-will, and your good welcome here.

Bal. I hold your dainties cheap, Sir, and your welcome dear.

Ant. E. O, Signior Balthazar, either at flesh or fish,
A table-full of welcome makes scarce one dainty dish.

Bal. Good meat, Sir, is common; that every churl affords.

Ant. E. And welcome more common; for that's nothing but words.

Bal. Small cheer, and great welcome, makes a merry feast.

Ant. E. Ay, to a niggardly host, and more sparing guest:
But though my cates be mean, take them in good part;
Better cheer may you have, but not with better heart.
But soft; my door is lock'd; Go bid them let us in.

---

[8] — *carkanet*,] seems to have been a necklace, or rather chain, perhaps hanging down double from the neck. JOHNSON.

"*Quarquan*, ornement d'or qu'on mit au col des damoiselles." *Le grand Dict. de Nicot.*—A *Carkanet* seems to have been a necklace set with stones, or strung with pearls. STEEVENS.

[9] *Marry, so it doth appear*
By the wrongs I suffer, and the blows I bear.] Mr. Theobald, instead of *doth*, reads—*don't*. MALONE.

I do not think this emendation necessary. He first says, that his *wrongs* and *blows* prove him an *ass*; but immediately, with a correction of his former sentiment, such as may be hourly observed in conversation, he observes that, if he had been an *ass*, he should, when he was *kicked*, have *kicked* again. JOHNSON.

Vol. IV.   C   *Dro. E.*

Dro. E. Maud, Bridget, Marian, Cicely, Gillian, Jen!
Dro. S. [*within*] Mome¹, malt-horse, capon, coxcomb, idiot, patch²!

Either get thee from the door, or sit down at the hatch:
Dost thou conjure for wenches, that thou call'st for such store,
When one is one too many? Go, get thee from the door.

Dro. E. What patch is made our porter? My master stays in the street.
Dro. S. Let him walk from whence he came, lest he catch cold on's feet.
Ant. E. Who talks within there? ho, open the door.
Dro. S. Right, Sir, I'll tell you when, an you'll tell me wherefore.
Ant. E. Wherefore? for my dinner; I have not din'd to-day.
Dro. S. Nor to-day here you must not; come again, when you may.
Ant. E. What art thou, that keep'st me out from the house I owe³?
Dro. S. The porter for this time, Sir, and my name is Dromio.
Dro. E. O villain, thou hast stolen both mine office and my name;

The one ne'er got me credit, the other mickle blame.
If thou hadst been Dromio to-day in my place,
Thou would'st have chang'd thy face for a name, or thy name for an ass.

Luce. [*within*] What a coil is there! Dromio, who are those at the gate?
Dro. E. Let my master in, Luce.
Luce. Faith no; he comes too late;
And so tell your master.
Dro. E. O Lord, I must laugh:—
Have at you with a proverb.—Shall I set in my staff?

---

¹ *Mome,*] a dull stupid blockhead, a stock, a post. This owes its original to the French word *Momon*, which signifies the gaming at dice in masquerade, the custom and rule of which is, that a strict silence is to be observed; whatever sum one stakes, another covers, but not a word is to be spoken; from hence also comes our word *mum!* for silence. HAWKINS.

² —*patch!*] i. e. fool. Alluding to the parti-colour'd coats worn by the licens'd fools or jesters of the age. STEEVENS.

³ —*I owe*] i. e. I own. STEEVENS.

Luce.

Luce. Have at you with another: that's—When? can you tell?

Dro. S. If thy name be called Luce, Luce, thou hast answer'd him well.

Ant. E. Do you hear, you minion? you'll let us in, I hope⁴?

Luce. I thought to have ask'd you.

Dro. S. And you said, no.

Dro. E. So, come, help; well struck; there was blow for blow.

Ant. E. Thou baggage, let me in.

Luce. Can you tell for whose sake?

Dro. E. Master, knock the door hard.

Luce. Let him knock till it ake.

Ant. E. You'll cry for this, minion, if I beat the door down.

Luce. What needs all that, and a pair of stocks in the town?

Adr. [*within*] Who is that at the door, that keeps all this noise?

Dro. S. By my troth, your town is troubled with unruly boys.

Ant. E. Are you there, wife? you might have come before.

Adr. Your wife, Sir knave! go get you from the door.

Dro. E. If you went in pain, master, this knave would go sore.

Ang. Here is neither cheer, Sir, nor welcome; we would fain have either.

Bal. In debating which was best, we shall part with neither⁵.

Dro. E. They stand at the door, master; bid them welcome hither.

Ant. E. There is something in the wind, that we cannot get in.

⁴ — *I hope?*] A line either preceding or following this, has, I believe, been lost. Mr. Theobald and the subsequent editors read—I *trow*; but that word, and *hope*, were not likely to be confounded by either the eye or the ear. MALONE.

⁵ — *we shall part with neither.*] In our old language, *to part* signified *to have part*. See Chaucer, Cant. Tales, ver. 9504:

"That no wight with his blisse *parten* shall."

The French use *partir* in the same sense. TYRWHITT.

Dro. E. You would say so master, if your garments were thin.

Your cake here is warm within; you stand here in the cold:
It would make a man mad as a buck, to be so bought and sold [6].

Ant. E. Go, fetch me something. I'll break ope the gate.

Dro. S. Break any thing here, and I'll break your knave's pate.

Dro. E. A man may break a word with you, Sir; and words are but wind;

Ay, and break it in your face, so he break it not behind.

Dro. S. It seems, thou wantest breaking; Out upon thee, hind!

Dro. E. Here's too much, out upon thee! I pray thee, let me in.

Dro. S. Ay, when fowls have no feathers, and fish have no fin.

Ant. E. Well, I'll break in; Go borrow me a crow.

Dro. E. A crow without feather; master mean you so?
For a fish without a fin, there's a fowl without a feather:
If a crow help us in, Sirrah, we'll pluck a crow together [7].

Ant. E. Go, get thee gone, fetch me an iron crow.

Bal. Have patience, Sir; O, let it not be so;
Herein you war against your reputation,
And draw within the compass of suspect
The unviolated honour of your wife.
Once this [8]—Your long experience of her wisdom,
Her sober virtue, years, and modesty,
Plead on her part [9] some cause to you unknown:

---

[6] — *bought and sold.*—] This is a proverbial phrase. "To be *bought and sold* in a company." See Ray's Collection, p. 179. edit. 1737. STEEVENS.

[7] — *we'll pluck a crow together*] We find the same quibble on a like occasion in one of the comedies of Plautus.—The children of distinction among the Greeks and Romans had usually birds of different kinds given them for their amusement. This custom Tyndarus in the *Captives* mentions, and says, that for his part he had *tantum upupam*. Upupa signifies both a *lapwing* and a *mattock*, or some instrument of the same kind, employed to dig stones from the quarries. STEEVENS.

[8] — *Once this,*—] This expression appears to me so singular, that I cannot help suspecting the passage to be corrupt. MALONE.

Once this may mean, Once for all, let me recommend *this* to your consideration. STEEVENS.

[9] *Your long experience of her wisdom—*
Plead on her part—] The old copy reads *year*, in both places. Corrected by Mr. Rowe. MALONE.

And

And doubt not, Sir, but she will well excuse
Why at this time the doors are made ¹ against you.
Be rul'd by me; depart in patience,
And let us to the Tyger all to dinner;
And, about evening come yourself alone,
To know the reason of this strange restraint.
If by strong hand you offer to break in,
Now in the stirring passage of the day,
A vulgar comment will be made of it;
And that supposed by the common rout ²
Against your yet ungalled estimation,
That may with foul intrusion enter in,
And dwell upon your grave when you are dead:
For slander lives upon succession ³;
For ever hous'd, where it gets possession.

Ant. E. You have prevail'd; I will depart in quiet,
And, in despight of mirth ⁴, mean to be merry.
I know a wench of excellent discourse—
Pretty and witty; wild, and, yet too, gentle;—
There will we dine: this woman that I mean,
My wife (but, I protest, without desert,)
Hath oftentimes upbraided me withal;
To her will we to dinner.—Get you home,
And fetch the chain; by this, I know, 'tis made:
Bring it, I pray you, to the Porcupine;
For there's the house; that chain will I bestow,
(Be it for nothing but to spight my wife,)
Upon mine hostess there: good Sir, make haste.
Since mine own doors refuse to entertain me,
I'll knock elsewhere, to see if they'll disdain me.

Ang. I'll meet you at that place, some hour hence.
Ant. E. Do so; This jest shall cost me some expence.
[*Exeunt.*

---

¹ —*the doors are made*—] To *make* the door, is the expression used to this day in some counties of England, instead of, *to bar the door*.
STEEVENS.

² —*supposed by the common rout*] Supposed is *founded on supposition*, made by conjecture. JOHNSON.

³ —*upon succession;*] Succession *is often used as a quadrisyllable by our author, and his contemporaries.* So below, p. 38, *satisfaction composes half a verse.*

⁴ *And, in despight of mirth,*—] Though mirth hath withdrawn herself from me, and seems determined to avoid me, yet in despight of her, and whether she will or not, I am resolved to be merry. HEATH.

C 3 SCENE

SCENE II.

The same.

Enter LUCIANA *and* ANTIPHOLUS *of Syracuse.*

Luc. And may it be, that you have quite forgot
A husband's office? Shall, Antipholus, hate,
Even in the spring of love, thy love-springs rot?
Shall love, in building, grow so ruinate⁵?

⁵ *And may it be, that you have quite forgot
An husband's office? Shall, Antipholus, hate
Even in the spring of love, thy love-springs rot?
Shall love in building grow so ruinate?*] So, in our author's 119th Sonnet:

"And ruin'd love, when it is built anew——."

The word *hate* at the end of the second line was supplied by Mr. Theobald; *building*, instead of *buildings*, is also his correction. In support of the former emendation, a passage in our author's 10th Sonnet may be produced:

"—— thou art so possess'd with murderous *hate*,
"That 'gainst thyself thou stick'st not to conspire,
"Seeking that beauteous roof to *ruinate*,
"Which to repair should be thy chief desire."

Again, in the *Rape of Lucrece*:

"To *ruinate* proud buildings with thy hours."

Stowe uses the adjective *ruinate* in his *Annales*, p. 892. "The last year at the taking down of the old *ruinate gate*——." MALONE.

The meaning is, Shall thy love-springs rot, even in the spring of love? and shall thy love grow ruinous, even while 'tis but building up?

Love-springs are what our poet, in *Romeo and Juliet*, called the *buds of love*.

The rhime which Mr. Theobald would restore, stands thus in the old edition:—Shall Antipholus——. If therefore instead of *ruinate* we should read *ruinous*, the passage may remain as it was originally written; and perhaps, indeed, throughout the play we should read *Antipholus*, a name which Shakspeare might have found in P. Holland's translation of Pliny, B. xxxv, and xxxvii. *Antipbilus* was a famous painter, and rival to Apelles.

Ruinous is justified by a passage in the *Two Gentlemen of Verona*, Act V. sc. iv:

"Lest growing *ruinous* the building fall."

Throughout the first folio, *Antipholus* occurs much more often than *Antipbolis*, even where the rhime is not concerned; and were the rhime defective here, such transgressions are accounted for in other places.
STEEVENS.

Antipholis occurs, I think, but thrice in the original copy. I have therefore adhered to the other spelling. MALONE.

If you did wed my sister for her wealth,
  Then, for her wealth's sake, use her with more kindness:
Or, if you like elsewhere, do it by stealth;
  Muffle your false love with some show of blindness:
Let not my sister read it in your eye;
  Be not thy tongue thy own shame's orator;
Look sweet, speak fair, become disloyalty;
  Apparel vice, like virtue's harbinger:
Bear a fair presence, though your heart be tainted;
  Teach sin the carriage of a holy saint;
Be secret-false; What need she be acquainted?
  What simple thief brags of his own attaint [6]?
'Tis double wrong, to truant with your bed,
  And let her read it in thy looks at board:
Shame hath a bastard fame, well managed;
  Ill deeds are doubled with an evil word.
Alas, poor women! make us but believe [7],
  Being compact of credit [8], that you love us;
Though others have the arm, shew us the sleeve;
  We in your motion turn, and you may move us.
Then, gentle brother, get you in again;
  Comfort my sister, cheer her, call her wife:
'Tis holy sport, to be a little [9] vain,
  When the sweet breath of flattery conquers strife.

Ant. S. Sweet mistress, (what your name is else, I
  know not,
Nor by what wonder you do hit of mine,)
Less, in your knowledge, and your grace, you show not,
  Than our earth's wonder; more than earth divine.
Teach me, dear creature, how to think and speak;
  Lay open to my earthly gross conceit,
Smother'd in errors, feeble, shallow, weak,
  The folded meaning of your words' deceit.
Against my soul's pure truth why labour you,
  To make it wander in an unknown field?
Are you a god? would you create me new?
  Transform me then, and to your power I'll yield.

[6] — *his own attaint?*] The old copy has—*attaine*. The emendation is Mr. Rowe's. MALONE.

[7] —*make us but believe.*] The old copy reads—*not believe*. It was corrected by Mr. Theobald. MALONE.

[8] *Being compact of credit,*] Means, *being made altogether of credulity.* STEEVENS.

[9] —*vain.*] Is *light of tongue, not vitious.* JOHNSON.

But

But if that I am I, then well I know,
  Your weeping sister is no wife of mine,
Nor to her bed no homage do I owe;
  Far more, far more, to you do I decline.
O, train me not, sweet mermaid¹, with thy note,
  To drown me in thy sister's flood² of tears;
Sing, syren, for thyself, and I will dote:
  Spread o'er the silver waves thy golden hairs,
And as a bed I'll take thee³, and there lie;
  And, in that glorious supposition, think
He gains by death, that hath such means to die:—
  Let love, being light, be drowned if she sink⁴!

Luc. What are you mad, that you do reason so?
Ant. S. Not mad, but mated⁵; how, I do not know.
Luc. It is a fault that springeth from your eye.
Ant. S. For gazing on your beams, fair sun, being by.
Luc. Gaze where⁶ you should, and that will clear your sight.

¹ — *mermaid*,] is only another name for *syren*. STEEVENS.

² — *in thy sister's flood* —] The old copy reads—*sister*. Corrected by the editor of the second folio. MALONE.

³ — *as a bed I'll take thee*,] *Bed,* which the word *lie* fully supports, was introduced in the second folio. The old copy has—*bud.* MALONE. Mr. Edwards suspects a mistake of one letter in the passage, and would read—I'll take *them.*—Perhaps, however, both the ancient readings may be right;—*as a bud I'll take thee,* &c. i. e. I like an insect, will take thy bosom for a rose, or some other flower, and,

    "——phœnix-like beneath thine eye
    "Involv'd in fragrance, burn and die."

It is common for Shakspeare to shift hastily from one image to another. Mr. Edwards's conjecture may, however, receive support from the following passage in the *Two Gentlemen of Verona,* Act i. sc. ii:

    "—— my bosom as a *bed*
    "Shall lodge thee." STEEVENS.

⁴ *Let love, being light, be drowned if she sink!*] *Love* means—the Queen of love. So, in *Antony and Cleopatra:*
    "Now for the love of *love,* and her soft hours—."
Again, more appositely in our author's *Venus and Adonis:*
    "Love is a spirit, all compact of fire,
    "Not gross to *sink,* but *light,* and will aspire."
Venus is here speaking of herself.
Again, *ibidem:*
    "*She's love,* she loves, and yet she is not lov'd." MALONE.

⁵ *Not mad, but mated,*] i. e. confounded.—So, in *Macbeth:*
    "My mind she has mated, and amaz'd my sight." STEEVENS.

⁶ *Gaze where*—] The old copy reads, *when.* STEEVENS.
The correction was made by Mr. Pope. MALONE.

Ant. S. As good to wink, sweet love, as look on night.
Luc. Why call you me love? call my sister so.
Ant. S. Thy sister's sister.
Luc. That's my sister.
Ant. S. No;
It is thyself, mine own self's better part;
Mine eye's clear eye, my dear heart's dearer heart;
My food, my fortune, and my sweet hope's aim,
My sole earth's heaven, and my heaven's claim [7].
Luc. All this my sister is, or else should be.
Ant. S. Call thyself sister, sweet, for I aim thee [8];
Thee will I love, and with thee lead my life;
Thou hast no husband yet, nor I no wife:
Give me thy hand.
Luc. O, soft, Sir, hold you still;
I'll fetch my sister, to get her good-will. [*Exit* Luc.

Enter, from the house of ANTIPHOLUS *of* Ephesus, DROMIO *of* Syracuse.

Ant. S. Why, how now, Dromio? where run'st thou so fast?
Dro. S. Do you know me, Sir? am I Dromio? am I your man? am I myself?
Ant. S. Thou art Dromio, thou art my man, thou art thyself.
Dro. S. I am an ass, I am a woman's man, and besides myself.
Ant. S. What woman's man? and how besides thyself?
Dro. S. Marry, Sir, besides myself, I am due to a woman; one that claims me, one that haunts me, one that will have me.
Ant. S. What claim lays she to thee?
Dro. S. Marry, Sir, such a claim as you would lay to your horse? and she would have me as a beast: not that, I

---

[7] *My sole earth's heaven, and my heaven's claim*] When he calls the girl his *only heaven on the earth*, he utters the common cant of lovers. When he calls her *his heaven's claim*, I cannot understand him. Perhaps he means that which he asks of heaven. JOHNSON.

[8] — *for I aim thee:*] The old copy reads—*for I am thee*. The emendation was suggested by Mr. Steevens. Antipholus has just told her, as the same gentleman observes—that she was his sweet hope's aim. MALONE.

C 5 being

being a beast, she would have me; but that she, being a very beastly creature, lays claim to me.

Ant. S. What is she?

Dro. S. A very reverent body; ay, such a one as a man may not speak of, without he say, sir-reverence: I have but lean luck in the match, and yet is she a wondrous fat marriage.

Ant. S. How dost thou mean, a fat marriage?

Dro. S. Marry, Sir, she's the kitchen-wench, and all grease; and I know not what use to put her to, but to make a lamp of her, and run from her by her own light. I warrant her rags, and the tallow in them, will burn a Poland winter: if she lives till doomsday, she'll burn a week longer than the whole world.

Ant. S. What complexion is she of?

Dro. S. Swart, like my shoe, but her face nothing like so clean kept; For why? she sweats, a man may go over shoes in the grime of it.

Ant. S. That's a fault that water will mend.

Dro. S. No, Sir, 'tis in grain; Noah's flood could not do it.

Ant. S. What's her name?

Dro. S. Nell, Sir;—but her name and three quarters [9], that is, an ell and three quarters, will not measure her from hip to hip.

Ant. S. Then she bears some breadth?

Dro. S. No longer from head to foot, than from hip to hip: she is spherical, like a globe; I could find out countries in her.

Ant. S. In what part of her body stands Ireland?

Dro. S. Marry, Sir, in her buttocks; I found it out by the bogs.

Ant. S. Where Scotland?

---

[9] *Nell, Sir; but her name* and *three quarters, &c.*] The old copy has —her name *is* three quarters, &c. The emendation was made by Dr. Thirlby. "This poor conundrum is borrowed by Massinger, in *The Old Law*, 1653:

"*Cook.* That *Nell* was Hellen of Greece.

"*Clown.* As long as she tarried with her husband she was *Ellen*, but after she came to Troy she was *Nell* of Troy.

"*Cook.* Why did she grow shorter when she came to Troy?

"*Clown.* She grew longer, if you mark the story, when she grew to be an *ell*, &c." MALONE.

Dro. S.

Dro. S. I found it by the barrenness; hard, in the palm of the hand.

Ant. S. Where France?

Dro. S. In her forehead; arm'd and reverted, making war against her hair [1].

Ant. S. Where England?

Dro. S. I look'd for the chalky cliffs, but I could find no whiteness in them: but I guess, it stood in her chin, by the salt rheum that ran between France and it.

Ant. S. Where Spain?

Dro. S. Faith, I saw it not; but I felt it, hot in her breath.

Ant. S. Where America, the Indies?

---

[1] *In her forehead; arm'd and reverted, making war against her hair.*] The old copy has—her *heir*. The present reading was introduced by the editor of the second folio. Mr. Theobald prefers the old reading, supposing the allusion to be to Henry IV. " whose claim, on the death of his father, in 1589, (and for several years afterwards) the States of France resisted, on account of his being a Protestant."

In *Macbeth*, folio, 1613, *heire* is printed for *hair*:

" Whose horrid image doth unfix my *heire*."

Again, in *Cymbeline*, folio, 1623:

" —— His meanest garment is dearer
" In my respect, than all the *heires* above thee." MALONE.

With this explication Dr. Warburton concurs; and Sir Thomas Hanmer thinks an equivocation was intended, though he retains *hair* in the text. Yet surely they have all lost the sense in looking beyond it. Our author, in my opinion, only sports with an allusion, in which he takes too much delight, and means that his mistress had the French disease. The ideas are rather too offensive to be dilated. By a forehead *armed*, he means covered with incrusted eruptions: by *reverted*, he means having the hair turning backward. An equivocal word must have senses applicable to both the subjects to which it is applied. Both *forehead* and *France* might in some sort make war against their *hair*, but how did the *forehead* make war against its *heir*? JOHNSON.

I think with Sir T. Hanmer, that an equivocation *may* have been intended. It is of little consequence which of the two words is preserved in the text, if the author meant that two senses should be couched under the same term.—Dr. Johnson's objection, that " an equivocal term must have senses applicable to both the subjects to which it is applied," appears to me not so well founded as his observations in general are; for, though a correct writer would observe that rule, our author is very seldom scrupulous in this particular, the terms which he uses in comparisons scarcely ever answering exactly on both sides. However, as *hair* affords the clearest and most obvious sense, I have placed it in the text. In *King Henry V*. 4to. 1600, we have—

" This your *heirs* of France hath blown this vice in me—" instead of *air*. MALONE.

Dro. S.

Dro. S. O, Sir, upon her nose, all o'er embellish'd with rubies, carbuncles, sapphires, declining their rich aspect to the hot breath of Spain; who sent whole armadoes of carracks to be ballast [1] at her nose.

Ant. S. Where stood Belgia, the Netherlands?

Dro. S. O, Sir, I did not look so low. To conclude, this drudge, or diviner, laid claim to me; call'd me Dromio; swore, I was assured to her [3]; told me what privy marks I had about me, as, the mark of my shoulder, the mole in my neck, the great wart on my left arm, that I amazed, ran from her as a witch: and, I think, if my breast had not been made of faith [4], and my heart of steel, she had transform'd me to a curtail-dog, and made me turn i' the wheel.

Ant. S. Go, hie thee presently post to the road;
And if the wind blow any way from shore,
I will not harbour in this town to-night.
If any bark put forth, come to the mart,
Where I will walk, till thou return to me.
If every one know us, and we know none,
'Tis time, I think, to trudge, pack, and be gone.

Dro. S. As from a bear a man would run for life,
So fly I from her that would be my wife. [*Exit.*

Ant. S. There's none but witches do inhabit here;
And therefore 'tis high time that I were hence.
She, that doth call me husband, even my soul
Doth for a wife abhor: but her fair sister,
Possess'd with such a gentle sovereign grace,
Of such inchanting presence and discourse,
Hath almost made me traitor to myself:
But, lest myself be guilty to self-wrong [5],
I'll stop mine ears against the mermaid's song.

Enter

---

[1] *— to be ballast*] i. e. ball fast. So, in *Hamlet*:
"―――― to have the engineer
" Hoist with his own petar." i. e. hoisted. STEEVENS.

[3] *— assured to her*;] i. e. affianced to her. STEEVENS.

[4] *— if my breast had not been made of* faith, &c.] Alluding to the superstition of the common people, that nothing could resist a witch's power of transforming men into animals, but a great share of *faith*.
WARBURTON.

[5] *— to self-wrong.*] I have met with other instances of this kind of phraseology. So, in *The Winter's Tale*:
" But

Enter ANGELO.

Ang. Master Antipholus?
Ant. S. Ay, that's my name.
Ang. I know it well, Sir: Lo, here is the chain;
I thought to have ta'en you at the Porcupine[d]:
The chain unfinish'd made me stay thus long.
Ant. S. What is your will, that I shall do with this?
Ang. What please yourself, Sir; I have made it for you.
Ant. S. Made it for me, Sir! I bespoke it not.
Ang. Not once, nor twice, but twenty times you have:
Go home with it, and please your wife withal;
And soon at supper-time I'll visit you,
And then receive my money for the chain.
Ant. S. I pray you, Sir, receive the money now,
For fear you ne'er see chain, nor money, more.
Ang. You are a merry man, Sir; fare you well. [*Exit.*
Ant. S. What I should think of this, I cannot tell:
But this I think, there's no man is so vain,
That would refuse so fair an offer'd chain.
I see, a man here needs not live by shifts,
When in the streets he meets such golden gifts.
I'll to the mart, and there for Dromio stay;
If any ship put out, then strait away. [*Exit.*

ACT IV. SCENE I.

The same.

Enter a Merchant, ANGELO, *and an Officer.*

Mer. You know, since pentecost the sum is due,
And since I have not much impórtun'd you;
Nor now I had not, but that I am bound

" But as the unthought-on accident is *guilty*
" To what we wildly do—."
Mr. Pope and the subsequent editors read—*of* self-wrong. MALONE.

[d] —*at the* Porcupine;] It is remarkable, that throughout the old editions of Shakspeare's plays, the word *Porpentine* is used instead of *Porcupine.* Perhaps it was so pronounced at that time. I have since observed the same spelling in the plays of our ancient authors. Mr. Tollet finds it likewise in p. 66. of Ascham's Works by Bennet, and in Stowe's Chronicle in the years 1117, 1135. STEEVENS.

To Persia, and want gilders [7] for my voyage:
Therefore make present satisfaction,
Or I'll attach you by this officer.

  Ang. Even just the sum, that I do owe to you,.
Is growing to me [8] by Antipholus:
And, in the instant that I met with you,
He had of me a chain; at five o'clock,
I shall receive the money for the same:
Pleaseth you walk with me down to his house,.
I will discharge my bond, and thank you too.

  Enter ANTIPHOLUS *of* Ephesus, *and* DROMIO *of* Ephesus.

  Off. That labour may you save; see where he comes.
  Ant. E. While I go to the goldsmith's house, go thou
And buy a rope's end; that will I bestow
Among my wife and her confederates [9],
For locking me out of my doors by day.—
But soft, I see the goldsmith:—get thee gone;
Buy thou a rope, and bring it home to me.

  Dro. E. I buy a thousand pound a year! I buy a rope!
                                                    [*Exit.* DROMIO.

  Ant. E. A man is well holp up, that trusts to you:
I promised your presence, and the chain;
But neither chain, nor goldsmith, came to me:
Belike, you thought our love would last too long,
If it were chain'd together; and therefore came not.
  Ang. Saving your merry humour, here's the note,
How much your chain weighs to the utmost carrat;
The fineness of the gold, and chargeful fashion;
Which doth amount to three odd ducats more
Than I stand debted to this gentleman:
I pray you, see him presently discharg'd,
For he is bound to sea, and stays but for it.
  Ant. E. I am not furnish'd with the present money;
Besides, I have some business in the town:
Good Signior, take the stranger to my house,

---

  [7] *— want gilders*] A *gilder* is a coin valued from one shilling and six-pence, to two shillings. STEEVENS.

  [8] *Is growing to me—*] i. e. accruing to me. STEEVENS.

  [9] *— and her confederates,*] The old copy has—*their* confederates. The emendation was made by Mr. Rowe. MALONE.

                                                                And

And with you take the chain, and bid my wife
Disburse the sum on the receipt thereof;
Perchance, I will be there as soon as you.

Ang. Then you will bring the chain to her yourself?

Ant. E. No; bear it with you, left I come not time enough.

Ang. Well, Sir, I will: Have you the chain about you?

Ant. E. An if I have not, Sir, I hope you have;
Or else you may return without your money.

Ang. Nay, come, I pray you, Sir, give me the chain;
Both wind and tide stays for this gentleman,
And I, to blame, have held him here too long.

Ant. E. Good Lord, you use this dalliance, to excuse
Your breach of promise to the Porcupine:
I should have chid you for not bringing it,
But, like a shrew, you first begin to brawl.

Mer. The hour steals on; I pray you, Sir, dispatch.

Ang. You hear, how he importunes me; the chain—

Ant. E. Why, give it to my wife, and fetch your money.

Ang. Come, come, you know, I gave it you even now;
Either send the chain, or send me by some token.

Ant. E. Fye, now you run this humour out of breath?
Come, where's the chain? I pray you, let me see it.

Mer. My business cannot brook this dalliance:
Good Sir, say, whe'r you'll answer me, or no;
If not, I'll leave him to the officer.

Ant. E. I answer you! what should I answer you?

Ang. The money, that you owe me for the chain.

Ant. E. I owe you none, till I receive the chain.

Ang. You know, I gave it you half an hour since.

Ant. E. You gave me none; you wrong me much to say so.

Ang. You wrong me more, Sir, in denying it;
Consider, how it stands upon my credit.

Mer. Well, officer, arrest him at my suit.

Off. I do;
And charge you in the duke's name to obey me.

Ang. This touches me in reputation:
Either consent to pay this sum for me,
Or I attach you by this officer.

Ant. E. Consent to pay thee that I never had!
Arrest me, foolish fellow, if thou dar'st.

Ang.

Ang. Here is thy fee; arrest him, officer;—
I would not spare my brother in this case,
If he should scorn me so apparently.

Off. I do arrest you, Sir; you hear the suit.

Ant. E. I do obey thee, till I give thee bail:—
But, Sirrah, you shall buy this sport as dear
As all the metal in your shop will answer.

Ang. Sir, Sir, I shall have law in Ephesus,
To your notorious shame, I doubt it not.

Enter DROMIO *of Syracuse.*

Dro. S. Master, there is a bark of Epidamnum,
That stays but till her owner comes aboard,
And then, Sir, she bears away: our fraughtage, Sir,
I have convey'd aboard; and I have bought
The oil, the balsamum, and aqua-vitæ.
The ship is in her trim; the merry wind
Blows fair from land: they stay for nought at all,
But for their owner, master, and yourself.

Ant. E. How now, a madman! Why, thou peevish sheep [1],
What ship of Epidamnum stays for me?

Dro. S. A ship you sent me to, to hire waftage.

Ant. E. Thou drunken slave, I sent thee for a rope;
And told thee to what purpose, and what end.

Dro. S. You sent me for a rope's end as soon [2]:
You sent me to the bay, Sir, for a bark.

Ant. E. I will debate this matter at more leisure,
And teach your ears to list me with more heed.
To Adriana, villain, hie thee straight;
Give her this key, and tell her, in the desk
That's cover'd o'er with Turkish tapestry,
There is a purse of ducats; let her send it;
Tell her, I am arrested in the street,
And that shall bail me: hie thee, slave, be gone.
On, officer, to prison till it come.

[*Exeunt* Merchant, ANGELO, *Officer, and* ANT. E.

---

[1] — *thou peevish sheep.*] *Peevish* is *silly.* So, in *Cymbeline:*
 "Desire my man's abode where I did leave him;
 "He's strange and *peevish.*" See a note on Act i. sc. vii.
 STEEVENS.

[2] *You sent me for a rope's end as soon:*] *Ropes* is here a dissyllable; the Saxon genitive case. MALONE.

Dro. S.

Dro. S. To Adriana! that is where we din'd,
Where Dowsabel² did claim me for her husband:
She is too big, I hope, for me to compass.
Thither I must, although against my will,
For servants must their masters' minds fulfil. [*Exit.*

SCENE II.

The same.

Enter ADRIANA *and* LUCIANA.

Adr. Ah, Luciana, did he tempt thee so?
Might'st thou perceive austerely in his eye
That he did plead in earnest, yea or no?
Look'd he or red, or pale; or sad, or merrily?
What observation mad'st thou in this case,
Of his heart's meteors⁴ tilting in his face?
Luc. First he deny'd you had in him no right.
Adr. He meant, he did me none; the more my spight.
Luc. Then swore he, that he was a stranger here.
Adr. And true he swore, though yet forsworn he were.
Luc. Then pleaded I for you.
Adr. And what said he?
Luc. That love I begg'd for you he begg'd of me.

---

² *Where Dowsabel—*] This name occurs in one of Drayton's Pastorals:
 "He had, as antique stories tell,
 "A daughter cleaped *Dowsabel*, &c." STEEVENS.

⁴ *Of his heart's meteors tilting in his face?*] Alluding to those meteors in the sky, which have the appearance of lines of armies meeting in the shock. To this appearance he compares civil wars in another place:
 "*Which like the meteors of a troubled heaven*,
 "*All of one nature, of one substance bred*,
 "*Did lately meet in the intestine shock*,
 "*And furious close of civil butchery.*" WARBURTON.

The allusion is more clearly explained by the following comparison in the second book of *Paradise Lost*:
 "As when, to warn proud cities, war appears
 "Wag'd in the troubled sky, and armies rush
 "To battle in the clouds, before each van
 "Prick forth the aery knights, and couch their spears,
 "Till thickest legions close; with feats of arms
 "From either end of heaven the welkin burns." STEEVENS.

The original copy reads—*Oh, his heart's meteors*, &c. The correction was made in the second folio. MALONE.

Adr.

Adr. With what persuasion did he tempt thy love?
Luc. With words, that in an honest suit might move.
First, he did praise my beauty; then, my speech.
Adr. Did'st speak him fair?
Luc. Have patience, I beseech.
Adr. I cannot, nor I will not, hold me still;
My tongue, though not my heart, shall have his will.
He is deformed, crooked, old, and sere⁵,
Ill-fac'd, worse-body'd, shapeless every where;
Vicious, ungentle, foolish, blunt, unkind;
Stigmatical in making⁶, worse in mind.
Luc. Who would be jealous then of such a one?
No evil lost is wail'd when it is gone.
Adr. Ah! but I think him better than I say,
And yet would herein others' eyes were worse:
Far from her nest the lapwing cries away⁷:
My heart prays for him, though my tongue do curse.

Enter DROMIO *of* Syracuse.

Dro. S. Here, go; the desk, the purse; sweet now, make haste.
Luc. How hast thou lost thy breath?
Dro. S. By running fast.
Adr. Where is thy master, Dromio? is he well?
Dro. S. No, he's in Tartar limbo, worse than hell;
A devil in an everlasting garment⁸ hath him,
One, whose hard heart is button'd up with steel;

---

⁵ —*sere,*] that is, *dry,* withered. JOHNSON.
⁶ *Stigmatical in making,*] That is, *marked or stigmatised* by nature with deformity, as a token of his vicious disposition. JOHNSON.
⁷ *Far from her nest the* lapwing, &c.] This expression seems to be proverbial. I have met with it in many of the old comic writers. Greene, in his Second Part of *Coney-catching,* 1592, says: " But again to our priggers, who, as before I said—*cry with the lapwing farthest from her nest,* and from their place of residence where their most abode is." Nash, speaking of Gabriel Harvey, says—" he withdraweth men, *lapwing-like,* from his nest, as much as might be." STEEVENS.
⁸ —*an* everlasting *garment*] *Everlasting* was in the time of Shakspeare as well as at present, the name of a kind of durable stuff. The quibble intended here, is likewise met with in B. and Fletcher's *Woman Hater:*

" ——— I'll quit this transitory
" Trade, and get me an *everlasting* robe,
" Sear up my conscience, and turn *serjeant.*" STEEVENS.

A fiend,

A fiend, a fairy, pitiless and rough?;
A wolf, nay, worse, a fellow all in buff;
A back-friend, a shoulder-clapper [1], one that countermands
The passages of alleys, creeks, and narrow lands;
A hound that runs counter, and yet draws dry-foot well [2];
One that, before the judgment, carries poor souls to hell [3].

Adr. Why, man, what is the matter?

Dro. S. I do not know the matter; he is 'rested on the case [4].

Adr. What, is he arrested? tell me, at whose suit.

Dro. S. I know not at whose suit he is arrested, well;
But he's in [5] a suit of buff, which 'rested him, that can I tell:
Will you send him, mistress, redemption, the money in his desk?

Adr. Go fetch it, sister.—This I wonder at,

[*Exit* LUCIANA.

---

[1] — *a fairy, pitiless and rough;*] There were fairies like hobgoblins, pitiless and rough, and described as malevolent and mischievous. JOHNSON.

So, Milton: " No goblin, or swart *fairy* of the mine,
" Hath hurtful power o'er true virginity." MALONE.

[1] — *a shoulder-clapper,*] is a bailiff. STEEVENS.

[2] *A hound that runs counter, and yet draws dry-foot well;*] To run counter is to run backward, by mistaking the course of the animal pursued; to draw *dry-foot* is, I believe, to pursue by the *track* or *prick* of the *foot*; to run *counter* and *draw dry-foot well* are, therefore, inconsistent. The jest consists in the ambiguity of the word *counter*, which means the *wrong way in the chase,* and a prison in London. The officer that arrested him was a serjeant of the *counter*. For the congruity of this jest with the scene of action, let our author answer. JOHNSON.

To draw *dry-foot,* is when the dog pursues the game by the scent of the foot; for which the blood hound is famed. GREY.

[3] — *to hell.*] Hell was the cant term for an obscure dungeon in any of our prisons. It is mentioned in the *Counter-rat,* a poem, 1658:
" In Wood-street's hole, or Poultry's *hell.*"

There was likewise a place of this name under the Exchequer chamber, where the king's debtors were confined till they had paid the uttermost farthing. STEEVENS.

[4] — *on the case.*] An action upon the case is a general action given for the redress of a wrong done any man without force, and not especially provided for by law. GREY.

Dromio, I believe, is still quibbling. His master's *case* was touched by the shoulder clapper. See p. 46:—" in a *case* of leather, &c." MALONE.

[5] *But he's in—*] The old copy reads—*But is in.* The emendation is Mr. Rowe's. MALONE.

That

That he [6], unknown to me, should be in debt:—
Tell me, was he arrested on a band??

Dro. S. Not on a band, but on a stronger thing;
A chain, a chain; do you not hear it ring?

Adr. What, the chain?

Dro. S. No, no, the bell; 'tis time, that I were gone.
It was two ere I left him, and now the clock strikes one.

Adr. The hours come back! that did I never hear.

Dro. S. O yes, If any hour meet a serjeant, 'a turns back for very fear.

Adr. As if time were in debt! how fondly dost thou reason?

Dro. S. Time is very a bankrout, and owes more than he's worth, to season.
Nay, he's a thief too: Have you not heard men say,
That time comes stealing on by night and day?
If he be in debt [8], and theft, and a serjeant in the way,
Hath he not reason to turn back an hour in a day?

Enter LUCIANA.

Adr. Go, Dromio; there's the money, bear it straight;
And bring thy master home immediately.—
Come, sister; I am press'd down with conceit;
Conceit, my comfort, and my injury. [*Exeunt.*

---

[6] *That he—*] The original copy has—*Thus he.* The emendation was made by the editor of the second folio. MALONE.

[7] —*was he arrested on a band?*] Thus the old copy, and I believe rightly, though the modern editors read *bond.* A *bond,* i. e. an obligatory writing to pay a sum of money, was anciently spelt *band.* A *band* is likewise a *neckcloth.* On this circumstance, I believe, the humour of the passage turns. STEEVENS.

See Minsheu's Dict. 1617, in v. "BAND or Obligation." In the same column is found "A BAND or thing to tie withal." Also, "A BAND for the neck, because it serves to *bind* about the neck." These sufficiently explain the equivoque.

Band is used in the sense which is couched under the words, "a stronger thing," in our author's *Venus and Adonis*:

"Sometimes her arms infold him, like a *band.*" MALONE.

[8] *If he be in debt*] The old edition reads—If *I* be in debt.
STEEVENS.

For the emendation now made the present editor is answerable. Mr. Rowe reads—If *time,* &c. but *I* could not have been confounded by the ear with *time,* though it might with *be.* MALONE.

SCENE.

COMEDY OF ERRORS.   45

SCENE III.

The same.

Enter ANTIPHOLUS *of Syracuse.*

Ant. S. There's not a man I meet, but doth falute me
As if I were their well acquainted friend;
And every one doth call me by my name,
Some tender money to me, some invite me;
Some other give me thanks for kindneſſes;
Some offer me commodities to buy;
Even now a tailor call'd me in his ſhop,
And ſhow'd me ſilks that he had bought for me,
And, therewithal, took meaſure of my body.
Sure, theſe are but imaginary wiles,
And Lapland ſorcerers inhabit here.

Enter DROMIO *of Syracuſe.*

Dro. S. Maſter, here's the gold you ſent me for: What, have you got the picture of old Adam new apparell'd?
Ant. S. What gold is this? What Adam doſt thou mean?
Dro. S. Not that Adam, that kept the paradiſe, but that Adam, that keeps the priſon: he that goes in the calf's-ſkin that was kill'd for the prodigal; he that came behind you, Sir, like an evil angel, and bid you forſake your liberty.

---

* *What, have you got the picture of old Adam new apparell'd?*] A ſhort word or two muſt have ſlipt out here, by ſome accident, in copying, or at preſs; otherwiſe I have no conception of the meaning of the paſſage. The caſe is this. Dromio's maſter had been arreſted, and ſent his ſervant home for money to redeem him: he running back with the money, meets the twin Antipholus, whom he miſtakes for his maſter, and ſeeing him clear of the officer before the money was come, he cries, in a ſurprize; *What, have you got rid of the picture of old Adam new apparell'd?* For ſo I have ventured to ſupply, by conjecture. But why is the officer call'd old Adam new apparell'd? The alluſion is to Adam in his ſtate of innocence going naked; and immediately after the fall being cloath'd in a frock of ſkins. Thus he was new apparell'd: and in like manner, the ſerjeants of the Counter were formerly clad in buff, or calf's ſkin, as the author humorouſly a little lower calls it. THEOBALD.

The explanation is very good, but the text does not require to be amended. JOHNSON.

Theſe jeſts on Adam's dreſs are common among our old writers. STEEVENS.

Ant. S.

Ant. S. I understand thee not.

Dro. S. No? why, 'tis a plain case: he that went like a base-viol, in a case of leather; the man, Sir, that, when gentlemen are tired, gives them a sob, and 'rests them; he, Sir, that takes pity on decayed men, and gives them suits of durance; he that sets up his rest to do more exploits with his mace, than a morris pike [1].

Ant. S. What! thou mean'st an officer?

Dro. S. Ay, Sir, the serjeant of the band; he, that brings any man to answer it, that breaks his band; one that thinks a man always going to bed, and says, *God give you good rest!*

Ant. S. Well, Sir, there rest in your foolery. Is there any ship puts forth to-night? may we be gone?

Dro. S. Why, Sir, I brought you word an hour since, that the bark Expedition put forth to-night; and then were you hindered by the serjeant, to tarry for the hoy, Delay: Here are the angels that you sent for, to deliver you.

Ant. S. The fellow is distract, and so am I;
And here we wander in illusions:
Some blessed power deliver us from hence!

Enter a Courtezan.

Cour. Well met, well met, master Antipholus.
I see, Sir, you have found the goldsmith now:
Is that the chain, you promis'd me to-day?

Ant. S. Satan, avoid! I charge thee, tempt me not!

Dro. S. Master, is this mistress Satan?

Ant. S. It is the devil.

---

[1] *— he that sets up his rest to do more exploits with his mace than a morris-pike.*] The *rest of a pike* was a common term, and signified, I believe, the manner in which it was fixed to receive the rush of the enemy. A *morris-pike* was a pike used in a *morris* or a military dance, and with which great exploits were done, that is, great feats of dexterity were shewn. JOHNSON.

A *morris-pike* is mentioned by the old writers as a formidable weapon. "*Morespikes* (says Langley, in his translation of *Polydore Virgil*) were used first in the siege of Capua." And in *Reynard's Deliverance of certain Christians from the Turks*, "The English mariners laid about them with brown bills, halberts, and *morris-pikes*." FARMER.

Polydore Virgil does not mention *morris-pikes* at the siege of Capua, though Langley's translation of him advances their antiquity so high. *Morris-pikes*, or the pikes of the Moors, were excellent formerly; and since the Spanish pikes have been equally famous. See Hartlib's legacy, p. 48. TOLLET.

Dro. S.

COMEDY OF ERRORS. 47

Dro. S. Nay, she is worse, she's the devil's dam; and here she comes in the habit of a light wench: and thereof comes, that the wenches say, *God damn me*, that's as much as to say, *God make me a light wench*. It is written, they appear to men like angels of light: light is an effect of fire, and fire will burn; *ergo*, light wenches will burn; Come not near her.

Cour. Your man and you are marvellous merry, Sir. Will you go with me? We'll mend our dinner here*.

Dro. S. Master, if you do expect spoon-meat, or bespeak a long spoon¹.

Ant. S. Why, Dromio?

Dro. S. Marry, he must have a long spoon, that must eat with the devil.

Ant. S. Avoid then, fiend! what tell'st thou me o. supping?
Thou art, as you are all, a sorceress:
I conjure thee to leave me, and be gone.

Cour. Give me the ring of mine you had at dinner,
Or, for my diamond, the chain you promis'd;
And I'll be gone, Sir, and not trouble you.

Dro. S. Some devils
Ask but the parings of one's nail, a rush,
A hair, a drop of blood, a pin, a nut,
A cherry-stone; but she, more covetous,
Would have a chain.
Master, be wise; and if you give it her,
The devil will shake her chain, and fright us with it.

Cour. I pray you, Sir, my ring, or else the chain;
I hope you do not mean to cheat me so.

Ant. S. Avaunt, thou witch? Come, Dromio, let us go.

---

* *We'll mend our dinner here.*] i. e. by purchasing something additional in the adjoining market. MALONE.

¹ — *if you do expect spoon-meat, or bespeak a long spoon.*] In the old copy *you* is accidentally omitted. It was supplied by the editor of the second folio. I believe some other words were passed over by the compositor—perhaps of this import:—" if you do expect spoon-meat, *either stay away*, or bespeak a long spoon." *Or* in the sense of *before*, which it signified in old Language, is hardly admissible here. In all the old writers, if I mistake not, when employed in this sense, it is joined with a personal pronoun,—" or ere *I* went,"—" or ere *he* spake;" &c. or with an article; as in the instance quoted by Mr. Steevens:

" He shall be murder'd *or* the guests come in."

I do not recollect to have ever met with it used as an adverb, for *beforehand*.—The proverb mentioned afterwards by Dromio, is again alluded to in *the Tempest*. MALONE.

Dro.

Dro. S. Fly pride, says the peacock: Mistress, that you
know. [*Exeunt.* ANT. *and* DRO.

Cour. Now, out of doubt, Antipholus is mad,
Else would he never so demean himself:
A ring he hath of mine worth forty ducats,
And for the same he promis'd me a chain;
Both one, and other, he denies me now.
The reason that I gather he is mad,
(Besides this present instance of his rage,)
Is a mad tale, he told to-day at dinner,
Of his own doors being shut against his entrance.
Belike, his wife, acquainted with his fits,
On purpose shut the doors against his way.
My way is now, to hie home to his house,
And tell his wife, that, being lunatic,
He rush'd into my house, and took perforce
My ring away: This course I fittest choose;
For forty ducats is too much to lose. [*Exit.*

SCENE II.

The same.

Enter ANTIPHOLUS *of* Ephesus, *and an* Officer.

Ant. E. Fear me not, man, I will not break away;
I'll give thee, ere I leave thee, so much money,
To warrant thee, as I am 'rested for.
My wife is in a wayward mood to-day;
And will not lightly trust the messenger,
That I should be attach'd in Ephesus:
I tell you, 'twill sound harshly in her ears.—

Enter DROMIO *of* Ephesus, *with a rope's-end.*

Here comes my man; I think he brings the money.
How now, Sir? have you that I sent you for?
Dro. E. Here's that, I warrant you, will pay them all*.
Ant. E. But where's the money?
Dro. E. Why, Sir, I gave the money for the rope!
Ant. E. Five hundred ducats, villain, for a rope?
Dro. E. I'll serve you, Sir, five hundred at the rate.
Ant. E. To what end did I bid thee hie thee home?

* — *will pay .b. a of.*] See Tempest, Vol. I. MALONE.

Dro. E.

COMEDY OF ERRORS. 49

Dro. E. To a rope's end, Sir; and to that end am I return'd.

Ant. E. And to that end, Sir, I will welcome you.
[*beating him.*

Off. Good Sir, be patient.

Dro. E. Nay, 'tis for me to be patient; I am in adversity.

Off. Good now, hold thy tongue.

Dro. E. Nay, rather persuade him to hold his hands.

Ant. E. Thou whoreson, senseless villain!

Dro. E. I would I were senseless, Sir, that I might not feel your blows.

Ant. E. Thou art sensible in nothing but blows, and so is an ass.

Dro. E. I am an ass, indeed; you may prove it by my long ears. I have serv'd him from the hour of my nativity to this instant, and have nothing at his hands for my service, but blows: when I am cold, he heats me with beating; when I am warm, he cools me with beating: I am wak'd with it, when I sleep; rais'd with it, when I sit; driven out of doors with it, when I go from home; welcomed home with it, when I return: nay, I bear it on my shoulders, as a beggar wont her brat; and, I think, when he hath lamed me, I shall beg with it from door to door.

Enter ADRIANA, LUCIANA, *and the* Courtezan, *with* PINCH[3], *and Others.*

Ant. E. Come, go along; my wife is coming yonder.

Dro. E. Mistress, *respice finem*, respect your end[4]; or rather the prophecy, like the parrot, *Beware the rope's end.*
Ant. E.

---

[3] — *Pinch.*] The direction in the old copy is,—" and a *school-master* called Pinch." In many country villages the pedagogue is still a reputed conjurer. So, in Ben Jonson's *Staple of News:* " I would have ne'er a cunning *school-master* in England, I mean a cunning man as a school-master; that is, a conjurer, &c." STEEVENS.

[4] *Mistress, respice finem, respect your end; or rather the prophecy, like the parrot, Beware the rope's end.*] These words seem to allude to a famous pamphlet of that time, wrote by Buchanan against the lord of Liddington, which ends with these words, *Respice funem, respice funem.* But to what purpose, unless our author would shew that he could quibble as well in English, as the other in Latin, I confess I know not. As for *prophesying like the parrot,* this alludes to people's teaching that

Ant. E. Wilt thou still talk? [*beats him.*
Cour. How say you now? is not your husband mad?
Adr. His incivility confirms no less.—
Good Doctor Pinch, you are a conjurer;
Establish him in his true sense again,
And I will please you what you will demand.
Luc. Alas, how fiery and how sharp he looks!
Cour. Mark, how he trembles in his ecstasy!
Pinch. Give me your hand, and let me feel your pulse.
Ant. E. There is my hand, and let it feel your ear.
Pinch. I charge thee, Satan, hous'd within this man,
To yield possession to my holy prayers,
And to thy state of darkness hie thee straight;
I conjure thee by all the saints in heaven.
Ant. E. Peace, doting wizard, peace; I am not mad.
Adr. O, that thou wert not, poor-distressed soul!
Ant. E. You minion, you, are these your customers*?
Did this companion with the saffron face
Revel and feast it at my house to day,
Whilst upon me the guilty doors were shut,
And I deny'd to enter in my house?
Adr. O, husband, God doth know you din'd at home,
Where 'would you had remain'd until this time,
Free from these slanders and this open shame!
Ant. E. I din'd at home⁴! Thou villain, what say'st thou?
Dro. Sir, sooth to say, you did not dine at home.
Ant. E. Were not my doors lock'd up, and I shut out?
Dro. E. Perdy, your doors were lock'd, and you shut out.
Ant. E. And did not she herself revile me there?
Dro. E. Sans fable, she herself revil'd you there.
Ant. E. Did not her kitchen-maid rail, taunt, and scorn me?

---

bird unlucky words; with which, when any passenger was offended, it was the standing joke of the wise owner to say, *Take heed, Sir, my parrot prophesies.* To this, Butler hints, where, speaking of Ralpho's skill in augury, he says:

 "Could tell what subtlest parrots mean,
 "That speak, and think contrary clean;
 "What member 'tis of whom they talk,
 "When they cry rope, and walk, knave, wa'k." WARB.

* —*your customers?*] A *customer* is used in Othello for a common woman. Here it seems to signify one who visits such women. MALONE.

⁴ *I din'd at home!*] *I* is not found in the old copy. It was inserted by Mr. Theobald. MALONE.

Dro. E.

Dro. E. Certes[5], she did; the kitchen-vestal[6] scorn'd you.
Ant. E. And did not I in rage depart from thence?
Dro. E. In verity, you did;—my bones bear witness,
That since have felt the vigour of his rage.
Adr. Is't good to sooth him in these contraries?
Pinch. It is no shame; the fellow finds his vein,
And, yielding to him, humours well his frenzy.
Ant. E. Thou hast suborn'd the goldsmith to arrest me.
Adr. Alas, I sent you money to redeem you,
By Dromio here, who came in haste for it.
Dro. E. Money by me? heart and good-will you might,
But, surely, Master, not a rag of money.
Ant. E. Went'st not thou to her for a purse of ducats?
Adr. He came to me, and I deliver'd it.
Luc. And I am witness with her, that she did.
Dro. E. God and the rope-maker, bear me witness,
That I was sent for nothing but a rope!
Pinch. Mistress, both man and master is possess'd;
I know it by their pale and deadly looks:
They must be bound, and laid in some dark room.
Ant. E. Say, wherefore didst thou lock me forth to-day,
And why dost thou deny the bag of gold?
Adr. I did not, gentle husband, lock thee forth.
Dro. E. And, gentle master, I receiv'd no gold;
But I confess, Sir, that we were lock'd out.
Adr. Dissembling villain, thou speak'st false in both.
Ant. E. Dissembling harlot, thou art false in all;
And art confederate with a damned pack,
To make a loathsome abject scorn of me:
But with these nails I'll pluck out these false eyes,
That would behold in me this shameful sport.

[PINCH *and his Assistants bind* ANT. *and* DROMIO.

Adr. O, bind him, bind him, let him not come near me.
Pinch. More company:—the fiend is strong within him.
Luc. Ah me, poor man, how pale and wan he looks!
Ant. E. What, will you murder me? Thou jailor, thou,
I am thy prisoner; wilt thou suffer them
To make a rescue?
Off. Masters, let him go:
He is my prisoner, and you shall not have him.

[5] — *Certes,*] i. e. *certainly.* STEEVENS.
[6] — *kitchen-vestal.*] Her charge being like that of the vestal virgins, to keep the fire burning. JOHNSON.

Pinch. Go, bind this man, for he is frantic too.
Adr. What wilt thou do, thou peevish officer[7]?
Hast thou delight to see a wretched man
Do outrage and displeasure to himself?
Off. He is my prisoner; if I let him go,
The debt he owes, will be requir'd of me.
Adr. I will discharge thee, ere I go from thee;
Bear me forthwith unto his creditor,
And, knowing how the debt grows, I will pay it.
Good Master Doctor, see him safe convey'd
Home to my house.—O most unhappy day!
Ant. E. O most unhappy strumpet[8]!
Dro. E. Master, I am here enter'd in bond for you.
Ant. E. Out on thee, villain! wherefore dost thou mad me?
Dro. E. Will you be bound for nothing? be mad,
Good Master; cry, the devil.—
Luc. God help, poor souls, how idly do they talk!
Adr. Go bear him hence.—Sister, go you with me.—
[*Exeunt* Pinch *and Assistants with* Ant. *and* Dro.
Say now, whose suit is he arrested at?
Off. One Angelo, a goldsmith: Do you know him?
Adr. I know the man: What is the sum he owes?
Off. Two hundred ducats.
Adr. Say, how grows it due?
Off. Due for a chain, your husband had of him.
Adr. He did bespeak a chain for me, but had it not.
Cour. When as your husband, all in rage, to-day
Came to my house, and took away my ring,
(The ring I saw upon his finger now,)
Straight after did I meet him with a chain.
Adr. It may be so, but I did never see it.—
Come jailer, bring me where the goldsmith is,
I long to know the truth hereof at large.

Enter Antipholus *of Syracuse with his rapier drawn, and*
Dromio *of Syracuse.*

Luc. God, for thy mercy! they are loose again.
Adr. And come with naked swords; let's call more help,

[7] — *thou peevish officer?*] This is the second time that in the course of this play, *peevish* has been used for *foolish.* Steevens.
[8] — *unhappy strumpet!*] Unhappy is here used in one of the senses of *unlucky;* i. e. *mischievous.* Steevens.

To

To have them bound again.

Off. Away, they'll kill us.

[*Exeunt Officer,* ADR. *and* LUC.

Ant. S. I see, these witches are afraid of swords.

Dro. S. She, that would be your wife, now ran from you.

Ant. S. Come to the Centaur; fetch our stuff[9] from thence:
I long, that we were safe and sound aboard.

Dro. S. Faith, stay here this night, they will surely do us no harm; you saw, they speak us fair, give us gold: methinks, they are such a gentle nation, that but for the mountain of mad flesh that claims marriage of me, I could find in my heart to stay here still, and turn witch.

Ant. S. I will not stay to-night for all the town;
Therefore away, to get our stuff aboard. [*Exeunt.*

ACT V. SCENE I.

The same.

Enter MERCHANT *and* ANGELO.

Ang. I am sorry, Sir, that I have hinder'd you;
But, I protest, he had the chain of me,
Though most dishonestly he doth deny it.

Mer. How is the man esteem'd here in the city?

Ang. Of very reverent reputation, Sir,
Of credit infinite, highly belov'd,
Second to none that lives here in the city;
His word might bear my wealth at any time.

Mer. Speak softly: yonder, as I think, he walks.

Enter ANTIPHOLUS *and* DROMIO *of* Syracuse.

Ang. 'Tis so; and that self-chain about his neck,
Which he forswore, most monstrously, to have.

---

9 — *our Stuff.*] i.e. our baggage. In the orders that were issued for the royal Progresses in the last century, the king's baggage was always thus denominated. MALONE.

D 3 Good

Good Sir, draw near to me, I'll speak to him.—
Signior Antipholus, I wonder much
That you would put me to this shame and trouble;
And not without some scandal to yourself,
With circumstance, and oaths, so to deny
This chain, which now you wear so openly:
Besides the charge, the shame, imprisonment,
You have done wrong to this my honest friend;
Who, but for staying on our controversy,
Had hoisted sail, and put to sea to-day:
This chain you had of me, can you deny it?

Ant. S. I think, I had; I never did deny it.

Mer. Yes, that you did, Sir; and forswore it too.

Ant. S. Who heard me to deny it, or forswear it?

Mer. These ears of mine, thou knowest, did hear thee:
Fy on thee, wretch! 'tis pity, that thou liv'st
To walk where any honest men resort.

Ant. S. Thou art a villain, to impeach me thus:
I'll prove mine honour and mine honesty
Against thee presently, if thou dar'st stand.

Mer. I dare, and do defy thee for a villain.

[*They draw.*

Enter ADRIANA, LUCIANA, *Courtezan, and Others.*

Adr. Hold, hurt him not, for God's sake; he is mad;—
Some get within him, take his sword away:
Bind Dromio too, and bear them to my house.

Dro. S. Run, master, run; for God's sake, take a house.
This is some priory;—In, or we are spoil'd.

[*Exeunt* ANTIPH. *and* DROMIO *to the Priory.*

Enter the Abbess.

Abb. Be quiet, people; Wherefore throng you hither?

Adr. To fetch my poor distracted husband hence:
Let us come in, that we may bind him fast,
And bear him home for his recovery.

Ang. I knew, he was not in his perfect wits.

Mer. I am sorry now, that I did draw on him.

Abb. How long hath this possession held the man?

Adr. This week he hath been heavy, sour, sad,
And much, much different from the man he was;
But, till this afternoon, his passion
Ne'er brake into extremity of rage.

Abb.

Abb. Hath he not lost much wealth by wreck of sea?
Bury'd some dear friend? Hath not else his eye
Stray'd his affection in unlawful love?
A sin prevailing much in youthful men,
Who give their eyes the liberty of gazing.
Which of these sorrows is he subject to?
Adr. To none of these, except it be the last;
Namely, some love, that drew him oft from home.
Abb. You should for that have reprehended him.
Adr. Why, so I did.
Abb. Ay, but not rough enough.
Adr. As roughly, as my modesty would let me.
Abb. Haply in private.
Adr. And in assemblies too.
Abb. Ay, but not enough.
Adr. It was the copy ¹ of our conference:
In bed, he slept not for my urging it;
At board, he fed not for my urging it;
Alone, it was the subject of my theme;
In company, I often glanced it;
Still did I tell him it was vile and bad.
Abb. And therefore came it, that the man was mad.
The venom clamours of a jealous woman
Poison more deadly than a mad dog's tooth.
It seems, his sleeps were hinder'd by thy railing:
And thereof comes it, that his head is light.
Thou say'st, his meat was sauc'd with thy upbraidings:
Unquiet meals make ill digestions,
Thereof the raging fire of fever bred;
And what's a fever but a fit of madness?
Thou say'st, his sports were hinder'd by thy brawls:
Sweet recreation barr'd, what doth ensue,
But moody and dull melancholy,
(Kinsman to grim and comfortless despair;)
And, at her heels ², a huge infectious troop

Of

¹ — *the copy*] i. e. the theme. We still talk of setting *a-pice* for boys. STEEVENS.

² *But moody and dull melancholy,*
(Kinsman to grim and comfortless despair;)
And, at her heels—] Mr. Heath, to remedy the defective metre of the first line, proposed to read—moody, *moping*, &c. and to obviate a female in the other, he would read—And at *their* heels—. The latter emendation is highly probable. In another place in this play, we have

Of pale diſtemperatures, and foes to life?
In food, in ſport, and life-preſerving reſt
To be diſturb'd, would mad or man, or beaſt:
The conſequence is then, thy jealous fits
Have ſcared thy huſband from the uſe of wits.

Luc. She never reprehended him but mildly,
When he demean'd himſelf rough, rude and wildly.
Why bear you theſe rebukes, and anſwer not?

Adr. She did betray me to my own reproof.—
Good people, enter, and lay hold on him.

Abb. No, not a creature enters in my houſe.

Adr. Then, let your ſervants bring my huſband forth.

Abb. Neither; he took this place for ſanctuary,
And it ſhall privilege him from your hands,
Till I have brought him to his wits again,
Or loſe my labour in aſſaying it.

Adr. I will attend my huſband, be his nurſe,
Diet his ſickneſs, for it is my office,
And will have no attorney but myſelf;
And therefore let me have him home with me.

Abb. Be patient; for I will not let him ſtir,
Till I have uſed the approved means I have,
With wholeſome ſyrups, drugs, and holy prayers,
To make of him a formal man again³:
It is a branch and parcel of mine oath,
A charitable duty of my order:
Therefore depart, and leave him here with me.

Adr. I will not hence, and leave my huſband here;
And ill it doth beſeem your holineſs,
To ſeparate the huſband and the wife.

Abb. Be quiet, and depart, thou ſhalt not have him.
[*Exit* Abbeſs.

Luc. Complain unto the Duke of this indignity.

Adr. Come, go; I will fall proſtrate at his feet,
And never riſe until my tears and prayers
Have won his grace to come in perſon hither,
And take perforce my huſband from the abbeſs.

have *their* for *her.* See p. 38. n. 9. *Kinſman,* however, (as an anonymous critic has obſerved,) might have been uſed by Shakſpeare in his licentious way, for *nearly related.* MALONE.

³ —*a formal man again;*] i. e. to bring him back to his ſenſes, and the forms of ſober behaviour. So, in *Meaſure for Meaſure,*—" *informal women,*" for juſt the contrary. STEEVENS.

Mer.

Mer. By this, I think, the dial points at five;
Anon, I am sure, the duke himself in person
Comes this way to the melancholy vale;
The place of death⁴ and sorry execution⁵,
Behind the ditches of the abbey here.
 Ang. Upon what cause?
 Mer. To see a reverend Syracusan merchant,
Who put unluckily into this bay
Against the laws and statutes of this town,
Beheaded publicly for his offence.
 Ang. See, where they come; we will behold his death.
 Luc. Kneel to the Duke, before he pass the abbey.

Enter DUKE *attended;* ÆGEON, *bare-headed; with the Heads-
 man and other Officers.*

 Duke. Yet once again proclaim it publicly,
If any friend will pay the sum for him,
He shall not die, so much we tender him.
 Adr. Justice, most sacred Duke, against the abbess!
 Duke. She is a virtuous and a reverend lady;
It cannot be, that she hath done thee wrong.
 Adr. May it please your grace, Antipholus, my husband—
Whom I made lord of me and all I had,
At your important letters⁶—this ill day
A most outrageous fit of madness took him;

---

⁴ *The place of* death—] The original copy has—*depth.* Mr. Rowe made the emendation. MALONE.

⁵ —*sorry execution*,] So, in *Macbeth:*
 " Of *sorriest* fancies your companions making."
Sorry had anciently a stronger meaning than at present. Thus, in Chaucer's *Prologue to The Sompnour's Tale,* v. 7283, late edit.:
 " This Frere, whan he loked had his fill
 " Upon the turments of this *sory* place."
Again, in the *Knightes Tale,* where the temple of Mars is described:
 " All full of chirking was that *sory* place." STEEVENS.

⁶ *Whom I made lord of me and all I had,
 At your* important *letters,*] Impo.t.nt for impo.tunate. JOHNSON.
So, in one of Shakspeare's Historical plays:
 "———— great France
 " My mourning and *important* tears hath ...e?."
Shakspeare, who gives to all nations the ..... f his own, seems from this passage to allude to a *court of w..* fo Ephesus. The *court of wards* was always considered as a griev... p.r ison. STEEVENS.
See a note on *King Henry IV.* P. ... Act III. Sc. v. MALONE.

D 5 'That

That defperately he hurry'd through the ftreet,
(With him his bondman, all as mad as he,)
Doing difpleafure to the citizens
By rufhing in their houfes, bearing thence
Rings, jewels, any thing his rage did like.
Once did I get him bound, and fent him home,
Whilft to take order[7] for the wrongs I went,
That here and there his fury had committed.
Anon, I wot not by what ftrong efcape[8],
He broke from thofe that had the guard of him;
And, with his mad attendant and himfelf[9],
Each one with ireful paffion, with drawn fwords,
Met us again, and, madly bent on us,
Chafed us away; till, raifing of more aid,
We came again to bind them: then they fled
Into this abbey, whither we purfued them;
And here the abbefs fhuts the gates on us,
And will not fuffer us to fetch him out,
Nor fend him forth, that we may bear him hence.
Therefore, moft gracious Duke, with thy command,
Let him be brought forth, and borne hence for help.

   Duke. Long fince, thy hufband ferv'd me in my wars;
And I to thee engag'd a prince's word,
When thou didft make him mafter of thy bed,
To do him all the grace and good I could.—
Go, fome of you, knock at the abbey-gate,
And bid the lady abbefs come to me;
I will determine this, before I ftir.

              Enter a Servant.

   Ser. O miftrefs, miftrefs, fhift and fave yourfelf!
My mafter and his man are both broke loofe,
Beaten the maids a-row[9], and bound the doctor,

---

[7] *— to take order*] i. e. to *take meafures.* STEEVENS.

[8] *— by what ftrong efcape,*] Though *ftrong* is not unintelligible, I fufpect we fhould read—*ftrange.* The two words are often confounded in the old copies. See p. 22. n. 1. MALONE.

[8] *And, with his mad attendant* and *himfelf,*] We fhould read—*mad himfelf.* WARBURTON.

We might read:
"*And here his mad attendant and himfelf.*" STEEVENS.
I fufpect, Shakfpeare is himfelf anfwerable for this inaccuracy.
                               MALONE.

[9] *— a-row*] i. e. fucceffively, one after another. STEEVENS.

Whose beard they have singed off with brands of fire';
And ever as it blazed, they threw on him
Great pails of puddled mire to quench the hair;
My master preaches patience to him, and the while
His man with scissars nicks him like a fool²:
And, sure, unless you send some present help,
Between them they will kill the conjurer.

Adr. Peace, fool, thy master and his man are here;
And that is false, thou dost report to us.

Sero. Mistress, upon my life, I tell you true;
I have not breath'd almost, since I did see it.
He cries for you, and vows, if he can take you,
To scorch your face³, and to disfigure you: [*Cry within.*
Hark, hark, I hear him, mistress; fly, be gone.

Duke. Come, stand by me, fear nothing: Guard with halberds.

---

¹ *Whose beard they have singed off with brands of fire:*] Such a ludicrous circumstance is not unworthy of the farce in which we find it introduced; but is rather out of place in an epic poem, amidst all the horrors and carnage of a battle:

"*Obvius ambustum torrem Corineus ab ara*
"*Corripit, et venienti Ebuso, plagamque ferenti,*
"*Occupat os flammis: Illi ingens barba reluxit,*
"*Nidoremque ambusta dedit.*"   Virg. Æneis, lib. xii.
    STEEVENS.

Shakspeare was a great reader of Plutarch, where he might have seen this method of shaving, in the life of Dion, p. 167. 4to. See North's Translation, in which ἐνδαλοῖς may be translated *brands*.   S. W.

² *His man with scissars nicks him like a fool:*] The force of this allusion I am unable to explain. Perhaps it was once the custom to cut the hair of idiots or jesters close to their heads. There is a proverbial simile—" Like crop the conjurer;" which might have been applied to either of these characters.   STEEVENS.

There is a penalty of ten shillings in one of king Alfred's ecclesiastical laws, if one opprobriously *shave* a common man like a *fool*.   TOLLET.

Fools undoubtedly were shav'd and nick'd in a particular manner, in our author's time, as is ascertained by the following passage in *The Choice of Change, containing the triplicitie of Divinitie, Philosophie, and Poetrie*, by S. R. Gent. 4to. 1598: "Three things used by monks, which provoke men to laugh at their follies, 1. They are *shoven and notched on the head, like fools*."

See also Florio's Italian Dictionary, 1598, in v. "*Zazzeato,* A shaven pate, a notted poule; a poule-pate; a gull, a ninnie."   MALONE.

³ *To scorch your face—*] We should read—*scotch,* i. e. hack, cut.
    WARBURTON.

To *scorch,* I believe, is right. He would have punished her as he had punished the conjurer before.   STEEVENS.

Adr. Ah me, it is my husband! Witness you,
That he is borne about invisible:
Even now we hous'd him in the abbey here;
And now he's there, past thought of human reason.

Enter ANTIPHOLUS *and* DROMIO *of Ephesus.*

Ant. E. Justice, most gracious Duke, oh, grant me
justice!
Even for the service that long since I did thee,
When I bestrid thee in the wars and took
Deep scars to save thy life: even for the blood
That then I lost for thee, now grant me justice.

Ege. Unless the fear of death doth make me dote,
I see my son Antipholus, and Dromio.

Ant. E. Justice, sweet prince, against that woman there.
She whom thou gav'st to me to be my wife;
That hath abused and dishonour'd me,
Even in the strength and height of injury!
Beyond imagination is the wrong,
That she this day hath shameless thrown on me.

Duke. Discover how, and thou shalt find me just.

Ant. E. This day, great Duke, she shut the doors upon
me,
While she with harlots [4] feasted in my house.

Duke. A grievous fault: Say, woman, didst thou so?

Adr. No, my good lord;—myself, he, and my sister,
To-day did dine together: So befal my soul,
As this is false, he burdens me withal!

Luc. Ne'er may I look on day, nor sleep on night,
But she tells to your highness simple truth!

Ang. O perjur'd woman! They are both forsworn.
In this the madman justly chargeth then.

Ant. E. My liege, I am advised [5] what I say;

---

[4] —*with harlots*] By this description he points out *Pinch* and his followers. *Harlot* was a term of reproach applied to cheats among men, as well as to wantons among women. Thus, in the *Fox*, Corbacchio says to Volpone,—" Out, harlot!"

Again, in the *Winter's Tale*;
" —— for the harlot king
" Is quite beyond mine arm."

The learned editor of *Chaucer's Canterbury Tales*, 4 vols. 8vo. 1775, observes, that in *The Romaunt of the Rose*, v 6068, *King of Harlots* is Chaucer's Translation of *Roy des ribauds*. STEEVENS.

[5] —*I am advised*—] i. e. I am not going to speak precipitately or rashly, but on reflexion and consideration. STEEVENS.

Neither

Neither disturb'd with the effect of wine,
Nor heady-rash, provok'd with raging ire,
Albeit, my wrongs might make one wiser mad.
This woman lock'd me out this day from dinner:
That goldsmith there, were he not pack'd with her,
Could witness it, for he was with me then;
Who parted with me to go fetch a chain,
Promising to bring it to the Porcupine,
Where Balthazar and I did dine together.
Our dinner done, and he not coming thither,
I went to seek him: in the street I met him;
And in his company, that gentleman.
There did this perjur'd goldsmith swear me down,
That I this day of him receiv'd the chain,
Which, God he knows, I saw not: for the which
He did arrest me with an officer.
I did obey; and sent my peasant home
For certain ducats; he with none return'd.
Then fairly I bespoke the officer,
To go in person with me to my house.
By the way we met
My wife, her sister, and a rabble more
Of vile confederates; along with them
They brought one Pinch; a hungry lean-faced villain,
A mere anatomy, a mountebank,
A thread-bare juggler, and a fortune-teller;
A needy, hollow-ey'd, sharp-looking wretch,
A living dead man: this pernicious slave,
Forsooth, took on him as a conjurer;
And, gazing in mine eyes, feeling my pulse,
And, with no face, as it were, out-facing me,
Cries out, I was possess'd: then altogether
They fell upon me, bound me, bore me thence;
And in a dark and dankish vault at home
There left me and my man, both bound together;
Till gnawing with my teeth my bonds in sunder,
I gain'd my freedom, and immediately
Ran hither to your grace; whom I beseech
To give me ample satisfaction
For these deep shames and great indignities.

   Ang. My Lord, in truth, thus far I witness with him;
That he dined not at home, but was lock'd out.
   Duke. But hath he such a chain of thee or no?

Ang. He had, my Lord: and when he ran in here,
Thefe people faw the chain about his neck.
  Mer. Befides, I will be fworn, thefe ears of mine
Heard you confefs, you had the chain of him,
After you firft forfwore it on the mart,
And, thereupon, I drew my fword on you;
And then you fled into this abbey here,
From whence, I think, you are come by miracle.
  Ant. E. I never came within thefe abbey walls,
Nor ever didft thou draw thy fword on me:
I never faw the chain, fo help me heaven!
And this is falfe, you burden me withal.
  Duke. Why, what an intricate impeach is this!
I think, you all have drunk of Circe's cup.
If here you hous'd him, here he would have been;
If he were mad, he would not plead fo coldly:—
You fay, he dined at home; the goldfmith here
Denies that faying:—Sirrah, what fay you?
  Dro. E. Sir, he dined with her there, at the Porcupine.
  Cour. He did; and from my finger fnatch'd that ring.
  Ant. E. 'Tis true, my liege, this ring I had of her.
  Duke. Saw'ft thou him enter at the abbey here?
  Cour. As fure, my liege, as I do fee your grace.
  Duke. Why, this is ftrange:—Go, call the abbefs hither;
I think you are all mated⁶, or ftark mad.
                                        [*Exit an Attendant.*
  Ege. Moft mighty Duke, vouchfafe me fpeak a word;
Haply, I fee a friend will fave my life,
And pay the fum that may deliver me.
  Duke. Speak freely, Syracufan, what thou wilt.
  Ege. Is not your name, Sir, call'd Antipholus?
And is not that your bondman Dromio?
  Dro. E. Within this hour I was his bondman, Sir,
But he, I thank him, gnaw'd in two my cords;
Now am I Dromio, and his man, unbound.
  Ege. I am fure, you both of you remember me.
  Dro. E. Ourfelves we do remember, Sir, by you;
For lately we were bound, as you are now.
You are not Pinch's patient, are you Sir?
  Ege. Why look you ftrange on me? you know me well.
  Ant. E. I never faw you in my life, till now.
  Ege. Oh! grief hath chang'd me, fince you faw me laft;

⁶ —————] See p. 32. n. 5. MALONE.

And

And careful hours, with Time's deformed ⁷ hand
Have written strange defeatures ⁸ in my face:
But tell me yet, dost thou not know my voice?

Ant. E. Neither?

Æge. Dromio, nor thou?

Dro. E. No, trust me, Sir, nor I.

Æge. I am sure, thou dost.

Dro. E. Ay, Sir? but I am sure, I do not; and whatsoever a man denies, you are now bound to believe him °.

Æge. Not know my voice! O, time's extremity!
Hast thou so crack'd and splitted my poor tongue,
In seven short years, that here my only son
Knows not my feeble key of untun'd cares?
Though now this grained face ⁹ of mine be hid
In sap-consuming winter's drizled snow,
And all the conduits of my blood froze up;
Yet hath my night of life some memory,
My wasting lamps some fading glimmer left,
My dull deaf ears a little use to hear:
All these old witnesses ¹ (I cannot err)
Tell me, thou art my son Antipholus.

Ant. E. I never saw my father in my life.

Æge. But seven years since, in Syracusa, boy,
Thou know'st, we parted: but, perhaps, my son,
Thou sham'st to acknowledge me in misery.

Ant. E. The Duke, and all that know me in the city,
Can witness with me that it is not so;
I ne'er saw Syracusa in my life.

Duke. I tell thee, Syracusan, twenty years
Have I been patron to Antipholus,

---

⁷ — *deformed*] for *deforming.* STEEVENS.

⁸ — *strange defeatures*] *defeature* is the privative of *feature.* The meaning is, time hath cancelled my features. JOHNSON.
Defeature is, I think, *alteration of feature, marks of deformity.* So, in our author's *Venus and Adonis:*
" —— to cross the curious workmanship of nature,
" To mingle beauty with infirmities,
" And pure perfection with impure *defeature.*" MALONE.

° — *you are now bound to believe him.*] Dromio is still quibbling on his favourite topic. See p. 61. MALONE.

⁹ — *this grained face*] i. e. furrow'd, like the *grain of wood.* So, in *Coriolanus:* " — my *grained* ash." STEEVENS.

¹ *All these old witnesses*—] By *old witnesses,* I believe, he means experienced, accustom'd ones, which are therefore less likely to err. So, in the *Tempest:*
" If these be *true spies* that I wear in my head."—. STEEVENS.

During

During which time he ne'er saw Syracusa:
I see, thy age and dangers make thee dote.

Enter Abbess, *with* ANTIPHOLUS *Syracusan and* DROMIO *Syracusan.*

Abb. Most mighty Duke, behold a man much wrong'd.
[*All gather to see him.*
Adr. I see two husbands, or mine eyes deceive me.
Duke. One of these men is Genius to the other;
And so of these: Which is the natural man,
And which the spirit? Who deciphers them?
Dro. S. I, Sir, am Dromio; command him away.
Dro. E. I, Sir, am Dromio; pray, let me stay.
Ant. S. Ægeon, art thou not? or else his ghost?
Dro. S. O, my old master! who hath bound him here?
Abb. Whoever bound him, I will loose his bonds,
And gain a husband by his liberty:—
Speak, old Ægeon, if thou be'st the man
That hadst a wife once call'd Æmilia,
That bore thee at a burden two fair sons:
O, if thou be'st the same Ægeon, speak,
And speak unto the same Æmilia!
Æge. If I dream not[1], thou art Æmilia;
If thou art she, tell me, where is that son
That floated with thee on the fatal raft?
Abb. By men of Epidamnum, he, and I,
And the twin Dromio, all were taken up;
But, by and by, rude fishermen of Corinth
By force took Dromio, and my son from them,
And me they left with those of Epidamnum:
What then became of them, I cannot tell;
I, to this fortune that you see me in.
Duke. Why, here begins his morning story right:
These two Antipholus's, these two so like,

---

[1] *If I dream not,*—] In the old copy this speech of Ægeon, and the subsequent one of the Abbess, follow the speech of the Duke, beginning with the words—" Why, here" &c. The transposition was suggested by Mr. Steevens. It scarcely requires any justification. Ægeon's answer to Æmilia's adjuration would necessarily immediately succeed to it. Besides, as Mr Steevens has observed, as these speeches stand in the old copy, the Duke comments on Æmilia's words before she has uttered them: The slight change now made renders the whole clear.
MALONE.

And

And these two Dromios, one in semblance [3]—
Besides her urging of her wreck at sea [4]—
These are the parents to these children,
Which accidentally are met together.
Antipholus, thou cam'st from Corinth first.

  Ant. S. No, Sir, not I; I came from Syracuse.
  Duke. Stay, stand apart; I know not which is which.
  Ant. E. I came from Corinth, my most gracious Lord.
  Dro. E. And I with him.
  Ant. E. Brought to this town by that most famous warrior,
Duke Menaphon, your most renown'd uncle.
  Adr. Which of you two did dine with me to-day?
  Ant. S. I, gentle Mistress.
  Adr. And are not you my husband?
  Ant. E. No, I say, nay, to that.
  Ant. S. And so do I, yet did she call me so;
And this fair gentlewoman, her sister here,
Did call me brother:—What I told you then,
I hope, I shall have leisure to make good:
If this be not a dream, I see, and hear.
  Ang. That is the chain, Sir, which you had of me.
  Ant. S. I think it be, Sir; I deny it not.
  Ant. E. And you, Sir, for this chain arrested me.
  Ang. I think, I did, Sir: I deny it not.
  Adr. I sent you money, Sir, to be your bail,
By Dromio; but I think, he brought it not.
  Dro. E. No, none by me.
  Ant. S. This purse of ducats I receiv'd from you.
And Dromio my man did bring them me:
I see, we still did meet each other's man,
And I was ta'en for him, and he for me,
And thereupon these Errors are arose.
  Ant. E. These ducats pawn I for my father here.
  Duke. It shall not need, thy father hath his life.
  Cour. Sir, I must have that diamond from you.
  Ant. E. There, take it; and much thanks for my good cheer.

---

[3] —*semblance,*] Is here a trisyllable. MALONE.

[4] —*of her wreck at sea*—] I suspect that a line following this has been lost; the import of which was, that *These circumstances all concurred to prove*—that These were the parents, &c. The line which I suppose to have been lost, and the following one, beginning perhaps with the same word, the omission might have been occasioned by the compositor's eye glancing from one to the other. MALONE.

Abb.

Abb. Renowned Duke, vouchsafe to take the pains
To go with us into the abbey here,
And hear at large discoursed all our fortunes:—
And all that are assembled in this place,
That by this sympathized one day's error
Have suffer'd wrong, go, keep us company,
And we shall make full satisfaction.—
Twenty-five years⁵ have I but gone in travail
Of you, my sons; nor, till this present hour⁶,
My heavy burdens are delivered:—
The Duke, my husband, and my children both,
And you the calendars of their nativity,
Go to a gossip's feast, and go with me;
After so long grief such nativity⁷!

Duke. With all my heart, I'll gossip at this feast.

[*Exeunt* DUKE, ABBESS, ÆGEON, COURTEZAN,
MERCHANT, ANGELO, *and Attendants.*

Dro. S. Master, shall I fetch your stuff from ship-board?
Ant. E. Dromio, what stuff of mine hast thou embark'd?
Dro. S. Your goods, that lay at host, Sir, in the Centaur.
Ant. S. He speaks to me; I am your master, Dromio:
Come, go with us; we'll look to that anon:
Embrace thy brother there, rejoice with him.

[*Exeunt* ANTIPHOLUS S. *and* E. ADR. *and* LUC.

Dro. S. There is a fat friend at your master's house,
That kitchen'd me for you to-day at dinner;
She now shall be my sister, not my wife.

Dro. E. Methinks, you are my glass, and not my brother;
I see by you, I am a sweet-faced youth.
Will you walk in to see their gossiping?

Dro. S. Not I, Sir, you are my elder.

---

⁵ Twenty-five *years*—] The old copy reads—*thirty-three*. The emendation, which is Mr. Theobald's, is supported by a passage in the first Act.—My youngest boy—At *eighteen* years, &c. compared with another in the present Act—But *seven* years since, &c. MALONE.

⁶ — nor, *till this present hour*,] The old copy reads—*and till*—. The emendation was made by Mr. Theobald. *Burden*, in the next line, was corrected by the editor of the second folio. MALONE.

⁷ *After so long grief such nativity!*] We should surely read—such *festivity*. Nativity lying so near, and the termination being the same of both words, the mistake was easy. JOHNSON.

The old reading may be right. She has just said, that to her, her sons were not *born* till now. STEEVENS.

Dro. E.

Dro. E. That's a question: how shall we try it?
Dro. S. We'll draw cuts for the senior: till then, lead thou first.
Dro. E. Nay, then, thus:
We came into the world, like brother and brother;
And now let's go hand in hand, not one before another⁹.

[*Exeunt.*

⁹ In this comedy we find more intricacy of plot than distinction of character; and our attention is less forcibly engaged, because we can guess in great measure how the denouement will be brought about. Yet the poet seems unwilling to part with his subject, even in this last and unnecessary scene, where the same mistakes are continued, till their power of affording entertainment is entirely lost. STEEVENS.

The long doggrel verses that Shakspeare has attributed in this play to the two Dromios, are written in that kind of metre which was usually attributed by the dramatic poets before his time, in their comic pieces, to some of their inferior characters; and this circumstance is one of many that authorize us to place the preceding comedy, as well as *Love's Labour's Lost*, and *The Taming of the Shrew*, (where the same kind of versification is likewise found), among our author's earliest productions; composed probably at a time when he was imperceptibly infected with the prevailing mode, and before he had completely learned "to deviate boldly from the common track." As these early pieces are now not easily met with, I shall subjoin a few extracts from some of them:

LIKE WILL TO LIKE.

1568.

" *Pryst.* If your name to me you will declare and showe,
" You may in this matter my minde the sooner knowe.
" *Tof.* Few wordes are best among friends, this is true,
" Wherefore I shall briefly show my name unto you.
" Tom Tospot it is, it need not to be printed,
" Wherefore I with Raife Roister must needs be acquainted." &c.

COMMON CONDITIONS.

[About 1570.]

" *Shift.* By gogs aloud, my maisters, we were not best longer here to
    " state,
" I thinke was never such a craftie knave before this daie. [*Ex.* Ambo.
" *Cond.* Are thei all gone? Ha, ha, well fare old Shift at a neede:
" By his wounden had I not devised this, I had hanged indeed.
" Tinkers, (qd you) tinke me no tinkers; I'll meddle with them no more.
" I thinke was never knave so used by a companie of tinkers before.
" By your leave I'll be so bolde as to looke about me and spie,
" Leaft any knaves for my coming down in ambush do lie.

" By

"By your licence I minde not to preache longer in this tree,
"My tinkerly slaves are packed hence, as farre as I maie see." &c.

PROMOS AND CASSANDRA.
1578.

" The wind is yl blowes no man's gaine; for cold I neede not care,
" Here is nine and twentie sutes of apparel for my share;
" And some, berlady, very good, for so standeth the case,
" As neither gentleman nor other Lord Promos sheweth any grace;
" But I marvel much, poore slaves, that they are hanged so soone,
" They were wont to staye a day or two, now scarce an afternoone," &c.

THE THREE LADIES OF LONDON.
1584.

" You think I am going to market to buy roll meate, do ye not?
" I thought so, but you are deceived, for I wot what I wot;
" I am neither going to the butchers, to buy veale, mutton, or beefe,
" But I am going to a bloodsucker, and who is it? saith Usurie, that
            theese."

THE COBLER'S PROPHECY.
1594.

" Quoth Nicenesse to Newfangle, thou art such a Jacke,
" That thou devisest sortie fashions for my ladie's backe.
" And thou, quoth he, art so possest with everie frantick toy,
" That following of my ladie's humour thou dost make her coy.
" For once a day for fashion-like my lady must be sicke,
" No meat but mutton, or at most the pinion of a chicket
" To-day her owne haire best becomes, which yellow is as gold,
" A periwig is better for to-morrow, blacke to behold:
" To-day in pumps and cheveril gloves to walk she will be bold,
" To-morrow cuffes and countenance, for feare of catching cold;
" Now is the barefast to be seene, straight on her muffer goes;
" Now is she buft up to the crowne, straight muffled to the nose."

See also *Gammer Gurton's Needle*, *Damon and Pythias*, &c. MALONE.

MUCH ADO ABOUT NOTHING.

PERSONS REPRESENTED.

Don Pedro, *Prince of* Arragon.
Don John, *his Bastard Brother.*
Claudio, *a young Lord of* Florence, *Favourite to Don* Pedro.
Benedick, *a young Lord of* Padua, *favoured likewise by Don Pedro.*
Leonato, *Governor of Messina.*
Antonio, *his Brother.*
Balthazar, *Servant to Don* Pedro.
Borachio, } *Followers of Don* John.
Conrade,
Dogberry, } *two foolish Officers.*
Verges,
A Sexton.
A Friar.
A Boy.

Hero, *Daughter to* Leonato.
Beatrice, *Niece to* Leonato.
Margaret, } *Gentlewomen attending on* Hero.
Ursula,

Messengers, Watch, and Attendants.

SCENE, Messina.

MUCH ADO ABOUT NOTHING[1].

ACT I. SCENE I.

Before Leonato's House.

Enter LEONATO, HERO, BEATRICE, *and Others, with a Messenger.*

Leon. I learn in this letter, that Don Pedro of Arragon comes this night to Messina.

Mess. He is very near by this; he was not three leagues off when I left him.

Leon.

---

[1] The story is from Ariosto, Orl. Fur. B. v. POPE.

It is true, as Mr. Pope has observed, that somewhat resembling the story of this play is to be found in the fifth book of the Orlando Furioso. In Spenser's Faery Queen, B. ii. c 4. as remote an original may be traced. A novel, however, of Belleforest, copied from another of Bandello, seems to have furnished Shakspeare with his fable, as it approaches nearer in all its particulars to the play before us, than any other performance known to be extant. I have seen so many versions from this once popular collection, that I entertain no doubt but that a great majority of the tales it comprehends, have made their appearance in an English dress. Of that particular story which I have just mentioned, viz. the 18th history in the third volume, no translation has hitherto been met with.

This play was entered at Stationer's Hall, Aug. 23, 1600. STEEVENS.

Ariosto is continually quoted for the fable of *Much Ado about Nothing*; but I suspect our poet to have been satisfied with the *Genevra* of Turberville. " The tale (says Harrington) is a pretie comical matter, and hath bin written in *English* verse some few years past, learnedly and with good grace, by M. George Turbervil." *Ariosto,* fol. 1591. p 39

FARMER.

I suppose

Leon. How many gentlemen have you loſt in this action?

Meſſ. But few of any ſort¹, and none of name.

Leon. A victory is twice itſelf, when the atchiever brings home full numbers. I find here, that Don Pedro hath beſtowed much honour on a young Florentine, call'd Claudio.

Meſſ. Much deſerved on his part, and equally remember'd by Don Pedro: He hath borne himſelf beyond the promiſe of his age; doing, in the figure of a lamb, the feats of a lion; he hath, indeed better better'd expectation, than you muſt expect of me to tell you how.

Leon. He hath an uncle here in Meſſina will be very much glad of it.

Meſſ. I have already delivered him letters, and there appears much joy in him; even ſo much, that joy could not ſhew itſelf modeſt enough, without a badge of bitterneſs³.

Leon. Did he break out into tears?

Meſſ. In great meaſure.

Leon. A kind overflow of kindneſs: There are no faces truer⁴ than thoſe that are ſo waſh'd. How much better is it to weep at joy, than to joy at weeping?

Bene. I pray you, is Signior Montanto return'd⁵ from the wars, or no?

---

¹ I ſuppoſe this comedy to have been written in 1600, in which year it was printed. See *An Attempt to aſcertain the order of Shakſpeare's plays*, Vol. i. MALONE.

² *— of any* ſort,] i. e. of any kind. *Sort*, in our author's age, was often uſed for *high rank*, (ſee p. 71.) but it ſeems from the context to have here the ſame ſignification as at preſent. MALONE.

³ *— joy could act ſhew itſelf modeſt enough, without a badge of bitterneſs.*] This is an idea which Shakſpeare ſeems to have been delighted to introduce. It occurs again in *Macbeth*:

"——— my plenteous joys,
"Wanton in fullneſs ſeek to hide themſelves
"In drops of ſorrow." STEEVENS.

A *badge* being the diſtinguiſhing *mark* worn in our author's time by the ſervants of noblemen, &c. on the ſleeve of their liveries, with his uſual licence he employs the word to ſignify a *mark* or *token* in general. So, in *Macbeth*:

"Their hands and faces were all *badg'd* with blood." MALONE.

⁴ *— no faces* truer] That is, none *honeſter*, none *more ſincere*.
JOHNSON.

⁵ *— is Signior* Montanto *return* — *Montanto* was one of the ancient terms of the fencing-ſchool. So, in the *Merry Wives of Windſor*: " — thy reverſe, thy diſtance, thy *montant*." STEEVENS.

Meſſ.

ABOUT NOTHING. 73

Mess. I know none of that name, lady; there was none such in the army of any sort⁶.

Leon. What is he that you ask for, niece?

Hero. My cousin means Signior Benedick of Padua.

Mess. O, he's return'd; and as pleasant as ever he was.

Beat. He set up his bills⁷ here in Messina, and challenged Cupid at the flight⁸; and my uncle's fool, reading the challenge, subscribed for Cupid, and challenged him at the bird-bolt⁹.—I pray you how many hath he kill'd and eaten in these wars? But how many hath he kill'd? for, indeed, I promise to eat all of his killing.

Leon. Faith, niece, you tax Signior Benedick too much; but he'll be meet with you¹, I doubt it not.

Mess. He hath done good service, lady, in these wars.

Beat. You had musty victual, and he hath holp to eat it: he's a very valiant trencher-man, he hath an excellent stomach.

Mess. And a good soldier too, lady.

Beat. And a good soldier to a lady;—But what is he to a lord?

Mess. A lord to a lord, a man to a man; stuff'd with all honourable virtues².

Beat.

⁶ —*of any sort*] i. e. of *any quality above the common*. WARBURTON.

⁷ *He set up his bills,* &c.] Beatrice means, that Benedick published a general challenge, like a prize-fighter. So, in Nashe's *Have with you to Saffron Walden,* &c. 1596: "—*setting up bills* like a bearward or fencer, what fights we shall have, and what weapons she will meet me at." STEEVENS.

⁸ —*challenged Cupid at the* flight:] To challenge at the *flight,* was a challenge to shoot with an *arrow. Flight* means an arrow. STEEV.

The *flight,* which in the Latin of the middle ages was called *flecta,* was a fleet arrow with narrow feathers, usually shot at rovers. See Blount's *Antient Tenures,* p. 64, edit. 1679. MALONE.

⁹ —*at the* bird-bolt.] A *bolt* seems to have been a general, though not an universal, term for an arrow. See Minshue's *Dict.* In v. The word is still used in the common proverb, "A fool's *bolt* is soon shot." That particular species of arrow which was employed in killing birds, was called a *bird*-bolt. MALONE.

The *bird-bolt* is a short thick arrow without point, and spreading at the extremity so much, as to leave a flat surface, about the breadth of a shilling. Such are to this day in use to kill rooks with, and are shot from a cross-bow. STEEVENS.

¹ —*he'll be meet with you,*] This a very common expression in the midland counties, and signifies *he'll be your match, he'll be even with you.* STEEVENS.

² —stuff'd *with all honourable virtues.*] Stuff'd, in this first instance, has no ridiculous meaning. Mr. Edwards observes, that *Mede,* in his

VOL. IV. E *Discourses*

Beat. It is so, indeed; he is no less than a stuff'd man: but for the stuffing—well, we are all mortal ³.

Leon. You must not, Sir, mistake my niece: there is a kind of merry war betwixt Signior Benedick and her: they never meet, but there's a skirmish of wit between them.

Beat. Alas, he gets nothing by that. In our last conflict, four of his five wits ⁴ went halting off, and now is the whole man govern'd with one: so that if he have wit enough to keep himself warm, let him bear it for a difference ⁵ between himself and his horse; for it is all the wealth that he hath left, to be known a reasonable creature.—Who is his companion now? he hath every month a new sworn brother.

Mess. Is it possible?

Beat. Very easily possible: he wears his faith ⁶ but as the fashion of his hat, it ever changes with the next block ⁷.

Mess. I see, lady, the gentleman is not in your books ⁸.

Beat.

Discourse on Scripture, speaking of Adam, says, "—he whom God had *stuffed* with so many excellent qualities." Edwards's MS. Again, in the *Winter's Tale*;

"———whom you know
"Of *stuff'd sufficiency.*" STEEVENS.

³ —*he is no less than a* stuff'd *man: but for the* stuffing—*well, we are all mortal.*] Beatrice starts an idea at the words *stuff'd man*; and prudently checks herself in the pursuit of it. A *stuff'd man* was one of the many cant phrases for a *cuckold*. FARMER.

⁴ —*four of his five wits*—] In our author's time *wit* was the general term for intellectual powers. The *wits* seem to have been reckoned five, by analogy to the five senses, or the five inlets of ideas.
JOHNSON.

⁵ —*if he hath wit enough to keep himself warm, let him bear it for a* difference, *&c.*] Such a one has *wit enough to keep himself warm*, is a proverbial expression. To bear any thing for a *difference*, is a term in heraldry. So, in *Hamlet*, Ophelia says: "—you may wear yours with a *difference.* STEEVENS.

⁶ —*he wears his* faith—] Not religious profession, but *profession of friendship.* WARBURTON.

⁷ —*with the next* block.] A *block* is the mould on which a hat is formed. The old writers sometimes use the word *block*, for the *hat itself.* STEEVENS.

⁸ —*the gentleman is not in your books.*] This is a phrase used, I believe, by more than understand it. *To be in one's books* is *to be in one's codicils or will, to be among friends set down for legacies.* JOHNSON.

I rather think that the *books* alluded to, are memorandum-books, like the visiting-books of the present age. It appears to have been anciently

Beat. No: an he were, I would burn my study. But, pray you, who is his companion? Is there no young squarer⁹ now, that will make a voyage with him to the devil?

Mess. He is most in the company of the right noble Claudio.

Beat. O lord! he will hang upon him like a disease: he is sooner caught than the pestilence, and the taker runs presently mad. God help the noble Claudio! if he have caught the Benedick, it will cost him a thousand pound ere he be cured.

Mess. I will hold friends with you, lady.
Beat. Do, good friend.
Leon. You'll ne'er run mad, niece.
Beat. No, not till a hot January.
Mess. Don Pedro is approach'd.

Enter Don PEDRO, *attended by* BALTHAZAR *and others;* Don JOHN, CLAUDIO, *and* BENEDICK.

D. Pedro. Good Signior Leonato, you are come to meet your trouble: the fashion of the world is to avoid cost, and you encounter it.

---

ciently the custom to *chronicle the small beer* of every occurrence, whether literary or domestic, in *Table-books.*

It should seem from the following passage in the *Taming of the Shrew,* that this phrase might have originated from the *Herald's Office:*

"A herald, Kate! oh, put me *in thy books!*"

After all, the following note in one of the Harleian MSS. No. 847, may be the best illustration:

"W. C. to Henry Pradsham, Gent. the owner of this book:
  'Some write their fantasies in verse
  "*In theire bookes* where they friendshippe shewe,
  "Wherein oft tymes they due rehearse
  "The great good will that they do owe, &c." STEEVENS.

To be in a man's books originally meant, to be in the list of his retainers. Sir John Mandeville tell us, "alle the mynstrelles that come before the great Chan ben witholden with him, as of his houshold, and entered in his *bookes,* as for his own men." FARMER.

A *servant* and a *lover,* in Cupid's Vocabulary, were synonymous. Hence perhaps the phrase—*to be in a person's books*—was applied equally to the lover and the menial attendant. MALONE.

⁹ —*young squarer*—] A *squarer* I take to be a choleric, quarrelsome fellow, for in this sense Shakspeare uses the word to *square.* So, in the *Midsummer Night's Dream,* it is said of Oberon and Titania, that they never meet but that they square. So the sense may be, *Is there no hot-blooded youth that will keep him company through all his mad pranks?* JOHNSON.

E 2   *Leon.*

Leon. Never came trouble to my house in the likeness of your grace: for trouble being gone, comfort should remain; but, when you depart from me, sorrow abides, and happiness takes his leave.

D. Pedro. You embrace your charge¹ too willingly.—I think, this is your daughter.

Leon. Her mother hath many times told me so.

Bene. Were you in doubt, Sir, that you ask'd her?

Leon. Signior Benedick, no; for then were you a child.

D. Pedro. You have it full, Benedick: we may guess by this what you are, being a man. Truly, the lady fathers herself²:—Be happy, lady! for you are like an honourable father.

Bene. If Signior Leonato be her father, she would not have his head on her shoulders for all Messina, as like him as she is.

Beat. I wonder, that you will still be talking, Signior Benedick; no body marks you.

Bene. What, my dear lady Disdain! are you yet living?

Beat. Is it possible, disdain should die, while she hath such meet food to feed it, as Signior Benedick³? Courtesy itself must convert to disdain, if you come in her presence.

Bene. Then is courtesy a turn-coat:—But it is certain, I am loved of all ladies, only you excepted: and I would I could find in my heart that I had not a hard heart; for, truly, I love none.

Beat. A dear happiness to women; they would else have been troubled with a pernicious suitor. I thank God, and my cold blood, I am of your humour for that; I had rather hear my dog bark at a crow, than a man swear he loves me.

Bene. God keep your ladyship still in that mind! so some gentleman or other shall 'scape a predestinate scratch'd face.

Beat. Scratching could not make it worse, an 'twere such a face as yours were.

¹ —*your charge*—] That is, your *burthen*, your *incumbrance*. JOHNSON.

² *Truly, the lady fathers herself*:]
  Sit suo similis patri
  Manlio, et facile inscis
  Noscitetur ab omnibus,
  Et pudicitiam suæ
  Matris indicet ore. *Catul.* 57. MALONE.

³ —*such meet food to feed it, as Signior Benedick?*] A kindred thought occurs in *Coriolanus,* Act II. sc. 1.: " Our very priests must become mockers, if they encounter such ridiculous subjects as you are." STEEV.

Bene.

Bene. Well, you are a rare parrot-teacher.

Beat. A bird of my tongue, is better than a beast of yours.

Bene. I would, my horse had the speed of your tongue; and so good a continuer: But keep your way o' God's name; I have done.

Beat. You always end with a jade's trick; I know you of old.

D. Pedro. This is the sum of all: Leonato—Signior Claudio, and Signior Benedick—my dear friend Leonato hath invited you all. I tell him, we shall stay here at the least a month; and he heartily prays, some occasion may detain us longer: I dare swear he is no hypocrite, but prays from his heart.

Leon. If you swear, my lord, you shall not be forsworn.—Let me bid you welcome, my lord: being reconciled to the prince your brother, I owe you all duty.

D. John. I thank you [4]: I am not of many words, but I thank you.

Leon. Please it your grace lead on?

D. Pedro. Your hand, Leonato; we will go together.

[*Exeunt all but* BENEDICK *and* CLAUDIO.

Claud. Benedick, didst thou note the daughter of Signior Leonato?

Bene. I noted her not; but I look'd on her.

Claud. Is she not a modest young lady?

Bene. Do you question me, as an honest man should do, for my simple true judgment? or would you have me speak after my custom, as being a professed tyrant to their sex?

Claud. No, I pray thee, speak in sober judgment.

Bene. Why, i'faith, methinks she is too low for a high praise, too brown for a fair praise, and too little for a great praise: only this commendation I can afford her; that were she other than she is, she were unhandsome; and being no other but as she is, I do not like her.

Claud. Thou think'st, I am in sport; I pray thee, tell me truly how thou likest her.

Bene. Would you buy her, that you enquire after her?

Claud. Can the world buy such a jewel?

Bene. Yea, and a case to put it into. But speak you this

---

[4] — *I thank you;*] The poet has judiciously marked the gloominess of Don John's character, by making him averse to the common forms of civility. Sir J. HAWKINS.

with a sad brow? or do you play the flouting Jack [5]; to tell us Cupid is a good hare-finder [6], and Vulcan a rare carpenter? Come, in what key shall a man take you, to go in the song? [7]

Claud. In mine eye, she is the sweetest lady that ever I looked on.

Bene. I can see yet without spectacles, and I see no such matter: there's her cousin, an she were not possess'd with a fury, exceeds her as much in beauty, as the first of May doth the last of December. But, I hope, you have no intent to turn husband; have you?

Claud. I would scarce trust myself, though I had sworn the contrary, if Hero would be my wife.

Bene. Is't come to this, i'faith? Hath not the world one man, but he will wear his cap with suspicion [8]? Shall I never

---

[5] *— the flouting Jack:*] *Jack*, in our author's time, I know not why, was a term of contempt. So, in *King Henry IV.* P. I. Act III. " — the prince is a *Jack*, a sneak-cup." Again, in the *Taming of the Shrew:*

"―――― rascal fidler,
" And twangling *Jack*, with such vile terms, &c."

See in *Minsheu's Dict.* 1617, " A *Jack* sauce, or saucie *Jack.*" See also Chaucer's *Cant. Tales*, ver. 14816, and the note, edit. Tyrwhitt. MALONE.

[6] *— to tell us Cupid is a good hair-finder,* &c.] I believe no more is meant by those ludicrous expressions than this—Do you mean, says Beuedick, to amuse us with improbable stories?

An ingenious correspondent, whose signature is R. W. explains the passage in the same sense, but more amply. " Do you mean to tell us that love is not blind, and that fire will not consume what is combustible?—for both these propositions are implied in making Cupid a *good hare-finder,* and Vulcan (the God of fire) *a good carpenter.* In other words, *would you convince me, whose opinion is this head is well known, that you can be in love without being blind, and can play with the flame of beauty without being scorched?* STEEVENS.

I explain the passage thus: *Do you scoff and mock in telling us that Cupid, who is blind, is a good hare-finder, which requires a quick eye-sight; and that Vulcan, a blacksmith, is a rare carpenter?* TOLLET.

After such attempts at decent illustration, I am afraid that he who wishes to know why Cupid is a good *hare-finder,* must discover it by the assistance of many quibbling allusions of the same sort, about *hair* and *bear,* in Mercutio's song in *Romeo and Juliet,* Act ii. COLLINS.

[7] *— to go in the song?*] i. e. to join with you in your song. STEEV.

[8] *— wear his cap with suspicion?*] That is, subject his head to the disquiet of jealousy. JOHNSON.

In the *Palace of Pleasure,* 8vo. 1566, p. 233, we have the following passage:

I never see a batchelor of threescore again? Go to, i'faith; an thou wilt needs thrust thy neck into a yoke, wear the print of it, and sigh away Sundays⁹. Look, Don Pedro is return'd to seek you.

Re-enter Don PEDRO.

D. Pedro. What secret hath held you here, that you followed not to Leonato's?

Bene. I would, your grace would constrain me to tell.

D. Pedro. I charge thee on thy allegiance.

Bene. You hear, Count Claudio: I can be secret as a dumb man, I would have you think so; but on my allegiance—mark you this, on my allegiance:—He is in love. With who?—now that is your grace's part.—Mark, how short his answer is:—With Hero, Leonato's short daughter.

Claud. If this were so, so were it uttered ¹.

Bene. Like the old tale, my lord: it is not so, nor 'twas not so; but, indeed, God forbid it should be so.

Claud. If my passion change not shortly, God forbid it should be otherwise.

D. Pedro. Amen, if you love her, for the lady is very well worthy.

Claud. You speak this to fetch me in, my lord.

D. Pedro. By my troth, I speak my thought.

Claud. And, in faith, my lord, I spoke mine.

---

passage: "All they that wear horns, be pardoned to wear their caps upon their heads." HENDERSON.

In our author's time none but the inferior classes wore caps, and such persons were termed in contempt *flat-caps*. All gentlemen wore hats. Perhaps therefore the meaning is, Is there not one man in the world prudent enough to keep out of that state where he must live in apprehension that his *night-cap* will be worn occasionally by another. So, in *Othello*:

"For I fear Cassio with my *night-cap* too." MALONE.

⁹ —*sigh away Sundays.*] A proverbial expression to signify that a man has no rest at all; when Sunday, a day formerly of ease and diversion, was passed so uncomfortably. WARBURTON.

The allusion is most probably to the strict manner in which the sabbath was observed by the *puritans*, who usually spent that day in *sighs* and *groanings*, and other hypocritical marks of devotion. STEEVENS.

¹ *Claud. If this were so, so were it uttered.*] Claudio, evading at first a confession of his passion, says; if I had really confided such a secret to him, yet he would have blabbed it in this manner. In his next speech, he thinks proper to avow his love; and when Benedick says, *God forbid it should be so,* i. e. God forbid he should even wish to marry her; Claudio replies, God forbid I should not wish it. STEEVENS.

Bene. And, by my two faiths and troths, my lord, I speak mine.

Claud. That I love her, I feel.

D. Pedro. That she is worthy, I know.

Bene. That I neither feel how she should be loved, nor know how she should be worthy, is the opinion that fire cannot melt out of me: I will die in it at the stake.

D. Pedro. Thou wilt ever an obstinate heretic in the despight of beauty.

Claud. And never could maintain his part, but in the force of his will [2].

Bene. That a woman conceived me, I thank her; that she brought me up, I likewise give her most humble thanks: but that I will have a rechcat winded in my forehead [3], or hang my bugle in an invisible baldric [4], all women shall pardon me: Because I will not do them the wrong to mistrust any, I will do myself the right to trust none; and the fine is, (for the which I may go the finer,) I will live a bachelor.

D. Pedro. I shall see thee, ere I die, look pale with love.

Bene. With anger, with sickness, or with hunger, my lord; not with love: prove, that ever I lose more blood with love, than I will get again with drinking, pick out mine eyes with a ballad-maker's pen, and hang me up at the door of a brothel-house for the sign of blind Cupid.

D. Pedro. Well, if ever thou dost fall from this faith, thou wilt prove a notable argument [5].

Bene. If I do, hang me in a bottle like a cat [6], and shoot at

---

[2] *— but in the force of his will.*] Alluding to the definition of a heretic in the schools. WARBURTON.

[3] *— but that I will have a rechcat winded in my forehead,*] That is, I will wear a horn on my forehead which the huntsman may blow. A *rechcat* is the sound by which dogs are called back. Shakspeare had no mercy upon the poor cuckold, his horn is an inexhaustible subject of merriment. JOHNSON.

A *rechcat* is a particular lesson upon the horn, to call dogs back from the scent; from the old French word *recet*. HANMER.

[4] *— hang my bugle in an invisible baldrick,*] *Bugle,* i. e. bugle-horn — hunting-horn. The meaning seems to be — or that I should be compelled to carry any horn that I must wish to remain invisible, and that I should be ashamed to hang openly in my belt or baldric. It is still said of the mercenary cuckold, that he *carries his horns in his pocket.* STEEV.

[5] *— notable argument.*] An eminent subject for satire. JOHNSON.

[6] *in a bottle like a cat,*] As to *the cat and bottle,* I can procure no better information than the following, which does not exactly suit with the text

at me; and he that hits me, let him be clap'd on the shoulder, and call'd Adam[7].

D. Pedro. Well, as time shall try:
In time the savage bull doth bear the yoke[8].

Bene. The savage bull may; but if ever the sensible Benedick bear it, pluck off the bull's horns, and set them in my forehead: and let me be vilely painted; and in such great letters as they write, *Here is good horse to hire,* let them signify under my *Sign*—*Here you may see Benedick the marry'd man.*

Claud. If this should ever happen, thou would'st be horn-mad.

D. Pedro. Nay, if Cupid have not spent all his quiver in Venice[9], thou wilt quake for this shortly.

Bene. I look for an earthquake too then.

D. Pedro. Well, you will temporize with the hours. In the mean time, good Signior Benedick, repair to Leonato's; commend me to him, and tell him, I will not fail him at supper; for, indeed, he hath made great preparation.

Bene. I have almost matter enough in me for such an embassage; and so I commit you——

Claud. To the tuition of God; from my house, (if I had it)——

tent. In some counties of England, a cat was formerly closed up with soot in a wooden bottle, (such as that in which shepherds carry their liquor) and was suspended on a line. He who beat out the bottom as he ran under it, and was nimble enough to escape its contents, was regarded as the hero of this inhuman diversion. STEEVENS.

To shoot at a cat in a wooden *bottle*; with its head only visible, might have been one of the cruel sports of our ancestors; for I find another kind of torment was formerly practised on this animal, at fairs, &c. So, in Braithwaithe's *Strappado for the Divell,* 8vo. 1615; p. 164:

"———who'd not thither runne,
"As 'twere to *whip the cat* at Abington?" MALONE.

[7] —*and call'd* Adam.] Adam Bell was a noted outlaw, and celebrated for his archery. MALONE.

See *Reliques of Anc. Eng. Poet.* Vol. i. p. 143. STEEVENS.

[8] *In time the savage bull doth bear the yoke.*] This line is taken from the *Spanish Tragedy,* or *Hieronymo,* &c. 1605. See a note on the last edit. of Dodsley's Old Plays, Vol. xii. p. 387. STEEVENS.

The *Spanish Tragedy* was written and acted before 1593. MALONE.

[9] —*if Cupid hath not spent all his quiver in* Venice.] All modern writers agree in representing Venice in the same light as the ancients did Cyprus. And it is this character of the people that is here alluded to. WARBURTON.

E 5   *D. Pedro.*

D. Pedro. The sixth of July; your loving friend, Benedick.

Bene. Nay mock not, mock not: The body of your discourse is sometimes guarded with fragments[1], and the guards are but slightly basted on neither: ere you flout old ends any further, examine your conscience[2]; and so I leave you. [*Exit* BENEDICK.

Claud. My liege, your highness now may do me good.

D. Pedro. My love is thine to teach; teach it but how, And thou shalt see how apt it is to learn Any hard lesson that may do thee good.

Claud. Hath Leonato any son, my lord?

D. Pedro. No child but Hero, she's his only heir: Dost thou affect her, Claudio?

Claud. O my lord,
When you went onward on this ended action,
I look'd upon her with a soldier's eye,

---

[1] — *guarded with fragments.*] Guards were ornamental laces or borders. STEEVENS.

[2] — *ere you flout old ends any farther, examine your conscience;*] Before you endeavour to distinguish yourself any more by antiquated allusions, examine whether you can fairly claim them for your own. This, I think, is the meaning; or it may be understood in another sense, *examine, if your sarcasms do not touch yourself.* JOHNSON.

Dr Johnson's latter explanation is, I believe, the true one. By *old ends* the speaker may mean the conclusion of letters commonly used in Shakspeare's time; "From my house this sixth of July, &c." So, in the conclusion of a letter which our author supposes Lucrece to write:

"So I commend me from our house in grief;
"My woes are tedious, though my words are brief."

See *the Rape of Lucrece*, p. 547, edit 1780, and the note there.

This kind of conclusion to letters was not obsolete in our author's time, as has been suggested. Michael Drayton concludes one of his letters to Drummond of Hawthornden in 1619, thus: "And so wishing you all happiness, *I commend you to God's tuition*, and rest your assured friend." So also Lord Salisbury concludes a letter to Sir Ralph Winwood, April 7th, 1610, "—And so I commit you to God's protection."
Winwood's *Memorials*, iii. 147.

Old ends, however, may refer to the quotation that D. Pedro had made from the *Spanish Tragedy.* "Ere you attack me on the subject of love, with fragments of old plays, examine whether you are yourself free from its power." So King Richard:

"With odd *old ends*, stol'n forth of holy writ." MALONE.

Barnaby Googe thus ends his dedication to the first edition of *Palingenius*, 12mo. 1560: And thus committing your Ladiship with all yours to the *tuition* of the most merciful God, I *ende*, From Staple-inne at London, the eighte and twenty of March." REED.

That

That lik'd, but had a rougher task in hand
Than to drive liking to the name of love:
But now I am return'd, and that war-thoughts
Have left their places vacant, in their room
Come thronging soft and delicate desires,
All prompting me how fair young Hero is,
Saying, I lik'd her ere I went to wars.

D. Pedro. Thou wilt be like a lover presently,
And tire the hearer with a book of words:
If thou dost love fair Hero, cherish it;
And I will break with her, and with her father,
And thou shalt have her: Was't not to this end,
That thou began'st to twist so fine a story?

Claud. How sweetly do you minister to love,
That know love's grief by his complexion!
But lest my liking might too sudden seem,
I would have salv'd it with a longer treatise.

D. Pedro. What need the bridge much broader than the flood?
The fairest grant is the necessity [3]:
Look, what will serve, is fit: 'tis once, thou lov'st [4];
And I will fit thee with the remedy.
I know, we shall have revelling to-night;
I will assume thy part in some disguise,
And tell fair Hero I am Claudio;
And in her bosom I'll unclasp my heart,
And take her hearing prisoner with the force
And strong encounter of my amorous tale:
Then, after, to her father will I break;
And, the conclusion is, she shall be thine:
In practice let us put it presently. [*Exeunt.*

SCENE II.

A Room in Leonato's *House.*

Enter LEONATO *and* ANTONIO.

Leo. How now, brother? Where is my cousin, your son? Hath he provided this music?

---

[3] *The fairest grant is the necessity.*] No one can have a better reason for granting a request than the necessity of its being granted. WARB.

[4] — *once, thou lov'st;*] Once has here, I believe, the force of—*once for all.* So, in *Coriolanus:* " Once, if he do require our voices, we ought not to deny him." MALONE.

Ant.

Ant. He is very busy about it. But, brother, I can tell you strange news that you yet dream'd not of.

Leon. Are they good?

Ant. As the event stamps them; but they have a good cover, they show well outward. The prince and Count Claudio, walking in a thick-pleached alley ⁵ in my orchard, were thus much overheard by a man of mine: The prince discover'd to Claudio, that he loved my niece your daughter, and meant to acknowledge it this night in a dance; and, if he found her accordant, he meant to take the present time by the top, and instantly break with you of it.

Leon. Hath the fellow any wit that told you this?

Ant. A good sharp fellow; I will send for him, and question him yourself.

Leon. No, no; we will hold it as a dream, till it appear itself:—but I will acquaint my daughter withal, that she may be the better prepared for an answer, if peradventure this be true: Go you and tell her of it. [*Several persons cross the stage here.*] Cousins, you know what you have to do.—O, I cry you mercy, friend; go you with me, and I will use your skill:—Good cousin, have a care this busy time. [*Exeunt.*

SCENE III.

Another Room in Leonato's *House.*

Enter Don JOHN *and* CONRADE.

Con. What the good-year⁶, my Lord! why are you thus out of measure sad?

D. John. There is no measure in the occasion that breeds it, therefore the sadness is without limit.

Con. You should hear reason.

D. John. And when I have heard it, what blessing bringeth it?

Con. If not a present remedy, yet a patient sufferance.

D. John. I wonder, that thou being (as thou say'st thou art) born under Saturn, goest about to apply a moral medicine to a mortifying mischief. I cannot hide what

---

⁵ —*a thick-pleached alley*] *Thick-pleached* is thickly interwoven.
STEEVENS.

⁶ —*good-year,*] A corruption of *goujeres*, lues venerea. MALONE.

I am:

I am⁷: I must be sad when I have cause, and smile at no man's jests; eat when I have stomach, and wait for no man's leisure; sleep when I am drowsy, and tend on no man's business; laugh when I am merry, and claw no man in his humour⁸.

Con. Yea, but you must not make the full show of this, till you may do it without controlment. You have of late stood out against your brother, and he hath ta'en you newly into his grace; where it is impossible you should take root, but by the fair weather that you make yourself: it is needful that you frame the season for your own harvest.

D. John. I had rather be a canker in a hedge than a rose in his grace⁹; and it better fits my blood to be disdain'd of all, than to fashion a carriage to rob love from any: in this, though I cannot be said to be a flattering honest man, it must not be deny'd but I am a plain-dealing villain. I am trusted with a muzzle, and infranchised with a clog; therefore I have decreed not to sing in my cage: If I had my mouth, I would bite; if I had my liberty, I would do my liking: in the mean time, let me be that I am, and seek not to alter me.

Con. Can you make no use of your discontent?

---

⁷ *I cannot hide what I am:*] This is one of our author's natural touches. An envious and unsocial mind, too proud to give pleasure, and too sullen to receive it, always endeavours to hide its malignity from the world and from itself, under the plainness of simple honesty, or the dignity of haughty independence. JOHNSON.

⁸ — *claw no man in his humour.*] To *claw* is to flatter. So *the pope's claw-backs*, in bishop Jewel, are the pope's *flatterers*. The sense is the same in the proverb, *Mulus mulum scabit.* JOHNSON.

⁹ *I had rather be a canker in a hedge, than a rose in his grace;*] A *canker* is the *canker* rose, *dog-rose*, *cynosbatus*, or *hip*. The sense is, I would rather live in obscurity the wild life of nature, than owe dignity or estimation to my brother. He still continues his wish of gloomy independence. But what is the meaning of *a rose in his grace?* JOHNSON.

The latter words are intended as an answer to what Conrade has just said—" he hath ta'en you newly into his *grace*, where it is impossible that you should take *root*, &c." In *Macbeth* we have a kindred expression:

"———— Welcome hither:
" I have begun to *plant* thee, and will labour
" To make thee full of *growing*."

Again, in *K. Henry VI. P. iii*:
" I'll *plant* Plantagenet, *root* him up who dares." MALONE.
So in Shakspeare's 54th Sonnet:
" The *canker* blooms have full as deep a d—,
" As the perfumed tincture of the *rose*." STEEVENS.

D. John.

D. John. I make all use of it, for I use it only. Who comes here? What news, Borachio?

Enter BORACHIO.

Bora. I came yonder from a great supper: the prince, your brother, is royally entertain'd by Leonato; and I can give you intelligence of an intended marriage.

D. John. Will it serve for any model to build mischief on? What is he for a fool, that betroths himself to unquietness?

Bora. Marry, it is your brother's right hand.

D. John. Who? the most exquisite Claudio?

Bora. Even he.

D. John. A proper squire! and who, and who? which way looks he?

Bora. Marry, on Hero, the daughter and heir of Leonato.

D. John. A very forward March-chick! How came you to this?

Bora. Being entertain'd for a perfumer, as I was smoking a musty room, comes me the prince and Claudio, hand in hand, in sad conference [1]: I whipt me behind the arras; and there heard it agreed upon, that the prince should woo Hero for himself, and having obtained her, give her to count Claudio.

D. John. Come, come, let us thither; this may prove food to my displeasure: that young start-up hath all the glory of my overthrow; if I can cross him any way, I bless myself every way: You are both sure [2], and will assist me.

Con. To the death, my lord.

D. John. Let us to the great supper; their cheer is the greater, that I am subdued: 'Would the cook were of my mind!—Shall we go prove what's to be done?

Bora. We'll wait upon your Lordship. [*Exeunt.*

---

[1] — *sad conference.*] Sad in this, as in a former instance, signifies serious. STEEVENS.

[2] — *both sure.*] i. e. 'to be depended on. STEEVENS.

ACT

ACT II. SCENE I.

A Hall in Leonato*'s House.*

Enter LEONATO, ANTONIO, HERO, BEATRICE, *and Others.*

Leo. Was not count John here at supper?

Ant. I saw him not.

Beat. How tartly that gentleman looks! I never can see him, but I am heart-burn'd an hour after[3].

Hero. He is of a very melancholy disposition.

Beat. He were an excellent man, that were made just in the mid-way between him and Benedick: the one is too like an image, and says nothing; and the other, too like my lady's eldest son, evermore tattling.

Leon. Then half Signior Benedick's tongue in count John's mouth, and half count John's melancholy in Signior Benedick's face—

Beat. With a good leg, and a good foot, uncle, and money enough in his purse. Such a man would win any woman in the world—if he could get her good will.

Leon. By my troth, niece, thou wilt never get thee a husband, if thou be so shrewd of thy tongue.

Ant. In faith, she's too curst.

Beat. Too curst is more than curst: I shall lessen God's sending that way: for it is said, *God sends a curst cow short horns*; but to a cow too curst he sends none.

Leon. So, by being too curst, God will send you no horns.

Beat. Just, if he send me no husband; for the which blessing, I am at him upon my knees every morning and evening: Lord! I could not endure a husband with a beard on his face; I had rather lie in the woollen.

Leon. You may light upon a husband, that hath no beard.

---

[3] — *heart-burn'd an hour after.*] The pain commonly called the *heart-burn*, proceeds from an *acid* humour in the stomach, and is therefore properly enough imputed to *tart* looks. JOHNSON.

Beat. What should I do with him? dress him in my apparel, and make him my waiting-gentlewoman? He that hath a beard, is more than a youth; and he that hath no beard, is less than a man: and he that is more than a youth, is not for me; and he that is less than a man, I am not for him: Therefore I will even take sixpence in earnest of the bear-herd, and lead his apes into hell.

Leon. Well then, go you into hell.

Beat. No; but to the gate: and there will the devil meet me, like an old cuckold, with horns on his head, and say, *Get you to heaven, Beatrice, get you to heaven; here's no place for you maids:* so deliver I up my apes, and away to Saint Peter for the heavens; he shews me where the bachelors sit, and there live we as merry as the day is long.

Ant. Well, niece, [*to Hero.*] I trust, you will be ruled by your father.

Beat. Yes, faith; it is my cousin's duty to make curt'sy, and say, *Father, as it pleaſe you:*—but yet for all that, cousin, let him be a handsome fellow, or else make another curt'sy, and say, *Father, as it pleaſe me.*

Leon. Well, niece, I hope to see you one day fitted with a husband.

Beat. Not till God make man of some other metal than earth. Would it not grieve a woman to be over-master'd with a piece of valiant dust? to make account of her life to a clod of wayward marle? No, uncle, I'll none: Adam's sons are my brethren, and truly, I hold it a sin to match in my kindred.

Leon. Daughter, remember, what I told you: if the prince do solicit you in that kind, you know your answer.

Beat. The fault will be in the music, cousin, if you be not woo'd in good time: if the prince be too important [4], tell him there is measure in every thing [5], and so dance out the answer. For hear me, Hero; Wooing, wedding and repenting, is a Scotch jig, a measure, and a cinque-pace: the first suit is hot and hasty, like a Scotch jig, and full as fantastical; the wedding, mannerly modest, as a measure, full of state and ancientry; and then comes repentance, and, with

---

[4] — *if the prince be too* important,] *Important* here, and in many other places, is *importunate.* See p. 22, n. 6. JOHNSON.

[5] — *there is* measure *in every thing.*] A *measure* in old language, beside its ordinary meaning, signified also a dance. MALONE.

his

his bad legs, falls into the cinque-pace faster and faster, till he sink into his grave.

Leon. Cousin, you apprehend passing shrewdly.

Beat. I have a good eye, uncle; I can see a church by day-light.

Leon. The revellers are entering; brother, make good room.

Enter Don PEDRO, CLAUDIO, BENEDICK, BALTHAZAR; *Don* JOHN, BORACHIO, MARGARET, URSULA, *and others, mask'd.*

Don Pedro. Lady, will you walk about with your friend⁵?

Hero. So you walk softly, and look sweetly, and say nothing, I am yours for the walk; and, especially, when I walk away.

D. Pedro. With me in your company?

Hero. I may say so, when I please.

D. Pedro. And when please you to say so?

Hero. When I like your favour; for God defend, the lute should be like the case⁶!

D. Pedro. My visor is Philemon's roof; within the house is Jove⁷.

Hero. Why, then your visor should be thatch'd.

D. Pedro. Speak low, if you speak love. [*takes her aside.*

Bene. Well, I would you did like me.

Marg. So would not I, for your own sake; for I have many ill qualities.

Bene. Which is one?

---

⁵ *— your friend?*] *Friend,* in our author's time, was the common term for a *lover.* So also in French and Italian. MALONE.

⁶ *— the lute should be like the case!*] i. e. that your face should be as homely and coarse as your mask. THEOBALD.

⁷ *— My visor is Philemon's roof; within the house is* Jove.] The poet alludes to the story of Baucis and Philemon, who, as Ovid describes it, lived in a thatched cottage, (stipulis et canna tecta palustri,) which received two gods (Jupiter and Mercury) under its roof. Don Pedro insinuates to Hero, that though his visor is but ordinary, he has something *godlike* within; alluding either to his dignity, or the qualities of his mind and person. THEOBALD.

The line of Ovid above quoted is thus translated by Golding, 1587:
" The *roofe* thereof was *thatched* all with straw and fennish reede."
MALONE.

Marg.

Marg. I say my prayers aloud.

Bene. I love you the better; the hearers may cry Amen [8].

Marg. God match me with a good dancer!

Balth. Amen.

Marg. And God keep him out of my sight when the dance is done!—Answer, clerk.

Balth. No more words; the clerk is answer'd.

Urs. I know you well enough; you are Signior Antonio.

Ant. At a word, I am not.

Urs. I know you by the wagling of your head.

Ant. To tell you true, I counterfeit him.

Urs. You could never do him so ill-well, unless you were the very man: Here's his dry hand [9] up and down; you are he, you are he.

Ant. At a word, I am not.

Urs. Come, come; do you think, I do not know you by your excellent wit? Can virtue hide itself? Go to, mum, you are he: graces will appear, and there's an end.

Beat. Will not you tell me who told you so?

Bene. No, you shall pardon me.

Beat. Nor will you not tell me who you are?

Bene. Not now.

Beat. That I was disdainful—and that I had my good wit out of the *Hundred Merry Tales* [1];—Well, this was Signior Benedick that said so.

Bene. What's he?

Beat.

[8] — *Amen.*] When Benedick says, *the bearers may cry, amen*, we must suppose that he leaves Margaret, and goes in search of some other sport. Margaret utters a wish for a good partner, Balthazar, who is represented as a man of the fewest words, repeats Benedick's *Amen*, and leads her off, desiring, as he says in the following short speech, to put himself to no greater expence of breath. STEEVENS.

[9] — *his dry hand*] A *dry* hand was anciently regarded as the sign of a cold constitution. To this Maria, in *Twelfth Night*, alludes; Act i. sc. iii. STEEVENS.

[1] — *Hundred Merry Tales*;] The book, to which Shakspeare alludes; was an old translation of *Les cent Nouvelles Nouvelles*. The original was published at Paris, in the black letter, before the year 1500, and is said to have been written by some of the royal family of France. Ames mentions a translation of it prior to the time of Shakspeare. Of this collection there are frequent entries in the register of the Stationers' Company. The first I met with was in Jan. 1581. STEEVENS.

This

Beat. I am sure, you know him well enough.
Bene. Not I, believe me.
Beat. Did he never make you laugh?
Bene. I pray you, what is he?
Beat. Why, he is the prince's jester: a very dull fool; only his gift is in devising impossible slanders [1]: none but libertines delight in him; and the commendation is not in his wit, but in his villainy [2]; for he both pleaseth men, and angers them, and then they laugh at him, and beat him: I am sure, he is in the fleet; I would he had boarded me.
Bene. When I know the gentleman, I'll tell him what you say.
Beat. Do, do: he'll but break a comparison or two on me; which, peradventure, not mark'd, or not laugh'd at, strikes him into melancholy; and then there's a partridge's wing saved, for the fool will eat no supper that night. [*Music within.*] We must follow the leaders.
Bene. In every good thing.
Beat. Nay, if they lead to any ill, I will leave them at the next turning. [*Dance. Then exeunt all but Don* JOHN, BORACHIO, *and* CLAUDIO.
D. John. Sure, my brother is amorous on Hero, and hath withdrawn her father to break with him about it: The ladies follow her, and but one visor remains.
Bora. And that is Claudio: I know him by his bearing [4].
D. John. Are you not Signior Benedick?
Claud. You know me well; I am he.

This book was certainly printed before the year 1575, and is much repute, as appears from the mention of it in Laneham's Letter [concerning the entertainment at Kenelworth Castle]. It has been suggested to me, that there is no other reason than the word *hundred* to suppose this book a translation of the *Cent Nouvelles Nouvelles*. REED.

[1] — *his gift is in devising* impossible *slanders:*] *Impossible* slanders are, I suppose, such slanders as, from their absurdity and impossibility, bring their own confutation with them. JOHNSON.

[2] — *his villainy;*] By which she means his malice and impiety. By his impious jests, she insinuates, *he pleased libertines*; and by his *devising slanders* of them, he angered them. WARBURTON.

[4] — *his bearing.*] i. e. his carriage, his demeanour. So, in *Measure for Measure:*

 " How I may formally in person *bear me*,
 " Like a true friar." STEEVENS.

D. John.

D. John. Signior, you are very near my brother in his love: he is enamour'd on Hero; I pray you, dissuade him from her, she is no equal for his birth: you may do the part of an honest man in it.

Claud. How know you he loves her?

D. John. I heard him swear his affection.

Bora. So did I too; and he swore he would marry her to-night.

D. John. Come, let us to the banquet.

[*Exeunt Don* JOHN *and* BORACHIO.

Claud. Thus answer I in name of Benedick,
'Tis certain so:—the prince woes for himself.
But hear these ill news with the ears of Claudio.—
Friendship is constant in all other things,
Save in the office and affairs of love:
Therefore, all hearts in love use their own tongues⁵;
Let every eye negotiate for itself,
And trust no agent: for beauty is a witch,
Against whose charms faith melteth into blood⁶.
This is an accident of hourly proof,
Which I mistrusted not: Farewell therefore, Hero.

Re-enter BENEDICK.

Bene. Count Claudio?

Claud. Yea, the same.

Bene. Come, will you go with me?

Claud. Whither?

Bene. Even to the next willow, about your own business, count. What fashion will you wear the garland of? About your neck, like an usurer's chain⁷? or under your arm,

---

⁵ *Therefore, all hearts in love,* &c.] *Let,* which is found in the next line, is understood here. MALONE.

⁶ ——— *beauty is a witch,*

Against whose charms faith melteth into blood.] i. e. as wax when opposed to the fire kindled by a witch, no longer preserves the figure of the person whom it was designed to represent, but flows into a shapeless lump; so fidelity, when confronted with beauty, dissolves into our ruling passion, and is lost there like a drop of water in the sea. STEEVENS.

Blood, I think, means here *amorous desire.* So also in *the Merchant of Venice:* " The brain may devise laws for the *blood,* &c. MALONE.

⁷ — *usurer's chain?*] Chains of gold, of considerable value, were in our author's time usually worn by wealthy citizens, and others, in the same manner as they are now by the aldermen of London. See *the Puritan,* Act iii. sc. iii; *Albumazar,* Act i. sc. iii. and other pieces. REED.

Usury

arm, like a lieutenant's scarf? You must wear it one way, for the prince hath got your Hero.

Claud. I wish him joy of her.

Bene. Why, that's spoken like an honest drover; so they sell bullocks. But did you think, the prince would have served you thus?

Claud. I pray you, leave me.

Bene. Ho! now you strike like the blind man; 'twas the boy that stole your meat, and you'll beat the post.

Claud. If it will not be, I'll leave you. [*Exit.*

Bene. Alas, poor hurt fowl! Now will he creep into sedges.—But, that my lady Beatrice should know me, and not know me! The prince's fool!—Ha? it may be, I go under that title, because I am merry.—Yea; but so [8]; I am apt to do myself wrong: I am not so reputed: it is the base, though bitter disposition of Beatrice, that puts the world into her person [9], and so gives me out. Well, I'll be revenged as I may.

Re-enter Don PEDRO, HERO, *and* LEONATO.

D. Pedro. Now, Signior, where's the count? Did you see him?

Bene. Troth, my Lord, I have play'd the part of lady Fame. I found him here as melancholy as a lodge in a warren [1]; I told him, and, I think, I told him true, that your

Usury seems about this time to have been a common topic of invective. I have three or four dialogues, pasquils, and discourses on the subject, printed before the year 1602. From every one of these it appears, that the merchants were the chief usurers of the age. STEEVENS.

So, in *The Choice of Change, containing the triplicitie of Divinitie, Philosophie, and Poetrie,* by S. R. Gent. 4to. 1598: "Three sortes of people, in respect of use in necessitie, may be accounted good :—*Merchants,* for they may play the *usurers,* instead of the Jewes." Again, ibid. "There is a scarcitie of Jewes because Christians make an occupation of *usurie.*" MALONE.

[8] — Yea, but so] But hold; softly ;—not so fast. MALONE.

[9] — *it is the base,* though bitter, *disposition of Beatrice, who puts the world into her person,*] That is, *It is the disposition of Beatrice, who takes upon her to personate the world, and therefore represents the world as saying what she only says herself.*

Base, though bitter. I do not understand how *base* and *bitter* are inconsistent, or why what is *bitter* should not be *base.* I believe, we may safely read, *It is the base,* the *bitter disposition.* JOHNSON.

The *base* though *bitter,* may mean, the *ill-natured, though witty.* STEEVENS.

[1] — *as melancholy as a lodge in a warren,*] A parallel thought occurs

your grace had got the good will of this young lady[1]; and I offered him my company to a willow tree, either to make him a garland, as being forsaken, or to bind him up a rod, as being worthy to be whipt.

D. Pedro. To be whipt! What's his fault?

Bene. The flat transgression of a school-boy; who, being overjoy'd with finding a bird's nest, shews it his companion, and he steals it.

D. Pedro. Wilt thou make a trust a transgression? The transgression is in the stealer.

Bene. Yet it had not been amiss, the rod had been made, and the garland too; for the garland he might have worn himself; and the rod he might have bestow'd on you, who, as I take it, have stol'n his bird's nest.

D. Pedro. I will but teach them to sing, and restore them to the owner.

Bene. If their singing answer your saying, by my faith, you say honestly.

D. Pedro. The lady Beatrice hath a quarrel to you; the gentleman, that danced with her, told her, she is much wrong'd by you.

Bene. O, she misused me past the endurance of a block; an oak, but with one green leaf on it, would have answer'd her; my very visor began to assume life and scold with her: She told me, not thinking I had been myself, that I was the prince's jester; and that I was duller than a great thaw; huddling jest upon jest, with such impossible conveyance[3], upon

---

curs in the first chapter of Isaiah, where the prophet describing the desolation of Judah, says: " The daughter of Zion is left as a cottage in a vineyard, as a lodge in a garden of cucumbers, &c." I am informed that near Aleppo, these lonely buildings are still made use of, it being necessary, that the fields where water-melons, cucumbers, &c. are raised, should be regularly watched. I learn from Thomas Newton's *Herball to the Bible*, 8vo. 1587, that " So soone as the cucumbers, &c. be gathered, these lodges are abandoned of the watchmen and keepers, and no more frequented." From these forsaken buildings, it should seem, the prophet takes his comparison. STEEVENS.

[2] —*of this young lady:*] Benedick speaks of Hero as if she were on the stage. Perhaps both she and Leonato were meant to make their entrance with Don Pedro. When Beatrice enters, she is spoken of as coming in with only Claudio. STEEVENS.

I have regulated the entries accordingly. MALONE.

[3] —*such impossible conveyance,*] I believe the meaning is—*with a rapidity equal to that of* jugglers, *who appear to perform* impossibilities.

We

upon me, that I stood like a man at a mark, with a whole army shooting at me: She speaks poniards, and every word stabs: if her breath were as terrible as her terminations, there were no living near her, she would infect to the north star. I would not marry her, though she were endowed with all that Adam had left him before he transgress'd: she would have made Hercules have turn'd spit; yea, and have cleft his club to make the fire too. Come, talk not of her; you shall find her the infernal Até⁴ in good apparel. I would to God, some scholar would conjure her: for, certainly, while she is here, a man may live as quiet in hell, as in a sanctuary; and people sin upon purpose, because they would go thither: so, indeed, all disquiet, horror, and perturbation follow her.

Enter CLAUDIO *and* BEATRICE.

D. Pedro. Look, here she comes.

Bene. Will your grace command me any service to the world's end? I will go on the slightest errand now to the Antipodes, that you can devise to send me on; I will fetch you a tooth-picker now from the farthest inch of Asia; bring you the length of Prester John's foot; fetch you a hair off the great Cham's beard⁵; do you any embassage to the Pigmies, rather than hold three words con-

---

We have the same epithet again in *Twelfth Night*:—"there is no christian can ever believe such *impossible* passages of grossness. "So, Ford says in the *Merry Wives of Windsor*, "I will examine *impossible* places." Again, in *Julius Cæsar*:

"—— Now bid me run,
"And I will strive with things *impossible*,
"And get the better of them."

Conversate was the common term in our author's time for *sight of hand*. MALONE.

Impossible may be licentiously used for *unaccountable*. Beatrice has already said, that Benedick invents *impossible* slanders. STEEVENS.

⁴ — *the infernal Ate*—The *goddess of revenge*. STEEVENS.

⁵ — *bring you the length of Prester John's foot; fetch you a hair off the great Cham's beard*;] i. e. I will undertake the hardest task, rather than have any conversation with lady Beatrice. Alluding to the difficulty of access to either of those monarchs, but more particularly to the former. STEEVENS.

"Thou must goe to the citie of Babylon to the Admiral Gaudiffe, to bring me thy hand full of the heare of his beard, and foure of his greatest teeth. Alas, my Lord, (quoth the Barrons) we see well you desire greatly his death, when you charge him with such a message." *Huon of Bourdeaux*, ch. 17. BOWLE.

ference

ference with this harpy: You have no employment for me?

D. Pedro. None, but to desire your good company.

Bene. O God, Sir, here's a dish I love not; I cannot endure my lady Tongue.

D. Pedro. Come, lady, come; you have lost the heart of Signior Benedick.

Beat. Indeed, my Lord, he lent it me a while; and I gave him use for it [6], a double heart for a single one: marry, once before he won it of me with falle dice, therefore your grace may well say, I have lost it.

D. Pedro. You have put him down, lady, you have put him down.

Beat. So I would not he should do me, my Lord, lest I should prove the mother of fools. I have brought count Claudio, whom you sent me to seek.

D. Pedro. Why, how now, count? wherefore are you sad?

Claud. Not sad, my Lord.

D. Pedro. How then? Sick?

Claud. Neither, my Lord.

Beat. The count is neither sad, nor sick, nor merry, nor well: but civil, count; civil as an orange [7], and something of that jealous complexion.

D. Pedro. I'faith, lady, I think your blazon to be true; though, I'll be sworn, if he be so, his conceit is false. Here, Claudio, I have wooed in thy name, and fair Hero is won; I have broke with her father, and his good will obtained: name the day of marriage, and God give thee joy!

Leon. Count, take of me my daughter, and with her my fortunes: his grace hath made the match, and all grace say Amen to it!

Beat. Speak, count, 'tis your cue.

Claud. Silence is the perfectest herald of joy: I were but little happy, if I could say how much.—Lady, as you are mine, I am yours: I give away myself for you, and dote upon the exchange.

[6] — *I gave him use for it.*] *Ule*, in our author's time, meant *interest* of money. MALONE.

[7] — *civil as an orange.*] This conceit likewise occurs in Nashe's *Four Letters confuted*, 1593:—" for the order of my life, it is as *civil as an orange.*" STEEVENS.

Beat.

Beat. Speak, cousin; or, if you cannot, stop his mouth with a kiss, and let him not speak neither.

D. Pedro. In faith, Lady, you have a merry heart.

Beat. Yea, my Lord; I thank it, poor fool [a], it keeps on the windy side of care: my cousin tells him in his ear, that he is in her heart.

Claud. And so she doth, cousin.

Beat. Good Lord, for alliance [b]!—Thus goes every one to the world but I, and I am sun-burn'd [c]; I may sit in a corner, and cry, heigh ho! for a husband.

D. Pedro. Lady Beatrice, I will get you one.

Beat. I would rather have one of your father's getting: Hath your grace ne'er a brother like you? Your father got excellent husbands, if a maid could come by them.

D. Pedro. Will you have me, Lady?

Beat. No, my Lord, unless I might have another for working days; your grace is too costly to wear every day:—But, I beseech your grace, pardon me; I was born to speak all mirth, and no matter.

D. Pedro. Your silence most offends me, and to be merry best becomes you; for, out of question, you were born in a merry hour.

Beat. No, sure, my Lord, my mother cry'd; but then there was a star danced, and under that was I born.—Cousins, God give you joy.

Leon. Niece, will you look to those things I told you of?

Beat. I cry you mercy, uncle.—By your grace's pardon.
[*Exit* BEATRICE.

D. Pedro. By my troth, a pleasant-spirited lady.

Leon. There's little of the melancholy element in her [d], my Lord: she is never sad, but when she sleeps; and not

---

[a] *— poor fool.*] This was formerly an expression of tenderness. See *King Lear*, last scene; "And my *poor fool* is hang'd." MALONE.

[b] *Good Lord for* alliance!] Claudio has just called Beatrice *cousin*. I suppose, therefore, the meaning is—Good Lord, here have I got a new kinsman by marriage. MALONE.

[c] *Thus goes every one to the world but I, and I am sun-burn'd.*] What is it, *to go to the world?* perhaps, to enter by marriage into a settled state. Shakspeare, in *All's Well that ends Well*, uses the phrase *to go to the world for marriage*. But why is the unmarri'd lady *sun-burn'd?* JOHNSON.

I am *sun-burnt* may mean, I have lost my beauty, and am consequently no longer such an object as can tempt a man to marry. STEEVENS.

[d] *There's little of the* melancholy *element in her*,] "Does not our life consist of the *four elements?*" says Sir Toby, in *Twelfth Night*. So, also in *King Henry V*: "He is pure air and fire, and the *dull elements* of earth and water never appear in him." MALONE.

VOL. IV. F

ever sad then; for I have heard my daughter say, she hath often dream'd of unhappiness[1], and waked herself with laughing.

D. Pedro. She cannot endure to hear tell of a husband.

Leon. O, by no means, she mocks all her wooers out of suit.

D. Pedro. She were an excellent wife for Benedick.

Leon. O Lord, my Lord, if they were but a week marry'd, they would talk themselves mad.

D. Pedro. Count Claudio, when mean you to go to church?

Claud. To-morrow, my Lord: Time goes on crutches, till love have all his rites.

Leon. Not till Monday, my dear son, which is hence a just seven-night; and a time too brief too, to have all things answer my mind.

D. Pedro. Come, you shake the head at so long a breathing; but, I warrant thee, Claudio, the time shall not go dully by us: I will, in the interim, undertake one of Hercules' labours; which is, to bring Signior Benedick, and the Lady Beatrice into a mountain of affection[2], the one with the other. I would fain have it a match; and I doubt not but to fashion it, if you three will but minister such assistance as I shall give you direction.

Leon. My Lord, I am for you, though it cost me ten nights' watchings.

Claud. And I, my Lord.

D. Pedro. And you too, gentle Hero?

Hero. I will do any modest office, my Lord, to help my cousin to a good husband.

D. Pedro. And Benedick is not the unhopefullest husband that I know: thus far can I praise him; he is of a no-

---

[1] *—she hath often dream'd of* unhappiness,] *Unhappiness* signifies a wild, wanton, unlucky trick. Thus Beaumont and Fletcher, in their comedy of the *Maid of the Mill*:

"My dreams *are like my thoughts, honest and innocent;*
"*Yours are* unhappy." WARBURTON.

[2] *— into a* mountain *of affection,*] by a *mountain of affection,* I believe, is meant *a great deal of* affection. Thus, in *King Henry VIII*, " a *sea* of glory;" in *Hamlet,* "a *sea* of troubles." Again, in Howel's *Hist. of Sicily:* "though they see *mountains* of miseries heaped on ones's back." Again, in the *Comedy of Errors:*—the mountain of mad flesh that claims marriage of me." STEEVENS.

Shakspeare has many phrases equally harsh. He who would hazard such expressions as *a storm of fortunes, a vale of years,* and *a tempest of prosecution,* would not scruple to write *a mountain of affection."* MALONE.

ble strain [4], of approved valour, and confirm'd honesty. I will teach you how to humour your cousin, that she shall fall in love with Benedick:—and I, with your two helps, will so practise on Benedick, that, in despight of his quick wit and his queasy stomach, he shall fall in love with Beatrice. If we can do this, Cupid is no longer an archer; his glory shall be ours, for we are the only love-gods. Go in with me, and I will tell you my drift. [*Exeunt.*

SCENE II.

Another Room in Leonato's *House.*

Enter Don JOHN *and* BORACHIO.

D. John. It is so; the Count Claudio shall marry the daughter of Leonato.

Bora. Yea, my Lord; but I can cross it.

D. John. Any bar, any cross, any impediment will be medicinable to me: I am sick in displeasure to him; and whatsoever comes athwart his affection, ranges evenly with mine. How canst thou cross this marriage?

Bora. Not honestly, my Lord: but so covertly that no dishonesty shall appear in me.

D. John. Shew me briefly how.

Bora. I think, I told your Lordship, a year since, how much I am in the favour of Margaret, the waiting gentlewoman to Hero.

D. John. I remember.

Bora. I can, at any unseasonable instant of the night, appoint her to look out at her lady's chamber window.

D. John. What life is in that, to be the death of this marriage?

Bora. The poison of that lies in you to temper. Go you to the prince your brother; spare not to tell him, that he hath wrong'd his honour in marrying the renown'd Claudio (whose estimation do you mightily hold up) to a contaminated stale, such a one as Hero.

D. John. What proof shall I make of that?

Bora. Proof enough to misuse the prince, to vex Claudio, to undo Hero, and kill Leonato: Look you for any other issue?

[4] —*of a noble strain*] i. e. descent, lineage. REED.

D. John

D. John. Only to despite them, I will endeavour any thing.

Bora. Go then, find me a meet hour to draw Don Pedro and the Count Claudio, alone: tell them that you know that Hero loves me; intend a kind of zeal * both to the prince and Claudio, as—in love of your brother's honour who hath made this match; and his friend's reputation, who is thus like to be cozen'd with the semblance of a maid—that you have discover'd thus. They will scarcely believe this without trial: offer them instances; which shall bear no less likelihood, than to see me at her chamber-window; hear me call Margaret, Hero; hear Margaret term me Claudio⁵; and bring them to see this, the very night before the intended wedding: for, in the mean time, I will so fashion the matter, that Hero shall be absent; and there shall appear such seeming truth of Hero's disloyalty, that jealousy shall be call'd assurance, and all the preparation overthrown.

D. John. Grow this to what adverse issue it can, I will put it in practice: Be cunning in the working this, and thy fee is a thousand ducats.

Bora. Be thou constant in the accusation, and my cunning shall not shame me.

D. John. I will presently go learn their day of marriage.   [*Exeunt.*

* —*intend a kind of zeal*—] To *intend* is often used by our author for to *pretend*. So, in *K. Rich. III*: —" intend some fear." MALONE.

⁵ —*term me* Claudio;] Mr. Theobald proposes to read *Borachio*, instead of *Claudio*. How, he asks, could it disgrace Claudio to hear his mistress making use of his name tenderly? Or how could her naming *Claudio* make the prince and Claudio believe that she l ved *Borachio?* MALONE.

I am not convinced that this exchange is necessary. *Claudio* would naturally resent the circumstance of hearing another called by his own name; because, in that case, baseness of treachery would appear to be aggravated by wantonness, of insult: and, at the same time he would imagine the person so distinguish'd to be *Borachio*, because *Don John* was previously to have informed both him and *Don Pedro*, that *Borachio* was the favoured lover. STEEVENS.

Claudio would naturally be enraged to find his mistress, Hero, (for such he wou'd imagine Margaret to be) address Borachio, or any other man, by his name, as he might suppose that she called him by the name of Claudio in consequence of a secret agreement between them, as a cover, in case she were overheard; and *he* would know, without a possibility of error, that it was not Claudio, with whom in fact she conversed. MALONE.

SCENE

SCENE III.

Leonato's Garden.

Enter BENEDICK *and a* BOY.

Bene. Boy,—

Boy. Signior.

Bene. In my chamber-window lies a book; bring it hither to me in the orchard [6].

Boy. I am here already, Sir.

Bene. I know that;—but I would have thee hence, and here again. [*Exit Boy.*]—I do much wonder, that one man, seeing how much another man is a fool when he dedicates his behaviour to love, will, after he hath laugh'd at such shallow follies in others, become the argument of his own scorn, by falling in love: And such a man is Claudio. I have known, when there was no mufic with him but the drum and the fife; and now had he rather hear the tabor and the pipe: I have known, when he would have walk'd ten mile a-foot, to see a good armour; and now will he lie ten nights awake, carving the fashion of a new doublet [7]. He was wont to speak plain, and to the purpose, like an honest man, and a soldier; and now is he turn'd orthographer [8]; his words are a very

---

[6] *—in the* orchard.] *Orchard* in our author's time signified a *garden*. MALONE.

[7] *—carving the fashion of a new doublet.*] This folly, so conspicuous in the gallants of former ages, is laughed at by all our comic writers. So in Greene's *Farewell to Folly*, 1617 :—" We are almost as fantastic as the English gentleman that is painted naked, with a pair of sheers in his hand, as not being resolved after what fashion to have his coat cut." STEEVENS.

The English gentleman in the above extract alludes to a plate in Borde's *Introduction to Knowledge*. REED.

He is represented naked, with a pair of tailor's sheers in one hand, and a piece of cloth on his arm, with the following verses:

" I am an Englishman, and naked I stand here,
" Musing in my mynde what rayment I shall were,
" For now I will ware this, and now I will were that,
" Now I will were I cannot tell what." &c.

See Camden's *Remaines*, 1614, p. 17. MALONE.

[8] *— orthographer.*] The old copies read—*orthography*. STEEVENS. Mr. Pope made the correction. MALONE.

fantastical

fantastical banquet, just so many strange dishes. May I be so converted, and see with these eyes? I cannot tell; I think not: I will not be sworn, but love may transform me to an oyster; but I'll take my oath on it, till he have made an oyster of me, he shall never make me such a fool. One woman is fair; yet I am well: another is wise; yet I am well: another virtuous; yet I am well: but till all graces be in one woman, one woman shall not come in my grace. Rich she shall be, that's certain; wise, or I'll none; virtuous, or I'll never cheapen her; fair, or I'll never look on her; mild, or come not near me; noble, or not I for an angel; of good discourse, an excellent musician, and her hair shall be of what colour it please God*. Ha! the prince and Monsieur Love! I will hide me in the arbour. [*withdraws.*

Enter Don Pedro, Leonato, Claudio, *and* Balthazar.

D. Pedro. Come, shall we hear this music?
Claud. Yea, my good Lord:—How still the evening is, As hush'd on purpose to grace harmony!
D. Pedro. See you where Benedick hath hid himself?
Claud. O, very well, my Lord: the music ended, We'll fit the kid-fox¹ with a penny-worth.

D. Pedro.

---

* *— and her hair shall be of what colour it pleas'd, &c.*] Perhaps Benedick alludes to a fashion, very common in the time of Shakspeare, that of dying the hair. Stubbs in his anatomy of Abuses, 1595, speaking of the attires of women's heads, says, " *If any have haire of her owne, naturall growing, which is not faire enough, then will they die it in divers colours.*" STEEVENS.

Or he may allude to the fashion of wearing *false* hair, " of whatever colour it pleased God." So, in a subsequent scene: " I like the new tire within, if the *hair* were a thought browner." Fines Moryson, describing the dress of the ladies of Shakspeare's time, says, Gentlewomen virgins wear gownes close to the body, and aprons of fine linnen, and go bareheaded, with their hair curiously knotted, and raised at the forehead, but *many* (against the cold, as they say,) weare cups of hair that *is not their own.*" See *the Two Gentlemen of Verona.* MALONE.

¹ — *we'll fit the kid-fox with a penny-worth*] i. e. we will be even with the fox now discovered. So the word *kid* or *kidde* signifies in Chaucer. *Rumaunt of the Rose*, 2172. GREY.

It is not impossible but that Shakspeare chose on this occasion to employ an antiquated word; and yet if any future editor should chuse
to

ABOUT NOTHING.

D. Pedro. Come, Balthazar, we'll hear that song again.
Balth. O good my Lord, tax not so bad a voice
To slander music any more than once.
  D. Pedro. It is the witness still of excellency,
To put a strange face on his own perfection:—
I pray thee, sing, and let me woo no more.
  Balth. Because you talk of wooing, I will sing:
Since many a wooer doth commence his suit
To her he thinks not worthy; yet he wooes;
Yet will he swear, he loves.
  D. Pedro. Nay, pray thee, come:
Or, if thou wilt hold longer argument,
Do it in notes.
  Balth. Note this before my notes,
There's not a note of mine that's worth the noting.
  D. Pedro. Why these are very crotchets that he speaks;
Note, notes, forsooth, and noting¹! [*musick*.
  Bene. Now, *Divine air!* now is his soul ravish'd—Is it
not strange, that sheeps guts should hale souls out of men's
bodies—Well, a horn for my money, when all's done.

Balth. sings.   Sigh no more, ladies, sigh no more,
        Men were deceivers ever;
      One foot in sea, and one on shore;
        To one thing constant never:
          Then sigh not so,
          But let them go,
        And be you blith and bonny;
      Converting all your sounds of woe
        Into, Hey nonny, nonny.

II.

      Sing no more ditties, sing no mo
        Of dumps so dull and heavy;
      The frauds of men were ever so,
        Since summer first was leavy.
          Then sigh not so, &c.

to read—*bid fox*, he may observe that Hamlet has said—"*Hide fox,
and all after.*" STEEVENS.
  Dr. Warburton reads, as Mr. Steevens proposes. MALONE.
  ¹ — *and* noting!] The old copies read—*nothing*. The correction was
made by Mr. Theobald. MALONE.

F 4   *D. Pedro.*

D. Pedro. By my troth, a good song.

Balth. And an ill singer, my Lord.

D. Pedro. Ha? no; no, faith; thou sing'st well enough for a shift.

Bene. [*aside.*] An he had been a dog, that should have howl'd thus, they would have hang'd him; and, I pray God, his bad voice bode no mischief! I had as lief have heard the night-raven, come what plague could have come after it.

D. Pedro. Yea, marry; [*to Claudio.*]—Dost thou hear, Balthazar? I pray thee, get us some excellent musick; for to-morrow night we would have it at the Lady Hero's chamber-window.

Balth. The best I can, my Lord. [*Exit* BALTHAZAR.

D. Pedro. Do so: farewell. Come hither, Leonato; What was it you told me of to-day, that your niece Beatrice was in love with Signior Benedick?

Claud. O, ay;—Stalk on, stalk on, the fowl sits[3]. [*aside to Don Pedro.*] I did never think that lady would have loved any man.

Leon. No, nor I neither; but most wonderful, that she should so dote on Signior Benedick, whom she hath in all outward behaviours seem'd ever to abhor.

Bene. Is't possible? Sits the wind in that corner? [*aside.*

Leon. By my troth, my Lord, I cannot tell what to think of it; but that she loves him with an enraged affection—it is past the infinite of thought[4].

D. Pedro. May be she doth but counterfeit.

Claud. 'Faith, like enough.

Leon. O God! counterfeit! There never was counterfeit

---

[3] —*Stalk on, stalk on, the fowl sits.*] This is an allusion to the *stalking horse*; a horse either real or factitious, by which the fowler anciently shelter'd himself from the sight of the game. STEEVENS.

So in *New Shreds of the Old Snare*, by John Gee, 4to. p. 13: "—Methinks I behold the cunning fowler, such as I have knowne in the fenne countries and else-where, that doo shoot at woodcockes, snipes, and wilde fowle, by sneaking behind a painted cloth, which they carrey before them, having pictured in it *the shape of a horse;* which while the silly fowle gazeth on is knockt downe with hale shot, and so put in the fowler's budget." REED.

[4] —*But that she loves him with an enraged affection—it is past the infinite of thought.*] The plain sense is, *I know not what to think otherwise, but that she loves him with* an enraged affection: It (this affection) is past the infinite of thought. *Infinite* is used by more careful writers for *indefinite*:

ABOUT NOTHING.

fit of passion came so near the life of passion as she discovers it.

D. Pedro. Why, what effects of passion shews she?

Claud. Bait the hook well; this fish will bite. [*aside.*

Leon. What effects, my Lord! She will sit you—You heard my daughter tell you how.

Claud. She did, indeed.

D. Pedro. How, how, I pray you? You amaze me: I would have thought her spirit had been invincible against all assaults of affection.

Leon. I would have sworn it had, my Lord: especially against Benedick.

Bene. [*aside.*] I should think this a gull, but that the white-bearded fellow speaks it: knavery cannot, sure, hide himself in such reverence.

Claud. He hath ta'en the infection; hold it up. [*aside.*

D. Pedro. Hath she made her affection known to Benedick?

Leon. No; and swears she never will: that's her torment.

Claud. 'Tis true, indeed; so your daughter says: *Shall I, says she, that have so often encounter'd him with scorn, write to him that I love him?*

Leon. This says she now when she is beginning to write to him: for she'll be up twenty times a night; and there will she sit in her smock, till she have writ a sheet of paper¹: —my daughter tells us all.

Claud. Now you talk of a sheet of paper, I remember a pretty jest your daughter told us of.

indefinite: and the speaker only means, that *thought*, though in itself unbounded, cannot reach or estimate the degree of her passion. JOHNSON.

The meaning, I think, is, *but with what an enraged affection she loves him, it is beyond the power of thought to conceive.* MALONE.

¹ *This says she now when she is beginning to write to him: for she'll be up twenty times a night; and there will she sit in her smock, till she have writ a sheet of paper.*] Shakspeare has more than once availed himself of such incidents as occurred to him from history, &c. to compliment the princes before whom his pieces were performed. A striking instance of flattery to James occurs in Macbeth; perhaps the passage here quoted was not less grateful to Elizabeth, as it apparently alludes to an extraordinary trait in one of the letters pretended to have been written by the hated Mary to Bothwell.

"I am *nakit*, and ganging to sleep, and zit I cease not to scribble all this paper, in so meikle as rest is thairof" *That is*, I am naked, and going to sleep, and yet I cease not to scribble to the end of my paper, much as there remains of it unwritten on. HENLEY.

Leon.

Leon. O,—When she had writ it, and was reading it over, she found Benedick and Beatrice between the sheet?—
Claud. That.
Leon. O, she tore the letter into a thousand half-pence [6]; rail'd at herself, that she should be so immodest to write to one that she knew would flout her: *I measure him*, says she, *by my own spirit; for, I should flout him, if he writ to me; yea, though I love him, I should.*
Claud. Then down upon her knees she falls, weeps, sobs, beats her heart, tears her hair, prays, curses;—*O sweet Benedick! God give me patience!*
Leon. She doth indeed: my daughter says so: and the ecstacy [a] hath so much overborne her, that my daughter is sometime afeard she will do desperate outrage to herself: It is very true.
D. Pedro. It were good, that Benedick knew of it by some other, if she will not discover it.
Claud. To what end? He would but make a sport of it, and torment the poor lady worse.
D. Pedro. An he should, it were an alms to hang him. She's an excellent sweet lady; and, out of all suspicion, she is virtuous.
Claud. And she is exceeding wise.
D. Pedro. In every thing but in loving Benedick.
Leon. O my Lord, wisdom and blood [7] combating in so tender a body, we have ten proofs to one, that blood hath the victory. I am sorry for her, as I have just cause, being her uncle and her guardian.

---

[6] *O, she tore the letter into a thousand half pence;*] i. e. into a thousand pieces of the same bigness. So, in *As you Like it:*—" they were all like one another, as half-pence are." THEOBALD.

See *Mortimeriados*, by Michael Drayton, 4to. 1596:

" She now begins to write unto her lover,—
" Then turning back to read what she had writ,
" She teyrs the paper, and condemns her wit."
                                                                MALONE.

A *farthing*, and perhaps a *half-penny*, was used to signify any small particle or division. So, in the character of the *Prioress* in *Chaucer:*

" That in hire cuppe was no ferthing sene
" Of grese, whan she dronken hadde hire draught."
            Prol. to the Cant. Tales, Late edit. v. 135. STEEVENS.

[a] —*and the ecstacy*] *Extasy* formerly signified a violent *perturbation of mind*. So, in *Macbeth:* "—in restless ecstacy." MALONE.

[7] —*wisdom and blood*—] *Blood* is here as in many other places used by our author in the sense of *passion*, or rather *temperament of body*.
                                                                MALONE.

D. Pedro.

D. Pedro. I would, she had bestow'd this dotage on me: I would have daff'd [a] all other respects, and made her half myself: I pray you, tell Benedick of it, and hear what he will say.

Leon. Were it good, think you?

Claud. Hero thinks surely, she will die: for, she says, she will die if he love her not; and she will die ere she make her love known; and she will die if he woo her, rather than she will 'bate one breath of her accustom'd crossness.

D. Pedro. She doth well: if she should make tender of her love, 'tis very possible, he'll scorn it; for the man, as you know all, hath a contemptible spirit [b].

Claud. He is a very proper man [c].

D. Pedro. He hath, indeed, a good outward happiness.

Claud. 'Fore God, and in my mind, very wise.

D. Pedro. He doth, indeed, shew some sparks that are like it.

Claud. And I take him to be valiant.

D. Pedro. As Hector, I assure you: and in the managing of quarrels you may say he is wise; for either he avoids them with great discretion, or undertakes them with a most Christian-like fear.

Leon. If he do fear God, he must necessarily keep peace; if he break the peace he ought to enter into a quarrel with fear and trembling.

D. Pedro. And so will he do; for the man doth fear God, howsoever it seems not in him, by some large jests he will make. Well, I am sorry for your niece: Shall we go seek Benedick, and tell him of her love?

Claud. Never tell him, my Lord; let her wear it out, with good counsel.

---

[a] — *have daff'd—*] To *daff* is the same as to *doff*, to *do off*, to put aside. STEEVENS.

[b] — *contemptible spirit.*] That is, a temper inclined to scorn and contempt. It has been before remarked, that our author uses his verbal adjectives with great licence. There is therefore no need of changing the word with Sir T. Hanmer to *contemptuous.* JOHNSON.
In the *argument* to *Darius,* a tragedy, by Lord Sterline, 1603, it is said, that Darius wrote to *Alexander* " in a proud and *contemptible* manner." In this place *contemptible* certainly means *contemptuous.*
STEEVENS.

[c] — *a very proper man.*] i. e. a very handsome man. MALONE.

Leon.

Leon. Nay, that's impossible; she may wear her heart out first.

D. Pedro. Well, we will hear further of it by your daughter; let it cool the while. I love Benedick well; and I could wish he would modestly examine himself, to see how much he is unworthy to have so good a lady.

Leon. My Lord, will you walk? dinner is ready.

Claud. If he do not dote on her upon this, I will never trust my expectation. [*aside.*

D. Pedro. Let there be the same net spread for her, and that must your daughter and her gentlewomen carry. The sport will be, when they hold one an opinion of another's dotage, and no such matter; that's the scene that I would see, which will be merely a dumb show. Let us send her to call him to dinner. [*aside.*

[*Exeunt Don* PEDRO, CLAUDIO, *and* LEONATO.

Bene. [*advancing.*] This can be no trick: The conference was sadly borne [1].—They have the truth of this from Hero. They seem to pity the lady; it seems, her affections have the full bent [2]. Love me! why, it must be requited. I hear how I am censured: they say, I will bear myself proudly, if I perceive the love come from her; they say too, that she will rather die than give any sign of affection.—I did never think to marry:—I must not seem proud:—happy are they that hear their detractions, and can put them to mending. They say, the lady is fair; 'tis a truth, I can bear them witness: and virtuous;—'tis so, I cannot reprove it: and wise, but for loving me;—By my troth, it is no addition to her wit;—nor no great argument of her folly, for I will be horribly in love with her.—I may chance have some odd quirks and remnants of wit broken on me, because I have rail'd so long against marriage: But doth not the appetite alter? A man loves the meat in his youth, that he cannot endure in his age: Shall quips, and sentences, and these paper bullets of the brain, awe a man from the career of his humour? No: The world must be peopled. When I said, I would die a batchelor, I did not think I should live till I were marry'd.—Here comes Beatrice: By this day, she's a fair lady: I do spy some marks of love in her.

---

[1] — *was sadly borne*] i. e. was seriously carried on. STEEVENS.

[2] — *have the full bent*] A metaphor from archery. So, in *Hamlet*: " They fool me to the top of my *bent*." MALONE.

Enter BEATRICE.

Beat. Against my will, I am sent to bid you come in to dinner.

Bene. Fair Beatrice, I thank you for your pains.

Beat. I took no more pains for those thanks, than you take pains to thank me; if it had been painful, I would not have come.

Bene. You take pleasure then in the message?

Beat. Yea, just so much as you may take upon a knife's point, and choke a daw withal:—You have no stomach, Signior; fare you well. [*Exit.*

Bene. Ha! *Against my will I am sent to bid you come in to dinner*—there's a double meaning in that. *I took no more pains for those thanks, than you took pains to thank me*—that's as much as to say, Any pains that I take for you is as easy as thanks:—If I do not take pity of her, I am a villain; if I do not love her, I am a Jew: I will go get her picture. [*Exit.*

ACT III. SCENE I.

Leonato's Garden.

Enter HERO, MARGARET, *and* URSULA.

Hero. Good Margaret, run thee into the parlour;
There shalt thou find my cousin Beatrice
Proposing with the prince and Claudio [1];
Whisper her ear, and tell her, I and Ursula
Walk in the orchard, and our whole discourse
Is all of her; say, that thou overheard'st us;
And bid her steal into the pleached bower,
Where honey-suckles, ripen'd by the sun,
Forbid the sun to enter;—like favourites,
Made proud by princes, that advance their pride

---

[1] Proposing *with the prince and Claudio:*] Proposing *is conversing, from the French word—*propos, *discourse, talk.* STEEVENS.

Against

Against that power that bred it:—there will she hide her,
To listen our propose [a] : This is thy office;
Bear thee well in it, and leave us alone.

 Marg. I'll make her come, I warrant you, presently.
               [*Exit.*

 Hero. Now, Ursula, when Beatrice doth come,
As we do trace this alley up and down,
Our talk must only be of Benedick:
When I do name him, let it be thy part
To praise him more than ever man did merit:
My talk to thee must be, how Benedick
Is sick in love with Beatrice: Of this matter
Is little Cupid's crafty arrow made,
That only wounds by hear-say. Now begin;

    Enter BEATRICE *behind.*

For look where Beatrice, like a lapwing, runs
Close by the ground, to hear our conference.
 Urs. The pleasant'st angling is to see the fish
Cut with her golden oars the silver stream,
And greedily devour the treacherous bait:
So angle we for Beatrice; who even now
Is couched in the woodbine coverture:
Fear you not my part of the dialogue.
 Hero. Then go we near her, that her ear lose nothing
Of the false sweet bait that we lay for it.—
        [*They advance to the bower.*
No, truly, Ursula, she is too disdainful;
I know her spirits are as coy and wild
As haggards [b] of the rock.

 Urs. But are you sure,
That Benedick loves Beatrice so entirely?
 Hero. So says the prince, and my new-trothed lord.
 Urs. And did they bid you tell her of it, Madam?
 Hero. They did intreat me to acquaint her of it;
But I persuaded them, if they lov'd Benedick,
To wish him wrestle with affection,
And never to let Beatrice know of it.
 Urs. Why did you so? Doth not the gentleman

---

[a] — *our propose:*] Thus the quarto. The folio reads—*our purpose.* *Propose* is right. See the preceding note. STEEVENS.
[b] — *as haggards*—] The wildest of the hawk species. MALONE.

               Deserve

ABOUT NOTHING. 111

Deserve as full, as fortunate a bed⁴,
As ever Beatrice shall couch upon?

Hero. O God of love! I know, he doth deserve
As much as may be yielded to a man:
But nature never fram'd a woman's heart
Of prouder stuff than that of Beatrice:
Disdain and scorn ride sparkling in her eyes,
Misprising⁵ what they look on; and her wit
Values itself so highly, that to her
All matter else seems weak: she cannot love,
Nor take no shape nor project of affection,
She is so self-endeared.

Urs. Sure, I think so;
And therefore, certainly, it were not good
She knew his love, lest she make sport at it.

Hero. Why, you speak truth: I never yet saw man,
How wise, how noble, young, how rarely featur'd,
But she would spell him backward⁶: if fair-faced,
She'd swear the gentleman should be her sister;
If black, why, nature, drawing of an antic,
Made a foul blot⁷: if tall, a lance ill-headed;

If

⁴ — *as full, as fortunate a bed.*] *Full* is used by our author and his contemporaries for *complete, perfect.* So, in *Antony and Cleopatra*, "the *full*-man was worthiest;" and in *Othello*, (as Mr. Steevens has observed,) "What a *full* fortune doth the thick-lips owe!" MALONE.

⁵ *Misprising*—] Despising, contemning. JOHNSON.
To *misprize* is to *undervalue*, or take in a wrong light. STEEVENS.

⁶ — *spell him backward.*] Alluding to the practice of witches in uttering prayers.
The following passage, containing a similar train of thought, is from Lilly's *Anatomy of Wit*, 1581, p. 44. b: — "if he be cleanly, they [women] term him proude; if meane in apparel, a sloven; if tall, a lungis; if shorte, a dwarfe; if bold, blunte; if shamefast, a coward; &c. P. 35. If she be well set, then call her a bosse; if slender, a hasil twig; if she be pleasant, then is she wanton; if sullen, a clowne; if honest, then is she coye." STEEVENS.

⁷ *If black, why, nature, drawing of an antic,
Made a foul blot.*] The *antic* was a buffoon character in the old English farces, with a *blacked face*, and a *patch-work habit.* What I would observe from hence is, that the name of *antic* or *antique*, given to this character, shews that the people had some traditional ideas of its being borrowed from the *ancient mimes*, who are thus described by Apuleius, "mimi centunculo, *fuligine faciem obducti.*" WARBURTON.
I believe what is here said of the old English farces, is said at random. Dr. Warburton was thinking, I imagine, of the modern Harlequin.

I have

If low, an agate very vilely cut [8]:
If speaking, why, a vane blown with all winds [9];
If silent, why, a block moved with none.
So turns she every man the wrong side out;
And never gives to truth and virtue, that
Which simpleness and merit purchaseth.

Urs. Sure, sure, such carping is not commendable.

Hero. No: not to be so odd, and from all fashions,
As Beatrice is, cannot be commendable;
But who dare tell her so? If I should speak,
She'd mock me into air; O, she would laugh me

I have met with no proof that the face of the antic or vice of the old English comedy was blackened. By the word *black* in the text, is only meant, as I conceive, swarthy, or dark brown. MALONE.

[8] *If low, an agate very vilely cut:*] Dr Warburton reads *aglet*, which was adopted, I think, too hastily, by the subsequent editors. I see no reason for departing from the old copy. Shakspeare's comparisons scarcely ever answer completely on both sides. Mr. Warburton asks, "What likeness is there between a little man and an *agate?*" No other than that both are *small*. Our author has himself in another place compared a *very little* man to an *agate*. "Thou whorson mandrake, (says Falstaff to his *page*,) thou art fitter to be worn in my cap, than to wait at my heels. I was never so *man'd* with an *agate* till now"— Hero means no more than this: "if a man be low, Beatrice will say that he is as diminutive and unhappily formed as an ill-cut agate."

It appears both from the passage just quoted, and from one of Sir John Harrington's epigrams, 4to. 1618, that agates were commonly worn in Shakspeare's time:

THE AUTHOR TO A DAUGHTER NINE YEARS OLD.

"Though pride in damsels is a hateful vice,
"Yet could I like a noble-minded girl,
"That would demand me things of costly price,
"Rich velvet gowns, pendents, and chains of pearle,
"Cark'nets of *agats, cut with rare device*," &c.

These lines, at the same time that they add support to the old reading, shew, I think, that the words "vilely *cut,*" are to be understood in their usual sense, when applied to precious stones, viz. *awkwardly wrought by a tool,* and not, as Mr. Steevens supposed, *grotesquely mixed* by nature. MALONE.

[9] —*a vane blown with all winds:*] This comparison might have been borrowed from an ancient black let. ballad, entitled *A comparison of the life of man:*

"I may compare a *man* againe
"Even like unto a *twining vaine*,
"That changeth even as doth the wind;
"Indeed so is man's feeble mind." STEEVENS.

Out

Out of myself, press me to death [1] with wit.
Therefore let Benedick, like cover'd fire,
Consume away in sighs, waste inwardly:
It were a better death than die with mocks [2];
Which is as bad as die with tickling [3].

Urs. Yet tell her of it; hear what she will say.

Hero. No; rather I will go to Benedick,
And counsel him to fight against his passion:
And, truly, I'll devise some honest slanders
To stain my cousin with: One doth not know,
How much an ill word may empoison liking.

Urs. O, do not do your cousin such a wrong.
She cannot be so much without true judgment,
(Having so swift and excellent a wit,
As she is priz'd to have,) as to refuse
So rare a gentleman as Signior Benedick.

Hero. He is the only man of Italy,
Always excepted my dear Claudio.

Urs. I pray you, be not angry with me, Madam,
Speaking my fancy; Signior Benedick,
For shape, for bearing, argument [4], and valour,
Goes foremost in report through Italy.

Hero. Indeed, he hath an excellent good name.

Urs. His excellence did earn it, ere he had it.—
When are you marry'd, Madam?

Hero. Why, every day;—to-morrow: Come, go in,
I'll shew thee some attires; and have thy counsel,
Which is the best to furnish me to-morrow.

---

[1] *—press me to death—*] The allusion is to an ancient punishment of our law, called *prius fort et dure*, which was formerly inflicted on those persons, who, being indicted, refused to plead. In consequence of their silence, they were pressed to death by a heavy weight laid upon their stomach. This punishment the good sense and humanity of the legislature have within these few years abolished. MALONE.

[2] *It were a better death than die with mocks;*] Thus the quarto. So before: "To wish him wrestle with affection." The folio reads—a better death *to* die with mocks. MALONE.

[3] *— with tickling.*] The author meant that *tickling* should be pronounced as a trisyllable; *tickeling.* So, in Spenser's F. Q. b. ii. c. 12.

"—— a strange kind of harmony;
"Which Guyon's senses softly tickeled, &c. MALONE.

[4] *—argument,*] This word seems here to signify *discourse*, or, the powers of reasoning. JOHNSON.

Urs. She's limed⁵, I warrant you; we have caught her, Madam.

Hero. If it prove so, then loving goes by haps:
Some Cupid kills with arrows, some with traps.

[*Exeunt* HERO *and* URSULA. BEATRICE *advances.*

Beat. What fire is in mine ears⁶? Can this be true?
Stand I condemn'd for pride and scorn so much?
Contempt, farewell! and maiden pride, adieu!
No glory lives behind the back of such.
And Benedick, love on, I will requite thee;
Taming my wild heart to thy loving hand⁷;
If thou dost love, my kindness shall incite thee
To bind our loves up in a holy band:
For others say, thou dost deserve: and I
Believe it better than reportingly.

SCENE II.

A Room in Leonato's *House.*

Enter Don PEDRO, CLAUDIO, BENEDICK, *and* LEONATO.

D. Pedro. I do but stay till your marriage be consummate, and then go I toward Arragon.

Claud. I'll bring you thither, my Lord, if you'll vouchsafe me.

D. Pedro. Nay, that would be as great a soil in the new gloss of your marriage, as to shew a child his new

---

⁵ *She's limed,*] She is ensnared and entangled, as a sparrow with birdlime. JOHNSON.
The folio reads—She's ta'en. STEEVENS.

⁶ *What fire is in mine ears?*] Alluding to a proverbial saying of the common people, that their ears burn when others are talking of them. WARBURTON

The opinion from whence this proverbial saying is derived, is of great antiquity, being thus mentioned by Pliny: "Moreover is not this an opinion generally received that when our *ears do glow and tingle,* some there be that in our absence doo talke of us." P. Holland's *Translation.* B. xxviii. p. 297. See also Brown's *Vulgar Errors.* REED.

⁷ *Taming my wild heart to thy loving hand;*] This image is taken from falconry. She had been charged with being as wild as *buzzards of the rock;* she therefore says, that *wild* as her *heart* is, she will *tame it to the hand.* JOHNSON.

coat,

coat, and forbid him to wear it⁸. I will only be bold with Benedick for his company; for, from the crown of his head to the sole of his foot, he is all mirth; he hath twice or thrice cut Cupid's bow-string, and the little hangman dare not shoot at him⁹; he hath a heart as sound as a bell, and his tongue is the clapper; for what his heart thinks, his tongue speaks¹.

Bene. Gallants, I am not as I have been.

Leon. So say I; methinks, you are sadder.

Claud. I hope, he be in love.

D. Pedro. Hang him, truant; there's no true drop of blood in him, to be truly touch'd with love; if he be sad, he wants money.

Bene. I have the tooth-ach.

D. Pedro. Draw it.

Bene. Hang it!

Claud. You must hang it first, and draw it afterwards.

D. Pedro. What? sigh for the tooth-ach?

Leon. Where is but a humour, or a worm?

Bene. Well, every one can master a grief² but he that has it.

Claud. Yet say I, he is in love.

D. Pedro. There is no appearance of fancy³ in him, un-

---

⁸ — *as to force a child his new coat, and forbid him to wear it,*] So, in *Romeo and Juliet:*
 "As is the night before some festival,
 "To an impatient child, that hath new robes,
 "And may not wear them." STEEVENS.

⁹ — *the little hangman dare not shoot at him:*] This character of Cupid came from the *Arcadia* of Sir Philip Sidney:
 "Millions of years this old drivel Cupid lives;
 "While still more wretch, more wicked he doth prove:
 "Till now at length that Jove him office gives,
 "(At Juno's suite, who much did Argus love,)
 "In this our world a hangman for to be.
 "Of all those fools that will have all they see."
  B. ii. ch. 14. FARMER.

¹ — *as a bell, and his tongue is the clapper,* &c.] A covert allusion to the old proverb:
 "As the fool thinketh,
 "So the bell clinketh." STEEVENS.

² — *can master a grief —*] The old copies read corruptly—*cannot*. The correction was made by Mr. Pope. MALONE.

³ *There is no appearance of* fancy, &c.] Here is a play upon the word *fancy,* which Shakspeare uses for *love* as well as for *humour, caprice,* or *affectation.* JOHNSON.

less it be a fancy that he hath to strange disguises; as to be a Dutchman to-day; a Frenchman to-morrow; or in the shape of two countries at once, as, a German from the waist downward, all slops⁴; and a Spaniard from the hip upward, no doublet⁵: Unless he have a fancy to this foolery, as it appears he hath, he is no fool for fancy, as you would have it to appear he is.

Claud. If he be not in love with some woman, there is no believing old signs; he brushes his hat o'mornings; What should that bode?

D. Pedro. Hath any man seen him at the barber's?

Claud. No but the barber's man hath been seen with him; and the old ornament of his cheek hath already stuff'd tennis-balls⁵.

Leon. Indeed, he looks younger than he did, by the loss of a beard.

D. Pedro. Nay, he rubs himself with civet; Can you smell him out by that?

Claud. That's as much as to say, The sweet youth's in love.

D. Pedro. The greatest note of it is his melancholy.

Claud. And when was he wont to wash his face?

D. Pedro. Yea, or to paint himself? for the which, I hear what they say of him.

Claud. Nay, but his jesting spirit; which is now crept into a lute-string⁶, and now govern'd by stops.

D. Pedro. Indeed, that tells a heavy tale for him: Conclude, conclude, he is in love.

Claud. Nay, but I know who loves him.

D. Pedro. That would I know too; I warrant, one that knows him not.

---

⁴ — *all slops;*] *Slops* are *loose breeches*. STEEVENS.

⁵ — *no doublet:*] Or, in other words, all cloak.

The words—" Or in the shape of two countries," &c. to "no doubt," were omitted in the folio, probably to avoid giving any offence to the Spaniards, with whom James became a friend in 1604. MALONE.

⁵ — *and the old ornament of his cheek hath already* stuff'd *tennis-balls.*] So, in *A Wonderful—Prognostication for this Year of our Lord* 1591, written by Nashe, in ridicule of Richard Harvey:—" they may sell their haire by the pound to *stuffe tennice balles.*" STEEVENS.

⁶ — *crept into a lute string*—] Love-songs in our author's time were generally sung to the music of the lute. So, in *King Henry IV. P. i.* " —as melancholy as an old lion, or *a lover's lute.*" MALONE.

Claud.

Claud. Yes, and his ill conditions[7]; and, in despight of all, dies for him.

D. Pedro. She shall be buried with her face upwards[8].

Bene. Yet is this no charm for the tooth-ach.—Old Signior, walk aside with me; I have studied eight or nine wise words to speak to you, which these hobby-horses must not hear. [*Exeunt* BENE. *and* LEONATO.

D. Pedro. For my life, to break with him about Beatrice.

Claud. 'Tis even so: Hero and Margaret have by this play'd their parts with Beatrice; and then the two bears will not bite one another, when they meet.

Enter Don JOHN.

D. John. My Lord and brother, God save you.

D. Pedro. Good den, brother.

D. John. If your leisure serv'd, I would speak with you.

D. Pedro. In private?

D. John. If it please you;—yet Count Claudio may hear; for what I would speak of, concerns him.

D. Pedro. What's the matter?

D. John. Means your Lordship to be marry'd to-morrow? [*To Claudio.*

D. Pedro. You know, he does.

[7] — *his ill conditions*:] i. e. qualities. MALONE.

[8] *She shall be buried with her face upwards*] Mr. Theobald's emendation (with her *heels* upwards) appears to be very specious. The meaning seems to be, that she who acted upon principles contrary to others, should be buried with the same contrariety. JOHNSON.

Theobald's conjecture may be supported by a passage in *The Wild Goose Chase* of Beaum. and Fletcher:

"—if I die o' th' first fit, I am unhappy,
"And worthy to be *buried with my heels upwards*."

The passage, indeed, may mean only—*She shall be buried in her lover's arms*. So, in *The Winter's Tale*:

"*Flo.* What? like a corse?
"*Per.* No, like a bank for love to lie and play on;
"Not like a corse:—or if,—not to be *buried*,
"But quick, and in my arms. STEEVENS.

This last is, I believe, the true interpretation. Our author often quotes Lilly's Grammar; (see p. 268.) and here perhaps he remembered a phrase that occurs in that book, p. 59, and is thus interpreted: —" Tu cubas supinus, thou liest *in bed with thy face upwards*."—Heels and *face* never could have been confounded by either the eye or the ear. Besides, Don Pedro is evidently playing on the word *dies* in Claudio's speech, which Claudio uses metaphorically, and of which Don Pedro avails himself to introduce an allusion to that consummation which he supposes Beatrice was *dying* for. MALONE.

D. John.

D. John. I know not that, when he knows what I know.

Claud. If there be any impediment, I pray you, discover it.

D. John. You may think, I love you not; let that appear hereafter, and aim better at me by that I now will manifest: For my brother, I think, he holds you well; and in dearness of heart hath holp to effect your ensuing marriage; surely, suit ill spent, and labour ill bestowed!

D. Pedro. Why, what's the matter?

D. John. I came hither to tell you, and, circumstances shorten'd, (for she hath been too long a talking of,) the lady is disloyal.

Claud. Who? Hero?

D. John. Even she; Leonato's Hero, your Hero, every man's Hero[*].

Claud. Disloyal?

D. John. The word is too good to paint out her wickedness; I could say, she were worse; think you of a worse title, and I will fit her to it. Wonder not till further warrant; go but with me to-night, you shall see her chamber-window enter'd; even the night before her wedding-day; if you love her then, to-morrow wed her; but it would better fit your honour to change your mind.

Claud. May this be so?

D. Pedro. I will not think it.

D. John. If you dare not trust that you see, confess not that you know; if you will follow me, I will shew you enough; and when you have seen more, and heard more, proceed accordingly.

Claud. If I see any thing to-night why I should not marry her; to-morrow, in the congregation, where I should wed, there will I shame her.

D. Pedro. And, as I wooed for thee to obtain her, I will join with thee to disgrace her.

D. John. I will disparage her no farther, till you are my witnesses: bear it coldly but till midnight, and let the issue shew itself.

D. Pedro. O day untowardly turned!

Claud. O mischief strangely thwarting!

---

[*] *Leonato's Hero, your Hero, every man's Hero.*] Dryden has transplanted this sarcasm into his *All for Love:* " Your Cleopatra; Dolabella's Cleopatra, every man's Cleopatra." STEEVENS.

D. John.

D. John. O plague right well prevented! So will you say, when you have seen the sequel. [*Exeunt.*

SCENE II.

A Street.

Enter DOGBERRY *and* VERGES, *with the* Watch.

Dog. Are you good men and true?

Ver. Yea, or else it were pity but they should suffer salvation, body and soul.

Dog. Nay, that were a punishment too good for them, if they should have any allegiance in them, being chosen for the prince's watch.

Ver. Well, give them their charge [1], neighbour Dogberry.

Dog. First, who think you the most desartless man to be constable?

1st. Watch. Hugh Oatcake, Sir, or George Seacoal; for they can write and read.

Dog. Come hither, neighbour Seacoal: God hath blessed you with a good name; to be a well-favoured man is the gift of fortune; but to write and read comes by nature.

2d. Watch. Both which, master constable,——

Dog. You have; I knew it would be your answer. Well, for your favour, Sir, why, give God thanks, and make no boast of it; and for your writing and reading, let that appear when there is no need of such vanity. You are thought here to be the most senseless and fit man for the constable of the watch; therefore bear you the lanthorn: This is your charge; you shall comprehend all vagrom men; you are to bid any man stand, in the prince's name.

2d. Watch. How if he will not stand?

Dog. Why then, take no note of him, but let him go; and presently call the rest of the watch together, and thank God you are rid of a knave.

Ver. If he will not stand when he is bidden, he is none of the prince's subjects.

Deg. True, and they are to meddle with none but the prince's subjects:—You shall also make no noise in the streets;

---

[1] *— give them their charge.*] It appears from several of our old comedies, that to *charge* his fellows was a regular part of the duty of the constable of the Watch. MALONE.

for, for the watch to babble and to talk, is moſt tolerable and not to be endured.

2d. Watch. We will rather ſleep than talk; we know what belongs to a watch.

Dog. Why, you ſpeak like an ancient and moſt quiet watchman; for I cannot ſee how ſleeping ſhould offend; only have a care that your bills be not ſtolen [a].—Well, you are to call at all the ale-houſes, and bid them that are drunk get them to bed.

2d. Watch. How if they will not?

Dog. Why then, let them alone till they are ſober; if they make you not then the better anſwer, you may ſay, they are not the men you took them for.

[a] *— bills be not ſtolen:*] A *bill* is ſtill carried by the watchmen at Litchfield. It was the old weapon of the Engliſh infantry, which, ſays Temple, gave the moſt ghaſtly and deplorable wounds. It may be called *fourth ſolaris.* JOHNSON.

The following are examples of ancient *bills.*

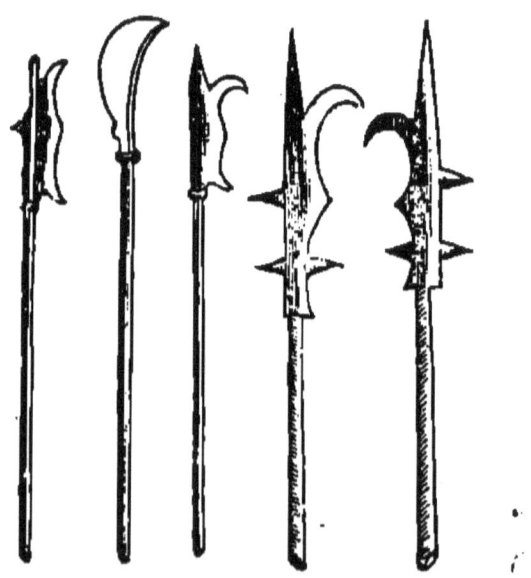

2. *Watch.*

2d. Watch. Well, Sir,

Dog. If you meet a thief, you may suspect him, by virtue of your office, to be no true man: and, for such kind of men, the less you meddle or make with them, why, the more is for your honesty.

2d. Watch. If we know him to be a thief, shall we not lay hands on him?

Dog. Truly, by your office you may; but, I think, they that touch pitch will be defiled; the most peaceable way for you, if you do take a thief, is, to let him shew himself what he is, and steal out of your company.

Ver. You have been always called a merciful man, partner.

Dog. Truly, I would not hang a dog by my will; much more a man who hath any honesty in him.

Ver. If you hear a child cry in the night [3], you must call to the nurse, and bid her still it.

2d. Watch. How if the nurse be asleep, and will not hear us?

Dog. Why then, depart in peace, and let the child wake her with crying: for the ewe that will not hear her lamb when it baes, will never answer a calf when he bleats.

Ver. 'Tis very true.

---

[3] *If you hear a child cry,* &c.] It is not impossible but that part of this scene was intended as a burlesque on *The Statutes of the Streets,* imprinted by Wolfe, in 1595. Among these I find the following:

22. "No man shall blowe any horne in the night, within this cittie, or whistle after the hour of nyne of the clock in the night, under paine of imprisonment.

23. "No man shall use to goe with visoures, or disguised by night, under like paine of imprisonment.

24. "Made, that night-walkers, and evisdroppers like punishment.

25. "No-hammar-man, as a smith, a pewterer, a founder, and all articicers making great sound, shall not worke after the houre of nyne at the night, &c.

30. "No man shall, after the houre of nyne at night, keepe any rule, whereby any such suddaine out-cry be made in the still of the night, as making any affray, or beating his wyfe, or servant, or singing, or revyling in his house, to the disturbance of his neighbours, under payne of ins. iiii d. &c. &c."

Ben Jonson appears to have ridiculed this scene in the Indoction to his *Bartholomew-Faire:* "And then a substantial *watch* to have stole in upon 'em and taken them away with *mistaking words,* as the fashion is in the stage practice." STEEVENS.

Dog. This is the end of the charge. You, constable, are to present the prince's own person; if you meet the prince in the night, you may stay him.

Ver. Nay, by'r-lady, that, I think, he cannot.

Dog. Five shillings to one on't, with any man that knows the statues, he may stay him: marry, not without the prince be willing: for, indeed, the watch ought to offend no man; and it is an offence to stay a man against his will.

Ver. By'r-lady, I think, it be so.

Dog. Ha, ha, ha! Well, masters, good night; an there be any matter of weight chances, call up me: keep your fellows' counsels and your own *, and good night.—Come, neighbour.

2d. Watch. Well, masters, we hear our charge: let us go sit here upon the church-bench till two, and then all to bed.

Dog. One word more, honest neighbours: I pray you, watch about Signior Leonato's door; for the wedding being there to-morrow, there is a great coil to-night: Adieu: be vigilant, I beseech you.

[*Exeunt* DOGBERRY *and* VERGES.

Enter BORACHIO *and* CONRADE.

Bora. What! Conrade—

2d. Watch. Peace, stir not. [*Aside.*

Bora. Conrade, I say!

Con. Here, man, I am at thy elbow.

Bora. Mass, and my elbow itch'd; I thought, there would a scab follow.

Con. I will owe thee an answer for that; and now forward with thy tale.

Bora. Stand thee close then under this pent-house, for it drizzles rain; and I will, like a true drunkard, utter all to thee.

2d. Watch. [*aside.*] Some treason, masters; yet stand close.

Bora. Therefore know, I have earned of Don John a thousand ducats.

Con. Is it possible that any villainy should be so dear?

---

* —*keep your fellows' counsels and your own.*] This is part of the oath of a grand juryman; and is one of many proofs of Shakspeare's having been very conversant, at some period of his life, with legal proceedings and courts of justice. MALONE.

Bora.

Bora. Thou should'st rather ask, if it were possible any villainy should be so rich; for when rich villains have need of poor ones, poor ones may make what price they will.

Con. I wonder at it.

Bora. That shews, thou art unconfirm'd[4]: Thou knowest, that the fashion of a doublet, or a hat, or a cloak, is nothing to a man.

Con. Yes, it is apparel.

Born. I mean, the fashion.

Con. Yes, the fashion is the fashion.

Bora. Tush! I may as well say the fool's the fool. But see'st thou not, what a deformed thief this fashion is?

1st. Watch. I know that Deformed; he has been a vile thief this seven year; he goes up and down like a gentleman: I remember his name.

Bora. Didst thou not hear some body?

Con. No; 'twas the vane on the house.

Bora. Seest thou not, I say, what a deformed thief this fashion is? how giddily he turns about all the hot bloods, between fourteen and five and thirty? sometime, fashioning them like Pharaoh's soldiers in the reechy painting[5]; sometime, like god Bel's priests in the old church-window; sometime, like the shaven Hercules[6] in the[7] smirch'd worm-eaten tapestry, where his cod-piece seems as massy as his club?

Con. All this I see; and see, that the fashion wears out more apparel than the man: But art not thou thyself giddy with the fashion too, that thou hast shifted out of thy tale into telling me of the fashion?

Bora. Not so neither: but know, that I have to-night woo'd Margaret, the Lady Hero's gentlewoman, by the name of Hero; she leans me out at her mistress' chamber-window,

---

[4] — *unconfirm'd:*] i. e. unpractised in the ways of the world.
WARBURTON.

[5] — *reechy painting:*] is painting stain'd by smoke; from *Recan*, Anglo-Saxon, *to rev', fumare.* STEEVENS.

[6] — *sometime, like the shaven Hercules,* &c.] I believe that Shakspeare by *the shaven Hercules* meant only *Hercules when shaven to make him look like a woman,* while he remained in the service of Omphale, his Lydian mistress. Had *the shaven Hercules* been meant to represent Samson, (as Dr. Warburton supposed,) he would probably have been equipped with a *jaw-bone* instead of a *club.* STEEVENS.

[7] — *smirch'd*] *Smirch'd*, is soiled, obscured. So, in *As you Like it:*

"And with a kind of umber *smirch* my face." STEEVENS.

124   MUCH ADO

bids me a thousand times good night,—I tell this tale vilely:
—I should first tell thee, how the Prince, Claudio and my
master, planted and placed, and possessed by master Don John,
saw afar off in the orchard this amiable encounter.

Con. And thought they, Margaret was Hero?

Bora. Two of them did, the Prince and Claudio; but the
devil my master knew she was Margaret; and partly by his
oaths, which first possessed them, partly by the dark night,
which did deceive them, but chiefly by my villainy, which did
confirm any slander that Don John had made, away went
Claudio enraged; swore he would meet her, as he was ap-
pointed, next morning at the temple, and there, before the
whole congregation, shame her with what he saw o'er night,
and send her home again without a husband.

1st. Watch. We charge you in the prince's name, stand.

2d. Watch. Call up the right master constable: We have
here recovered the most dangerous piece of lechery that ever
was known in the common-wealth.

1st. Watch. And one Deformed is one of them; I know
him, he wears a lock [8].

Con. Masters, masters—

2d. Watch. You'll be made bring Deformed forth, I war-
rant you.

Con. Masters,—

1st. Watch. Never speak; we charge you: let us obey you
to go with us [9].

Bora. We are like to prove a goodly commodity, being
taken up of these mens bills [*].

Con. A commodity in question, I warrant you. Come,
we'll obey you.   [*Exeunt.*

[8] — *wears a lock.*] See Dr. Warburton's Note, Act v. sc. i.
                                                    STEEVENS.

[9] *Never speak; &c.*] These words in the old copies are by the mistake
of the transcriber or printer given to Conrade. The present regulation
is Mr. Theobald's.   MALONE.

[*] *a goodly commodity, being taken up of these men's bills.*] Here is a
cluster of conceits. *Commodity* was formerly as now, the usual term for
an article of merchandise. *To take up,* besides its common meaning,
(*to apprehend*), was the phrase for obtaining goods on credit. "If a
man is thorough with them in honest *taking up,* (says Falstaff,) then
they must stand upon *security.*" *Bill,* was the term both for a single
bond, and a halberd.

We have the same conceit in *K. Henry VI.* P. ii. "My Lord, when
shall we go to Cheapside, and *take up commodities* upon our *bills.*"
                                                    MALONE.

SCENE

SCENE IV.

A Room in Leonato's *House.*

Enter HERO, MARGARET, *and* URSULA.

Hero. Good Ursula, wake my cousin Beatrice, and desire her to rise.
Urs. I will, Lady.
Hero. And bid her come hither.
Urs. Well. [*Exit* URSULA.
Mar. Troth, I think, your other rabato [1] were better.
Hero. No, pray thee, good Meg, I'll wear this.
Mar. By my troth, it's not so good: and I warrant, your cousin will say so.
Hero. My cousin's a fool, and thou art another; I'll wear none but this.
Mar. I like the new tire within excellently, if the hair were a thought browner [2]: and your gown's a most rare fashion, i'faith. I saw the dutchess of Milan's gown, that they praise so.
Hero. O, that exceeds, they say.
Mar. By my troth it's but a night-gown in respect of yours: Cloth of gold, and cuts, and laced with silver; set with pearls, down sleeves, side sleeves, and skirts round, underborne with a blueish tinsel: but for a fine, quaint, graceful, and excellent fashion, your's is worth ten on't.
Hero. God give me joy to wear it, for my heart is exceeding heavy!
Mar. 'Twill be heavier soon, by the weight of a man.
Hero. Fie upon thee! art not ashamed?
Mar. Of what, Lady? of speaking honourably? Is not marriage honourable in a beggar? Is not your lord honourable without marriage? I think you would have me say, saving your reverence,—*a husband:* an bad thinking do not wrest true speaking, I'll offend no body: Is there any harm in——

---

[1] *—— rabato?*] An ornament for the neck, a collar-band or kind of ruff. Fr. *Rabat.* Menage saith it comes from *rabattre,* to put back, because it was at first nothing but the collar of the shirt or shift turned backwards the shoulders. T. HAWKINS.
[2] *—— if the hair were a thought browner:*] See p. 102, note 9.
MALONE.

the heavier for a hufband? None, I think, an it be the right hufband, and the right wife; otherwife, 'tis light and not heavy: Afk my Lady Beatrice elfe, here fhe comes.

Re-enter BEATRICE.

Hero. Good morrow, coz.
Beat. Good morrow, fweet Hero.
Hero. Why, how now! do you fpeak in the fick tune?
Beat. I am out of all other tune, methinks.
Mar. Clap us into *Light o'love*[1]; that goes without a burden; do you fing it, and I'll dance it.
Beat. Yea, *Light o'love*, with your heels!—then if your hufband have ftables enough, you'll look he fhall lack no barns[2].
Mar. O illegitimate conftruction! I fcorn that with my heels.
Beat. 'Tis almoft five o'clock, coufin; 'tis time you were ready. By my troth, I am exceeding ill;—hey ho!

[1] *Light o'love;*] This is the name of an old dance tune which has occurred already in the *Two Gentlemen of Verona*.

I have lately recovered it from an ancient MS. and it is as follows:

SIR JOHN HAWKINS.

[2] *—no barns,*] A quibble between *barns*, repofitories of corn, and *bairns*, the old word for children. JOHNSON.

Mar.

Mar. For a hawk, a horse, or a husband⁴?

Beat. For the letter that begins them all, H⁵.

Mar. Well, an you be not turn'd Turk⁶, there's no more sailing by the star.

Beat. What means the fool, trow?

Mar. Nothing I; but God send every one their heart's desire!

Hero. These gloves the count sent me, they are an excellent perfume.

Beat. I am stuff'd, cousin, I cannot smell.

Mar. A maid, and stuff'd! there's goodly catching of cold!

Beat. O, God help me! God help me! how long have you profess'd apprehension?

Mar. Ever since you left it: Doth not my wit become me rarely?

Beat. It is not seen enough, you should wear it in your cap.—By my troth, I am sick.

Mar. Get you some of this distill'd Cardinus Benedictus, and lay it to your heart; it is the only thing for a qualm.

Hero. There thou prick'd her with a thistle.

Beat. Benedictus! why Benedictus? you have some moral⁷ in this Benedictus.

⁴ ——— hey ho!
Mar. For *a hawk, a horse, or a husband?*] "*Heigh ho for a husband, or the willing maid's wants made known,*" is the title of an old ballad in the Pepysian Collection, in Magdalen College, Cambridge.
MALONE.

⁵ *For the letter that begins them all, H.*] This is a poor jest, somewhat obscured, and not worth the trouble of elucidation. Margaret asks Beatrice for what she cries, *hey ho*; Beatrice answers, for an *H*, that is, for an *ache* or *pain*. JOHNSON.

⁶ —*turn'd Turk.*] Hamlet uses the same expression, and talks of his *fortune's turning Turk*. *To turn Turk* was a common phrase for a change of condition or opinion. STEEVENS.

⁷ —*some moral*—] That is, some secret meaning, like the *moral* of a fable. JOHNSON.
Dr. Johnson's explanation is certainly the true one, though it has been doubted. In the *Rape of Lucrece* our author uses the verb to *moralize* in the same sense:
"Nor could she *moralize* his wanton sight."
i. e. investigate the *latent meaning* of his looks.
Again, in *The Taming of the Shrew*: "— and has left me here behind, to expound the meaning or *moral* of his signs and tokens."
MALONE.

Mar.

Mar. Moral? no, by my troth, I have no moral meaning; I meant, plain holy-thistle. You may think, perchance, that I think you are in love: nay, by'r-lady, I am not such a fool to think what I list; nor I list not to think what I can; nor, indeed, I cannot think, if I would think my heart out o'thinking, that you are in love, or that you will be in love, or that you can be in love: yet Benedick was such another, and now is he become a man: he swore he would never marry; and yet now, in despight of his heart, he eats his meat without grudging⁸: and how you may be converted, I know not; but, methinks, you look with your eyes as other women do.

Beat. What pace is this that thy tongue keeps?
Mar. Not a false gallop.

Re-enter URSULA.

Urs. Madam, withdraw; the Prince, the Count, Signior Benedick, Don John, and all the gallants of the town, are come to fetch you to church.

Hero. Help to dress me, good coz, good Meg, good Ursula. [*Exeunt.*

SCENE V.

Another Room in Leonato's *House.*

Enter LEONATO, DOGBERRY, *and* VERGES.

Leon. What would you with me, honest neighbour?
Dog. Marry, Sir, I would have some confidence with you, that decerns you nearly.
Leon. Brief, I pray you; for you see, 'tis a busy time with me.
Dog. Marry, this it is, Sir.
Ver. Yes, in truth, it is, Sir.
Leon. What is it, my good friends?
Dog. Goodman Verges, Sir, speaks a little of the matter:

---

⁸ — *he eats his meat without grudging:*] Perhaps, *to eat meat without grudging,* was the same as *to do as others do,* and the meaning is, *he is content to live by eating like other mortals, and will be content, notwithstanding his boasts, like other mortals, to have a wife.* JOHNSON.

The meaning, I think, is, "and yet now, in spight of his resolution to the contrary, he *feeds* on *love,* and likes his food." MALONE.

an old man, Sir, and his wits are not so blunt, as, God help, I would desire they were! but, in faith, honest, as the skin between his brows⁰.

Ver. Yes, I thank God, I am as honest as any man living, that is an old man, and no honester than I.

Dog. Comparisons are odorous: *palabras*¹, neighbour Verges.

Leon. Neighbours, you are tedious.

Dog. It pleases your worship to say so, but we are the poor duke's officers; but, truly, for mine own part, if I were as tedious as a king, I could find in my heart to bestow it all of your worship.

Leon. All thy tediousness on me! ha!

Dog. Yea, an 'twere a thousand times more than 'tis: for I hear as good exclamation on your worship, as of any man in the city; and though I be but a poor man, I am glad to hear it.

Ver. And so am I.

Leon. I would fain know what you have to say.

Ver. Marry, Sir, our watch to-night, excepting your worship's presence, have ta'en a couple of as arrant knaves as any in Messina.

Dog. A good old man, Sir; he will be talking; as they say, When the age is in, the wit is out; God help us! it is a world to see²!—Well said, i'faith, neighbour Verges:—well God's a good man³; An two men ride of a horse, one must ride behind⁴:—An honest soul, i'faith, Sir; by my

---

⁰ — *honest as the skin between his brows.*] This is a proverbial expression. STEEVENS.

¹ — *palabras.*] So, in the *Taming of the Shrew*, the Tinker says, *pocas palabras*, i. e. few words. A scrap of Spanish, which might once have been current among the vulgar. STEEVENS.

² *It is a world to see!*] i. e. it is wonderful to see. The same phrase often occurs with the same meaning in Holinshed. STEEVENS.

³ — *well, God's a good man;*] This expression (as Mr. Steevens has shewn) frequently occurs in the old *Moralities.* MALONE.

⁴ *An two men ride,* &c.] This is not out of place, or without meaning. Dogberry, in his vanity of superior parts, apologising for his neighbour, observes, that *of two men on an horse, one must ride behind.* The first place of rank or understanding can belong but to one, and that happy one ought not to despise his inferior. JOHNSON.

Shakspeare might have caught this idea from the common seal of the Knights Templars; the device of which was *two riding upon one horse.* An engraving of the seal is preserved at the end of Matt. Paris Hist. Ang. 1640. STEEVENS.

truth he is, as ever broke bread: but, God is to be worshipp'd: All men are not alike; alas, good neighbour!

Leon. Indeed, neighbour, he comes too short of you.

Dog. Gifts, that God gives.

Leon. I must leave you.

Dog. One word, Sir: our watch, Sir, have, indeed, comprehended two aspicious persons, and we would have them this morning examined before your worship.

Leon. Take their examination yourself, and bring it me; I am now in great haste, as may appear unto you.

Dog. It shall be suffigance.

Leon. Drink some wine ere you go: fare you well.

Enter a Messenger.

Mess. My Lord, they stay for you to give your daughter to her husband.

Leon. I will wait upon them; I am ready.

[*Exeunt* LEONATO *and* Messenger.

Dog. Go, good partner, go, get you to Francis Seacoal, bid him bring his pen and inkhorn to the jail; we are now to examination these men.

Ver. And we must do it wisely.

Dog. We will spare for no wit, I warrant you; here's that [*touching his forehead.*] shall drive some of them to a *non-com*[5]: only get the learned writer to set down our excommunication, and meet me at the jail. [*Exeunt.*

ACT IV. SCENE I.

A Church.

Enter Don PEDRO, *Don* JOHN, LEONATO, Friar, CLAUDIO, BENEDICK, HERO, *and* BEATRICE.

Leon. Come, Friar Francis, be brief; only to the plain form of marriage, and you shall recount their particular duties afterwards.

[5] — *to a non-com:*] i. e. to a *non compos mentis*; put them out of their wits;—or perhaps he confounds the term with *non-plus*. MALONE.

Fria.

Friar. You come hither, my Lord, to marry this lady?
Claud. No.
Leon. To be marry'd to her, Friar; you come to marry her.
Friar. Lady, you come hither to be marry'd to this count?
Hero. I do.
Friar. If either of you know any inward impediment why you should not be conjoined, I charge you, on your souls, to utter it.
Claud. Know you any, Hero?
Hero. None, my Lord.
Friar. Know you any, Count?
Leon. I dare make his answer, none.
Claud. O, what men dare do! what men may do! what men daily do! not knowing what they do.
Bene. How now! Interjections? Why, then some be of laughing [1], as, ha! ha! he!
Claud. Stand thee by, Friar:—Father, by your leave; Will you with free and unconstrained soul Give me this maid your daughter?
Leon. As freely, son, as God did give her me.
Claud. And what have I to give you back, whose worth May counterpoise this rich and precious gift?
D. Pedro. Nothing, unless you render her again.
Claud. Sweet Prince, you learn me noble thankfulness.—
There Leonato, take her back again;
Give not this rotten orange to your friend;
She's but the sign and semblance of her honour:—
Behold, how like a maid she blushes here:
O, what authority and shew of truth
Can cunning sin cover itself withal!
Comes not that blood, as modest evidence,
To witness simple virtue? Would you not swear,
All you that see her, that she were a maid,
By these exterior shews? But she is none:
She knows the heat of a luxurious bed [2]:
Her blush is guiltiness, not modesty.

---

[1] *— some be of laughing.*] This is a quotation from the *Accidence*. JOHNSON.

[2] *— luxurious bed.*] That is, *lascivious*. *Luxury* is the confessor's term for unlawful pleasures of the sex. JOHNSON.

So, in *King Lear*:
"To't, *luxury*, pell-mell, for I lack soldiers." STEEVENS.

Leon.

Leon. What do you mean, my Lord?
Claud. Not to be marry'd,
Not to knit my soul to an approved wanton.
Leon. Dear my Lord, if you in your own proof [3]
Have vanquish'd the resistance of her youth,
And made defeat of her virginity—
Claud. I know what you would say; If I have known her,
You'll say, she did embrace me as a husband,
And so extenuate the 'forehand sin:
No, Leonato,
I never tempted her with word too large [4]:
But, as a brother to his sister, shew'd
Bashful sincerity, and comely love.
Hero. And seem'd I ever otherwise to you?
Claud. Out on thy seeming [5]! I will write against it [6]:
You seem to me as Dian in her orb;
As chaste as is the bud [7] ere it be blown;
But you are more intemperate in your blood
Than Venus, or those pamper'd animals
That rage in savage sensuality.
Hero. Is my Lord well, that he doth speak so wide?
Leon. Sweet prince, why speak not you?
D. Pedro. What should I speak?
I stand dishonour'd, that have gone about
To link my dear friend to a common stale.
Leon. Are these things spoken, or do I but dream?
D. John. Sir, they are spoken, and these things are true.
Bene. This looks not like a nuptial.
Hero. True! O God!

---

[3] *Dear my Lord, if you in your own proof:*] In *your own proof* may signify *in your own trial* of her. TYRWHITT.

Dear, like *deer, fire, hour,* and many similar words, is here used as a dissyllable. MALONE.

[4] *— word too large:*] So he uses *large jests* in this play, for *licentious, not restrained within due bounds.* JOHNSON.

[5] *— thy seeming.*] The old copies have *thee*. The emendation is Mr. Pope's. In the next line Shakspeare probably wrote—*seem'd.*
MALONE.

[6] *I will write against it:*] So in *Cymbeline* Posthumus, speaking of women, says,
"—— I'll *write against* them,
" Detest them, curse them." STEEVENS.

[7] *— chaste as is the bud*] Before the air has tasted its sweetness.
JOHNSON.

Claud.

Claud. Leonato, stand I here?
Is this the prince? Is this the prince's brother?
Is this face Hero's? Are our eyes our own?
Leon. All this is so: But what of this, my Lord?
Claud. Let me but move one question to your daughter;
And, by that fatherly and kindly power [*]
That you have in her, bid her answer truly.
Leon. I charge thee do so, as thou art my child.
Hero. O God defend me! how am I beset!—
What kind of catechizing call you this?
Claud. To make you answer truly to your name.
Hero. Is it not Hero? Who can blot that name
With any just reproach?
Claud. Marry, that can Hero;
Hero itself can blot out Hero's virtue.
What man was he talk'd with you yesternight
Out at your window, betwixt twelve and one?
Now, if you are a maid, answer to this.
Hero. I talk'd with no man at that hour, my Lord.
D. Pedro. Why, then are you no maiden.—Leonato,
I am sorry you must hear; Upon mine honour,
Myself, my brother, and this grieved Count,
Did see her, hear her, at that hour last night,
Talk with a ruffian at her chamber-window;
Who hath, indeed, most like a liberal villain [9],
Confess'd the vile encounters they have had
A thousand times in secret.
D. John. Fie, fie! they are
Not to be nam'd, my Lord, not to be spoke of;
There is not chastity enough in language,
Without offence, to utter them: Thus, pretty Lady,
I am sorry for thy much misgovernment.
Claud. O Hero! what a Hero hadst thou been [*]
If half thy outward graces had been placed
About the thoughts and counsels of thy heart!
But, fare thee well, most foul, most fair! farewell!
Thou pure impiety, and impious purity!
For thee I'll lock up all the gates of love,

---

[*] *—kindly power*] That is, *natural power. Kind* is *nature.* JOHNS.

[9] *—liberal villain,*] *Liberal* here, as in many places of these plays, means, *frank beyond modesty* or *decency. Free of tongue.* JOHNSON.

[*] *What a Hero hadst thou been*] I am afraid here is intended a poor conceit upon the word *Hero.* JOHNSON.

And on my eye-lids shall conjecture hang [2],
To turn all beauty into thoughts of harm,
And never shall it more be gracious [3].

Leon. Hath no man's dagger here a point for me [4]?

[*Hero swoons.*

Beat. Why, how now, cousin, wherefore sink you down?

D. John. Come, let us go; these things, come thus to light,
Smother her spirits up.

[*Exeunt Don* Pedro, *Don* John, *and* Claudio.

Bene. How doth the Lady?

Beat. Dead, I think;—Help, uncle;—
Hero! why, Hero!—Uncle!—Signior Benedick!—
Friar!

Leon. O fate, take not away thy heavy hand!
Death is the fairest cover for her shame,
That may be wish'd for.

Beat. How now, cousin Hero?

Friar. Have comfort, Lady.

Leon. Dost thou look up?

Friar. Yea; Wherefore should she not?

Leon. Wherefore? Why, doth not every earthly thing
Cry shame upon her? Could she here deny
The story that is printed in her blood [5]?—
Do not live, Hero; do not ope thine eyes:
For did I think, thou would'st not quickly die,
Thought I, thy spirits were stronger than thy shames,
Myself would, on the rearward of reproaches,
Strike at thy life. Griev'd I, I had but one?
Chid I for that at frugal nature's frame [6]?

---

[2] *—shall conjecture hang.*] Conjecture is here used for *suspicion*.
MALONE.

[3] *And never shall it more be gracious.*] i. e. lovely, attractive.
MALONE.

[4] *Hath no man's dagger here a point for me?*]
  " A thousand daggers, all in honest hands!
  " And have not I friend to stick one here!"
Venice Preserv'd. STEEVENS.

[5] *The story that is printed in her blood?*] That is, the story which her blushes discover to be true. JOHNSON.

[6] *—frugal nature's frame?*] *Frame* is contrivance, order, disposition of things. So afterwards: " *—in frame* of villanies." STEEVENS.
The meaning, I think, is,—Grieved I at Nature's being *so frugal* as to have *framed* for me only one child? MALONE.

O, one

O, one too much by thee! Why had I one?
Why ever wast thou lovely in my eyes?
Why had I not, with charitable hand,
Took up a beggar's issue at my gates;
Who smeared thus, and mired with infamy,
I might have said, *No part of it is mine,*
This shame derives itself from unknown loins?
But mine, and mine I lov'd [7], and mine I prais'd,
And mine that I was proud on; mine so much,
That I myself was to myself not mine,
Valuing of her; why, she.—O, she, is fallen
Into a pit of ink! that the wide sea
Hath drops too few to wash her clean again;
And salt too little, which may season give
To her foul tainted flesh!

  Bene. Sir, Sir, be patient:
For my part I am so attir'd in wonder,
I know not what to say.

  Beat. O, on my soul, my cousin is bely'd!

  Bene. Lady, were you her bedfellow last night?

  Beat. No, truly, not; although, until last night,
I have this twelvemonth been her bedfellow.

  Leon. Confirm'd, confirm'd! O, that is stronger made,
Which was before barr'd up with ribs of iron!
Would the two Princes lie? and Claudio lie?
Who lov'd her so, that speaking of her foulness,
Wash'd it with tears? Hence from her; let her die.

  Friar. Hear me a little;
For I have only been silent so long,
And given way unto this course of fortune,
By noting of the lady: I have mark'd
A thousand blushing apparitions
To start into her face; a thousand innocent shames
In angel whiteness bear away those blushes;
And in her eye there hath appear'd a fire,
To burn the errors that these princes hold
Against her maiden truth:—Call me a fool;
Trust not my reading, nor my observations,
Which with experimental seal do warrant
The tenor of my book [8]; trust not my age,

---

[7] *—and mine I lov'd,*] i. e. mine *that* I loved. JOHNSON.
[8] *—of my book;*] i. e. of what I have read. MALONE.

My reverence, calling, nor divinity,
If this sweet Lady lie not guiltless here
Under some biting error.

   Leon. Friar, it cannot be:
Thou seest, that all the grace that she hath left,
Is, that she will not add to her damnation
A sin of perjury; she not denies it:—
Why seek'st thou then to cover with excuse
That which appears in proper nakedness?

   Friar. Lady, what man is he you are accus'd of?

   Hero. They know that do accuse me; I know none:
If I know more of any man alive,
Than that which maiden modesty doth warrant,
Let all my sins lack mercy! O my father,
Prove you that any man with me convers'd
At hours unmeet, or that I yesternight
Maintain'd the change of words with any creature,
Refuse me, hate me, or torture me to death.

   Friar. There is some strange misprision in the princes.

   Bene. Two of them have the very bent of honour [9];
And if their wisdoms be misled in this,
The practice of it lives in John the bastard,
Whose spirits toil in frame of villainies.

   Leon. I know not; if they speak but truth of her,
These hands shall tear her; if they wrong her honour,
The proudest of them shall well hear of it.
Time hath not yet so dry'd this blood of mine,
Nor age so eat up my invention,
Nor fortune made such havoc of my means,
Nor my bad life reft me so much of friends,
But they shall find, awak'd in such a kind,
Both strength of limb, and policy of mind,
Ability in means, and choice of friends,
To quit me of them thoroughly.

   Friar. Pause a while,
And let my counsel sway you in this cause.
Your daughter here the princes left for dead [1];

---

[9] — *bent of honour*;] *Bent* is used by our author for the utmost degree of any passion, or mental quality. In this play before, Benedick says of Beatrice, *her affection has its full bent.* The expression is derived from archery; the bow has its *bent,* when it is drawn as far as it can be. JOHNSON.

[1] *Your daughter here the princes left for dead;*] The old copies have *princess.* The correction was made by Mr. Theobald. MALONE.

Let

Let her awhile be secretly kept in,
And publish it, that she is dead indeed:
Maintain a mourning ostentation [a];
And on your family's old monument
Hang mournful epitaphs, and do all rites
That appertain unto a burial.

Leon. What shall become of this? What will this do?

Friar. Marry, this, well carry'd, shall on her behalf
Change slander to remorse; that is some good:
But not for that dream I on this strange course,
But on this travail look for greater birth.
She dying, as it must be so maintain'd,
Upon the instant that she was accus'd,
Shall be lamented, pity'd, and excus'd,
Of every hearer: for it so falls out,
That what we have we prize not to the worth,
Whiles we enjoy it; but being lack'd and lost,
Why, then we rack the value [3]; then we find
The virtue that possession would not shew us
Whiles it was ours:—So will it fare with Claudio:
When he shall hear she dy'd upon his words,
The idea of her life shall sweetly creep
Into his study of imagination;
And every lovely organ of her life
Shall come apparel'd in more precious habit,
More moving-delicate, and full of life,
Into the eye and prospect of his soul,
Than when she liv'd indeed:—then shall he mourn,
(If ever love had interest in his liver,)
And wish he had not so accused her;
No, though he thought his accusation true.
Let this be so, and doubt not but success
Will fashion the event in better shape
Than I can lay it down in likelihood.
But if all aim but this be levell'd false,
The supposition of the Lady's death
Will quench the wonder of her infamy:

---

[a] — *ostentation*;] Show; appearance. JOHNSON.

[3] — *we rack the value*;] We exaggerate the value. The allusion is to *rack-rents*. The same kind of thought occurs in *Antony and Cleopatra*:

" What our contempts do often hurl from us,
" We wish it ours again." STEEVENS.

And, if it fort not well, you may conceal her
(As beſt befits her wounded reputation,)
In ſome recluſive and religious life,
Out of all eyes, tongues, minds, and injuries.

Bene. Signior Leonato, let the Friar adviſe you:
And though, you know, my inwardneſs and love
Is very much unto the Prince and Claudio,
Yet, by mine honour, I will deal in this
As ſecretly, and juſtly, as your ſoul
Should with your body.

Leon. Being that
I flow in grief, the ſmalleſt twine may lead me [4].

Friar. 'Tis well conſented; preſently away;
For to ſtrange ſores ſtrangely they ſtrain the cure.—
Come, Lady, die to live: this wedding day,
Perhaps, is but prolong'd; have patience, and endure.

[*Exeunt* Friar, Hero, *and* Leonato [5].

Bene. Lady Beatrice, have you wept all this while?
Beat. Yea, and I will weep a while longer.
Bene. I will not deſire that.
Beat. You have no reaſon, I do it freely.
Bene. Surely, I do believe your fair couſin is wrong'd.
Beat. Ah, how much might the man deſerve of me, that would right her!
Bene. Is there any way to ſhew ſuch friendſhip?
Beat. A very even way, but no ſuch friend.
Bene. May a man do it?

---

[4] — *the ſmalleſt twine may lead me.*] This is one of our author's obſervations upon life. Men overpowered with diſtreſs, eagerly liſten to the firſt offers of relief, cloſe with every ſcheme, and believe every promiſe. He that has no longer any confidence in himſelf, is glad to repoſe his truſt in any other that will undertake to guide him. JOHNSON.

[5] *Exeunt, &c.*] The poet, in my opinion, has ſhewn a great deal of addreſs in this ſcene. Beatrice here engages her lover to revenge the injury done her couſin Hero: and without this very natural incident, conſidering the character of Beatrice, and that the ſtory of her paſſion for Benedick was all a fable, ſhe could never have been eaſily or naturally brought to confeſs ſhe loved him, notwithſtanding all the foregoing preparation. And yet, on this confeſſion, in this very place, depended the whole ſucceſs of the plot upon her and Beardick. For had ſhe not owned her love here, they muſt have ſoon found out the trick, and then the deſign of bringing them together had been defeated; and ſhe would never have owned a paſſion ſhe had been only tricked into, had not her deſire of revenging her couſin's wrong made her drop her capricious humour at once. WARBURTON.

Beat.

Beat. It is a man's office, but not yours.

Bene. I do love nothing in the world so well as you; is not that strange?

Beat. As strange as the thing I know not: It were as possible for me to say, I loved nothing so well as you; you believe me not; and yet I lie not; I confess nothing, nor I deny nothing:—I am sorry for my cousin.

Bene. By my sword, Beatrice, thou lovest me.

Beat. Do not swear by it, and eat it.

Bene. I will swear by it, that you love me; and I will make him eat it, that says, I love not you.

Beat. Will you not eat your word?

Bene. With no sauce that can be devised to it: I protest, I love thee.

Beat. Why then, God forgive me!

Bene. What offence, sweet Beatrice?

Beat. You have staid me in an happy hour; I was about to protest, I loved you.

Bene. And do it with all thy heart.

Beat. I love you with so much of my heart, that none is left to protest.

Bene. Come, bid me do any thing for thee.

Beat. Kill Claudio.

Bene. Ha! not for the wide world.

Beat. You kill me to deny it: Farewel.

Bene. Tarry, sweet Beatrice.

Beat. I am gone, though I am here [6];—There is no love in you:—nay, I pray you, let me go.

Bene. Beatrice—

Beat. In faith, I will go.

Bene. We'll be friends first.

Beat. You dare easier be friends with me, than fight with mine enemy.

Bene. Is Claudio thine enemy?

Beat. Is he not approved in the height a villain [7], that hath slander'd, scorn'd, dishonour'd my kinswoman?—O,

---

[6] *I am gone, though I am here:*] i. e. I am out of your mind already, though I remain here in person before you. STEEVENS.

Or, perhaps, my affection is withdrawn from you, thorgh I am yet here. MALONE.

[7] *— in the height a villain,*] So, in *King Henry VIII.*

"He's traitor to the *height.*"

In *præcipiti* vitium stetit. STEEVENS.

that I were a man!—What, bear her in hand until they come to take hands; and then with public accusation, uncover'd slander, unmitigated rancour—O God, that I were a man! I would eat his heart in the market-place.

Bene. Hear me, Beatrice.

Beat. Talk with a man out at a window?—a proper saying!

Bene. Nay, but Beatrice;—

Beat. Sweet Hero! she is wrong'd, she is slander'd, she is undone.

Bene. Beat—

Beat. Princes and counties [9]! Surely, a princely testimony, a goodly count-comfect [9]; a sweet gallant, surely! O that I were a man for his sake! or that I had any friend would be a man for my sake! But manhood is melted into courtesies, valour into compliment, and men are only turned into tongue, and trim ones too [1]: he is now as valiant as Hercules, that only tells a lie, and swears it:—I cannot be a man with wishing, therefore I will die a woman with grieving.

Bene. Tarry, good Beatrice: By this hand, I love thee.

Beat. Use it for my love some other way than swearing by it.

Bene. Think you in your soul, the Count Claudio hath wrong'd Hero?

Beat. Yea, as sure as I have a thought, or a soul.

Bene. Enough, I am engaged, I will challenge him; I will kiss your hand, and so leave you: By this hand, Claudio shall render me a dear account: As you hear of me, so think of me. Go, comfort your cousin: I must say she is dead; and so farewel. [*Exeunt.*

---

[9] — *and counties!*] *County* was the ancient general term for a nobleman. See note on the *County* Paris in *Romeo and Juliet*. STEEVENS.

[9] — *a goodly count-comfect*] i. e. a specious nobleman made out of sugar. STEEVENS.

[1] — *and men are only turned into* tongue, *and trim ones too*;] Mr. Heath would read *tongues*, but he mistakes the construction of the sentence, which is—not only men, but trim ones, are turned into tongue, i. e. not only *common* but *clever* men, &c. STEEVENS.

SCENE

SCENE II.

A Prison.

Enter DOGBERRY, VERGES, *and* SEXTON, *in gowns*[2]: BORACHIO, CONRADE, *and the* Watch.

Dog. Is our whole diſſembly appear'd?
Ver. O, a ſtool and a cuſhion for the ſexton.[*]
Sex. Which be the malefactors?
Dog. Marry, that am I and my partner.
Ver. Nay that's certain; we have the exhibition to examine.
Sex. But which are the offenders that are to be examined; let them come before maſter conſtable.
Dog. Yea, marry, let them come before me.—What is your name, friend?
Bora. Borachio.
Dog. Pray write down—Borachio.—Yours, Sirrah?
Con. I am a gentleman, Sir, and my name is Conrade.
Dog. Write down—maſter gentleman Conrade.——Maſters, do you ſerve God?
Con. Bora. Yea, Sir, we hope.
Dog. Write down—that they hope they ſerve God:—and write God firſt; for God defend but God ſhould go before ſuch villains[3]!—Maſters, it is proved already that you are little

---

[2] — *in gowns*;] It appears from *The Black Dog*, 4to, 1604, that this was the dreſs of a conſtable in our author's time: "— when they miſt their *conſtable*, and ſawe the *black gowne* of his office lye full in a puddle—"

The *ſexton* (as Mr. Tyrwhitt obſerved) is ſtyled in this ſtage-direction, in the old copies, *the Towne-clerk,* "probably from his doing the duty of ſuch an officer." But this error has only happened here; for throughout the ſcene itſelf he is deſcribed by his proper title. By miſtake alſo in the quarto, and the folio, which appears to have been printed from it, the name of Kempe (an actor in our author's theatre) throughout this ſcene is prefixed to the ſpeeches of Dogberry, and that of Cowley to thoſe of Verges, except in two or three inſtances, where either *Conſtable* or *Andrew* are ſubſtituted for Kempe. MALONE.

[*] O, a ſtool and a cuſhion *for the Sexton*.] Perhaps a ridicule was here aimed at *The Spaniſh Tragedy:*
"*Hieron.* What, are you ready?
"*Balth.* Bring a *chaire* and a *cuſhion* for the king." MALONE.

[3] *Write down, &c.* This paſſage, which was omitted in the folio, was reſtored by Mr. Theobald. MALONE.

The

little better than false knaves, and it will go near to be thought so shortly; How answer you for yourselves?

Con. Marry, Sir, we say we are none.

Dog. A marvellous witty fellow, I assure you; but I will go about with him.—Come you hither, Sirrah; a word in your ear, Sir; I say to you, it is thought you are false knaves.

Bora. Sir, I say to you, we are none.

Dog. Well, stand aside.—'Fore God, they are both in a tale:—Have you writ down—that they are none?

Sex. Master Constable, you go not the way to examine; you must call forth the watch that are their accusers.

Dog. Yea, marry, that's the eftest way ⁴:—Let the watch come forth:—Masters, I charge you in the prince's name accuse these men.

1st. Watch. This man said, Sir, that Don John, the prince's brother, was a villain.

Dog. Write down—prince John a villain:—Why this is flat perjury, to call a prince's brother—villain.

Bora. Master Constable—

Dog. Pray thee, fellow, peace! I do not like thy look, I promise thee.

Sex. What heard you him say else?

2d. Watch. Marry that he had received a thousand ducats of Don John, for accusing the Lady Hero wrongfully.

Dog. Flat burglary, as ever was committed.

Ver. Yea, by the mass, that it is.

Sex. What else, fellow?

1st. Watch. And that Count Claudio did mean, upon his words, to disgrace Hero before the whole assembly, and not marry her.

Dog. O villain! thou wilt be condemned into everlasting redemption for this.

Sex. What else?

2d. Watch. This is all.

Sex. And this is more, masters, than you can deny. Prince John is this morning secretly stolen away; Hero was in this manner accused, in this manner refused, and upon the grief of this, suddenly died.—Mas-

---

⁵ The omission of this passage since the edition of 1600, may be accounted for from the stat. 3 Jac. I. c. 21. the sacred name being jestingly used four times in one line. BLACKSTONE.

⁴ — *the eftest way.*] Dogberry means *deftest*; i. e. the most fit and commodious way. MALONE.

ter Constable, let these men be bound, and brought to Leonato's; I will go before, and shew him their examination. [*Exit.*

Dog. Come, let them be opinion'd.
Ver. Let them be in the hands—
Con. Off, coxcomb!⁵
Dog. God's my life! where's the sexton? let him write down—the prince's officer, coxcomb.—Come, bind them:—Thou naughty varlet!
Con. Away! you are an ass, you are an ass.
Dog. Dost thou not suspect my place? Dost thou not suspect my years?—O that he were here to write me down—an ass!—but, masters, remember, that I am an ass; though it be not written down, yet forget not that I am an ass:——No, thou villain, thou art full of piety as shall be proved upon thee by good witness: I am a wise fellow, and, which is more, an officer; and, which is more, a householder; and, which is more, as pretty a piece of flesh as any in Messina; and one that knows the law, go to; and a rich fellow enough, go to; and a fellow that hath had losses; and one that hath two gowns, and every thing handsome about him:—Bring him away. O, that I had been writ down—an ass! [*Exeunt.*

⁵ *Off, coxcomb!*] The old copies read—*of*, and these words make a part of the last speech, "Let them be in the hand *of coxcomb.*" The present regulation was made by Dr. Warburton, and has been adopted by the subsequent editors. *Off* was formerly spelt *of.* See p. 149, n. 1. In the early editions of these plays a broken sentence (like that before us, "Let them be in the hands"—) is almost always corrupted by being tacked, through the ignorance of the transcriber or printer, to the subsequent words. So in *Coriolanus*, instead of
You shames of Rome! you herd of—Boils and plagues
Plaister you o'er!
we have in the folio, 1623, and the subsequent copies,
You shames of Rome, you! Herd of boils and plagues, &c.
See also *Measure for Measure.*
Perhaps however we should read and regulate the passage thus:
Ver. Let them be in the hands of—[*the law,* he might have intended to say.]
Con. Coxcomb! MALONE.

ACT

ACT V. SCENE I.

Before Leonato's House.

Enter LEONATO *and* ANTONIO.

Ant. If you go on thus, you will kill yourself;
And 'tis not wisdom, thus to second grief
Against yourself.
    Leon. I pray thee, cease thy counsel,
Which falls into mine ears as profitless
As water in a sieve: give not me counsel;
Nor let no comforter delight mine ear,
But such a one whose wrongs do suit with mine.
Bring me a father, that so lov'd his child,
Whose joy of her is overwhelm'd like mine,
And bid him speak of patience;
Measure his woe the length and breadth of mine,
And let it answer every strain for strain;
As thus for thus, and such a grief for such,
In every lineament, branch, shape, and form:
If such a one will smile, and stroke his beard;
In sorrow wag; cry hem, when he should groan¹;

Patch

---

¹ *In sorrow wag; cry hem, when he should groan;*] This is one of those passages from which an editor can hardly escape without censure. The old copies read:

    And sorrow, wag, cry hem, when he should groan.

To print absolute nonsense is surely no part of his duty. To substitute any word in the room of those furnished by ancient copies (though sanctioned in some measure by the numerous emendations which at various times have been happily made,) is certainly undesirable; yet at all hazards one would wish for some glimmering of meaning. To obtain this, Dr. Johnson printed this line thus (in which he has been followed in the late editions):

    And, sorrow, wag, cry; hem when he should groan;

but this punctuation (to say nothing of the *unexampled* harshness of such a phraseology) is certainly inadmissible; it appearing from a passage in *K. Henry IV.* and from other examples, that to "*cry hem*" was in our author's time a cant term of festivity. See Mr. Tyrwhitt's note below. Again, in *As you Like it:*—"If I could *cry hem*, and have him." On the other hand, to *cry woe* is used in the *Winter's Tale* to denote grief. So also, in *K. Richard III:*

    " You

Patch grief with proverbs; make misfortune drunk
With candle-wasters [2]; bring him yet to me,
                                                    And

"You live, that shall cry woe for this hereafter."
For the emendation now made the present editor is answerable. *And* and *In*, hastily or indistinctly pronounced, might have been easily confounded, supposing (what there is great reason to believe) that these plays were copied for the press by the ear; and by this slight change a clear sense is given, the latter part of the line being a paraphrase on the foregoing. So afterwards: "Charm ach with air, and agony, &c."
This emendation may derive some support from *K. Henry V.* edit. 1623, where we find

So many a thousand actions once a foot
And in one purpose—

instead of—*End* in one purpose; the transcriber's ear having deceived him, as I suppose it did in the present instance.

With respect to the word *wag*, the using it as a verb, in the sense of *to play the wag*, is entirely in Shakspeare's manner. There is scarcely one of his plays in which we do not find substantives used as verbs. Thus we have—to testimony, to boy, to couch, to grave, to bench, to voice, to paper, to page, to dram, to stage, to fever, to fool, to palate, to mountebank, to god, to virgin, to passion, to monster, to history, to fable, to wall, to period, to spaniel, to stranger, &c. &c.

I shall subjoin the conjectures of Mr. Tyrwhitt and Mr. Steevens on this difficult passage, as the emendations suggested by them depart very little from the old copies. The reading proposed by the latter gentleman (And, *sorry wag*, &c.) appears so probable, that I know not whether it has not as good a title to a place in the text as that which I have adopted. Let me however observe, that, though the punctuation of the old copies is of no great authority, yet in so doubtful a matter as the present it may be worth attending to. In both the quarto and folio there is a comma after *sorrow*, which, though unnecessary, is not inconsistent with the emendation now made, but entirely adverse to the supposition that that word was a misprint for any epithet applied to *wag*.

For the latter word Mr. Theobald reads *wage*, and Sir T. Hanmer and Dr. Warburton *waive*.

The following errors of the press, in the old copies, which I had not observed, when this note was written, incline me to prefer Mr. Steevens's emendation of this passage (And, *sorry wag*, &c.) to my own. In *Cymbeline*, Act. v. sc. ult. we find in the original copy, "I am *sorrow* for thee," instead of "I am *sorry*," &c. And in one of the quarto copies of *K. Lear*, printed in 1608, the same misprint is found in Act iv. sc. vii.

"——— I am only *sorrow*
"He had no other deathsman."

The other quarto, printed in the same year, and also the folio, read rightly,

"I am only *sorry*," &c.

The word *wag*, as a substantive, however unsuitable to the gravity of the speaker, may be also confirmed by a passage in *Cymbeline*:

Vol. IV.   H   "——— change

And I of him will gather patience.
But there is no such man: For, brother, men
Can counsel, and speak comfort to that grief

"———— change fear and niceness
"————————— into a *waggish* courage,
" Ready in *gibes*, quick-answer'd, saucy," &c.

i. e. to the courage of a gay, lively, young fellow, one who would "*cry hem*, when he should groan. MALONE.

I think we might read—

And sorrow *gagge*; cry hem, when he should groan;"— but leaving this conjecture to shift for itself, I will say a few words on the phrase, *cry hem*. It is used again by our author in the *First Part of Henry IV*. Act ii. sc. vii. "They call drinking deep, dying scarlet; and when you breathe in your watering, they *cry hem*, and bid you play it off."—In both places to *cry hem*, seems to signify the same as *to cry courage*; in which sense the interjection *hem* was sometimes also used by the Latins. TYRWHITT.

What will be said of the conceit I shall now offer, I know not; let it, however, take its chance. We might read:

If such a one will smile, and stroke his beard:
And, *sorry wag!* cry hem, when he should groan.—

i. e. *unfeeling humourist!* to employ a *note of festivity, when his sighs ought to express concern*. Both the words I would introduce, are used by Shakspeare. Falstaff calls the prince, *sweet wag!* and the epithet *sorry* is applied, even at this time, to denote any moderate deviation from propriety or morality; as, for instance, a *sorry fellow*. Othello speaks of a salt and *sorry* rheum. STEEVENS.

² ———— *made misfortune drunk*.

With candle-wasters;] This may mean, either wash away his sorrow among those who sit up all night to drink, and in that sense may be styled *wasters of candles*; or overpower his misfortunes by swallowing flap-dragons in his glass, which are described by Falstaff as made of *candles' ends*. STEEVENS.

This is a very difficult passage, and hath not, I think, been satisfactorily explained. The explanation I shall offer, will give, I believe, as little satisfaction; but I will, however, venture it. *Candle-wasters* is a term of contempt for scholars; thus Jonson in *Cynthia's Revels*, Act iii. sc. ii.—" spoiled by a whoreson book-worm, a *candle-waster*." In the *Antiquary*, Act iii. is a like term of ridicule: " He should there catch your delicate court-ear, than all your head-scratchers, thumb-biters, *lamp-wasters* of them all." The sense then, which I would assign to Shakspeare, is this: " If such a one will patch grief with proverbs,—*ease or cover the wounds of his grief with proverbial sayings*;— make misfortune drunk with candle-wasters,—*stupify misfortune, or render himself insensible to the strokes of it, by the conversation or lucubrations of scholars; the production of the lamp, but not fitted to human nature*. *Patch*, in the sense of mending a defect or breach, occurs in *Hamlet*, Act v. sc. i:

O that the earth which kept the world in awe,
Should *patch* a wall, to expel the winter's flaw. WHALLEY.

Which

Which they themselves not feel; but, tasting it,
Their counsel turns to passion, which before
Would give preceptial medicine to rage,
Fetter strong madness in a silken thread,
Charm ach with air, and agony with words:
No, no; 'tis all men's office to speak patience
To those that wring under the load of sorrow;
But no man's virtue, nor sufficiency,
To be so moral, when he shall endure
The like himself: therefore give me no counsel:
My griefs cry louder than advertisement [3].

Ant. Therein do men from children nothing differ.

Leon. I pray thee peace; I will be flesh and blood;
For there was never yet philosopher,
That could endure the tooth-ach patiently;
However they have writ the style of gods [4],
And made a pish at chance and sufferance [5].

Ant. Yet bend not all the harm upon yourself;
Make those, that do offend you, suffer too.

Leon. There thou speak'st reason: nay, I will do so:
My soul doth tell me, Hero is bely'd;
And that shall Claudio know, so shall the Prince,
And all of them, that thus dishonour her.

Enter Don PEDRO *and* CLAUDIO.

Ant. Here comes the Prince, and Claudio, hastily.

Don Pedro. Good den, good den.

Claud. Good day to both of you.

Leon. Hear you, my Lords—

Don Pedro. We have some haste, Leonato.

Leon. Some haste, my Lord?—well, fare you well, my Lord:—
Are you so hasty now?—well, all is one.

[3] — *than advertisement.*] That is, than admonition, than moral instruction. JOHNSON.

[4] *However they have writ the style of gods.*] This alludes to the extravagant titles the Stoicks gave their wise men. WARBURTON.

Shakspeare might have used this expression, without any acquaintance with the hyperboles of stoicism. By the *style of gods*, he meant an exalted language; such as we may suppose would be written by beings superior to human calamities, and therefore regarding them with neglect and coldness. STEEVENS.

[5] *And made a pish at chance and sufferance.*] Alludes to their famous apathy. WARBURTON.

Old Copies—*push.* Corrected by Mr. Pope. MALONE.

H 2 *D. Pedro.*

Don Pedro. Nay, do not quarrel with us, good old man.
Ant. If he could right himself with quarreling,
Some of us would lie low.
Claud. Who wrongs him?
Leon. Marry,
Thou dost wrong me, thou dissembler, thou:—
Nay, never lay thy hand upon thy sword,
I fear thee not.
Claud. Marry, beshrew my hand,
If it should give your age such cause of fear:
In faith my hand meant nothing to my sword.
Leon. Tush, tush, man, never fleer and jest at me:
I speak not like a dotard, nor a fool;
As, under privilege of age, to brag
What I have done being young, or what would do,
Were I not old: Know, Claudio, to thy head,
Thou hast so wrong'd my innocent child, and me,
That I am forc'd to lay my reverence by;
And, with grey hairs, and bruise of many days,
Do challenge thee to trial of a man.
I say, thou hast bely'd mine innocent child;
Thy slander hath gone through and through her heart,
And she lies bury'd with her ancestors:
O, in a tomb where never scandal slept,
Save this of hers, fram'd by thy villainy!
Claud. My villainy?
Leon. Thine, Claudio; thine I say.
Don Pedro. You say not right, old man.
Leon. My Lord, my Lord;
I'll prove it on his body, if he dare;
Despight his nice fence, and his active practice,
His May of youth, and bloom of lustihood.
Claud. Away, I will not have to do with you.
Leon. Canst thou so duffe me⁶? Thou hast kill'd my child;
If thou kill'st me, boy, thou shalt kill a man.
Ant. He shall kill two of us, and men indeed⁷:

But

---

⁶ *Canst thou so daffe me?*] To *daffe* and *doffe* are synonimous terms, that mean to *put off*. THEOBALD.

⁷ Ant. *He shall kill two of us*, &c.] This *brother Anthony* is the truest picture imaginable of human nature. He had assumed the character of a sage to comfort his brother, o'erwhelmed with grief for his only daughter's affront and dishonour; and had severely reproved him for not
commanding

But that's no matter; let him kill one first;—
Win me and wear me—let him answer me;—
Come, follow me, boy; come, Sir boy, come, follow me:
Sir boy, I'll whip you from your foining fence;
Nay, as I am a gentleman, I will.

Leon. Brother—

Ant. Content yourself; God knows, I lov'd my niece;
And she is dead, slander'd to death by villains;
That dare as well answer a man, indeed,
As I dare take a serpent by the tongue:
Boys, apes, braggarts, Jacks [8], milksops!—

Leon. Brother Anthony—

Ant. Hold you content; What, man! I know them, yea,
And what they weigh, even to the utmost scruple?
Scambling [9], out-facing, fashion-mong'ring boys,
That lie, and cog, and flout, deprave and slander,
Go antickly, and show outward hideousness,
And speak off [1] half a dozen dangerous words,
How they might hurt their enemies, if they durst,
And this is all.

Leon. But, brother Antony—

Ant. Come 'tis no matter;
Do not you meddle, let me deal in this.

D. Pedro. Gentlemen both, we will not wake your patience [2].

commanding his passion better on so trying an occasion. Ἀ is immediately after this, no sooner does he begin to suspect that his son and valour are slighted, but he falls into the most intemperate fit of rage himself; and all he can do or say is not of power to pacify him. This is copying nature with a penetration and exactness of judgment peculiar to Shakspeare. As to the expression, too, of his passion, nothing can be more highly painted. WARBURTON.

[8] —*braggarts*, Jacks,] See p. 78. n. 3. MALONE.

[9] *Scambling.*]—i. e. *scrambling.* The word is more than once used by Shakspeare. See Dr. Percy's note on the first speech of the play of K. *Henry* V. and likewise the Scots proverb "It is well ken'd your father's son was never a *scambler.*" A *scambler*, in its literal sense, is one who goes about among his friends to get a dinner, by the Irish call'd a *cosherer*. STEEVENS.

[1] *And speak off*—] The old copies have—*of.* Mr. Theobald made the correction. In the books of our author's age, *of* is very frequently printed instead of *off*. MALONE.

[2] *we will not wake your patience.*] The old men have been both very angry and outrageous; the Prince tells them that he and Claudio will *not wake their patience*, will not any longer force them to *endure* the presence of those whom, though they look on them as enemies, they cannot resist. JOHNSON.

My heart is sorry for your daughter's death;
But on my honour, she was charg'd with nothing
But what was true, and very full of proof.

Leon. My Lord, my Lord—

D. Pedro. I will not hear you.

Leon. No?
Come, brother, away:—I will be heard;—

Ant. And shall,
Or some of us will smart for it.

Enter BENEDICK.

D. Pedro. See, see,
Here comes the man we went to seek.

[*Exeunt* LEONATO *and* ANTONIO.

Claud. Now, Signior!
What news?

Bene. Good day, my Lord.

D. Pedro. Welcome, Signior:
You are almost come to part almost a fray.

Claud. We had like to have had our two noses snapt off
with two old men without teeth.

D. Pedro. Leonato and his brother: What think'st
thou? Had we fought, I doubt, we should have been too
young for them.

Bene. In a false quarrel there is no true valour.
I came to seek you both.

Claud. We have been up and down to seek thee; for we
are high-proof melancholy, and would fain have it beaten
away: Wilt thou use thy wit?

Bene. It is in my scabbard; Shall I draw it?

D. Pedro. Dost thou wear thy wit by thy side?

Claud. Never any did so, though very many have been
beside their wit.—I will bid thee draw, as we do the min-
strels; draw, to pleasure us.

D. Pedro. As I am an honest man, he looks pale:—
Art thou sick, or angry?

Claud. What! courage, man! What though care kill'd
a cat, thou hast mettle enough in thee to kill care.

Bene. Sir, I shall meet your wit in the career, an you
charge it against me:—I pray you choose another subject.

Claud. Nay, then give him another staff; this last was
broke cross³.

³ *Nay, then give him another staff*; &c] An allusion to *tilting*. See
note, *As you Like it*, Act iii. sc. iv. WARBURTON.

D. Pedro.

ABOUT NOTHING.

D. Pedro. By this light, he changes more and more; I think, he be angry indeed.

Claud. If he be, he knows how to turn his girdle [4].

Bene. Shall I speak a word in your ear?

Claud. God bless me from a challenge!

Bene. You are a villain;—I jest not:—I will make it good how you dare, with what you dare, and when you dare:—Do me right, or I will protest your cowardice. You have kill'd a sweet lady, and her death shall fall heavy on you: Let me hear from you.

Claud. Well, I will meet you, so I may have good cheer.

D. Pedro. What, a feast? a feast?

Claud. I'faith, I thank him; he hath bid [5] me to a calf's-head and a capon; the which if I do not carve most curiously, say, my knife's naught.—Shall I not find a woodcock too [6]?

Bene. Sir, your wit ambles well; it goes easily.

D. Pedro. I'll tell thee how Beatrice prais'd thy wit the other day: I said, thou hadst a fine wit; *True,* says she, *a fine little one:* No, said I, *a great wit; Right,* said she, *a great gross one;* Nay, said I, *a good wit; Just,* said she, *it hurts no body:* Nay, said I, *the gentleman is wise; Certain,* said she, *a wise gentleman* [7]; Nay, said I, *he hath the tongues; That I*

[4] *—to turn his girdle.*] We have a proverbial speech, *If he be angry, let him turn the buckle of his girdle.* But I do not know its original or meaning. JOHNSON.

A corresponding expression is used to this day in Ireland.—*If he be angry, let him tie up his brogues.* Neither proverb, I believe, has any other meaning than this: If he is in a bad humour, let him employ himself till he is in a better. STEEVENS.

I believe the meaning is—If he be angry, he knows how to prepare himself for combat, and to obtain redress. Wrestlers (as is observed in the *Gentleman's Magazine,* 1782) formerly before they engaged, probably turned the buckle of their girdle behind.—In a letter from Sir Ralph Winwood to Secretary Cecil, dated Dec. 17, 1602, we meet with the expression mentioned by Dr. Johnson: "I said, what I spake was not to make him angry. He replied, *If I were angry, I might turn the buckle of my girdle behind me.*" MALONE.

[5] *—bid—*] i. e. invited. REED

[6] *Shall I not find a woodcock too?*] A woodcock, being supposed to have no brains, was a proverbial term for a foolish fellow. See the *London Prodigal,* 1605, and other comedies. MALONE.

[7] *—a wise gentleman;*] This jest depending on the colloquial use of words is now obscure; perhaps we should read *a wise gentleman,* or *a man wise enough to be a coward.* Perhaps *wise gentleman* was in that age used ironically, and always stood for *silly fellow.* JOHNSON,

believe,

believe, said she, *for he swore a thing to me on Monday night, which he forswore on Tuesday morning; there's a double tongue, there's two tongues.* Thus did she, an hour together, transhape thy particular virtues; yet, at last, she concluded with a sigh, thou wast the properest man in Italy.

Claud. For the which she wept heartily, and said, she cared not.

D. Pedro. Yea, that she did; but yet, for all that, an if she did not hate him deadly, she would love him dearly; the old man's daughter told us all.

Claud. All, all; and moreover, *God saw him when he was hid in the garden.*

D. Pedro. But when shall we set the savage bull's horns on the sensible Benedick's head?

Claud. Yea, and text underneath, *Here dwells Benedick the married man?*

Bene. Fare you well, boy; you know my mind; I will leave you now to your gossip-like humour: you break jests as braggarts do their blades, which, God be thanked, hurt not.—My Lord, for your many courtesies I thank you; I must discontinue your company: your brother, the bastard, is fled from Messina; you have, among you, kill'd a sweet and innocent lady: For my Lord Lack-beard there, he and I shall meet; and till then, peace be with him!

[*Exit* BENEDICK.

D. Pedro. He is in earnest.

Claud. In most profound earnest; and, I'll warrant you, for the love of Beatrice.

D. Pedro. And hath challeng'd thee?

Claud. Most sincerely.

D. Pedro. What a pretty thing man is, when he goes in his doublet and hose, and leaves off his wita!

Enter

ᵃ *What a pretty thing man is, when he goes in his doublet and hose, and leaves off his wit!*] It was esteemed a mark of levity and want of becoming gravity, at that time, *to go in the doublet and hose, and leave off the cloak;* to which this well turned expression alludes. The thought is, that love makes a man as ridiculous, and exposes him as naked as being in the doublet and hose without a cloak. WARBURTON.

I doubt much concerning this interpretation, yet am by no means confident that my own is right. I believe, however, these words refer to what Don Pedro had said just before—" And hath *challeng'd* thee?" —and that the meaning is, What a pretty thing a man is, when he is silly enough to throw off his cloak, and go in his doublet and hose, to *fight* for a woman! In the *Merry Wives of Windsor,* when Sir Hugh

Enter Dogberry, Verges, *and the* Watch, *with* Conrade *and* Borachio.

Claud. He is then a giant to an ape: but then is an ape a doctor to such a man.

D. Pedro. But, soft you, let be⁹; pluck up my heart, and be sad: Did he not say, my brother was fled?

Dog. Come, you, Sir; if justice cannot tame you, she shall ne'er weigh more reasons in her balance: nay, an you be a cursing hypocrite once, you must be look'd to.

D. Pedro. How now, two of my brother's men bound! Borachio, one!

Claud. Harken after their offence, my Lord!

D. Pedro. Officers, what offence have these men done?

Dog. Marry, Sir, they have committed false report; moreover, they have spoken untruths: secondarily, they are slanders; sixth and lastly, they have bely'd a lady; thirdly, they have verify'd unjust things; and, to conclude, they are lying knaves.

D. Pedro. First, I ask thee what they have done; thirdly, I ask thee what's their offence; sixth and lastly, why they are committed; and, to conclude, what you lay to their charge?

---

is going to engage with Dr. Caius, he walks about in his doublet and hose. "Page. And youthful still in your *doublet and hose*, this raw rheumatic day!" — "There is reasons and causes for it," says Sir Hugh, alluding to the duel he was going to fight.—I am aware that there was a particular species of single combat, called *Rapier and cloak*; but I suppose, nevertheless, that when the small sword came into common use, the cloak was generally laid aside in duels, as tending to embarrass the combatants. Malone.

⁹ *But, soft you, let be;*] The quarto and first folio read corruptly—*let me be*, which the editor of the second folio, in order to obtain some sense, converted to—*let me see.* I was once idle enough to suppose that copy was of some authority; but a minute examination of it has shewn me that all the alterations made in it were merely arbitrary, and generally very injudicious. *Let be* were without doubt the author's words. The same expression occurs again in *K. Henry VIII*:

"——— and they were ratified,
"As he cried, thus *let be.*"

Again, in *Antony and Cleopatra*, Act iv. sc. iv.
"What's this for? Ah, *let be, let be.*" Malone.
Again, in *The Winter's Tale*, Leonato says, "*let be, let be.*" Reed.

Let be is the true reading. It means, *let things remain as they are*. I have heard the phrase used by Dr. Johnson himself. Steevens.

Claud. Rightly reasoned, and in his own division; and, by my troth, there's one meaning well suited [1].

D. Pedro. Whom have you offended, masters, that you are thus bound to your answer? this learned constable is too cunning to be understood: What's your offence?

Bora. Sweet Prince, let me go no farther to mine answer; do you hear me, and let this Count kill me. I have deceived even your very eyes: what your wisdoms could not discover, these shallow fools have brought to light; who, in the night, overheard me confessing to this man, how Don John your brother incens'd me [*] to slander the Lady Hero; how you were brought into the orchard, and saw me court Margaret in Hero's garments; how you disgraced her, when you should marry her: my villainy they have upon record; which I had rather seal with my death than repeat over to my shame: the lady is dead upon mine and my master's false accusation; and briefly, I desire nothing but the reward of a villain.

D. Pedro. Runs not this speech like iron through your blood?

Claud. I have drunk poison, whiles he utter'd it.

D. Pedro. But did my brother set thee on this?

Bora. Yea, and paid me richly for the practice of it.

D. Pedro. He is compos'd and fram'd of treachery:— And fled he is upon this villainy.

Claud. Sweet Hero! now thy image doth appear
In the rare semblance that I lov'd it first.

Dog. Come, bring away the plaintiffs; by this time our Sexton hath reform'd Signior Leonato of the matter: And masters, do not forget to specify, when time and place shall serve, that I am an ass.

Verg. Here, here comes master Signior Leonato, and the Sexton too.

Re-enter LEONATO, *and* ANTONIO *with the* SEXTON.

Leon. Which is the villain? Let me see his eyes;
That when I note another man like him,
I may avoid him: Which of these is he?

---

[1] *— one meaning well suited.*] That is, *one meaning is put into many different dresses*; the Prince having asked the same question in four modes of speech. JOHNSON.

[*] *incens'd me—*] instigated me. See Minsheu's Dict. In v. MALONE.

Bora.

Bora. If you would know your wronger, look on me.
Leon. Art thou the slave, that with thy breath hast kill'd
Mine innocent child?
Bora. Yea, even I alone.
Leon. No, not so, villain; thou bely'st thyself;
Here stand a pair of honourable men,
A third is fled, that had a hand in it:—
I thank you, Princes, for my daughter's death!
Record it with your high and worthy deeds;
'Twas bravely done, if you bethink you of it.
Claud. I know not how to pray your patience,
Yet I must speak: Choose your revenge yourself;
Impose me to what penance [2] your invention
Can lay upon my sin: yet sinn'd I not,
But in mistaking.
D. Pedro. By my soul, nor I;
And yet, to satisfy this good old man,
I would bend under any heavy weight
That he'll enjoin me to.
Leon. I cannot bid you bid my daughter live,
That were impossible; but, I pray you both,
Possess the people in Messina here
How innocent she dy'd: and, if your love
Can labour aught in sad invention,
Hang her an epitaph upon her tomb,
And sing it to her bones; sing it to-night:—
To-morrow morning come you to my house;
And since you could not be my son-in-law,
Be yet my nephew; my brother hath a daughter,
Almost the copy of my child that's dead,
And she alone is heir to both of us [3];
Give her the right you should have given her cousin,
And so dies my revenge.
Claud. O noble Sir,
Your over-kindness doth wring tears from me!

---

[2] *Impose me to what penance*—] i. e. *command* me to undergo whatever penance, &c. A task or exercise prescribed by way of punishment for a fault committed at the universities, is yet called (as Mr. Steevens has observed in a former note) an *impositio*. MALONE.

[3] *And she alone is heir to both of us;*] Shakspeare seems to have forgot what he had made Leonato say in the fifth scene of the first act to Antonio, "*How now, brother; where is my cousin your son? hath he provided the musick?*" ANONYMOUS.

I do embrace your offer; and difpofe
For henceforth of poor Claudio.

Leon. To-morrow then I will expect your coming;
To-night I take my leave.—This naughty man
Shall face to face be brought to Margaret,
Who, I believe, was pack'd in all this wrong [4],
Hir'd to it by your brother.

Bora. No, by my foul, fhe was not;
Nor knew not what fhe did, when fhe fpoke to me;
But always had been juft and virtuous,
In any thing that I do know by her.

Dog. Moreover, Sir, (which, indeed, is not under white
and black,) this plaintiff here, the offender, did call me afs:
I befeech you, let it be remember'd in his punifhment:
And alfo, the watch heard them talk of one Deformed:
they fay, he wears a key in his ear, and a lock hanging by
it; and borrows money in God's name [5]; the which he hath
ufed fo long, and never paid, that now men grow hard-hearted,
and will lend nothing for God's fake: Pray you, examine him
upon that point.

---

[4] — *pack'd in all this wrong,*] i. e combined; an accomplice.
MALONE.

[5] — *he wears a key in his ear, and hath a lock hanging by it; and borrows money in God's name:*] The allufion is to a fantaftical fafhion of that time, the men's wearing rings in their ears, and indulging a favourite lock of hair which was brought before, and ty'd with ribbons, and called a *love-lock.* Againft this fafhion William Prynne wrote his treatife, called, *The Unlovelinefs of Love-locks.* WARBURTON.

Dr. Warburton, I believe, has here (as he frequently does,) refined a little too much. There is no allufion, I conceive, to the fafhion of wearing rings in the ears (a fafhion which our author himfelf followed). The pleafantry feems to confift in Dogberry's fuppofing that the *lock* which DEFORMED wore, muft have a key to it.

Fynes Moryfon, in a very particular account that he has given of the drefs of Lord Mountjoy, (the rival, and afterwards the friend of Robert Earl of Effex,) fays, that his hair was " thinne on the head, where he wore it fhort, except a *lock under his left eare*, which he nourifhed the time of this warre, [the Irifh War in 1599,] and being woven up, hid it in his neck under his ruffe." ITINERARY, P. ii. p. 45. When he was not on fervice, he probably wore it in a different fafhion.—The portrait of Sir Edward Sackville, Earl of Dorfet, painted by Vandyck, (now at Knowle) exhibits this lock with a large knotted ribband at the end of it. It hangs under the ear on the left fide, and reaches as low as where the ftar is now worn by the knights of the garter.

The fame fafhion is alluded to in an epigram quoted in Vol. I.:
" Or what he doth with fuch a horfe-tail-*lock*," &c. MALONE.

Leon.

Leon. I thank thee for thy care and honeſt pains.

Dog. Your worſhip ſpeaks like a moſt thankful and reverend youth: and I praiſe God for you.

Leon. There's for thy pains.

Dog. God ſave the foundation!

Leon. Go, I diſcharge thee of thy priſoner, and I thank thee.

Dog. I leave an errant knave with your worſhip; which, I beſeech your worſhip, to correct yourſelf, for the example of others. God keep your worſhip; I wiſh your worſhip well; God reſtore you to health: I humbly give you leave to depart; and if a merry meeting may be wiſh'd God, prohibit it.—Come, neighbour.

[*Exeunt* DOGBERRY, VERGES, *and* Watch.

Leon. Until to-morrow morning, Lords, farewel.

Ant. Farewel, my Lords; we look for you to-morrow.

D. Pedro. We will not fail.

Claud. To-night I'll mourn with Hero.

[*Exeunt* DON PEDRO *and* CLAUDIO.

Leon. Bring you theſe fellows on; we'll talk with Margaret,
How her acquaintance grew with this lewd fellow. [*Exeunt.*

SCENE II.

A Room in Leonato's *Houſe.*

Enter BENEDICK, *and* MARGARET, *meeting.*

Bene. Pray thee, ſweet miſtreſs Margaret, deſerve well at my hands, by helping me to the ſpeech of Beatrice.

Mar. Will you then write me a ſonnet in praiſe of my beauty?

Bene. In ſo high a ſtyle, Margaret, that no man living ſhall come over it; for, in moſt comely truth, thou deſerveſt it.

Mar. 'To have no man come over me? why, ſhall I always keep below ſtairs[d]?

Bene.

---

[d] *To have no man come over me? why, ſhall I always keep below ſtairs?*] Theobald with ſome probability reads—*above* ſtairs; yet *below* and *above* were not likely to be confounded either by the tranſcriber or compoſitor. MALONE.

I ſuppoſe

158   MUCH ADO

Bene. Thy wit is as quick as the greyhound's mouth; it catches.

Mar. And your's as blunt as the fencer's foils, which hit, but hurt not.

Bene. A moſt manly wit, Margaret, it will not hurt a woman; and ſo, I pray thee, call Beatrice: I give thee the bucklers [7].

Mar. Give us the ſwords, we have bucklers of our own.

Bene. If you uſe them, Margaret, you muſt put in the pikes with a vice; and they are dangerous weapons for maids.

Mar. Well, I will call Beatrice to you, who, I think, hath legs.   [*Exit* MARGARET.

Bene. And therefore will come.

> *The god of love,*   [ſinging.
> *That ſits above,*
> *And knows me, and knows me,*
> *How pitiful I deſerve*—

I mean in ſinging; but in loving—Leander the good ſwimmer, Troilus the firſt employer of pandars, and a whole book full of theſe quondam carpet-mongers, whoſe names yet run ſmoothly in the even road of a blank verſe, why they were never ſo truly turn'd over and over, as my poor ſelf, in love: Marry, I cannot ſhew it in rhime; I have try'd; I can find out no rhime to *lady* but *baby,* an innocent rhime; for *ſcorn, born,* a hard rhime; for *ſchool, fool,* a babbling rhime: very ominous endings: No, I was not born under a rhiming planet, nor I cannot woo in feſtival terms.—

Enter BEATRICE.

Sweet Beatrice, would'ſt thou come when I call'd thee?

I ſuppoſe every reader will find the meaning. JOHNSON.

Leſt he ſhould not, the following inſtance from Sir Aſhton Cockayne's *Poems* is at his ſervice:

"But to prove rather he was not beguil'd,
"Her he o'ercame, for he got her with child."

And another, more appoſite, from Marſton's *Inſatiate Counteſs,* 1613:

"Alas! when we are once o' the falling hand,
"A man may eaſily come over us." COLLINS.

[7] *I give thee the bucklers*] I ſuppoſe that *to give the bucklers* is, to yield or to lay by all thoughts of defence; ſo *clypeum abjicere.* The reſt deſerves no comment. JOHNSON.

The expreſſion (as Mr Steevens has ſhewn) occurs very frequently in our old comedies. MALONE.

Beat.

Beat. Yea, Signior, and depart when you bid me.
Bene. O, stay but till then!
Beat. Then is spoken; fare you well now:—and yet ere I go, let me go with that I came for [8], which is, with knowing what hath pass'd between you and Claudio.
Bene. Only foul words; and thereupon I will kiss thee.
Beat. Foul words are but foul wind, and foul wind is but foul breath, and foul breath is noisome; therefore I will depart unkiss'd.
Bene. Thou hast frighted the word out of his right sense, so forcible is thy wit: But I must tell thee plainly, Claudio undergoes my challenge; and either I must shortly hear from him, or I will subscribe him a coward. And, I pray thee now, tell me, for which of my bad parts didst thou fall in love with me?
Beat. For them all together; which maintain'd so politic a state of evil, that they will not admit any good part to intermingle with them. But for which of my good parts did you first suffer love for me?
Bene. *Suffer love*; a good epithet! I do suffer love, indeed, for I love thee against my will.
Beat. In spight of your heart, I think; alas! poor heart! If you spight it for my sake, I will spight it for yours; for I will never love that, which my friend hates.
Bene. Thou and I are too wise to woo peaceably.
Beat. It appears not in this confession: there's not one wise man among twenty, that will praise himself.
Bene. An old, an old instance, Beatrice, that lived in the time of good neighbours [9]: if a man do not erect in this age his own tomb ere he dies, he shall live no longer in monument, than the bell rings, and the widow weeps.
Beat. And how long is that, think you?
Bene. Question [1]? Why an hour in clamour, and a quarter in rheum: Therefore it is most expedient for the wise, (if Don Worm, his conscience, find no impediment to the contrary,) to be the trumpet of his own virtues, as I am to myself: So much for praising myself, (who, I myself

---

[8] —— *with that I came for.*] *For*, which is wanting in the old copy, was inserted by Mr. Rowe. MALONE.

[9] —— *in the time of good neighbours:*] i. e. When men were not envious, but every one gave another his due. WARBURTON.

[1] *Question? why, an hour,* &c.] i. e. What a question's there?
WARBURTON.

will

will bear witness, is praise worthy,)—and now tell me, how doth your cousin?

Beat. Very ill.

Bene. And how do you?

Beat. Very ill too.

Bene. Serve God, love me, and mend: there will I leave you too, for here comes one in haste.

Enter URSULA.

Urs. Madam, you must come to your uncle; yonder's old coil at home: it is proved, my Lady Hero hath been falsely accused, the Prince and Claudio mightily abused; and Don John is the author of all, who is fled and gone: Will you come presently?

Beat. Will you go hear this news, Signior?

Bene. I will live in thy heart, die in thy lap, and be bury'd in thy eyes; and, moreover, I will go with thee to thy uncle's. [*Exeunt.*

SCENE III.

A Church.

Enter Don PEDRO, CLAUDIO, *and Attendants with music and tapers.*

Claudio. Is this the monument of Leonato?

Atten. It is, my Lord.

Claud. [*reads from a scroll.*]
Done to death [2] *by slanderous tongues*
 Was the Hero that here lies:
Death, in guerdon of her wrongs,
 Gives her fame which never dies:
So the life, that dy'd with shame,
Lives in death with glorious fame.

Hang thou there upon the tomb, [*affixing it.*
Praising her when I am dumb.—

---

[2] *Done to death*] This obsolete phrase occurs frequently in our ancient dramas. Thus, in Marlowe's *Lust's Dominion:*
 " His mother's hand shall stop thy breath,
 " Thinking her own son is *done to death*." MALONE.

Now

Now, music, sound, and sing your solemn hymn.

SONG.

Pardon, Goddess of the night,
Those that slew thy virgin knight [3];
For the which, with songs of woe,
Round about her tomb they go.
Midnight, assist our moan;
Help us to sigh and groan,
Heavily, heavily:
Graves, yawn, and yield your dead,
Till death be uttered,
Heavily, heavily.

Claud. Now [4], unto thy bones good night!
Yearly will I do this rite.

---

[3] *Those that slew thy virgin knight:*] Knight, in its original signification, means *follower* or *pupil*, and in this sense may be feminine. Helena, in *All's Well that Ends Well*, uses knight in the same signification. JOHNSON.

Virgin *knight* is virgin hero. In the times of chivalry, a *virgin knight* was one who had as yet achieved no adventure. A *hero* had as yet achieved no matrimonial one. It may be added, that a *virgin knight* wore no device on his shield, having no right to any till he had deserved it.—On the books of the Stationer's Company in the year 1594, is entered, "— Pheander the *mayden knight*."

It appears, however, from several passages in Spenser's *Faerie Queen*, B. i. c. 7. that an *ideal order* of this name was supposed, as a compliment to Queen Elizabeth's virginity:

"Of doughtie knights whom faery land did raise
"That noble order hight of *maidenhed*."
Again, B. ii. c. 2. STEEVENS.

I do not believe that any allusion was here intended to Hero's having yet atchieved "no matrimonial adventure." *Diana's knight*, or *Virgin knight*, was the common poetical appellation of virgins, in Shakspeare's time.

So, in The Two Noble Kinsmen, 1634:

"O sacred, shadowy, cold and constant queen,
"———————— who to thy *female knights*
"Allow'st no more blood than will make a blush,
"Which is their order's robe——."

Again, more appositely in Spenser's *Faery Queene*, B. iii. c. 12.

"Soon as that *virgin knight* he saw in place,
"His wicked bookes in hast he overthrew." MALONE.

[4] *Claud. Now, &c.*] In the old copy these lines, by a mistake of the transcriber or compositor, are given to an attendant. Mr. Rowe made the correction now adopted. MALONE.

D. Pedro.

MUCH ADO

D. Pedro. Good morrow, masters; put your torches out:
The wolves have prey'd; and look, the gentle day,
Before the wheels of Phœbus, round about
Dapples the drowsy east with spots of grey:
Thanks to you all, and leave us; fare you well.
Claud. Good morrow, masters; each his several way.
D. Pedro. Come, let us hence, and put on other weeds;
And then to Leonato's we will go.
Claud. And Hymen now with luckier issue speed's [5],
Than this, from whom we render'd up this woe! [*Exeunt.*

SCENE IV.

A Room in Leonato's *House.*

Enter LEONATO, ANTONIO, BENEDICK, BEATRICE, MARGARET, URSULA, FRIAR, *and* HERO.

Friar. Did I not tell you she was innocent?
Leon. So are the Prince and Claudio, who accus'd her,
Upon the error that you have heard debated:
But Margaret was in some fault for this;
Although against her will, as it appears
In the true course of all the question.
Ant. Well, I am glad that all things sort so well.
Bene. And so am I, being else by faith enforc'd
To call young Claudio to a reckoning for it.
Leon. Well, daughter, and you gentlewomen all,
Withdraw into a chamber by yourselves;
And, when I send for you, come hither mask'd:
The prince and Claudio promis'd by this hour
To visit me:—You know your office, brother;
You must be father to your brother's daughter,
And give her to young Claudio. [*Exeunt Ladies.*
Ant. Which I will do with confirm'd countenance.
Bene. Friar, I must entreat your pains, I think.

---

[5] —*speed's,*] i. e. *speed us!* The old copy reads—*speeds*. Corrected and explained by Dr Thirlby. Claudio, as he observes, could not know that the proposed match would have any luckier event than that designed with Hero. Yet I confess, the contraction introduced is so extremely harsh, that I doubt whether it was intended by the author. However I have followed former editors in adopting it. MALONE.

Friar.

Friar. To do what, Signior?

Bene. To bind me, or undo me, one of them.—
Signior Leonato, truth it is, good Signior,
Your niece regards me with an eye of favour.

Leon. That eye my daughter lent her; 'Tis most true.

Bene. And I do with an eye of love requite her.

Leon. The fight whereof, I think, you had from me,
From Claudio, and the Prince; But what's your will?

Bene. Your answer, Sir, is enigmatical:
But, for my will, my will is, your good will
May stand with ours, this day to be conjoin'd
In the estate of honourable marriage;—
In which, good Friar, I shall desire your help.

Leon. My heart is with your liking.

Friar. And my help.
Here comes the Prince, and Claudio.

Enter Don PEDRO, CLAUDIO, *and Attendants.*

D. Pedro. Good morrow to this fair assembly.

Leon. Good morrow, Prince; good morrow, Claudio;
We here attend you; Are you yet determin'd
To-day to marry with my brother's daughter?

Claud. I'll hold my mind, were she an Ethiope.

Leon. Call her forth, brother, here's the Friar ready.

[*Exit* ANTONIO.

D. Pedro. Good morrow, Benedick: Why, what's the matter,
That you have such a February face,
So full of frost, of storm, and cloudiness?

Claud. I think, he thinks upon the savage bull * :—
Tush, fear not, man, we'll tip thy horns with gold,
And all Europa shall rejoice at thee;
As once Europa did at lusty Jove,
When he would play the noble beast in love.

Bene. Bull Jove, Sir, had an amiable low;
And some such strange bull leapt your father's cow,
And got a calf in that same noble feat,
Much like to you, for you have just his bleat.

* — *upon the savage bull:*] See p. 91. n. 8. MALONE.

Re-enter

Re-enter ANTONIO, *with the Ladies mask'd.*

Claud. For this I owe you: here come other reck'nings.
Which is the lady I must seize upon?
Ant. This same is she, and I do give you her [6].
Claud. Why, then she's mine: Sweet, let me see your face.
Leon. No, that you shall not, till you take her hand
Before this Friar, and swear to marry her.
Claud. Give me your hand before this holy Friar;
I am your husband, if you like of me.
Hero. And when I liv'd, I was your other wife:

[*unmasking.*

And when you lov'd, you were my other husband.
Claud. Another Hero?
Hero. Nothing certainer:
One Hero dy'd desil'd; but I do live,
And, surely as I live, I am a maid.
D. Pedro. The former Hero! Hero that is dead!
Leon. She dy'd, my Lord, but whiles her slander liv'd.
Friar. All this amazement can I qualify;
When, after that the holy rites are ended,
I'll tell you largely of fair Hero's death:
Mean time let wonder seem familiar,
And to the chapel let us presently.
Bene. Soft and fair, Friar:—Which is Beatrice?
Beat. I answer to that name; [*unmasking.*] what is your will?
Bene. Do not you love me?
Beat. Why, no, no more than reason.
Bene. Why, then your uncle, and the Prince, and Claudio,
Have been deceived; for they swore you did [7].
Beat. Do not you love me?
Bene. Troth, no, no more than reason.

---

[6] Ant. *This same, &c.*] This speech is in the old copies given to Leonato. Mr. Theobald first assigned it to the right owner. Leonato has in a former part of this scene told Antonio,—that *he* "must be father to his brother's daughter, and *give her* to young Claudio." MALONE.

[7] — *for they swore you did.*] *For*, which both the sense and metre require, was inserted by Sir Thomas Hanmer. So below:
"Are much deceiv'd; *for* they did swear you did." MALONE.

Beat.

Beat. Why, then my cousin, Margaret, and Ursula,
Are much deceiv'd; for they did swear you did.
Bene. They swore that you were almost sick for me.
Beat. They swore that you were well-nigh dead for me.
Bene. 'Tis no such matter:— Then, you do not love me.
Beat. No, truly, but in friendly recompence.
Leon. Come, cousin, I am sure you love the gentleman.
Claud. And I'll be sworn upon't, that he loves her;
For here's a paper written in his hand,
A halting sonnet of his own pure brain,
Fashion'd to Beatrice.
Hero. And here's another,
Writ in my cousin's hand, stolen from her pocket,
Containing her affection unto Benedick.
Bene. A miracle! here's our own hands against our hearts!
—Come, I will have thee; but, by this light, I take thee for pity.
Beat. I would not deny you⁸;—but, by this good day, I yield upon great persuasion; and, partly, to save your life, for I was told you were in a consumption.
Bene. Peace, I will stop your mouth⁹. [*kissing her.*
D. Pedro. How dost thou, Benedick the married man?
Bene. I'll tell thee what, Prince; a college of wit-crackers cannot flout me out of my humour: Dost thou think, I care for a satire, or an epigram? No: if a man will be beaten with brains, he shall wear nothing handsome about him: In brief, since I do purpose to marry, I will think nothing to any purpose that the world can say against it; and therefore never flout at me for what I have said against it; for man is a giddy thing, and this is my conclusion.—For thy part, Claudio, I did think to have beaten thee; but in that thou art like to be my kinsman, live unbruis'd and love my cousin.
Claud. I had well hoped, thou wouldst have denied Beatrice, that I might have cudgell'd thee out of thy single life, to make thee a double dealer; which, out of ques-

---

⁸ *I would not deny you, &c.*] I cannot find in my heart to deny you, but for all that I yield, after having stood out great persuasions to submission. He had said, *I take thee for pity*; she replies, *I would not deny thee*, i. e. I take thee for pity too: but as I live, I am won to this compliance by importunity of friends. WARBURTON.

⁹ Bene. *Peace, I will stop your mouth.*] In the old copies these words are by mistake given to Leonato. The present regulation was made by Mr. Theobald. MALONE.

tion, thou wilt be, if my cousin do not look exceeding narrowly to thee.

Bene. Come, come, we are friends:—let's have a dance ere we are marry'd, that we may lighten our own hearts, and our wives' heels.

Leon. We'll have dancing afterward.

Bene. First, o' my word; therefore, play music.—Prince, thou art sad; get thee a wife, get thee a wife: there is no staff more reverend than one tipp'd with horn [1].

[1] *— no staff more reverend than one tipp'd with horn.*] This passage may admit of some explanation that I am unable to furnish. By accident I lost several instances I had collected for the purpose of throwing light on it. The following however may assist the future commentator. Mss. Sloan, 1691. "THAT A FELON MAY WAGE BATTAILE, WITH THE ORDER THEREOF." "—by order of the lawe both the parties must at theire own charge be armed withoute any yron or long armoure, and theire heades bare, and bare-handed, and bare-footed, every one of them having a *baston burned* at ech ende, of one length."
STEEVENS.

Mr. Steevens's explanation is undoubtedly the true one. The allusion is certainly to the antient trial by *wager of battel*, in suits both criminal and civil. The quotation above given recites the form in the former case,—viz. an appeal of felony. The practice was nearly similar in civil cases, upon issue joined in a writ of right. Of the last trial of this kind in England, (which was in the thirteenth year of Queen Elizabeth,) our author might have read a particular account in Stowe's *Annales*. Henry Nailor, master of defence, was champion for the demandants, Simon Low and John Kyme; and George Thorne for the tenant, (or defendant,) Thomas Paramoure. The combat was appointed to be fought in Tuthill fields, and the Judges of the Common Pleas and Serjeants at Law attended. But a compromise was entered into between the parties, the evening before the appointed day, and they only went through the forms, for the greater security of the tenant. Among other ceremonies Stowe mentions, that " the gauntlet that was cast down by George Thorne was borne before the sayd Nailor, in his passage through London, upon a sword's point, and his baston (a *staff* of an ell-long, made taper-wise, *tipt with horn*,) with his shield of hard leather, was borne after him, &c." See also Minsheu's Dict. 1617, in v. *Combat*; from which it appears that Nailor on this occasion was introduced to the Judges, with " *three solemn congies*," by a very *reverend* person, " Sir Jerome Bowes, ambassador from Queen Elizabeth into Russia, who carried a red *baston* of an ell-long, *tipped with horne*."—In a very ancient law-book entitled *Britton*, the manner in which the combatants are to be armed is particularly mentioned. The quotation from the Sloanian MS. is a translation from thence. By a ridiculous mistake the words, " sauns loge arme," are rendered in the modern translation of that book, printed a few years ago,—" without *linen* armour;" and " a mains nues & pies" (bare-handed and bare-footed) is translated, " and their hands naked, and *on feet*." MALONE.

Enter

Enter a Messenger.

Mess. My Lord, your brother John is ta'en in flight,
And brought with armed men back to Messina.

Bene. Think not on him till to-morrow; I'll devise thee brave punishments for him.—Strike up, pipers.
[*Dance. Exeunt* [2].

[2] This play may be justly said to contain two of the most sprightly characters that Shakspeare ever drew. The wit, the humourist, the gentleman and the soldier, are combined in Benedick. It is to be lamented, indeed, that the first and most splendid of these distinctions is disgraced by unnecessary profaneness; for the goodness of his heart is hardly sufficient to atone for the licence of his tongue. The too sarcastic levity, which flashes out in the conversation of Beatrice, may be excused on account of the steadiness and friendship so apparent in her behaviour, when she urges her lover to risque his life by a challenge to Claudio. In the conduct of the fable, however, there is an imperfection similar to that which Dr. Johnson has pointed out in the *Merry Wives of Windsor:*—the second contrivance is less ingenious than the first:—or, to speak more plainly, the same incident is become stale by repetition. I wish some other method had been found to entrap Beatrice, than that very one which before had been successfully practised on Benedick.

Much Ado about Nothing, (as I understand from one of Mr. Vertue's MSS.) formerly passed under the title of Benedick and Beatrix. Hemming the player received, on the 20th of May, 1613, the sum of forty pounds, and twenty pounds more as his majesty's gratuity, for exhibiting six plays at Hampton-Court, among which was this comedy.

STEEVENS.

LOVE'S

LOVE'S LABOUR'S LOST.

PERSONS REPRESENTED.

Ferdinand, *King of* Navarre.
Biron,
Longaville, } *Lords, attending on the King.*
Dumain,
Boyet,
Mercade, } *Lords, attending on the Princess of* France.
Don Adriano de Armado, *a fantastical* Spaniard.
Sir Nathaniel, *a Curate.*
Holofernes, *a Schoolmaster.*
Dull, *a Constable.*
Costard, *a Clown.*
Moth, *Page to* Armado.
A Forester.

Princess *of France.*
Rosaline,
Maria, } *Ladies, attending on the Princess.*
Catharine,
Jaquenetta, *a Country Wench.*

Officers, *and others, attendants on the King and Princess.*

SCENE, Navarre.

LOVE'S LABOUR'S LOST[1].

ACT I. SCENE I.

Navarre. A Park, with a Palace in it.

Enter the KING, BIRON, LONGAVILLE, *and* DUMAIN.

King. Let fame, that all hunt after in their lives,
Live register'd upon our brazen tombs,
And then grace us in the disgrace of death;
When, spight of cormorant devouring time,
The endeavour of this present breath may buy
That honour, which shall bate his scythe's keen edge,
And make us heirs of all eternity.
Therefore, brave conquerors—for so you are,
That war against your own affections,
And the huge army of the world's desires,—
Our late edict shall strongly stand in force:
Navarre shall be the wonder of the world;
Our court shall be a little Academe,
Still and contemplative in living art.
You three, Birón, Dumain, and Longaville,
Have sworn for three years' term to live with me,
My fellow-scholars, and to keep those statutes,
That are recorded in this schedule here:

---

[1] I have not hitherto discovered any novel on which this comedy appears to have been founded; and yet the story of it has most of the features of an ancient romance. STEEVENS.

Love's Labour's Lost I conjecture to have been written in 1594. See *An Attempt to ascertain the order of Shakspeare's Plays.* Vol. I. MALONE.

Your oaths are past, and now subscribe your names;
That his own hand may strike his honour down,
That violates the smallest branch herein:
If you are arm'd to do, as sworn to do,
Subscribe to your deep oath [1], and keep it too.

Long. I am resolv'd: 'tis but a three years' fast;
The mind shall banquet, though the body pine:
Fat paunches have lean pates; and dainty bits
Make rich the ribs, but bank'rout quite the wits.
[*subscribes.*

Dum. My loving Lord, Dumain is mortify'd;
The grosser manner of these world's delights
He throws upon the gross world's baser slaves:
To love, to wealth, to pomp, I pine and die;
With all these living in philosophy [2]. [*subscribes.*

Bir. I can but say their protestation over,
So much, dear liege, I have already sworn,
That is, to live and study here three years.
But there are other strict observances:
As, not to see a woman in that term;
Which, I hope well, is not enrolled there:
And, one day in a week to touch no food;
And but one meal on every day beside;
The which, I hope, is not enrolled there:
And then, to sleep but three hours in the night,
And not be seen to wink of all the day;
(When I was wont to think no harm all night,
And make a dark night too of half the day;)
Which, I hope well, is not enrolled there.
O, these are barren tasks, too hard to keep;
Not to see ladies, study, fast, not sleep [3].

King. Your oath is pass'd to pass away from these.
Bir. Let me say, no, my liege, an if you please;

---

[1] *— your deep oath,*] The old copies have—*oaths*. Corrected by Mr. Steevens. MALONE.

[2] *With all these living in philosop'y.*] The style of the rhyming scenes in this play is often entangled and obscure. I know not certainly to what *all these* is to be referred; I suppose he means, that he finds *love, pomp,* and *wealth* in *philosophy.* JOHNSON.

By *all these* Dumain means the King, Biron, &c. to whom he may be supposed to point, and with whom he is going to live in philosophical retirement. A. C.

[3] *Not to see ladies, study, fast, not sleep.*] That is, to see no ladies, to study, to fast, and not to sleep. MALONE.

I only

I only swore, to study with your grace,
And stay here in your court for three years' space.
  Long. You swore to that, Biron, and to the rest.
  Bir. By yea and nay, Sir, then I swore in jest.—
What is the end of study? let me know.
  King. Why, that to know, which else we should not know.
  Bir. Things hid and barr'd, you mean, from common
    sense?
  King. Ay, that is study's god-like recompence.
  Bir. Come on then, I will swear to study so,
To know the thing I am forbid to know:
As thus—To study where I well may dine,
  When I to feast expressly am forbid [5];
Or, study where to meet some mistress fine,
  When mistresses from common sense are hid:
Or, having sworn too hard-a-keeping oath,
Study to break it, and not break my troth.
If study's gain be thus, and this be so,
Study knows that, which yet it doth not know:
Swear me to this, and I will ne'er say, no.
  King. These be the stops that hinder study quite,
And train our intellects to vain delight.
  Bir. Why, all delights are vain; but that most vain,
Which, with pain purchas'd, doth inherit pain:
As, painfully to pore upon a book,
  To seek the light of truth; while truth the while
Doth falsly blind the eye-sight of his look [6]:
  Light, seeking light, doth light of light beguile:
So, ere you find where light in darkness lies,
Your light grows dark by losing of your eyes.
Study me how to please the eye indeed,
  By fixing it upon a fairer eye;
Who dazzling so, that eye shall be his heed,
  And give him light that was it blinded by [7].

Study

---

[5] *When I to feast expressly am forbid;*] The old copy has—*to fast*. This necessary emendation was made by Mr. Theobald. MALONE.

[6] ———*while truth the while*
Doth falsly blind, &c.] *Falsly* is here, and in many other places, the same as *dishonestly* or *treacherously*. The whole sense of this gingling declamation is only this, *that a man by too close study may read himself blind*, which might have been told with less obscurity in fewer words. JOHNSON.

[7] *Who dazzling so, that eye shall be his heed,*
And give him light that was it blinded by.] This is another passage unnecessarily

Study is like the heaven's glorious sun,
  That will not be deep search'd with saucy looks;
Small have continual plodders ever won,
  Save base authority from others' books.
These earthly godfathers of heaven's lights,
  That give a name to every fixed star,
Have no more profit of their shining nights,
  Than those that walk and wot not what they are.
Too much to know, is, to know nought but fame;
And every godfather can give a name ⁸.

King. How well he's read, to reason against reading!
Dum. Proceeded well, to stop all good proceeding⁹!
Long. He weeds the corn, and still lets grow the weeding.
Bir. The spring is near, when green geese are a breeding.
Dum. How follows that?
Bir. Fit in his place and time.
Dum. In reason nothing.
Bir. Something then in rhime.
King. Biron is like an envious sneaping frost ¹,
  That bites the first-born infants of the spring.
Bir. Well, say I am; why should proud summer boast,
  Before the birds have any cause to sing?
Why should I joy in an abortive birth?
At Christmas I no more desire a rose,
Than wish a snow in May's new-fangled shows ²;

But

---

unnecessarily obscure: the meaning is, that when he *dazzles*, that is, has his eye made weak, *by fixing his eye upon a fairer eye, that fairer eye shall be his heed*, his *direction* or *lode-star*, (See Midsummer Night's Dream,) and *give him light that was blinded by it.* JOHNSON.
The old copies read—*it was*. Corrected by Mr. Steevens. MALONE.

⁸ *Too much to know, is to know nought but fame;*
And every godfather can give a name.] The consequence, says Biron, of *too much knowledge*, is not any real solution of doubts, but mere empty reputation. That is, *too much knowledge gives only fame, a name, which every godfather can give likewise.* JOHNSON.

⁹ *Proceeded well, to stop all good proceeding!*] To *proceed* is an academical term, meaning, *to take a degree*; as *he proceeded batchelor in physic.* The sense is, *he has taken his degrees in the art of hindering the degrees of others.* JOHNSON.

¹ — *sneaping frost,*] So *sneaping winds* in the *Winter's Tale.* To *sneap* is to *check*, to *rebuke*. STEEVENS.

² — *May's new-fangled shows*;] Mr. Theobald reads—new-fangled *earth*, in order to rhyme with the last line but one. I rather suspect a line to have been lost after " an abortive birth."—For *an* in that line the old copies have *any*. Corrected by Mr. Pope.

Mr.

But like of each thing, that in season grows.
So you, to study now it is too late,
Climb o'er the house to unlock the little gate ³.

King. Well, fit you out ⁺: go home, Biron; adieu!

Bir. No, my good Lord; I have sworn to stay with you:
And, though I have for barbarism spoke more,
Than for that angel knowledge you can say,
Yet confident I'll keep what I have swore,
And bide the penance of each three years' day.
Give me the paper, let me read the same;
And to the strict'st decrees I'll write my name.

King. How well this yielding rescues thee from shame!

Bir. [*reads.*] Item, *That no woman shall come within a mile of my court;*—Hath this been proclaimed?

Long. Four days ago.

Bir. Let's see the penalty. [*reads.*]—*on pain of losing her tongue.* Who devised this penalty?

Long. Marry, that did I.

Bir. Sweet Lord, and why?

Long. To fright them hence with that dread penalty.

Bir. A dangerous law against gentility ⁴!——[*reads.*]
Item, *If any man be seen to talk with a woman within the term of three*

Mr. Wharton is of opinion that Shakspeare here alludes to the May games. But I have no doubt that the more obvious interpretation is the true one. So, in Chaucer's *Knightes Tale:*
"And fresher than *May* with *floures* new,"—.
So also in our poet's *K. Richard II.*
" She came *adorned* hither, like sweet *May.*"
i. e. as the ground is in that month enamelled by the gay diversity of flowers which the spring produces.
Again, in *The Destruction of Troy*, 1619: " At the entry of the month of May, when the earth is attired and adorned with diverse flowers," &c. MALONE.

³ *Climb o'er the house, &c.*] This is the reading of the quarto, 1598, and much preferable to that of the folio—
That were to climb o'er the house to unlock the gate. MALONE.

⁺ — *fit you out:*] This may mean, *hold you out, continue refractory.* But I suspect, we should read—*fit you out.* MALONE.

⁴ *A dangerous law against* gentility!] This and the four following lines, which in the old copy are given to Longaville, were properly attributed to Biron by Mr. Theobald. MALONE.

Gentility, here, does not signify that rank of people called, *gentry*; but what the French express by, *gentilesse*, i. e. *elegantia*, *urbanitas*. And the meaning is this: Such a law for banishing women from the court, is

I 4   dangerous

three years, be shall endure such public shame as the rest of the court can possibly devise.—
  This article, my liege, yourself must break;
    For, well you know, here comes in embassy
The French king's daughter, with yourself to speak—
    A maid of grace, and cómplete majesty—
About surrender up of Aquitain
    To her decrepit, sick, and bed-rid father:
Therefore this article is made in vain,
    Or vainly comes the admired princess hither.
  King. What say you, Lords? why, this was quite forgot.
  Bir. So study evermore is overshot;
While it doth study to have what it would,
It doth forget to do the thing it should:
And when it hath the thing it hunteth most,
'Tis won, as towns with fire; so won, so lost.
  King. We must, of force, dispense with this decree,
She must lie here⁵ on mere necessity.
  Bir. Necessity will make us all forsworn
Three thousand times within this three years' space:
For every man with his affects is born;
    Not by might master'd, but by special grace⁶:
If I break faith, this word shall speak for me,
I am forsworn on mere necessity.—
So to the laws at large I write my name: [*subscribes.*
    And he, that breaks them in the least degree,
Stands in attainder of eternal shame:
    Suggestions⁷ are to others, as to me;
But, I believe, although I seem so loth,
I am the last that will last keep his oath.
But is there no quick recreation⁸ granted?
  King. Ay, that there is: our court, you know, is haunted

dangerous, or injurious, to *politeness, urbanity,* and the more refined pleasures of life. For men without women would turn brutal, and savage, in their natures and behaviour. THEOBALD.

⁵ *She must lie here—*] To *lie* in old language is to *sojourn*. MALONE.

⁶ *Not by might master'd, but by special grace:*] Biron, amidst his extravagancies, speaks with great justness against the folly of vows. They are made without sufficient regard to the variations of life, and are therefore broken by some unforeseen necessity. They proceed commonly from a presumptuous confidence, and a false estimate of human power.
JOHNSON.

⁷ *Suggestions—*] Temptations. JOHNSON.

⁸ *— quick recreation—*] Lively sport, sprightly diversion. JOHNSON.

With

With a refined traveller of Spain;
A man in all the world's new fashion planted,
  That hath a mint of phrases in his brain:
One, whom the musick of his own vain tongue
  Doth ravish, like enchanting harmony;
A man of complements, whom right and wrong
  Have chose as umpire of their mutiny ⁹:
This child of fancy ¹, that Armado hight ²,
  For interim to our studies, shall relate,
In high-born words, the worth of many a knight
  From tawny Spain, lost in the world's debate ³.
How you delight, my Lords, I know not, I;
But, I protest, I love to hear him lie,
And I will use him for my minstrelsy.

⁹ *A man of complements, whom right and wrong*
Have chose as umpire of their mutiny:] This passage, I believe, means no more than that Don Armado was a man nicely versed in ceremonial distinctions, one who could distinguish in the most delicate questions of honour the exact boundaries of right and wrong. *Compliment,* in Shakspeare's time, did not signify, at least did not only signify verbal civility, or phrases of courtesy, but, according to its original meaning, the trappings, or ornamental appendages of a character, in the same manner, and on the same principles of speech with *accomplishment.* *Compliment* is, as Armado well expresses it, *the varnish of a compleat man.*
JOHNSON.

So, in the title-page to R. Braithwaite's *English Gentlewoman:* "—what ornaments do best adorn her, and what *complements* do best accomplish her." Again, in *Sir Giles Goosecap,* 1606:—" adorned with the exactest *complements* belonging to everlasting nobleness." STEEVENS.

¹ *This child of fancy,*] This fantastic. The expression, in another sense, has been adopted by Milton in his *L'Allegro:*
  "Or sweetest Shakspeare, *Fancy's child—*." MALONE.

² *— that Armado hight,*] Who is *called* Armado. MALONE.

³ *From tawny Spain, lost in the world's debate.*] i. e. he shall relate to us the celebrated stories recorded in the old romances, and in their very style. Why he says *from tawny Spain* is, because these romances, being of Spanish original, the heroes and the scene were originally of that country. Why he says, *lost in the world's debate,* is, because the subject of those romances were the crusades of the European Christians against the Saracens of Asia and Africa. WARBURTON.

I have suffered this note to hold its place, though Mr. Tyrwhitt has shewn that it is wholly unfounded, because Dr. Warburton refers to it in his Dissertation at the end of this play. MALONE.

— *in the world's debate.*] The world seems to be used in a monastic sense by the king, now devoted for a time to a monastic life. *In the world, in seculo,* in the hustle of human affairs, from which we are now happily sequestered, *in the world,* to which the votaries of solitude have no relation. JOHNSON.

Bir. Armado is a most illustrious wight,
A man of fire-new words, fashion's own knight.
Long. Costard the swain, and he, shall be our sport;
And, so to study, three years is but short.

Enter DULL, *with a letter, and* COSTARD.

Dull. Which is the Duke's own person⁴?
Bir. This, fellow; What would'st?
Dull. I myself reprehend his own person: for I am his grace's tharborough⁵: but I would see his own person in flesh and blood.
Bir. This is he.
Dull. Signior Arme—Arme—commends you. There's villainy abroad; this letter will tell you more.
Cost. Sir, the contempts thereof are as touching me.
King. A letter from the magnificent Armado.
Bir. How low soever the matter, I hope in God for high words.
Long. A high hope for a low having⁶: God grant us patience!
Bir. To hear; or forbear hearing⁷?
Long. To hear meekly, Sir, and to laugh moderately; or to forbear both.
Bir. Well, Sir, be it as the stile shall give us cause to climb in the merriness.
Cost. The matter is to me, Sir, as concerning Jaquenetta. The manner of it is, I was taken with the manner⁸.

Bir.

---

⁴ — *the Duke's own person?*] Theobald, without any necessity, reads —*king's* own person. The princess in the next act calls the king—" this virtuous duke;" a word which, in our author's time, seems to have been used with great laxity. And indeed, though this were not the case, such a fellow as Costard may well be supposed ignorant of his true title. MALONE.

⁵ —*tharborough;*] i. e. *Third-borough*, a peace officer, alike in authority with a headborough or a constable. SIR J. HAWKINS.

⁶ *A high hope for a low having;*] The old copies read—*havves*. The emendation was made by Mr. Theobald, and has been adopted by all the subsequent editors. *Having* is *acquisition*. MALONE.
Heaven, however, may be the true reading, in allusion to the gradation of happiness promised by *Mahommed* to his followers. So, in the comedy of *Old Fortunatus*, 1600:
" Oh, how my soul is rapt to a *third heaven!*" STEEVENS.

⁷ *To hear; or forbear hearing?*] One of the modern editors, plausibly enough, reads,—*To hear; or forbear laughing?"* MALONE.

⁸ — *taken with the manner.*] A forensic term. A thief is said to be
taken

Bir. In what manner?

Coſt. In manner and form following, Sir; all thoſe three: I was ſeen with her in the manor houſe, ſitting with her upon the form, and taken following her into the park; which put together, is, in manner and form following. Now, Sir, for the manner—it is the manner of a man to ſpeak to a woman: for the form—in ſome form.

Bir. For the following, Sir?

Coſt. As it ſhall follow in my correction: And God defend the right!

King. Will you hear this letter with attention?

Bir. As we would hear an oracle.

Coſt. Such is the ſimplicity of man to hearken after the fleſh.

King. [reads.] *Great deputy, the welkin's vice-gerent, and ſole dominator of Navarre, my ſoul's earth's God, and body's foſtering patron—*

Coſt. Not a word of Coſtard yet.

King. So it is—

Coſt. It may be ſo: but if he ſay it is ſo, he is, in telling true, but ſo, ſo [9].

King. Peace.

Coſt. —be to me, and every man that dares not fight!

King. No words.

Coſt. —of other men's ſecrets, I beſeech you.

King. *So it is, beſieged with ſable-colour'd melancholy, I did commend the black oppreſſing humour to the moſt wholſome phyſic of thy health-giving air; and, as I am a gentleman, betook myſelf to walk. The time, when? About the ſixth hour; when beaſts moſt graze, birds beſt peck, and men ſit down to that nouriſhment which is called ſupper. So much for the time when: Now for the ground which; which, I mean, I walk'd upon: it is y-cleped, thy park. Then for the place where; where, I mean, I did encounter that obſcene and moſt prepoſterous event, that draweth from my ſnow-white pen the ebon-colour'd ink, which here thou vieweſt, beholdeſt, ſurveyeſt, or ſeeſt: But to the place, where— It ſtandeth north-north-eaſt and by eaſt from the weſt corner of thy*

---

taken with the manner, i. e. *w[itneſs]* or *mainour*, (for ſo it is written in our old law-books,) when he is apprehended with the thing ſtolen in his poſſeſſion. The thing that he has taken was called *mainour*, from the Fr. *manier*, manu tractare. MALONE.

9 —*but ſo, ſo.*] The ſecond *ſo* was added by Sir T. Hanmer, and adopted by the ſubſequent editors. MALONE.

curious-

curious-knotted garden: There did I see that low-spirited swain, that base minnow of thy mirth[1].

Cost. Me.

King.—*that unletter'd small-knowing soul,*

Cost. Me.

King.—*that shallow vassal,*

Cost. Still me.

King.—*which, as I remember, hight Costard,*

Cost. O me!

King.—*sorted and consorted, contrary to thy established proclaimed edict and continent canon, with—with*[2]—*O with—but with this I passion to say wherewith.*

Cost. With a wench.

King.—*with a child of our grandmother Eve, a female; or, for thy more sweet understanding, a woman. Him I (as my everesteemed duty pricks me on) have sent to thee, to receive the meed of punishment, by thy sweet Grace's officer, Anthony Dull; a man of good repute, carriage, bearing, and estimation.*

Dull. Me, an't shall please you; I am Anthony Dull.

King. For *Jacquenetta,* (so is the weaker vessel called, which I apprehended with the aforesaid swain,) I keep her as a vessel of thy law's fury; and shall, at the least of thy sweet notice, bring her to trial. Thine, in all compliments of devoted and heart-burning heat of duty,

Don Adriano de Armado.

Bir. This is not so well as I look'd for, but the best that ever I heard.

King. Ay, the best for the worst. But, Sirrah, what say you to this?

Cost. Sir, I confess the wench.

King. Did you hear the proclamation?

Cost. I do confess much of the hearing it, but little of the marking of it[3].

---

[1] *—base minnow of thy mirth.*] The base *minnow* of thy mirth, is the contemptibly little object that contributes to thy entertainment. Shakspeare makes Coriolanus characterise the tribunitian insolence of Sicinius, under the same figure:

"——— hear you not

"This Triton of the *minnows?*"

Again, in *Have with you to Saffron Walden,* &c. 1596: "Let him denie that there was another shewe made of the little *minnow,* his brother," &c. STEEVENS.

[2] —with —*with*—] The old copy reads—*which* with. The correction is Mr. Theobald's. MALONE.

— *King.*

LOVE'S LABOUR'S LOST.

King. It was proclaim'd a year's imprisonment to be taken with a wench.

Cost. I was taken with none, Sir; I was taken with a damosel.

King. Well, it was proclaim'd damosel.

Cost. This was no damosel neither, Sir; she was a virgin.

King. It is so varied too; for it was proclaim'd, virgin.

Cost. If it were, I deny her virginity; I was taken with a maid.

King. This maid will not serve your turn, Sir.

Cost. This maid will serve my turn, Sir.

King. Sir, I will pronounce your sentence: You shall fast a week with bran and water.

Cost. I had rather pray a month with mutton and porridge.

King. And Don Armado shall be your keeper.—
My Lord Biron, see him deliver'd o'er.—
And go we, lords, to put in practice that
Which each to other hath so strongly sworn.

[*Exeunt* KING, LONGAVILLE, *and* DUMAIN.

Bir. I'll lay my head to any good man's hat,
These oaths and laws will prove an idle scorn.—
Sirrah, come on.

Cost. I suffer for the truth, Sir: for true it is, I was taken with Jaquenetta, and Jaquenetta is a true girl; and therefore, Welcome the sour cup of prosperity! Affliction may one day smile again, and till then, Sit thee down, sorrow!

[*Exeunt.*

SCENE II.

Another part of the same. A Room in Armado's *House.*

Enter ARMADO *and* MOTH.

Arm. Boy, what sign is it, when a man of great spirit grows melancholy?

Moth. A great sign, Sir, that he will look sad.

---

³ *I do confess much of the bearing it, but little of the marking of it.*] So *Falstaff,* in *K. Henry* IV. P. ii.: "—it is the disease of not listening, the malady of not marking, that I am troubled withal." STEEVENS.

Arm.

Arm. Why, sadness is one and the self-same thing, dear imp [4].

Moth. No, no; O Lord, Sir, no.

Arm. How can'st thou part sadness and melancholy, my tender juvenal [5]?

Moth. By a familiar demonstration of the working, my tough senior?

Arm. Why tough Senior? why tough Senior?

Moth. Why tender Juvenal? why tender Juvenal?

Arm. I spoke it, tender Juvenal as a congruent epitheton, appertaining to thy young days, which we may nominate tender.

Moth. And I, tough Senior, as an appertinent title to your old time [6], which we may name tough [7].

Arm. Pretty, and apt.

Moth. How mean you, Sir? I pretty, and my saying apt? or I apt, and my saying pretty?

Arm. Thou pretty, because little.

Moth. Little pretty, because little: Wherefore apt?

Arm. And therefore apt, because quick.

Moth. Speak you this in my praise, master?

Arm. In thy condign praise.

Moth. I will praise an eel with the same praise.

Arm. What? that an eel is ingenious?

Moth. That an eel is quick.

Arm. I do say, thou art quick in answers: Thou heat'st my blood.

Moth. I am answer'd, Sir.

Arm. I love not to be cross'd.

---

[4] — *dear imp.*] Imp was anciently a term of dignity. Lord Cromwell, in his last letter to Henry VIII. prays for *the imp his son*. It is now used only in contempt or abhorrence; perhaps in our author's time it was ambiguous, in which state it suits well with this dialogue. JOHNSON.

Pistol salutes King Henry V. by the same title. STEEVENS.

[5] — *my tender juvenal?*] Juvenal is youth. STEEVENS.

[6] — *tough Senior, as an appertinent title to your old time,*] Here, and in two speeches above, the old copies have *senior*, which appears to have been the old spelling of *junior*. So, in the last scene *of the Comedy of Errors,* edit. 1623: "We will draw cuts for the *signior*; till then, lead thou first." In that play the spelling has been corrected properly by the modern editors, who yet, I know not why, have retained the old spelling in the passage before us. MALONE.

[7] — *tough.*] Old and tough, young and tender, is one of the proverbial phrases collected by Ray. STEEVENS.

Moth.

Moth. He speaks the mere contrary, crosses love not him [8].   [*aside.*
Arm. I have promised to study three years with the Duke.
Moth. You may do it in an hour, Sir.
Arm. Impossible.
Moth. How many is one thrice told?
Arm. I am ill at reckoning, it fitteth the spirit of a tapster.
Moth. You are a gentleman and a gamester, Sir.
Arm. I confess both; they are both the varnish of a complete man.
Moth. Then, I am sure, you know how much the gross sum of deuce-ace amounts to.
Arm. It doth amount to one more than two.
Moth. Which the base vulgar do call, three.
Arm. True.
Moth. Why, Sir, is this such a piece of study? Now here is three studied, ere you'll thrice wink: and how easy it is to put years to the word three, and study three years in two words, the dancing horse will tell you [9].

Arm.

---

[8] — *crosses love not him.*] By *crosses* he means money. So, in *As you Like it,* the Clown says to Celia, "*if I should bear you, I should bear no cross.*" JOHNSON.

[9] — *and how easy it is to put years to the word three, and study three years in two words, the dancing horse will tell you.*] Bankes's *horse,* which play'd many remarkable pranks. Sir Kenelm Digby (*A Treatise of Bodies,* ch. xxxviii. p. 323.) observes, "That his horse would restore a glove to the due owner, after the master had whispered the man's name in his ear; would tell the just number of pence in any piece of silver coin, newly shewed him by his master; and even obey presently his command, in discharging himself of his excrements, whensoever he had bade him." GREY.

See also *Chrestoleros,* or Seven Bookes of Epigrames, written by T. B. [Thomas Bastard] 1598, lib. iii. ep. 17:

"*Of Bankes's Horse.*
" *Bankes* hath a horse of wondrous qualitie,
" For he can fight, and pisse, and daunce, and lie,
" And finde your purse, and tell what coyne ye have:
" But *Bankes,* who taught your horse to smel a knave?"

Among other exploits of this celebrated beast, it is said that he went up to the top of St. Paul's.

Among the entries at Stationers'-Hall is the following: Nov. 14, 1595, "A Ballad shewing the strange qualities of a young nagg called *Morocco.*" STEEVENS.

Arm. A most fine figure!

Moth. To prove you a cypher. [*aside.*

Arm. I will hereupon confess, I am in love: and, as it is base for a soldier to love, so am I in love with a base wench. If drawing my sword against the humour of affection would deliver me from the reprobate thought of it, I would take desire prisoner; and ransom him to any French courtier for a new devised court'sy. I think scorn to sigh; methinks, I should out-swear Cupid. Comfort me, boy; What great men have been in love?

In 1595 was published a pamphlet entitled *Morocco, extaticus, or Bankes' bay horse in a trance. A discourse set downe in a merry dialogue between Bankes and his horse; anatomizing some abuses and bad tricks of the age*, 4to. Ben Jonson hints at the unfortunate catastrophe of both man and horse, which, I find, happened at Rome, where to the disgrace of the age, of the country, and of humanity, they were burnt by order of the pope, for magicians. See *Don Zara del Fogo*, 12mo, 1660, p. 114. REED.

Underneath is a representation of Bankes and his horse, copied from the pamphlet above mentioned.

MALONE.

Meth.

Moth. Hercules, master.

Arm. Most sweet Hercules!—More authority, dear boy, name more; and, sweet my child, let them be men of good repute and carriage.

Moth. Sampson, master: he was a man of good carriage, great carriage; for he carried the town-gates on his back, like a porter: and he was in love.

Arm. O well-knit Sampson! strong-jointed Sampson! I do excel thee in my rapier, as much as thou didst me in carrying gates. I am in love too. Who was Sampson's love, my dear Moth?

Moth. A woman, master.

Arm. Of what complexion?

Moth. Of all the four, or the three, or the two; or one of the four.

Arm. Tell me, precisely, of what complexion?

Moth. Of the sea-water green, Sir.

Arm. Is that one of the four complexions?

Moth. As I have read, Sir; and the best of them too.

Arm. Green, indeed, is the colour of lovers [1]: but to have a love of that colour, methinks, Sampson had small reason for it. He, surely, affected her for her wit.

Moth. It was so, Sir; for she had a green wit.

Arm. My love is most immaculate white and red.

Moth. Most maculate thoughts [2], master, are mask'd under such colours.

Arm. Define, define, well-educated infant.

Moth. My father's wit, and my mother's tongue assist me!

Arm. Sweet invocation of a child; most pretty, and pathetical!

---

[1] *Green, indeed, is the colour of lovers*:] I do not know whether our author alludes to "the rare green eye, which in his time seems to have been thought a beauty, or to that frequent attendant on love, jealousy, to which, in *The Merchant of Venice*, and in *Othello*, he has applied the epithet *green-ey'd*. MALONE.

[2] *Most maculate thoughts,*—] So the first quarto, 1598. The folio has *immaculate*. To avoid such notes for the future, it may be proper to apprize the reader, that where the reading of the text does not correspond with the folio, without any reason being assigned for the deviation, it is always warranted by the authority of the first quarto.
MALONE.

Moth. If she be made of white and red,
  Her faults will ne'er be known;
 For blushing³ cheeks by faults are bred,
  And fears by pale-white shown:
 Then, if she fear, or be to blame,
  By this you shall not know;
 For still her cheeks possess the same,
  Which native she doth owe.

A dangerous rhime, master, against the reason of white and red.

Arm. Is there not a ballad, boy, of the King and the Beggar⁴?

Moth. The world was very guilty of such a ballad some three ages since: but, I think, now 'tis not to be found; or, if it were, it would neither serve for the writing, nor the tune.

Arm. I will have that subject newly writ o'er, that I may example my digression⁵ by some mighty precedent. Boy, I do love that country girl, that I took in the park with the rational hind Costard⁶; she deserves well.

Moth. To be whipp'd; and yet a better love than my master. [*aside.*

Arm. Sing, boy; my spirit grows heavy in love.

Moth. And that's great marvel, loving a light wench.

Arm. I say, sing.

Moth. Forbear, till this company be past.

---

³ *For* blushing—] The original copy has—*blush in.* The emendation was made by the editor of the second folio. MALONE.

⁴ *—the King and the Beggar?*] See Dr. Percy's *Collection of old Ballads,* in three vols. STEEVENS.

⁵ *—my* digression] *Digression* on this occasion signifies the act of going out of the right way. So, in *Romeo and Juliet:*

"Thy noble shape is but a form of wax,
"Digressing from the valour of a man." STEEVENS.

Again, in our author's *Rape of Lucrece:*

"——— my *digression* is so vile, so base,
"That it will live engraven in my face." MALONE.

⁶ *—the* rational hind *Costard;*] The *reasoning brute,* the *animal with some share of reason.* STEEVENS.

I have always read *irrational hind:* if *hind* be taken in its *bestial* sense, Armado makes Costard a *female.* FARMER.

Shakspeare uses it in its *bestial* sense in *Julius Cæsar,* Act i. sc. iii. and as of the masculine gender:

"He were no *lion,* were not Romans *hinds.*"

Again, in *K. Henry* IV. sc. iii.:—" —you are a shallow cowardly *hind,* and you lye. STEEVENS.

Enter

LOVE'S LABOUR'S LOST.

Enter DULL, COSTARD, *and* JAQUENETTA.

Dull. Sir, the Duke's pleasure is, that you keep Costard safe; and you must let him take no delight, nor no penance; but a' must fast three days a-week. For this damsel, I must keep her at the park; she is allow'd for the day-woman. Fare you well.

Arm. I do betray myself with blushing.—Maid.
Jaq. Man.
Arm. I will visit thee at the lodge.
Jaq. That's hereby.
Arm. I know where it is situate.
Jaq. Lord, how wise you are!
Arm. I will tell thee wonders.
Jaq. With that face?
Arm. I love thee.
Jaq. So I heard you say.
Arm. And so, farewel.
Jaq. Fair weather after you!
Dull. Come, Jaquenetta, away [7].

[*Exeunt* DULL *and* JAQUENETTA.

Arm. Villain, thou shalt fast for thy offences, ere thou be pardoned.
Cost. Well, Sir, I hope, when I do it, I shall do it on a full stomach.
Arm. Thou shalt be heavily punished.
Cost. I am more bound to you, than your fellows, for they are but lightly rewarded.
Arm. Take away this villain; shut him up.
Moth. Come, you transgressing slave; away.
Cost. Let me not be pent up, Sir: I will fast, being loose.
Moth. No, Sir; that were fast and loose: thou shalt to prison.
Cost. Well, if ever I do see the merry days of desolation that I have seen, some shall see—
Moth. What shall some see?
Cost. Nay, nothing, Master Moth, but what they look upon. It is not for prisoners to be too silent in their words;

---

[7] *Come, &c.*] To this line in the first quarto, and the first folio, *Clo.* by an error of the press is prefixed, instead of *Con.* i. e. Constable, or Dull. Mr. Theobald made the necessary correction. MALONE.

and,

and, therefore, I will say nothing: I thank God, I have as little patience as another man; and, therefore I can be quiet.

[*Exeunt* MOTH *and* COSTARD.

Arm. I do affect [a] the very ground, which is base, where her shoe, which is baser, guided by her foot, which is basest, doth tread. I shall be forsworn, (which is a great argument of falshood,) if I love: And how can that be true love, which is falsly attempted? Love is a familiar; love is a devil: there is no evil angel but love. Yet Sampson was so tempted; and he had an excellent strength; yet was Solomon so seduced; and he had a very good wit. Cupid's but-shaft is too hard for Hercules' club, and therefore too much odds for a Spaniard's rapier. The first and second cause will not serve my turn [9]; the passado he respects not, the duello he regards not; his disgrace is to be call'd boy; but his glory is, to subdue men. Adieu, valour! rust, rapier! be still, drum! for your manager is in love; yea, he loveth. Assist me some extemporal god of rhime, for, I am sure, I shall turn sonneteer [1]. Devise, wit; write, pen; for I am for whole volumes in folio. [*Exit.*

ACT II. SCENE I.

Another part of the same. A Pavilion and Tents at a distance.

Enter the Princess of France, ROSALINE, MARIA, CATHARINE, BOYET, *Lords, and other Attendants.*

Boy. Now, Madam, summon up your dearest spirits:
Consider who the king your father sends;
To whom he sends; and what's his embassy:
Yourself, held precious in the world's esteem;
To parly with the sole inheritor
Of all perfections that a man may owe,

---

[a] —*affect*—] i. e. love. STEEVENS.
[9] *The first and second cause will not serve my turn;*] See the last act of *As you Like it*, with the notes. JOHNSON.
[1] —*sonneteer.*] The old copies read only—*sonnet.* STEEVENS. The emendation is Sir T. Hanmer's. MALONE.

Matchless

Matchless Navarre; the plea of no less weight
Than Aquitain, a dowry for a queen.
Be now as prodigal of all dear grace,
As nature was in making graces dear,
When she did starve the general world beside,
And prodigally gave them all to you.

 Prin. Good Lord Boyet, my beauty, though but mean,
Needs not the painted flourish of your praise;
Beauty is bought by judgment of the eye,
Not utter'd by base sale of chapmen's tongues [a]:
I am less proud to hear you tell my worth,
Than you much willing to be counted wise
In spending your wit in the praise of mine.
But now to task the tasker—Good Boyet,
You are not ignorant, all-telling fame
Doth noise abroad, Navarre hath made a vow,
Till painful study shall out-wear three years,
No woman may approach his silent court:
Therefore to us seemeth it a needful course,
Before we enter his forbidden gates,
To know his pleasure; and in that behalf,
Bold of your worthiness we single you
As our best-moving fair solicitor:
Tell him, the daughter of the king of France,
On serious business, craving quick dispatch,
Importunes personal conference with his grace.
Haste, signify so much; while we attend,
Like humble-visag'd suitors, his high will.

 Boy. Proud of employment, willingly I go.   [*Exit.*
 Prin. All pride is willing pride, and yours is so.—
Who are the votaries, my loving lords,
That are vow-fellows with this virtuous Duke?
 1st. Lord. Longaville is one.
 Prin. Know you the man?

---

[a] *Beauty is bought by judgment of the eye,*
Not utter'd by base sale of chapmen's *tongues.*] So, in our author's 102d Sonnet:
 "That love is merchandiz'd, whose rich esteeming
 "The owner's tongue doth publish every where." MALONE.

Chapman here seems to signify the *seller*, not, as now commonly, the *buyer*. *Cheap* or *cheaping* was anciently the *market*; *chapman* therefore is *marketman*. The meaning is, that *the estimation of beauty depends not on the uttering or proclamation of the seller, but on the eye of the buyer.*
          JOHNSON.

Mar.

Mar. I know him, Madam; at a marriage feast,
Between Lord Perigort and the beauteous heir
Of Jaques Faulconbridge solémnized,
In Normandy saw I this Longaville:
A man of sovereign parts he is esteem'd ³;
Well fitted in the arts ⁴, glorious in arms:
Nothing becomes him ill, that he would well.
The only soil of his fair virtue's gloss,
(If virtue's gloss will stain with any soil,)
Is a sharp wit match'd with ⁵ too blunt a will; -
Whose edge hath power to cut, whose will still wills
It should none spare that come within his power.
  Prin. Some merry mocking Lord, belike; is't so?
  Mar. They say so most, that most his humours know.
  Prin. Such short-liv'd wits do wither as they grow.
Who are the rest?
  Cath. The young Dumain, a well-accomplish'd youth,
Of all that virtue love for virtue lov'd:
Most power to do most harm, least knowing ill;
For he hath wit to make an ill shape good,
And shape to win grace though he had no wit.
I saw him at the Duke Alençon's once;
And much too little of that good I saw,
Is my report, to his great worthiness ⁶.

---

³ *A man of sovereign parts he is esteem'd;*] Thus the folio. The first quarto, 1598, has the line thus:
"A man of sovereign peerless he is esteem'd."
I believe, the author wrote
"A man of,—sovereign, peerless, he's esteem'd.
A man of extraordinary accomplishments, the speaker perhaps would have said, but suddenly checks himself; and adds—" sovereign, peerless he's esteem'd." So, before: " Matchless Navarre." Again, in the *Tempest*:
———" but you, O you,
"So perfect, and so peerless are created."
In the old copies no attention seems to have been given to abrupt sentences. They are, almost uniformly printed corruptly, without any mark of abruption. Thus, in *Much Ado about Nothing*, we find both in the folio and quarto, "—but for the stuffing well, we are all mortal." MALONE.

⁴ *Well fitted in the arts,*—] *Well fitted*, is *well qualified*. JOHNSON.
The, which is not in the old copies, was added for the sake of the metre, by the editor of the second folio. MALONE.

⁵ — *match'd with*—] i. *combined* or *joined* with. JOHNSON.

⁶ *And much too little,* &c.} i. e. And my report of the good I saw, is much too little, *compared* to his great worthiness. HEATH.

Ros.

Ros. Another of these students at that time
Was there with him, if I have heard a truth;
Biron they call him; but a merrier man,
Within the limit of becoming mirth,
I never spent an hour's talk withal:
His eye begets occasion for his wit;
For every object that the one doth catch,
The other turns to a mirth-moving jest;
Which his fair tongue (conceit's expositor)
Delivers in such apt and gracious words,
That aged ears play truant at his tales,
And younger hearings are quite ravished;
So sweet and voluble is his discourse.

Prin. God bless my ladies! are they all in love;
That every one her own hath garnished
With such bedecking ornaments of praise?

1st. Lord. Here comes Boyet.

Re-enter BOYET.

Prin. Now, what admittance, Lord?

Boy. Navarre had notice of your fair approach;
And he and his competitors[7] in oath
Were all address'd[8] to meet you, gentle Lady,
Before I came. Marry, thus much I have learnt,
He rather means to lodge you in the field,
(Like one that comes here to besiege his court,)
Than seek a dispensation for his oath,
To let you enter his unpeopled house.
Here comes Navarre. [*The ladies mask.*

Enter KING, LONGAVILLE, DUMAIN, BIRON, *and Attendants.*

King. Fair Princess, welcome to the court of Navarre.

Prin. Fair, I give you back again; and welcome I have not yet: the roof of this court is too high to be yours; and welcome to the wide fields too base to be mine.

King. You shall be welcome, Madam, to my court.

Prin. I will be welcome then; conduct me thither.

---

[7] — *his competitors*—] That is, his confederates. MALONE.
[8] *Were all address'd*—] To *address* is to *prepare*. So, in *Hamlet:*
"—— it lifted up its head, and did *address*
"Itself to motion." STEEVENS.

King. Hear me, dear Lady; I have sworn an oath.
Prin. Our Lady help my Lord! he'll be forsworn.
King. Not for the world, fair Madam, by my will.
Prin. Why, will shall break it; will, and nothing else.
King. Your ladyship is ignorant what it is.
Prin. Were my Lord so, his ignorance were wise,
Where now his knowledge must prove ignorance.
I hear, your grace hath sworn-out house-keeping:
'Tis deadly sin to keep that oath, my Lord,
And sin to break it [9]:
But pardon me, I am too sudden bold;
To teach a teacher ill beseemeth me.
Vouchsafe to read the purpose of my coming,
And suddenly resolve me in my suit. [*gives a paper.*
King. Madam, I will, if suddenly I may.
Prin. You will the sooner, that I were away:
For you'll prove perjur'd, if you make me stay.
Bir. Did not I dance with you in Brabant once [1]?
Ros. Did not I dance with you in Brabant once?
Bir. I know, you did.
Ros. How needless was it then
To ask the question!
Bir. You must not be so quick.
Ros. 'Tis long of you that spur me with such questions.
Bir. Your wit's too hot, it speeds too fast, 'twill tire.
Ros. Not till it leave the rider in the mire.
Bir. What time o' day?
Ros. The hour that fools should ask.
Bir. Now fair befal your mask!
Ros. Fair fall the face it covers!
Bir. And send you many lovers!
Ros. Amen, so you be none.
Bir. Nay, then will I be gone.
King. Madam, your father here doth intimate
The payment of a hundred thousand crowns;
Being but the one half of an entire sum,

---

[9] *And sin to break it:*] Sir T. Hanmer reads—"*Not sin to break it?*"
—I believe erroneously. The princess shews an inconvenience very frequently attending rash oaths, which, whether kept or broken, produce guilt. JOHNSON.

[1] Ros. *Did not I dance with you in Brabant once?*] Thus the folio. In the first quarto, this dialogue passes between *Catharine* and Biron. It is a matter of little consequence. MALONE.

Disbursed

Disbursed by my father in his wars.
But say, that he, or we, (as neither have,)
Receiv'd that sum; yet there remains unpaid
A hundred thousand more; in surety of the which,
One part of Aquitain is bound to us,
Although not valued to the money's worth.
If then the king your father will restore
But that one half which is unsatisfy'd,
We will give up our right in Aquitain,
And hold fair friendship with his majesty.
But that, it seems, he little purposeth,
For here he doth demand to have repaid
An hundred thousand crowns; and not demands,
On payment of a hundred thousand crowns[2],
To have his title live in Aquitain;
Which we much rather had depart withal[3],
And have the money by our father lent,
Than Aquitain so gelded as it is.
Dear Princess, were not his requests so far
From reason's yielding, your fair self should make
A yielding, 'gainst some reason, in my breast,
And go well satisfied to France again.

Prin. You do the king my father too much wrong,
And wrong the reputation of your name,
In so unseeming to confess receipt
Of that which hath so faithfully been paid.

King. I do protest, I never heard of it;
And, if you prove it, I'll repay it back,
Or yield up Aquitain.

Prin. We arrest your word:
Boyet, you can produce acquittances,
For such a sum, from special officers
Of Charles his father.

King. Satisfy me so.

Boy. So please your grace, the packet is not come,
Where that and other specialties are bound;
To-morrow you shall have a sight of them.

[2] *On payment—*] This is Mr. Theobald's correction. The old copies have—*One payment.* The two words are frequently confounded in the books of our author's age. See a note on *King John,* Act iii. sc. iii. MALONE.

[3] *—depart withal*] To *depart* and to *part* were anciently synonymous. So, in *K. John:*
"Hath willingly *departed* with a part." STEEVENS.

King. It shall suffice me: at which interview,
All liberal reason I will yield unto.
Mean time, receive such welcome at my hand,
As honour, without breach of honour, may
Make tender of to thy true worthiness:
You may not come, fair Princess, in my gates;
But here without you shall be so receiv'd,
As you shall deem yourself lodg'd in my heart,
Though so deny'd fair harbour in my house.
Your own good thoughts excuse me, and farewel:
To-morrow shall we visit you again.

  Prin. Sweet health and fair desires comfort your grace!
  King. Thy own wish wish I thee in every place!

[*Exeunt* KING *and his Train.*

  Bir. Lady, I will commend you to my own heart.
  Ros. Pray you, do my commendations; I would be glad to see it.
  Bir. I would, you heard it groan.
  Ros. Is the fool sick [4]?
  Bir. Sick at the heart.
  Ros. Alack, let it blood.
  Bir. Would that do it good?
  Ros. My physic says, I [5].
  Bir. Will you prick't with your eye?
  Ros. No, *point*, with my knife.
  Bir. Now, God save thy life!
  Ros. And yours from long living!
  Bir. I cannot stay thanksgiving. [*retiring.*
  Dum. Sir, I pray you, a word; What lady is that same [6]?

---

[4] *Is the fool sick?*] She means perhaps his *heart.* So, in *Much Ado about Nothing:* (ante, p. 83.) "*D. Pedro.* In faith, lady, you have a merry *heart. Beat.* Yes, my Lord; I thank it, poor *fool*, it keeps on the windy side of care." MALONE.

[5] *My physic says,* I.] She means to say, *ay.* The old spelling of the affirmative particle has been retained here for the sake of the rhime.
  MALONE.

[6] *What lady is that same?*] It is odd that Shakspeare should make *Dumain* enquire after *Rosaline*, who was the mistress of *Biron*, and neglect *Catharine*, who was his own. *Biron* behaves in the same manner. No advantage would be gained by an exchange of names, because the last speech is determined to *Biron* by *Maria*, who gives a character of him after he has made his exit. Perhaps *all* the ladies wore masks but the princess. STEEVENS.

They certainly did. See p. 192, where Biron says to Rosaline— "Now fair befal your *mask!*" MALONE.

Boy.

Boy. The heir of Alençon, Rosaline her name.
Dum. A gallant lady! Monsieur, fare you well.
　　　　　　　　　　　　　　　　　　[*Exit* DUMAIN.
Long. I beseech you a word; What is she in the white?
Boy. A woman sometimes, an you saw her in the light.
Long. Perchance, light in the light: I desire her name.
Boy. She hath but one for herself; to desire that, were
　　a shame.
Long. Pray you Sir, whose daughter?
Boy. Her mother's I have heard.
Long. God's blessing on your beard[7]!
Boy. Good Sir, be not offended:
She is an heir of Faulconbridge.
Long. Nay, my choler is ended.
She is a most sweet lady.
Boy. Not unlike, Sir; that may be.　　[*Exit* LONG.
Bir. What's her name in the cap?
Boy. Catharine, by good hap.
Bir. Is she wedded, or no?
Boy. To her will, Sir, or so.
Bir. You are welcome, Sir; adieu!
Boy. Farewel to me, Sir, and welcome to you.
　　　　　　　　　　　　　[*Exit* BIRON. *Ladies unmask.*
Mar. That last is Biron, the merry mad-cap Lord;
Not a word with him but a jest.
Boy. And every jest but a word.
Prin. It was well done of you, to take him at his word.
Boy. I was as willing to grapple; as he was to board.
Mar. Two hot sheeps, marry!
Boy. And wherefore not ships?
No sheep, sweet lamb, unless we feed on your lips[8].
Mar. You sheep, and I pasture; Shall that finish the jest?
Boy. So you grant pasture for me.　　[*offering to kiss her.*
Mar. Not so, gentle beast;

[7] *God's blessing on your beard!*] That is, may'st thou have sense and seriousness more proportionate to thy beard, the length of which suits ill with such idle catches of wit　　JOHNSON.
　I doubt whether so much meaning was intended to be conveyed by these words.　MALONE.

[8] *— unless we feed on your lips*] Our author has the same expression in his *Venus and Adonis*:
　　" *Feed* where thou wilt, on mountain or on dale;
　　" *Graze on my lips.*"　MALONE.

K 3

My lips are no common, though several they be [9].
Boy. Belonging to whom?
Mar. To my fortunes and me.
Prin. Good wits will be jangling: but, gentles, agree:
The civil war of wits were much better used
On Navarre and his book-men; for here 'tis abused.
Boy. If my observation, (which very seldom lies,)
By the heart's still rhetoric, disclosed with eyes [a],
Deceive me not now, Navarre is infected.
Prin. With what?
Boy. With that which we lovers intitle, affected.
Prin. Your reason?
Boy. Why, all his behaviours did make their retire
To the court of his eye, peeping thorough desire:
His heart, like an agate, with your print impressed,
Proud with his form, in his eye pride expressed:
His tongue, all impatient to speak and not see [1],
Did stumble with haste in his eye-sight to be;
All senses to that sense did make their repair,
To feel only looking [2] on fairest of fair:
Methought, all his senses were lock'd in his eye,
As jewels in crystal for some prince to buy;
Who, tend'ring their own worth, from where they were
     glass'd,
Did point you to buy them, along as you pass'd.

[9] *My lips are no common, though several they be.*] A play on the word *several*, which, besides its ordinary signification of *separate, distinct*, likewise signifies in uninclosed lands, a certain portion of ground appropriated to either corn or meadow, adjoining the *common* field. In Minsheu's Dictionary, 1617, is the following article: " To *sever* from others. Hinc nos pascua et campos seorsim ab aliis separatos *Severals* dicimus." In the margin he spells the word as Shakspeare does—*severals*.—Our author is seldom careful that his comparisons should answer on both sides. If *several* be understood in its rustic sense, the adversative particle stands but awkwardly. To say, that *though* land is *several*, it is not a *common*, seems as unjustifiable as to assert, that *though* a house is a cottage, it is not a palace. MALONE.

[a] *By the heart's still rhetoric, disclosed with eyes*,] So in Daniel's *Complaint of Rosamond*, 1594:
" Sweet *silent rhetoric* of persuading *eyes*;
" *Dumb eloquence*——." MALONE.

[1] *His tongue all impatient to speak and not see*,] That is, his tongue being impatiently desirous to see as well as speak. JOHNSON.

[2] *To feel only looking*——] Perhaps we may better read:
    To feel *only by looking*. JOHNSON.

His

His face's own margent did quote ³ such amazes,
That all eyes saw his eyes enchanted with gazes:
I'll give you Aquitain, and all that is his,
An you give him for my sake but one loving kiss.
 Prin. Come, to our pavilion: Boyet is dispos'd—
 Boy. But to speak that in words, which his eye hath
  disclos'd:
I only have made a mouth of his eye,
By adding a tongue which I know will not lie.
 Ros. Thou art an old love-monger, and speak'st skilfully.
 Mar. He is Cupid's grandfather, and learns news of him.
 Ros. Then was Venus like her mother; for her father is
  but grim.
 Boy. Do you hear, my mad wenches?
 Mar. No.
 Boy. What then, do you see?
 Ros. Ay, our way to be gone.
 Boy. You are too hard for me.   [*Exeunt.*

ACT III. SCENE I.

Another part of the same.

Enter ARMADO *and* MOTH.

 Arm. Warble, child; make passionate my sense of hearing.
 Moth. Concolinel—¹   [*singing.*
 Arm.

---

³ *His face's own margent did quote, &c.*] In our author's time, notes, quotations, &c. were usually printed in the exterior margin of books. So, in *Romeo and Juliet*:
  " And what obscur'd in this fair *volume* lies,
  " Find written in the *margin* of his eyes."
Again in *Hamlet:* " I knew you must be edified by the *margent*."
         MALONE.

¹ *Concolinel*—] Here is apparently a song lost. JOHNSON.
I have observed in the old comedies, that the songs are frequently omitted. On this occasion the stage-direction is generally—*Here they sing*—or, *Cantant*. Probably the performer was left to chuse his own ditty, and therefore it could not with propriety be exhibited as part of

K 3   a new

Arm. Sweet air!—Go, tenderness of years; take this key, give enlargement to the swain, bring him festinately hither[1]; I must employ him in a letter to my love.

Moth. Master, will you win your love with a French brawl[3]?

Arm. How mean'st thou? brawling in French?

Moth. No, my complete master: but to jig off a tune at the tongue's end, canary to it with your feet[4], humour it with turning up your eye-lids; sigh a note, and sing a note; sometime through the throat, as if you swallow'd love with singing love; sometime through the nose, as if you snuff'd up love by smelling love; with your hat penthouse-like, o'er the shop of your eyes; with your arms cross'd on your thin belly-doublet, like a rabbit on a spit; or your hands in your pocket, like a man after the old painting[5]; and keep not too long in one tune, but a snip and away: These are complements[6], these are humours; these betray nice wenches—that would be betray'd without these; and make them men of note, (do you note, men?) that most are affected to these[7].

Arm. How hast thou purchased this experience?

Moth. By my penny of observation[8].

Arm.

a new performance. Sometimes yet more was left to the discretion of the ancient comedians, as I learn from the following circumstance in A. *Edward IV* 2d p. 1619:—"Jockey is led whipping over the stage, speaking some words, but of no importance." Again, in Decker's *Honest Whore*, 1635: "He places all things in order, *singing* with the ends of old ballads as he does it." STEEVENS.

[1] — *festinately hither*] i. e. hastily. Shakspeare uses the adjective *festinate*, in another of his plays. STEEVENS.

[3] — *a French brawl?*] A *brawl* is a kind of *dance*. STEEVENS.

[4] — *canary to it with your feet*.] *Canary* was the name of a sprightly nimble dance. THEOBALD.

[5] — *like a man after the old painting*;] It was a common trick among some of the most indolent of the ancient masters, to place the hands in the bosom or the pockets, or conceal them in some other part of the drapery, to avoid the labour of representing them, or to disguise their own want of skill to employ them with grace and propriety. STEEVENS.

[6] — *complements*] i. e. accomplishments. See p. 177, n. 9. MALONE.

[7] — *and make them men of note, (do you note, men?) that are most affected to these*] i. e. and make those men who are most affected to such accomplishments, men of note.—Mr. Theobald, without any necessity, reads—and make *the* men of note, &c. which was, I think, too hastily adopted in the subsequent editions. One of the modern editors, instead of—" do you note, men?" with great probability reads—do you note *me?* MALONE.

[8] *By my penny of observation.*] The old copy reads—*pen*. The emendation is Sir T. Hanmer's. MALONE.

It

Arm. But O—but O—

Moth. —the hobby-horse is forgot.

Arm. Call'st thou my love, hobby-horse?

Moth. No, master, the hobby-horse is but a colt, and your love, perhaps, a hackney. But have you forgot your love?

Arm. Almost I had.

Moth. Negligent student! learn her by heart.

Arm. By heart, and in heart, boy.

Moth. And out of heart, master; all those three I will prove.

Arm. What wilt thou prove?

Moth. A man, if I live; and this, by, in, and without, upon the instant: By heart you love her, because your heart cannot come by her: in heart you love her, because your heart is in love with her; and out of heart you love her, being out of heart that you cannot enjoy her.

Arm. I am all these three.

Moth. And three times as much more, and yet nothing at all.

Arm. Fetch hither the swain; he must carry me a letter.

Moth. A message well sympathised; a horse to be embassador for an ass!

Arm. Ha, ha; what sayest thou?

Moth. Marry, Sir, you must send the ass upon the horse, for he is very slow-gaited: But I go.

It is certainly right. The allusion is to the famous old piece, called *A Pennyworth of Wit.* FARMER.

Arm. But O—but O—

Moth.—*the hobby-horse is forgot.*] In the celebration of May-day, besides the sports now used of hanging a pole with garlands, and dancing round it, formerly a boy was dressed up representing Maid Marian; another like a fryar; and another rude on a hobby-horse, with bells jingling, and painted streamers. After the reformation took place, and precisians multiplied, these latter rites were looked upon to favour of paganism; and then Maid Marian, the friar, and the poor hobby-horse, were turned out of the games. Some who were not so wisely precise, but regretted the disuse of the hobby-horse, no doubt, satirized this suspicion of idolatry, and archly wrote the epitaph above alluded to. Now Moth, hearing Armado groan ridiculously, and cry out, *But oh! but oh!*—humourously pieces out his exclamation with the sequel of this epitaph. THEOBALD.

The same line is repeated in *Hamlet.* See the note on Act iii. sc. ii.
STEEVENS.

— but a colt.] *Colt* is a hot, mad-brained, unbroken young fellow; or sometimes an old fellow with youthful desires. JOHNSON.

K 4 *Arm.*

Arm. The way is but short; away.
Moth. As swift as lead, Sir.
Arm. Thy meaning, pretty ingenious?
Is not lead a metal, heavy, dull, and slow?
Moth. Minime, honest master, or rather, master, no.
Arm. I say, lead is slow.
Moth. You are too swift, Sir, to say so [2]:
Is that lead slow which is fir'd from a gun?
Arm. Sweet smoke of rhetoric!
He reputes me a cannon; and the bullet, that's he:—
I shoot thee at the swain.
Moth. Thump then, and I flee.   [*Exit.*
Arm. A most acute juvenal; voluble and free of grace!
By thy favour, sweet welkin [3], I must sigh in thy face;
Most rude melancholy, valour gives thee place.
My herald is return'd.

Re-enter MOTH *and* COSTARD.

Moth. A wonder, master; here's a Costard [4] broken in a shin.
Arm. Some enigma, some riddle: come,—thy l'envoy; —begin.
Cost. No egma, no riddle, no l'envoy [5]; no salve in the

---

[2] *You are too swift, Sir, to say so:*] The meaning, I believe, is, *You do not give yourself time to think, if you say so.* Swift, however, means ready at replies. STEEVENS.

Swift is here used, as in other places, synonymously with witty.
                                                    FARMER.
So, in *As you Like it*: " He is very *swift* and sententious." Again in *Much Ado about Nothing*:
    " Having so *swift* and excellent a wit."
On reading the letter which contained an intimation of the Gunpowder-plot in 1605, King James said, that " the style was more *quick* and pithie than was usual in pasquils and libels." MALONE.

[3] *By thy favour, sweet welkin,*] Welkin is the sky, to which Armado, with the false dignity of a Spaniard, makes an apology for sighing in its face. JOHNSON.

[4] — *here's a Costard broken* —] i. e. a head. STEEVENS.

[5] — *no l'envoy;*] The *l'envoy* is a term borrowed from the old French poetry. It appeared always at the head of a few concluding verses to each piece, which either served to convey the moral, or to address the poem to some particular person. It was frequently adopted by the ancient English writers. STEEVENS.

mail,

mail, Sir[6]: O Sir, plantain, a plain plantain; no *l'envoy*, no *l'envoy*, no falve, Sir, but a plantain!

Arm. By virtue, thou enforceſt laughter; thy ſilly thought, my ſpleen; the heaving of my lungs provokes me to ridiculous ſmiling: O, pardon me, my ſtars! Doth the inconſiderate take ſalve for *l'envoy*, and the word, *l'envoy*, for a ſalve?

Moth. Do the wiſe think them other? is not *l'envoy* a ſalve?

Arm. No, page: it is an epilogue or diſcourſe, to make plain
Some obſcure precedence that hath tofore been ſain.
I will example it[7]:
    The fox, the ape, and the humble bee,
    Were ſtill at odds, being but three.
There's the moral: Now the *l'envoy*.

Moth. I will add the *l'envoy*: Say the moral again.

Arm. The fox, the ape, and the humble bee,
    Were ſtill at odds, being but three:

Moth. Until the gooſe came out of door,
    And ſtay'd the odds by adding four.
Now will I begin your moral, and do you follow with my *l'envoy*.
    The fox, the ape, and the humble bee,
    Were ſtill at odds, being but three:

Arm. Until the gooſe came out of door,
    Staying the odds by adding four.

Moth. A good *l'envoy*, ending in the gooſe: Would you deſire more?

---

[6] — *no ſalve in the mail, Sir.*] *No ſalve in the mail,* may mean, no ſalve in the mountebank's budget. JOHNSON.

Male, which is the reading of the old copies, is only the old ſpelling of *mail.* So, in Taylor the Water-Poet's Works, *(Character of a Bawd)* 1630:—"the cloathe-bag of counſel, the toy-ſenſe, ſarſle, pack, *male,* of friendly toleration." The quarto 1598, and the firſt folio, have—*thee* male. Corrected by the editor of the ſecond folio. MALONE.

I can ſcarcely think that Shakſpeare had ſo far forgotten his little ſchool-learning, as to ſuppoſe that the Latin verb *ſalve,* and the Engliſh ſubſtantive, *ſalve,* had the ſame pronunciation, and yet, without this, the quibble cannot be preſerved. FARMER.

The ſame quibble occurs in *Ariſtippus, or the Jovial Philoſopher,* 1630:
    " *Salve,* Maſter Simplicius.
    " *Salve* me; 'tis but a ſurgeon's compliment." STEEVENS.

[7] *I will example it:*] This and the following eight lines are omitted in the folio. MALONE.

Cost. The boy hath sold him a bargain, a goose, that's flat:—

Sir, your penny-worth is good, an your goose be fat.—
To sell a bargain well, is as cunning as fast and loose:
Let me see a fat *l'envoy*; ay, that's a fat goose.

Arm. Come hither, come hither; how did this argument begin?

Moth. By saying, that a *Costard* was broken in a shin. Then call'd you for the *l'envoy*.

Cost. True, and I for a plantain; Thus came your argument in:

Then the boy's fat *l'envoy*, the goose that you bought;
And he ended the market [a].

Arm. But tell me; how was there a Costard broken in a shin [b]?

Moth. I will tell you sensibly.

Cost. Thou hast no feeling of it, Moth: I will speak that *l'envoy*:—

I, Costard, running out, that was safely within,
Fell over the threshold, and broke my shin.

Arm. We will talk no more of this matter.

Cost. Till there be more matter in the shin.

Arm. Sirrah Costard, I will enfranchise thee.

Cost. O, marry me to one Frances;—I smell some *l'envoy*, some goose, in this.

Arm. By my sweet soul, I mean setting thee at liberty, enfreedoming thy person; thou wert immur'd, restrained, captivated, bound.

Cost. True, true; and now you will be my purgation, and let me loose.

Arm. I give thee thy liberty, set thee from durance; and, in lieu thereof, impose on thee nothing but this: Bear this significant to the country maid Jaquenetta: there is remuneration; [*giving him money*] for the best ward of mine honour, is rewarding my dependants. Moth, follow. [*Exit.*

Moth. Like the sequel, I [c].—Signior Costard, adieu.

Cost.

---

[a] *And he ended the market*] Alluding to the proverb—*Three women and a goose make a market. Tre donne ed un' oca fan un mercato.* Ital. Ray's Proverbs. STEEVENS.

[b] *—how was there a* Costard *broken in a shin?*] It has been already observed that the *head* was anciently called the *Costard*. STEEVENS.

[c] *Like the* sequel, *I.*] I follow you as close as the sequel does the premises. HEATH.

Moth

Cost. My sweet ounce of man's flesh! my incony Jew [1]—
 [*Exit* MOTH.
Now will I look to his remuneration. Remuneration! O, that's the Latin word for three farthings; three farthings—remuneration. *What's the price of this inkle? a penny? No, I'll give you a remuneration:* why, it carries it.—Remuneration!—why, it is a fairer name than French crown. I will never buy and sell out of this word.

Enter BIRON.

Bir. O, my good knave Costard! exceedingly well met.

Cost. Pray you, Sir, how much carnation ribbon may a man buy for a remuneration?

Bir. What is a remuneration?

Cost. Marry, Sir, half-penny farthing.

Bir. O, why then, three-farthings-worth of silk.

Cost. I thank your worship: God be wi' you!

Bir. O, stay, slave; I must employ thee:
As thou wilt win my favour, good my knave,
Do one thing for me that I shall entreat.

Cost. When would you have it done, Sir?

Bir. O, this afternoon.

Cost. Well, I will do it, Sir: Fare you well.

Bir. O, thou knowest not what it is.

Cost. I shall know, Sir, when I have done it.

Bir. Why, villain, thou must know first.

Cost. I will come to your worship to-morrow morning.

Bir. It must be done this afternoon. Hark, slave, it is but this:—
The Princess comes to hunt here in the park,

---

[1] Moth alludes to the sequel of any story which follows a preceding part, and was in the old story-books introduced in this manner:—"Here followeth the sequel of such a story or adventure." So Hamlet says—" But is there no *sequel* at the heels of this mother's admonition?" MASON.

[2] — *my incony, Jew!*] *Incony* or *kony* in the north signifies, fine, delicate;—as *a kony thing,* a fine thing. WARBURTON.

Jew, in our author's time, was, for whatever reason, apparently a word of endearment. So, in the *Midsummer-Night's Dream:*
 "*Most briskey Juvenal, and eke most lovely* Jew." JOHNSON.
In the old comedy called *Blurt Master Constable,* 1602, I meet with this word. A maid is speaking to her mistress about a gown:—" it makes you have a most *incony* body." Again, in Marlowe's *Jew of Malta,* 1633:
 " While I in thy *incony* lap do tumble." STEEVENS.

And

And in her train there is a gentle lady;
When tongues speak sweetly, then they name her name,
And Rosaline they call her: ask for her;
And to her white hand see thou do commend
This seal'd-up counsel. There's thy guerdon; go.

[gives him money.

Cost. Guerdon—O sweet guerdon! better than remuneration; eleven-pence farthing better³: Most sweet guerdon!—I will do it, Sir, in print⁴.—Guerdon—remuneration.

[Exit.

Bir. O!—And I, forsooth, in love! I, that have been
    love's whip;
A very beadle to a humourous sigh;
A critic; nay, a night-watch constable;
A domineering pedant o'er the boy,
Than whom no mortal so magnificent!

---

³ *Cost. Guerdon—O sweet* guerdon! *better than* remuneration; eleven-pence farthing better, &c.] *Guerdon.* i. e. reward.

The following parallel passage in *A Health to the Gentlemanly Profession of Serving-men, or the Serving-man's Comfort*, &c. 1598, was pointed out to me by Dr. Farmer:

"There was, sayth he, a man, (but of what estate, degree, or calling, I will not name, least thereby I might incurre displeasure of anie) that coming to his friendes house, who was a gentleman of good reckoning, and being there kindly entertained, and well used, as well of his friende the gentleman as of his servantes; one of the sayde servantes doing him some extraordinarie pleasure during his abode there, at his departure he comes unto the sayde servante, and saith unto him, Holde thee, here is a *remuneration* for thy paynes, which the servante receiving, gave him utterly for it (besides his paynes) thankes, for it was but a *three-farthings* peece: and I holde thankes for the same a small price, howsoever the market goes. Now an other comming to the sayd gentleman's house, it was the forefayd servant's good hap to be neare him at his going away, who calling the servant unto him, say'd, Holde thee, here is a *guerdon* for thy desertes: now the servant payd no dearer for the guerdon than he did for the *remuneration*; though the *guerdon* was sixd. farthing better; for it was a *shilling*, and the other but a *three-farthinges*."

Whether Shakspeare or the auther of this pamphlet was the borrower, cannot be known, till the time, when *Love's Labour's Lost* was written, and the date of the earliest edition of the *Serving man's Comfort*, &c. shall be ascertained by circumstances which are at present beyond our reach. STEEVENS.

⁴ —*in print.*] i. e. with the utmost nicety. STEEVENS.

The expression, as Mr. Steevens and Mr. Tyrwhitt have shewn, often occurs in our old English comedies. MALONE.

This

This wimpled [5], whining, purblind, wayward boy;
This Signior Junio's giant-dwarf, Dan Cupid [6];
Regent of love-rhimes, lord of folded arms,

[5] *This wimpled—*] The *wimple* was a hood or veil which fell over the face. Had Shakspeare been acquainted with the *fammum* of the Romans, or the gem which represents the marriage of Cupid and Psyche, his choice of the epithet would have been much applauded by all the advocates in favour of his learning. STEEVENS.

[6] *This signior* Junio's *giant-dwarf, Dan Cupid;*] Mr. Theobald says, that some one proposed to him to read—
This *senior junior*, giant-dwarf, Dan Cupid;
That is, "this old young man." So, afterwards:
 "That was the way to make his godhead wax,
 "For he hath been five thousand years a boy."
If the old copies had exhibited *Junior*, I should have had no doubt that the second word in the line was only the old spelling of *senior*, as in a former passage, (p. 182,) and in one in the *Comedy of Errors* quoted below by Mr. Tollet; but as the text appears both in the quarto 1598, and the folio, Cupid is not himself called *signior*, or *senior* Junio, but a giant-dwarf *to* [that is, attending upon] Signior Junio, and therefore we must endeavour to explain the words as they stand. In both these copies *Junio's* is printed in Italics as a proper name. For the reasons already mentioned, I suppose *signior* here to have been the Italian title of honour, and Cupid to be described as uniting in his person the characters of both a giant, and a dwarf; a giant on account of his power over mankind, and a dwarf on account of his size; [So afterwards: "Of his (Cupid's) *almighty*, dreadful, *little* might"] and as attending in this double capacity on youth, (personified under the name of Signior Junio,) the age in which the passion of love has most dominion over the heart. In characterizing youth by the name of *Junio*, our author may be countenanced by Ovid, who ascribes to the month of June a similar etymology:

Junius a juvenum *nomine dictus adest*.

Dr. Warburton was likewise of opinion that by *Junio* is meant youth in general. Mr. Upton would read—'This signior *Julio's* giant-dwarf;—supposing that our author meant *Julio Romano*, and that that painter had drawn Cupid in the character of a giant dwarf. But "who (as Mr. Tollet justly observes) will ascertain that Julio Romano ever drew Cupid as a giant-dwarf?" MALONE.

In the exaggeration of poetry we might call Cupid a giant-dwarf; but how a giant-dwarf should be represented in painting, I cannot well conceive. MASON.

Shakspeare, in *K. Richard* III. A&. iv. sc. iv. uses *signory* for *seniority*; and Stowe's Chronicle, p. 149, edit. 1614, speaks of Edward the *signior*, i. e. the elder. I can therefore suppose that *signor* here means *senior*, and not the Italian title of honour. Thus in the first folio, at the end of the *Comedy of Errors*:

 "S. *Dro.* Not I, Sir, you are my *elder*.
 "E. *Dro.* That's a question: how shall we try it?
 "S. *Dro.* We'll draw cuts for the *signior.*" TOLLET.

The

The anointed sovereign of sighs and groans,
Liege of all loiterers and malecontents,
Dread prince of plackets, king of codpieces,
Sole imperator, and great general
Of trotting paritors⁷,—O my little heart!—
And I to be a corporal of his field⁸,
And wear his colours like a tumbler's hoop⁹!
What? I! I love! I sue! I seek a wife!
A woman that is like a German clock,
Still a repairing²; ever out of frame;

            And

---

⁷ *Of trotting paritors.*] An *apparitor*, or *paritor*, is an officer of the bishop's court, who carries out citations: as citations are most frequently issued for fornication, the paritor is put under Cupid's government.
            JOHNSON.

⁸ *And I to be a corporal of his field.*] Giles Clayton in his *Martial Discipline*, 1591, has a chapter on the office and duty of a *corporal of the field*. Brokesby tells us, that " Mr. Dodwell's father was in an office then known by the name of *corporal of the field*, which he said was equal to that of a captain of horse." FARMER.

It appears from Lord Stafford's *Letters*, vol. ii. p. 199, that a *corporal of the field* was employed as an aid-de-camp is now, " in taking and carrying to and fro the directions of the general, or other the higher officers of the field." TYRWHITT.

⁹ *And wear his colours like a tumbler's hoop!*] The notion is not that the *hoop wears colours*, but that the colours are worn as a *tumbler* carries his *hoop*, hanging on one shoulder, and falling under the opposite arm. JOHNSON.

Perhaps the *tumbler's hoops* were adorned with their master's colours, or with ribbands. To *wear his colours*, means to wear his *badge* or *cognisance*, or to be his servant or retainer. So, in Stowe's *Annals*, p. 274: " All that *ware* the Duke's sign, or *colours*, were fain to hide them, conveying them from their necks into their bosoms." TOLLET.

It was once a mark of gallantry to wear a *lady's colours*. I am informed by a lady who remembers morris-dancing, that the character who tumbled, always carried his *hoop* dressed out with ribbands, and in the position described by Dr. Johnson. STEEVENS.

¹ *What? I! I love?*] The first *I*, which is not in the old copies, has been supplied by Mr. Tyrwhitt. There is no mistake more common at the press than the omission of a word, when it happens to be repeated in the same line, and the two words join. Mr. Tyrwhitt's emendation is supported by the first line of the present speech:

  And I forsooth in love! *I*, that have been love's whip—.

Sir T. Hanmer supplied the metre by repeating the word *What*.
            MALONE.

² —— *like a German clock*,

Still a repairing;] The same allusion occurs in *Westward Hoe*, by Decker and Webster 1607: —no German clock, no mathematical engine

And never going aright, being a watch,
But being watch'd that it may still go right?
Nay, to be perjur'd which is worst of all;
And, among three, to love the worst of all;
A whitely wanton with a velvet brow,
With two pitch balls stuck in her face for eyes;
Ay, and, by heaven, one that will do the deed,
Though Argus were her eunuch and her guard:
And I to sigh for her! to watch for her!
To pray for her! Go to; it is a plague
That Cupid will impose for my neglect
Of his almighty dreadful little might.
Well, I will love, write, sigh, pray, sue, and groan³;
Some men must love my lady, and some Joan⁴. [*Exit.*

gine whatsoever, requires so much reparation, &c."—The following extract is taken from a book called *The Artificial Clock-maker*, 3d edit. 1714: " Clock-making was supposed to have had its beginning in Germany within less than these two hundred years. It is very probable, that our balance-clocks or watches, and some other automata, might have had their beginning there; &c." Again, p. 91.—" Little worth remark is to be found till towards the 16th century; and then clockwork was revived or wholly invented anew in Germany, as is generally thought, because the ancient pieces are of German work."

A skilful watch-maker informs me, that clocks have not been commonly made in England much more than one hundred years backward.

To the inartificial construction of these first pieces of mechanism executed in Germany, we may suppose Shakspeare alludes. The clock at Hampton-Court, which was set up in 1540, (as appears from the inscription affixed to it,) is said to be the first ever fabricated in England. STEEVENS.

" In some towns in Germany (says Dr. Powel, in his *Human Industry*, 8vo. 1661,) there are very rare and elaborate clocks to be seen in their town-halls, wherein a man may read astronomy, and never look up to the skies.—In the town hall of Prague there is a clock that shews the annual motions of the sun and moon, the names and numbers of the months, days, and festivals of the whole year, the time of the sun rising and setting throughout the year, the equinoxes, the length of the days and nights, the rising and setting of the twelve signs of the Zodiac, &c.—But the town of Strasburgh carries the bell of all other steeples of Germany in this point." These elaborate clocks were probably often " out of frame." MALONE.

³ *— and groan;*] *And*, which is not in either of the authentic copies of this play, the quarto 1598, and the folio 1623, was added to supply the metre, by the editor of the second folio. MALONE.

⁴ *Some men must love my lady, and some Joan.*] To this line Mr. Theobald extends his second act, not injudiciously, but, without sufficient authority. JOHNSON.

ACT

ACT IV. SCENE I.

Another part of the same.

Enter the PRINCESS, ROSALINE, MARIA, CATHARINE, BOYET, *Lords, Attendants, and a Forester.*

Prin. Was that the king, that fpur'd his horfe fo hard
Againft the fteep-uprifing of the hill?
　Boy. I know not; but, I think, it was not he.
　Prin. Whoe'er he was, he fhew'd a mounting mind.
Well, lords, to-day we fhall have our difpatch;
On Saturday we will return to France —
Then, Forefter, my friend, where is the bufh,
That we muft ftand and play the murderer in?
　For. Here by, upon the edge of yonder coppice;
A ftand, where you may make the faireft fhoot.
　Prin. I thank my beauty, I am fair that fhoot,
And thereupon thou fpeak'ft, the faireft fhoot.
　For. Pardon me, Madam, for I meant not fo.
　Prin. What, what? firft praife me, and again fay, no?
O fhort-liv'd pride! Not fair? alack for woe!
　For. Yes, Madam, fair.
　Prin. Nay, never paint me now;
Where fair is not, praife cannot mend the brow.
Here, good my glafs¹, take this for telling true;
　　　　　　　　　　　　　[*giving him money.*
Fair payment for foul words is more than due.
　For. Nothing but fair is that which you inherit.
　Prin. See, fee, my beauty will be fav'd by merit.
O herefy in fair, fit for thefe days!
A giving hand, though foul, fhall have fair praife.—
But come, the bow:—Now mercy goes to kill,
And fhooting well is then accounted ill.
Thus will I fave my credit in the fhoot:
Not wounding, pity would not let me do't:

---

¹ *Here, good my glafs,*—] She rewards the Forefter for having fhewn her to herfelf as in a mirror. STEEVENS.

If wounding, then it was to shew my skill;
That more for praise, than purpose, meant to kill.
And, out of question, so it is sometimes;
Glory grows guilty of detected crimes;
When, for fame's sake, for praise, an outward part,
We bend to that the working of the heart:
As I, for praise alone, now seek to spill
The poor deer's blood, that my heart means no ill [1].

Boy. Do not curst wives hold that self-sovereignty [2]
Only for praise' sake, when they strive to be
Lords o'er their lords?

Prin. Only for praise: and praise we may afford
To any lady that subdues a lord.

Enter COSTARD.

Prin. Here comes a member of the commonwealth [3].

Cost. God dig-you-den [4] all! Pray you, which is the head lady?

Prin. Thou shalt know her, fellow, by the rest that have no heads.

Cost. Which is the greatest lady, the highest?

Prin. The thickest, and the tallest.

Cost. The thickest and the tallest! it is so: truth is truth.
An your waist, mistress, were as slender as my wit,
One of these maids' girdles for your waist should be fit.
Are not you the chief woman? you are the thickest here.

Prin. What's your will, Sir? what's your will?

Cost. I have a letter from Monsieur Biron, to one Lady Rosaline.

Prin. O, thy letter, thy letter; he's a good friend of mine:

---

[1] — *that my heart means no ill*] i. e. *to whom my heart means no ill.* The common phrase suppresses the particle, as *I mean him* [not *to him*] *no harm*. JOHNSON.

[2] — *that self-sovereignty,*—] Not a sovereignty *over,* but *in,* themselves: —so *self*-sufficiency, *self*-confequence, &c. MALONE.

[3] — *a member of the commonwealth.*] Here, I believe, is a kind of jest intended: a member of the *common*-wealth is put for one of the *common* people, one of the meanest. JOHNSON.

[4] *God dig-you-den*—] A corruption of—*God give you good even.*
MALONE.

Stand

Stand aside, good bearer.—Boyet, you can carve;
Break up this capon [6].

Boy. I am bound to serve.—
This letter is mistook, it importeth none here;
It is writ to Jaquenetta.

Prin. We will read it, I swear:
Break the neck of the wax [7], and every one give ear.

Boy. [reads.] "By heaven, that thou art fair, is most
"infallible; true, that thou art beauteous; truth itself, that
"thou art lovely: More fairer than fair, beautiful than
"beauteous, truer than truth itself, have commiseration on
"thy heroical vassal! The magnanimous and most illustrate [8]
"king *Cophetua* [9] set eye upon the pernicious and indubitate
"beggar *Zenelophon*; and he it was that might rightly say,
"*veni, vidi, vici*, which to anatomize, in the vulgar, (O
"base and obscure vulgar!) *videlicet*, he came, saw, and
"overcame: he came, one; saw [1] two; overcame, three.
"Who came? the king? why did he come? to see; Why
"did he see? to overcome: To whom came he? to the beg-
"gar: What saw he? the beggar? Who overcame he? the

---

[6] *— Boyet, you can carve;*
Break up this capon.] i. e. open this letter.
Our poet uses this metaphor as the French do their *poulet*; which signifies both a young fowl and a love-letter. THEOBALD.

One of Lord Chesterfield's letters, 8vo. vol. iii. p. 114, gives us the reason why *poulet* means *amatoria litera*. TOLLET.

Henry IV. consulting with Sully about his marriage, says, "my niece of Guise would please me best, notwithstanding the malicious reports, that she loves *poulets* in paper, better than in a *fricasee*."—A message is called *a cold pigeon*, in the letter concerning the entertainments at Killingworth Castle. FARMER.

To *break up* was a peculiar phrase in carving. PERCY.

[7] *Break the neck of the wax,*] Still alluding to the *capon*. JOHNSON.

[8] *— illustrate*] for *illustrious*. It is often used by Chapman in his translation of Homer. STEEVENS.

[9] *— king Cophetua*] This story is again alluded to in *Henry* IV:
"*Let king Cophetua know the truth thereof.*"
But of this king and beggar, the story, then doubtless well known, is, I am afraid, lost. JOHNSON.

The ballad of *King Cophetua and the Beggar-Maid*, may be seen in the *Reliques of Antient Poetry*, vol. i. The beggar's name was Penelophon, here corrupted. PERCY.

The poet alludes to this song in *Romeo and Juliet*, *Henry* IV. 2d Part, and *Richard* II. STEEVENS.

[1] *— saw*] The old copies here and in the preceding line have—*see*. Mr. Rowe made the correction. MALONE.

"beggar;

" beggar: The conclusion is victory; On whose side? the
" king's: the captive is enrich'd; On whose side? the beg-
" gar's; The catastrophe is a nuptial; On whose side? the
" king's?—no; on both in one, or one in both. I am the
" king; for so stands the comparison: thou the beggar; for
" so witnesseth thy lowliness. Shall I command thy love? I
" may: Shall I enforce thy love? I could: Shall I en-
" treat thy love? I will. What shalt thou exchange for
" rags? robes; For titles? titles; For thyself? me. Thus,
" expecting thy reply, I prophane my lips on thy foot, my
" eyes on thy picture, and my heart on thy every part.

" Thine, in the dearest design of industry,
                        " DON ADRIANO DE ARMADO."

Thus dost thou hear the Nemean lion roar [2]
'Gainst thee, thou lamb, that standest as his prey;
Submissive fall his princely feet before,
And he from forage will incline to play:
But if thou strive, poor soul, what art thou then?
Food for his rage, repasture for his den.
   Prin. What plume of feathers is he, that indited this
     letter?
What vane? what weather-cock? Did you ever hear better?
   Boy. I am much deceived, but I remember the stile.
   Prin. Else your memory is bad, going o'er it [3] ere-
     while [4].
   Boy. This Armado is a Spaniard, that keeps here in
     court;
A phantasm [5], a *Monarcho* [6]; and one that makes sport
To the prince, and his book-mates.
                                             Prin.

[2] *Thus dost thou hear, &c.*] These six lines appear to be a quotation from some ridiculous poem of that time. WARBURTON.
[3] —*going o'er it.*] A pun upon the word *stile.* MUSGRAVE.
[4] *erewhile.*] Just now; a little while ago. JOHNSON.
[5] *A phantasm,*] On the books of the Stationers' Company, Feb. 6, 1608, is entered, " A book called *Phantasm,* the *Italian Taylor and his Boy*; made by Mr. Armin, servant to his majesty." It probably contains the history of *Monarcho,* of whom Dr. Farmer speaks in the following note, to which I have subjoined an additional instance.
                                             STEEVENS.
[6] —*a Monarcho;*] The allusion is to a fantastical character of the time.—" Popular applause (says Meres) doth nourish some, neither " do they gape after any other thing, but vaine praise and glorie—as " in our age Peter Shakerlye of Paules, and *Monarcho* that lived about " the court." FARMER.

                                             In

Prin. Thou, fellow, a word:
Who gave thee this letter?
Cost. I told you; my Lord.
Prin. To whom should'st thou give it?
Cost. From my lord to my lady.
Prin. From which lord to which lady?
Cost. From my Lord Biron, a good master of mine,
To a lady of France, that he call'd Rosaline.
Prin. Thou hast mistaken his letter. Come, lords, away [7].
Here, sweet, put up this; 'twill be thine another day.
　　　　　　　　　　　　[*Exeunt Princess, and Train.*
Boy. Who is the shooter? who is the shooter [8]?
　　　　　　　　　　　　　　　　　　　　　Ros.

In Nash's *Have with you to Saffron Walden*, &c. 1595, I meet with the same allusion:—"but now he was an insulting monarch above "Monarcho the Italian, that wore crownes in his shoes, and quite re- "nounced his natural English accents and gestures, and wrested him- "self wholly to the Italian puntilios, &c."

A local allusion employed by a poet like Shakspeare, resembles the mortal steed that drew in the chariot of Achilles. But short services could be expected from either. STEEVENS.

From a pamphlet, entitled *A brief Discourse of the Spanish State*, &c. 4to. 1590, (quoted by Mr. Reed,) it appears that Monarcho figured in London so early in the reign of Queen Elizabeth as the year 1566.
　　　　　　　　　　　　　　　　　　　　　MALONE.

[7] *Come, lords, away.*] Perhaps the Princess said rather—*Come, ladies, away.* The rest of the scene deserves no care. JOHNSON.

[8] *Who is the shooter?*] It should be, *Who is the suitor?*—and this occasions the quibble. "*Finely put on, &c.*" seem only marginal obser- vations. FARMER.

It appears th t *suiter* was anciently pronounced *shooter*. So, in *The Puritan*, 1607, the maid informs her mistress that some *archers* are come to wait on her. She supposes them to be *fletchers*, or arrow-smiths.
　　　　　　　　　Enter the *suiters*, &c.
"Why do you not see them before you? are not these *archers*, what do you call them, *shooters? Shooters* and *archers* are all one, I hope."
　　　　　　　　　　　　　　　　　　　　　STEEVENS.

Wherever Shakspeare uses words equivocally, as in the present in- stance, he lays his editor under some embarrassment. When he told Ben Jonson he would stand Godfather to his child, "and give him a dozen *latten* spoons," if we write the word as I have now done, the conceit, such as it is, is lost, at least does not at once appear; if we write it *Latin*, it becomes absurd. So, in *Much Ado about Nothing*, Dogberry says, "if justice cannot tame you, she shall ne'er weigh more *reasons* in her balance." If we write the word thus, the constable's *equivoque*, poor as it is, is lost, at least to the eye. If we write *rai- sins*, (between which word and *reasons* there was, I believe, no differ- ence at that time in pronunciation,) we write nonsense. In the passage before us an equivoque was certainly intended; the words *shooter* and
　　　　　　　　　　　　　　　　　　　　　　　　　　suiter

LOVE'S LABOUR'S LOST.

Ros. Shall I teach you to know?
Boy. Ay, my continent of beauty.
Ros. Why, she that bears the bow.
Finely put off!
Boy. My lady goes to kill horns; but, if thou marry,
Hang me by the neck, if horns that year miscarry.
Finely put on!
Ros. Well then, I am the shooter.
Boy. And who is your deer?
Ros. If we choose by the horns, yourself: come not near.
Finely put on, indeed!—
Mar. You still wrangle with her, Boyet, and she strikes at the brow.
Boy. But she herself is hit lower: Have I hit her now?
Ros. Shall I come upon thee with an old saying, that was a man when king Pepin of France was a little boy, as touching the hit it?
Boy. So I may answer thee with one as old, that was a woman when queen Guinever [1] of Britain was a little wench, as touching the hit it.
Ros. *Thou can'st not hit it, hit it, hit it,* [singing.
Thou can'st not hit it, my good man.
Boy. *An I cannot, cannot, cannot,*
An I cannot, another can. [*Exeunt* Ros. *and* Cat.

---

suitor being (as Mr. Steevens has observed) pronounced alike in Shakspeare's time. So, in *Essays and Characters of a Prison and Prisoners,* by G. M. 1618: "The king's guard are counted the strongest *archers*, but here are better *suitors.*" Again, in *Antony and Cleopatra,* edit. 1623, (owing probably to the transcriber's ear having deceived him)—

"—— a grief that *suits*
" My very heart at root——."

instead of—a grief that *shoots.*

In Ireland, where, I believe, much of the pronunciation of Queen Elizabeth's age is yet retained, the word *suitor* is at this day pronounced by the vulgar as if it were written *shooter.* However, I have followed the spelling of the old copy, as it is sufficiently intelligible. MALONE.

[*And who is your deer?*] Our author has the same play on this word in the *Merry Wives of Windsor,* Act. v. Again, in his *Venus and Adonis:*

"I'll be thy park, and thou shalt be my *deer.*" MALONE.

[1] *—queen Guinever*] This was king Arthur's queen, not over famous for fidelity to her husband. See the song of the *Boy and the Mantle,* in Dr. Percy's collection.—In Beaumont and Fletcher's *Scornful Lady,* the elder Loveless addresses Abigail, the old incontinent waiting-woman, by this name. STEEVENS.

Cost.

Cost. By my troth, most pleasant! how both did fit it!
Mar. A mark marvellous well shot; for they both did hit it.
Boy. A mark! O, mark but that mark: A mark, says my lady!
Let the mark have a prick in't, to mete at, if it may be.
Mar. Wide o' the bow hand! I'faith, your hand is out.
Cost. Indeed, a' must shoot nearer, or he'll ne'er hit the clout [1].
Boy. An if my hand be out, then, belike your hand is in.
Cost. Then will she get the upshot by cleaving the pin [2].
Mar. Come, come, you talk greasily, your lips grow foul.
Cost. She's too hard for you at pricks, Sir; challenge her to bowl.
Boy. I fear too much rubbing [3]; Good night, my good owl. [*Exeunt* Boyet *and* Maria.
Cost. By my soul, a swain! a most simple clown!
Lord, lord! how the ladies and I have put him down!
O' my troth, most sweet jests! most incony vulgar wit!
When it comes so smoothly off, so obscenely, as it were, so fit.
Armatho o' the one side—O, a most dainty man!
To see him walk before a lady, and to bear her fan [4]!
To see him kiss his hand! and how most sweetly a' will swear [5]!—
And his page o' t'other side, that handful of wit!
Ah heavens, it is a most pathetical nit! [*Shouting within.*
Sola, sola! [*Exit* Costard, *running.*

[1] *— the clout.*] The *clout* was the white mark at which archers took their aim. The *pin* was the wooden nail that upheld it. STEEVENS.

[2] *— by cleaving the pin.*] Honest Costard might have befriended Dean Milles, whose note on a song in the *Pseudo-Rowley's* Ella has exposed him to so much ridicule. See his book, p. 213. Costard's application of the word *pin* might here lead the Dean to suspect the qualities of the basket. But what has mirth to do with archæology? STEEVENS.

[3] *I fear too much* rubbing;] To *rub* is one of the terms of the bowling-green. Boyet's further meaning needs no comment. MALONE.

[4] *— to bear her fan!*] See a note on *Romeo and Juliet*, Act ii. sc. iv. where Nurse asks Peter for her *fan*. STEEVENS.

[5] *— a' will swear!—*] A line following this seems to have been lost. MALONE.

SCENE

SCENE II.

The same.

Enter Holofernes[7], *Sir* Nathaniel, *and* Dull.

Nath. Very reverent sport, truly; and done in the testimony of a good conscience.

Hol.

[7] *Enter* Holofernes.] There is very little personal reflection in Shakspeare. Either the virtue of those times, or the candour of our author, has so effected, that his satire is, for the most part, general, and, as himself says,

—— *his taxing like a wildgoose flies,*
Unclaim'd of any man.

The place before us seems to be an exception. For by Holofernes is designed a particular character, a pedant and school-master of our author's time, one John Florio, a teacher of the Italian tongue in London, who has given us a small dictionary of that language under the title of *A World of Words*, folio, 1598. From the ferocity of this man's temper it was, that Shakspeare chose for him the name which Rabelais gives to his pedant of Thubal Holoferne. Warburton.

I have omitted the passages which Dr. Warburton has quoted from the preface to Florio's Dictionary in support of his hypothesis, because, though that writer may perhaps have been pointed at, they do not appear to me at all to prove the point. Malone.

I am not of the learned commentator's opinion, that the satire of Shakspeare is so seldom personal. It is of the nature of personal invectives to be soon unintelligible; and the author that gratifies private malice, *animum in vulnere ponit*, destroys the future efficacy of his own writings, and sacrifices the esteem of succeeding times to the laughter of a day. It is no wonder, therefore, that the sarcasms, which, perhaps, in the author's time, *set the playhouse in a roar*, are now lost among general reflections. Yet whether the character of Holofernes was pointed at any particular man, I am, notwithstanding the plausibility of Dr. Warburton's conjecture, inclined to doubt. Every man adheres as long as he can to his own pre-conceptions. Before I read this note I considered the character of Holofernes as borrowed from the *Rhombus* of Sir Philip Sidney, who, in a kind of pastoral entertainment, exhibited to queen Elizabeth, has introduced a school-master so called, speaking *a leash of languages at once*, and puzzling himself and his auditors with a jargon like that of Holofernes in the present play. Sidney himself might bring the character from Italy; for, as Peacham observes, the school-master has long been one of the ridiculous personages in the farces of that country. Johnson.

Dr. Warburton is certainly right in his supposition, that *Florio* is meant by the character of *Holofernes*. Florio had given the first affront. "The plaies, says he, [in his *Second Frutes*, 4to. 1591,] that they plaie in England, are neither right comedies, nor right tragedies; but representa-

Hol. The deer was, as you know, in *sanguis*—blood[8]; ripe as a pomewater[9], who now hangeth like a jewel in the ear of *cælo*[1]—the sky, the welkin, the heaven; and anon falleth like a crab, on the face of *terra*—the soil, the land, the earth.

Nath. Truly, Master Holofernes, the epithets are sweetly varied, like a scholar at the least; But, Sir, I assure ye, it was a buck of the first head[2].

Hol. Sir Nathaniel, *haud credo*.

Dull. 'Twas not a *haud credo*, 'twas a pricket.

Hol. Most barbarous intimation! yet a kind of insinuation, as it were, *in via*, in way of explication; *facere*, as it were, replication; or, rather *ostentare*, to show, as it were, his inclination—after his undressed, unpolished, uneducated, unpruned, untrained, or rather unlettered, or, ratherest, unconfirmed fashion—to insert again my *haud credo* for a deer.

---

tions of *histories* without any decorum."—The scraps of Latin and Italian are transcribed from his works, particularly the proverb about *Venice*, which has been corrupted so much. The *affectation of the letter*, which argues *facilitie*, is likewise a copy of his manner. We meet with much of it in the sonnets to his patrons.

"In Italic your lordship well hath scene
"Their manners, monuments, magnificence,
"Their language learnt, in sound, in stile, in sense,
"Proving by profiting where you have beene.
"—— To adde to fore-learn'd facultie, *facilitie*."

Mr. Warton informs us, in his Life of Sir *Tho. Pope*, that there was an old play of *Holophernes* acted before the Princess Elizabeth in the year 1556. FARMER.

The verses above cited are prefixed to Florio's DICT. 1598. MALONE.

[8] — *in sanguis, blood*;] The old copies read—*sanguis, in blood*. The transposition was proposed by Mr. Steevens, and is, I think, warranted by the following words, which are arranged in the same manner: "— in the ear of *cælo*, the sky," &c. The same expression occurs in *King Henry IV*. P. i.
"If we be English deer, be then *in blood*." MALONE.

[9] — *as a pomewater*,] A species of apple, formerly much esteemed. *Malus Carbonaria.* See Gerard's Herbal, edit. 1597, p. 1273. STEEVENS.

[1] — *in the ear of* cælo, &c.] In Florio's Italian Dictionary, *Cielo* is defined "*heaven*, the *skie*, firmament, or *welkin*;" and *terra* is explained thus: "The element called *earth*; anie ground, earth, countrie, —*land, soile*, &c. If there was any edition of this Dictionary prior to the appearance of *Love's Labour's Lost*, this might add some little strength to Dr. Warburton's conjecture, (see p. 216, n. 7.) though it would by no means be decisive; but my edition is dated 1598 (posterior to the exhibition of this play,) and it appears to be the first. MALONE.

[2] — *a buck of the first head.*] i. e. a buck five years o'd. When this animal is in his second year, he is called a *pricket*. MALONE.

Dull.

Dull. I said, the deer was not a *haud credo*; 'twas a pricket.

Hol. Twice sod simplicity, *bis coctus!* O thou monster ignorance, how deformed dost thou look!

Nath. Sir, he hath never fed of the dainties that are bred in a book; he hath not eat paper, as it were; he hath not drunk ink: his intellect is not replenished; he is only an animal, only sensible in the duller parts;
And such barren plants are set before us, that we thankful should be
(Which we of taste and feeling are,) for those parts that do fructify in us more than he [3].
For as it would ill become me to be vain, indiscreet, or a fool.
So were there a patch set on learning, to see him in a school [4]:
But *omne bene*, say I; being of an old father's mind,
Many can brook the weather, that love not the wind.

Dull. You two are book-men; Can you tell by your wit,

---

[3] *And such barren plants are set before us, that we thankful should be, (Which we of taste and feeling are) for those parts that do fructify in us more than he.*] The length of these lines was no novelty on the English stage. The Moralities afford scenes of the like measure. JOHNSON.

In the old copies the word *of* is wanting, "Which we *of* taste," &c. Mr. Tyrwhitt's last observation is fully supported by a subsequent passage:
"—— and then we,
"Following the sign, woo'd but the sign of *she*."
This stubborn piece of nonsense, as somebody has called it, wants only a particle, I think, to make it sense. I would read:
"And such barren plants are set before us, that we thankful should be
"(Which we *of* taste and feeling are) for those parts, that do fructify in us more than he."
Which in this passage has the force of *as*, according to an idiom of our language, not uncommon, though not strictly grammatical. What follows is still more irregular: for I am afraid our poet, for the sake of his rhime, has put *he* for *him*, or rather *in him*. If he had been writing prose, he would have expressed his meaning, I believe, more clearly thus—*that do fructify in us more than in him.* TYRWHITT.

I have adopted Mr. Tyrwhitt's emendation. Some examples confirming Dr. Johnson's observation may be found at the end of the *Comedy of Errors.* MALONE.

[4] *For as it would ill become me to be vain, indiscreet, or a fool: So, were there a patch set on learning, to see him in a school.*] The meaning is, to be in a school would as ill become a patch, or low fellow, as folly would become me. JOHNSON.

What was a month old at Cain's birth, that's not five weeks old as yet?

Hol. Dictynna⁵, good man Dull; Dictynna, good man Dull.

Dull. What is Dictynna?

Nath. A title to Phœbe, to Luna, to the moon.

Hol. The moon was a month old, when Adam was no more;

And raught not ⁶ to five weeks, when he came to five score. The allusion holds in the exchange ⁷.

Dull. 'Tis true, indeed; the collusion holds in the exchange.

Hol. God comfort thy capacity! I say, the allusion holds in the exchange.

Dull. And I say, the pollution holds in the exchange; for the moon is never but a month old: and I say beside, that 'twas a pricket that the princess kill'd.

Hol. Sir Nathaniel, will you hear an extemporal epitaph on the death of the deer? and, to humour the ignorant, I have * call'd the deer the princess kill'd, a pricket.

Nath. Perge, good Master Holofernes, perge; so it shall please you to abrogate scurrillity.

Hol. I will something affect the letter: for it argues facility.
The praiseful princess ⁸ *pierc'd and prick'd a pretty pleasing pricket;*
Some say, a sore; but not a sore, till now made sore with shooting.
The dogs did yell; put l to sore, then sorel jumps from thicket;
Or pricket, sore, or else sorel; the people fall a hooting.

---

⁵ *Dictynna,*] Old Copies—*Dictisima.* Corrected by Mr. Rowe.
                                                              MALONE.

⁶ *And* raught *not*] i. e. reach'd not. STEEVENS.

⁷ *The allusion holds in the exchange*] i. e. the riddle is as good when I use the name of Adam, as when you use the name of Cain. WARB.

* — *I have*—] These words were inserted by Mr. Rowe. MALONE.

⁸ *The* praiseful princess—] This emendation was made by the editor of the second folio. The quarto, 1598, and folio, 1623, read corruptly *prayful.* MALONE.

The ridicule designed in this passage may not be unhappily illustrated by the alliteration in the following lines of *Ulpian Fulwell,* in his Commemoration of Queen Anne Bullayne, which makes part of a collection called, *The Flower of Fame,* printed 1575:

" Whose princely praise hath pearst the pricke,
" And price of endless fame, &c." STEEVENS.

If

LOVE'S LABOUR'S LOST

If sore be sore, then L to sore makes fifty sores; O sore I.⁹ !
Of one sore I an hundred make, by adding but one more L.

Nath. A rare talent!

Dull. If a talent be a claw, * look how he claws him with a talent.

Hol. This is a gift that I have, simple, simple; a foolish extravagant spirit, full of forms, figures, shapes, objects, ideas, apprehensions, motions, revolutions: these are begot in the ventricle of memory, nourished in the womb of *pia mater*, and deliver'd upon the mellowing of occasion: but the gift is good in those in whom it is acute, and I am thankful for it.

Nath. Sir, I praise the Lord for you; and so may my parishioners; for their sons are well tutor'd by you, and their daughters profit very greatly under you: you are a good member of the commonwealth.

Hol. Mehercle, if their sons be ingenious, they shall want no instruction: if their daughters be capable ¹, I will put it to them: But, *vir sapit, qui pauca loquitur:* a soul feminine saluteth us.

Enter JAQUENETTA *and* COSTARD.

Jac. God give you good morrow, master person ².

Hol.

---

⁹ *O sore I.!*] In the old copies—*O sorel.* The correction was suggested by Dr. Warburton. The rhime confirms it. The allusion (as Dr. Warburton observes) is to L, being the numeral for fifty.

A deer during his third year is called a sorel. MALONE.

* *If a talent be a claw,* &c.] In our author's time the *talon* of a bird was frequently written *talent.* Hence the quibble here, and in *Twelfth Night,* "— let them use their *talents.*" So, in *The First Part of the Contention between the Houses of York and Lancaster,* 1600:

"Are you the kite, Beaufort? where's your *talents?*"

Again, in Marlowe's *Tamberlaine,* 1590:

"—— and now doth ghastly death

"With greedy *tallents* gripe my bleeding heart." MALONE.

¹ — *if their daughters be capable,* &c.] Of this double *entendre*, despicable as it is, Mr. Pope and his coadjutors availed themselves, in their unsuccessful comedy called, *Three Hours after Marriage.* STEEVENS.

Capable is used equivocally. One of its senses was *reasonable*; endowed with a ready capacity to learn. So, in *King Richard III:*

"O 'tis a parlous boy,

"Bold, quick, ingenious, forward, *capable.*"

The other wants no explanation. MALONE.

² — *master person.*] Thus the quarto, 1598, and the first folio. The editor of the second folio, not understanding the passage, reads — *parson*, which renders what follows nonsense. *Person*, as Sir William Blackstone observes,

220   LOVE'S LABOUR'S LOST.

Hol. Master person—*quasi* pers-on *. And if one should be pierced, which is the one?

Cost. Marry, master school-master, be that is likest to a hogshead.

Hol. Of piercing a hogshead! a good lustre of conceit in a turf of earth; fire enough for a flint, pearl enough for a swine: 'tis pretty; it is well.

Jaq. Good master parson, be so good as read me this letter; it was given me by Costard, and sent me from Don Armatho: I beseech you, read it.

Hol. *Fauste, precor gelidâ* ³ *quando pecus omne sub umbrâ Ruminat*—and so forth. Ah, good old Mantuan! I may speak of thee as the traveller doth of Venice;

————*Vinegia, Vinegia,*
Chi non te vede, ei non te pregia ⁴.

Old observer, in his *Commentaries*, is the original and proper term; *persona ecclesiæ*. So, in *Hollinshed*, p. 953, (the quotation is Mr. Steevens's,) "Jeroun was vicar of Stepnie, and Garard was *pusin* of Honie-lane." It is here necessary to retain the old spelling. MALONE.

* *—quasi* pers-on.] I believe we should write the word—pers-*one*. The same play on the word *pierce* is put into the mouth of *Falstaff*.
                                                    STEEVENS.

The words *on* and *one* were, I believe, pronounced nearly alike, at least in some counties, in our author's time; the quibble, therefore, that Mr. Steevens has noted, may have been intended as the text now stands. In the same style afterwards Moth says, " Offer'd by a child to an old man, which is *wit old*." MALONE.

³ *Fauste, precor gelidâ*, &c.] Though all the editions concur to give this speech to Sir Nathaniel, yet, as Dr. Thirlby ingeniously observed to me, it is evident it must belong to Holofernes. The Curate is employed in reading the letter to himself; and while he is doing so, that the stage may not stand still, Holofernes either pulls out a book, or, repeating some verse by heart from Mantuanus, comments upon the character of that poet. Baptista Spagnolus (surnamed Mantuanus, from the place of his birth) was a writer of poems, who flourished towards the latter end of the 15th century. THEOBALD.

The *Eclogues* of Mantuanus the Carmelite were translated before the time of Shakspeare, and the Latin printed on the opposite side of the page. STEEVENS.

From a passage in Nashe's *Apologie of Pierce Pennilesse*, 1593, the *Eclogues* of Mantuanus appear to have been a school-book in our author's time: " With the first and second leafe he plaies very prettilie, and, in ordinarie terms of extenuating, verdits *Pierce Pennilesse* for a grammar-school wit; faies, his margine is as deeply learned as *Fauste precor gelida*." A translation of Mantuanus by George Turberville was printed in 8vo. in 1567. MALONE.

⁴ ———*Vinegia, Vinegia,*
Chi non te vede, ei non te pregia.] Our author is applying the
                                                            praises

Old Mantuan! old Mantuan! Who underſtandeth thee not, loves thee not.—*Ut, re, fol, la, mi, fa.*—Under pardon, Sir, what are the contents? or, rather, as Horace ſays in his— What, my ſoul, verſes?

Nath. Ay, Sir, and very learned.

Hol. Let me hear a ſtaff, a ſtanza, a verſe: *Lege, domine.*

Nath. If love make me forſworn [5], how ſhall I ſwear to love?
Ah, never faith could hold, if not to beauty vowed!
Though to myſelf forſworn, to thee I'll faithful prove;
Thoſe thoughts to me were oaks, to thee like oſiers bowed.
Study his bias leaves, and makes his book thine eyes;
Where all thoſe pleaſures live, that art would compre- hend:
If knowledge be the mark, to know thee ſhall ſuffice;
Well learned is that tongue, that well can thee commend:
All ignorant that ſoul, that ſees thee without wonder;
(Which is to me ſome praiſe, that I thy parts admire:
Thy eye Jove's lightning bears, thy voice his dreadful thunder,
Which, not to anger bent, is muſic, and ſweet fire [6].

Celeſtial

praiſes of Mantuanus to a common proverbial ſentence, ſaid of Venice, *Vinegia, Vinegia! qui non te vedi, ci non te pregia.* O Venice, Venice, he who has never ſeen thee, has thee not in eſteem. THEOBALD.

The proverb ſtands thus in Howell's *Letters*, book i. ſect. 1. L 36.

*Venetia, Venetia, chi non te vede, non te pregia,
Ma chi t' ha troppo veduto, te diſpregia.*

Venice, Venice, none thee unſeen can prize;
Who thee hath ſeen too much, will thee deſpiſe.

The players in their edition, have thus printed the firſt line:

"*Vemchie, vencha, que non le unde que non te perreche.*" STEEVENS.

The editors of the firſt folio here, as in many other inſtances, implicitly copied the preceding quarto. The text was corrected by Mr. Theobald.

Our author, I believe, found this Italian proverb in Florio's *Second Frutes*, 4to. 1591, where it ſtands thus:

"*Venetia, chi non ti vede, non ti pretia;*
"*Ma chi ti vede, ben gli coſta.*" MALONE.

[5] *If love make me forſworn, &c.*] Theſe verſes are printed with ſome variations in a book entitled, the *Paſſionate Pilgrim*, 8vo. 1599. MALONE.

[6] *— thy voice his dreadful* thunder.
Which not to anger bent, is muſic *and* ſweet *fire.*] So, in *Antony and Cleopatra:*

Celestial as thou art, oh pardon, love, this wrong,
That sings heaven's praise with such an earthly tongue!

Hol. You find not the apostrophes, and so miss the accent:— let me supervise the canzonet. Here are only numbers ratify'd[7]; but, for the elegancy, facility, and golden cadence of poesy, *caret*. Ovidius Naso was the man: and why, indeed, Naso; but for smelling out the odoriferous flowers of fancy, the jerks of invention? *Imitari*, is nothing: so doth the hound his master, the ape his keeper, the tired horse[8] his rider. But, damosella virgin, was this directed to you?

Jaq. Ay, Sir, from one Monsieur Biron[9], one of the strange queen's lords.

Hol. I will overglance the superscript. *To the snow-white hand of the most beauteous Lady Rosaline.* I will look again on the intellect of the letter, for the nomination of the party writing[1] to the person written unto:

Your Ladyship's in all desired employment, BIRON.

Sir Nathaniel, this Biron is one of the votaries with the king; and here he hath framed a letter to a sequent of the stranger queen's, which, accidentally, or by the way of progression, hath miscarry'd.—Trip and go, my sweet[2]; deliver

"——— his voice was *propertied*
" As all the *tuned spheres,* and that to friends;
" But when he meant to quail, and shake the orb,
" He was as rutling *thunder*." MALONE.

[7] *Here are only numbers ratify'd;*] These words and the following lines of this speech, which in the old copy are given to Sir Nathaniel, were rightly attributed to Holofernes by Mr. Theobald. MALONE.

[8] *— the tired horse,*] was the horse adorned with ribbands—the famous *Banks's horse,* so often alluded to. Lilly, in his *Mother Bombie,* brings in a *Hackneyman* and Ms. *Halfpenny* at cross-purposes with this word; " Why didst thou bowre the horse through the—" " — It was for *tiring*." " He would never *tire*," replies the other. FARMER.

Again, in *What you will,* by Marston, 1607:
" My love hath *tyr'd* some fidler like Albano." MALONE.

[9] *Ay, Sir, from one Monsieur Biron,*] Shakspeare forgot himself in this passage. Jaquenetta knew nothing of Biron, and had said just before that the letter had been " sent to her from Don Armatho, and given to her by Costard." MASON.

[1] *—writing*] Old Copies—*written*. Corrected by Mr. Rowe. The first five lines of this speech were restored to the right owner by Mr. Theobald. Instead of Sir *Nathaniel,* the old copies have—Sir *Holofernes.* Corrected by Mr. Steevens. MALONE.

[2] *Trip and go, my sweet;*] Perhaps originally the burthen of a song. So, in *Summer's Last Will and Testament,* by T. Nashe, 1600:

" *Trip*

liver this paper into the royal hand of the king; it may concern much: Stay not thy compliment; I forgive thy duty: adieu.

Jaq. Good Coſtard, go with me.—Sir, God ſave your life!

Coſt. Have with thee, my girl. [*Exeunt* Cost. *and* Jaq.

Nath. Sir, you have done this in the fear of God, very religiouſly; and, as a certain father ſaith—

Hol. Sir, tell not me of the father, I do fear colourable colours [3]. But, to return to the verſes; Did they pleaſe you, Sir Nathaniel?

Nath. Marvellous well for the pen.

Hol. I do dine to-day at the father's of a certain pupil of mine; where if, before repaſt [4], it ſhall pleaſe you to gratify the table with a grace, I will, on my privilege I have with the parents of the foreſaid child or pupil, undertake your *ben venuto*; where I will prove thoſe verſes to be very unlearned, neither ſavouring of poetry, wit, nor invention: I beſeech your ſociety.

Nath. And thank you too: for ſociety (ſaith the text) is the happineſs of life.

Hol. And, certes, the text moſt infallibly concludes it.— Sir, [*to* Dull.] I do invite you too; you ſhall not ſay me, nay: *pauca verba*. Away; the gentles are at their game, and we will to our recreation. [*Exeunt.*

SCENE III.

Another part of the ſame.

Enter Biron, *with a paper.*

Bir. The king he is hunting the deer; I am courſing myſelf: they have pitch'd a toil; I am toiling in a pitch [5]; pitch, that defiles; defile! a foul word. Well, ſet thee down, ſorrow! for ſo, they ſay, the fool ſaid, and ſo ſay I, and I

" *Trip and go*, heave and hoe,
" Up and down, to and fro.—" Malone.

[3] — *colourable colours.*] That is, ſpecious, or fair ſeeming appearances. Johnson.

[4] — *before repaſt.*] Thus the quarto, 1598. Folio—*being* repaſt. Malone.

[5] *I am toiling in a pitch.*] Alluding to Lady Roſaline's complexion, who is through the whole play repreſented as a black beauty. Johnson.

the fool. Well proved, wit! By the lord, this love is as mad as Ajax: it kills sheep; it kills me, I a sheep: Well proved again on my side! I will not love: if I do, hang me; i'faith, I will not. O, but her eye—by this light, but for her eye, I would not love her; yes, for her two eyes. Well, I do nothing in the world but lie, and lie in my throat. By heaven, I do love: and it hath taught me to rhime, and to be melancholy; and here is part of my rhime, and here my melancholy. Well, she hath one o' my sonnets already; the clown bore it, the fool sent it, and the lady hath it: sweet clown, sweeter fool, sweetest lady! By the world, I would not care a pin, if the other three were in: Here comes one with a paper; God give him grace to groan! [*gets up into a tree.*

Enter the King, *with a paper.*

King. Ah me!
Bir. [*aside.*] Shot, by heaven!—Proceed, sweet Cupid: thou hast thump'd him with thy bird-bolt under the left pap: —I'faith secrets.—
King. [*reads.*] *So sweet a kiss the golden sun gives not*
To those fresh morning drops upon the rose,
As thy eye-beams, when their fresh rays have smote
The night of dew that on my cheeks down flows [6]*;*
Nor shines the silver moon one half so bright [7]
Through the transparent bosom of the deep,
As doth thy face through tears of mine give light;
Thou shin'st in every tear that I do weep:
No drop but as a coach doth carry thee,
So ridest thou triumphing in my woe;
Do but behold the tears that swell in me,
And they thy glory through my grief will show:
But do not love thyself; then thou wilt keep
My tears for glasses, and still make me weep.
O queen of queens, how far dost thou excel!
No thought can think, nor tongue of mortal tell.—

[6] *The night of dew that on my cheeks down flows*;] This phrase, however quaint, is the poet's own. He means, *the dew that nightly flows down his cheeks.* Shakspeare, in one of his other plays, uses *night of dew,* for *dewy night,* but I cannot at present recollect, in which.
STEEVENS.

[7] *Nor shines the silver moon,*" &c.] So in our poet's *Venus and Adonis*:
" But hers, which *through the crystal tears gave light,*
" Shone, *like the moon in water, seen by night.*" MALONE.

How

How shall she know my griefs? I'll drop the paper;
Sweet leaves, shade folly. Who is he comes here?
[steps aside.

Enter LONGAVILLE, *with a paper.*

What, Longaville! and reading! listen, ear.
 Bir. Now, in thy likeness, one more fool, appear! [*aside.*
 Long. Ah me! I am forsworn.
 Bir. Why, he comes in like a perjure, wearing papers[7].
              [*aside.*
 King. In love, I hope[8]; Sweet fellowship in shame!
               [*aside.*
 Bir. One drunkard loves another of the name. [*aside.*
 Long. Am I the first that have been perjur'd so? [*aside.*
 Bir. I could put thee in comfort; not by two, that I
  know: [*aside.*
Thou mak'st the triumviry, the corner-cap of society,
The shape of love's Tyburn that hangs up simplicity.
 Long. I fear, these stubborn lines lack power to move:
O sweet Maria, empress of my love!
These numbers will I tear, and write in prose.
 Bir. O, rhimes are guards on wanton Cupid's hose:
Disfigure not his flop[9]. [*aside.*
 Long. This same shall go.

Did not the heavenly rhetoric of thine eye [*reads.*
 ('Gainst whom the world cannot hold argument,)
Persuade my heart to this false perjury?
 Vows, for thee broke, deserve not punishment.

---

[7] — *becomes in like a perjure*, &c.] The punishment of perjury is to wear on the breast a paper expressing the crime. JOHNSON.

[8] *In love, I hope*; &c.] In the old copy this line is given to Longaville. The present regulation was made by Mr. Pope. MALONE.

[9] *O, rhimes are guards on wanton Cupid's hose:*
Disfigure not his flop.] I suppose this alludes to the usual tawdry dress of Cupid, when he appeared on the stage. In an old translation of *Cebes's Galtire* is this precept: " Thou shalt wear no garments that be over much doubled with *gardings*: that men may not say, thou hast *Ganimedes* hosen, or *Cupides doublet*." FARMER.

Slops are large and wide-kneed breeches, the garb in fashion in our author's time. THEOBALD.

The old copy reads—*flop*. The emendation was made by Mr. Theobald. *Guards* have been already explained. MALONE.

L 5

A woman I forswore; but, I will prove,
  Thou being a goddess, I forswore not thee:
My vow was earthly, thou a heavenly love;
  Thy grace being gain'd, cures all disgrace in me.
Vows are but breath, and breath a vapour is:
  Then thou, fair sun, which on my earth dost shine,
Exhal'st this vapour-vow; in thee it is:
  If broken then, it is no fault of mine;
If by me broke, What fool is not so wise,
To lose an oath to win a paradise [1] *?*

Bir. [*aside.*] This is the liver vein [2], which makes flesh
  a deity;
A green goose, a goddess: pure, pure idolatry.
God amend us, God amend! we are much out o' the way.

  Enter DUMAIN, *with a paper.*

Long. By whom shall I send this?—Company! stay.
            [*stepping aside.*
  Bir. [*aside.*] All hid, all hid [3], an old infant play;
Like a demy-god here sit I in the sky,
And wretched fools' secrets heedfully o'er-eye.
More sacks to the mill! O heavens, I have my wish;
Dumain, transform'd: four woodcocks in a dish [4]!
  Dum. O most divine Kate!
  Bir. O most prophane coxcomb!   [*aside.*
  Dum. By heaven, the wonder of a mortal eye!
  Bir. By earth she is not, corporal; there you lie [5]. [*aside.*
                                                      Dum.

---

[1] *To lose an oath to win a paradise?*] The *Passionate Pilgrim*, 1599, in which this sonnet is also found, reads—To *break* an oath. But the opposition between *lose* and *win* is much in our author's manner.
                                                      MALONE.

[2] — *the liver vein,*] The liver was anciently supposed to be the seat of love. JOHNSON.

[3] *All hid, all hid,*) The children's cry at *hide and seek.* MUSGRAVE.

[4] — *four woodcocks in a dish.*] A *woodcock* was a proverbial term for a silly fellow. See p. 151. n. 6. MALONE

[5] *By earth she is not, corporal; there you lie.*] Mr. Theobald says that Dumain had no post in the army, and therefore reads—she *is but* corporal, understanding the latter word in the sense of *corporeal*: but it should be remembered that Biron in a former scene, when he perceives that he is in love, exclaims—

  And I to be a *corporal* of his field,
  And wear his colours——!
                                                      Why

Dum. Her amber hairs for foul have amber quoted⁶.
Bir. An amber-colour'd raven was well noted. [*aside.*
Dum. As upright as the cedar.
Bir. Stoop, I say:
Her shoulder is with child. [*aside.*
Dum. As fair as day.
Bir. Ay, as some days; but then no sun must shine. [*aside.*
Dum. O that I had my wish!
Long. And I had mine! [*aside.*
King. And I mine too, good Lord! [*aside.*
Bir. Amen, so I had mine; is not that a good word? [*aside.*
Dum. I would forget her; but a fever she
Reigns in my blood⁷, and will remember'd be.
Bir. A fever in your blood! why, then incision
Would let her out in sawcers; Sweet misprision! [*aside.*
Dum. Once more I'll read the ode that I have writ.
Bir. Once more I'll mark how love can vary wit. [*aside.*

Why then may he not in jest apply that appellation to another, which he has already given to himself? He only means by the title, that Dumain is one of Cupid's *Aid-du-camps*, as well as himself.

If *corporal* is to be considered as an adjective, Theobald's emendation appears to me to be absolutely necessary.

I have no doubt that Theobald's emendation is right. In the text therefore, for *not*, read *but*.

The word *corporal* in Shakspeare's time was used for *corporeal*. So, in *Macbeth,* " each *corporal* agent." Again:

"——— and what seem'd *corporal,* melted
" As breath into the wind."

Again, in *Julius Cæsar:*

" His *corporal* motion govern'd by my spirit."

This adjective is found in Bullokar's *Expositor,* 8vo. 1616, but *corporeal* is not.

Not is again printed for *but* in the original copy of *The Comedy of Errors,* (See p. 31, n. 7.) and in other places. MALONE.

⁶ *—for foul have amber quoted.*] *Quote* here, I think, signifies, *marked, written down.* So, in *All's Well that Ends Well:*

" He's *quoted* for a most perfidious slave."

The word in the old copies is *coted;* but that (as Dr. Johnson has observed, in the last scene of this play,) is only the old spelling of *quoted,* owing to the transcriber's trusting to his ear, and following the pronunciation. To *cote* is elsewhere used by our author, with the signification of *overtake,* but that will by no means suit here. MALONE.

⁷ *— but a fever she*
Reigns in my blood.] So, in *Hamlet:*

" For, like the hectic, in my blood he rages." STEEVENS.

Dum. On a day, (alack the day!)
    Love, whose month is ever May,
    Spy'd a blossom, passing fair,
    Playing in the wanton air:
    Through the velvet leaves the wind,
    All unseen, 'gan passage find [8];
    That the lover, sick to death,
    Wish'd himself the heaven's breath.
    Air, quoth he, thy cheeks may blow;
    Air, would I might triumph so!
    But alack, my hand is sworn [9],
    Ne'er to pluck thee from thy thorn [1]:
    Vow, alack, for youth unmeet;
    Youth so apt to pluck a sweet.
    Do not call it sin in me,
    That I am forsworn for thee:
    Thou for whom Jove would swear [2],
    Juno but an Ethiope were;
    And deny himself for Jove,
    Turning mortal for thy love.—
This will I send, and something else more plain,
That shall express my true love's fasting pain [3].
O, would the King, Biron, and Longaville,
Were lovers too! Ill, to example ill,
Would from my forehead wipe a perjur'd note;
For none offend, where all alike do dote.

Long. Dumain, [*advancing.*] thy love is far from charity,
That in love's grief desir'st society:

---

[8] — *'gan passage find*] The quarto, 1598, and the first folio, have *ran.* Corrected by Mr. Theobald. In the line next but one, *Wish* (the reading of the old copies) was corrected by the editor of the second folio. MALONE.

[9] — *my hand is sworn,*] A copy of this sonnet is printed in *England's Helicon*, 1614, and reads:
"But, alas! my hand hath sworn."
It is likewise printed as Shakspeare's, in Jaggard's *Collection*, 1599.
STEEVENS.

[1] —*from thy thorn:*] So Mr. Pope. The original copy reads *throne.* MALONE.

[2] — *Jove would swear,*] *Swear* is here used as a dissyllable. Mr. Pope, not attending to this, reads—*so's* Jove—which has been adopted by the subsequent editors. MALONE.

[3] — *my true love's fasting pain.*] *Fasting* is longing, hungry, wanting. JOHNSON.

You may look pale, but I should blush, I know,
To be o'er-heard, and taken napping so.
　　King. Come, Sir, [*advancing.*] you blush; as his, your
　　　　case is such;
You chide at him, offending twice as much:
You do not love Maria; Longaville
Did never sonnet for her sake compile;
Nor never lay his wreathed arms athwart
His loving bosom, to keep down his heart.
I have been closely shrowded in this bush,
And mark'd you both, and for you both did blush.
I heard your guilty rhimes, observ'd your fashion;
Saw sighs reek from you, noted well your passion:
Ah me! says one; O Jove! the other cries;
One, her hairs were gold⁴, crystal the other's eyes:
You would for paradise break faith and troth;　[*to Long.*
And Jove, for your love, would infringe an oath.
　　　　　　　　　　　　　　　　　　　　　[*to Dumain.*

What will Birón say, when that he shall hear
Faith infringed, which such zeal did swear⁵?
How will he scorn? how will he spend his wit?
How will he triumph, leap, and laugh at it?
For all the wealth that ever I did see,
I would not have him know so much by me.
　　Bir. Now step I forth to whip hypocrify.— 　[*descends.*
Ah, good my liege, I pray thee, pardon me:
Good heart, what grace hast thou, thus to reprove
These worms for loving, that art most in love?
Your eyes do make no coaches⁶; in your tears
There is no certain princess that appears;
You'll not be perjur'd, 'tis a hateful thing;
Tush, none but minstrels like of sonneting.

---

⁴ *One, her hairs—*] the folio reads—*One her hairs, &c.* I some years ago conjectured that we should read, *One her hairs were gold, &c.* i. e. *the hairs of one of the ladies were of the colour of gold, and the eyes of the other as clear as crystal.* The king is speaking of the panegyricks pronounced by the two lovers on their mistresses. On examining the first quarto, 1598, I have found my conjecture confirmed; for so it reads. *One* and *on* are frequently confounded in the old copies of our author's plays. See a note on *K. John,* Act. iii. sc. iii.　MALONE.

⁵ —*which such zeal did swear?*] See p. 218. n. 2　MALONE.

⁶ *Your eyes do make no coaches;*] Alluding to a passage in the king's sonnet:

　　　"No drop but as a *coach* doth carry thee:"　STEEVENS.

The old copy has—*couches.* Mr. Pope corrected it.　MALONE.

But

But are you not asham'd? nay, are you not,
All three of you, to be thus much o'er-shot?
You found his mote; the king your mote did see;
But I a beam do find in each of three.
O, what a scene of foolery have I seen,
Of sighs, of groans, of sorrow, and of teen!
O me, with what strict patience have I sat,
To see a king transformed to a gnat⁷!
To see great Hercules whipping a gig,
And profound Solomon to tune a jig,
And Nestor play at push-pin with the boys,
And critic Timon laugh at idle toys⁸!
Where lies thy grief, O tell me, good Dumain?
And, gentle Longaville, where lies thy pain?
And where my liege's? all about the breast:—
A caudle, ho!

King. Too bitter is thy jest.
Are we betray'd thus to thy over-view?

---

⁷ *To see a king transformed to a gnat!*] Alluding to the singing of that insect, suggested by the poetry the King had been detected in. HEATH.

Mr. Tollet seems to think it contains an allusion to St. *Matthew*, ch. xxiii. v. 24. where the metaphorical term of a *gnat* means a thing of least importance, or what is proverbially small. The smallness of a *gnat* is likewise mentioned in *Cymbeline*. STEEVENS.

Mr. Theobald and the succeeding editors read—to a *knot*. The original reading, and Mr. Heath's explanation of it, are confirmed by a passage in Spenser's *Fairy Queen*, B. ii. c. ix.:

"As when a swarme of *gnats* at even-tide
"Out of the fennes of Allan doe arise,
"Their *murmuring* small *trompetts sounden* wide," &c. MALONE.

A *knot* is, I believe, a *true lover's knot*, meaning that the King

——— lay'd his *enwreathed arms athwart*
His loving bosom———

so long, i. e. remained so long in the lover's posture, that he seemed actually transformed into a *knot*. The word *sat* is in some counties pronounced *set*. This may account for the seeming want of exact rhime. In the *Tempest* the same thought occurs:

"——— sitting,
"His arms in this sad *knot*." STEEVENS.

⁸ —*critic Timon*—] *Critic* and *critical* are used by our author in the same sense as *cynic* and *cynical*. Iago, speaking of the fair sex as harshly as is sometimes the practice of Dr. Warburton, declares he is *nothing if not critical*. STEEVENS.

Mr. Steevens's observation is supported by our author's 112th Sonnet:

"——— my adder's sense
"To *critic* and to *flatterer* stopped are." MALONE.

Bir.

Bir. Not you by me, but I betray'd to you;
I that am honeſt; I, that hold it ſin
To break the vow I am engaged in;
I am betray'd, by keeping company
With men like men, of ſtrange inconſtancy [9].
When ſhall you ſee me write a thing in rhime?
Or groan for Joan? or ſpend a minute's time
In pruning me [1]? When ſhall you hear that I
Will praiſe a hand, a foot, a face, an eye,
A gait, a ſtate, a brow, a breaſt, a waiſt,
A leg, a limb?—
King. Soft; Whither away ſo faſt?
A true man, or a thief, that gallops ſo?
Bir. I poſt from love; good lover, let me go.

Enter JAQUENETTA *and* COSTARD.

Jaq. God bleſs the King! *offers him a paper.*
King. What preſent haſt thou there?

[9] *With* men *like* men, *of* ſtrange inconſtancy.] Thus the old copies. Sir Thomas Hanmer reads, With *vane*-like men. The following paſſage in *K. Henry VI.* P. iii adds ſome ſupport to his conjecture:

"Look, as I blow this *feather* from my face,
"And as the air blows it to me again,
"Obeying with my *wind* when I do blow,
"And yielding to another when it blows,
"Commanded always by the greater guſt;
"Such is the lightneſs of your common men."

Mr. Maſon, whoſe remarks on our author's plays have juſt reached my hands, propoſes, with great acuteneſs, to read,

With *moon*-like men, of ſtrange inconſtancy.
So, Juliet:
"O ſwear not by the moon, the *inconſtant moon.*"
Again, more appoſitely, in *As you Like It:* "—I being but a *moniſh* youth, changeable,"—*inconſtant,* &c.

Dr. Johnſon thinks the poet might have meant—" *With* men *like* common men." So alſo Mr. Heath: "With men of ſtrange inconſtancy, as men in general are."

Strange, which is not in the quarto or firſt folio, was added by the editor of the ſecond folio, and conſequently any other word as well as that may have been the author's; for all the additions in that copy were maniſeſtly arbitrary, and are generally injudicious. MALONE.

I believe the emendation [*vane* like] is proper. So, in *Much Ado about Nothing:*

"Heſpeaking, why a *vane* blown with all winds." STEEVENS.

[1] *In pruning me?*] A bird is ſaid to *prune* himſelf when he pricks and ſleeks his feathers. So, in *K. Henry IV.* Part i:

"Which makes him *prune* himſelf, and briſtle up
"The creſt of youth." STEEVENS.

Coſt.

Coſt. Some certain treaſon.
King. What makes treaſon here?
Coſt. Nay, it makes nothing, Sir.
King. If it mar nothing neither,
The treaſon, and you, go in peace away together.
Jaq. I beſeech your grace, let this letter be read;
Our parſon * miſdoubts it; 'twas treaſon he ſaid.
King. Biron, read it over.— [*giving him the letter.*
Where hadſt thou it?
Jaq. Of Coſtard.
King. Where hadſt thou it?
Coſt. Of Don Adramadio, Don Adramadio.
King. How now! what is in you? why doſt thou tear it?
Bir. A toy, my liege, a toy; your grace needs not fear it.
Long. It did move him to paſſion, and therefore let's hear it.
Dum. It is Biron's writing, and here is his name.
[*picks up the pieces.*
Bir. Ah, you whoreſon loggerhead, [*to Coſt.*] you were born to do me ſhame —
Guilty, my Lord, guilty; I confeſs, I confeſs.
King. What?
Bir. That you three fools lack'd me fool to make up the meſs:
He, he, and you, and you, my liege, and I,
Are prick-purſes in love, and we deſerve to die.
O, diſmiſs this audience, and I ſhall tell you more.
Dum. Now the number is even.
Bir. True, true; we are four:—
Will theſe turtles be gone?
King. Hence, Sirs; away.
Coſt. Walk aſide the true folk, and let the traitors ſtay.
[*Exeunt* Costard *and* Jaquenetta.
Bir. Sweet lords, ſweet lovers, O let us embrace!
As true we are, as fleſh and blood can be:
The ſea will ebb and flow, heaven ſhew his face;
Young blood doth not obey an old decree:
We cannot croſs the cauſe why we were born,
Therefore, of all hands muſt we be forſworn.

* *Our parſon—*] Here, as in a former inſtance, (ſee p. 239) in the authentic copies of this play, this word is ſpelt *perſon*; but there being no reaſon for adhering here to the old ſpelling, the modern in conformity to the rule generally obſerved in this edition, is preferred. Steevens.

King.

King. What, did these rent lines shew some love of thine?
Bir. Did they, quoth you? Who sees the heavenly Ro-
saline,
That, like a rude and savage man of Inde,
  At the first opening of the gorgeous east,
Bows not his vassal head; and, strucken blind,
  Kisses the base ground with obedient breast?
What peremptory eagle-sighted eye
  Dares look upon the heaven of her brow,
That is not blinded by her majesty?
  King. What zeal, what fury hath inspir'd thee now?
My love, her mistress, is a gracious moon;
  She, an attending star[2], scarce seen a light.
  Bir. My eyes are then no eyes, nor I Birón[3]:
O, but for my love, day would turn to night!
Of all complexions the cull'd sovereignty
  Do meet, as at a fair, in her fair cheek;
Where several worthies make one dignity;
  Where nothing wants, that want itself doth seek.
Lend me the flourish of all gentle tongues—
  Fye, painted rhetoric! O, she needs it not:
To things of sale a seller's praise belongs[4];
  She passes praise; then praise too short doth blot.

[2] *My love, her mistress, is a gracious* moon,
  She, an attending star,—]
  ——— Micat inter omnes
  Julium sidus, velut inter ignes
  Luna minores. Hor. MALONE.

Something like this is a stanza of Sir Henry Wotton, of which the poetical reader will forgive the insertion:

  You meaner beauties of the night,
    That poorly satisfy our eyes
  More by your number than your light,
    You common people of the skies,
  What are you when the sun shall rise? JOHNSON.

[3] *My eyes are then no eyes, nor I* Birón:] Here, and indeed throughout this play, the name of Biron is accented on the second syllable. In the first quarto, 1598, and the folio 1623, he is always called *Berowne*. From the line before us it appears, that in our author's time the name was pronounced *Biroon*. MALONE.

[4] *T; things of sale a seller's* praise *belongs;*] So in our author's 21st Sonnet:
  " I will not *praise*, that purpose not to *sell*." MALONE.

A wither'd

A wither'd hermit, fivescore winters worn,
    Might shake off fifty, looking in her eye:
Beauty doth varnish age, as if new born,
    And gives the crutch the cradle's infancy.
O 'tis the sun that maketh all things shine!
    King. By heaven thy love is black as ebony.
    Bir. Is ebony like her? O wood divine⁵!
A wife of such wood were felicity.
O, who can give an oath? where is a book?
That I may swear, beauty doth beauty lack,
If that she learn not of her eye to look:
No face is fair, that is not full as black⁶.
    King. O paradox! Black is the badge of hell,
The hue of dungeons; and the scowl of night⁶;
And beauty's crest becomes the heavens well⁷.
    Bir. Devils soonest tempt, resembling spirits of light.

⁵ — *O wood divine!*] The old copies read—*O word.* The emendation is Mr. Theobald's; and has been adopted by the subsequent editors. MALONE.

⁶ —— *beauty doth beauty lack,*
If that she learn not of her eye to look:
No face is fair, that is not full as black.] So, in our poet's 132d Sonnet:

" — *those two mourning eyes become thy face:*—
" *O, let it then as well beseem thy heart*
" *To mourn for me;*—
" *Then will I swear, beauty herself is black,*
" *And all they foul, that thy complexion lack."*

See also his 127th Sonnet. MALONE.

⁶ —— *Black is the badge of hell,*
—— *the scowl of night,*) This is Dr. Warburton's emendation. Old copies—*school.* In our author's 148th Sonnet we have

" *Who art as black as hell, as dark as night.* MALONE.

⁷ *And beauty's crest becomes the heavens well*] *Crest* is here properly opposed to *badge*. *Black*, says the King, is the *badge of hell,* but that which graces the heaven is the *crest of beauty*. *Black* darkens hell, and is therefore hateful: *white* adorns heaven, and is therefore lovely. JOHNSON.

And beauty's crest becomes the heavens well,] i. e the very *top*, the *bright* of beauty, or the utmost degree of fairness, becomes the heavens. So, the word *crest* is explained by the poet himself in *King John*:

" ———— *This is the very top,*
" *The bright, the crest, or crest unto the crest*
" *Of murder's arm."*

In heraldry, a *crest* is a device placed above a coat of arms. Shakspeare therefore assumes the liberty to use it in a sense equivalent to *top* or *utmost bright,* as he has used *spire* in *Coriolanus*:

" *to the spire and top of praises vouch'd."* TOLLET.

O, if

LOVE'S LABOUR'S LOST. 235

O, if in black my Lady's brows be deckt,
  It mourns, that painting, and usurping hair [a],
Should ravish doters with a false aspect;
  And therefore is she born to make black fair.
Her favour turns the fashion of the days;
  For native blood is counted painting now;
And therefore red that would avoid dispraise,
  Paints itself black, to imitate her brow.
Dum. To look like her, are chimney-sweepers black.
Long. And, since her time, are colliers counted bright.
King. And Ethiops of their sweet complexion crack.
Dum. Dark needs no candles now, for dark is light.
Bir. Your mistresses dare never come in rain,
For fear their colours should be wash'd away.
King. 'Twere good, yours did; for, Sir, to tell you plain,
  I'll find a fairer face not wash'd to-day.
Bir. I'll prove her fair, or talk till dooms-day here.
King. No devil will fright thee then so much as she.
Dum. I never knew man hold vile stuff so dear.
Long. Look, here's thy love: my foot and her face see.
                                    [shewing his shoe.
Bir. O, if the streets were paved with thine eyes,
  Her feet were much too dainty for such tread!
Dum. O vile! then as she goes, what upward lies
  The street should see as she walk'd over head.
King. But what of this? Are we not all in love?
Bir. O nothing so sure; and thereby all forsworn.
King. Then leave this chat; and, good Birón, now prove
  Our loving lawful, and our faith not torn.
Dum. Ay, marry, there;—some flattery for this evil.
Long. O some authority how to proceed;
  Some tricks, some quillets [b], how to cheat the devil.

---

[a] *— and usurping hair,*] *And,* which is wanting in the old copies, was supplied by the editor of the second folio. *Usurping hair* alludes to the fashion, which prevailed among ladies in our author's time, of wearing false hair, or *periwigs,* as they were then called, before that kind of covering for the head was worn by men. The sentiments here uttered by Biron may be found, in nearly the same words, in our author's 127th Sonnet. MALONE.

[b] *— some* quillets—] *Quillet* is the peculiar word applied to law-chicane. I imagine the original to be this. In the French pleadings, every several allegation in the plaintiff's charge, and every distinct plea in the defendant's answer, began with the words *qu'il est;*—from whence was formed the word *quillet,* to signify a false charge or an evasive answer. WARBURTON.

Dum.

Dum. Some salve for perjury.

Bir. O, 'tis more than need!—
Have at you then, affection's men at arms[1];
Consider, what you first did swear unto;—
To fast—to study—and to see no woman;—
Flat treason 'gainst the kingly state of youth.
Say, can you fast? your stomachs are too young:
And abstinence engenders maladies.
And where that you have vow'd to study, Lords,
In that each of you hath forsworn[2] his book:
Can you still dream, and pore, and thereon look?
For when would you, my Lord, or you, or you,
Have found the ground of study's excellence,
Without the beauty of a woman's face?
From women's eyes this doctrine I derive;
They are the ground, the books, the academes,
From whence doth spring the true Promethean fire.
Why, universal plodding prisons up[3]
The nimble spirits in the arteries[4];
As motion, and long-during action, tires
The sinewy vigour of the traveller.
Now, for not looking on a woman's face,
You have in that forsworn the use of eyes;
And study too the causer of your vow:
For where is any author in the world,
Teaches such beauty as a woman's eye[5]?
Learning is but an adjunct to ourself,
And where we are, our learning likewise is.

---

[1] —*affection's* men at arms:] *A* man *at* arms is a soldier armed at all points, both offensively and defensively. It is no more than *Te soldiers of affection.* JOHNSON.

[2] —hath *forsworn*—] Old Copies—*bow*. Corrected by Mr. Pope.
MALONE.

[3] —prisons *up*—] The quarto 1598, and the folio 1623, read—*poisons* up. The emendation was made by Mr. Theobald. A passage in *King John* may add some support to it:
"Or, if that surly spirit, melancholy,
"Had bak'd thy blood, and made it *heavy, thick,*
"Which 'else *runs trickling* up and down the veins, &c." MALONE.

[4] *The nimble* spirits in the arteries;] In the old system of physic they gave the same office to the *arteries* as is now given to the nerves; as appears from the name, which is derived from ἀηρ τηρεῖν.
WARBURTON.

[5] *Teaches such* beauty *as a woman's eye?*] I. e. a lady's eyes give a fuller notion of beauty than any author. JOHNSON.

Then

Then, when ourselves we see in ladies' eyes,
Do we not likewise see our learning there?
O, we have made a vow to study, Lords;
And in that vow we have forsworn our books[6];
For when would you, my liege, or you, or you,
In leaden contemplation, have found out
Such fiery numbers[7], as the prompting eyes
Of beauteous tutors[8] have enrich'd you with?
Other slow arts entirely keep the brain;
And therefore finding barren practisers,
Scarce shew a harvest of their heavy toil;
But love, first learned in a lady's eyes,
Lives not alone immured in the brain;
But with the motion of all elements,
Courses as swift as thought in every power;
And gives to every power a double power,
Above their functions and their offices:
It adds a precious seeing to the eye;
A lover's eyes will gaze an eagle blind;
A lover's ear will hear the lowest sound,
When the suspicious head of theft is stopp'd[9];
Love's feeling is more soft, and sensible,
Than are the tender horns of cockled snails;
Love's tongue proves dainty Bacchus gross in taste:
For valour, is not love a Hercules,

---

[6] — *our books;*] i. e. our true books, from which we derive most information;—the *eyes* of women. MALONE.

[7] *In leaden contemplation have found out*
Such fiery numbers——] *Numbers* are, in this passage, nothing more than *poetical measures.* Could you, says Biron, *by solitary contemplation, have attained such poetical fire, such spritely numbers, as have been prompted by the eyes of beauty?* JOHNSON.

[8] *Of beauteous tutors*——] Old Copies *beauty's*. Corrected by Sir T. Hanmer. MALONE.

[9] — *the suspicious head of theft is stopp'd.*] i. e. a lover in pursuit of his mistress has his senses of hearing quicker than a thief (who suspects every sound he hears) in pursuit of his prey. WARBURTON.

"*The suspicious head of theft*" is the *head suspicious* of theft. "He watches like one that fears robbing," says Speed, in the *Two Gentlemen of Verona*. This transposition of the adjective is sometimes met with. Grimme tells us, in *Damon and Pythias:*

"A heavy pouch with golde makes a light heart." FARMER.

I rather incline to Dr. Warburton's interpretation, in support of which Mr. M. Mason observes, that "the thief is as watchful on his part as the person who fears to be robbed; and Biron poetically makes theft a person." MALONE.

Still

Still climbing trees in the Hesperides⁹?
Subtle as sphinx; as sweet, and musical,
As bright Apollo's lute, strung with his hair¹;
And, when love speaks, the voice of all the gods
Makes ² heaven drowsy with the harmony ³.

Never

⁹ *Still climbing trees in the Hesperides?*] The *Hesperides* were the daughters of Hesperus, who, according to some writers, were possessed of those golden apples which Hercules carried away, though they were guarded by a dragon. More ancient mythologists suppose them to have been possessed of some very beautiful sheep. Our author had heard or read of " the gardens of the Hesperides," and seems to have thought that the latter word, was the name of the garden in which the golden apples were kept; as we say, the gardens of the *Tuilleries*, &c.

Our poet's contemporaries, I have lately observed, are chargeable with the same inaccuracy. So, in *Friar Lucas and Friar Bungay*, by Robert Greene, 1598:

"Shew thee the tree, leav'd with refined gold,
"Whereon the fearful dragon held his seat,
"That watch *the garden*, call'd HESPERIDES."

The word may have been used in the same sense in *The Legend of Orpheus and Eurydice*, a poem, 1597:

"And, like the dragon of the Hesperides,
"Shutteth the garden's gate—." MALONE.

¹ *As bright Apollo's lute, strung with his hair;*] These words are to be taken in their literal sense; and, in the stile of Italian imagery, the thought is highly elegant. The very same sort of conception occurs in Lilly's *Mydas*, (1592) Act. IV. sc. i. Pan tells Apollo, " Had thy lute been of laurel, and the *strings* of Daphne's *hair*, thy tunes might have been compared to my noies." T. WARTON.

The same thought occurs in *How to chuse a good Wife from a bad*, 1608:

"Hath he not torn those gold wires from thy head,
"Wherewith Apollo would have strung his harp,
"And kept them to play music to the gods." STEEVENS.

² For *makes*, read *make*, for the reason assigned in the note. So, in *Twelfth Night*: " — for every one of these *letters are* in my name."

Again, in *K. Henry V.*:

" The *venom* of such *looks*, we fairly hope
" *Have* lost their quality."

Again, in *Julius Cæsar*:

" The *posture* of your *blows are* yet unknown."

Again, more appositely, in *K. John*:

" How oft the *sight of means* to do ill deeds
" *Make* ill deeds done."

So Marlowe, in his *Hero and Leander*:

" The *outside* of her *garments were* of lawn."

See also, the sacred writings: " The *number of the names together were* about an hundred and twenty." Acts i. 15. MALONE.

³ *And when love speaks, the voice of all the gods*
Makes heaven drowsy with the harmony.] The old copies read—*make.*

The

LOVE'S LABOUR'S LOST.

Never durst poet touch a pen to write,
Until his ink were temper'd with love's sighs;
O, then his lines would ravish savage ears,
And plant in tyrants mild humility.
From women's eyes this doctrine I derive [3]:

          They,

The emendation was made by Sir T. Hanmer. More correct writers than Shakspeare often fall into the same inaccuracy when a noun of multitude has preceded the verb. In a former part of this speech the same error occurs: "— each of you *have* forsworn—." MALONE.

The meaning is, whenever love speaks, all the gods join their voices with his in harmonious concert. HEATH.

When Love speaks (says Biron) *the assembled gods reduce the element of the sky to a calm, by their harmonious applauses of this favoured orator.*
              STEEVENS.

Few passages have been more canvassed than this. I believe it wants no alteration of the words, but only of the pointing:

  And, when love speaks, (the voice of all,) the gods
  Make heaven drowsy with the harmony.

Love, I apprehend, is called the *voice of all*, as gold, in *Timon*, is said to *speak with every tongue*; and *the gods* (being drowsy themselves *with the harmony*) are supposed to make heaven drowsy. If one could possibly suspect Shakspeare of having read *Pindar*, one should say, that the idea of music making the hearers drowsy, was borrowed from the first Pythian. TYRWHITT.

Perhaps here is an accidental transposition. We may read, as, I think, some one has proposed before;

  ——— the voice *makes* all the gods
  Of heaven drowsy with the harmony." FARMER.

That harmony had the power to make the hearers drowsy, the present commentator might infer from the effect it usually produces on himself. In *Cinthia's Revenge*, 1613, however, is an instance which should weigh more with the reader:

  "Howl forth some ditty, that vast hell may ring
  "With charms all-potent, earth *asleep to bring*."

Again, in the *Midsummer Night's Dream*:

  "——— music call, and strike more dead
  "Than common *sleep*, of all these five the sense." STEEVENS.

So also in *K. Henry IV.* P. ii:

  "——— softly, pray;
  "Let there be no noise made, my gentle friends;
  "Unless some *dull* and favourable hand
  "Will whisper *music* to my wearied spirit."

Again, in *Pericles*, 1609:

  "Most *heavenly music!*
  "It nips me into listening, and *thick slumber*
  "Hangs on mine eyes; let me rest." MALONE.

[3] *From women's eyes this doctrine I derive:*] In this speech I suspect a more than common instance of the inaccuracy of the first publishers:

From women's eyes this doctrine I derive,

and several other lines, are as unnecessarily repeated. Dr. Warburton

They sparkle still the right Promethean fire;
They are the books, the arts, the academes,
That shew, contain, and nourish all the world;
Else none at all in aught proves excellent:
Then fools you were, these women to forswear:
Or, keeping what is sworn, you will prove fools.
For wisdom's sake, a word that all men love;
Or for love's sake, a word that loves all men;
Or for men's sake, the authors * of these women;
Or women's sake, by whom we men are men;
Let us once lose our oaths, to find ourselves,
Or else we lose ourselves to keep our oaths:
It is religion, to be thus forsworn;
For charity itself fulfils the law;
And who can sever love from charity?

King. Saint Cupid, then! and, soldiers, to the field!
Bir. Advance your standards, and upon them, Lords:
Pell-mell, down with them! but be first advis'd,
In conflict that you get the sun of them †.

was aware of this, and omitted two verses, which Dr. Johnson has since inserted. Perhaps the players printed from piece-meal parts, or retained what the author had rejected, as well as what had undergone his revisal. It is here given according to the regulation of the old copies. STEEVENS.

Biron repeats the principal topics of his argument, as preachers do their text, in order to recal the attention of the auditors to the subject of their discourse. MASON.

‡ — *a word that loves all men*;] i. e. that is pleasing to all men. So, in the language of our author's time—*it likes me well*, for *it pleases me*. Shakspeare uses the word thus licentiously, merely for the sake of the antithesis. *Men*, in the following line, are with sufficient propriety said to be authors of women, and these again of men, the aid of both being necessary to the continuance of human kind. There is surely, therefore, no need of any of the alterations that have been proposed to be made in these lines. MALONE.

I think no alteration should be admitted in these four lines, that destroys the artificial structure of them, in which, as has been observed by the author of the *Revisal*, the word which terminates every line, is prefixed to the word *sake* in that immediately following. TOLLET.

* — *the* authors—] Old Copies—*author*. The emendation was suggested by Dr. Johnson. MALONE.

† — *but be first advis'd*,
In conflict that you get the sun of them.] In the days of archery, it was of consequence to have the sun at the back of the bowmen, and in the face of the enemy. This circumstance was of great advantage to our Henry the Fifth, at the battle of Azincourt.—Our poet, however, I believe, had also an equivoque in his thoughts. MALONE.

Long.

Long. Now to plain-dealing; lay these glozes by:
Shall we resolve to woo these girls of France?

King. And win them too: therefore let us devise
Some entertainment for them in their tents.

Bir. First, from the park let us conduct them thither;
Then, homeward, every man attach the hand
Of his fair mistress: in the afternoon
We will with some strange pastime solace them,
Such as the shortness of the time can shape;
For revels, dances, masks, and merry hours,
Fore-run fair Love⁵, strewing her way with flowers.

King. Away, away! no time shall be omitted.
That will be time, and may by us be fitted.

Bir. Allons! allons!—Sow'd cockle reap'd no corn⁶;
And justice always whirls in equal measure:
Light wenches may prove plagues to men forsworn;
If so, our copper buys no better treasure⁷. [*Exeunt.*

ACT V. SCENE I.

Another part of the same.

Enter HOLOFERNES, *Sir* NATHANIEL, *and* DULL.

Hol. Satis quod sufficit⁸.

Nath. I praise God for you, Sir: your reasons at dinner have been sharp and sententious⁹; pleasant without scurrility, witty

---

⁵ *Fore-run fair Love,*] i. e. Venus. So, in *Antony and Cleopatra:*
"Now for the love of *Love,* and *her* soft hours—." MALONE.

⁶ *— sow'd cockle reap'd no corn;*] This proverbial expression intimates, that beginning with perjury, they can expect to reap nothing but falsehood. The following lines lead us to this sense. WARBURTON.

Dr. Warburton's first interpretation of this passage, which is preferred in Mr. Theobald's edition—" if we don't take the proper measures for winning these ladies, we shall never achieve them,"—is undoubtedly the true one. HEATH.

Mr. Edwards, however, approves of Dr. Warburton's second thoughts. MALONE.

⁷ Here Mr. Theobald ends the third act. JOHNSON.

⁸ *Satis quod sufficit.*] i. e. Enough's as good as a feast. STEEVENS.

⁹ *Your reasons at dinner have been, &c.*] I know not well what degree

witty without affection¹, audacious without impudency, learned without opinion, and strange without heresy. I did converse this *quondam* day with a companion of the king's, who is intituled, nominated, or called, Don Adriano de Armado.

Hol. *Novi hominem tanquam te:* His humour is lofty, his discourse peremptory, his tongue filed², his eye ambitious, his gait majestical, and his general behaviour vain, ridiculous, and thrasonical³. He is too picked⁴, too spruce, too affected, too odd, as it were, too peregrinate, as I may call it.

Nath. A most singular and choice epithet.

                                                  [*takes out his table-book.*

Hol. He draweth out the thread of his verbosity finer than the staple of his argument. I abhor such fanatical phantasms†, such insociable and point-devise⁵ companions; such rackers of orthography, as to speak, dout, fine, when he should say, doubt; det, when he should pronounce, debt; d, e, b, t; not d, e, t: he clepeth a calf, cauf; half, hauf;

---

of respect Shakspeare intends to obtain for this vicar, but he has here put into his mouth a finished representation of colloquial excellence. It is very difficult to add any thing to this character of the schoolmaster's table-talk, and perhaps all the precepts of Castiglione will scarcely be found to comprehend a rule for conversation so justly delineated, so widely dilated, and so nicely limited.

It may be proper just to note, that *refer* here, and in many other places, signifies *discourse*; and that *audacious* is used in a good sense for spirited, animated, confident. Opinion is the same with *obstinacy* or *opiniatreté.* JOHNSON.

So, again in this play:
     " Yet fear not thou, but speak *audaciously.*" STEEVENS.
¹ —*without affection*,] i. e. without affectation. So, in *Hamlet*:
     " No matter that might indite the author of *affection.*"
So, in *Twelfth Night,* Malvolio is call'd " an *affection'd* ass. STEEVENS.
² —*his tongue* filed,] Chaucer, Skelton, and Spenser, are frequent in their use of this phrase. Ben Jonson has it likewise. STEEVENS.
³ —*thrasonical*] The use of the word *thrasonical* is no argument that the author had read Terence. It was introduced to our language long before Shakspeare's time. FARMER.
⁴ —*too picked,*] i. e. nicely dressed. The substantive *pickedness* is used by Ben Jonson for *nicety in dress.* *Discoveries*—" too much pickedness is not manly." TYRWHITT.
Again, in Nashe's *Apologie of Pierce Pennilefs,* 1593: "—he might have shewed a *picked* effeminate carpet knight, under the fictionate person of Hermaphroditus." MALONE.
† —*such fanatical* phantasms,] See p. 211. n. 5. MALONE.
⁵ —*point-devise*—] A French expression for the utmost, or finical exactness. STEEVENS.

neighbour,

neighbour, *vocatur*, nebour; neigh, abbreviated, ne: This is abhominable⁶, (which he would call abominable,) it infinuateth me of infanie⁷; *Ne intelligis, domine?* to make frantic, lunatic.

Nath. *Laus deo, bone intelligo.*

Hol. *Bone?*—*bone,* for *bene: Prifcian*⁸ a little fcratch'd; 'twill ferve.

Enter ARMADO, MOTH, *and* COSTARD.

Nath. *Videfne quis venit?*

Hol. *Video & gaudeo.*

Arm. Chirra!   [*to Moth.*

Hol. *Quare* Chirra, not Sirrah?

Arm. Men of peace, well encounter'd.

Hol. Moſt military Sir, falutation.

Moth. They have been at a great feaſt of languages, and ſtolen the ſcraps †.   [*to Coſtard afide.*

Coſt. O, they have lived long on the alms-baſket of words⁹! I marvel, thy maſter hath not eaten thee for a word; for thou art not ſo long by the head as *honorificabilitudinitatibus*¹: thou art eaſier ſwallow'd than a flap-dragon².

⁶ — *abhominable*,] So the word is conſtantly ſpelt in the old moralities and other antiquated books. STEEVENS.

⁷ — *it infinuateth me of* infanie;] The old copies read—*infanie.* This emendation, as well as that in the next ſpeech (*bone*, inſtead of *bene,*) is Mr. Theobald's. Dr. Farmer with great probability propoſes to read—it infinuateth *men* of infanie. MALONE.

Infanie appears to have been a word anciently uſed. STEEVENS.

⁸ *Bone?—bone for bene: Prifcian a little fcratch'd*;—] *Diminuit Priſciani caput*—is applied to ſuch as ſpeak falſe Latin. THEOBALD.

This paſſage, which in the old copies is very corrupt, was amended by the commentator above-mentioned. MALONE.

⁹ — *the* alms-baſket *of words?*] i. e. the refuſe of words. STEEVENS.

† *They have been at a great feaſt of languages, and ſtolen the ſcraps*] So, in *Chriſt's Tears over Jeruſalem,* by Thomas Naſhe, 1594: " The phraſe of ſermons, as it ought to agree with the ſcripture, ſo heed muſt be taken, that their whole ſermon ſeem not *a banquet of the broken fragments of* ſcripture." MALONE.

The refuſe meat of families was put into a *buſket* in our author's time, and given to the poor. So, in Florio's *Second Fruits,* 1591: " Take away the table, fould up the cloth, and put all thoſe pieces of broken meat into the *buſket* for the *poor.*" MALONE.

¹ *Honorificabilitudinitatibus*:] This word, whenceſoever it comes, is often mentioned as the longeſt word known. JOHNSON.

² — *a* flap-dragon.] A *flap-dragon* is a ſmall inflammable ſubſtance which topers ſwallow in a glaſs of wine. See a note on *King Henry IV.* Part ii. Act ii. ſc. *ult.* STEEVENS.

M 2   *Moth.*

Moth. Peace; the peal begins.
Arm. Monsieur, [*to Hol.*] are you not letter'd?
Moth. Yes, yes; he teaches boys the horn-book:—What is a, b, spelt backward with a horn on his head?
Hol. Ba, *pueritia*, with a horn added.
Moth. Ba, most silly sheep, with a horn:—You hear his learning.
Hol. *Quis, quis,* thou consonant?
Moth. The third of the five vowels[3] if you repeat them; or the fifth, if I.
Hol. I will repeat them; a, e, i—
Moth. The sheep: the other two concludes it; o, u[4].
Arm. Now, by the salt wave of the Mediterraneum, a sweet touch, a quick venew of wit[5]: snip, snap, quick and home; it rejoiceth my intellect: true wit.
Moth. Offer'd by a child to an old man; which is wit-old.
Hol. What is the figure? what is the figure?
Moth. Horns.
Hol. Thou disputest like an infant: go, whip thy gig.
Moth. Lend me your horn to make one, and I will whip about your infamy *circùm circà*[6]; A gig of a cuckold's horn!
Cost. An I had but one penny in the world, thou should'st have it to buy ginger-bread: hold, there is the very remuneration I had of thy master, thou half-penny purse of wit, thou pigeon-egg of discretion. O, an the heavens were so pleased, that thou wert but my bastard! what a joyful father would'st thou make me! Go to; thou hast it *ad dunghill*, at the fingers' ends, as they say.
Hol. O, I smell false Latin; dunghill for *unguem*.
Arm. Arts-man, *preambula*; we will be singled from the

[3] *The third of the five vowels—*] The old copies read—the *last.* The emendation is Mr. Theobald's. MALONE.

[4] *—the other two concludes it; o, u.*] By o, u, Moth would mean *Oh you;* i. e. you are the sheep still, either way; no matter which of us repeats them. THEOBALD.

[5] *—a quick venew of wit*·] A *venew* is the technical term for *a bout* at the fencing-school. STEEVENS.

A *venue*, as has already been observed, is not a *bout* at fencing, but " A sweet touch of wit, (says Armado) a smart *hit.*" So, in *The Famous History of Captain Thomas Stukeley,* bl. l. 1605: "—for forfeits, and *venues* given, upon a wager, at the ninth button of your doublet, thirty crowns." MALONE.

[6] —*circùm circà.*] Old Copies—*unum cita.* Corrected by Mr. Theobald. MALONE.

barbarous.

barbarous. Do you not educate youth at the charge-house[7] on the top of the mountain?

Hol. Or, *mons*, the hill.

Arm. At your sweet pleasure, for the mountain.

Hol. I do, sans question.

Arm. Sir, it is the king's most sweet pleasure and affection, to congratulate the princess at her pavilion, in the posteriors of this day; which the rude multitude call, the afternoon.

Hol. The posterior of the day, most generous Sir, is liable, congruent, and measurable for the afternoon: the word is well cull'd, chose; sweet and apt, I do assure you, Sir, I do assure.

Arm. Sir, the king is a noble gentleman; and my familiar, I do assure you, very good friend:—For what is inward between us, let it pass—I do beseech thee, remember thy courtesy;—I beseech thee, apparel thy head[8]:—and among other importunate and most serious designs—and of great import indeed, too;—but let that pass:—for I must tell thee, it will please his grace (by the world) sometime to lean upon my poor shoulder; and with his royal finger, thus, dally with

---

[7] — *the* charge-house] I suppose, is the *free-school.* STEEVENS.

[8] *I do beseech thee*, remember thy courtesy;—*I beseech thee, apparel thy head*:] I believe the word *not* was inadvertently omitted by the transcriber or compositor; and that we should read—I do beseech thee, remember *not* thy courtesy.—Armado is boasting of the familiarity with which the king treats him, and intimates (" but let that pass,") that when he and his Majesty converse, the king lays aside all state, and makes him wear his hat: " *I do beseech thee*, (will he say to me) *remember not thy courtesy*; do not observe any ceremony with me; *be covered*." " The putting off the hat at the table (says Florio in his *Second Fruites*, 1591, is a kind of *courtesie* or ceremonie rather to be avoided than otherwise."

These words may, however, be addressed by Armado to Holofernes, whom we may suppose to have stood uncovered from respect to the Spaniard.

If this was the poet's intention, they ought to be included in a parenthesis. To whomsoever the words are supposed to be addressed, the emendation appears to me equally necessary. It is confirmed by a passage in *A Midsummer Night's Dream:* " Give me your neif, Mounsieur Mustardseed. Pray you, *leave your courtesie*, Mounsieur."

In *Hamlet*, the prince, when he desires Osrick to " put his bonnet to the right use," begins his address with the same words which Armado uses: but unluckily is interrupted by the courtier, and prevented (as I believe) from using the very word which I suppose to have been accidentally omitted here:

" *Ham. I beseech you remember*—

" *Ofr.* Nay, good my Lord, for my ease, in good faith."

M 3

with my excrement⁹, with my muſtachio: but ſweet heart, let that paſs. By the world, I recount no fable; ſome certain ſpecial honours it pleaſeth his greatneſs to impart to Armado, a ſoldier, a man of travel, that hath ſeen the world: but let that paſs.—The very all of all is—but, ſweet heart, I do implore ſecreſy—that the King would have me preſent the Princeſs, ſweet chuck, with ſome delightful oſtentation, or ſhow, or pageant, or antic, or fire-work. Now underſtanding that the curate, and your ſweet ſelf, are good at ſuch eruptions, and ſudden breaking out of mirth, as it were, I have acquainted you withal, to the end to crave your aſſiſtance.

Hol. Sir, you ſhall preſent before her the nine worthies.—Sir Nathaniel, as concerning ſome entertainment of time, ſome ſhow in the poſterior of this day, to be render'd by our aſſiſtance—the king's command, and this moſt gallant, illuſtrate, and learned gentleman—before the Princeſs; I ſay, none ſo fit as to preſent the nine worthies.

Nath. Where will you find men worthy enough to preſent them?

Hol. Joſhua, yourſelf; myſelf, or this gallant gentleman¹, Judas Maccabæus; this ſwain, becauſe of his great limb or joint, ſhall paſs Pompey the great; the page, Hercules.

Arm. Pardon, Sir, error; he is not quantity enough for that worthy's thumb: he is not ſo big as the end of his club.

Hol. Shall I have audience? he ſhall preſent Hercules in minority: his *enter* and *exit* ſhall be ſtrangling a ſnake; and I will have an apology for that purpoſe.

Moth. An excellent device! ſo, if any of the audience hiſs, you may cry; *well done, Hercules! now thou cruſheſt the ſnake!* that is the way to make an offence gracious; though few have the grace to do it.

Arm. For the reſt of the worthies?—

In the folio copy of this play, we find in the next ſcene:
" O, that your face were ſo full of o's—"
inſtead of—were not ſo full, &c. MALONE.

⁹ — *dally with my excrement*,—] The author calls the beard *valour's excrement* in the *Merchant of Venice*. JOHNSON.

¹ — *myſelf*, or *this gallant gentleman*—] The old copy has *and* this, &c. The correction was made by Mr. Steevens. We ought, I believe, to read in the next line—ſhall paſs *for* Pompey the great. If the text be right, the ſpeaker muſt mean that the ſwain ſhall, in repreſenting Pompey, *ſurpaſs* him, " becauſe of his great limb." MALONE.

Hol.

Hol. I will play three myself.
Moth. Thrice-worthy gentleman!
Arm. Shall I tell you a thing?
Hol. We attend.
Arm. We will have, if this fadge not [1], an antic. I beseech you, follow.
Hol. Via [3], goodman Dull! thou hast spoken no word all this while.
Dull. Nor understood none neither, Sir.
Hol. Allons! we will employ thee.
Dull. I'll make one in a dance or so: or I will play on the tabor to the worthies, and let them dance the hay.
Hol. Most dull, honest Dull, to our sport, away. [*Exeunt.*

SCENE II.

Another part of the same. Before the Princess's *Pavilion.*

Enter the PRINCESS, CATHARINE, ROSALINE, *and* MARIA.

Prin. Sweet hearts, we shall be rich ere we depart,
If fairings come thus plentifully in:
A lady wall'd about with diamonds!—
Look you, what I have from the loving King.
    Ros. Madam, came nothing else along with that?
    Prin. Nothing but this? yes, as much love in rhime,
As would be cramm'd up in a sheet of paper,
Writ on both sides the leaf, margent and all;
That he was fain to seal on Cupid's name.
    Ros. That was the way to make his god-head wax [4];
For he hath been five thousand years a boy.
    Cath. Ay, and a shrewd unhappy gallows too.
    Ros. You'll ne'er be friends with him; he kill'd your sister.
    Cath. He made her melancholy, sad, and heavy;
And so she died: had she been light, like you,
Of such a merry, nimble, stirring spirit,

---

[1] — *if this fadge not*] i. e. suit not. STEEVENS.
[3] *Via*—] An Italian exclamation, signifying, *Courage! come on!*
STEEVENS.
[4] — *to make his god-head wax*;] To *wax* anciently signified to *grow.* It is yet said of the moon, that she *waxes* and *wanes.* STEEVENS.

She

Rof. 'Ware pencils[1]! How? let me not die your debtor,
My red dominical, my golden letter:
O, that your face were not so full of O's[2]!
   Cath. A pox of that jest[3]! and beshrew all shrows!
   Prin. But what was sent to you from fair Dumain?
   Cath. Madam, this glove.
   Prin. Did he not send you twain?
   Cath. Yes, Madam; and moreover,
Some thousand verses of a faithful lover:
A huge translation of hypocrisy,
Vilely compil'd, profound simplicity.
   Mar. This, and these pearls, to me sent Longaville;
The letter is too long by half a mile.
   Prin. I think no less; Dost thou not wish in heart,
The chain were longer, and the letter short?
   Mar. Ay, or I would these hands might never part.
   Prin. We are wise girls, to mock our lovers so.
   Rof. They are worse fools, to purchase mocking so.
That same Biron I'll torture ere I go.
O, that I knew he were but in by the week[4]!

                                                    How

---

[1] *'Ware pencils!*] Rosaline, a black beauty, reproaches the fair Catharine for painting. JOHNSON.

Dr. Johnson mistakes the meaning of this sentence; it is not a reproach, but a cautionary threat. Rosaline says that Biron had drawn her picture in his letter; and afterwards playing on the word *letter*, Catharine compares her to a text B. Rosaline, in reply, advises her to beware of pencils, that is of drawing likenesses, lest she should retaliate; which she afterwards does, by comparing her to a red dominical letter, and calling her marks of the small pox oes. MASON.

[2] *—so full of O's*] i. e. pimples. Shakspeare talks of "—fiery O's and eyes of light." in another play. STEEVENS.

[3] *A pox of that jest!* &c] This line which in the old copies is given to the Princess, Mr. Theobald rightly attributed to Catharine. The metre, as well as the mode of expression, shew that—"*I* beshrew," the reading of those copies, was a mistake of the transcriber. MALONE.

Mr. Theobald is scandalized at this language from a Princess. But there needs no alarm—the *small pox* only is alluded to; with which, it seems, Catharine was pitted; or, as it is quaintly expressed, "her face was full of O's." Davison has a canzonnet on his lady's sickness of the *pox*; and Dr. Donne writes to his sister: "—at my return from Kent, I found *Pegge* had the *pox*—I humbly thank God, it hath not much disfigured her." FARMER.

[4] *—in by the week!*] This I suppose to be an expression taken from hiring servants or artificers; meaning, I wish I was as sure of his service for any time limited, as if I had hired him. The expression was a common one. So, in *Vittoria Corombona*, 1612: "What, are you in

How I would make him fawn, and beg, and seek;
And wait the season, and observe the times,
And spend his prodigal wits in bootless rhimes:
And shape his service wholly to my behests ³,
And make him proud to make me proud that jests!
So portent-like would I o'erfway his state ⁴,
That he should be my fool, and I his fate.

Prin. None are so ⁵ surely caught, when they are catch'd,
As wit turn'd fool: folly, in wisdom hatch'd,
Hath wisdom's warrant, and the help of school;
And wit's own grace to grace a learned fool.

Ros. The blood of youth burns not with such excess,
As gravity's revolt to wantonness ⁶.

Mar. Folly in fools bears not so strong a note,
As foolery in the wise, when wit doth dote;
Since all the power thereof it doth apply,
To prove, by wit, worth in simplicity.

Enter BOYET.

Prin. Here comes Boyet, and mirth is in his face.

by the week? So; I will try now whether thy wit be close prisoner."
Again, in the *Wit of a Woman*, 1604:
"Since I am in by the week, let me look to the year."
STEEVENS.

³ —*wholly to my behests;*] The quarto 1598, and the first folio,
read—*to my device.* The emendation, which the rhime confirms, was
made by the editor of the second folio, and is one of the very few cor-
rections of any value to be found in that copy. MALONE.

⁴ *So portent-like, &c.*] In former copies—*So pertaunt-like, &c.* In
old farces, to shew the inevitable approaches of death and destiny, the
Fool of the farce is made to employ all his stratagems, to avoid Death or
Fate; which very stratagems, as they are ordered, bring the *Fool,* at
every turn, into the very jaws of *Fate.* To this Shakspeare alludes again
in *Measure for Measure.*
"———— *merely thou art* Death's Fool;
"For him thou labour'st by thy flight to shun,
"And yet run'st towards him still."
It is plain from all this, that the nonsense of *pertaunt-like,* should be
read, *portent like,* i.e. I would be his fate or destiny, and, like a por-
tent, hang over, and influence his fortunes. For *portents* were not only
thought to *forebode,* but to *influence.* So the Latins called a person
destined to bring mischief, *fatale portentum.* WARBURTON.
This emendation appeared first in the Oxford Edition. MALONE.

⁵ *None are so, &c.*] These are observations worthy of a man who has
surveyed human nature with the closest attention. JOHNSON.

⁶ —*to wantonness.*] The quarto 1598, and the first folio have—to
wantons be. For this emendation we are likewise indebted to the second
folio. MALONE.

Boy.

Boy. O, I am stabb'd with laughter! Where's her grace?
Prin. Thy news, Boyet?
Boy. Prepare, Madam, prepare!—
Arm, wenches, arm! encounters mounted are
Against your peace: Love doth approach disguis'd,
Armed in arguments; you'll be surpris'd:
Muster your wits; stand in your own defence;
Or hide your heads like cowards, and fly hence.
   Prin. Saint Dennis to Saint Cupid⁷! What are they,
That charge their breath against us? say, scout, say.
   Boy. Under the cool shade of a sycamore,
I thought to close mine eyes some half an hour:
When, lo, to interrupt my purpos'd rest,
Toward that shade I might behold addrest
The king and his companions: warily
I stole into a neighbouring thicket by,
And overheard what you shall overhear;
That, by and by, disguis'd they will be here.
Their herald is a pretty knavish page,
That well by heart hath conn'd his embassage:
Action, and accent, did they teach him there;
Thus must thou speak, and thus thy body bear:
And ever and anon they made a doubt,
Presence majestical would put him out;
For, quoth the King, *an angel shalt thou see;
Yet fear not thou, but speak audaciously;*
The boy reply'd, *An angel is not evil;
I should have fear'd her, had she been a devil.*
With that all laugh'd, and clap'd him on the shoulder;
Making the bold wag by their praises bolder.
One rubb'd his elbow thus; and fleer'd, and swore,
A better speech was never spoke before:
Another, with his finger and his thumb,
Cry'd, *Via! we will do't, come what will come:*
The third he caper'd, and cry'd, *All goes well:*
The fourth turn'd on the toe, and down he fell.
With that, they all did tumble on the ground,
With such a zealous laughter, so profound,
That in this spleen ridiculous⁸ appears,

---

⁷ *Saint Dennis to Saint Cupid!*] The princess of France invokes with too much levity, the patron of her country, to oppose his power to that of Cupid. JOHNSON.

⁸ —*spleen ridiculous—*] is, a ridiculous *fit.* JOHNSON.

252   LOVE'S LABOUR'S LOST.

To check their folly, passion's solemn tears [*].
  Prin. But what, but what, come they to visit us?
  Boy. They do, they do; and are apparel'd thus—
Like Muscovites, or Russians: as I guess [9],
Their purpose is, to parle, to court, and dance;
And every one his love-feat will advance
Unto his several mistress; which they'll know
By favours several, which they did bestow.
  Prin. And will they so? the gallants shall be task'd:—
For, ladies, we will every one be mask'd;
And not a man of them shall have the grace,
Despight of suit, to see a lady's face.
Hold, Rosaline, this favour thou shalt wear;
And then the king will court thee for his dear;
Hold, take thou this, my sweet, and give me thine;
So shall Biron take me for Rosaline—
And change you favours too; so shall your loves
Woo contrary, deceiv'd by these removes.
  Ros. Come on then; wear the favours most in sight.
  Cath. But, in this changing, what is your intent?
  Prin. The effect of my intent is, to cross theirs:
They do it but in mocking merriment;
And mock for mock is only my intent.
Their several counsels they unbosom shall
To loves mislook; and so be mock'd withal,
Upon the next occasion that we meet,
With visages display'd, to talk, and greet.
  Ros. But shall we dance, if they desire us to't?
  Prin. No; to the death, we will not move a foot:
Nor to their penn'd speech render we no grace;
But, while 'tis spoke, each turn away her face [1].
  Boy. Why, that contempt will kill the speaker's heart,
And quite divorce his memory from his part.

---

[*] —*passion's solemn tears.*] So, in *A Midsummer Night's Dream;*
  "Made mine eyes water, but more merry tears
  "The passion of loud laughter never shed." MALONE.

[9] *Like Muscovites, or Russians:*] The settling commerce in Russia was, at that time, a matter that much ingrossed the concern and conversation of the public. There had been several embassies employed thither on that occasion; and several tracts of the manners and state of that nation written: so that a mask of Muscovites was as good an entertainment to the audience of that time, as a coronation has been since. WARBURTON.

[1] —*her face.*] The first folio, and the quarto 1598, have—*his* face. Corrected by the editor of the second folio. MALONE.

Prin.

Prin. Therefore I do it; and, I make no doubt,
The rest will ne'er come in [2], if he be out.
There's no such sport, as sport by sport o'erthrown;
To make theirs ours, and ours none but our own:
So shall we stay, mocking intended game;
And they, well mock'd, depart away with shame.

[*Trumpets sound within.*

Boy. The trumpet sounds; be mask'd, the maskers come.

[*The ladies mask.*

Enter the KING, BIRON, LONGAVILLE, *and* DUMAIN, *in Russian habits, and masked;* MOTH, *Musicians, and Attendants.*

Moth. All hail, the richest beauties on the earth!
Boy. Beauties no richer than rich taffata [3].
Moth. A holy parcel of the fairest dames,

[*The ladies turn their backs to him.*

That ever turn'd their —backs— to mortal views.
Bir. Their eyes, villain, their eyes.
Moth. That ever turn'd their eyes to mortal views!
Out—
Boy. True, out, indeed.
Moth. Out of your favours, heavenly spirits, vouchsafe
Not to behold—
Bir. Once to behold, rogue.
Moth. Once to behold with your sun-beamed eyes,
—— with your sun-beamed eyes——
Boy. They will not answer to that epithet;
You were best call it, daughter-beamed eyes.
Moth. They do not mark me, and that brings me out.
Bir. Is this your perfectness? begone, you rogue.
Ros. What would these strangers? know their minds,
Boyet:
If they do speak our language, 'tis our will
That some plain man recount their purposes:
Know what they would.

---

[2] — *will ne'er come in*] The quarto, 1598, and the folio, 1623, read— will e'er. The correction was made in the second folio. MALONE.

[3] — *than rich taffata*.] i. e. the taffata masks they wore to conceal themselves. Boyet is sneering at the absurdity of complimenting the beauty of the ladies, when they were mask'd. THEOBALD.

This line is given in the old copies to Biron. The present regulation is Mr. Theobald's. MALONE.

Boy.

Boy. What would you with the Princess?
Bir. Nothing but peace, and gentle visitation.
Ros. What would they, say they?
Boy. Nothing but peace, and gentle visitation.
Ros. Why, that they have; and bid them so be gone.
Boy. She says, you have it, and you may be gone.
King. Say to her, we have measur'd many miles,
To tread a measure with her on this grass.
Boy. They say that they have measur'd many a mile,
To tread a measure * with you on this grass.
Ros. It is not so: ask them, how many inches
Is in one mile: if they have measur'd many,
The measure then of one is easily told.
Boy. If, to come hither you have measur'd miles,
And many miles; the Princess bids you tell,
How many inches do fill up one mile.
Bir. Tell her, we measure them by weary steps.
Boy. She hears herself.
Ros. How many weary steps,
Of many weary miles you have o'ergone,
Are number'd in the travel of one mile?
Bir. We number nothing that we spend for you;
Our duty is so rich, so infinite,
That we may do it still without accompt.
Vouchsafe to shew the sunshine of your face,
That we, like savages, may worship it.
Ros. My face is but a moon, and clouded too.
King. Blessed are clouds, that do as such clouds do!

---

* *To tread a measure,*] The *measures* were dances solemn and slow. So in *Orchestra*, a poem by Sir John Davies, 1622:

"———— all the feet whereon these *measures* go,
"Are only spondees, solemn, grave, and slow."

They were performed at Court, and at public entertainments of the societies of law and equity, at their halls, on particular occasions. It was formerly not deemed inconsistent with propriety even for the gravest persons to join in them; and accordingly at the revels which were celebrated at the inns of court, it has not been unusual for the first characters of the law to become performers in *treading the measures.* See Dugdale's *Origines Judiciales.* REED.

See Beatrice's description of this dance in *Much Ado About Nothing,* p. 118. MALONE.

§ *Vouchsafe, bright moon, and these thy stars—*] When Queen Elizabeth asked an ambassador how he liked her ladies, *It is hard,* said he, *to judge of stars, in presence of the sun.* JOHNSON.

Vouchsafe,

Vouchsafe, bright moon, and these thy stars¹, to shine
(Those clouds remov'd) upon our watry eyne.

Ros. O vain petitioner! beg a greater matter;
Thou now request'st but moon-shine in the water.

King. Then in our measure do but vouchsafe one change:
Thou bid'st me beg; this begging is not strange.

Ros. Play, music, then; nay you must do it soon.
                                        [*Music plays.*
Not yet;—no dance:—thus change I like the moon.

King. Will you not dance? How come you thus estrang'd?

Ros. You took the moon at full; but now she's chang'd.

King. Yet still she is the moon, and I the man ᵈ.

The music plays; vouchsafe some motion to it.

Ros. Our ears vouchsafe it.

King. But your legs should do it.

Ros. Since you are strangers, and come here by chance,
We'll not be nice: take hands;—we will not dance.

King. Why take we hands then?

Ros. Only to part friends:
Court'sy, sweet hearts; and so the measure ends.

King. More measure of this measure; be not nice.

Ros. We can afford no more at such a price.

King. Prize you yourselves; What buys your company?

Ros. Your absence only.

King. That can never be.

Ros. Then cannot we be bought: and so adieu;
Twice to your visor, and half once to you!

King. If you deny to dance, let's hold more chat.

Ros. In private then.

King. I am best pleas'd with that. [*They converse apart.*

Bir. White-handed mistress, one sweet word with thee.

Prin. Honey, and milk, and sugar; there is three.

Bir. Nay, then, two treys, (an if you grow so nice,)
Metheglin, wort, and malmsey;—Well run, dice!
There's half a dozen sweets.

Prin. Seventh sweet, adieu!
Since you can cog⁷, I'll play no more with you.

Bir. One word in secret.

ᵈ *— the man.*] I suspect, that a line which rhimed with this, has been lost. MALONE.

⁷ *Since you can cog,*] To *cog*, signifies *to falsify the dice*, and *to falsify a narrative, or to lye.* JOHNSON.

                                                Prin.

Prin. Let it not be sweet.
Bir. Thou griev'st my gall.
Prin. Gall? bitter.
Bir. Therefore meet.   [*They converse apart.*
Dum. Will you vouchsafe with me to change a word?
Mar. Name it.
Dum. Fair lady—
Mar. Say you so? Fair lord—
Take that for your fair lady.
Dum. Please it you,
As much in private, and I'll bid adieu.

                                 [*They converse apart.*

Cath. What, was your vizor made without a tongue?
Long. I know the reason, Lady, why you ask.
Cath. O, for your reason! quickly, Sir; I long.
Long. You have a double tongue within your mask,
And would afford my speechless vizor half.
Cath. Veal, quoth the Dutchman²; Is not veal a calf?
Long. A calf, fair Lady?
Cath. No, a fair Lord calf.
Long. Let's part the word.
Cath. No, I'll not be your half:
Take all, and wean it; it may prove an ox.
Long. Look, how you butt yourself in these sharp mocks!
Will you give horns, chaste Lady? do not so.
Cath. Then die a calf, before your horns do grow.
Long. One word in private with you, ere I die.
Cath. Bleat softly then, the butcher hears you cry.

                                 [*They converse apart.*

Boy. The tongues of mocking wenches are as keen
As is the razor's edge invisible,
Cutting a smaller hair than may be seen;
Above the sense of sense: so sensible
Seemeth their conference; their conceits have wings,
Fleeter than arrows, bullets, wind, thought, swifter things.
Ros. Not one word more, my maids; break off, break off.
Bir. By heaven, all dry-beaten with pure scoff!
King. Farewel, mad wenches; you have simple wits.

---

² *Veal, quoth the Dutchman;*—] I suppose by *veal*, she means *well*, founded as foreigners usually pronounce that word; and introduced merely for the sake of the subsequent question. MALONE.

Prin.

LOVE'S LABOUR'S LOST. 257

Prin. Twenty adieus, my frozen Muscovites.—

[*Exeunt* King, Lords, Moth, *Music, and Attendants.*

Are these the breed of wits so wonder'd at?

Boy. Tapers they are, with your sweet breaths puff'd out.

Ros. Well-liking wits⁹ they have; gross, gross; fat, fat.

Prin. O poverty in wit, kingly-poor flout!
Will they not, think you, hang themselves to night?
Or ever, but in vizors, shew their faces?
This pert Biron was out of countenance quite.

Ros. O, they were all in lamentable cases¹!
The king was weeping-ripe for a good word.

Prin. Biron did swear himself out of all suit.

Mar. Dumain was at my service, and his sword:
No *point*, quoth I²; my servant straight was mute.

Cath. Lord Longaville said, I came o'er his heart;
And trow you, what he call'd me?

Prin. Qualm, perhaps.

Cath. Yes, in good faith.

Prin. Go, sickness as thou art!

Ros. Well, better wits have worn plain statute-caps³.
But will you hear? the King is my love sworn.

Prin.

---

⁹ *Well-liking wits—*] *Well-liking* is the same as *embonpoint*. So, in *Job, ch.* xxxix. v. 4. " Their young ones are in *good-liking*." STEEVENS.

¹ O! *they were all,* &c.] O, which is not found in the first quarto or folio, was added by the editor of the second folio. MALONE.

² *No point, quoth I*;] *Point* in French is an adverb of negation; but, if properly spoken, is not sounded like the point of a sword. A quibble, however, is intended. From this, and other passages, it appears, that either our author was not well acquainted with the pronunciation of the French language, or it was different formerly from what it is at present

The former supposition appears to me much the more probable of the two.

In the *Return from Parnassus* 1606, Philomusus says:—" Tit, tit, tit, non poynte; non debet fieri," &c. See also Florio's Italian Dict. 1598, in v. " Punto—never a whit;—*no point*, as the Frenchmen say."

MALONE.

³ —*better wits have worn plain statute-caps.*] This line is not universally understood, because every reader does not know that a statute-cap is part of the academical habit. Lady Rosaline declares that her expectation was disappointed by these courtly students, and that *better wits* might be found in the common places of education. JOHNSON.

Woollen caps were enjoined by act of parliament, in the year 1571, the 13th of queen Elizabeth, to be worn by all above six years of age (except the nobility and some others) on sabbath days and holy-days, under the penalty of ten groats. GREY.

I think

Prin. And quick Birón hath plighted faith to me.
Cath. And Longaville was for my service born.
Mar. Dumain is mine, as sure as bark on tree.
Boy. Madam, and pretty mistresses, give ear:
Immediately they will again be here
In their own shapes; for it can never be,
They will digest this harsh indignity.
Prin. Will they return?
Boy. They will, they will, God knows;
And leap for joy, though they are lame with blows:
Therefore, change favours; and, when they repair,
Blow like sweet roses in this summer air.
Prin. How blow? how blow? speak to be understood.
Boy. Fair ladies, mask'd, are roses in their bud:
Dismask'd, their damask sweet commixture shewn,
Are angels vailing clouds, or roses blown [4].
Prin. Avaunt, perplexity! What shall we do,
If they return in their own shapes to woo?
R-f. Good Madam, if by me you'll be advis'd,
Let's mock them still, as well known, as disguis'd:
Let us complain to them what fools were here,
Disguis'd like Muscovites, in shapeless gear [5];

I think my own interpretation of this is right. JOHNSON.
Probably the meaning is—*letter exits may be found among the citizens*, who are not in general remarkable for sallies of imagination. In Marston's *Dutch Courtezan*, 1605, Mrs. Mulligrub say—" though my husband be a citizen, and his *cap's made of wool*, yet I have wit." Again, in the *Family of Love*, 1608: " 'Tis a law enacted by the common council of *statute-caps*." Again, in *Newes from Hell, brought by the Devil's carrier*, 1606: " —in a bowling alley, in a *flat-cap*, like a *shop-keeper*." STEEVENS.
The statute mentioned by Dr. Grey was repealed in the year 1597. The epithet by which these statute-caps are described, " *plain* statute caps," induces me to believe the interpretation given in the preceding note by Mr. Steevens, the true one. The king and his lords probably wore *hats* adorned with feathers. So they are represented in the print prefixed to this play in Mr. Rowe's edition, probably from some stage tradition. MALONE.

[4] *Are angels vailing clouds, or roses blown.*] *Ladies unmask'd*, says Boyet, *are like angels vailing clouds*, or letting those clouds which obscured their brightness, sink from before them. JOHNSON.
To *avale* comes from the Fr. *aval*, (Terme de batelier) down, downward, down the stream. So, in Lancham's *Narative of Queen Elizabeth's Entertainment at Kenelworth-Castle*, 1575: " —as on a sea-shore when the water is *avail'd*." STEEVENS.
[5] *—shapeless gear;*] *Shapeless* for uncouth. WARBURTON.

And

LOVE'S LABOUR'S LOST.

And wonder, what they were; and to what end
Their shallow shows, and prologue vilely penn'd,
And their rough carriage so ridiculous,
Should be presented at our tent to us.

Boy. Ladies, withdraw; the gallants are at hand.
Prin. Whip to our tents, as roes run over land.

[*Exeunt* PRINCESS[4], ROS. CAT. *and* MAR.

Enter the KING, BIRON, LONGAVILLE, *and* DUMAIN, *in their proper habits.*

King. Fair Sir, God save you! Where's the Princess?
Boy. Gone to her tent: Please it your Majesty,
Command me any service to her thither?
King. That she vouchsafe me audience for one word.
Boy. I will; and so will she, I know, my Lord. [*Exit.*
Bir. This fellow pecks[7] up wit, as pigeons peas[8];
And utters it again when God doth please!
He is wit's pedler; and retails his wares
At wakes, and wassels[9], meetings, markets, fairs;
And we that sell by gross, the Lord doth know,
Have not the grace to grace it with such show.
This gallant pins the wenches on his sleeve;
Had he been Adam, he had tempted Eve:
He can carve too, and lisp[1]: Why, this is he,

That

---

[4] *Exeunt* Princess, &c.] Mr. Theobald ends the fourth act here. JOHNSON.

[7] *This fellow* pecks—] This is the reading of the first quarto. The folio has—*picks*.

That the original is the true reading, is ascertained by one of Nashe's tracts; *Christ's Tears over Jerusalem*, 1594: "The sower scattered some seeds by the highway side, which the foules of the ayre *peck'd up*." MALONE.

[8] — *as pigeons peas*;] This expression is proverbial:

"Children pick up words *as pigeons peas*,
"And utter them again as God shall please."

See *Ray's Collection*. STEEVENS.

[9] — wassels,] *Wassels* were meetings of rustic mirth and intemperance. STEEVENS.

Wees heal, that is, be of health, was a salutation first used by the Lady Rowena to King Vortiger. Afterwards it became a custom in villages, on new year's eve and twelfth night, to carry a *Wassel* or *Wassail* bowl from house to house, which was presented with the Saxon words above mentioned. Hence in process of time *wassel* signified intemperance in drinking, and also a meeting for the purposes of festivity. MALONE.

[1] *He can* carve *too, and* lisp:] I cannot cog, (says Falstaff, in the *Merry Wives*

That kiss'd his hand away in courtesy;
This is the ape of form, Monsieur the nice,
That, when he plays at tables, chides the dice
In honourable terms: nay, he can sing
A mean [2] most meanly; and in ushering,
Mend him who can: the ladies call him, sweet;
The stairs, as he treads on them, kiss his feet:
This is the flower that smiles on every one,
To shew his teeth as white as whales-bone [3]:
And consciences, that will not die in debt,
Pay him the due of honey-tongued Boyet.

King. A blister on his sweet tongue, with my heart,
That put Armado's page out of his part!

Enter the PRINCESS, *usher'd by* BOYET; ROSALINE, MARIA,
 CATHARINE, *and Attendants.*

Boy. See, where it comes!—Behaviour, what wert thou [4],
Till this mad man shew'd thee? and what art thou now?
King. All hail, sweet Madam, and fair time of day!
Prin. Fair, in all hail, is foul, as I conceive.
King. Construe my speeches better, if you may.
Prin. Then wish me better, I will give you leave.
King. We came to visit you: and purpose now
 To lead you to our court: vouchsafe it then.
Prin. This field shall hold me; and so hold your vow:
 Nor God, nor I, delight in perjur'd men.
King. Rebuke me not for that which you provoke;
 The virtue of your eye must break my oath [5].
                                                    Prin.

Wives of Windsor,] and say then art this and that, like many of those
lisping hawthorn buds, that come like women in men's apparel—."
                                                    MALONE.
[2] *A mean*—] The *mean*, in music, is the tenor. STEEVENS.
[3] — *as whales bone;*] The Saxon genitive case. So, in the *Mid-
summer Night's Dream*:
 " Swifter than the *moones* sphere."
It should be remembered that some of our ancient writers suppose ivory
to be part of the *bones of a whale.* The *same* simile occurs in the black
letter romance of *Sir Eglamoure of Artoys,* in that of *Sir Isumbras,* and in
The Squire of Low Degree. STEEVENS
 As white as whales bone, is a proverbial comparison in the old poets.
See Spenser's *Faery Queen,* b. iii. c. 1. st. 15; and Lord Surrey, folio
14. edit. 1567. T. WARTON.
[4] — Behaviour, *what wert thou,*] *Behaviour* here signifies—courtly or
studied manners. MALONE.
[5] *The virtue of your eye must break my oath.*] I believe the author
                                                    means

Prin. You nick-name virtue; vice you should have spoke;
   For virtue's office never breaks men's troth.
Now, by my maiden honour, yet as pure
   As the unsully'd lily, I protest,
A world of torments though I should endure,
   I would not yield to be your house's guest:
So much I hate a breaking cause to be
Of heavenly oaths, vow'd with integrity.
   King. O, you have liv'd in desolation here,
   Unseen, unvisited, much to our shame.
   Prin. Not so, my Lord; it is not so, I swear;
   We have had pastimes here, and pleasant game:
A mess of Russians left us but of late.
   King. How, Madam? Russians?
   Prin. Ay, in truth, my Lord;
Trim gallants, full of courtship, and of state.
   Ros. Madam, speak true:—It is not so, my Lord:
My Lady, (to the manner of the days,)
In courtesy, gives undeserving praise.
We four, indeed, confronted were with four
In Russian habit; here they stay'd an hour,
And talk'd apace; and in that hour, my Lord,
They did not bless us with one happy word.
I dare not call them fools; but this I think,
When they are thirsty, fools would fain have drink.
   Bir. This jest is dry to me.—My gentle sweet⁶,
Your wit makes wise things foolish: when we greet⁷
With eyes best seeing heaven's fiery eye,
By light we lose light: Your capacity

means that the *virtue,* in which word *goodness* and *power* are both comprised, *must dispense* the obligation of the oath. The Princess, in her answer, takes the most invidious part of the ambiguity. JOHNSON.

⁶ *My gentle sweet.*] The word *my,* which is wanting in the first quarto, and folio, I have supplied. *Sweet* is generally used as a substantive by our author, in his addresses to ladies. So, in *The Winter's Tale:*
   " —— When you speak, *sweet,*
   " I'd have you do it ever."
Again, in the *Merchant of Venice:*
   " And now, good *sweet,* say thy opinion."
Again, in *Othello:*
   " O, my *sweet,*
   " I prattle out of tune."
The editor of the second folio, with less probability, (as it appears to me,) reads—*fair,* gentle, sweet. MALONE.

⁷ —— *when we greet,* &c.] This is a very lofty and elegant compliment. JOHNSON.

I s

Is of that nature, that to your huge store
Wise things seem foolish, and rich things but poor.

Ros. This proves you wise and rich; for in my eye—
Bir. I am a fool, and full of poverty.
Ros. But that you take what doth to you belong,
It were a fault to snatch words from my tongue.
Bir. O, I am yours, and all that I possess.
Ros. All the fool mine?
Bir. I cannot give you less.
Ros. Which of the vizors was it, that you wore?
Bir. Where? when? what vizor? why demand you this?
Ros. There, then, that vizor; that superfluous case,
That hid the worse, and shew'd the better face.
King. We are descry'd: they'll mock us now downright.
Dum. Let us confess, and turn it to a jest.
Prin. Amaz'd, my Lord? Why looks your highness sad?
Ros. Help, hold his brows! he'll swoon! Why look you pale?—
Sea-sick, I think, coming from Muscovy.
Bir. Thus pour the stars down plagues for perjury.
Can any face of brass hold longer out?—
Here stand I, Lady; dart thy skill at me;
Bruise me with scorn, confound me with a flout;
Thrust thy sharp wit quite through my ignorance;
Cut me to pieces with thy keen conceit;
And I will wish thee never more to dance,
Nor never more in Russian habit wait.
O! never will I trust to speeches penn'd,
Nor to the motion of a school-boy's tongue;
Nor never come in vizor to my friend;
Nor woo in rhime, like a blind harper's song:
Taffata phrases, silken terms precise,
Three-pil'd hyperboles, spruce affection *,
Figures pedantical; these summer-flies
Have blown me full of maggot ostentation:

---

* *Three-pil'd hyperboles, spruce affection,*] The modern editors read —*affectation.* There is no need of change. We already in this play have had *affection* for *affectation;*—" witty without *affection."* The word was used by our author and his contemporaries, as a quadrisyllable; and the rhime such as they thought sufficient. MALONE.

† *Three-pil'd hyperboles,*] A metaphor from the *pile* of velvet. So, in the *Winter's Tale,* Autolycus says, " I have worn *three-pile."* STEEVENS.

I do

I do forswear them: and I here protest,
  By this white glove, (how white the hand, God knows!)
Henceforth my wooing mind shall be express'd
  In russet yeas, and honest kersey noes:
And, to begin, wench—so God help me, la!—
My love to thee is found, sans crack or flaw.

Ros. Sans *sans*, I pray you⁹.
Bir. Yet I have a trick
Of the old rage:—bear with me, I am sick;
I'll leave it by degrees. Soft, let us see;—
Write, *Lord have mercy upon us*¹, on those three;
They are infected, in their hearts it lies;
They have the plague, and caught it of your eyes:
These lords are visited; you are not free.
For the Lord's tokens on you do I see.

Prin. No, they are free, that gave these tokens to us.
Bir. Our states are forfeit, seek not to undo us.
Ros. It is not so; for how can this be true,
That you stand forfeit, being those that sue²?
Bir. Peace: for I will not have to do with you.
Ros. Nor shall not, if I do as I intend.
Bir. Speak for yourselves, my wit is at an end.
King. Teach us, sweet Madam, for our rude transgression
Some fair excuse.
Prin. The fairest is confession.
Were you not here, but even now, disguis'd?

---

⁹ Sans, *sans, I pray you.*] It is scarce worth remarking, that the conceit here is obscured by the punctuation. It should be written *Sans* SANS, i. e. without SANS; without French words: an affectation of which Biron had been guilty in the last line of his speech, though just before he had *forsworn* all *affectation* in phrases, terms, &c. TYRWHITT.

¹ *Write,* Lord have mercy on us—] This was the inscription put upon the door of the houses infected with the plague, to which Biron compares the love of himself and his companions, and pursuing the metaphor finds the *tokens* likewise on the ladies. The *tokens* of the plague are the first spots or discolorations, by which the infection is known to be received. JOHNSON.

So, in Sir Thomas Overbury's *Characters*, 1616: " *Lord have mercy on us* may well stand over their doors, for debt is a most dangerous city *pestilence.* MALONE.

² ———— *how can this be true,*
  That you should forfeit, being those that sue?] That is, how can those be liable to forfeiture that begin the process? The jest lies in the ambiguity of *sue*, which signifies *to prosecute by law*, or *to offer a petition.* JOHNSON.

King.

King. Madam, I was.
Prin. And were you well advis'd?
King. I was, fair Madam.
Prin. When you then were here,
What did you whisper in your Lady's ear?
King. That more than all the world I did respect her.
Prin. When she shall challenge this, you will reject her.
King. Upon mine honour, no.
Prin. Peace, peace, forbear;
Your oath once broke, you force not to forswear [3].
King. Despise me, when I break this oath of mine.
Prin. I will; and therefore keep it:—Rosaline,
What did the Russian whisper in your ear?
Ros. Madam, he swore, that he did hold me dear
As precious eye-sight; and did value me
Above this world: adding thereto, moreover,
That he would wed me, or else die my lover.
Prin. God give thee joy of him! the noble Lord
Most honourably doth uphold his word.
King. What mean you, Madam? by my life, my troth,
I never swore this lady such an oath.
Ros. By heaven, you did; and to confirm it plain,
You gave me this: but take it, Sir, again.
King. My faith, and this, the Princess I did give;
I knew her by this jewel on her sleeve.
Prin. Pardon me, Sir, this jewel did she wear;
And Lord Birón, I thank him, is my dear:—
What; will you have me, or your pearl again?
Bir. Neither of either [4]; I remit both twain.—
I see the trick on't; here was a consent [5],
(Knowing aforehand of our merriment,)

---

[3] *—you force not to forswear.*] *You force not* is the same with *you make no difficulty.* This is a very just observation. The crime which has been once committed, is committed again with less reluctance. JOHNSON.

So, in Warner's *Albion's England*, b. 2. ch. 59:
"— he *forced* not to hide how he did err." STEEVENS.
[4] *Neither of either;*] This seems to have been a common expression in our author's time. It occurs, in the *London Prodigal*, 1605, and other comedies. MALONE.
[5] *—a consent!* i. e. *a conspiracy.* So, in *K. Henry VI.* Part i.:
"——— the stars
" That have *consented* to King Henry's death." STEEVENS.

To dash it like a Christmas comedy:
Some carry-tale, some please-man, some slight zany⁶,
Some mumble-news, some trencher-knight⁷, some Dick—
That smiles his cheek in jeers⁸; and knows the trick
To make my lady laugh, when she's dispos'd—
Told our intents before: which once disclos'd,
The ladies did change favours; and then we,
Following the signs, woo'd but the sign of she.
Now, to our perjury to add more terror,
We are again forsworn; in will, and error.

⁶ *—zany.*] A zany is a buffoon, a Merry Andrew, a gross mimick.
STEEVENS.

⁷ *—some* trencher-knight,] See below:
"And stand between her back, Sir, and the fire,
"Holding a *trencher*, &c." MALONE.

⁸ *———— some* Dick,

That smiles his cheek in jeers;] The old copies read—in *yeeres*. The present emendation, which I proposed some time ago, I have since observed, was made by Mr. Theobald. Dr. Warburton endeavours to support the old reading, by explaining *years* to mean *wrinkles*, which belong alike to laughter and old age. But allowing the word to be used in that licentious sense, surely our author would have written, not *in*, but *into*, years—i. e. *into* wrinkles, as in a passage quoted by Mr. Steevens from *Twelfth Night:* "— he does *smile his cheek into* more *lines* than is in the new map, &c." The change being only that of a single letter for another nearly resembling it, I have placed *jeers* (formerly spelt *jeeres*) in the text. The words—*jeer, flout*, and *nod*, were much more in use in our author's time than at present.

In *Othello*, 1622, the former word is used exactly as here:
"And mark the *jeers*, the gibes, and notable scorns,
"That dwell in every region of his *face*."

At the end add—Again, in *The Epistle Dedicatorie* to Nashe's *Have with you to Saffron Walden*, 1596: "— nor Dick Swash, or *Desperate Dick*, that's such a terrible cutter at a chine of beefe, and devoures more meat at ordinaries in discoursing of his fraies, and deep acting of his slashing and hewing, than would serve half a dozen brewers draymen." MALONE.

Out-roaring Dick was a celebrated singer, who, with W. Wimbars, is said by Henry Chettle, in his KIND HARTS DREAME, to have got twenty shillings a day by singing at Braintree fair, in Essex. Perhaps this itinerant droll was here in our author's thoughts. This circumstance adds some support to the emendation now made. From the following passage in *Sir John Oldcastle*, 1600, it seems to have been a common term for a noisy swaggerer:
"O ho, Sir, he's a desperate *Dick* indeed;
"Bar him your house."
Again, in Kemp's *Nine Daies Wonder*, &c. 4to. 1600:
"A boy arm'd with a poking stick
"Will dare to challenge *cutting Dick*." MALONE.

Much upon this it is ᵖ:—And might not you,   [*to* Boyet.
Forestal our sport, to make us thus untrue?
Do not you know my lady's foot by the squire¹?
  And laugh upon the apple of her eye?
And stand between her back, Sir, and the fire,
  Holding a trencher, jesting merrily?
You put our page out: Go, you are allow'd²;
Die when you will, a smock shall be your shrewd.
You leer upon me, do you; there's an eye,
Wounds like a leaden sword.
  Boy. Full merrily
Hath this brave manage³, this career been run.
  Bir. Lo, he is tilting straight! Peace; I have done.

Enter COSTARD.

Welcome, pure wit! thou partest a fair fray.
  Cost. O Lord, Sir, they would know,
Whether the three worthies shall come in, or no.
  Bir. What, are there but three?
  Cost. No, Sir; but it is vara fine,
For every one pursents three.
  Bir. And three times thrice is nine.
  Cost. Not so, Sir; under correction, Sir; I hope, it is
    not so:
You cannot beg us⁴, Sir, I can assure you, Sir; we know
    what we know:
I hope, Sir, three times thrice, Sir—
  Bir. Is not nine.

ᵖ *Much upon this it is:*] Dr. Johnson would give these words to Boyet. MALONE.

¹ *—by the squire?*] From *esquierre*, Fr. a *rule* or *square*. The sense is nearly the same as that of the proverbial expression in our own language, *he hath got the length of her foot*; i. e. he hath humoured her so long, that he can persuade her to what he pleases. HEATH.

Squire in our author's time was the common term for a *rule*. See Minshen's *Dict.* in v. The word occurs again in the *Winter's Tale*. MALONE.

² *—Go, you are allow'd;*] i. e. you may say what you will; you are a licensed fool, a common jester. So, in *Twelfth Night*:

   "*There is no slander in an* allow'd *fool.*" WARBURTON.

³ *Hath this brave* manage—] The old copy has *manager*. Corrected by Mr. Theobald. MALONE.

⁴ *You cannot beg us*—] That is, we are not fools; our next relations cannot *beg* the wardship of our persons and fortunes. One of the legal tests of a *natural* is to try whether he can number. JOHNSON.

Cost.

Cost. Under correction, Sir, we know whereuntil it doth amount.

Bir. By Jove, I always took three threes for nine.

Cost. O Lord, Sir, it were pity you should get your living by reckoning, Sir

Bir. How much is it?

Cost. O Lord, Sir, the parties themselves, the actors, Sir, will shew whereuntill it doth amount: for mine own part, I am as they say, but to parfect one man—e'en one poor man⁵; Pompion the great, Sir.

Bir. Art thou one of the worthies?

Cost. It pleased them, to think me worthy of Pompey the Great: for mine own part, I know not the degree of the worthy; but I am to stand for him⁶.

Bir. Go, bid them prepare.

Cost. We will turn it finely off, Sir; we will take some care. [*Exit* Costard.

King. Biron, they will shame us, let them not approach.

Bir. We are shame-proof, my Lord: and 'tis some policy To have one show worse than the King's and his company.

King. I say, they shall not come.

Prin. Nay, my good Lord, let me o'er-rule you now; That sport best pleases, that doth least know how: Where zeal strives to content, and the contents Die in the zeal of them which it presents⁷,

Their

---

⁵ *— one man, e'en one poor man.*] The old copies read—*in* one poor man. For the emendation I am answerable. The same mistake has happened in several places in our author's plays. See my note on *All's Well that Ends Well,* Act. i. sc. iii. " You are shallow, madam," &c.
MALONE.

⁶ *I know not the degree of the worthy,* &c.] This is a stroke of satire which, to this hour, has lost nothing of its force. Few performers are sick us about the history of the character they are to represent.
STEEVENS.

⁷ *That sport best pleases, that doth least know how:*
Where zeal strives to content, and the contents
Die in the zeal of them which it presents, &c.] The quarto 1598, and the folio 1623, read—*of that* which it presents. The context, I think, clearly shews that *them* (which, as the passage is unintelligible in its original form, I have ventured to substitute,) was the poet's word. *Which* for *who* is common in our author; So, (to give one instance out of many,) in *the Merchant of Venice*:

" —— a civil doctor,
" *Which* did refuse three thousand ducats of me."

Their form confounded makes most form in mirth;
When great things labouring perish in their birth [*].
   Bir. A right description of our sport, my Lord.

Enter ARMADO.

   Arm. Anointed, I implore so much expence of thy royal sweet breath as will utter a brace of words.
   [*Arm. converses with the King, and delivers him a paper.*
   Prin. Doth this man serve God?
   Bir. Why ask you?
   Prin. He speaks not like a man of God's making.

---

and y^m and y^t were easily confounded: nor is the false concord introduced by this reading (of them who presents it,) any objection to it; for every page of these plays furnishes us with examples of the kind: So *dies* in the present line, for, thus the old copy reads; though here, and in almost every other passage where a singular corruption occurs, I have followed the example of my predecessors, and corrected the error. Where rhimes or metre, however, are concerned, it is impossible. Thus we must still read in *Cymbeline*, *lies*, as in the line before us, *presents*:

   " And Phœbus 'gins to *rise*,
   " His steeds to water at those springs
   " On chalic'd flowers that *lies*.
Again, in the play before us:
   " That in this spleen ridiculous *appears*,
   " To check their folly, passion's solemn *tears*.
Again in *the Merchant of Venice*:
   " Whose own hard dealings teaches them suspect."
Dr. Johnson would read—
   Die in the zeal of *him* which *them* presents.
But *him* was not, I believe, abbreviated in old MSS. and therefore not likely to have been confounded with *that*.
The word *it*, I believe, refers to *sport*. *That sport*, says the Princess, *pleases best, where the actors are least skilful; where zeal strives to please, and the contents*, or, (as these exhibitions are immediately afterwards called) *great things, great attempts, perish in the very act of being produced, from the ardent zeal of those who present the sportive entertainment*. To " *present* a play" is still the phrase of the theatre. *It* however may refer to *contents*, and that word may mean the most material part of their exhibition.
                                                MALONE.

This sentiment of the Princess is very natural, but less generous than that of the Amazonian Queen, who says, on a like occasion, in the *Midsummer Night's Dream*:
   " I love not to see wretchedness o'ercharg'd,
   " Nor duty in his service perishing." JOHNSON.

[*] — *labouring perish in their birth*.] *Labouring* here means, *in the act of parturition.* So Roscommon:
   " The mountains labour'd, and a mouse was born." MALONE.

                                                      Arm.

Arm. That's all one, my fair, sweet, honey monarch: for, I protest, the school-master is exceeding fantastical; too, too vain; too, too vain: But we will put it, as they say, to *fortuna della guerra.* I wish you the peace of mind, most royal couplement⁹! [*Exit* ARMADO.

King. Here is like to be a good presence of worthies: He presents Hector of Troy; the swain, Pompey the great; the parish curate, Alexander; Armado's page, Hercules; the pedant, Judas Machabæus.
And if these four worthies¹ in their first show thrive,
These four will change habits, and present the other five.

Bir. There is five in the first show.

King. You are deceiv'd, 'tis not so.

Bir. The pedant, the braggart, the hedge-priest, the fool, and the boy:—
Abate a throw at novum², and the whole world again
Cannot prick out³ five such, take each one in his vein.

King. The ship is under sail, and here she comes amain.
[*Seats brought for the King, Princess, &c.*

Pageant

---

⁹ *I wish you the peace of mind, most royal* couplement!] This singular word is again used by our author in his 21st Sonnet:
"Making a *couplement* of proud compare—." MALONE.

¹ *And if these four worthies,* &c.] These two lines might have been designed as a ridicule on the conclusion of *Selimus,* a tragedy, 1594:
"If this first part, gentles, do like you well,
"The second part shall greater murders tell." STEEVENS.

I rather think Shakspeare alludes to the shifts to which the actors were reduced in the old theatres, one person often performing two or three parts. MALONE.

² *Abate a throw at novum*—] *Abate* throw—is the reading of the original and authentic copies; the quarto 1598, and the folio, 1623. A *bare* throw, &c. was an arbitrary alteration made by the editor of the second folio. I have added only the article, which seems to have been inadvertently omitted. I suppose the meaning is, Except or put the chance of the dice out of the question, and the world cannot produce five such as these. *Abate,* from the Fr. *abatre,* is used again by our author, in the same sense, in *All's Well that Ends Well:*
"——— those *'bated,* that inherit but the fall
"Of the last monarchy."
"A *bare* throw at novum" is to me unintelligible. MALONE.

Novum (or *Novem*) appears to have been some game at dice. STEEV.

³ *Cannot* prick *out,* &c.] Dr. Grey proposes to read, *pick* out. So, in *K. Henry IV.* P. i.: "Could the world *pick* thee out three such enemies again?" The old reading, however, may be right. To *prick out,* is a phrase still in use among gardeners. To *prick* may likewise have reference to *vein.* STEEVENS.

Pageant of the Nine Worthies.

Enter COSTARD *arm'd, for* Pompey.

Cost. I Pompey am—
Bir. You lie, you are not he.
Cost. I Pompey am—
Boy. With libbard's head on knee.
Bir. Well said, old mocker; I must needs be friends with thee.
Cost. I Pompey am, Pompey surnam'd the big—
Dum. The great.
Cost. It is great, Sir;—Pompey surnamed the great;
That oft in field, with targe and shield, did make my foe to sweat:
And, travelling along this coast, I here am come by chance;
And lay my arms before the legs of this sweet lass of France.
If your ladyship would say, *Thanks, Pompey,* I had done.
Prin. Great thanks, great Pompey.
Cost. 'Tis not so much worth; but, I hope, I was perfect: I made a little fault in, *great*.
Bir. My hat to a halfpenny, Pompey proves the best worthy.

Pied is the reading of the quarto, 1598; *Cannot* pick out—that of the folio, 1623. Our author uses the same phrase in his 20th Sonnet, in the same sense;—*cannot* paint out *by a picture or mark*. Again, in *Julius Cæsar*:

" Will you be *prick'd* in number of our friends?" MALONE.

4 *Pageant of the nine worthies.*] In MS. Harl. 2057, p. 31, is " The order of a showe intended to be made Aug. 1, 1621."

" First 2 woodmen, &c.

" St. George fighting with the dragon.

" The 9 worthies in compleat armour with crownes of gould on their heads, every one having his esquires to beare before him his sheild and penon of armes dressed according as these lords were accustomed to be: 3 Assaralits, 3 Infidels, 3 Christians.

" After them, a Fame, to declare the rare virtues and noble deedes of the 9 worthye women."

Such a pageant as this, we may suppose it was the design of Shakspeare to ridicule. STEEVENS.

5 *With* libbard's *head on knee*] This alludes to the old heroic habits, which on the knees and shoulders had usually, by way of ornament, the resemblance of a leopard's or lion's head. WARBURTON.

See *Masquine* in Cotgrave's *Dictionary:* The representation of a lyon's head, &c. upon the elbow or knee of some old-fashioned garments."
TOLLET.

The *libbard*, as some of the old English glossaries inform us, is the *male* of the *panther*. STEEVENS.

Enter

Enter NATHANIEL *arm'd, for Alexander.*

Nath. When in the world I liv'd, I was the world's commander;
By east, west, north, and south, I spread my conquering might:
My 'scutcheon plain declares, that I am Alisander.

Boy. Your nose says, no, you are not; for it stands too right [6].

Bir. Your nose smells, no, in his most tender-smelling knight.

Prin. The conqueror is dismay'd: Proceed, good Alexander.

Nath. When in the world I liv'd, I was the world's commander;

Boy. Most true, 'tis right; you were so, Alisander.

Bir. Pompey the great—

Cost. Your servant, and Costard.

Bir. Take away the conqueror, take away Alisander.

Cost. O, Sir, [*to* Nath.] you have overthrown Alisander the conqueror! You will be scraped out of the painted cloth for this: your lion, that holds his poll-ax sitting on a close-stool [7], will be given to A-jax [8]: he will be the ninth worthy. A conqueror, and afeard to speak! run away for shame, Alisander. [*Nath. retires.*] There,

---

[6] —*it stands too right.*] It should be remembered, to relish this jake, that the head of Alexander was obliquely placed on his shoulders.
STEEVENS.

[7] —*lion, that holds his poll-ax, sitting on a close-stool,*] This alludes to the arms given in the old history of the *Nine Worthies*, to " Alexander, the which did beare geules, a lion or, *seiante in a chayer*, holding a battell-ax argent." Leigh's *Accidence of Armoury,* 1597. p. 23. TOLLET.

[8] *A-jax;*] There is a conceit of Ajax and *a jakes.* JOHNSON.
This conceit, paltry as it is, was used by Ben Jonson, and Camden the antiquary. Ben, among his *Epigrams,* has those two lines:
" And I could wish, for their eternis'd sakes,
" My muse had plough'd with his that sung *A-jax.*"
So, Camden, in his *Remains,* having mentioned the French word *pet,* says, " Enquire, if you understand it not, of Cloacina's chaplains, or such as are well read in *A-jax.*"
See also Sir John Harrington's *New Discourse of a stale Subject, called, the Metamorphosis of Ajax,* 1596; his *Anatomie of the metamorphosed Ajax,* no date; and *Ulysses upon Ajax,* 1596. All these performances are founded on the same conceit, of Ajax and *A-jakes.* To the first of them a licence was refused, and the author was forbid the court for writing it. STEEVENS.

an't shall please you; a foolish mild man; an honest man, look you, and soon dash'd! He is a marvellous good neighbour, insooth; and a very good bowler: but, for Alisander, alas, you see, how 'tis;—a little o'er-parted⁹:—But there are worthies a coming will speak their mind in some other sort.

Prin. Stand aside, good Pompey.

Enter HOLOFERNES *arm'd, for* Judas, *and* MOTH *arm'd, for* Hercules.

Hol. Great Hercules is presented by this imp,
  Whose club kill'd Cerberus, that three-headed canus;
And, when he was a babe, a child, a shrimp,
  Thus did he strangle serpents in his manus:
Quoniam, he seemeth in minority;
Ergo, I come with this apology.—
Keep some state in thy exit, and vanish. [*Exit* MOTH.
Judas I am—

Dum. A Judas!

Hol. Not Iscariot, Sir.—
Judas I am, yclept Machabæus.

Dum. Judas Machabæus clipt, is plain Judas.

Bir. A kissing traitor:—How art thou prov'd Judas?

Hol. Judas I am—

Dum. The more shame for you, Judas.

Hol. What mean you, Sir?

Boy. To make Judas hang himself.

Hol. Begin, Sir; you are my elder.

Bir. Well follow'd: Judas was hang'd on an elder.

Hol. I will not be put out of countenance.

Bir. Because thou hast no face.

Hol. What is this?

Boy. A cittern head¹

Dum. The head of a bodkin.

Bir. A death's face in a ring.

Long. The face of an old Roman coin, scarce seen.

Boy. The pummel of Cæsar's faulchion.

Dum. The carv'd-bone face on a flask².

---

⁹ — *a little o'er-parted:*] That is, the *part* or character allotted to him in this piece is too considerable. MALONE.

¹ *A cittern head.*] So, in Decker's *Match me in London*, 1631:—"fiddling on a *cittern* with a man's broken *head* at it." STEEVENS.

² — *on a flask.*] i.e. a soldier's powder-horn. STEEVENS.

Bir.

LOVE'S LABOUR'S LOST.

Bir. St. George's half cheek in a brooch.
Dum. Ay, and in a brooch of lead.
Bir. Ay, and worn in the cap of a tooth-drawer: And now, forward; for we have put thee in countenance.
Hol. You have put me out of countenance.
Bir. False; we have given thee faces.
Hol. But you have out-fac'd them all.
Bir. An thou wert a lion we would do so.
Boy. Therefore, as he is an ass, let him go.
And so adieu, sweet Jude! nay, why dost thou stay?
Dum. For the latter end of his name.
Bir. For the ass to the Jude; give it him:—Jud-as, away.
Hol. This is not generous, not gentle, not humble.
Boy. A light for Monsieur Judas: it grows dark, he may stumble. [*Holofernes retires.*
Prin. Alas, poor Machabæus, how hath he been baited!

Enter ARMADO *arm'd, for* Hector.

Bir. Hide thy head, Achilles; here comes Hector in arms.
Dum. Though my mocks come home by me, I will now be merry.
King. Hector was but a Trojan³ in respect of this.
Boy. But is this Hector?
Dum. I think, Hector was not so clean-timber'd.
Long. His leg is too big for Hector.
Dum. More calf, certain.
Boy. No; he is best indued in the small.
Bir. This cannot be Hector.
Dum. He's a god or a painter; for he makes faces.
Arm. The armipotent Mars, of lances the almighty,
Gave Hector a gift—
Dum. A gilt nutmeg⁴.
Bir. A lemon.
Long. Stuck with cloves⁵.

Dum.

³ *Hector was but a Trojan—*] A *Trojan*, I believe, was in the time of Shakspeare, a cant term for a *thief*. So, in *K. Henry IV.* Part I.: "Tut there are other *Trojans* that thou dream'st not of, &c." Again, in this scene, "—unless you play the *honest* Trojan, &c." STEEVENS.

⁴ *A gilt nutmeg.*] The quarto, 1598, reads—A *gift* nutmeg; and if a gift nutmeg had not been mentioned by Ben Jonson, (see Mr. Steevens's next note,) I should have thought it right. So, we say, a *gift horse*, &c. MALONE.

⁵ *Stuck with cloves.*] An orange stuck with cloves appears to have been a common new-year's gift. So, Ben Johnson, in his *Christmas Masque:*

Dum. No, cloven.
Arm. Peace!
The armipotent Mars, of lances [6] *the almighty,*
Gave Hector a gift, the heir of Ilion;
A man so breath'd, that certain he would fight, yea [7],
From morn till night, out of his pavilion.
I am that flower—
Dum. That mint.
Long. That columbine.
Arm. Sweet Lord Longaville, rein thy tongue.
Long. I must rather give it the rein; for it runs against Hector.
Dum. Ay, and Hector's a greyhound.
Arm. The sweet war-man is dead and rotten; sweet chucks, beat not the bones of the buried: when he breath'd, he was a man—But I will forward with my device; sweet royalty, [*to the Princess.*] bestow on me the sense of hearing.   [Biron *whispers* Costard.
Prin. Speak, brave Hector; we are much delighted.
Arm. I do adore thy sweet grace's slipper.
Boy. Loves her by the foot.
Dum. He may not by the yard.
Arm. This Hector far surmounted Hannibal—
Cost. The party is gone, fellow Hector, she is gone; she is two months on her way.
Arm. What mean'st thou?
Cost. 'Faith, unless you play the honest Trojan, the poor wench is cast away: she's quick; the child brags in her belly already; 'tis yours.
Arm. Dost thou infamonize me among potentates? thou shalt die.
Cost. Then shall Hector be whipp'd, for Jaquenetta that is quick by him; and hang'd, for Pompey that is dead by him.
Dum. Most rare Pompey!
Boy. Renowned Pompey!
Bir. Greater than great, great, great, great, Pompey! Pompey the huge!

Masque: " he has an orange and rosemary, but not a clove to stick in it. A gilt nutmeg is mentioned in the same piece, and on the same occasion. STEEVENS.

[4] *— of lances*] i. e. of lance men STEEVENS.

[7] *— he would fight, yea,*] Thus all the old copies. Pope very plausibly reads—he would *fight ye*; a common vulgarism. STEEVENS.

Dum.

Dum. Hector trembles.

Bir. Pompey is mov'd:—More Ates, more Ates[8], stir them on, stir them on!

Dum. Hector will challenge him.

Bir. Ay, if he have no more man's blood in's belly than will sup a flea.

Arm. By the north pole, I do challenge thee.

Cost. I will not fight with a pole, like a northern man[9]; I'll slash; I'd do it by the sword:—I pray you, let me borrow my arms[1] again.

Dum. Room for the incensed worthies.

Cost. I'll do it in my shirt.

Dum. Most resolute Pompey!

Moth. Master, let me take you a button-hole lower. Do you not see, Pompey is uncasing for the combat? What mean you? you will lose your reputation.

Arm. Gentlemen, and soldiers, pardon me; I will not combat in my shirt.

Dum. You may not deny it; Pompey hath made the challenge.

Arm. Sweet bloods, I both may and will.

Bir. What reason have you for't?

Arm. The naked truth of it is, I have no shirt; I go woolward for penance.

Moth. True, and it was enjoin'd him in Rome for want of linen[2]: since when, I'll be sworn, he wore none, but a dish-

---

[8] — *more Ates:*] That is, more instigation. Ate was the mischievous goddess that incited bloodshed. JOHNSON.

So, in *K. John*:

"An *Ate*, stirring him to war and strife." STEEVENS.

[9] — *like a northern man*;] *Vir Borealis*, a clown. See Glossary to Urry's Chaucer. FARMER.

[1] — *my arms*] The weapons and armour which he wore in the character of Pompey. JOHNSON.

[2] — *it was enjoin'd him in Rome for want of linen:* &c.] To go woolward, I believe, was a phrase appropriated to pilgrims and penitentiaries. In this sense it seems to be used in *Pierce Plowman's Vision*, Pass. xviii fol. 96. b. edit. 1550. It means *cloathd in wool, and not in linen.* T. WARTON.

The same custom is alluded to in Powel's *History of Wales*, 1584: "The Angles and Saxons slew 1000 priests and monks of Bangor, with a great number of lay-brethren, &c. who were come barefooted and *woolward* to crave mercy, &c." STEEVENS.

In Lodge's *Incarnate Devils*, 1596, we have the character of a dish-clout of Jaquenetta's; and that 'a wears next his heart for a favour.

Enter MERCADE.

Mer. God save you, Madam!
Prin. Welcome, Mercade;
But that thou interrupt'st our merriment.
Mer. I am sorry, Madam; for the news I bring,
Is heavy in my tongue. The King your father—
Prin. Dead, for my life.
Mer. Even so; my tale is told.
Bir. Worthies, away; the scene begins to cloud.
Arm. For mine own part, I breath free breath; I have seen the day of wrong through the little hole of discretion [3], and I will right myself like a soldier. [*Exeunt Worthies.*
King. How fares your majesty?
Prin. Boyet, prepare; I will away to-night.
King. Madam, not so; I do beseech you, stay.
Prin. Prepare, I say.—I thank you, gracious Lords,
For all your fair endeavours; and entreat,
Out of a new-sad soul, that you vouchsafe
In your rich wisdom, to excuse, or hide,
The liberal [4] opposition of our spirits:
If over-boldly we have borne ourselves
In the converse of breath [5], your gentleness
  guilty of it.—Farewel, worthy Lord!

---

swashbuckler: "His common course is to go always untrust; except when his shirt is a-washing, and then he goes woolward." FARMER.

To this speech in the oldest copy *Boy.* is prefixed, by which designation most of Moth's speeches are marked. The name of *Boyet* is generally printed at length. It seems better suited to Armado's page than to Boyet, to whom it has been given in the modern editions. MALONE.

[3] *I have seen the day of wrong through the little hole of discretion,*] I believe he means, *I have hitherto looked on the indignities I have received, with the eyes of discretion,* (i. e. not been too forward to resent them,) *and will insist on such satisfaction as will not disgrace my character, which is that of a soldier.* To have decided the quarrel in the manner proposed by his antagonist would have been at once a derogation from the honour of a soldier, and the pride of a spaniard.

"One may see day at a little hole," is a proverb in Ray's Collection: "Daylight will peep through a little hole," in Kelly's. STEEVENS.

[4] —*liberal*—] Free to excess. See p. 131. n. 9. STEEVENS.

[5] *In the converse of breath*—] Perhaps *converse* may, in this line, mean interchange. JOHNSON.

A heavy

A heavy heart bears not an humble tongue⁶:
Excuse me so, coming too short of thanks
For my great suit so easily obtain'd.

King. The extreme parts of time extremely form
All causes to the purpose of his speed;
And often, at his very loose⁷, decides
That which long process could not arbitrate:
And though the mourning brow of progeny
Forbid the smiling courtesy of love,
The holy suit which fain it would convince⁸;
Yet since love's argument was first on foot,
Let not the cloud of sorrow justle it
From what it purpos'd; since, to wail friends lost,
Is not by much so wholesome, profitable,
As to rejoice at friends but newly found.

Prin. I understand you not; my griefs are double⁹.

Bir. Honest plain words¹ best pierce the ear of grief;—
And by these badges understand the King.

For

---

⁶ *An heavy heart bears not an* humble *tongue:*] By *humble*, the Princess seems to mean *obsequiously thankful.* STEEVENS.

So, in the *Merchant of Venice:*
 " Shall I bend low, and in a bondman's key
 " With 'bated breath, and whispering *humbleness*," &c.
A heavy heart, says the Princess, does not admit of that verbal obeisance which is paid by the humble to those whom they address. Farewel therefore at once. MALONE.

⁷ —*at his very loose*] *At his very loose* may mean, *at the moment of his parting,* i. e. of his *getting loose*, or away from us. STEEVENS.

⁸ —*which fain it would convince;*] We must read—*which fain* would it *convince*; that is, the entreaties of love which would fain over-power grief. So Lady Macbeth declares, " *That she will* convince *the chamberlains with wine,*" JOHNSON.

⁹ *I understand you not; my griefs are* double.] I suppose, she means, 1. on account of the death of her father; 2. on account of not understanding the King's meaning.—A modern editor, instead of *double*, reads *deaf*; but the former is not at all likely to have been mistaken, either by the eye or the ear, for the latter. MALONE.

¹ *Honest plain words, &c.*] As it seems not very proper for Biron to court the Princess for the King in the King's presence at this critical moment, I believe the speech is given to a wrong person. I read thus:

 Prin. *I understand you not; my griefs are double:*
 Honest plain words best pierce the ear of grief.
 King. *And by these badges,* &c. JOHNSON.

Too many authors sacrifice propriety to the consequence of their principal character, into whose mouth they are willing to put more than justly belongs to him, or at least the best things they have to say. The

original

178   LOVE'S LABOUR'S LOST.

For your fair fakes have we neglected time,
Play'd foul play with our oaths; your beauty, ladies,
Hath much deform'd us, fashioning our humours
Even to the oppofed end of our intents:
And what in us hath feem'd ridiculous—
As love is full of unbefitting ftrains;
All wanton as a child, fkipping, and vain;
Form'd by the eye, and therefore like the eye,
Full of ftrange fhapes, of habits, and of forms²,
Varying in fubjects as the eye doth roll
To every varied object in his glance:
Which party-coated prefence of loofe love,
Put on by us, if, in your heavenly eyes,
Have mifbecom'd our oaths and gravities,
Thofe heavenly eyes, that look into thefe faults,
Suggefted us to make ³: Therefore, ladies,
Our love being yours, the error that love makes
Is likewife yours: we to ourfelves prove falfe,
By being once falfe for ever to be true

original actor of Biron, however, like *Bottom* in the *Midfummer Night's Dream*, might have taken this fpeech out of the mouth of an inferior performer. STEEVENS.

In a former part of this fcene Biron fpeaks for the King and the other lords, and being at length exhaufted, tells them, they muft wou for themfelves. I believe, therefore, the old copies are right in this refpect; but think with Dr. Johnfon that the line " Honeft, &c." belongs to the Princefs. MALONE.

² *Full of ftrange fhapes, of habits and of forms,*] The old copies read —Full of *ftraying* fhapes. Both the fenfe and the metre appear to me to require the emendation which I fuggefted fome time ago, "*ftrange* fhapes" might have been eafily confounded by the ear with the words that have been fubftituted in their room. In *Coriolanus* we meet with a corruption of the fame kind, which could only have arifen in this way:

" —— Better to ftarve
" Than crave the *higher* [hire] which firft we do deferve."

The following paffages of our author will, I apprehend, fully fupport the correction that has been made:

" In him a plenitude of fubtle matter,
" Applied to cautels, all *ftrange forms* receives." *Lover's Complaint.*

Again, in the *Rape of Lucrece:*

" —— the *impreffion* of *ftrange* kinds
" Is *form'd* in them, by force, by fraud, or fkill."

In *K. Henry V.* 4to. 1600, we have—*Forraging* blood of French nobility, inftead of *Forrage* in blood, &c. Mr. Capell, I find, has made the fame emendation. MALONE.

³ *Suggefted us—*] That is, *tempted us.* JOHNSON.

To

LOVE'S LABOUR'S LOST.

To those that make us both—fair ladies, you:
And even that falsehood, in itself a sin,
Thus purifies itself, and turns to grace.

  Prin. We have receiv'd your letters, full of love:
Your favours, the embassadors of love;
And, in our maiden council, rated them
At courtship, pleasant jest, and courtesy,
As bombast and as lining to the time⁴:
But more devout than this, in our respects⁵,
Have we not been; and therefore met your loves
In their own fashion, like a merriment.

  Dum. Our letters, Madam, shew'd much more than jest.
  Long. So did our looks.
  Ros. We did not quote them so⁶.
  King. Now, at the latest minute of the hour,
Grant us your loves.
  Prin A time, methinks, too short
To make a world-without-end bargain in⁷:
No, no, my Lord, your grace is perjur'd much,
Full of dear guiltiness; and, therefore, this—

---

⁴ *As bombast and as lining to the time:*] This line is obscure. Bombast was a kind of loose texture not unlike what is now called wadding, used to give the dresses of that time bulk and protuberance, without much increase of weight; whence the same name is given to a tumour of words unsupported by solid sentiment. The Princess, therefore, says, that they considered this courtship as but bombast, as something to fill out life, which not being closely united with it, might be thrown away at pleasure. JOHNSON.

Prince Henry calls Falstaff, "my sweet creature of bombast." STEEVENS.

⁵ *But more devout than this, in our respects*] *In*, which is wanting in the old copies, was added by Sir Thomas Hanmer. MALONE.

⁶ *We did not quote them so.*] In the old copies—*cote* 'them. It is only the old spelling of *quote*. So again, in our poet's *Rape of Lucrece*, 1594:

"Yea, the illiterate—
"Will *cote* my loathed trespass in my looks." MALONE.

We should read *quote*, esteem, reckon, though our old writers spelling by the ear, probably wrote *cote*, as it was pronounced. JOHNSON.

We did not *quote* 'em so, i. e. *we did not regard them as such.* So, in *Hamlet:*

"I'm sorry that with better heed and judgment
"I had not *quoted* him." See Act ii. sc. i. STEEVENS.

⁷ *To make a world-without-end bargain in:*] This singular phrase, which Shakspeare borrowed probably from our Liturgy, occurs again in his 57th Sonnet

"Nor dare I chide the *world-without-end* hour." MALONE.

If for my love (as there is no such cause)
You will do aught, this shall you do for me:
Your oath I will not trust; but go with speed
To some forlorn and naked hermitage,
Remote from all the pleasures of the world;
There stay, until the twelve celestial signs
Have brought about their annual reckoning:
If this austere insociable life
Change not your offer made in heat of blood;
If frosts, and fasts, hard lodging, and thin weeds [8],
Nip not the gaudy blossoms of your love,
But that it bear this trial, and last love [9];
Then, at the expiration of the year,
Come challenge, challenge me by these deserts [1],
And, by this virgin palm, now kissing thine,
I will be thine; and, till that instant, shut
My woeful self up in a mourning house;
Raining the tears of lamentation,
For the remembrance of my father's death.
If this thou do deny, let our hands part;
Neither intitled in the other's heart [2].

  King. If this, or more than this, I would deny,
    To flatter up these powers of mine with rest,
The sudden hand of death close up mine eye!
    Hence ever then my heart is in thy breast.

---

[8] —*and thin weeds,*] i.e. cloathing. MALONE.

[9] —*and last love;*] I suspect that the compositor caught this word from the preceding line, and that Shakspeare wrote—*last still.* If the present reading be right, it must mean—"if it continue still to deserve the name of love." MALONE.

[1] *Come challenge, challenge me*—] The old copies read (probably by the compositor's eye glancing on a wrong part of the line) Come challenge *me*, challenge me, &c. Corrected by Sir T. Hanmer. MALONE.

[2] *Neither intitled in the other's heart.*] Thus the folio. The quarto, 1598, reads *intikd*, which may be right; neither of us having a *dwelling* in the heart of the other.

Our author has the same kind of imagery in many other places. Thus, in the *Comedy of Errors:*

  " Shall *love* in *building* grow so ruinate?"

Again, in his *Love's Complaint:*

  " *Love* lack'd a *dwelling*, and made him her place."

Again, in the *Two Gentlemen of Verona:*

  " O thou, that dust *inhabit in my breast*,
  " Leave not the *mansion* so long tenantless,
  " Lest growing ruinous the *building* fall." MALONE.

Bir.

Bir. And what to me, my love? and what to me!
Rof. You muſt be purged too, your ſins are rack'd[3];
You are attaint with faults and perjury:
Therefore, if you my favour mean to get,
A twelve-month ſhall you ſpend, and never reſt,
But ſeek the weary beds of people ſick[4].
Dum. But what to me, my love? but what to me?
Cath. A wife!—A beard, fair health, and honeſty;
With three-fold love I wiſh you all theſe three.
Dum. O, ſhall I ſay, I thank you, gentle wife?
Cath. Not ſo, my Lord;—a twelve-month and a day
I'll mark no words that ſmooth-fac'd wooers ſay:
Come when the King doth to my lady come,
Then, if I have much love, I'll give you ſome.
Dum. I'll ſerve thee true and faithfully till then.
Cath. Yet, ſwear not, leſt you be forſworn again.
Long. What ſays Maria?
Mar. At the twelve-month's end,
I'll change my black gown for a faithful friend.
Long. I'll ſtay with patience; but the time is long.
Mar. The liker you; few taller are ſo young.
Boy. Studies my Lady? Miſtreſs, look on me,
Behold the window of my heart, mine eye,
What humble ſuit attends thy anſwer there;
Impoſe ſome ſervice on me for thy love.
Roſ. Oft have I heard of you, my Lord Birón,
Before I ſaw you: and the world's large tongue
Proclaims you for a man replete with mocks;
Full of compariſons, and wounding flouts;
Which you on all eſtates will execute,
That lie within the mercy of your wit:
To weed this wormwood from your fruitful brain,
And, therewithal, to win me, if you pleaſe,
(Without the which I am not to be won,)
You ſhall this twelve-month term from day to day

---

[3] — *your fins are* rack'd;] i. e. *extended* "to the top of their bent."
So, in *Much Ado About Nothing:*
 "Why, then we *raiſ* the value."
Mr. Rowe and the ſubſequent editors read—are *rouſ*. MALONE.

[4] — *of people ſick.*] Mr. Theobald and Dr. Warburton were of opinion that this and the five preceding lines, though written by Shakſpeare, were rejected by him, "he having executed the ſame thought a little lower with more ſpirit and elegance." MALONE.

Viſit

Visit the speechless sick, and still converse
With groaning wretches; and your task shall be,
With all the fierce endeavour of your wit [5],
To enforce the pained impotent to smile.

Bir. To move wild laughter in the throat of death?
It cannot be; it is impossible:
Mirth cannot move a soul in agony.

Ros. Why that's the way to choke a gibing spirit,
Whose influence is begot of that loose grace,
Which shallow laughing hearers give to fools:
A jest's prosperity lies in the ear
Of him that hears it, never in the tongue
Of him that makes it: then if sickly ears,
Deaf'd with the clamours of their own dear groans [6],
Will hear your idle scorns, continue then,
And I will have you, and that fault withal;
But, if they will not, throw away that spirit,
And I shall find you empty of that fault,
Right joyful of your reformation.

Bir. A twelve-month? well, befal what will befal,
I'll jest a twelve-month in an hospital [7].

Prin. Ay, sweet my Lord; and so I take my leave.
[*To the King.*

King. No, Madam: we will bring you on your way.

Bir. Our wooing doth not end like an old play;
Jack hath not Jill: these ladies' courtesy
Might well have made our sport a comedy.

King. Come, Sir, it wants a twelve-month and a day,
And then 'twill end.

---

[5] —*fierce endeavour*] *Fierce* is *vehement, rapid*. So, in *King John:*
"——*fierce extremes* of sickness." STEEVENS.

[6] — *dear groans,*] *Dear* should here, as in many other places, be *dere,* sad, odious. JOHNSON.
I believe *dear* in this place, as in many others, means only *immediate, consequential.* So, already in this scene:
"——full of *dear* guiltiness. STEEVENS.

[7] The characters of *Biron* and *Rosaline* suffer much by comparison with those of *Benedick* and *Beatrice.* We know that *Love's Labour's Lost* was the elder performance; and as our author grew more experienced in dramatic writing, he might have seen how much he could improve on his own originals. To this circumstance, perhaps, we are indebted for the more perfect comedy of *Much Ado About Nothing.*
STEEVENS.

Bir.

Bir. That's too long for a play.

Enter ARMADO.

Arm. Sweet Majesty, vouchsafe me—
Prin. Was not that Hector?
Dum. The worthy knight of Troy.
Arm. I will kiss thy royal finger, and take leave: I am a votary; I have vow'd to Jaquenetta to hold the plough for her sweet love three years. But, most esteemed greatness, will you hear the dialogue that the two learned men have compiled, in praise of the owl and the cuckoo? it should have follow'd in the end of our show.
Long. Call them forth quickly, we will do so.
Arm. Holla! approach.—

Enter HOLOFERNES, NATHANIEL, MOTH, COSTARD, *and others.*

This side is Hiems, winter; this Ver, the spring; the one maintain'd by the owl, the other by the cuckoo. Ver, begin.

S O N G.

Spr. When daisies pied, and violets blue [8],
And lady-smocks all silver-white,
And cuckoo-buds [9] *of yellow hue,*
Do paint the meadows with delight,

The

---

[8] *When daisies pied, &c.*] The first lines of this song that were transposed, have been replaced by Mr. Theobald. JOHNSON.

[9] *Cuckoo-buds—*] Gerrard in his *Herbal*, 1597, says that the *flos cuculi, cardamins*, &c. are called " in English *cuckow-flowers*, in Norfolk *Canterbury-bells*, and at *Namptwich* in Cheshire *ladie-smocks*." Shakspeare, however, might not have been sufficiently skilled in botany to be aware of this particular.

Mr. Tollet has observed, that Lyte in his *Herbal*, 1578 and 1579, remarks, that *cowslips* are in French, of some called *coqus*, prime vere, and brayes de coqu. This he thinks will sufficiently account for our author's *cuckoo-buds*, by which he supposes *cowslip-buds* to be meant; and further directs the reader to Cotgrave's *Dictionary*, under the articles—*Coqu*, and *herbe a coqu*. STEEVENS.

Cuckoo-buds must be wrong. I believe *cowslip-buds*, the true reading. FARMER.

Mr. Whalley, the learned editor of B. Jonson's works, many years ago proposed to read—*crocus* buds. The cuckoo-flower, he observed, could not be called *yellow*, it rather approaching to the colour of white,

The cuckoo, then, on every tree,
Mocks marry'd men, for thus sings he,
   Cuckoo;
Cuckoo, cuckoo—O word of fear,
Unpleasing to a married ear!

II.

When shepherds pipe on oaten straws,
 And merry larks are plowmen's clocks,
When turtles tread, and rooks, and daws,
 And maidens bleach their summer smocks,
The cuckoo, then, on every tree,
 Mocks married men, for thus sings he,
   Cuckoo;
Cuckoo, cuckoo—O word of fear,
Unpleasing to a marry'd ear!

III.

Win. *When icicles hang by the wall* [1],
 And Dick *the shepherd blows his nail,*
And Tom *bears logs into the hall,*
 And milk comes frozen home in pail,
When blood is nipt, and ways be foul,
Then nightly sings the staring owl,
   To-who;
Tu-wit, to-who, a merry note;
While greasy Joan *doth keel the pot* [2].

IV. *When*

by which epithet, Cowley, who was himself no mean botanist, has distinguished it:

 Albaque cardamine, &c. MALONE.

[1] *When icicles hang by the wall,*] i. e. from the eaves of the thatch or other roofing, from which in the morning icicles are found depending in great abundance, after a night of frost. So, in *K. Henry IV*:
  " Let us not *hang* like roping *icicles,*
  " Upon our *houses thatch.*"
 Our author (whose images are all taken from nature) has alluded in *the Tempest,* to the drops of water that after rain flow from such coverings, in their natural unfrozen state:
  " His tears run down his beard, like *winter's drops*
  " *From eves of reeds.*" MALONE.

[2] — *doth keel the pot.*] To *keel* the pot, is to *cool it,* but in a particular manner: it is to stir the pottage with the ladle to prevent the *boiling over.* FARMER.

So, in Marston's *What You Will,* 1607: " 'Faith, Doricus, thy braine boyles; *keel* it, *keel* it, or all the fat's i'the fire."

         Ibidem.

IV.

When all aloud the wind doth blow,
    And coughing drowns the parson's saw [3],
And birds sit brooding in the snow,
    And Marian's nose looks red and raw,
When roasted crabs hiss in the bowl [4],
Then nightly sings the staring owl,
        To who;
Tu-whit, to-who, a merry note;
While greasy Joan doth keel the pot.

Arm. The words of Mercury are harsh after the songs of Apollo. You, that way; we, this way [5]. *Exeunt.*

[ ] *Ibidem. And Dick the shepherd blows his nail.*] So, in *King Henry VI.* P. iii.
"What time *the shepherd, blowing of his nails,*
"Can neither call it perfect day nor night." MALONE.

Mr. Lambe observes in his notes on the ancient metrical History of the *Battle of Flodden*, that it is a common thing in the North "for a maid servant to take out of a boiling pot a *wheen*, i. e. a small quantity, viz. a porringer or two of broth, and then to fill up the pot with cold water. The broth thus taken out, is called the *keeling wheen*. In this manner greasy Joan keeled the pot." STEEVENS.

[3] — *the parson's saw.*] *Saw* seems anciently to have meant, not as at present, a proverb, a sentence, but the whole tenor of any instructive discourse.

So, in the *Tragedies of John Bochas*, translated by Lidgate, b. i. c. 4.
"These old poetes in their *sawes* swete
"Full covertly in their verses do fayne, &c." STEEVENS.

Yet, in *As You Like It*, our author uses this word in the sense of a sentence, or maxim: "Dead shepherd, now I find thy *saw* of might, &c." It is, I believe, so used here. MALONE.

[4] *When roasted crabs, &c.] Crabs* are crab-apples. The bowl must be supposed to be filled with ale; a toast and some spice and sugar being added, what is called *Lamb's-wool* is produced. So, in *K. Henry V.* 1598, (not our author's play):
"Yet we will have in store a *crab in the fire*,
"With nut-brown ale, that is full stale," &c. MALONE.
So, in the *Midsummer Night's Dream:*
"And sometimes lurk I *in a gossip's bowl*,
"In very likeness of a *roasted crab*." STEEVENS.

[5] In this play, which all the editors have concurred to censure, and some have rejected as unworthy of our poet, it must be confessed that there are many passages mean, childish, and vulgar: and some which ought not to have been exhibited, as we are told they were, to a maiden queen. But there are scattered through the whole many sparks of genius; nor is there any play that has more evident marks of the hand of Shakspeare. JOHNSON.

ACT

ACT I. SCENE I. Page 171.

This child of fancy, that Armado hight, &c.] This, as I have shewn in the note in its place, relates to the stories in the books of chivalry. A few words, therefore, concerning their origin and nature, may not be unacceptable to the reader. As I don't know of any writer who has given any tolerable account of this matter: and especially as Monsieur Huet, the bishop of Avranches, who wrote a formal treatise of the Origin of Romances, has said little or nothing of these in that superficial work. For having brought down the account of romances to the later Greeks, and entered upon those composed by the barbarous western writers, which have now the name of Romances almost appropriated to them, he puts the change upon his reader, and instead of giving us an account of these books of chivalry, one of the most curious and interesting parts of the subject he promised to treat of, he contents himself with a long account of the poems of the Provincial writers, called likewise romances; and so, under the *equivoque* of a common term, drops his proper subject, and entertains us with another, that had no relation to it more than in the name.

The Spaniards were of all others the fondest of these fables, as suiting best their extravagant turn to gallantry and bravery; which in time grew so excessive, as to need all the efficacy of Cervantes's incomparable satire to bring them back to their senses. The French suffered an easier cure from their Doctor Rabelais, who enough discredited the books of chivalry, by only using the extravagant stories of its giants, &c. as a cover for another kind of satire against the *refined politics* of his countrymen; of which they were as much possessed as the Spaniards of their *romantic bravery: in a word*, our Shakspeare makes their characteristic in this description of a Spanish gentleman:

> *A man of compliments, whom right and wrong*
> *Have chose as umpire of their mutiny:*
> *This child of fancy, that Armado hight,*
> *For interim to our studies, shall relate,*
> *In high-born words, the worth of many a knight,*
> *From tawny Spain, lost in the world's debate.*

The sense of which is to this effect: *This gentleman*, says the speaker, *shall relate to us the celebrated stories recorded in the old romances, and in their very stile.* Why he says *from tawny Spain*, is because these romances, being of the Spanish original, the heroes and the scene were generally of that country. He says, *lost in the world's debate*, because the subjects of those romances were the crusades of the European Christians against the Saracens of Asia and Africa.

Indeed, the wars of the Christians against the Pagans were the general subject of the romances of chivalry. They all seem to have had their ground-work in two fabulous monkish historians: the one, who under the name of Turpin, archbishop of Rheims, wrote the History and Achievements of Charlemagne and his Twelve Peers; to whom, instead of his father, they assigned the task of driving the Saracens out of France and the south part of Spain: the other, our Geoffry of Monmouth.

Two of these peers, whom the old romances have rendered most famous, were Oliver and Rowland. Hence Shakspeare makes Alençon,

in the first part of Henry VI. ay; " Froissard, a countryman of ours,
" records, England all Olivers and Rowlands bred, during the time Ed-
" ward the Third did reign." In the Spanish romance of *Bernardo del
Carpio*, and in that of *Roncefvalles*, the feats of Roland are recorded un-
der the name of *Roldan el encantador*; and in that of *Palmerin de Oliva* ‖,
or simply *Oliva*, those of Oliver: for *Oliva* is the same in Spanish as
Olivier is in French. The account of their exploits is in the highest
degree monstrous and extravagant, as appears from the judgment passed
upon them by the priest in Don Quixote, when he delivers the knight's
library to the secular arm of the house-keeper, " Desuendo á un Ber-
" nardo del Carpio que anda por ay, à otro llamado Roncesvalles; que
" estos en llegando à mis manos, an de estar en las de la ama, y dellas
" en las del fuego sin remission alguna*." And. of Oliver he says,
" essa Oliva se haga luego rajas, y se queme, que aun no queden della
" las cenizas †." The reasonableness of this sentence may be partly
seen from one story in the *Bernardo del Carpio*, which tells us, that the
cleft called Roldan, to be seen in the summit of an high mountain in
the kingdom of Valencia, near the town of Alicant, was made with a
single back-stroke of that hero's broad-sword. Hence came the pro-
verbial expression of our plain and sensible ancestors, who were much
cooler readers of these extravagances than the Spaniards, *of giving one a
Rowland for his Oliver*, that is, of matching one impossible lye with
another: as, in French, *faire le Roland* means, *to swagger*. This
driving the Saracens out of France and Spain, was, as we say, the sub-
ject of the elder romances. And the first that was printed in Spain was
the famous *Amadis de Gaula*, of which the inquisitor priest says: " se-
" gun he oydo dezir, este libro fué el primero de Cavallerias que se im-
" primió en Espana, y todos los demás an tomado principio y origen
" deste §;" and for which he humorously condemns it to the fire,
even à Dogmatizador de una sesta tan mala. When this subject was
well exhausted, the affairs of Europe afforded them another of the same
nature. For after that the western parts had pretty well cleared them-
selves of these inhospitable guests; by the excitements of the popes,
they carried their arms against them into Greece and Asia, to support the
Byzantine empire, and recover the holy sepulchre. This gave birth to
a new tribe of romances, which we may call of the *second* race or class.
And as *Amadis de Gaula* was at the head of the first, so, correspondently
to the subject, *Amadis de Gracia* was at the head of the latter. Hence
it is, we find, that Trebizonde is as celebrated in these romances as Ron-
cesvalles is in the other. It may be worth observing, that the two fa-
mous Italian epic poets, Ariosto and Tasso, have borrowed, from each
of these classes of old romances, the scenes and subjects of their several
stories: Ariosto choosing the first, *the Saracens in France and Spain*; and

---

‖ Dr. Warburton is quite mistaken in deriving Oliver from (Palmerin de) Oliva,
which is utterly incompatible with the genius of the Spanish language. The old
romance, of which Oliver was the hero, is entitled in Spanish, " Historia de los
nobles Cavalleros universos de Castilla, y Artus de Algarbe, in fol. en Vallad-lid 1501,
in fol. en Sevilla, 1507 :" and in French thus, " Histoire d'Olivier de Castille, &
Artus d'Algarve, son loyal compagnon, & de Heleine, fille au Roy d'Angleterre,
&c. translatée de Latin par Phil. Kamus," in fol. Gothique. It has also appeared in
English. See Ames's Typography, p. 94, 47. Percy.

* B. I. c. 6. † Ibid. § Ibid.

Tasso,

Tasso, the latter, *the Crusade against them in Asia*: Ariosto's hero being Orlando, or the French *Roland*: for as the Spaniards, by one way of transposing the letters, had made it *Roldan*, so the Italians, by another, make it *Orland*.

The main subject of these fooleries, as we have said, had its original in Turpin's famous History of Charlemagne and his Twelve Peers. Nor were the monstrous embellishments of enchantments, &c. the invention of the romancers, but formed upon eastern tales, brought thence by travellers from their crusades and pilgrimages; which indeed have a cast peculiar to the wild imaginations of the eastern people. We have a proof of this in the travels of Sir J. Maundevile, whose excessive superstition and credulity, together with an impudent monkish addition to his genuine work, have made his veracity thought much worse of than it deserved. This voyager, speaking of the isle of Cos in the Archipelago, tells the following story of an enchanted dragon. "And also "a zonge man, that wist not of the dragoun, went out of the schipp, "and went through the isle, till that he cam to the castelle, and cam "into the cave; and went so long till that he found a chambre, and "there he saughe a damysell, that kembed hire hede, and lokede "in a myrour, and sche hadde moche tresoure abouten hire: and "he trowed that sche hadde ben a comoun woman, that dwelled there "to receive men to folye. And he abode till the damysell saughe the "schadowe of him in the myrour. And sche turned hire toward him, "and asked him what he wolde. And he seyde, he wolde ben hire "lemman or paramour. And sche asked him, if that he were a knyghte. "And he sayde, nay. And then sche sayde, that he might not ben hire "lemman. But sche bad him gon azen unto his felowes, and make him "knyghte, and come azen upon the morwe, and sche scholde come out "of her cave before him; and thanne come and kysse hire on the "mowth and have no drede. For I schall do the no manner harm, alle "be it that thou see me in lykenesse of a dragoun. For thoughe thou "see me hideouse and horrible to loken onne, I do the to wytene that "it is made be enchauntement. For withouten doubte, I am none "other than thou seest now a woman; and herefore drede the noughte. "And zyf thou kysse me, thou schalt have all this tresoure, and be my "lord, and lord also of all that isle. And he departed, &c. p. 27, 30. ed. 1725. Here we see the very spirit of a romance adventure. This honest traveller believed it all, and so, it seems, did the people of the isle. "And some men seyne (says he) that in the isle of Lango is zit "the doughtre of Ypocras in form and lykenesse of a gret dragoun, "that is an hundred fadame in lengthe, as men seyn; for I have not "seen hire. And they of the isles callen hire, lady of the land." We are not to think then, these kind of stories, believed by pilgrims and travellers, would have less credit either with the writers or readers of romances: which humour of the times therefore may well account for their birth and favourable reception in the world.

The other monkish historian, who supplied the romancers with materials, was our Geoffry of Monmouth. For it is not to be supposed, that these *children of fancy* (as Shakspeare in the place quoted above, finely calls them, insinuating that *fancy* hath its *infancy* as well as *manhood*,) should stop in the midst of so extraordinary a career, or confine themselves within the lists of the *terra firma*. From *him* therefore the

Spanish romances took the story of the British Arthur, and the knights of his round table, his wife Gueniver, and his conjurer Merlin. But still it was the same subject, (essential to books of chivalry,) the wars of Christians against Infidels. And, whether it was by blunder or design, they changed the Saxons into Saracens. I suspect by design; for chivalry without a Saracen was so very lame and imperfect a thing, that even the wooden image, which turned round on an axis, and served the knights to try their swords, and break their lances upon, was called by the Italians and Spaniards, *Sarkino* and *Sarasino*; so closely were these two ideas connected.

In these old romances there was much religious superstition mixed with their other extravagancies; as appears even from their very names and titles. The first romance of Lancelot of the Lake and King Arthur and his Knights, is called the History of Saint Greaal. This Saint Greaal was the famous relic of the holy blood pretended to be collected into a vessel by Joseph of Arimathea. So another is called Kyrie Eleison of Montauban. For in those days Deuteronomy & Paralipomenon were supposed to be the names of holy men. And as they made saints of their knights-errant, so they made knights-errant of their tutelary saints; and each nation advanced its own into the order of chivalry. Thus every thing in those times being either a saint or a devil, they never wanted for the *marvellous*. In the old romance of Launcelot of the Lake, we have the doctrine and discipline of the church as formally delivered as in Bellarmine himself. " La confession " (says the preacher) ne vaut rien si le cœur n'est repentant; et si tu es " mouli & eloigné de l'amour de nostre Seigneur, tu ne peus estre re- " cordé si non par trois choses: premierement par la confession de " bouche; secondement par une contrition de cœur; tiercement par " peine de cœur, & par œuvre d'aumône & charité. Telle est la droite " voye d'aimer Dieu. Or va & si te confesse en cette maniere & recois " la discipline des mains de tes confesseurs, car c'est le signe de merite. " —Or mande le roy ses evesques, dont grandepartie avoit en l'ost, & vin- " rent tous en sa chapelle. Le roy vint devant eux tout nud en pleurant, " & tenant son plein point de vint menuës verges, si les jetta devant eux, " & leur dit en soupirant, qu'ils prissent de luy vengeance, car je suis le " plus vil pecheur, &c.—Apres print discipline de d'eux & moult douce- " ment la receut." Hence we find the divinity lectures of Don Quixote and the penance of his 'squire, are both of them in the ritual of chivalry. Lastly, we find the knight-errant, after much turmoil to himself, and disturbance to the world, frequently ended his course, like Charles V, of Spain, in a monastery; or turned hermit, and became a saint in good earnest. And this again will let us into the spirit of those dialogues between Sancho and his master, where it is gravely debated whether he should not turn saint or archbishop.

There were several causes of this strange jamble of nonsense and religion. As, first, the nature of the subject, which was a religious war or crusade: secondly, the quality of the first writers, who were religious men; and, thirdly, the end of writing many of them, which was to carry on a religious purpose. We learn, that Clement V. interdicted justs and tournaments, because he understood they had much hindered the crusade decreed in the council of Vienna. " Torneamenta ipsa & " hastiludia sive juxtas in regnis Franciæ, Angliæ, & Almanniæ, & " aliis

"aliis nonnullis provinciis, in quibus ea consuevere frequentiús exerceri,
"specialiter interdixit." *Extrav. de Tormentis C. unic. temp. Ed. I.*
Religious men, I conceive, therefore, might think to forward the design of the crusades by turning the fondness for tilts and tournaments into that channel. Hence we see the books of knight-errantry so full of solemn justs and torreaments held at Trebizonde, Bizance, Tripoly, &c. Which wise project, I apprehend, it was Cervantes's intention to ridicule, where he makes his knight propose it as the best means of subduing the Turk, to assemble all the knights-errant together by proclamation*. WARBURTON.

It is generally agreed, I believe, that this long note of Dr. Warburton's is, at least, very much misplaced. There is not a single passage in the character of *Armado*, that has the least relation to *any story in any romance of chivalry*. With what propriety therefore a dissertation *upon the origin and nature of these romances* is here introduced, I cannot see; and I should humbly advise the next editor of Shakspeare to omit it. That he may have the less scruple upon that head, I shall take this opportunity of throwing out a few remarks, which, I think, will be sufficient to shew, that the learned writer's hypothesis was formed upon a very hasty and imperfect view of the subject.

At setting out, in order to give a greater value to the information which is to follow, he tells us, that no other writer has given any tolerable account of this matter; and particularly—that *Monsieur Huet, the bishop of Avranches, who wrote a formal treatise of the Origin of Romances, has said little or nothing of these* [books of chivalry] *in that superficial work*."—The fact is true, that *Monsieur Huet* has said very little of Romances of chivalry; but the imputation, with which Dr. W. proceeds to load him, of—"*putting the change upon his reader,*" and "*dropping his proper subject*" for another, "*that had no relation to it more than in the name,*" is unfounded.

It appears plainly from *Huet*'s introductory address to *De Segrais*, that his object was to give some account of those romances which were then popular in France, such as the *Astrée* of D'Urfé, the *Grand Cyrus* of *De Scuderi*, &c. He defines the Romances of which he means to treat, to be "*fictions des avantures amoureuses;*" and he excludes epic poems from the number, because—"*Enfin les poëmes ont pour sujet une action militaire ou politique, et ne traitent d'amour que par occasion; les Romans au contraire ont l'amour pour sujet principal, et ne traitent la politique et la guerre que par incident. Je parle des Romans réguliers; car la plûpart des vieux Romans François, Italiens, et Espagnols sont bien moins amoureux que militaires.*" After this declaration, surely no one has a right to complain of the author for not treating more at large of the old romances of chivalry, or to stigmatise his work as superficial, upon account of that omission. I shall have occasion to remark below, that Dr. W. who, in turning over this *superficial work*, (as he is pleased to call it,) seems to have shut his eyes against every ray of good sense and just observation, has condescended to borrow from it a very gross mistake.

Dr. W's own positions, to the support of which his subsequent facts and arguments might be expected to apply, are two; 1. *That Romances*

* See Part II. L. 5. c. 1.

of chivalry being of Spanish original, the heroes, and the scene were generally of that country; 2. That the subject of these romances were the crusades of the European Christians against the Saracens of Asia and Africa. The first position, being complicated, should be divided into the two following; 1. That romances of chivalry were of Spanish original; 2. That the heroes and the scene of them were generally of that country.

Here are therefore three positions, to which I shall say a few words in their order; but I think it proper to premise a sort of definition of a Romance of Chivalry. If Dr. W. had done the same, he must have seen the hazard of systematizing in a subject of such extent, upon a cursory perusal of a few modern books, which indeed ought not to have been quoted in the discussion of a question of antiquity.

A romance of chivalry therefore, according to my notion, is any fabulous narration, in verse or prose, in which the principal characters are knights, conducting themselves, in the several situations and adventures, agreeably to the institutions and customs of Chivalry. Whatever names the characters may bear, whether historical or fictitious; and in whatever country, or age, the scene of the action may be laid, if the actors are represented as knights, I should call such a fable a Romance of Chivalry.

I am not aware that this definition is more comprehensive than it ought to be: but, let it be narrowed ever so much; let any other be substituted in its room; Dr. W's *first* position, *that romances of chivalry were of Spanish original*, cannot be maintained. *Monsieur Huet* would have taught him better. He says very truly, that "*les plus vieux*," of the Spanish romances, "*sont posterieurs à nos* Tristans *et à nos* Lancelots, *de quelques centaines d'années*." Indeed the fact is indisputable. *Cervantes*, in a passage quoted by Dr. W. speaks of *Amadis de Gaula* (the first four books) as the *first book of chivalry printed in Spain*. Though he says only *printed*, it is plain that he means *written*. And indeed there is no good reason to believe that *Amadis* was written long before it was printed. It is unnecessary to enlarge upon a system, which places the original of romances of chivalry in a nation, which has none to produce older than the art of printing.

Dr. W's *second* position, *that the heroes and the scene of these romances were generally of the country of Spain*, is as unfortunate as the former. Whoever will take the second volume of *Du Fresnoy's Bibliotheque des Romans*, and look over his lists of *Romans de Chevalerie*, will see that not one of the celebrated heroes of the old romances was a Spaniard. With respect to the general scene of such irregular and capricious fictions, the writers of which were used, literally, to "give to airy nothing, a local habitation and a name," I am sensible of the impropriety of asserting any thing positively, without an accurate examination of many more of them than have fallen in my way. I think, however, I might venture to assert, in direct contradiction to Dr. W. that the scene of them was *not generally* in Spain. My own notion is, that it was very rarely there: except in those few romances which treat expressly of the affair at Roncesvalles.

His *last* position, *that the subject of these romances were the crusades of the European Christians against the Saracens of Asia and Africa*, might be admitted with a small amendment. If it stood thus; *the subject of some, or a few, of these romances were the crusades*, &c. the position would have been incontrovertible; but then it would not have been either new, or fit to support a system.

After this state of Dr. W.'s hypothesis, one must be curious to see what he himself has offered in proof of it. Upon the *two first* positions he says not one word: I suppose he intended that they should be received as axioms. He begins his illustration of his *third* position, by repeating it (*with a little change of terms*, for a reason, which will appear). " *Indeed the wars of the Christians against* the Pagans *were the general subject of the romances of chivalry. They all seem to have had their ground-work in two fabulous monkish historians, the one, who, under the name of* Turpin, *archbishop of Rheims, wrote* the History and Atchievements of Charlemagne and his twelve Peers;—*the other, our* Geoffry *of Monmouth*." Here we see the reason for changing the terms of *crusades* and *Saracens* into *wars* and *Pagans*; for, though the expedition of Charles into Spain, as related by the Pseudo-Turpin, might be called a crusade against the Saracens, yet, unluckily, our Geoffry has nothing like a crusade, nor a single Saracen in his whole history: which indeed ends before Mahomet was born. I must observe too, that the speaking of Turpin's history under the title of " *the History of the Atchievements of Charlemagne and his twelve Peers*," is inaccurate and unscholarlike, as the fiction of a limited number of twelve peers is of a much later date than that history.

However, the ground-work of the romances of chivalry being thus marked out and determined, one might naturally expect some account of the first builders and their edifices; but instead of that we have a digression upon *Oliver* and *Roland*, in which an attempt is made to say something of those two famous characters, not from the old romances, but from Shakspeare, and Don Quixote, and some modern Spanish romances. My learned friend, the dean of Carlisle, has taken notice of the strange mistake of Dr. W. in supposing that the feats of *Oliver* were recorded under the name of *Palmerin de Oliva*; a mistake, into which no one could have fallen, who had read the first page of the book. And I very much suspect that there is a mistake, though of less magnitude, in the assertion, that, " *in the Spanish romance of* Bernardo del Carpio, *and in that of* Roncesvalles, *the feats of* Roland *are recorded under the name of* Roldan el Encantador." Dr. W.'s authority for this assertion was, I apprehend, the following passage of Cervantes, in the first chapter of Don Quixote. " *Mejor estava con* Bernardo del Carpio *porque en Roncesvalles avia muerto à* Roldan el Encantado, *valiendose de la industria de Hercules, quando ahogò à* Anteon el hijo de la Tierra *entre los braços*." Where is is observable, that *Cervantes* does not appear to speak of more than one romance; he calls Roldan *el encantado*, and not *el encantador*; and moreover the word *encantado* is not to be understood as an addition to Roldan's name, but merely as a participle, expressing that he was *enchanted*, or *made invulnerable by enchantment*.

But this is a small matter. And perhaps *encantador* may be an error of the press for *encantado*. From this digression Dr. W. returns to the subject of the old romances in the following manner. " *This driving the Saracens out of France and Spain was, as we say, the subject of the elder romances. And the first that was printed in Spain was the famous* Amadis de Gaula." According to all common rules of construction, I think the latter sentence must be understood to imply, that *Amadis de Gaula*

Gaula was *one of the elder romances*, and that the subject of it was the driving the *Saracens out of France or Spain*; whereas, for the reasons already given, *Amadis*, in comparison with many other romances, must be considered as *a very modern one*; and the subject of it has not the least connexion with *any driving of the Saracens whatsoever.*—But what follows, is still more extraordinary. "*When this subject was well exhausted, the affairs of Europe afforded them another of the same nature. For after that the western parts had pretty well cleared themselves of those inhospitable guests, by the excitements of the popes, they carried their arms against them into Greece and Asia, to support the Byzantine empire, and recover the holy sepulchre. This gave birth to a new tribe of romances, which we may call of the second race or class. And as* Amadis de Gaula *was at the head of the first, so, correspondently to the subject,* Amadis de Græcia *was at the head of the latter.*"—It is impossible, I apprehend, to refer *this subject* to any antecedent but that in the paragraph last quoted, viz. *the driving of the Saracens out of France and Spain.* So that, according to one part of the hypothesis here laid down, the subject *of the driving of the Saracens out of France and Spain* was well exhausted by the old romances (with *Amadis de Gaula* at the head of them) *before the crusades*: the first of which is generally placed in the year 1095: and, according to the latter part, the crusades happened in the interval between *Amadis de Gaula*, and *Amadis de Græcia*; a space of twenty, thirty, or at most fifty years, to be reckoned backwards from the year 1532, in which year an edition of *Amadis de Græcia* is mentioned by *Du Fresnoy*. What induced Dr. W. to place *Amadis de Græcia* at the head of his *second race or class* of romances, I cannot guess. The fact is, that *Amadis de Græcia* is no more concerned in *supporting the Byzantine empire, and recovering the holy sepulchre*, than *Amadis de Gaula* in driving the Saracens *out of France and Spain*. And a still more pleasant circumstance is, that *Amadis de Græcia*, through more than nine-tenths of his history, is himself a declared Pagan.

And here ends Dr. W.'s account of the old romances of chivalry, which he supposes to have had their ground-work in *Turpin's* history. Before he proceeds to the others, which had their ground-work in our *Geoffry*, he interposes a curious solution of a puzzling question concerning the origin of lying in romances.—"*Nor were the monstrous embellishments of enchantments, &c. the invention of their romancers, but formed upon eastern tales, brought thence by travellers from their crusades and pilgrimages, which, indeed, have a cast peculiar to the wild imaginations of the eastern people. We have a proof of this in the Travels of Sir J. Maundeville.*"—He then gives us a story of an enchanting dragon in the isle of Cos, from Sir. *J. Maundevile*, who wrote his Travels in 1356; by way of *proof*, that the tales of enchantments, &c. which had been current here in romances of chivalry for about two hundred years before, were brought by travellers from the East! The proof is certainly not conclusive. On the other hand, I believe it would be easy to shew, that at the time when romances of chivalry began, our Europe had a very sufficient stock of lies of her own growth, to furnish materials for every variety of *monstrous embellishment*. At most times, I conceive, and in most countries, imported lies are rather for luxury than necessity.

Dr. W.

Dr. W. comes now to that other ground-work of the old romances, our *Geoffry of Monmouth*. And him he dispatches very shortly, because, as has been observed before, it is impossible to find any thing in him to the purpose of *crusades* or *Saracens*. Indeed, in treating of Spanish romances, it must be quite unnecessary to say much of *Geoffry*, as, whatever they have of "*the British Arthur and his conjurer Merlin*," is of so late a fabric, that, in all probability, they took it from the more modern Italian romances, and not from *Geoffry*'s own book. As to the doubt, "*whether it was by blunder or design that they changed the Saxons into Saracens*," I should wish to postpone the consideration of it, till we have some Spanish romance before us, in which King *Arthur* is introduced carrying on a war against *Saracens*.

And thus, I think, I have gone through the several facts and arguments, which Dr. W. has advanced in support of his *third* position. In support of his *two first* positions, as I have observed already, he has said nothing; and indeed nothing can be said. The remainder of his note contains another hypothesis concerning *the strange jumble of nonsense and religion in the old romances*, which I shall not examine. The reader, I presume, by this time is well aware, that Dr. W.'s information upon this subject is to be received with caution. I shall only take a little notice of one or two facts, with which he sets out—"*In these old romances there was much religious superstition mixed with their other extravagancies; as appears even from their very names and titles*. The first romance of *Lancelot of the Lake and King Arthur and his Knights* is called *the* History of Saint Graal—So another is call'd Kyrie eleison of *Montauban*. For in those days *Deuteronomy and Paralipomenon were supposed to be the names of holy men*.—I believe no one, who has ever looked into the common romance of King *Arthur*, will be of opinion, that the part relating to the *Saint Graal* was the *first* romance of *Lancelot of the Lake and King Arthur and his Knights*. And as to the other supposed to be called *Kyrie eleison of Montauban*, there is no reason to believe that any romance with that title ever entitled. This is the mistake, which, as was hinted above, Dr. W. appears to have borrowed from *Huet*. The reader will judge. Huet is giving an account of the romances in Don Quixote's library, which the curate and barber saved from the flames.—"*Ceux qu' ils jugent dignes d'etre gardes sont les quatre livres d' Amadis de Gaule—Palmerin d'Angleterre—Don Belianis; le miroir de chevalerie; Tirante le Blanc, et Kyrie éleison de Montauban (car au bon vieux temps, on croyoit que Kyrie éleison et Paralipomenon etoient les noms de quelques saints) où les subtilitez de la Damoiselle Plaisir-de-ma-vie, et les tromperies de la Veuve reposée, sont fort louées.*"—It is plain, I think, that Dr. W. copied what he says of *Kyrie eleison of Montauban*, as well as the witticism in his last sentence, from this passage of Huet, though he has improved upon his original by introducing a *saint Deuteronomy*, upon what authority I know not. It is still more evident (from the passage of *Cervantes*, which is quoted below*) that

---

* Don Quix. lib. 1. c. 6. "Valame Dios, dixo el Cura, dando una gran voz, que aqui esté *Tirante el Blanco*! Dadmele aca, compadre, que hago cuenta que he hallado en él un tesoro de contento, y una mina de passatiempos. Aqui está Don Quirieleyson de Montalvan, valeroso Cavallero, y su hermano Tomas de Montalvan, y el Cavallero Fonseca, con la batalla que el valiente Detriante [r. de Tirante] hizo con el alano, y las agudezas de la Donzella Plazer de mi vida, con

that *Huet* was mistaken in supposing *Kyrie eleison de Montauban* to be the name of a separate romance. He might as well have made *La Damoiselle Plaisir-de-ma-vie* and *La Veuve reposée* the names of separate romances. All three are merely characters in the romance of *Tirante le Blanc*.—And so much for Dr. W.'s account of the origin and nature of romances of chivalry. TYRWHITT.

No future editor of Shakspeare will, I believe, readily consent to omit the dissertation here examined, though it certainly has no more relation to the play before us, than any other of our author's dramas. Mr. Tyrwhitt's judicious observations upon it have given it a value which it certainly had not before; and I think I may venture to foretel, that Dr. Warburton's futile performance, like the pismire which Martial tells us was accidentally incrusted with amber, will be ever preserved, for the sake of the admirable comment in which it is now *enshrined*.

——quæ fuerat vitâ contempta manente,
Funeribus facta est nunc pretiosa suis. MALONE.

A MIDSUMMER-NIGHT'S DREAM.

PERSONS REPRESENTED.

Theseus, *Duke of Athens.*
Egeus, *Father to Hermia.*
Lysander, } *in love with Hermia.*
Demetrius,
Philostrate, *Master of the Revels to Theseus.*
Quince, *the Carpenter.*
Snug, *the Joiner.*
Bottom, *the Weaver.*
Flute, *the Bellows-mender.*
Snowt, *the Tinker.*
Starveling, *the Tailor.*

Hippolita, *Queen of the Amazons, betrothed to Theseus.*
Hermia, *Daughter to Egeus, in love with Lysander.*
Helena, *in love with Demetrius.*

Oberon, *King of the Fairies.*
Titania, *Queen of the Fairies.*
Puck, or Robin-goodfellow, *a Fairy.*
Peaseblossom,
Cobweb,
Moth,   } *Fairies.*
Mustard-seed,

Pyramus,
Thisbe,
Wall,   } *Characters in the Interlude performed by*
Moonshine,   *the Clowns.*
Lion,

Other Fairies attending their King and Queen.
Attendants on Theseus *and* Hippolita.

SCENE, Athens, *and a Wood not far from it.*

MIDSUMMER-NIGHT'S DREAM[1].

ACT I. SCENE I.

Athens. *A Room in the Palace of* Theseus.

Enter THESEUS, HIPPOLITA, PHILOSTRATE, *and Attendants.*

The. Now, fair Hippolita, our nuptial hour
Draws on apace; four happy days bring in
Another moon: but, oh, methinks, how slow
This old moon wanes; she lingers my desires,

                                      Like

---

[1] This play was entered at Stationers' Hall, Oct. 8, 1600, by Thomas Fisher. It is probable that the hint for it was received from Chaucer's *Knight's Tale.* Thence it is, that our author speaks of Theseus as *Duke* of Athens. The tale begins thus; late edit. v. 861:
    "Whilom as olde stories tellen us,
    "There was a *Duk* that highte Theseus,
    "Of Athenes he was lord and governor, &c."
Lidgate too, the monk of Bury, in his translation of the *Tragedies of John Bochas*, calls him by the same title, chap. xii. L 21.
    "*Duke* Theseus had the victorye."
Creon, in the tragedy of *Jocasta,* translated from *Euripides* in 1566, is called *Duke Creon.* So likewise Skelton:
    "Not lyke *Duke* Hamilcar,
    "Not like *Duke* Arsdruball."
I have been informed that the originals of Shakspeare's *Oberon* and *Titania* are to be sought in the ancient French Romance of *Huon de Bourdeaux*. STEEVENS.

    Mr. Warton remarks, (*Observat.* on Spenser's F. Q. v. ii. 138,) that " this romance is mentioned among other old histories of the same kind in Lancham's Letter, concerning Queen Elizabeth's Entertainment at Kenelworth Castle. It is entitled, *The famous exploits of Sir Huon of Bourdeaux,* and was translated from the French by John Bourchier, Lord Berners, in the reign of Henry VIII."

                                      The

Like to a step-dame, or a dowager,
Long withering out a young man's revenue [1].
   Hip. Four days will quickly steep themselves in nights;
Four nights will quickly dream away the time;
And then the moon, like to a silver bow
New bent [3] in heaven, shall behold the night
Of our solemnities.
   The. Go, Philostrate,
Stir up the Athenian youth to merriments;
Awake the pert and nimble spirit of mirth;
Turn melancholy forth to funerals,
The pale companion is not for our pomp.—   [*Exit Phi.*
Hippolita, I woo'd thee with my sword,
And won thy love, doing thee injuries;
But I will wed thee in another key,
With pomp, with triumph, and with revelling [4].

   Enter EGEUS, HERMIA, LYSANDER, *and* DEMETRIUS.

   Ege. Happy be Theseus, our renowned Duke!
   The. Thanks, good Egeus: What's the news with thee?
   Ege. Full of vexation come I, with complaint

The *Midsummer-Night's Dream* I suppose to have been written in 1592. See *An Attempt to ascertain the order of Shakspeare's Plays*, Vol. I.
   MALONE.

[2] *Like to a step-dame, or a dowager,*
   Long withering out a young man's revenue.]
         —— Ut piger annus
      Pupillis, quos dura premit custodia matrum,
      Sic mihi tarda fluunt ingrataque tempora. HOR. MALONE.

[3] *New bent*—] The old copies read—*Now bent.* Corrected by Mr. Rowe. MALONE.

[4] *With pomp, with triumph, and with revelling.*] By triumph, as Mr. Warton has observed in his late edition of Milton's POEMS, p. 56, we are to understand *shews*, such as masks, revels, &c. So, again in *King Henry VI.* P. iii:
   " And now what rests, but that we spend the time
   " With stately *triumphs*, mirthful comic shews,
   " Such as befits the pleasures of the court."
Again, in the preface to Burton's *Anatomie of Melancholy*, 1624: " Now come tidings of weddings, maskings, mummeries, entertainments, trophies, *triumphs*, revels, sports, playes:" Jonson, as the same gentleman observes, in the title of his masque called *Love's* triumph through *Callipolis*, by *triumph* seems to have meant a grand procession; and in one of the stage-directions, it is said, " the triumph is seen far off." MALONE.

Against

Against my child, my daughter Hermia.—
Stand forth, Demetrius;—My noble Lord,
This man hath my consent to marry her:—
Stand forth, Lysander;—and, my gracious Duke,
This hath bewitch'd⁵ the bosom of my child:
Thou, thou, Lysander, thou hast given her rhimes,
And interchang'd love-tokens with my child:
Thou hast by moon-light at her window sung,
With feigning voice, verses of feigning love;
And stol'n the impression of her fantasy
With bracelets of thy hair, rings, gawds⁶, conceits,
Knacks, trifles, nosegays, sweet-meats; messengers
Of strong prevailment in unharden'd youth:
With cunning hast thou filch'd my daughter's heart;
Turn'd her obedience which is due to me,
To stubborn harshness:—And, my gracious Duke,
Be it so she will not here before your grace
Consent to marry with Demetrius,
I beg the ancient privilege of Athens;
As she is mine, I may dispose of her:
Which shall be either to this gentleman,
Or to her death; according to our law⁷,
Immediately provided in that case.

The. What say you, Hermia? be advis'd, fair maid:
To you your father should be as a god;
One that compos'd your beauties; yea, and one
To whom you are but as a form in wax,
By him imprinted, and within his power
To leave the figure, or disfigure it.
Demetrius is a worthy gentleman.

⁵ *This hath bewitch'd—*] The old copies read—This *man* hath bewitch'd— The emendation was made for the sake of the metre, by the editor of the second folio. It is very probable that the compositor caught the word *man* from the line above. MALONE.

⁶ —*gawds—*] i. e. baubles, toys, trifles. Our author has the word frequently. The Rev Mr. Lambe in his notes on the ancient metrical history of the *Battle of Flodden*, observes that a *gawd* is *a child's toy*, and that the children in the North call their play-things *gawdys*, and their baby-house a *gawdy-house*. STEEVENS.

⁷ *Or to her death; according to our law*] By a law of Solon's, parents had an absolute power of life and death over their children. So it suited the poet's purpose well enough, to suppose the Athenians had it before.—Or perhaps he neither thought nor knew any thing of the matter. WARBURTON.

Her.

Her. So is Lysander.

The. In himself he is:
But, in this kind, wanting your father's voice,
The other must be held the worthier.

Her. I would, my father look'd but with my eyes.

The. Rather your eyes must with his judgment look.

Her. I do entreat your grace to pardon me.
I know not by what power I am made bold;
Nor how it may concern my modesty,
In such a presence here, to plead my thoughts:
But I beseech your grace, that I may know
The worst that may befal me in this case,
If I refuse to wed Demetrius.

The. Either to die the death [8], or to abjure
For ever the society of men.
Therefore, fair Hermia, question your desires,
Know of your youth [9], examine well your blood,
Whether if you yield not to your father's choice,
You can endure the livery of a nun;
For aye [1] to be in shady cloister mew'd,
To live a barren sister all your life,
Chanting faint hymns to the cold fruitless moon.
Thrice blessed they, that master so their blood,
To undergo such maiden pilgrimage:
But earthlier happy is the rose distill'd [2],
Than that, which, withering on the virgin thorn,
Grows, lives, and dies, in single blessedness.

Her. So will I grow, so live, so die, my Lord,
Ere I will yield my virgin patent up
Unto his lordship, whose unwished yoke [3]
My soul consents not to give sovereignty.

The.

---

[9] *Know of your youth*] Bring your youth to the question. Consider your youth. JOHNSON.

[1] *For aye*—] i. e. for ever. STEEVENS.

[2] *But earthlier happy is the rose distill'd*] Thus all the copies: yet *earthlier* is so harsh a word, and *earthlier happy* for *happier earthly*, a mode of speech so unusual, that I wonder none of the editors have proposed *earlier happy*. JOHNSON.

It has since been observed, that Mr. Pope did propose *earlier.* We might read, *earthly happier.* STEEVENS.

This is a thought in which Shakspeare seems to have much delighted. We meet with it again in his 5th, 6th, and 54th Sonnet. MALONE.

[3] — *whose unwished yoke,* &c.) I have adhered to the old copies in this passage. The editor of the second folio has rendered it—" to whose

The. Take time to pause: and, by the next new moon,
(The sealing-day betwixt my love and me,
For everlasting bond of fellowship,)
Upon that day either prepare to die,
For disobedience to your father's will;
Or else to wed Demetrius, as he would;
Or on Diana's altar to protest,
For aye, austerity and single life.

Dem. Relent, sweet Hermia;—And, Lysander, yield
Thy crazed title to my certain right.

Lys. You have her father's love, Demetrius;
Let me have Hermia's: do you marry him [4].

Ege. Scornful Lysander! true, he hath my love;
And what is mine, my love shall render him;
And she is mine; and all my right of her
I do estate unto Demetrius.

Lys. I am, my Lord, as well deriv'd as he,
As well possess'd; my love is more than his;
My fortunes every way as fairly rank'd,
If not with vantage, as Demetrius';
And, which is more than all these boasts can be,
I am belov'd of beauteous Hermia:
Why should not I then prosecute my right?
Demetrius, I'll avouch it to his head,
Made love to Nedar's daughter, Helena,
And won her soul; and she, sweet lady, dotes,
Devoutly dotes, dotes in idolatry,
Upon this spotted [5] and inconstant man.

The. I must confess, that I have heard so much,
And with Demetrius thought to have spoke thereof;
But, being over-full of self-affairs,
My mind did lose it.—But, Demetrius, come;
And come, Egeus; you shall go with me,—
I have some private schooling for you both.—
For you, fair Hermia, look you arm yourself
To fit your fancies to your father's will;
Or else the law of Athens yields you up

whose unwish'd yoke;" but this was a dangerous innovation, arising from the editor's ignorance of Shakspeare's phraseology. MALONE.

[4] *Let me have Hermia's: do you marry him*] I suspect that Shakspeare wrote:
"Let me have Hermia; do you marry him." TYRWHITT.

[5] —*spotted—*] As *spotless* is innocent, so *spotted* is wicked. JOHNSON.

(Which by no means we may extenuate)
To death, or to a vow of single life.—
Come, my Hippolita; What cheer, my love?—
Demetrius, and Egeus, go along;
I must employ you in some business
Against our nuptial; and confer with you
Of something nearly that concerns yourselves.

 Ege. With duty, and desire, we follow you.
    [*Exeunt* THES. HIP. EGE. DEM. *and Train.*
 Lys. How now, my love? Why is your cheek so pale?
How chance the roses there do fade so fast?
 Her. Belike, for want of rain; which I could well
Beteem them [6] from the tempest of mine eyes.
 Lys. Ah me! for aught that I could ever read,
Could ever hear by tale or history,
The course of true love never did run smooth [7]:
But, either it was different in blood;
 Her. O cross! too high to be enthrall'd to low [8]!
 Lys. Or else misgraffed, in respect of years;
 Her. O spight! too old to be engag'd to young!
 Lys. Or else it stood upon the choice of friends;
 Her. O hell! to choose love by another's eye!
 Lys. Or, if there were a sympathy in choice,
War, death, or sickness did lay siege to it;
Making it momentany [9] as a sound,

---

[6] *Beteem them*] Give them, bestow upon them. The word is used by Spenser.
  " So would I, said the enchanter, glad and fain
  " *Beteem* to you this sword, you to defend." JOHNSON.
Again, in *The Case is Altered; How! Ask Dollie and Millo*, 1604:
  " I could *beteem* her a better match."
I rather think that to *beteem* in this place signifies (as in the northern countries) to *pour out*; from *tœmmer*, Danish. STEEVENS.

[7] *The course of true love*, &c.] This passage seems to have been imitated by Milton. *Paradise Lost*, B. 10.—898, et seqq. MALONE.

[8] —*too high to be enthrall'd to low*!] The old copies read—*to love*. The emendation is Mr. Theobald's. It is fully supported, not only by the tenour of the preceding lines, but by a passage in our author's *Venus and Adonis*, in which the former predicts that the course of love never shall run smooth."
  " Sorrow on love hereafter shall attend,
  " Ne'er settled equally, *too high, or low*, &c." MALONE.

[9] *Making it momentany*—] Thus the quartos. The folio reads—*momentary*. MALONE.
Momentany is the old and proper word. JOHNSON.

Swift

Swift as a shadow, short as any dream;
Brief as the lightning in the coll,'d night [1],
That, in a spleen, unfolds both heaven and earth,
And ere a man hath power to say—Behold!
The jaws of darkness do devour it up:
So quick bright things come to confusion.

Her. If then true lovers have been ever cross'd,
It stands as an edict in destiny:
Then let us teach our trial patience,
Because it is a customary cross;
As due to love, as thoughts, and dreams, and sighs,
Wishes, and tears, poor fancy's followers [2].

Lys. A good persuasion; therefore, hear me, Hermia,
I have a widow aunt, a dowager
Of great revenue, and she hath no child:
From Athens is her house remote seven leagues;
And she respects me as her only son.
There, gentle Hermia, may I marry thee;
And to that place the sharp Athenian law
Cannot pursue us: If thou lov'st me then,
Steal forth thy father's house to-morrow-night:
And in the wood, a league without the town,
Where I did meet thee once with Helena,
To do observance to a morn of May,
There will I stay for thee.

---

[1] *Brief as the lightning in the* colly'd *night,*
That, in a spleen, unfolds both heaven and earth] Though the word *spleen* be here employed oddly enough, yet I believe it right. Shakspeare, always hurried on by the grandeur and multitude of his ideas, assumes every now and then, an uncommon licence in the use of his words. Particularly in complex moral modes it is usual with him to employ one, only to express a very few *ideas* of that number of which it is composed. Thus wanting here to express the ideas—of a sudden, or —*in a trice,* he uses the word *spleen*; which, partially considered, signifying a hasty sudden fit, is enough for him, and he never troubles himself about the further or fuller signification of the word. Here, he uses the word *spleen* for a *sudden hasty fit*; so just the contrary, in the *Two Gentlemen of Verona,* he uses *sudden* for *splenetic:*—" sudden quips." And it must be owned this sort of conversation adds a force to the diction.
WARBURTON.

— *the* colly'd *night,*] colly'd, i. e. black, smutted with coal, a word still used in the midland counties. STEEVENS.

[2] — *poor* fancy's *followers.*] *Fancy* here, and in many other places in these plays, signifies *love.* MALONE.

Her.

Her. My good Lysander!
I swear to thee, by Cupid's strongest bow;
By his best arrow with the golden head;
By the simplicity of Venus' doves;
By that which knitteth souls, and prospers loves;
And by that fire which burn'd the Carthage queen³,
When the false Trojan under sail was seen;
By all the vows that ever men have broke,
In number more than ever women spoke;—
In that same place thou hast appointed me,
To-morrow truly will I meet with thee.

Lys. Keep promise, love: Look, here comes Helena.

Enter HELENA.

Her. God speed, fair Helena! Whither away?
Hel. Call you me fair? that fair again unsay.
Demetrius loves your fair⁴. O happy fair!
Your eyes are lode-stars⁵! and your tongue's sweet air
More tuneable than lark to shepherd's ear,
When wheat is green, when haw-thorn buds appear.
Sickness is catching; O, were favour so⁶!

---

³ — *by that fire that burn'd the Carthage queen*] Shakspeare had forgot that Theseus performed his exploits before the Trojan war, and consequently long before the death of Dido. STEEVENS.

⁴ — *your fair:*] *Fair* is used again as a substantive in the *Comedy of Errors*:

"——— My decayed *fair*,
"A sunny look of his would soon repair."

See p. 15. n. 6. STEEVENS.

⁵ *Your eyes are lode-stars;*] This was a compliment not unfrequent among the old poets. The lode-star is the *leading* or guiding star, that is, the pole-star. The magnet is, for the same reason, called the *lode-stone*, either because it leads iron, or because it guides the sailor. Milton has the same thought in *L'Allegro:*

"*Tow'rs and battlements he sees*
"*Bosom'd high in tufted trees,*
"*Where perhaps some beauty lies,*
"*The cynosure of neigh'ring eyes.*"

Davies calls Elizabeth, "*lode-stone* to hearts and *lode-stars* to all eyes." JOHNSON.

⁶ — *O, were favour so!*] *Favour* is *feature*, *countenance*. So, in *Twelfth-Night*, Act ii. sc. iv:

"——— thine eye
"Hath stay'd upon some *favour* that it loves." STEEVENS.

Your

Your words I'd catch[7], fair Hermia, ere I go;
My ear should catch your voice, my eye your eye,
My tongue should catch your tongue's sweet melody.
Were the world mine, Demetrius being bated,
The rest I'll give to be to you translated[8].
O, teach me how you look; and with what art
You sway the motion of Demetrius' heart.

Her. I frown upon him, yet he loves me still.
Hel. O, that your frowns would teach my smiles such skill!
Her. I give him curses, yet he gives me love.
Hel. O, that my prayers could such affection move!
Her. The more I hate, the more he follows me.
Hel. The more I love, the more he hateth me.
Her. His folly, Helena, is no fault of mine.
Hel. None, but your beauty; 'would that fault were mine!
Her. Take comfort; he no more shall see my face;
Lysander and myself will fly this place.—
Before the time I did Lysander see[9],
Seem'd Athens as a paradise to me:
O then, what graces in my love do dwell,
That he hath turn'd a heaven unto a hell!

Lys. Helen to you our minds we will unfold:
To-morrow night when Phœbe doth behold
Her silver visage in the watry glass,
Decking with liquid pearl the bladed grass,
(A time that lovers' flights doth still conceal,)
Through Athens' gates have we devis'd to steal.

---

[7] *Your words I'd catch—*] The old copies read—I *catch.* The emendation was made by the editor of the second folio. Sir Thomas Hanmer reads—Yours *would* I catch; in which he has been followed by the subsequent editors. As the old reading *(words)* is intelligible, I have adhered to the ancient copies. MALONE.

[8] —— *to be to you* translated.] To *translate,* in our author, sometimes signifies to *change,* to *transform.* So, in *Timon:*

"—— to present slaves and servants
"*Translates* his rivals." STEEVENS.

[9] Perhaps every reader may not discover the propriety of these lines. Hermia is willing to comfort Helena, and to avoid all appearance of triumph over her. She therefore bids her not to consider the power of pleasing, as an advantage to be much envied or much desired, since Hermia, whom she considers as possessing it in the supreme degree, has found no other effect of it than the loss of happiness. JOHNSON.

Her.

Her. And in the wood where often you and I
Upon faint primrose-beds were wont to lie,
Emptying our bosoms of their counsel sweet¹;
There my Lysander and myself shall meet:
And thence, from Athens, turn away our eyes,
To seek new friends and stranger companies.
Farewel, sweet play-fellow; pray thou for us,
And good luck grant thee thy Demetrius!—
Keep word, Lysander: we must starve our sight
From lovers' food, 'till morrow deep midnight ².

[*Exit* HERMIA.

Lys. I will, my Hermia.—Helena, adieu:
As you on him, Demetrius dote on you! [*Exit* LYS.

Hel. How happy some, o'er other some, can be!
Through Athens I am thought as fair as she.
But what of that? Demetrius thinks not so;
He will not know what all but he do know.
And as he errs, doting on Hermia's eyes,
So I, admiring of his qualities.

---

¹ *Emptying our bosoms of their counsel sweet;*] That is, emptying our bosoms of those secrets upon which we were wont to consult each other with so sweet a satisfaction. HEATH.

The old copies read—*farewell'd*; and in the line next but one *strange companions*. Both emendations were made by Mr. Theobald, who supports them by observing that " this whole scene is in rhime. *Sweet* was easily corrupted into *farewell'd*, because that made an antithesis to *emptying*; and " strange companions" our editors thought was plain English, but " *stranger companies*" a little quaint and unintelligible." Our author very often uses the substantive, *stranger*, adjectively, and *companies*, to signify *companions*. So, in *K. Richard II.* Act i.:
" To tread the *stranger* paths of banishment."
And in *King Henry V*:
" His *companies* unletter'd, rude, and shallow."

The latter of Mr. Theobald's emendations is likewise supported by Stowe's *Annales*, p. 991, edit. 1615: " The prince himself was faine to get upon the high altar, to girt his aforesaid *companies* with the order of knighthood." Mr. Heath observes, that our author seems to have had the following passage in the 55th Psalm, (v. 14, 15.) in his thoughts: " But it was even thou, my companion, my guide, and mine own familiar friend. We took *sweet counsel* together, and walked in the house of God as friends." MALONE.

² —— *when Phœbe doth behold*, &c.
—— *deep midnight.*] Shakspeare has a little forgotten himself. It appears from page 299, that to-morrow night would be within three nights of the new moon, when there is no moonshine at all, much less at deep midnight. The same oversight occurs in Act iii. sc. i.

BLACKSTONE.

Things

Things base and vile, holding no quantity³,
Love can transpose to form and dignity.
Love looks not with the eyes, but with the mind;
And therefore is wing'd Cupid painted blind:
Nor hath love's mind of any judgment taste;
Wings, and no eyes, figure unheedy haste:
And therefore is love said to be a child,
Because in choice he is so oft beguil'd.
As waggish boys in game⁴ themselves forswear,
So the boy love is perjur'd every where:
For ere Demetrius look'd on Hermia's eyne⁵,
He hail'd down oaths, that he was only mine;
And when this hail some heat from Hermia felt,
So he dissolv'd, and showers of oaths did melt.
I will go tell him of fair Hermia's flight:
Then to the wood will he, to-morrow-night,
Pursue her; and for this intelligence
If I have thanks, it is a dear expence:
But herein mean I to enrich my pain,
To have his sight thither, and back again. [*Exit.*

SCENE II.

The same. A Room in a Cottage.

Enter SNUG, BOTTOM, FLUTE, SNOUT, QUINCE, *and* STARVELING⁶.

Quin. Is all our company here?

---

³ — *as quantity*,] *Quality* seems a word more suitable to the sense than *quantity*, but either may serve. JOHNSON.

⁴ — *in game*;] *Game* here signifies not contentious play, but *sport, jest*. So Spenser: " 'twixt earnest and 'twixt game." JOHNSON.

⁵ — *Hermia's* eyne,] This plural is common both in Chaucer and Spenser. STEEVENS.

⁶ In this scene Shakspeare takes advantage of his knowledge of the theatre, to ridicule the prejudices and competitions of the players. Bottom, who is generally acknowledged the principal actor, declares his inclination to be for a tyrant, for a part of fury, tumult and noise, such as every young man pants to perform when he first steps upon the stage. The same Bottom, who seems bred in a tiring-room, has another histrionical passion. He is for engrossing every part, and would exclude his inferiors from all possibility of distinction. He is therefore desirous to play Pyramus, Thisbe, and the Lyon, at the same time. JOHNSON.

Ett.

Bot. You were best to call them generally, man by man, according to the scrip [7].

Quin. Here is the scroll of every man's name, which is thought fit, through all Athens, to play in our interlude before the Duke and Dutchess, on his wedding-day at night.

Bot. First, good Peter Quince, say what the play treats on; then read the names of the actors; and so grow to a point [8].

Quin. Marry, our play is—The most lamentable comedy, and most cruel death of Pyramus and Thisby [9].

Bot. A very good piece of work, I assure you, and a merry [1].—Now, good Peter Quince, call forth your actors by the scroll: Masters, spread yourselves.

Quin. Answer, as I call you.—Nick Bottom the weaver.

Bot. Ready: Name what part I am for, and proceed.

Quin. You, Nick Bottom, are set down for Pyramus.

Bot. What is Pyramus? a lover, or a tyrant?

Quin. A lover, that kills himself most gallantly for love.

Bot. That will ask some tears in the true performing of it: If I do it, let the audience look to their eyes; I will move storms, I will condole in some measure. To the rest:— Yet my chief humour is for a tyrant: I could play Ercles rarely [2], or a part to tear a cat in [3], to make all split [3].

" The

---

[7] *—the scrip.*] A *scrip.* Fr. *script*, now written *ecrit.* STEEVENS.

[8] *—grow to a point.*] So, in *the Arraignment of Paris*, 1584:

"Our reasons will be infinite, I trow,

"Unless unto some other point we grow." STEEVENS.

[9] *The most lamentable comedy,* &c.] This is very probably a burlesque on the title-page of Cambyses: "A lamentable tragedie, mixed full of pleasant mirth, containing, *The Life of Cambyses, King of Persia,* &c." By Thomas Preston, bl. l. no date. On the registers of the stationers' Company however appears " the duke of *Pyramus* and *Thisbye*, 1562." Perhaps Shakspeare copied some part of his interlude from it. STEEV.

A poem entitled *Pyramus and Thisbe* by Dr. Gale, was published in 4to. in 1597; but this, I believe, was posterior to the *Midsummer-Night's Dream.* MALONE.

[1] *A very good piece of work—and a merry.*] This is designed as a ridicule on the titles of our ancient moralities and interludes. Thus Skelton's *Magnificence* is called " a goodly interlude and a merry." STEEVENS.

[2] *I could play Ercles rarely, or a part to tear a cat in.*] In the old comedy of the *Roaring Girl,* 1611, there is a character called *Tear-cat,* who says, " I am called, by those who have seen my valour, *Tear-cat.*" In an anonymous piece called *Histriomastix,* or *The Player whipt,* 1610, in six acts, a parcel of soldiers drag a company of players on the stage, and

"The raging rocks,
"And shivering shocks,
"Shall break the locks
"Of prison-gates;
"And Phibbus' car
"Shall shine from far,
"And make and mar
"The foolish fates."

This was lofty!—Now name the rest of the players.—This is Ercles' vein, a tyrant's vein; a lover is more condoling.

Quin. Francis Flute, the bellows-mender [2].
Flu. Here, Peter Quince.
Quin. You must take Thisby on you.
Flu. What is Thisby? a wandering knight?
Quin. It is the Lady that Pyramus must love.
Flu. Nay, faith, let me not play a woman; I have a beard coming.
Quin. That's all one; you shall play it in a mask, and you may speak as small as you will [4].

Bot.

and the captain says, "Sirrah, this is you that would rend and *tear a cat* upon a stage, &c." Again, in *The isle of Gulls*, a comedy by J. Day, 1606: "I had rather hear two such jests, than a whole play of such *Tearcat* thunder-claps." STEEVENS.

[2] —*to make all split.*] This is to be connected with the previous part of the speech; not with the subsequent rhymes. It was the description of a bully. In the second act of the *Scornful Lady*, we meet with "two *roaring boys* of Rome, that *made all split*." FARMER.

The same expression is used by Chapman in his *Widow's Tears*, 1612. MALONE.

[3] —*the bellows-mender.*] In Ben Jonson's masque of *Pan's Anniversary*, &c. a man of the same profession is introduced. I have been told that a *bellows-mender* was one who had the care of *organs, regals*, &c. STEEVENS.

[4] —*as small as you will.*] This passage shews how the want of women on the old stage was supplied. If they had not a young man who could perform the part with a face that might pass for feminine, the character was acted in a mask, which was at that time a part of a lady's dress so much in use that it did not give any unusual appearance to the scene, and he that could modulate his voice in a female tone might play the woman very successfully. It is observed in Down's *Memoirs of the Playhouse*, that one of these counterfeit heroines moved the passions more strongly than the women that have since been brought upon the stage. Some of the catastrophes of the old comedies, which make lovers marry the wrong women, are, by recollection of the common use of masks, brought nearer to probability. JOHNSON.

Pyram,

Bot. An I may hide my face, let me play Thisby too: I'll speak in a monstrous little voice;—*Thisne, Thisne—Ah, Pyramus, my lover dear; thy Thisby dear! and lady dear!*

Quin. No, no; you must play Pyramus, and, Flute, you Thisby.

Bot. Well, proceed.

Quin. Robin Starveling, the tailor.

Star. Here, Peter Quince.

Quin. Robin Starveling, you must play Thisby's mother⁵. —Tom Snout, the tinker.

Snout. Here, Peter Quince.

Quin. You, Pyramus's father; myself, Thisby's father; —Snug, the joiner, you, the lion's part:—and, I hope, here is a play fitted.

Snug. Have you the lion's part written? pray you, if it be, give it me, for I am slow of study⁶.

Quin. You may do it extempore, for it is nothing but roaring.

Bot. Let me play the lion too: I will roar, that I will do any man's heart good to hear me; I will roar, that I will make the Duke say, *Let him roar again, let him roar again.*

Quin. An you should do it too terribly, you would fright the Dutchess and the ladies, that they would shriek; and that were enough to hang us all.

All. That would hang us every mother's son.

Bot. I grant you, friends, if that you should fright the ladies out of their wits, they would have no more discretion but to hang us: but I will aggravate my voice so, that I will roar you as gently as any sucking dove; I will roar you an 'twere any nightingale.

Quin. You can play no part but Pyramus: for Pyramus

Prynne, in his *Histriomastix*, exclaims with great vehemence through several pages, because a woman acted a part in a play at Black-fryars in the year 1628. STEEVENS.

⁵ —*you must play Thisby's mother.*] There seems a double forgetfulness of our poet, in relation to the characters of this interlude. The father and mother of Thisbe, and the father of Pyramus, are here mentioned, who do not appear at all in the interlude; but Wall and Moonshine are both employed in it, of whom there is not the least notice taken here. THEOBALD.

Theobald is wrong in this last particular. The introduction of *Wall* and *Moonshine* was an after-thought. See Act iii. sc. i. It may be observed, however, that no part of what is rehearsed is afterwards repeated, when the piece is acted before Theseus. STEEVENS.

is a sweet-faced man; a proper man, as one shall see in a summer's-day; a most lovely, gentleman-like man; therefore you must needs play Pyramus.

Bot. Well, I will undertake it. What beard were I best to play it in?

Quin. Why, what you will.

Bot. I will discharge it in either your straw-colour'd beard, your orange-tawny beard, your purple-in-grain beard, or your French crown-colour beard, your perfect yellow [7].

Quin. Some of your French crowns [8] have no hair at all, and then you will play barefaced.—But, masters, here are your parts: and I am to entreat you, request you, and desire you, to con them by to-morrow night; and meet me in the palace wood a mile without the town, by moon-light; there will we rehearse: for if we meet in the city, we shall be dog'd with company, and our devices known. In the mean time, I will draw a bill of properties [9], such as our play wants. I pray you, fail me not.

Bot. We will meet; and there we may rehearse more obscenely, and courageously. Take pains; be perfect; adieu.

Quin. At the Duke's oak we meet.

Bot. Enough; hold, or cut bow-strings [1]. [*Exeunt.*

ACT

---

[6] —*slow of study.*] *Study* is still the cant term used in a theatre for getting any nonsense by rote. Hamlet asks the player if he can "*study*" a speech. STEEVENS.

[7] —*your perfect yellow.*] Here Bottom again discovers a true genius for the stage by his solicitude for propriety of dress, and his deliberation which beard to chuse among many beards, all unnatural.
JOHNSON.

It was the custom formerly to wear coloured beards. So in the old comedy of *Ram-Alley*, 1611:

"What *colour'd beard* comes next by the window?
"A black man's, I think;
"I think a *red*, for that is most in fashion." STEEVENS.

[8] —*French crowns,* &c.] That is, a head from which the hair has fallen in one of the last stages of the *lues venerea*, called the *corona veneris*. To this our poet has frequent allusions. STEEVENS.

[9] —*properties.*] *Properties* are whatever little articles are wanted in a play- for the actors, according to their respective parts, dresses and scenes excepted. The person who delivers them out is to this day called the *property-man*. STEEVENS.

[1] —*Hold, or cut bow-strings.*] To meet, *whether bow-strings hold or are cut,* is to meet in all events. To cut the bowstring, when bows were in use, was probably a common practice of those who bore enmity

ACT V. SCENE I.

A Wood near Athens.

Enter a FAIRY *at one Door, and* PUCK *at another.*

Puck. How now spirit! whither wander you?
Fai. Over hill, over dale [1],
 Thorough bush, thorough briar,
Over park, over pale,
 Thorough flood, thorough fire,
I do wander every where,
Swifter than the moones sphere [3];

[1] to the archer. "He hath twice or thrice cut Cupid's bow-string, (says Don Pedro in *Much Ado About Nothing*,) and the little hangman dare not shoot at him." MALONE.
Hold, or cut cod-piece point, is a proverb to be found in Ray's Collection, p. 57. edit. 1737. COLLINS.

[2] *Over hill, over dale*, &c.] So Drayton in his *Court of Fairy*;
 "Thorough brake, thorough brier,
 " Thorough muck, thorough mire,
 " Thorough water, thorough fire." JOHNSON.

[3] — *the moones sphere*;] Unless we suppose this to be the Saxon genitive case, (as it is here printed,) the metre will be defective. So, in a letter from Gabriel Harvey to Spenser, 1580: "Have we not *God bys wrath*, for Goddes wrath, and a thousand of the same stampe, wherein the corrupt orthography in the moste, hath been the sole or principal cause of corrupte prosodye in over-many?" STEEVENS.

[4] *To dew her orbs upon the green*:] The orbs here mentioned are the circles supposed to be made by the fairies on the ground, whose verdure proceeds from the fairy's care to water them. Thus Drayton:
 "They in their courses make that round,
 " In meadows and in marshes found,
 " Of them so called the fairy ground." JOHNSON.

Thus in *Olaus Magnus de Gentibus Septentrionalibus*: "— similes illis spectris, quæ in multis locis, præsertim nocturno tempore, suum saltatorium orbem cum omnium musarum concentu versare solent." It appears from the same author, that these dancers always patched up the grass, and therefore it is properly made the office of *Puck* to refresh it.
STEEVENS.

And

And I serve the fairy queen,
To dew her orbs⁴ upon the green:
The cowslips tall her pensioners be⁵;
In their gold coats spots you see⁶;
Those be rubies, fairy favours,
In those freckles live their favours:
I must go seek some dew-drops here,
And hang a pearl in every cowslip's ear⁷.
Farewel, thou lob of spirits⁸, I'll be gone;
Our queen and all her elves come here anon.

Puck. The King doth keep his revels here to-night;
Take heed, the Queen come not within his sight.
For Oberon is passing fell and wrath,
Because that she, as her attendant, hath
A lovely boy, stol'n from an Indian king;
She never had so sweet a changeling⁹;
And jealous Oberon would have the child
Knight of his train, to trace the forests wild:

---

⁵ *The cowslips tall her* pensioners *be;*] i. e. her guards. The golden-coated cowslips were chosen by the author as *pensioners* to the Fairy Queen, the dress of the Band of Gentlemen Pensioners being in the time of Queen Elizabeth very splendid, and (as we learn from Osborne) the *tallest* and handsomest men being generally chosen by her for that office. The allusion was pointed out by Mr. Steevens. MALONE.

The cowslip was a favourite among the Fairies. JOHNSON.

⁶ *In their gold coats spots you see;*] Shakspeare, in *Cymbeline*, refers to the same red spots:

"A mole cinque-spotted, like the crimson drops
"I' the bottom of a cowslip." PERCY.

⁷ *And hang a pearl in every cowslip's ear.*] The same thought occurs in an old comedy call'd the *Wisdom of Doctor Dodypoll*, 1600. An enchanter says:

"'Twas I that led you through the painted meads
"Where the light fairies danc'd upon the flowers,
"Hanging on every leaf an orient pearl." STEEVENS.

⁸ — *lob of spirits.*] Lob, lubber, looby, lobcock, all denote both inactivity of body and dullness of mind. JOHNSON.

So, in the *Knight of the Burning Pestle*, by B. and Fletcher: "There is a pretty tale of a witch that had the devil's mark about her, that had a giant to her son, that was called *Lob-lye-by-the-fire*." This being seems to be of kin to the *lubbar-fiend* of Milton, as Mr. Warton has remarked in his *Observations on the Faery Queen.* STEEVENS.

⁹ — *changeling;*] Changeling is commonly used for the child supposed to be left by the fairies, but here for the child taken away. JOHNSON.

P 2

But

But she, perforce, withholds the loved boy,
Crowns him with flowers, and makes him all her joy:
And now they never meet in grove, or green,
By fountain clear, or spangled star-light sheen [1],
But they do square [2]; that all their elves, for fear,
Creep into acorn cups, and hide them there.

Fai. Either I mistake your shape and making quite,
Or else you are that shrewd and knavish sprite,
Call'd Robin Good-fellow [3]: are you not he,
That fright [4] the maidens of the villagery;
Skim milk; and sometimes labour in the quern [5],
And bootless make the breathless housewife churn;

And

---

[1] *—sheen,*] Shining, bright, gay. JOHNSON.

[2] *But they do square;*] To *square* here is to quarrel. The French word *contrecarrer* has the same import. JOHNSON.

So, in *Jack Drum's Entertainment*, 1601:
" — pray let me go, for he'll begin to *square*." STEEVENS.

It is somewhat whimsical, that the glaziers use the words *square* and *quarrel* as synonymous terms, for a pane of glass. BLACKSTONE.

[3] *— Robin Goodfellow;*] This account of Robin Good-fellow corresponds, in every article, with that given of him in *Harsnet's Declaration*, ch. xx. p. 134: " And if that the bowle of curds and creame were not duly set out for Robin Good-fellow, the frier, and Sisse, the dairy-maid, why then either the pottage was burnt to next day in the pot, or the cheeses would not curdle, or the butter would not come, or the ale in the fat never would have good head. But if a Peeter-penny or an house-egge were behind, or a patch of tythe unpaid—then 'ware — of hull-beggars, spirits, &c." He is mentioned by Cartwright (*Ordinary*, Act iii. sc. i.) as a spirit particularly fond of disconcerting and disturbing domestic peace and œconomy. T. WARTON.

Reginald Scot gives the same account of this frolicsome spirit, in his *Discovery of Witchcraft*, Lond. 1588. 4to. p. 66. " Your grandames maids, were wont to set a bowl of milk for him, for his pains in grinding of malt and mustard, and sweeping the house at midnight—this white bread and bread and milk, was his standing fee." STEEVENS.

[4] *That fright—*] The old copies read *frights*; and in grammatical propriety, I believe, this verb, as well as those that follow, should agree with the personal pronoun *he*, rather than with *you*. If so, our author ought to have written—*frights, skims, labours, makes*, and *misleads*. The other, however, being the more common usage, and that which he has preferred, I have corrected the former word. MALONE.

[5] *Skim milk; and sometimes labour in the quern,*
And bootless make the breathless housewife churn;] The sense of these lines is confused. *Are not you he,* says the fairy, *that fright the country girls, that skim milk, work in the hand-mill, and make the tired dairy-woman churn without effect?* The mention of the mill seems out of place, for she is not now telling the good but the evil that he does. JOHNSON.

Perhaps

And sometime make the drink to bear no barm⁶;
Mislead night-wanderers, laughing at their harm?
Those that Hobgoblin call you, and sweet Puck⁷,
You do their work, and they shall have good luck:
Are not you he?

Puck. Thou speak'st aright⁸;
I am that merry wanderer of the night.

> Perhaps the construction is—and sometimes make the breathless housewife labour in the quern, and bootless churn. This would obviate the objection made by Dr. Johnson, viz. that "the mention of the mill is out of place, for she is not now telling the good but the evil that he does." MALONE.
>
> A *Quern* is a hand-mill, kuerna, *wola*. Islandic. STEEVENS.
>
> ⁶ — no barm;] *Barme* is a name for *yeast*, yet used in our midland countries, and universally in Ireland. STEEVENS.
>
> ⁷ *Those that Hobgoblin call you, and sweet Puck,* &c.] To those traditionary opinions Milton has reference in *L'Allegro*. A like account of Puck is given by Drayton, in his *Nymphidia*.—Whether Drayton or Shakspeare wrote first, I cannot discover. JOHNSON.
>
> The editor of the *Canterbury Tales of Chaucer,* in 4 vols 8vo. 1775, has incontrovertibly proved Drayton to have been the follower of Shakspeare; for, says he, "*Don Quixote* (which was not published till 1605.) is cited in the *Nymphidia,* whereas we have an edition of the *Midsummer-Night's Dream* in 1600." STEEVENS.
>
> *Don Quixote,* though published in Spain in 1605, was probably little known in England till Shelton's translation appeared in 1612. Drayton's poem was, I have no doubt, subsequent to that year. The earliest edition of it that I have seen, was printed 1619. MALONE.
>
> — sweet Puck,] The epithet is by no means superfluous; as *Puck* alone was far from being an endearing appellation. It signified nothing better than *fiend* or *devil*. So, the author of *Pierce Ploughman* puts *the puck for the devil.* fol. lxxxi. b. v. penult. See also fol. lxvii v. 15. "*nane belle powke.*"
>
> It seems to have been an old Gothic word. *Puke, puken*; Sathanas. *Gudm. And. Lexicon. Island.* TYRWHITT.
>
> So, in Spenser's *Epithalamion,* 1595:
> "Ne let house-fyres, nor lightning's helpelesse harme,
> "Ne let the *pouke,* nor other evil spright,
> "Ne let mischievous witches with their charms,
> "Ne let hobgoblins, &c." STEEVENS.
>
> ⁸ *Puck. Thou speak'st aright;*] I would fill up the verse which I suppose the author left complete: *I am,* thou speak'st aright.
>
> It seems that in the Fairy mythology Puck, or Hobgoblin, was the trusty servant of Oberon, and always employed to watch or detect the intrigues of Queen Mab, called by Shakspeare Titania. For in Drayton's *Nymphidia,* the same fairies are engaged in the same business. Mab has an amour with Pigwiggen; Oberon being jealous, sends Hobgoblin to catch them, and one of Mab's nymphs opposes him by a spell.
>   JOHNSON.

I jest to Oberon, and make him smile,
When I a fat and bean-fed horse beguile,
Neighing in likeness of a filly foal:
And sometime lurk I in a gossip's bowl,
In very likeness of a roasted crab [9];
And, when she drinks, against her lips I bob,
And on her wither'd dew-lap pour the ale.
The wisest aunt [1], telling the saddest tale,
Sometime for three-foot stool mistaketh me;
Then slip I from her bum, down topples she,
And *tailor* cries [2], and falls into a cough;
And then the whole quire hold their hips, and loffe [3];
And waxen [4] in their mirth, and neeze, and swear
A merrier hour was never wasted there.—
But room, Faery [5], here comes Oberon.

Fai. And here my mistress:—'Would that he were gone!

Enter OBERON [6], *at one door, with his train, and* TITANIA [7],
at another, with hers.

Obe. Ill met by moon-light, proud Titania.

[9] — *a roasted crab*,] i. e. a crab apple. So again in *Love's Labour's Lost*:
"When roasted crabs hiss in the bowl." MALONE.

[1] *The wisest aunt*,] Though *aunt* in many ancient English books means a *procuress*, I believe it here only signifies an old woman in general. MALONE.

[2] *And tailor cries*,] The custom of crying *tailor* at a sudden fall backwards, I think I remember to have observed. He that slips beside his chair, falls as a taylor squats upon his board. The Oxford editor, and Dr. Warburton after him, read *and rails* or *cries*, plausibly, but I believe not rightly. Besides, the trick of the fairy is represented as producing rather merriment than anger. JOHNSON.
This phrase perhaps originated in a pun. *Your tail is now on the ground.* See Camden's Remaines, 1614. PROVERBS. "Between two stools the tayle goeth to the ground. MALONE.

[3] — *hold their hips, and loffe*;)
"And Laughter holding both his sides." *Milton.* STEEVENS.

[4] *And waxen*,] And *encrease*, as the *moon waxes*. JOHNSON.

[5] *But room*, Faery.] The word Fairy or Faery, was sometimes of three syllables, as often in Spenser. JOHNSON.

[6] *Enter* Oberon,] The judicious editor of the *Canterbury Tales* of Chaucer, in his *Introductory Discourse*, (See vol. iv. p. 161,) observes, that " *Pluto* and *Proserpina* in the *Merchant's Tale*, appear to have been the true progenitors of Shakspeare's *Oberon* and *Titania*. STEEVENS.

[7] *Titania*.] As to the *Fairy Queen*, (says Mr. Warton in his *Observations on Spenser*,) considered apart from the race of fairies, the notion of such an imaginary personage was very common. Chaucer, in his *Rime of Sir Thopas*, mentions her, together with a Fairy land. STEEVENS.

Tita.

Tita. What, jealous Oberon? Fairy, skip hence;
I have forsworn his bed and company.
　Obe. Tarry, rash wanton; Am not I thy lord?
　Tita. Then I must be thy lady: But I know
When thou hast stol'n away from fairy land,
And in the shape of Corin sate all day,
Playing on pipes of corn, and versing love
To amorous Phillida. Why art thou here,
Come from the farthest steep of India?
But that, forsooth, the bouncing Amazon,
Your buskin'd mistress, and your warrior love,
To Theseus must be wedded; and you come
To give their bed joy and prosperity.
　Ob. How canst thou thus, for shame, Titania,
Glance at my credit with Hippolita,
Knowing I know thy love to Theseus?
Didst thou not lead him through the glimmering night [8]
From Perigenia, whom he ravished [9]?
And make him with fair Ægle break his faith,
With Ariadne, and Antiopa?
　Tita. These are the forgeries of jealousy:
And never, since the middle summer's spring [1],
Met we on hill, in dale, forest, or mead,
By paved fountain [2], or by rushy brook,
Or on the beached margent [3] of the sea,

---

[8] *— through the* glimmering *night*] The *glimmering night* is the night faintly illuminated by stars. In *Macbeth* our author says,
　"The west yet *glimmers* with some streaks of day." STEEV.

[9] *From* Perigenia, *whom he ravished?*] In North's translation of Plutarch (Life of Theseus) this lady is called *Perigouna.* The alteration was probably intentional, for the sake of harmony. Her real name was *Perigune.* MALONE.

[1] *And never, since the middle summer's* spring, &c.] By the *middle summer's spring,* our author seems to mean the *beginning of middle* or *mid* summer. *Spring* for *beginning* he uses again; *Henry IV.* P. ii.
　"As flaws congealed in the spring *of day.*" STEEVENS.
So Holinshed, p. 474:—" the morowe after about the *spring* of the daie"—. MALONE.

[2] *paved fountain;*] A fountain laid round the edge with stone. JOHNS.
Perhaps *paved* at the bottom So, Lord Bacon in his *Essay on Gardens:* " As for the other kind of *fountains,* which we may call a bathing-pool, it may admit much curiosity and beauty. ... As that the bottom be finely *paved.* ... the *sides* likewise, &c." STEEVENS.

[3] *Or on the beached margent*—] The old copies read—*Or in.* Corrected by Mr. Pope. MALONE.

To dance our ringlets to the whistling wind,
But with thy brawls thou hast disturb'd our sport.
Therefore the winds, piping to us in vain⁴,
As in revenge have suck'd up from the sea
Contagious fogs; which falling in the land,
Have every pelting river⁵ made so proud,
That they have overborne their continents⁶:
The ox hath therefore stretch'd his yoke in vain,
The ploughman lost his sweat; and the green corn
Hath rotted, ere his youth attain'd a beard⁷:
The fold stands empty in the drowned field,
And crows are fatted with the murrain flock⁸;
The nine-men's morris is fill'd up with mud⁹;

And

⁴ — *the winds, piping*] So, Milton:
   "*While rocking* winds *are piping loud.*" JOHNSON.

⁵ — *pelting river*] Thus the quarto: the folio reads *petty*. Shakspeare has in *Lear* the same word—*low pelting farms*. The meaning is, I think, *despicable, mean, forry, wretched*; but as it is a word without any reasonable etymology, I should be glad to dismiss it for *petty*; yet it is undoubtedly right. We have "*petty pelting officer* in *Measure for Measure*." JOHNSON.

This word is always used as a term of contempt. So, in Gascoigne's *Glass of Government*, 1575: "Doway is a *pelting* town, pack'd full of poor scholars." STEEVENS.

⁶ — *overborne their continents:*] Borne down the banks that contained them. So, in *Lear*:
   "——— *close pent-up guilts,*
   "*Rive your concealing continents!*" JOHNSON.

⁷ ——— *and the green corn*
   Hath rotted, ere his youth attain'd a beard:] So, in our author's 12th Sonnet:
   "And summer's *green* all girded up in *sheaves,*
   "Borne on the bier with white and bristly *beard.*" MALONE.

⁸ — *murrain flock:*] The *murrain* is the plague in cattle. It is here used by Shakspeare as an adjective; as a substantive by others.
   STEEVENS.

⁹ *The nine men's morris is fill'd up with mud;*] In that part of Warwickshire where Shakspeare was educated, and the neighbouring parts of Northamptonshire, the shepherds and other boys dig up the turf with their knives to represent a sort of imperfect chess-board. It consists of a square, sometimes only a foot diameter, sometimes three or four yards. Within this is another square, every side of which is parallel to the external square, and these squares are joined by lines drawn from each corner of both squares, and the middle of each line. One party, or player, has wooden pegs, the other stones, which they move in such a manner as to take up each other's men as they are called, and the area of the inner square is called the Pound, in which the men taken up are

And the quaint mazes in the wanton green,
For lack of tread, are undistinguishable:
The human mortals [1] want their winter here [2];
No night is now with hymn or carol blest [3];—
Therefore the moon, the governess of floods [4],

Pale

are impounded. These figures are by the country people called *Nine Men's Morris*, or *Merrils*, and are so called, because each party has nine men. These figures are always cut upon the green turf or leys, as they are called, or upon the grass at the end of ploughed lands, and in rainy seasons never fail to be *choaked up with mud*. JAMES.

Nine men's morris is a game still play'd by the shepherds, cow-keepers, &c. in the midland counties, as follows:

A figure is made on the ground, by cutting out the turf; and two persons take each nine stones, which they place by turns in the angles, and afterwards move alternately, as at chess or draughts. He who can place three in a straight line, may then take off any one of his adversary's, where he pleases, till one, having lost all his men, loses the game.
—ALCHORNE.

In Cotgrave's *Dictionary*, under the article *Merelles*, is the following explanation. "Le Jeu des Merelles. The boyish game called Merils, or fivepenny morris; played here most commonly with stones, but in France with pawns, or men made on purpose, and termed *merelles*."
TOLLET.

The foregoing explanation is probably the true one. Some, however, have thought that "the nine men's morris" here means the ground marked out for a morris dance performed by nine persons. MALONE.

[1] *The human mortals.*] Shakspeare might have employed this epithet, which, at first sight, appears redundant, to mark the difference between *men* and *fairies*. Fairies were not *human*, but they were yet *subject to mortality*. STEEVENS.

See the *Fairy Queen*, B. ii. c. 10; and Warton's OBSERVATIONS on Spenser, vol i. p 55. REED.

[2] —*their winter here*;] *Here*, in this country.—I once inclined to receive the emendation proposed by Mr. Theobald, and adopted by Sir T. Hanmer—their winter *cheer*; but perhaps alteration is unnecessary. "Their winter" may mean those sports with which country people are wont to beguile a winter's evening, at the season of Christmas, which it appears from the next line was particularly in our author's contemplation:

"The very *winter* nights restore the *Christmas games*.
"And now the season doth invite to banquet townish dames."

Romeus and Juliet, 1562. MALONE.

[3] *No night is now with hymn or carol blest*;] Since the coming of Christianity, this season, (winter) in commemoration of the birth of Christ, has been particularly devoted to festivity. And to this custom, notwithstanding the impropriety, *hymn*, or *carol blest* certainly alludes.
WARBURTON.

[4] *Therefore the moon, the governess of floods*, &c.] This line has no immediate connection with that preceding it (as Dr. Johnson seems to

have

Pale in her anger, washes all the air,
That rheumatic diseases do abound : *

have thought). It does not refer to the omission of hymns or carols, but of the fairy rites, which were disturbed in consequence of Oberon's quarrel with Titania. The moon is with peculiar propriety represented as incensed at the cessation—not of the Christian carols, (as Dr. Warburton thinks,) nor of the heathen rites of adoration, (as Dr. Johnson supposes,) but of those sports, which have been always reputed to be celebrated by her light.

As the whole passage has been much misunderstood, it may be proper to observe that Titania begins with saying,

And never, since the middle summer's spring,
Met we on hill, in dale, forest, or mead—
But with thy brawls thou hast disturb'd our sport.

She then particularly enumerates the several consequences that have flowed from their contention. The whole is divided into four clauses :

1. *Therefore* the winds, &c.
   That they have overborne their continents :
2. The Ox hath *therefore* stretch'd his yoke in vain ;
   The ploughman lost his sweat;———
   No night is now with hymn or carol blest :
3. *Therefore* the Moon—washes all the air,
   That rheumatic diseases do abound :
4. And, *through* this distemperature, we see,
   The seasons alter ;———
   ——— and the mazed world,
   By their increase, now knows not which is which :
   And this same progeny of evils comes
   From *our* debate, from *our* dissension.

In all this there is no difficulty. All these calamities are the consequences of the dissention between Oberon and Titania; as seems to be sufficiently pointed out by the word *therefore*, so often repeated. Those lines which have it not, are evidently put in apposition with the preceding line in which that word is found. MALONE.

The repeated adverb *therefore*, throughout this speech, I suppose to have constant reference to the first time when it is used—All these irregularities of season happened in consequence of the disagreement between the king and queen of the fairies, and not in consequence of each other.—Ideas crowded fast on Shakspeare, and as he committed them to paper, he did not attend to the distance of the leading object from whom they took their rise.

That the festivity and hospitality attending Christmas, decreased, was the subject of complaint to many of our ludicrous writers. Among the rest, to Nash, whose comedy called *Summer's Last Will and Testament*, made its first appearance in the same year with this play, viz. 1600. The confusion of seasons here described, is no more than a poetical account of the weather, which happened in England about the time when this play was first published. For this information I am indebted to chance, which furnished me with a few leaves of an old meteorological history. STEEVENS.

* *That* rheumatic diseases *do abound.*] *Rheumatic diseases*, signified in Shakspeare's time, not what we now call *rheumatism*, but distillations

And, thorough this distemperature⁵, we see
The seasons alter: hoary-headed frosts
Fall in the fresh lap of the crimson rose⁶;
And on old Hyems' chin⁷, and icy crown,
An odorous chaplet of sweet summer buds
Is, as in mockery, set: The spring, the summer,
The childing autumn, angry winter, change
Their wonted liveries and the 'mazed world,

from the head, catarrhs, &c. So, in a paper entitled, " The State of Sir H. Sydney's Bodie, &c. Feb. 1567;" *Sydney's Memorials*, Vol. i. p. 94: "—he hath verie much distempered diverse parts of his bodie, as namely, his hedde, his stomach, &c. and thereby is always subject to coughes, distillations, and other *rumatic diseases*." MALONE.

⁵ — *this distemperature*,] By *distemperature*, I imagine is meant in this place, the perturbed state in which the king and queen had lived for some time past. Mr. Steevens thinks it means " the perturbation of the *elements*." MALONE.

⁶ — *hoary headed frosts*
Fall in the fresh lap of the crimson rose;] Shakspeare, in *Coriolanus*, talks of the " consecrated snow that lies on Dian's *lap*;" and Spenser in his *Fairy Queen*, B. ii. c. 2. has—

" And fils with flow're fair Flora's painted *lap*." STEEVENS.

This thought is elegantly expressed by Goldsmith, in his *Traveller*:

" And winter lingering chills the lap of May." MALONE.

⁷ — Hyems' *chin*] Dr. Grey, not inelegantly conjectures that the poet wrote, " —on old Hyems' *chill* and icy crown." It is not indeed easy to discover how a chaplet can be placed on *the chin*. STEEV.

It should be rather for *thin*, i. e. thin-hair'd. TYRWHITT.

So Cordelia speaking of Lear:

" —— to watch, poor perdu!
" With this *thin* helm." STEEVENS.

Thinne is nearer to *chinne* (the spelling of the old copies) than *chill*, and therefore, I think, more likely to have been the author's word.

This singular image was, I believe, suggested to our poet by Golding's translation of Ovid, Book ii.

" And lastly, quaking for the colde, stood *Winter* all forlorne,
" With rugged head as white as dove, and garments all to-torne,
' Forladen with the isycles, that dangled up and downe
" Upon his gray and *hoary head*, and showie *frozen crown*."

MALONE.

I believe this peculiar image of Hyems' chin must have come from Virgil, (Æneid iv. 253) through the medium of the translation of the day:

—— tum flumine mento

Precipitant senis, et glacie riget horrida barba." S. W.

Thus translated by Phaer, 1562:

" —— and from his hoary beard adowne,
" The streames of waters fall; with yce and frost his face doth frowne."

MALONE.

By

MIDSUMMER-NIGHT'S DREAM.

By their increase [8], now knows not which is which:
And this same progeny of evils comes
From our debate, from our dissention;
We are their parents and original.

Obe. Do you amend it then; it lies in you:
Why should Titania cross her Oberon?
I do but beg a little changeling boy,
To be my henchman [9].

Tita. Set your heart at rest,
The fairy land buys not the child of me.
His mother was a vot'ress of my order:
And, in the spiced Indian air, by night,
Full often hath she gossip'd by my side;
And sat with me on Neptune's yellow sands,
Marking the embarked traders on the flood;
When we have laugh'd to see the sails conceive,
And grow big-bellied, with the wanton wind:
Which she, with pretty and with swimming gait,
(Following her womb then rich with my young 'squire,)
Would imitate [1]; and sail upon the land,

To

---

[8] *The chilling autumn, angry winter, change*
Their wonted liveries, and the 'mazed world
By their increase, *&c.*] The *chilling* autumn is the *pregnant* autumn, *fructifer autumnus.* STEEVENS.

By their increase, is, by their produce. JOHNSON.

So, in our author's 97th Sonnet:
"The *teeming* autumn, big with rich *increase*,
"Bearing the wanton burthen of the prime."

The latter expression is scriptural: "Then shall the earth bring forth her *increase*, and God, even our God, shall give us his blessing." PSALM lxvii. MALONE.

[9] — *henchman*] Page of honour. GREY.

Henchman. Quasi haunch-man. One that goes behind another. *Podiseguus.* BLACKSTONE.

The learned commentator might have given his etymology some support from the following passage in *K. Henry IV. P. ii.*
"O Westmoreland, thou art a summer bird,
"Which ever in the *haunch* of winter sings
"The lifting up of day." STEEVENS.

[1] *Which she, with pretty and with swimming gait,*
Following, (her womb then rich with my young 'squire,)
Would imitate;—] Perhaps the parenthesis should begin sooner; as I think Mr. Kenrick observes:
(*Following her womb,* then rich with my young 'squire.)
So, in Trolla's combat with Hudibras:
"————— She press'd so home,
"That he retired, and *follow'd's* bum."

And

To fetch me trifles, and return again,
As from a voyage, rich with merchandize.
But she, being mortal, of that boy did die;
And, for her sake, do I rear up her boy;
And, for her sake, I will not part with him.

Obe. How long within this wood intend you stay?

Tita. Perchance, till after Theseus' wedding-day.
If you will patiently dance in our round,
And see our moon-light revels, go with us;
If not, shun me, and I will spare your haunts.

Obe. Give me that boy, and I will go with thee.

Tita. Not for thy fairy kingdom.—Fairies, away:
We shall chide down-right, if I longer stay.

[*Exeunt* TITANIA, *and her Train.*

Obe. Well, go thy way: thou shalt not from this grove,
Till I torment thee for this injury.—
My gentle Puck, come hither: Thou remember'st
Since once I sat upon a promontory,
And heard a mermaid on a dolphin's back [3],

Uttering

And Dryden says of his *Spanish Friar*, "his great belly walks in state before him, and his gouty legs come limping *after it.*" PARMER.

I have followed this regulation, (which was likewise adopted by Mr. Steevens,) though I do not think that of the old copy at all liable to the objection made to it by Dr. Warburton. "She did not, (he says) follow the ship whose motion she imitated; for that sailed on the water, she on land." But might she not on land move in the same direction with the ship at sea, which certainly would outstrip her? and what is this but *following?*

Which, according to the present regulation, must mean—*which motion of the ship with swelling sails,* &c. according to the old regulation it must refer to "embarked traders." MALONE.

[3] *And heard a mermaid on a dolphin's back,* &c.] By the *mermaid* in this passage says Dr Warburton, the poet meant Mary Queen of Scots; by the *dolphin*, her husband, the Dauphin of France (formerly spelt *Dolphi*). Mary is called a mermaid, to denote, 1. her reign over a kingdom situated in the sea; 2. her beauty and intemperate lust. *Such dulcet and harmonious breath* alludes to her genius and learning, more particularly to her sweet and graceful elocution. *The rude sea* alludes to Scotland, which in her absence rose up in arms against the Regent, and the disorder which she, on her return home, found means to quiet. The Earls of Northumberland and Westmoreland, who fell in her quarrel, and the Duke of Norfolk, whose projected marriage with her was attended with such fatal consequences, are imagined by *the stars that shot madly from their spheres.* In the latter part of the imagery there is a peculiar justness, the vulgar opinion being that the mermaid allured men to destruction by her songs.

The

Uttering such dulcet and harmonious breath,
That the rude sea grew civil at her song;
And certain stars shot madly from their spheres [4],
To hear the sea-maid's music.
  Puck. I remember.
  Obe. That very time I saw, (but thou could'st not,)
Flying between the cold moon and the earth,
Cupid all arm'd [5]: a certain aim he took
At a fair vestal, throned by the west [6];
And loos'd his love-shaft smartly from his bow,
As it should pierce a hundred thousand hearts:
But I might see young Cupid's fiery shaft
Quench'd in the chaste beams of the watery moon;
And the imperial vot'ress passed on,
In maiden meditation, fancy-free.
Yet mark'd I where the bolt of Cupid fell:
It fell upon a little western flower—
Before, milk-white; now purple with love's wound—;
And maidens call it, love-in-idleness [7].

The learned commentator's note is here considerably abridged, but I have endeavoured to preserve the substance of it. MALONE.

[4] *And certain stars shot madly from their spheres.*] So, in our author's *Rape of Lucrece*:
  "And little stars shot from their fixed places." MALONE.

[5] *Cupid all arm'd.*] *All arm'd*, does not signify *dressed in panoply*, but only enforces the word *armed*, as we might say *all booted*. JOHNSON.
So, in Green's *Never Too Late*, 1616:
  "Or where proud Cupid sat *all arm'd* with fire."
So, in Lord Surrey's translation of the fourth book of the *Æneid*:
  "*All utterly* I could not seem forsaken." STEEVENS.

[6] *At a fair vestal, throned by the west;*] A compliment to Queen Elizabeth. POPE.
It was no uncommon thing to introduce a compliment to Queen Elizabeth in the body of a play. So, again in *Tancred and Gismunda*, 1592:
  "There lives a virgin, one without compare,
  "Who of all graces hath her heavenly share;
  "In whose renowne, and for whose happie days,
  "Let us record this Pæan of her praise." *Cantant.* STEEVENS.

[7] *And maidens call it love-in-idleness.*] It is scarce necessary to mention that *love-in-idleness* is a flower. STEEVENS.
The flower or violet commonly called pansies, or heart's-ease, is named *love-in-idleness* in Warwickshire, and in Lyte's Herbal. There is a reason why Shakspeare says it is "*now purple* with love's wound," because one or two of its petals are of a purple colour. TOLLET.
It is called in other countries the *Three colour'd violet*, the *Herb of Trinity*, *Three faces in a hood*, *Cuddle me to you*, &c. STEEVENS.

Fetch

Fetch me that flower; the herb I shew'd thee once;
The juice of it, on sleeping eye-lids laid,
Will make or man or woman madly dote
Upon the next live creature that it sees.
Fetch me this herb; and be thou here again,
Ere the leviathan can swim a league.

Puck. I'll put a girdle round about the earth [a]
In forty minutes. [*Exit.*

Obe. Having once this juice,
I'll watch Titania when she is asleep,
And drop the liquor of it in her eyes:
The next thing then she waking looks upon,
(Be it on lion, bear, or wolf, or bull,
On meddling monkey, or on busy ape,)
She shall pursue it with the soul of love.
And ere I take this charm off from her sight,
(As I can take it with another herb,)
I'll make her render up her page to me.
But who comes here? I am invisible [b];
And I will over-hear their conference.

Enter DEMETRIUS, HELENA *following him.*

Dem. I love thee not, therefore pursue me not.
Where is Lysander, and fair Hermia?
The one I'll slay, the other slayeth me [c].
Thou told'st me, they were stol'n into this wood;
And here am I, and wood within this wood [d],
Because I cannot meet with Hermia.
Hence, get thee gone, and follow me no more.

---

[a] *I'll put a girdle round about the earth*] This expression (as Mr. Steevens has shewn) occurs in many of our old plays. MALONE.

[b] *I am invisible;*] I thought proper here to observe, that, as Oberon and Puck his attendant may be frequently observed to speak, when there is no mention of their entering, they are designed by the poet to be supposed on the stage during the greatest part of the remainder of the play; and to mix, as they please, as spirits, with the other actors; and embroil the plot, by their interposition, without being seen, or heard, but when to their own purpose. THEOBALD.

[c] *The one I'll slay, the other slayeth me*] The old copies read—*slay* and *slayeth*. Corrected by Dr. Thirlby. MALONE.

[d] — *and wood within this wood,*] *Wood*, or mad, wild, raving. POPE. In the third part of the Countess of Pembroke's *Ivy Church*, 1591, is the same quibble on the word:

"Daphne goes to the *woods*, and vowes herself to Diana;
"Phœbus grows stark *wood* for love and fancie to Daphne." STEEV.

Hel.

Hel. You draw me, you hard-hearted adamant;
But yet you draw not iron [3], for my heart
Is true as steel: Leave you your power to draw,
And I shall have no power to follow you.
　Dem. Do I entice you? Do I speak you fair?
Or, rather, do I not in plainest truth
Tell you—I do not, nor I cannot love you?
　Hel. And even for that do I love you the more.
I am your spaniel; and, Demetrius,
The more you beat me, I will fawn on you:
Use me but as your spaniel, spurn me, strike me,
Neglect me, lose me; only give me leave,
Unworthy as I am, to follow you.
What worser place can I beg in your love;
(And yet a place of high respect with me,)
Than to be used as you use your dog?
　Dem. Tempt not too much the hatred of my spirit;
For I am sick, when I do look on thee.
　Hel. And I am sick, when I look not on you.
　Dem. You do impeach your modesty too much,
To leave the city, and commit yourself
Into the hands of one that loves you not;
To trust the opportunity of night,
And the ill counsel of a desert place,
With the rich worth of your virginity.
　Hel. Your virtue is my privilege for that [4].
It is not night, when I do see your face [5],
Therefore I think I am not in the night:
Nor doth this wood lack worlds of company;
For you, in my respect, are all the world [6]:

Then

---

[3] *You draw me, you hard-hearted adamant;*
But yet you draw not iron,] I learn from Edward Fenton's *Certaine Secrete Wonders of Nature*, bl. l. 1569, that "— there is now a dayes a kinde of adamant, which draweth unto it flesh, and the same so strongly, that it hath power to knit and tie together two mouthes of contrary persons, and draw the heart of a man out of his bodie without offending any part of him." STEEVENS.

[4] — *for that.*] i. e. for leaving the city, &c. TYRWHITT.

[5] *It is not night, when I do see your face, &c.*] This passage is paraphrased from two lines of an ancient poet ("Tibullus]*e*
"　　　　　—— *Te nocte vel atra*
"*Lumen, et in solis tu mihi turba locis.*" JOHNSON.

[6] *Nor doth this wood lack worlds of company, &c.*] The same thought occurs in K. Henry VI. P. ii.

" A wilder-

Then how can it be said, I am alone,
When all the world is here to look on me?

Dem. I'll run from thee, and hide me in the brakes,
And leave thee to the mercy of wild beasts.

Hel. The wildest hath not such a heart as you⁷.
Run when you will, the story shall be chang'd:
Apollo flies, and Daphne holds the chase.
The dove pursues the griffin; the mild hind
Makes speed to catch the tyger: Bootless speed!
When cowardice pursues, and valour flies.

Dem. I will not stay thy questions; let me go:
Or, if thou follow me, do not believe
But I shall do thee mischief in the wood.

Hel. Ay, in the temple, in the town, the field,
You do me mischief. Fie, Demetrius!
Your wrongs do set a scandal on my sex:
We cannot fight for love as men may do;
We should be woo'd, and were not made to woo.
I'll follow thee, and make a heaven of hell,
To die upon the hand I love so well. [*Exeunt* DEM. *and* HEL.

Ob. Fare thee well, nymph: ere he do leave this grove,
Thou shalt fly him, and he shall seek thy love.—

Re-enter PUCK.

Hast thou the flower there? Welcome, wanderer.

Puck. Ay, there it is.

Ob. I pray thee, give it me.
I know a bank where⁸ the wild thyme blows,
Where ox-lips⁸ and the nodding violet grows;
Quite over-canopy'd with luscious woodbine⁹,

With

" A wilderness is populous enough,
" So Suffolk had thy heavenly company." MALONE.
⁷ *The wildest hath not such a heart as you.*]
Mitius inveni quam te genus omne ferarum. *Ovid.*
See *Timon of Athens,* Act iv. sc. i.
" — where he shall find
" The unkindest beasts more kinder than mankind." S. W.
⁸ — *where—*] is here used as dissyllable. The modern editors unnecessarily read—*whereon.* MALONE.
⁸ *Where* oxlips] The *oxlip* is the greater *cowslip.* STEEVENS.
⁹ *Quite over-canopy'd with luscious woodbine,*] On the margin of one of my folio's, an unknown hand has written—*lush* woodbine, which, I think is right.

This

With sweet musk-roses, and with eglantine:
There sleeps Titania, some time of the night,
Lull'd in these flowers with dances and delight;
And there the snake throws her enamel'd skin,
Weed wide enough to wrap a fairy in:
And with the juice of this I'll streak her eyes,
And make her full of hateful fantasies.
Take thou some of it, and seek through this grove:
A sweet Athenian lady is in love
With a disdainful youth: anoint his eyes;
But do it, when the next thing he espies
May be the lady: Thou shalt know the man
By the Athenian garments he hath on.
Effect it with some care; that he may prove
More fond on her, than she upon her love:
And look thou meet me ere the first cock crow.

Puck. Fear not, my Lord, your servant shall do so.
[*Exeunt.*

SCENE III.

Another Part of the Wood.

Enter TITANIA, *with her train.*

Tita. Come, now a roundel, and a fairy song¹:
Then for the third part of a minute, hence²:
Some, to kill cankers in the musk-rose buds;

This hand I have since discovered to be Theobald's. JOHNSON.
Shakspeare uses the word *lush* in *The Tempest*, Act ii. 1
" How *lush* and lusty the grass looks? how green!" STEEVENS.
¹ — *a roundel,*] A *roundel;* that is, as I suppose, *a circular dance.* Ben Jonson seems to call *the rings* which such dances are supposed to make in the grass, *roundels.* Vol. V. *Tale of a Tub,* p. 23:
" I'll have no *roundels,* I, in the queen's paths." TYRWHITT.
Rounds or *roundels* were like the present country dances. See *Orchestra,* by Sir John Davis, 1622. REED.
² *Then for the third part of a minute, hence:*] Dr. Warburton reads—*for the third part of* the midnight—.
The persons employed are *fairies,* to whom the third part of a minute might not be a very short time to do such work in. The critic might as well have objected to the epithet *tall,* which the fairy bestows on the *cowslip.* But Shakspeare, throughout the play, has preserved the proportion of other things in respect of these tiny beings, compared with whose size, a cowslip might be tall, and to whose powers of execution, a minute might be equivalent to an age. STEEVENS.

Some

Some, war with rear-mice [3] for their leathern wings,
To make my small elves coats; and some, keep back
The clamorous owl, that nightly hoots, and wonders
At our quaint spirits [4]: Sing me now asleep;
Then to your offices, and let me rest.

SONG.

1. *Fai.* *You spotted snakes, with double tongue,*
   Thorny hedge-hogs, be not seen;
   Newts, and blind-worms, do no wrong;
   Come not near our fairy queen:

Chorus.

Philomel, with melody,
Sing in our sweet lullaby;
Lulla, lulla, lullaby; lulla, lulla, lullaby:
Never harm, nor spell nor charm,
Come our lovely lady nigh;
So, good night, with lullaby.

II.

2. *Fai.* *Weaving spiders, come not here;*
   Hence, you long-legg'd spinners, hence:
   Beetles black, approach not near;
   Worm, nor snail, do no offence.

Chorus.

Philomel, with melody, &c.

1. *Fa.* Hence, away; now all is well [5]:
   One, aloof, stand sentinel.

[*Exeunt* Fairies. TITANIA *sleeps.*

[3] — *with rear-mice*] A *rear mouse* is a bat; a *mouse* that *rears* from the ground by the aid of wings. STEEVENS.

[4] — *quaint spirits:*] For this Dr. Warburton reads against all authority—*quaint sports*. But Prospero, in *The Tempest*, applies *quaint* to Ariel. JOHNSON.

Dr. Johnson is right in the word, and Dr. Warburton in the interpretation. A *spirit* was sometimes used for a *sport*. In Decker's play, *If it be not good the devil is in it,* the king of Naples says to the devil Ruffman, disguised in the character of Shalcan: "Now Shalcan, some new *spirit*? Ruff. A thousand wenches stark-naked to play at leap-frog. O *meee*. O rare sight!" FARMER.

[5] *Hence, away*, &c.] This, according to all the editions, is made part of the song; but I think without sufficient reason, as it appears to be spoken after the song is over. In the quarto 1600, it is given to the 2d Fairy; but the other division is better. STEEVENS.

Enter

MIDSUMMER-NIGHT'S DREAM.

Enter OBERON.

Obe. What thou seeſt, when thou doſt wake,
  [*ſqueezes the flower on Titania's eye-lids.*
Do it for thy true love take;
Love, and languiſh for his ſake:
Be it ounce [6], or cat, or bear,
Pard, or boar with briſtled hair,
In thy eye that ſhall appear
When thou wak'ſt, it is thy dear;
Wake, when ſome vile thing is near.   [*Exit.*

Enter LYSANDER *and* HERMIA.

Lyſ. Fair love, you faint with wandering in the wood;
And to ſpeak troth, I have forgot our way:
We'll reſt us, Hermia, if you think it good,
And tarry for the comfort of the day.

Her. Be it ſo, Lyſander: find you out a bed,
For I upon this bank will reſt my head.

Lyſ. One turf ſhall ſerve as pillow for us both;
One heart, one bed, two boſoms, and one troth.

Her. Nay, good Lyſander; for my ſake, my dear,
Lie further off yet, do not lie ſo near.

Lyſ. O, take the ſenſe, ſweet, of my innocence [7];
Love takes the meaning, in love's conference [8].
I mean, that my heart unto yours is knit;
So that but one heart we can make of it:
Two boſoms interchained with an oath;
So then, two boſoms, and a ſingle troth.
Then, by your ſide no bed-room me deny,
For, lying ſo, Hermia, I do not lie.

---

[6] *Be it ounce.*] The ounce is a ſmall tiger, or tiger-cat. JOHNSON.

[7] *O, take the ſenſe, ſweet, of my innocence;*] Underſtand *the meaning of my innocence,* or *my innocent meaning.* Let no ſuſpicion of ill enter thy mind. JOHNSON.

[8] *Love takes the meaning, in love's conference.*] In the converſation of thoſe who are aſſured of each other's kindneſs, not *ſuſpicion* but *love takes the meaning.* No malevolent interpretation is to be made, but all is to be received in the ſenſe which *love* can find, and which *love* can dictate. JOHNSON.

This line is certainly intelligible as Dr. Johnſon has explained it; but I think it requires a ſlight alteration to make it connect well with the former. I would read:
  Love take the meaning in love's conference.
That is, Let *love take the meaning.* TYRWHITT.

Her.

Her. Lysander, riddles very prettily:—
Now much beshrew [9] my manners and my pride,
If Hermia meant to say, Lysander lied.
But, gentle friend, for love and courtesy
Lie further off; in human modesty
Such separation, as, may well be said,
Becomes a virtuous bachelor and a maid:
So far be distant; and good night, sweet friend:
Thy love ne'er alter, till thy sweet life end!
  Lys. Amen, amen, to that fair prayer, say I:
And then end life, when I end loyalty!
Here is my bed: sleep give thee all his rest!
  Her. With half that wish the wisher's eyes be press'd!
                                    [*They sleep.*

              Enter PUCK.

  Puck. Through the forest have I gone,
     But Athenian found I none,
     On whose eyes I might approve
     This flower's force in stirring love.
     Night and silence! who is here?
     Weeds of Athens he doth wear:
     This is he, my master said,
     Despised the Athenian maid;
     And here the maiden sleeping found,
     On the dank and dirty ground.
     Pretty soul! she durst not lie
     Near this lack-love, this kill-court'sy [1].
     Churl, upon thy eyes I throw
     All the power this charm doth owe:
     When thou wak'st, let love forbid
     Sleep his seat on thy eye-lid.
     So awake, when I am gone;
     For I must now to Oberon.   [*Exit.*

---

[9] *Now much beshrew, &c.*] This word, of which the etymology is not exactly known, implies a sinister wish, and means the same as if she had said, " now ill *befall* my manners, &c." STEEVENS.
  See Minsheu's etymology of it, which seems to be an imprecation or wish of such evil to one, as the venomous biting of the *shrew-mouse*.
                                                  TOLLET.

[1] *— this kill-court'sy.*] We meet with the same abbreviation in our author's *Venus and Adonis*:
  " They all strain *court'sy*, who shall cope him first." MALONE.

Enter

Enter DEMETRIUS, *and* HELENA, *running.*

Hel. Stay, though thou kill me, sweet Demetrius.
Dem. I charge thee, hence, and do not haunt me thus.
Hel. O, wilt thou darkling leave me? do not so.
Dem. Stay on thy peril; I alone will go. [*Exit* DEM.
Hel. O, I am out of breath, in this fond chace!
The more my prayer, the lesser is my grace [2].
Happy is Hermia, wheresoe'er she lies;
For she hath blessed, and attractive eyes.
How came her eyes so bright? Not with salt tears;
If so, my eyes are oftner wash'd than hers.
No, no, I am as ugly as a bear;
For beasts that meet me, run away for fear:
Therefore, no marvel, though Demetrius
Do, as a monster, fly my presence thus.
What wicked and dissembling glass of mine
Made me compare with Hermia's sphery eyne?—
But who is here? Lysander! on the ground!
Dead? or asleep? I see no blood, no wound:—
Lysander, if you live, good Sir, awake.

Lys. And run through fire I will, for thy sweet sake
[*waking.*

Transparent Helena! Nature shews art [3],
That through thy bosom makes me see thy heart.
Where is Demetrius? O, how fit a word
Is that vile name, to perish on my sword!

Hel. Do not say so, Lysander; say not so:
What though he love your Hermia? Lord, what though?
Yet Hermia still loves you: then be content.

Lys. Content with Hermia? No: I do repent
The tedious minutes I with her have spent.
Not Hermia, but Helena I love:
Who will not change a raven for a dove?
The will of man is by his reason sway'd;
And reason says you are the worthier maid.
Things growing are not ripe until their season:
So, I, being young, till now ripe not to reason;

---

[2] — *my grace.*] My acceptableness, the favour that I can gain. JOHNS.
[3] — *Nature shews art,*] Thus the quarto. The folio reads—Nature *her shews art*—perhaps an error of the press for—Nature *shews her art.* The editor of the second folio changed *her* to *here.* MALONE.

And

MIDSUMMER-NIGHT'S DREAM. 335

And touching now the point of human skill⁴,
Reason becomes the marshal to my will⁵,
And leads me to your eyes; where I o'erlook
Love's stories, written in love's richest book.
 Hel. Wherefore was I to this keen mockery born?
When, at your hands, did I deserve this scorn?
Is't not enough, is't not enough, young man,
That I did never, no, nor never can,
Deserve a sweet look from Demetrius' eye,
But you must flout my insufficiency?
Good troth, you do me wrong, good sooth, you do,
In such disdainful manner me to woo.
But fare you well: perforce I must confess,
I thought you lord of more true gentleness⁶.
O, that a lady, of one man refus'd,
Should, of another, therefore be abus'd! [*Exit.*
 Lys. She sees not Hermia:—Hermia, sleep thou there;
And never may'st thou come Lysander near!
For, as a surfeit of the sweetest things
The deepest loathing to the stomach brings;
Or, as the heresies, that men do leave,
Are hated most of those they did deceive;

---

⁴ *— touching now the point of human skill,*] i. e. my senses being now at their utmost height of perfection. So, in *K. Henry VIII*:
 " I have touch'd the highest *point* of all my greatness." STEEV.
⁵ *Reason becomes the marshal to my will,*] That is, My will now follows reason. JOHNSON.
So, in *Macbeth*:
 " Thou *marshal'st* me the way that I was going." STEEVENS.
 A modern writer [*Letters of Literature*, 8vo. 1785,] contends that Dr. Johnson's explanation is inaccurate. The meaning, says he, is, " my will now obeys the command of my reason, not my will follows my reason. *Marshal* is a director of an army, of a turney, of a feast. Sydney has used *marshal* for *herald* or poursuivant, but improperly."
 Of such flimsy materials are many of the *hyper-criticisms* composed, to which the labours of the editors and commentators on Shakspeare have given rise. Who does not at once perceive, that Dr. Johnson, when he speaks of the will *following* reason, uses the word not literally, but metaphorically? " My will *follows* or obeys *the dictates* of reason." Or that if this were the case, he would not yet be justified by the context, (And *leads* me—) and by the passage quoted from *Macbeth*.—The heralds, distinguished by the names of " *poursuivants* at arms," were likewise called *marshals.* See Minsheu's DICT. 1617, in v. MALONE.
⁶ *— true gentleness.*] *Gentleness* is equivalent to what, in modern language, we should call the *spirit of a gentleman.* PERCY.

So

So thou, my surfeit, and my herefy,
Of all be hated; but the moſt of me!
And all my powers, addreſs your love and might,
To honour Helen, and to be her knight! [*Exit.*
Her. [*ſtarting.*] Help me, Lyſander, help me! do thy beſt,
To pluck this crawling ſerpent from my breaſt!
Ah me, for pity!—what a dream was here?
Lyſander, look, how I do quake with fear:
Methought, a ſerpent eat my heart away,
And you ſat ſmiling at his cruel prey:—
Lyſander! what, remov'd? Lyſander! Lord!
What out of hearing? gone? no ſound, no word?
Alack, where are you? ſpeak, an if you hear;
Speak, of all loves; I ſwoon almoſt with fear.
No?—then I well perceive you are not nigh:
Either death, or you, I'll find immediately. * [*Exit.*

⁷ *Speak, of all loves;—*] *Of all loves* is an adjuration more than once uſed by our author. So, in the *Merry Wives of Windſor*, Act ii. ſc. iii.
" —— to ſend her your little page, *of all loves.*" STEEVENS.
Either death, or you, I'll find immediately.] Thus the ancient copies, and ſuch was Shakſpeare's uſage. He frequently employs *either* and other ſimilar words, as monoſyllables. So, in *K. Henry IV*. P. ii.:
" *Either* from the king, or in the preſent time."
Again, in *K. Henry V.*
" *Either* paſt, or not arriv'd to pith and puiſſance."
Again, in *Julius Cæſar:*
" *Either* led or driven, as we point the way."
Again, in *K. Richard III.:*
" *Either* thou will die by God's juſt ordinance—."
Again, in *Othello:*
" *Either* in diſcourſe of thought, or actual deed."
So alſo Marlowe in his *Edward II.* 1598:
" *Either* baniſh him that was the cauſe thereof—."
The modern editors read—*Or death or you,* &c. MALONE

A C T

ACT III. SCENE I[1].

The same. The Queen of Fairies lying asleep.

Enter QUINCE, SNUG, BOTTOM, FLUTE, SNOUT, *and* STARVELING.

Bot. Are we all met?

Quin. Pat, pat; and here's a marvellous convenient place for our rehearsal: This green plot shall be our stage, this hawthorn brake our tyring-house; and we will do it in action, as we will do it before the Duke.

Bot. Peter Quince—

Quin. What say'st thou, bully Bottom?

Bot. There are things in this comedy of *Pyramus and Thisby*, that will never please. First, Pyramus must draw a sword to kill himself; which the ladies cannot abide. How answer you that?

Snout. By'rlakin[2], a parlous fear.

Star. I believe, we must leave the killing out, when all is done.

Bot. Not a whit; I have a device to make all well. Write me a prologue: and let the prologue seem to say, we will do no harm with our swords; and that Pyramus is not kill'd indeed: and, for the more better assurance, tell them, that I Pyramus am not Pyramus, but Bottom the weaver: This will put them out of fear.

Quin. Well, we will have such a prologue; and it shall be written in eight and six[3].

---

[1] In the time of Shakspeare, there were many companies of players, sometimes five at the same time, contending for the favour of the public. Of these some were undoubtedly very unskilful and very poor, and it is probable that the design of this scene was to ridicule their ignorance, and the odd expedients to which they might be driven by the want of proper decorations. Bottom was perhaps the head of a rival house, and is therefore honoured with an ass's head. JOHNSON.

[2] *By'rlakin, a parlous fear.*] By *our lady'kin*, or *little lady*, as *ifakins* is a corruption of, *by my faith*. *Parlous*, a word corrupted from *perilous*, i. e. dangerous. STEEVENS.

[3] *—in eight an! six.*] i. e. in alternate verses of eight and six syllables. MALONE.

Bot. No, make it two more; let it be written in eight and eight.

Snout. Will not the ladies be afeard of the lion?

Star. I fear it, I promise you.

Bot. Masters, you ought to consider with yourselves: to bring in, God shield us! a lion among ladies, is a most dreadful thing: * for there is not a more fearful wild-fowl, than your lion, living; and we ought to look to it.

Snout. Therefore, another prologue must tell, he is not a lion.

Bot. Nay, you must name his name, and half his face must be seen through the lion's neck; and he himself must speak through, saying thus, or to the same defect—Ladies, or fair ladies, I would wish you, or, I would request you, or, I would entreat you, not to fear, not to tremble: my life for yours. If you think I come hither as a lion, it were pity of my life: No, I am no such thing; I am a man as other men are:—and there, indeed, let him name his name; and tell them plainly, he is Snug the joiner⁴.

Quin.

* *God shield us! A lion among ladies is a most dreadful thing.*] There is an odd coincidence between what our author has here written for Bottom, and a real occurrence at the Scottish court in the year 1594. Prince Henry, the eldest son of James the First, was christened in August in that year. While the King and Queen, &c. were at dinner, a triumphal chariot (the frame of which, we are told, was ten feet long and seven broad) with several allegorical personages on it, was drawn in by " a black-moore. This chariot should have been drawn in by a lyon, but because his presence might have brought some feare to the neerest, or that the sight of the lighted torches might have commoved his tameness, it was thought meete that the Moore should supply that room." A true account of the most triumphal and royal accomplishment of the baptism of the most excellent, right high, and mighty prince, Henry Frederick, &c. as it was solemnized the 30th day of August, 1594. 8vo. 1603. MALONE.

⁴ *No, I am no such thing; I am a man, as other men are:—and there, indeed, let him name his name; and tell them plainly he is Snug the joiner.*] There are probably many temporary allusions to particular incidents and characters scattered through our author's plays, which gave a poignancy to certain passages, while the events were recent, and the persons pointed at, yet living.—In the speech before us, I think it not improbable that he meant to allude to a fact which happened in his time, at an entertainment exhibited before Queen Elizabeth. It is recorded in a manuscript collection of anecdotes, stories, &c. entitled, *Merry Passages and Jeasts*, MS. Harl. 6395:

" There was a spectacle presented to Queen Elizabeth upon the water.

Quin. Well it shall be so. But there is two hard things; that is, to bring the moon-light into a chamber: for you know, Pyramus and Thisby meet by moon-light.

Snug. Doth the moon shine that night we play our play?

Bot. A calendar, a calendar! look in the almanack: find out moon-shine, find out moon-shine.

Quin. Yes, it doth shine that night.

Bot. Why, then you may leave a casement of the great chamber window, where we play, open; and the moon may shine in at the casement.

Quin. Ay; or else one must come in with a bush of thorns and a lanthorn, and say, he comes to disfigure, or to present, the person of moon-shine. Then, there is another thing: we must have a wall in the great chamber; for Pyramus and Thisby, says the story, did talk through the chink of a wall.

Snug. You can never bring in a wall—What say you, Bottom?

Bot. Some man or other must present wall; and let him have some plaister, or some lome, or some rough cast about him, to signify wall; or let him hold his fingers thus, and through that cranny shall Pyramus and Thisby whisper.

Quin. If that may be, then all is well. Come, sit down, every mother's son, and rehearse your parts. Pyramus, you begin: when you have spoken your speech, enter into that brake [5]; and so every one according to his cue.

Enter PUCK *behind.*

Puck. What hempen home-spuns have we swaggering here,
So near the cradle of the fairy queen?

ter, and among others *Harry Goldingham* was to represent *Arion* upon the dolphin's backe; but finding his voice to be very hoarse and unpleasant, when he came to perform it, he tears off his disguise, and swears he was none of *Arion*, not he, but even honest *Harry Goldingham*; which blunt discoverie pleased the Queen better than if it had gone through in the right way:—yet he could order his voice to an instrument exceeding well."

The collector of these *Merry Passages* appears to have been nephew to Sir Roger L'Estrange. MALONE.

[5] — *that brake*;] *Brake* anciently signified a *thicket* or *bush*. STEEVENS.

Brake in the West of England is used to express a large extent of ground overgrown with furze, and appears both here and in the next scene to convey the same idea. HENLEY.

What, a play toward? I'll be an auditor;
An actor too, perhaps, if I see 'cause.

Quin. Speak, Pyramus:—Thisby, stand forth.
Pyr. *Thisby, the flowers of odious favours sweet,—*
Quin. Odours, odours.
Pyr. ———— *odours favours sweet:*
So hath thy breath[6], *my dearest Thisby dear.—*
But, hark, a voice! stay thou but here a while[7],
And by and by I will to thee appear. [*Exit.*
Puck. A stranger Pyramus than e'er play'd here[8]!
[*aside.—Exit.*

Thif. Must I speak now?
Quin. Ay, marry, must you: for you must understand, he goes but to see a noise that he heard, and is to come again.

Thif. *Most radiant Pyramus, most lilly-white of hue,*
Of colour like the red rose on triumphant brier,
Most brisky juvenal[9], *and eke most lovely Jew,*
As true as truest horse, that yet would never tire.
I'll meet thee, Pyramus, at Ninny's tomb.

Quin. Ninus' tomb, man: Why, you must not speak that yet; that you answer to Pyramus: you speak all your part at once, cues and all[9].—Pyramus enter; your cue is past; it is, *never tire.*

Re-enter PUCK, *and* BOTTOM *with an ass's head.*

Thif. O,—*As true as truest horse, that yet would never tire.*
Pyr. *If I were fair*[1], *Thisby, I were only thine:—*
Quin. O monstrous! O strange! we are haunted. Pray masters! fly, masters! help! [*Exeunt Clowns.*

[6] *So hath thy breath,—*] Mr. Pope reads—*So doth,* instead of—*So hath,* but nothing, I think, is got by the change. I suspect two lines to have been lost; the first of which rhymed with "favours sweet," and the other with "here a while." The line before us appears to me to refer to some thing that has been lost. MALONE.

[7] — *a while,*] Thus the old copies. Mr. Theobald reads *a while;* but this is no rhyme to *sweet.* The corruption arose, I believe, from a different cause. See the last note. MALONE.

[8] — *than e'er play'd here!*] I suppose he means in that theatre where the piece was acting. STEEVENS.

[9] *juvenal,*] i. e. a young man So, Falstaff, "—the *juvenal* thy master." STEEVENS.

[9] — *cues and all.*] A *cue,* in stage cant, is the last words of the preceding speech, and serves as a hint to him who is to speak next. STEEVENS.

[1] *If I were fair,* &c.] Perhaps we ought to point out thus: If I were, [i. e. as true, &c.] fair Thisby, I were only thine. MALONE.

Puck.

Puck. I'll follow you, I'll lead you about a round,
Through bog, through bush, through brake, through brier[1];
Sometime a horse I'll be, sometime a hound,
A hog, a headless bear, sometime a fire;
And neigh, and bark, and grunt, and roar and burn,
Like horse, hound, hog, bear, fire, at every turn. [*Exit.*

Bot. Why do they run away? this is a knavery of them, to make me afeard[2].

Re-enter SNOUT.

Snout. O Bottom, thou art changed! what do I see on thee[3]?

Bot. What do you see? you see an ass' head of your own; Do you?

Re-enter QUINCE.

Quin. Bless thee, Bottom! bless thee! thou art translated. [*Exit.*

Bot. I see their knavery: this is to make an ass of me; to fright me, if they could. But I will not stir from this place, do what they can: I will walk up and down here, and I will sing, that they shall hear I am not afraid. [*Sings.*

The ousel-cock, so black of hue[4],
With orange-tawny bill,

---

[1] *Through bog, through bush, through brake, through brier;*] Here are two syllables wanting. Perhaps it was written:—*Through bog, through mire—.* JOHNSON.

So, in Spenser's *Faery Queen*, B. vi. c. viii.

"Through hills, through dales, *through bushes, and through briars,*

"Long thus she bled," &c. MALONE.

[2] — *to make me afeard*] *Afeard* is from *to fear*, by the old form of the language, as *an hungered*, from *to hunger*. So *adry*, for *thirsty*. JOHNSON.

[3] *O Bottom, thou art changed! what do I see on thee?*] It is plain by Bottom's answer, that Snout mentioned an *ass's head*. Therefore we should read:

Snout. O *Bottom, thou art changed! what do I see on thee? An ass's head?* JOHNSON.

[4] *The ousel cock, so black of hue*, &c.] In *The Arbor of Amorous Devises* 4to. bl. l. are the following lines:

"The chattering pie, the jay, and eke the quaile,

"The thrustle-cock that was so black of hewe."

The former leaf and the title-page being torn out of the copy I consulted, I am unable either to give the two preceding lines of the stanza, or to ascertaine the date of the book.

The throstle with his note so true[6],
The wren with little quill;

Tita. What angel wakes me from my flowery bed?[7]

[*waking*

Bot. *The finch, the sparrow, and the lark,*
The plain-song cuckoo[8] *gray,*
Whose note full many a man doth mark,
And dares not answer, nay;—

for indeed, who would set his wit to so foolish a bird? who would give a bird the lie, though he cry, *cuckoo*, never so.

Tita. I pray thee, gentle mortal, sing again:
Mine ear is much enamour'd of thy note,
So is mine eye enthralled to thy shape;
And thy fair virtue's force perforce doth move me,
On the first view, to say, to swear, I love thee.

Bot. Methinks, mistress, you should have little reason for that: And yet to say the truth, reason and love keep little company together now-a-days: The more the pity, that some

---

The *ouzel-cock* is generally understood to be the cock blackbird. P. Holland, however, in his translation of Pliny's *Nat. Hist.* b. 1. ch. 14. re: refents the *ouzel* and the *blackbird* as different birds. See also Mr. Lever's *Museum*. STEEVENS.

[d] *The* throstle—] It appears from the following passage in Thomas Newton's *Herball to the Bible*, 8vo. 1587, that the *throstle* is a distinct bird from the *thrush*: "There is also another sorte of myrtle, or myrtle, which is wild; whose berries the mavises, *throstels*, owsells, and *thrushes* delite much to eate." STEEVENS.

7 *What angel wakes me from my flowery bed?*] Perhaps a parody on a line in the *Spanish Tragedy*, often ridiculed by the poets of our author's time:

"What outcry calls me from my naked bed?"

The *Spanish Tragedy* was entered on the Stationers' books in 1592.
MALONE.

8 *plain-song cuckoo*, &c.] That is, the cuckoo, who, having no variety of strains, sings in *plain-song*, or in *plano cantu*; by which expression the uniform modulation or simplicity of the *chant* was anciently distinguished, in opposition to *prick-song* or variegated music sung by note. Skelton introduces the birds singing the different parts of the service at the funeral of his favourite sparrow: among the rest is the cuckoo, p. 227. edit. Lond. 1736:

"But with a large and a long
"To kepe just *playne songe*,
"Our chanter shall be your *cuckow*." T. WARTON.

honest

honest neighbours will not make them friends. Nay, I can gleek [9], upon occasion.

Tita. Thou art as wise as thou art beautiful.

Bot. Not so, neither: but if I had wit enough to get out of this wood, I have enough to serve mine own turn.

Tita. Out of this wood do not desire to go;
Thou shalt remain here whether thou wilt or no.
I am a spirit, of no common rate;
The summer still doth tend upon my state,
And I do love thee: therefore, go with me;
I'll give thee fairies to attend on thee;
And they shall fetch thee jewels from the deep,
And sing, while thou on pressed flowers dost sleep;
And I will purge thy mortal grossness so,
That thou shalt like an airy spirit go.—
Pease-blossom! Cobweb! Moth! and Mustard-seed!

Enter four Fairies.

1. *Fair.* Ready.
2. *Fair.* And I.
3. *Fair.* And I.
4. *Fair.* And I.

All. Where shall we go?

Tita. Be kind and courteous to this gentleman;
Hop in his walks, and gambol in his eyes;
Feed him with apricocks, and dewberries [1],
With purple grapes, green figs, and mulberries;
The honey-bags steal from the humble-bees,

---

[9] —*gleek*,] Joke or scoff. POPE.

Gleek was originally a game at cards. The word is often used by our ancient comic writers in the same sense as by our author. Mr. Lambe observes in his notes on the ancient metrical history of the *Battle of Flodden*, that in the North to *gleek* is to *deceive*, or *beguile*; and that the reply made by the Queen of the Fairies, proves this to be the meaning of it. STEEVENS.

[1] — dewberries,] *Dewberries* strictly and properly are the fruit of one of the species of wild bramble called the creeping or the lesser bramble: but as they stand here among the more delicate fruits, they must be understood to mean *raspberries*, which are also of the bramble kind.
HAWKINS.

Dewberries are *gooseberries*, which are still so called in several parts of the kingdom. HENLEY.

And, for night tapers, crop their waxen thighs,
And light them at the fiery glow-worm's eyes [2],
To have my love to bed, and to arise;
And pluck the wings from painted butterflies,
To fan the moon-beams from his sleeping eyes:
Nod to him, elves, and do him courtesies.

1. *Fai.* Hail, mortal [3]!
2. *Fai.* Hail!
3. *Fai.* Hail!
4. *Fai.* Hail!

Bot. I cry your worship's mercy, heartily.—I beseech, your worship's name?

Cob. Cobweb.

Bot. I shall desire you of more acquaintance [4], good

---

[2] *—the fiery glow-worm's eyes,*] I know not how Shakspeare, who commonly derived his knowledge of nature from his own observation, happened to place the glow-worm's light in his eyes, which is only in his tail. JOHNSON.

The blunder is not in Shakspeare, but in those who have construed too literally a poetical expression. It appears from every line of his writings that he had studied with attention the book of nature, and was an accurate observer of every object that fell within his notice. He must have known that the light of the glow-worm was seated in the tail; but surely a poet is justified in calling the luminous part of a glow-worm its eye. It is a liberty we take in plain prose; for the point of greatest brightness in a furnace is commonly called the eye of it.

Dr. Johnson might have arraigned him with equal propriety for sending his fairies to *light* their tapers at the fire of the glow-worm, which, in *Hamlet*, he terms *uneffectual*:

" The glow-worm shews the matin to be near,
" And 'gins to pale his uneffectual fire." MASON.

[3] *Hail, mortal!*] The old copies read—Hail, mortal, hail! The second *hail* was clearly intended for another of the fairies, for as at each of them should address Bottom. The regulation now adopted was proposed by Mr. Steevens. MALONE.

[4] *I shall desire you of more acquaintance,*] This line has been very unnecessarily altered. Such phraseology was very common to many of our ancient writers. So in *Lusty Juventus*, a morality, 1561: " I shall desire you *of* better acquaintance." Again in *An Humorous Day's Mirth*, 1599: " I desire you *of* more acquaintance." STEEVENS.

The alteration in the modern editions was made on the authority of the first folio, which reads in the next speech but one—' I shall desire *of you* more acquaintance.' But the old reading is undoubtedly the true one. So, in Spenser's *Faery Queen*, B. ii. c. ix.:

" If it be I, *of* pardon I you pray." MALONE.

Master

Mafter Cobweb: If I cut my finger, I fhall make bold with you.— Your name, honeft gentleman¹?

Peafe. Peafe-bloffom.

Bot. I pray you, commend me to Miftrefs Squafh, your mother⁶, and to Mafter Peafcod, your father. Good Mafter Peafe-bloffom, I fhall defire you of more acquaintance too.— Your name, I befeech you, Sir?

Muf. Muftard-feed.

Bot. Good Mafter Muftard-feed, I know your patience⁷ well: that fame cowardly, giant-like, ox-beef hath devoured many a gentleman of your houfe: I promife you your kindred hath made my eyes water ere now. I defire you, more acquaintance, good mafter Muftard-feed.

Tita. Come, wait upon him; lead him to my bower.
The moon, methinks, looks with a watery eye;
And when fhe weeps, weeps every little flower,
Lamenting fome enforced chaftity.
Tie up my lover's tongue⁸, bring him filently. [*Exeunt.*

---

¹ *— good Mafter Cobweb: If I cut my finger, I fhall make bold with you.—Your name, honeft gentleman?*] In *The Mayde's Metamorphofis,* a comedy by Lilly, there is a dialogue between fome forefters and a troop of fairies, very fimilar to the prefent:

"*Mo.* I pray, Sir, what might I call you?
"1. *Fai.* My name is Penny.
"*Mop.* I am forry I cannot purfe you.
"*Frifco.* I pray you, Sir, what might I call you?
"2. *Fai.* My name is Cricket.
"*Frif.* I would I were a chimney for your fake."

The *Maid's Metamorphofis,* was not printed till 1600, but was probably written fome years before. Mr Warton fays, (*Hiftory of Englifh Poetry,* vol. ii. p. 373.) that Lilly's laft play appeared in 1597.
MALONE.

⁶ — *Miftrefs Squafh, your mother,*] A *fquafh* is an immature peafcod. So, in *Twelfth Night,* Act i. fc. v.: "—as a *fquafh* is, before 'tis a peafcod." STEEVENS.

⁷ — *patience.*] By *patience* is meant, ftanding ftill in a muftard pot to be eaten with the beef, on which it was a conftant attendant.
COLLINS.

⁸ *my lover's tongue,*] The old copies read—my *lover's* tongue, and they are certainly right. Mr. Pope had made it—my *love's* tongue. Our poet has again ufed lover as a monofyllable in *Twelfth Night:*
"Sad true *lover* never find my grave." MALONE.

Q5 SCENE

SCENE II.

Another part of the Wood.

Enter OBERON.

Obe. I wonder, if Titania be awak'd;
Then, what it was that next came in her eye,
Which she must dote on in extremity.

Enter PUCK.

Here comes my messenger.—How now, mad spirit?
What night-rule [a] now about this haunted grove?
 Puck. My mistress with a monster is in love.
Near to her close and consecrated bower,
While she was in her dull and sleeping hour,
A crew of patches [1], rude mechanicals,
That work for bread upon Athenian stalls,
Were met together to rehearse a play,
Intended for great Theseus' nuptial day.
The shallowest thick-skin of that barren sort [2],
Who Pyramus presented, in their sport
Forsook his scene, and enter'd in a brake:
When I did him at this advantage take,

---

[a] *What night-rule—*] Night-rule in this place should seem to mean, what frolic of the night, what revelry is going forward? So, in *Tom Tyler and his Wife*, 1661: "Marry, here is good rule." It appears, from the old song of *Robin Goodfellow*, in the third volume of Dr. Percy's *Reliques of Ancient English Poetry*, that it was the office of this waggish spirit "to viewe the nighte-sports." STEEVENS.

[1] *—patches,*] Patch was in old language used as a term of opprobry; perhaps with much the same import as we use *raggamuffin*, or *tatterdemalion*. JOHNSON.

This common opprobrious term, probably took its rise from Patch, Cardinal Wolsey's fool. In the western counties, *cross-patch* is still used for *perverse, ill-natured fool*. T. WARTON.

The name was rather taken from the *patch'd* or *pyed* coats worn by the fools or jesters of those times. STEEVENS.

I should suppose *patch* to be merely a corruption of the Italian *pazzo*, which signifies properly a *fool*. So, in the *Merchant of Venice*, Act ii. sc. v. Shylock says of Launcelot, *The* patch *is kind enough*;—after having just called him, *that fool of Hagar's offspring*. TYRWHITT.

[2] *—sort,*] See note 5. MALONE.

An ass's nowl [3] I fixed on his head;
Anon, his Thisbe must be answered,
And forth my mimic [4] comes: When they him spy,
As wild geese that the creeping fowler eye,
Or russet-pated choughs, many in sort [5],
Rising and cawing at the gun's report,
Sever themselves, and madly sweep the sky;
So, at his sight, away his fellows fly:
And, at our stamp [6], here o'er and o'er one falls;
He murder cries, and help from Athens calls.

Their

[3] —*nowl*—] A head. Saxon. JOHNSON.

[4] —*my mimic*—] This is the reading of the folio. The quarto printed by Fisher has —*minnic*; that by Roberts *minnow*: both evidently corruptions. The line has been explained as if it related to Thisbe; but it does not relate to her, but to Pyramus. Bottom had just been playing that part, and had retired into a brake; (according to Quince's direction: " When you have spoken your speech, enter into that brake.") " Anon his Thisbe must be answered, And forth my mimic (i. e. my actor) *comes*." In this there seems no difficulty.

Mimic is used as synonymous to *actor*, by Decker, in his Gul's Hornbook, 1609: " Draw what troop you can from the stage after you; the mimics are beholden to you for allowing them elbow room." Again, in his Satiromastix, 1602: " Thou [Ben Jonson] hast forgot how thou amblest in a leather pilch by a play-waggon in the highway, and took'st mad Jeronymo's part; to get service amongst the *mimics*." MALONE.

[5] —*sort*,] Company. So above: " — *that barren* sort; and in Waller;
" A *sort of lusty shepherds strive*." JOHNSON.

[6] And, at our *stamp*,—] This seems to be a vicious reading. Fairies are never represented stamping, or of a size that should give force to a thump, nor could they have distinguished the stamps of Puck from those of their own companies; I read:

And at a *stump* here o'er and o'er one falls." JOHNSON.

I adhere to the old reading. The *stamp* of a fairy might be efficacious, though not loud; neither is it necessary to suppose, when supernatural beings are spoken of, that the size of the agent determines the force of the action. That fairies did *stamp* to some purpose, may be known from the following passage in Olaus Magnus de Gentibus Septentrionalibus.—" Vero saltum *aho profundè* in terram impresserunt, ut locus insigni ardore orbiculariter peresus, non pariat arenti redivivum cespite gramen." Shakspeare's own authority, however, is most decisive. See the conclusion of the first scene of the fourth act;

" Come, my queen, take hand with me,
" And *rock* the ground whereon these sleepers be." STEEVENS.

Our " grandams maides were woont to set a boll of milke before Incubus, and his cousin Robin Goodfellow, for grinding of malt or mustard, and sweeping the house at midnight; and—he would chafe exceedingly if the maid or good wife of the house, having compassion of his nakedness, laid anie clothes for him, besides his messe of white bread

and

Their sense, thus weak, lost with their fears, thus strong,
Made senseless things begin to do them wrong:
For briers and thorns at their apparel snatch;
Some sleeves; some hats: from yielders all things catch.
I led them on in this distracted fear,
And left sweet Pyramus translated there:
When in that moment (so it came to pass)
Titania wak'd, and straightway lov'd an ass.

Obe. This falls out better than I could devise.
But hast thou yet latch'd [7] the Athenian's eyes
With the love-juice, as I did bid thee do?

Puck. I took him sleeping—that is finish'd too—
And the Athenian woman by his side;
That, when he wak'd, of force she must be ey'd.

Enter DEMETRIUS *and* HERMIA.

Obe. Stand close; this is the same Athenian.
Puck. This is the woman, but not this the man.
Dem. O, why rebuke you him that loves you so?
Lay breath so bitter on your bitter foe.
Her. Now I but chide, but I should use thee worse;
For thou, I fear, hast given me cause to curse.
If thou hast slain Lysander in his sleep,
Being o'er shoes in blood [8], plunge in the deep,
And kill me too.
The sun was not so true unto the day,
As he to me: Would he have stol'n away
From sleeping Hermia? I'll believe as soon,
This whole earth may be bor'd; and that the moon
May through the center creep, and so displease
Her brother's noon-tide with the Antipodes.[9]
It cannot be, but thou hast murder'd him;
So should a murderer look; so dead [1], so grim.

Dem.

and miller, which was his standing fee; for in that case he saith, What have we here? Henton haunten, here will I never more tread, nor stampen." *Discoveries of Witchcraft*, by Reginald Scott, 1584. p 85.
ANONYMOUS.

[7] ——*latch'd*] or ketch'd, lick'd over; *lecher*, to lick, French.
HANMER.

In the North, it signifies to *infect*. STEEVENS.

[8] *Being o'er shoes in blood*,] An allusion to the proverb, *Over shoes, over boots*. JOHNSON.

[9] —— *with the Antipodes.*] i. e. on the other side of the globe. EDWARDS.

[1] —— *so dead*,] So again in *K. Henry IV*. P. ii. Act. i. sc. iii.

"*Ev'n*

Dem. So should the murder'd look; and so should I,
Pierc'd through the heart with your stern cruelty:
Yet you, the murderer, look as bright, as clear,
As yonder Venus in her glimmering sphere.
  Her. What's this to my Lysander? where is he?
Ah, good Demetrius, wilt thou give him me?
  Dem. I had rather give his carcase to my hounds.
  Her. Out, dog! out, cur! thou driv'st me past the bounds
Of maiden's patience. Hast thou slain him then?
Henceforth be never number'd among men!
O! once tell true, tell true, even for my sake;
Durst thou have look'd upon him, being awake,
And hast thou kill'd him sleeping³? O brave touch³!
Could not a worm, an adder, do so much?
An adder did it; for with doubler tongue
Than thine, thou serpent, never adder stung.
  Dem. You spend your passion on a mispris'd mood⁴:
I am not guilty of Lysander's blood;
Nor is he dead, for aught that I can tell.
  Her. I pray thee tell me then that he is well.
  Dem. An if I could, what should I get therefore?
  Her. A privilege, never to see me more.——
And from thy hated presence part I so⁵:
See me no more, whether he be dead or no.   [*Exit.*
  Dem. There is no following her in this fierce vein:
Here, therefore, for a while I will remain.

   " *Even such a man, so faint, so spiritless,*
   " *So dull, so dead in look, so woe-begone.*   STEEVENS.
So also in Lodge's *Rosalind and Euphues:* "—if thou marry in age,
thy wife's fresh colours will breed in thee dead thoughts and suspicion."
                                                MALONE.

³ *Durst thou have look'd upon him, being awake,*
   And hast thou kill'd him sleeping?] She means, Hast thou kill'd him
sleeping, whom, when awake, thou didst not dare to look upon?

³ — *O brave touch!*] *Touch* in Shakspeare's time was the same with
our *exploit*, or rather *stroke.* A brave *touch*, a noble stroke, *un grand
coup.*   JOHNSON.
   A *touch* anciently signified a *trick.* In the old black letter story of
Howleglas, it is always used in that sense.   STEEVENS.

⁴ — *mispris'd mood:*] Mistaken; as below *misprision* is mistake.
                                                JOHNSON.
   Mood is *anger*, or perhaps rather in this place, *caprision fancy.*
                                                MALONE.

⁵ — *part I so:*] *So*, which is not in the old copy, was inserted for the
sake of both metre and rhime, by Mr. Pope.   MALONE.

                                                So

So sorrow's heaviness doth heavier grow,
For debt that bankrupt sleep doth sorrow owe;
Which now in some slight measure it will pay,
If for his tender here I make some stay. [*lies down.*

Obe. What hast thou done? thou hast mistaken quite,
And laid the love-juice on some true love's sight:
Of thy misprision must perforce ensue
Some true love turn'd, and not a false turn'd true.

Puck. Then fate o'er-rules; that, one man holding troth,
A million fail, confounding oath on oath.

Obe. About the wood go swifter than the wind,
And Helena of Athens look thou find:
All fancy-sick she is, and pale of cheer
With sighs of love, that cost the fresh blood dear:
By some illusion see thou bring her here;
I'll charm his eyes, against she do appear.

Puck. I go, I go; look, how I go;
Swifter than arrow from the Tartar's bow. [*Exit.*

Obe. Flower of this purple dye,
Hit with Cupid's archery [6],
Sink in apple of his eye!
When his love he doth espy,
Let her shine as gloriously
As the Venus of the sky.—
When thou wak'st, if she be by,
Beg of her for remedy.

Re-enter PUCK.

Puck. Captain of our fairy band,
Helena is here at hand;
And the youth mistook by me,
Pleading for a lover's fee;
Shall we their fond pageant see?
Lord, what fools these mortals be!

Obe. Stand aside: the noise they make
Will cause Demetrius to awake.

Puck. Then will two, at once, woo one;
That must needs be sport alone:
And those things do best please me,
That befal preposterously.

---

[6] *Hit with Cupid's archery,*] This alludes to what was said before:
——— the bolt of Cupid fell,
It fell upon a little western flower,
Before milk-white, now purple with love's wound. STEEV.

Enter LYSANDER *and* HELENA.

Lyf. Why should you think, that I should woo in scorn?
Scorn and derision never come in tears:
Look, when I vow, I weep; and vows so born,
In their nativity all truth appears.
How can these things in me seem scorn to you,
Bearing the badge of faith to prove them true?

Hel. You do advance your cunning more and more.
When truth kills truth, O devilish-holy fray!
These vows are Hermia's; Will you give her o'er?
Weigh oath with oath, and you will nothing weigh:
Your vows, to her and me, put in two scales,
Will even weigh; and both as light as tales.

Lyf. I had no judgment, when to her I swore.

Hel. Nor none, in my mind, now you give her o'er.

Lyf. Demetrius loves her, and he loves not you.

Dem. [*awaking.*] O Helen, goddess, nymph, perfect, divine!
To what, my love, shall I compare thine eyne?
Crystal is muddy. O, how ripe in show
Thy lips, those kissing cherries, tempting grow!
That pure congealed white, high Taurus' snow [7],
Fann'd with the eastern wind, turns to a crow,
When thou hold'st up thy hand: O let me kiss
This princess of pure white [8], this seal of bliss [9]!

Hel. O spight! O hell! I see you all are bent
To set against me, for your merriment.
If you were civil, and knew courtesy,
You would not do me thus much injury.
Can you not hate me, as I know you do,
But you must join, in souls [1], to mock me too?

If

[7] *Taurus' snow.*] Taurus is the name of a range of mountains in Asia. JOHNSON.

[8] *This princess of pure white*—] So in Wyat's poems:
"— of beauty princess chief." STEEVENS.
In the *Winter's Tale* we meet with a similar expression:
"—— good sooth, she is
"The Queen of curds and cream." MALONE.

[9] *—seal of bliss!*] He has, in *Measure for Measure*, the same image:
"But my kisses bring again,
"Seals of love, but seal'd in vain." JOHNSON.

[1] *— join in souls.*] i. e. join heartily, unite in the same mind. Shakspeare in *Henry V.* uses an expression not unlike this:

"For

If you were men, as men you are in show,
You would not use a gentle lady so;
To vow, and swear, and superpraise my parts,
When, I am sure, you hate me with your hearts.
You both are rivals, and love Hermia;
And now both rivals, to mock Helena:
A trim exploit, a manly enterprize [2],
To conjure tears up in a poor maid's eyes,
With your derision! None, of noble sort [3],
Would so offend a virgin; and extort [4]
A poor soul's patience [4], all to make you sport.

Lys. You are unkind, Demetrius; be not so;
For you love Hermia; this, you know, I know:
And here, with all good will, with all my heart,
In Hermia's love I yield you up my part;
And yours of Helena to me bequeath,
Whom I do love, and will do to my death.

Hel. Never did mockers waste more idle breath.

"*For we will hear, note, and believe* in heart;"
i. e. heartily believe; and, in *Measure for Measure*, he talks of electing with *special soul*. In *Troilus and Cressida*, Ulysses, relating the character of Hector as given him by Æneas, says,
  "——— with *private soul*
  "Did in great Ilion thus translate him to me."
And, in *All Fools*, by Chapman, 1605, is the same expression as that in the text:
  "Happy, *in soul*, only by winning her."
Again in *Pierce Pennilesse his supplication to the Devil*, 1592:—" whose subversion *in soul* they have vow'd." STEEVENS.

A similar phraseology is found in *Measure for Measure*:
  "Is't not enough thou hast suborn'd these women
  "To accuse this worthy man, but in foul mouth
  "To call him villain!" MALONE.
I rather believe the line should be read thus:
  "But you must join, *ill* souls, to mock me too." TYRWHITT.

[2] *A trim exploit, a manly enterprize, &c.*] This is written much in the manner and spirit of Juno's reproach to Venus in the 4th book of the *Æneid*:
  "Egregiam vero laudem et spolia ampla refertis,
  "Tuque puerque tuus; magnum et memorabile nomen,
  "Una dolo divôm si fœmina victa duorum est." STEEVENS.

[3] —— *none, of noble* sort,] *Sort,* is here used for *degree* or *quality.* So in the old ballad of *Jane Shore:*
  "Long time I lived in the court,
  "With lords and ladies of great *sort*." MALONE.

[4] —— *extort a poor soul's patience.*] Harrass, torment. JOHNSON.

Dem.

Dem. Lysander, keep thy Hermia; I will none:
If e'er I lov'd her, all that love is gone.
My heart with her but, as guest-wise, sojourn'd;
And now to Helen is it home return'd [5],
There to remain.
　Lys. Helen, it is not so.
　Dem. Disparage not the faith thou dost not know,
Lest, to thy peril, thou aby it dear.—
Look, where thy love comes; yonder is thy dear.

Enter HERMIA.

　Her. Dark night, that from the eye his function takes,
The ear more quick of apprehension makes;
Wherein it doth impair the seeing sense,
It pays the hearing double recompence:—
Thou art not by mine eye, Lysander, found;
Mine ear, I think it, brought me to thy sound.
But why unkindly did'st thou leave me so?
　Lys. Why should he stay, whom love doth press to go?
　Her. What love could press Lysander from my side?
　Lys. Lysander's love, that would not let him bide,
Fair Helena; who more engilds the night
Than all yon fiery oes [6] and eyes of light.
Why seek'st thou me? could not this make thee know,
The hate I bare thee made me leave thee so?
　Her. You speak not as you think; it cannot be.
　Hel. Lo, she is one of this confederacy!
Now I perceive they have conjoin'd, all three,

---

[5] *My heart with her but, as guest-wise, sojourn'd;*
And now to Helen is it home return'd,] So, in our author's 109th Sonnet:

"This is my *home* of love; if I have rang'd,
"Like him that travels, I *return again*."

The old copies read—*to her.* Corrected by Dr. Johnson. MALONE.

My heart, &c.] So Prior:

"No matter what beauties I saw in my way,
"They were but my visits, but thou art my home." JOHNSON.

[6] *— all you fiery oes*] Shakspeare uses O for a circle. So, in the prologue to *King Henry V.*

"———— can we crowd
"Within this little *O*, the very casques
"That did affright the air at Agincourt?" STEEVENS.

D'Ewes's *Journal of Queen Elizabeth's Parliaments*, p. 650, mentions a patent to make spangles and *oes* of gold; and I think haberdashers call small curtain rings, O's as being circular. TOLLET.

To

To fashion this false sport in spight of me.
Injurious Hermia! most ungrateful maid?
Have you conspir'd, have you with these contriv'd
To bait me with this foul derision?
Is all the counsel that we two have shar'd,
The sisters' vows⁷, the hours that we have spent,
When we have chid the hasty-footed time
For parting us—O, is all now forgot⁸?
All school-days' friendship, childhood innocence?
We, Hermia, like two artificial gods⁹,
Have with our needls¹ created both one flower,
Both on one sampler, sitting on one cushion,
Both warbling of one song, both in one key;
As if our hands, our sides, voices, and minds,
Had been incorporate. So we grew together,
Like to a double cherry, seeming parted;
But yet an union in partition,

⁷ *The sisters' vows*—] We might read more elegantly—*The sister' vows*, and a few lines lower—*All school-day friendship*. The latter emendation was made by Mr. Pope; but changes merely for the sake of elegance ought to be admitted with great caution. MALONE.

⁸ *For parting us—O, is all now forgot?*] The word *now* is not in the old copies. For the emendation the present editor is answerable. The editor of the second folio, to complete the metre, introduced the word *and*;—*O, and is all forgot?* It stands so awkwardly, that I am persuaded it was not the author's word. MALONE.

⁹ —*artificial gods,*] *Artificial* is ingenious, artful. STEEVENS.

¹ *Have with our needls, &c.*] In the old copies the word is written *needles*. MALONE.

It was probably written by Shakspeare *needls*, (a common contraction in the inland counties at this day), otherwise the verse will be inharmonious. See Gammer Gurton's *Needle*. The same idea occurs in *Pericles, Prince of Tyre*, 1609:

"————she
" Would ever with Marina be;
" Be't when they weav'd the sleded silk,
" With fingers long, small, white as milk,
" Or when she would with sharp *nyld* wound
" The cambrick, &c."

In the age of Shakspeare many contractions were used. Ben Jonson has *wher* for *whether* in the prologue to his *Sad Shepherd*; and in Lord Sterline's *Darius* is *sport* for *support*, and *twards* for *towards*. STEEVENS.

In the old editions of these plays many words of two syllables are printed at length, though intended to be pronounced as one. Thus *spirit* is almost always so written, though often used as a monosyllable; and *whether*, though intended often to be contracted, is always (I think, improperly,) written at length. MALONE.

Two

Two lovely berries moulded on one stem:
So, with two seeming bodies, but one heart;
Two of the first, like coats in heraldry,
Due but to one, and crowned with one crest [2].
And will you rent our ancient love asunder,
To join with men in scorning your poor friend?
It is not friendly, 'tis not maidenly:
Our sex, as well as I, may chide you for it;
Though I alone do feel the injury.

Her. I am amazed at your passionate words:
I scorn you not; it seems that you scorn me.

Hel. Have you not set Lysander, as in scorn,
To follow me, and praise my eyes and face?
And made your other love, Demetrius,
(Who even but now did spurn me with his foot,)
To call me goddess, nymph, divine, and rare,
Precious, celestial? Wherefore speaks he this
To her he hates? and wherefore doth Lysander
Deny your love, so rich within his soul,
And tender me, forsooth, affection;
But by your setting on, by your consent?
What though I be not so in grace as you,
So hung upon with love, so fortunate;
But miserable most, to love unlov'd?
This you should pity, rather than despise.

Her. I understand not what you mean by this.

Hel. Ay, do, persever [3], counterfeit sad looks,
Make mouths upon me when I turn my back;
Wink at each other; hold the sweet jest up:

---

[2] *Two of the first, like coats in heraldry,*
Due but to one, and crowned with one crest.] The old copy reads—*life coats*, &c. Corrected by Mr. Martin Folkes.
According to the rules of heraldry, the *first* house only, (e. g. a father who has a son living, or an elder brother as distinguished from a younger,) has a right to bear the family coat. The son's coat is distinguished from the father's by a label; the younger brother's from the elder's by a mullet. The same crest is common to both. Helena therefore means to say, that she and her friend were as closely united, as much *one* person, as if they were *both of the first* house; as if they both had the privilege *due but to one* person, (viz. to him of the first house,) the right of bearing the family coat without any distinguishing mark. MALONE.

[3] — persever,] The word was formerly so pronounced. So, in *All's Well that Ends Well*, Act iv. sc. ii.:
" ———— say, thou art mine, and ever
" My love, as it begins, so shall persever." STEEVENS.

This sport, well carry'd, shall be chronicled.
If you have any pity, grace, or manners,
You would not make me such an argument [4].
But, fare ye well: 'tis partly mine own fault;
Which death, or absence, soon shall remedy.
  Lys. Stay, gentle Helena; hear my excuse;
My love, my life, my soul, fair Helena!
  Hel. O excellent!
  Her. Sweet, do not scorn her so.
  Dem. If she cannot entreat, I can compel.
  Lys. Thou canst compel no more than she entreat;
Thy threats have no more strength, than her weak prays [5].—
Helen, I love thee; by my life, I do;
I swear by that which I will lose for thee,
To prove him false, that says I love thee not.
  Dem. I say, I love thee more than he can do.
  Lys. If thou say so, withdraw, and prove it too.
  Dem. Quick, come—
  Her. Lysander, whereto tends all this?
  Lys. Away, you Ethiop!
  Dem. No, no; he'll——Sir [6],
Seem to break loose; take on, as you would follow;
But yet come not: you are a tame man, go!
  Lys. Hang off, thou cat, thou burr; vile thing, let loose;
Or I will shake thee from me, like a serpent.
  Her. Why are you grown so rude? what change is this,
Sweet love?
  Lys. Thy love? out, tawny Tartar, out!

---

[4] *—such an argument.*] Such a *subject* of light merriment. JOHNSON. So, in the first part of *King Henry IV.* Act ii. sc. ii.
  " — it would be *argument* for a week, &c." STEEVENS.

[5] *—than her weak prays.*] i. e. prayers, entreaties. The old copies read—*her weak praise.* Mr. Theobald proposed the reading now adopted. A noun thus formed from the verb, to *pray*, is much in our author's manner; and the transcriber's ear might have been easily deceived by the similarity of sounds. MALONE.

[6] *No, no, he'll——Sir,*] This passage, like almost all those in these plays in which there is a sudden transition, or the sense is hastily broken off, is much corrupted in the old copies. The present text is formed from the quarto printed by Fisher and the first folio. The words "*he'll*" are not in the folio, and *Sir* is not in the quarto. Demetrius, I suppose, would say, *No, no;* he'll *not have resolution to disengage* himself *from Hermia.* But turning abruptly to Lysander, he addresses him ironically:—Sir, seem to break loose; &c. MALONE.

Out,

Out, loathed medicine! hated potion, hence[7]!

Her. Do you not jeſt?

Hel. Yes, 'footh; and ſo do you.

Lyſ. Demetrius, I will keep my word with thee.

Dem. I would, I had your bond: for I perceive,
A weak bond holds you; I'll not truſt your word.

Lyſ. What, ſhould I hurt her, ſtrike her, kill her dead?
Although I hate her, I'll not harm her ſo.

Her. What, can you do me greater harm, than hate?
Hate me! wherefore? O me! what news, my love?
Am not I Hermia? Are not you Lyſander?
I am as fair now, as I was erewhile.
Since night, you lov'd me; yet, ſince night, you left me:
Why, then you left me—O, the gods forbid!—
In earneſt, ſhall I ſay?

Lyſ. Ay, by my life;
And never did deſire to ſee thee more.
Therefore, be out of hope, of queſtion, doubt[8],
Be certain, nothing truer; 'tis no jeſt,
That I do hate thee, and love Helena.

Her. O me! you juggler! you canker-bloſſom[9]!
You thief of love! what, have you come by night,
And ſtol'n my love's heart from him?

Hel. Fine, i'faith!
Have you no modeſty, no maiden ſhame,
No touch of baſhfulneſs? What, will you tear
Impatient anſwers from my gentle tongue?
Fie, fie! you counterfeit, you puppet, you!

Her. Puppet! why ſo? Ay, that way goes the game.
Now I perceive that ſhe hath made compare
Between our ſtatures, ſhe hath urg'd her height;
And with her perſonage, her tall perſonage,

---

[7] — *hated potion, hence!*] The old copies have *O* before *hated.* Corrected by Mr. Pope. MALONE.

[8] — *of queſtion, doubt,*] The old copies read—*of doubt.* The correction was made by Mr. Pope. MALONE.

[9] *O me! you juggler! you canker-bloſſom!*] *Juggler,* in this line, is uſed as a triſyllable; So again, in *King Henry VI.* P. i.:

"She and the dauphin have been *juggling.*"
So alſo *tickling, wreſtler,* and many more. MALONE.

By the *canker bloſſom* is here meant a worm that preys on the leaves or buds of flowers, always beginning in the middle. So, in this play, Act ii. ſc. iii.:

"Some to kill *cankers* in the muſk-roſe buds." STEEVENS.

Her height, forsooth, she hath prevail'd with him.—
And are you grown so high in his esteem,
Because I am so dwarfish, and so low?
How low am I, thou painted maypole? speak;
How low am I? I am not yet so low,
But that my nails can reach unto thine eyes.

Hel. I pray you, though you mock me, gentlemen,
Let her not hurt me: I was never curst [1];
I have no gift at all in shrewishness;
I am a right maid for my cowardice;
Let her not strike me: You, perhaps, may think,
Because she's something lower than myself,
That I can match her.

Her. Lower! hark, again.

Hel. Good Hermia, do not be so bitter with me.
I evermore did love you, Hermia,
Did ever keep your counsels, never wrong'd you;
Save that, in love unto Demetrius,
I told him of your stealth unto this wood:
He follow'd you; for love, I follow'd him.
But he hath chid me hence; and threaten'd me
To strike me, spurn me, nay, to kill me too:
And now, so you will let me quiet go,
To Athens will I bear my folly back,
And follow you no further: Let me go:
You see how simple and how fond I am [2].

Her. Why, get you gone: Who is't that hinders you?
Hel. A foolish heart, that I leave here behind.
Her. What, with Lysander?
Hel. With Demetrius.
Lys. Be not afraid: she shall not harm thee, Helena.
Dem. No, Sir; she shall not, though you take her part.
Hel. O, when she's angry, she is keen and shrew'd:
She was a vixen when she went to school;
And, though she be but little, she is fierce.

Her. Little again? nothing but low and little?—
Why will you suffer her to flout me thus?
Let me come to her.

Lys. Get you gone, you dwarf;

---

[1] *— I was never curst*] Perverse; wicked. MALONE.
[2] *— how fond*] i. e. foolish. STEEVENS.

You

You minimus, of hind'ring knot-grass made³;
You bead, you acorn.
  Dem. You are too officious,
In her behalf that scorns your services.
Let her alone; speak not of Helena;
Take not her part: for if thou dost intend
Never so little shew of love to her,
Thou shalt aby it⁴.
  Lys. Now she holds me not;
Now follow, if thou dar'st, to try whose right,
Or thine or mine⁵, is most in Helena.
  Dem. Follow? nay, I'll go with thee, check by jole.
                    [*Exeunt* LYSANDER *and* DEMETRIUS.
  Her. You, mistress, all this coil is 'long of you:
Nay, go not back.
  Hel. I will not trust you, I;
Nor longer stay in your curst company.
Your hands, than mine, are quicker for a fray;
My legs are longer though, to run away.   [*Exit.*
  Her. I am amaz'd, and know not what to say.
                    [*Exit, pursuing* HELENA.
  Obe. This is thy negligence: still thou mistak'st,
Or else commit'st thy knaveries wilfully.
  Puck. Believe me, king of shadows, I mistook.
Did not you tell me, I should know the man
By the Athenian garments he had on?
And so far blameless proves my enterprize,
That I have 'nointed an Athenian's eyes:
And so far am I glad it so did sort⁶,
As this their jangling I esteem a sport.

---

³ *—of hind'ring knot-grass made;*] It appears that knot-grass was anciently supposed to prevent the growth of any animal or child. Beaumont and Fletcher mention this property of it in the *Knight of the Burning Pestle*, and in the *Coxcomb*. Daisy roots were supposed to have the same effect. STEEVENS.

⁴ *Thou shalt aby it.*] To *aby* is to pay dear for, to suffer. STEEVENS.

⁵ *Or thine or mine—*] The old copies read—*Of* thine. The emendation is Mr. Theobald's. I am not sure that the old reading is corrupt. If the line had run—" Of mine or thine," I should have suspected that the phrase was borrowed from the Latin:—Now follow, to try whose right of *property*—of *meum* or *tuum*—is the greatest in Helena.
                                                        MALONE.

⁶ *—so did sort,*] So happen in the issue. JOHNSON.

Obe. Thou seest, these lovers seek a place to fight:
Hie therefore, Robin, overcast the night;
The starry welkin cover thou anon
With drooping fog, as black as Acheron;
And lead these testy rivals so astray,
As one come not within another's way.
Like to Lysander sometime frame thy tongue,
Then stir Demetrius up with bitter wrong;
And sometime rail thou like Demetrius;
And from each other look thou lead them thus,
Till o'er their brows death counterfeiting sleep
With leaden legs and batty wings doth creep:
Then crush this herb into Lysander's eye;
Whose liquor hath this virtuous property [7],
To take from thence all error, with his might,
And make his eye-balls roll with wonted sight.
When they next wake, all this derision
Shall seem a dream, and fruitless vision;
And back to Athens shall the lovers wend,
With league, whose date till death shall never end.
Whiles I in this affair do thee employ,
I'll to my queen, and beg her Indian boy;
And then I will her charmed eye release
From monster's view, and all things shall be peace.

Puck. My fairy Lord, this must be done with haste;
For night's swift dragons cut the clouds full fast [8],
And yonder shines Aurora's harbinger;
At whose approach, ghosts, wandering here and there,
Troop home to church-yards: damned spirits all,
That in cross-ways and floods have burial [9],

Already

---

[7] — *virtuous property,*] Salutiferous. So he calls, in the *Tempest, poisonous dew, wicked dew.* JOHNSON.

[8] — *night's swift dragons cut the clouds full fast.*] "The image of dragons drawing the chariot of the night is derived" (as a late writer has observed,) "from the watchfulness of that fabled animal." LETTERS OF LITERATURE, 8vo. 1785.

This circumstance Shakspeare might have learned from a passage in Golding's translation of Ovid, which he has imitated in the *Tempest:*
"Among the earth-bred brothers you a mortal war did set,
"And brought asleep the *dragon* fell, *whose eyes were never shet.*"
MALONE.

[9] — *damned spirits all,
That in cross-ways and floods have burial,*] i. e. The ghosts of self-murderers, who are buried in cross-roads; and of those who being drowned,

Already to their wormy beds are gone;
For fear lest day should look their shames upon,
They wilfully themselves exile from light,
And must for aye consort with black-brow'd night.

Obe. But we are spirits of another sort:
I with the morning's love have oft made sport [1];
And, like a forester, the groves may tread,
Even till the eastern gate, all fiery-red,
Opening on Neptune with fair blessed beams,
Turns into yellow gold his salt-green streams.
But, notwithstanding, haste; make no delay:
We may effect this business yet ere day. [*Exit* OBE.

Puck. Up and down, up and down;
I will lead them up and down;
I am fear'd in field and town;
Goblin, lead them up and down,
Here comes one.

Enter LYSANDER.

Lys. Where art thou, proud Demetrius? speak thou now.
Puck. Here villain; drawn and ready. Where art thou?
Lys. I will be with thee straight.
Puck. Follow me then.
To plainer ground. [*Exit* LYS. *as following the voice.*

Enter DEMETRIUS.

Dem. Lysander! speak again.

---

drowned, were condemned (according to the opinion of the ancients) to wander for a hundred years, as the rites of sepulture had never been regularly bestowed on their bodies. That the waters were sometimes the place of residence for *damned spirits,* we learn from the ancient bl. L. Romance of *Syr Eglamoure of Artoys,* no date:

"Let seme preest a gospel saye,
"For doute of *fendes in the flode.*" STEEVENS.

[1] *I with the morning's love have oft made sport;*] Thus all the old copies, and I think, rightly. Tithonus was the husband of Aurora, and Tithonus was no *young* deity. So, in Spenser's *Fairy Queen,* b. iii. c. 3:

"As faire *Aurora* rising hastily,
"Doth by her blushing tell that she did lye
"All night in *old Tithones*' frozen bed."

How such a waggish spirit as the King of the Fairies might make sport with an antiquated lover, or his mistress in his absence, may be easily understood. Dr. Johnson reads with all the modern editors, " I with the morning's *light,* &c." STEEVENS.

Thou runaway, thou coward, art thou fled?
Speak. In some bush? Where dost thou hide thy head?
　Puck. Thou coward, art thou bragging to the stars,
Telling the bushes that thou look'st for wars,
And wilt not come? Come, recreant; come, thou child;
I'll whip thee with a rod: He is defil'd,
That draws a sword on thee.
　Dem. Yea; art thou there?
　Puck. Follow my voice; we'll try no manhood here.
　　　　　　　　　　　　[*Exeunt* PUCK *and* DEMETRIUS.

　　　　　Re-enter LYSANDER.

　Lys. He goes before me, and still dares me on;
When I come where he calls, then he is gone.
The villain is much lighter heel'd, than I:
I follow'd fast, but faster he did fly;
That fall'n am I in dark uneven way,
And here will rest me. Come, thou gentle day!
　　　　　　　　　　　　　　　　[*lies down.*
For if but once thou shew me thy grey light,
I'll find Demetrius, and revenge this spight. [*sleeps.*

　　　　Re-enter PUCK *and* DEMETRIUS.

　Puck. Ho, ho, ho! coward, why comest thou not [2]?
　Dem. Abide me, if thou dar'st; for well I wot,
Thou runn'st before me, shifting every place;
And dar'st not stand, nor look me in the face.
Were art thou?
　Puck. Come hither; I am here.
　Dem. Nay, then thou mock'st me. Thou shalt buy this
dear [3],
If ever I thy face by day-light see:
Now, go thy way. Faintness constraineth me

---

[2] Ho, ho, ho! *coward, why comest thou not?*] It may be remarked that this exclamation is peculiar to *Puck.* In the old song printed by Peck, in which he relates all his gambols, he concludes every verse with *ho, ho, ho!* He here forgets his assumed character. ANONYMOUS.
　The song above alluded to may be found in Percy's *Reliques of Ancient Poetry,* vol. iii. p. 203. MALONE.
[3] — *buy this dear,*] i. e. *thou shalt dearly pay for this.* Though this is sense, and may well enough stand, yet the poet perhaps wrote *thou shalt 'by it dear.* So, in another place, *thou shalt aby it.* So, *Milton:*
　"*How* dearly I abide that boast so vain." JOHNSON.

To-

To measure out my length on this cold bed.—
By day's approach look to be visited. [*lies down and sleeps.*

Enter HELENA.

Hel. O weary night, O long and tedious night,
Abate thy hours: shine, comforts, from the east;
That I may back to Athens, by day-light,
From these that my poor company detest:—
And, sleep, that sometime shuts up sorrow's eye,
Steal me a while from mine own company. [*sleeps.*
 Puck. Yet but three? Come one more;
Two of both kinds make up four.
Here she comes, curst, and sad:—
Cupid is a knavish lad,
Thus to make poor females mad.

Enter HERMIA.

Her. Never so weary, never so in woe,
Bedabbled with the dew, and torn with briers;
I can no further crawl, no further go;
My legs can keep no pace with my desires.
Here will I rest me, till the break of day.
Heavens shield Lysander, if they mean a fray! [*lies down.*
 Puck. On the ground
   Sleep found:
    I'll apply
     To your eye,
Gentle lover, remedy.
     [*squeezing the juice on* Lysander's *eye.*
    When thou wak'st,
    Thou tak'st *
    True delight
    In the sight
Of thy former lady's eye:
And the country proverb known,
That every man should take his own,
In your waking shall be shown;

---

* *When thou wak'st,*
 Thou tak'st] The second line would be improved, I think, both in
its measure and construction, if it were written thus:
 When thou wak'st,
 See thou tak'st
 True delight, &c. TYRWHITT.

Jack shall have Jill [5]:
Nought shall go ill;
The man shall have his mare again, and all shall be well.
[*Exit* Puck.—Dem. Hel. &c. *sleep.*

ACT IV. SCENE I[6].

The same.

Enter Titania, *and* Bottom, *Fairies attending;* Oberon *behind, unseen.*

Tita. Come sit thee down upon this flowery bed,
 While I thy amiable cheeks do coy[7],
And stick musk-roses in thy sleek smooth head,
 And kiss thy fair large ears, my gentle joy.
Bot. Where's Pease-blossom?
Peafe. Ready.
Bot. Scratch my head, Pease-blossom.—Where's Monsieur Cobweb?
Cob. Ready.
Bot. Monsieur Cobweb; good Monsieur, get your weapons in your hand, and kill me a red-hip'd humble bee on the top of a thistle; and, good Monsieur, bring me the honey-bag. Do not fret yourself too much in the action, Monsieur; and, good Monsieur, have a care the honey-bag break not; I would be loth to have you over-flown[8] with a honey-bag, Signior.—Where's Monsieur Mustard-seed?

---

[5] *Jack shall have Jill,* &c.] These three last lines are to be found among *Heywood's Epigrams on three hundred Proverbs.* STEEVENS.

[6] I see no reason why the fourth act should begin here, when there seems no interruption of the action. In the old quartos of 1600, there is no division of acts, which seems to have been afterwards arbitrarily made in the first folio, and may therefore be altered at pleasure.
JOHNSON.

[7] *— do coy,*] To *coy,* is to sooth, to stroke. So, in Warner's *Albion's England,* 1602, B. vi. c. 30.:
 "And whilst she *coys* his footy cheeks, or curls his sweaty top.—"
STEEVENS.

[8] *— over-flown —*] It should be *over-flow'd;* but it appears from a rhyme in another play that the mistake was our author's. MALONE.

Must.

Muſt. Ready.
Bot. Give me your neif [9], Monſieur Muſtard-ſeed. Pray you, leave your courteſy, good Monſieur.
Muſt. What's your will?
Bot. Nothing, good Monſieur, but to help Cavalero Cobweb [1] to ſcratch. I muſt to the barber's, Monſieur; for, methinks, I am marvellous hairy about the face; and I am ſuch a tender aſs, if my hair do but tickle me, I muſt ſcratch.
Tita. What, wilt thou hear ſome muſic, my ſweet love?
Bot. I have a reaſonable good ear in muſic: let us have the tongs [2] and the bones.
Tita. Or, ſay, ſweet love, what thou deſir'ſt to eat.
Bot. Truly, a peck of provender; I could munch your good dry oats. Methinks I have a great deſire to a bottle of hay: good hay, ſweet hay, hath no fellow.
Tita. I have a venturous fairy that ſhall ſeek
The ſquirrel's hoard, and fetch thee new nuts.
Bot. I had rather have a handful, or two of dried peaſe. But, I pray you, let none of your people ſtir me; I have an expoſition of ſleep come upon me.
Tita. Sleep thou, and I will wind thee in my arms.
Fairies, be gone, and be all ways away [3].
So doth the woodbine [4], the ſweet honey-ſuckle,

Gently

---

[9] — *neif.*] i. e. fiſt. *Henry IV.* Act ii. ſc. v. 1
" *Sweet knight, I kiſs thy neif.*" GREY.

[1] — *Cavalero Cobweb*—! Without doubt it ſhould be *Cavalero* Peaſe-bloſſom; as for *Cavalero Cobweb*, he had juſt been diſpatched upon a perilous adventure. GREY.

[2] — *the tongs*—] The old ruſtic muſic of the *tongs and key.* The folio has this ſtage direction.—" *Muſicle Tongs, Rurall Muſicke.*"
STEEVENS.

[3] — *and be all ways away.*] i. e. diſperſe yourſelves, and ſcout out ſeverally, in your *watch*, that danger approach us from no quarter.
THEOBALD.
The old copies read—be *always*. Corrected by Mr. Theobald.
MALONE.

[4] *So doth the woodbine, the ſweet honey-ſuckle,*
Gently entwiſt—the female ivy ſo
Enrings, the barky fingers of the elm.] Dr. Warburton objects, that the wood-bine and the honey-ſuckle are the ſame plant, and that therefore it is abſurd to make one of them entwine the other. But the interpretation of either Dr. Johnſon or Mr. Steevens removes all difficulty. The following paſſage in *The Fatal Union,* 1640, in which the honey-ſuckle is ſpoken of as the flower, and the woodbine as the plant, adds ſome ſupport to Dr. Johnſon's expoſition :

Gently entwift—the female ivy [5] fo
Enrings, the barkey fingers of the elm.
O, how I love thee! how I dote on thee! [*They sleep.*

OBERON *advances.* *Enter* PUCK.

Obe. Welcome, good Robin. See'ft thou this fweet fight?
Her dotage now I do begin to pity.
For meeting her of late, behind the wood,
Seeking fweet favours for this hateful fool,
I did upbraid her, and fall out with her:
For fhe his hairy temples then had rounded.

" —— as fit a gift
" As this were for a lord—a *honey-fuckle,*
" The amorous *woodbine's offspring*."
But Minfhieu in v. *Woodbind,* fuppofes them the fame : " Alio nomine nobis Anglis *Honyfuckle* dictus." If Dr. Johnfon's explanation be right, there fhould be no point after *woodbine, honey-fuckle,* or *enrings.* MALONE.

Shakfpeare perhaps only meant, fo the leaves involve the flower, ufing *woodbine* for the plant, and *honey-fuckle* for the flower or perhaps Shakfpeare made a blunder. JOHNSON.

The thought is Chaucer's. See his *Troilus and Creffeide,* v. 1336, lib. III.
" And as about a tree with many a twift
" Bitrent and writhin is the fwete *woodbinde,*
" Gan eche of hem in armis other winde."

What Shakfpeare feems to mean, is this—*So the woodbine,* i. e. the *fweet honey-fuckle, doth gently entwift the barky fingers of the elm, and fo does the female ivy enring the fame fingers.* It is not unfrequent in the poets, as well as other writers, to explain one word by another which is better known. The reafon why Shakfpeare thought *woodbine* wanted illuftration, perhaps is this. In fome countries, by *woodbine* or *woodbind* would have been generally underftood the ivy, which he had occafion to mention in the very next line. STEEVENS.

It is certain that the *woodbine* and the *honey-fuckle* were fometimes confidered as different plants. But I think Mr. Steevens's interpretation the true one. The old writers did not always carry the auxiliary verb forward, as the late editor feems to have thought by his alteration of *enring* to *enring.* So Bifhop Lowth, in his excellent *Introduction to Grammar,* p. 126, has without reafon corrected a fimilar miftake in *St. Matthew.* FARMER.

5 — *the female ivy*] Shakfpeare calls it *female* ivy, becaufe it always requires fome fupport, which is poetically called its hufband. So Milton:
" —— led the vine
" To wed *her* elm; fhe fpous'd, about him twines
" Her marriageable arms."
Ulmo conjuncta marito. Catull.
Platanufque cœlebs
Evincet ulmos. Hor. STEEVENS.

With

With coronet of fresh and fragrant flowers;
And that same dew, which sometime on the buds
Was wont to swell, like round and orient pearls,
Stood now within the pretty flouret's eyes,
Like tears that did their own disgrace bewail.
When I had, at my pleasure, taunted her,
And she, in mild terms, begg'd my patience,
I then did ask of her her changeling child;
Which straight she gave me, and her fairy sent
To bear him to my bower in fairy land.
And now I have the boy, I will undo
This hateful imperfection of her eyes.
And, gentle Puck, take this transformed scalp
From off the head of this Athenian swain;
That he awaking when the others do [*],
May all to Athens back again repair;
And think no more of this night's accidents,
But as the fierce vexation of a dream.
But first I will release the fairy queen.
  Be, as thou wast wont to be;
            [*touching her eyes with an herb.*
  See, as thou wast wont to see:
  Dian's bud o'er Cupid's flower [6]
  Hath such force and blessed power.
Now, my Titania; wake you, my sweet queen.

Tita. My Oberon! what visions have I seen!
Methought, I was enamour'd of an ass.

Obe. There lies your love.

Tita. How came these things to pass?
O, how mine eyes do loath his visage now!

---

[*] *That he awaking when the other do,*] Such is the reading of the old copies, and such was the phraseology of Shakspeare's age; though the modern editors have rendered it—when the *others* do.
So, in *King Henry IV.* P. i.
  "— and unbound the rest, and then came in the *other*."
Again, in *King Henry IV.* P. ii. " For the *other*, Sir John, let me see," &c.
So, in the Epistle prefixed to *Pierce Pennilesse his Supplication to the Devil*, by Thomas Nashe, 4to. 1592; " I hope they will give me leave to think there be fooles of that art, as well as of all *other*." MALONE.

[6] *Dian's bud o'er Cupid's flower*] The old copies read—*or* Cupid's. Corrected by Dr. Thirlby. The herb now employed is styled *Diana's bud*, because it is applied as an antidote to that charm which had constrained Titania to dote on Bottom with " the soul of *love*." MALONE.

Obe. Silence, a while.—Robin, take off this head.
Titania, music call; and strike more dead
Than common sleep, of all these five the sense[7].
   Tita. Music, ho! music; such as charmeth sleep.
   Puck. Now, when thou wak'st, with thine own fool's eyes
      peep.
   Obe. Sound, music. [*Still music.*] Come, my queen, take
      hands with me,
And rock the ground whereon these sleepers be.
Now thou and I are new in amity;
And will, to-morrow midnight, solemnly,
Dance in Duke Theseus' house triumphantly,
And bless it to all fair prosperity[8]:
There shall the pairs of faithful lovers be
Wedded, with Theseus, all in jollity.
   Puck. Fairy king, attend, and mark;
   I do hear the morning lark.
   Obe. Then, my Queen, in silence sad,
   Trip we after the night's shade[9]:
   We the globe can compass soon,
   Swifter than the wand'ring moon.
   Tita. Come, my Lord; and in our flight,
   Tell me how it came this night,
   That I sleeping here was found,
   With these mortals on the ground.   [*Exeunt.*

---

[7] — *all these five the sense.*] The old copies read—these *fine*; the *u* being accidentally reversed at the press. The emendation was made by Mr. Theobald. MALONE.

The five that lay asleep on the stage were Demetrius, Lysander, Hermia, Helena, and Bottom. THEOBALD.

[8] — *to all fair* prosperity!] I have preferred this, which is the reading of the first and best quarto, printed by Fisher, to that of the other quarto and the folio, (*posterity,*) induced by the following lines in a former scene:

   "———— your warrior love
   "To Theseus must be wedded, and you come
   "To give their bed joy and *prosperity.*" MALONE.

[9] *Then, my Queen, in silence sad,*
Trip we after the night's shade:] Sad signifies grave, sober; and is opposed to their dances and revels, which were now ended at the singing of the morning lark. So, *Winter's Tale,* Act iv.: " *My father and the gentlemen are in sad talk.*" WARBURTON.

A statute 3 Hen. VII. c. 14. directs certain offences committed in the king's palace, to be tried by twelve *sad* men of the king's household.
                                BLACKSTONE.

Horns sound within.

Enter Theseus, Hippolita, Egeus, *and Train.*

The. Go, one of you, find out the forester;—
For now our observation is perform'd¹:
And since we have the vaward of the day,
My love shall hear the music of my hounds.—
Uncouple in the western valley; go:
Dispatch, I say, and find the forester.—
We will, fair Queen, up to the mountain's top,
And mark the musical confusion
Of hounds and echo in conjunction.

Hip. I was with Hercules, and Cadmus, once,
When in a wood of Crete they bay'd the bear²
With hounds of Sparta; never did I hear
Such gallant chiding³; for, besides the groves,

---

¹ — *our observation is perform'd:*] The honours due to the morning of *May.* I know not why Shakspeare calls this play a *Midsummer-Night's Dream*, when he so carefully informs us that it happened on the night preceding *May-day.* JOHNSON.

The title of this play seems no more intended to denote the precise *time of the action*, than that of *The Winter's Tale*; which we find, was at the season of sheep-shearing. FARMER.

The same phrase has been used in a former scene;
" To do *observance* to a morn of May."
I imagine that the title of this play was suggested by the time it was first introduced on the stage, which was probably at *Midsummer.* " A Dream for the *entertainment* of a Midsummer-night." *Twelfth Night* and *The Winter's Tale* had probably their titles from a similar circumstance. MALONE.

² — *they bay'd the bear*] Thus all the old copies. And thus in Chaucer's *Knightes Tale*, v. 2020, late edit:
" The hunte ystrangled with the wilde *beres.*" STEEVENS.

In *The Winter's Tale*, Antigonus is destroyed by a *bear*, who is chased by hunters. See also, our poet's *Venus and Adonis*:
" For now she hears it is no gentle chase,
" But the blunt boar, rough *bear*, or lion proud." MALONE.

Holinshed, with whose histories our poet was well acquainted, says, " the *bear* is a beast commonlie hunted in the East countries." See vol. i. p. 2065 and in p. 226, he says, " Alexander at vacant times hunted the tiger, the pard, the *bore*, and the *beare*." Pliny, Plutarch, &c. mention bear-hunting. Turberville, in his *Book of Hunting*, has two chapters on hunting the *bear*. As the persons mentioned by the poet are foreigners of the heroic strain, he might perhaps think it nobler sport for them to hunt the *bear* than the *boar*. TOLLET.

³ *Such gallant chiding;*] *Chiding* in this instance means only *sound.* So, in *King Henry VIII:*
" As doth a rock against the *chiding* flood." STEEVENS.

The skies, the fountains [4], every region near
Seem all one mutual cry: I never heard
So musical a discord, such sweet thunder.

The. My hounds are bred out of the Spartan kind [5],
So flew'd [6], so sanded [7]; and their heads are hung
With ears that sweep away the morning dew;
Crook-knee'd, and dew-lap'd like Thessalian bulls;
Slow in pursuit, but match'd in mouth like bells,
Each under each. A cry more tuneable
Was never holla'd to, nor cheer'd with horn,
In Crete, in Sparta, nor in Thessaly:
Judge, when you hear.—But, soft; what nymphs are these?

Ege. My Lord, this is my daughter here asleep;
And this, Lysander; this Demetrius is;
This Helena, old Nedar's Helena:
I wonder of [8] their being here together.

The.

[4] ———— *for, besides the groves.*

The skies, the fountains——] Instead of *fountains*, Mr. Heath would read *mountains*. The change had been proposed to Mr. Theobald, who has well supported the old reading, by observing that Virgil and other poets have made rivers, lakes, &c. responsive to sound:

Tum vero exoritur clamor, ripæque lacus que
Responsant circa, et cœlum tonat omne tumultu. MALONE.

[5] *My hounds are bred,* &c.] This passage has been imitated by Lee in his *Theseus:*

[6] "Then through the woods we chac'd the foaming boar,
"With hounds that open'd like Thessalian bulls;
"Like tygers flew'd, and sanded as the shore;
"With ears and cheils that dash'd the morning dew." MALONE.

[6] *So flew'd,*] i. e. so mouthed. *Flews* are the large chaps of a deep-mouthed hound. HANMER.

Arthur Golding uses this word in his translation of Ovid's *Metamorphoses,* finished 1567, a book with which Shakspeare appears to have been well acquainted. The poet is describing Actæon's hounds, b. iii. p. 33, b. 1603. 'Two of them, like our author's, were of Spartan kind; bred from a Spartan bitch and a Cretan dog:

" ——— with other twaine, that had a sire of Crete,
" And dam of Sparte: th' one of them called Jollyboy, a grete
" And large-flew'd hound."

Shakspeare mentions Cretan hounds (with Spartan) afterwards in this speech of Theseus. And Ovid's translator, Golding, in the same description, has them both in one verse, ibid. p. 33, a:

" This latter was a hound of Crete, the other was of Spart."
T. WARTON.

[7] *So sanded*] So marked with small spots. JOHNSON.

Sandy'd means of a sandy colour, which is one of the true denotements of a blood-hound. STEEVENS.

[8] *I wonder of—*] The modern editors read—I wonder at, &c. But changes

The. No doubt, they rose up early, to observe
The rite of May; and, hearing our intent,
Came here in grace of our solemnity.
But, speak, Egeus; is not this the day
That Hermia should give answer of her choice?
 Ege. It is: my Lord.
 The. Go, bid the huntsmen wake them with their horns.

Horns, and shout within. DEMETRIUS, LYSANDER, HERMIA,
and HELENA, *wake and start up.*

 The. Good-morrow, friends. Saint Valentine is past [9];
Begin these wood-birds but to couple now?
 Lys. Pardon, my Lord. [*He and the rest kneel to* Theseus.
 The. I pray you all, stand up.
I know, you two are rival enemies;
How comes this gentle concord in the world,
That hatred is so far from jealousy,
To sleep by hate, and fear no enmity?
 Lys. My Lord, I shall reply amazedly,
Half asleep, half waking: But as yet, I swear,
I cannot truly say how I came here:
But, as I think, (for truly would I speak—
And now I do bethink me, so it is;)
I came with Hermia hither: our intent
Was to be gone from Athens, where we might be
Without the peril of the Athenian law.
 Ege. Enough, enough, my Lord; you have enough;
I beg the law, the law, upon his head.—
They would have stol'n away, they would, Demetrius,
Thereby to have defeated you and me:
You, of your wife; and me, of my consent;
Of my consent that she should be your wife.
 Dem. My Lord, fair Helen told me of their stealth,
Of this their purpose hither to this wood;
And I in fury hither follow'd them;

changes of this kind ought, I conceive, to be made with great caution; for the writings of our author's contemporaries furnish us with abundant proofs that many modes of speech, which now seem harsh to our ears, were justified by the phraseology of former times. In *All's Well that Ends Well*, we have:
  " ——— thou dislik'st
  " Of virtue, for the name" MALONE.
 [9] — *Saint Valentine is past:*] Alluding to the old saying, that birds begin to couple on St. Valentine's day. STEEVENS.

Fair

Fair Helena in fancy following me [1].
But, my good Lord, I wot not by what power,
(But by some power it is,) my love to Hermia,
Melted as doth the snow [2], seems to me now
As the remembrance of an idle gawd,
Which in my childhood I did dote upon:
And all the faith, the virtue of my heart,
The object, and the pleasure of mine eye,
Is only Helena. To her, my Lord,
Was I betroth'd ere I did see [3] Hermia:
But, like a sickness, did I loath this food:
But, as in health, come to my natural taste,
Now do I wish it, love it, long for it,
And will for evermore be true to it.

The. Fair lovers, you are fortunately met:
Of this discourse we will hear more anon.—
Egeus, I will over-bear your will;
For in the temple, by and by with us,
These couples shall eternally be knit.
And, for the morning now is something worn,
Our purpos'd hunting shall be set aside.—
Away, with us, to Athens: Three and three,
We'll hold a feast in great solemnity.—
Come, Hippolita.   [*Exeunt* THE. HIP. EGE. *and Train.*

Dem. These things seem small, and undistinguishable,
Like far-off mountains turned into clouds.

Her. Methinks I see these things with parted eye,
When every thing seems double.

Hel. So methinks:

---

[1] *Fair Helena* in fancy *following me.*] Fancy is here taken for *love* or *affection*, and is opposed to *fury*, as before:
   . *Sighs and tears, poor* Fancy's *followers.*
Some now call that which a man takes particular delight in, his *fancy.* *Flower-fancier,* for a florist, and *bird-fancier,* for a lover and feeder of birds, are colloquial words.   JOHNSON.
So, in our author's *Rape of Lucrece:*
   " A martial man to be soft *fancy's* slave!"   MALONE.

[2] — *as doth the snow,*] The word *doth* which seems to have been inadvertently omitted, was supplied by Mr. Capell.
The emendation here made is confirmed by a passage in *K. Henry V.*
   " ———— as *doth* the melted snow.
   " Upon the vallies."   MALONE.

[3] — *ere I did see*—] *Did,* which is wanting in the old copies, was supplied by Mr. Rowe.   MALONE.

And

And I have found Demetrius like a jewel,
Mine own, and not mine own [4].

Dem. Are you sure
That we are awake [5]?—It seems to me,
That yet we sleep, we dream.—Do not you think,
The Duke was here, and bid us follow him?

Her. Yea; and my father.

Hel. And Hippolita.

Lys. And he did bid us follow to the temple.

Dem. Why then, we are awake: let's follow him;
And, by the way, let us recount our dreams.   [*Exeunt.*

As they go out, Bottom *awakes.*

Bot. When my cue comes, call me, and I will answer:
—my next is, *Most fair Pyramus*—Hey, ho!—Peter
Quince! Flute, the bellows-mender! Snout, the tinker!
Starveling! God's my life! stolen hence, and left me asleep!
I have had a most rare vision. I have had a dream—past the
wit of man to say what dream it was: Man is but an ass,
if he go about to expound this dream. Methought I was—
there is no man can tell what. Methought I was, and me-
thought I had—But man is but a patch'd fool [6], if he will
offer to say what methought I had. The eye of man hath not
heard, the ear of man hath not seen; man's hand is not able
to taste, his tongue to conceive, nor his heart to report, what

[4] *And I have found Demetrius like a jewel,*
 Mine own, and not mine own.] Helena, I think, means to say,
that having found Demetrius *unexpectedly,* she considered her property
in him as insecure as that which a person has in a jewel that he has
found by *accident*; which he knows not whether he shall retain, and
which therefore may properly enough be called *his own and not his own.*
She does not say, as Dr. Warburton has represented, that Demetrius *was
like a jewel,* but that she had *found* him, like a jewel, &c.
 A kindred thought occurs in *Antony and Cleopatra:*
 "——— by starts,
 " His fretted fortunes give him hope and fear
 " Of what he has, and has not."
The same kind of expression is found also in *The Merchant of Venice:*
 " Where every something, being blent together,
 " Turns to a wild of nothing, save of joy,
 " *Exprest,* and not *exprest.*" MALONE.

[5] *Are you sure*
That we are awake?] *Sure* is here used as a dissyllable: so *fire,
fire, hour,* &c. The word *now* [That we are *now* awake?] seems to be
wanting, to complete the metre of the next line. MALONE.

[6] *—patch'd fool.*] That is, a fool in a partycolour'd coat. JOHNSON.

my

my dream was. I will get Peter Quince to write a ballad of this dream: it shall be call'd Bottom's Dream, because it hath no bottom; and I will sing it in the latter end of a play, before the Duke: Peradventure, to make it the more gracious, I shall sing it at her death⁷. [*Exit.*

SCENE II.

Athens. *A Room in Quince's House.*

Enter QUINCE, FLUTE, SNOUT, *and* STARVELING.

Quin. Have you sent to Bottom's house? is he come home yet?

Star. He cannot be heard of. Out of doubt, he is transported.

Flu. If he come not, then the play is marr'd: It goes not forward, doth it?

Quin. It is not possible: you have not a man in all Athens able to discharge Pyramus, but he.

Flu. No; he hath simply the best wit of any handycraft man in Athens.

Quin. Yea, and the best person too; and he is a very paramour, for a sweet voice.

Flu. You must say, paragon: a paramour is, God bless us! a thing of nought⁸.

Enter SNUG.

Snug. Masters, the Duke is coming from the temple, and

---

⁷ — *at her death.*] He means *the death of Thisbe*, which is what his head is at present full of. STEEVENS.

Theobald reads—*after death.* He might have quoted the following passage in the *Tempest*, in support of his emendation. "This is a very scurvy tune (says Trinculo,) for a man to *sing at his funeral*."—Yet I believe the text is right. MALONE.

⁸ —*a thing of nought.*] This Mr. Theobald changes with great pomp, to *a thing of naught*; i. e. a *good for nothing thing*. JOHNSON.

A thing of nought is the true reading. So in *Hamlet*:

"*Ham.* The King is a *thing*—
"*Guil.* A *thing*, my Lord?
"*Ham.* Of *nothing.*"

See the note on this passage. STEEVENS.

there

there is two or three lords and ladies more married: if our sport had gone forward, we had all been made men [1].

Flu. O sweet bully Bottom! Thus hath he lost six-pence a-day during his life; he could not have 'scaped six-pence a-day: an the Duke had not given him six-pence a-day for playing Pyramus, I'll be hang'd; he would have deserv'd it: six-pence a-day, in Pyramus, or nothing.

Enter BOTTOM.

Bot. Where are these lads? where are these hearts?

Quin. Bottom?—O most courageous day! O most happy hour!

Bot. Masters, I am to discourse wonders: but ask me not what; for, if I tell you, I am no true Athenian. I will tell you every thing, right as it fell out.

Quin. Let us hear, sweet Bottom.

Bot. Not a word of me. All that I will tell you, is, that the Duke hath dined: Get your apparel together; good strings to your beards [2]; new ribbons to your pumps; meet presently at the palace; every man look o'er his part; for, the short and the long is, our play is preferr'd [3]. In any case, let Thisby have clean linen; and let not him, that plays the lion, pare his nails, for they shall hang out for the lion's claws. And, most dear actors, eat no onions, nor garlick, for we are to utter sweet breath; and I do not doubt but to hear them say, it is a sweet comedy. No more words; away; go, away. [*Exeunt.*

[1] — *made men*] In the same sense as in the *Tempest*, "any monster in England makes a man." JOHNSON.

[2] — *good strings to your beards*] i. e. to prevent the false beards, which they were to wear, from falling off. MALONE.

[3] — *our play is preferr'd.*] This word is not to be understood in its most common acceptation here, as if their play was chosen in preference to the others; (for that appears afterwards not to be the fact;) but, means, that it was given in among others for the Duke's option. So, in *Julius Cæsar*, Decius says,

"Where is Metellus Cimber? Let him go
"And presently *prefer his suit* to Cæsar." THEOBALD.

ACT

ACT V. SCENE I.

The same. An Apartment in the Palace of Theseus.

Enter THESEUS, HIPPOLITA, PHILOSTRATE, *Lords, and Attendants.*

Hip. 'Tis strange, my Theseus, that these lovers speak of.
The. More strange than true. I never may believe
These antique fables, nor these fairy toys.
Lovers, and madmen, have such seething brains [1],
Such shaping fantasies, that apprehend
More than cool reason ever comprehends.
The lunatic, the lover, and the poet [2],
Are of imagination all compact [3]:
One sees more devils than vast hell can hold;
That is, the madman: the lover, all as frantic,
Sees Helen's beauty in a brow of Egypt:
The poet's eye, in a fine frenzy rolling [4],
Doth glance from heaven to earth, from earth to heaven;
And, as imagination bodies forth

---

[1] *— such seething brains,*] We meet with the same expression in *The Winter's Tale:* " Would any but these boil'd brains of three and twenty hunt this weather?" MALONE.

[2] *The lunatic, the lover, and the poet,*] An ingenious modern writer supposes that our author had here in contemplation Orestes, Mark Antony, and himself; but I do not recollect any passage in his works that shows him to have been acquainted with the story of Agamemnon's son—*siderum furiis agitatus Orestes:* and indeed, if even such were found, the supposed allusion would still remain very problematical. MALONE.

[3] *Are of imagination all compact:*] i. e. made up of mere imagination. So, in *As You Like It:*
" If he, compact of jars, grow musical." STEEVENS.

[4] *— in a fine frenzy rolling,*] This seems to have been imitated by Drayton, in his *Epistle to J. Reynolds on Poets and Poetry:* describing Marlowe, he says,
" —— that fine madness still he did retain,
" Which rightly should possess a *poet's* brain." MALONE.

The forms of things unknown, the poet's pen
Turns them to shapes, and gives to airy nothing
A local habitation, and a name.
Such tricks hath strong imagination;
That, if it would but apprehend some joy,
It comprehends some bringer of that joy;
Or, in the night, imagining some fear,
How easy is a bush suppos'd a bear?

Hip. But all the story of the night told over,
And all their minds transfigur'd so together,
More witnesseth than fancy's images,
And grows to something of great constancy⁵;
But, howsoever, strange, and admirable.

Enter LYSANDER, DEMETRIUS, HERMIA, *and*
HELENA.

The. Here come the lovers, full of joy and mirth.—
Joy, gentle friends! joy, and fresh days of love,
Accompany your hearts!

Lys. More than to us
Wait on ⁶ your royal walks, your board, your bed!

The. Come now; what masks, what dances shall we have,
To wear away this long age of three hours,
Between our after-supper, and bed-time?
Where is our usual manager of mirth?
What revels are in hand? Is there no play,
To ease the anguish of a torturing hour?
Call Philostrate ⁷.

Philost. Here, mighty Theseus.

The. Say, what abridgement ⁸ have you for this evening?
What mask? what music? How shall we beguile
The lazy time, if not with some delight?

---

⁵ —*constancy;*] Consistency, stability, certainty. JOHNSON.

⁶ *Wait on—*] The old copies have—wait *in.* Corrected by Mr. Rowe. MALONE.

⁷ *Call Philostrate.*] In the *Knight's Tale* of Chaucer, Arcite, under the name of *Philostrate,* is squire of the chamber to *Theseus.* STEEVENS.

⁸ *Say, what abridgement,* &c.] By *abridgement* our author means a dramatic performance, which crowds the events of years into a few hours. So, in *Hamlet,* Act. ii. sc. vii. he calls the players " *abridgements, abstracts,* and *brief chronicles of the time.*" Again, in *King Henry V.*
" Then brook *abridgement;* and your eyes advance
" After your thoughts." STEEVENS.

Philost.

Philost. There is a brief⁹, how many sports are ripe;
          [*giving a paper.*
Make choice of which your highness will see first.
    The. *The battle with the Centaurs, to be sung*   [reads.
By an Athenian eunuch to the harp.
We'll none of that: that have I told my love,
In glory of my kinsman Hercules.
    The riot of the tipsy Bacchanals,
    Tearing the Thracian singer in their rage.
That is an old device; and it was play'd
When I from Thebes came last a conqueror.
    The thrice three Muses mourning for the death
    Of learning, late deceas'd in beggary ¹.
That is some satire, keen, and critical ²,
Not sorting with a nuptial ceremony.
    A tedious brief scene of young Pyramus,
    And his love Thisbe; very tragical mirth.
Merry and tragical ³? Tedious and brief?
That is, hot ice, and wondrous strange snow ⁴.
                                                How

⁹ — brief.] i. e. a short account or enumeration. STEEVENS.

¹ *The thrice three Muses mourning for the death*
Of learning, &c.] I do not know whether it has been observed, that Shakspeare here, perhaps, alluded to Spenser's poem, entitled *The Tears of the Muses,* on the neglect and contempt of learning. This piece first appeared in quarto, with others, 1591. T. WARTON.

This pretended title of a dramatic performance might be designed as a covert stroke of satire on those who had permitted Spenser to die through absolute want of bread, in the year 1598:—" *late deceas'd in beggary,*" seems to refer to this circumstance. STEEVENS.

If such an allusion was intended, this passage must have been added after the original appearance of this play; for we know that it was written in or before the year 1598, and Spenser did not die till 1599.
                                                            MALONE.

² — *keen and critical,*] *Critical* here means *criticising, censuring.* So in *Othello:* " O, I am nothing if not critical." STEEVENS.

³ *Merry and tragical ?*—] Our poet is still harping on *Cambyses.*
                                                            STEEVENS.

⁴ *That is, hot ice, and wondrous strange snow.*] Mr. Upton reads, not improbably:
    — *and wondrous strange black snow.* JOHNSON.

I think the passage needs no change on account of the versification; for *wonderous* is as often used as *three,* as it is as *two* syllables. The meaning of the line is—" That is, *hot ice* and *snow* of *as strange a quality.*" STEEVENS.

How shall we find the concord of this discord?

Philost. A play there is, my Lord, some ten words long:
Which is as brief as I have known a play;
But by ten words, my Lord, it is too long;
Which makes it tedious: for in all the play
There is not one word apt, one player fitted.
And tragical, my noble Lord, it is;
For Pyramus therein doth kill himself.
Which, when I saw rehears'd, I must confess,
Made mine eyes water; but more merry tears
The passion of loud laughter never shed.

The. What are they, that do play it?

Philost. Hard-handed men, that work in Athens here,
Which never labour'd in their minds till now;
And now have toil'd their unbreath'd memories ⁵
With this same play against your nuptial.

The. And we will hear it.

Philost. No, my noble Lord,
It is not for you; I have heard it over,
And it is nothing, nothing in the world;
Unless you can find sport in their intents⁶,
Extremely stretch'd, and conn'd with cruel pain,
To do you service.

The. I will hear that play:
For never any thing can be amiss,
When simpleness and duty tender it.

As there is no antithesis between *strange* and *snow*, as there is between *hot* and *ice*, I believe we should read—" and wonderous *strong* snow."
MASON.

In support of Mr. Mason's conjecture it may be observed that the words *strong* and *strange* are often confounded in our old plays.

Mr. Upton's emendation may derive some support from a passage in *Macbeth*;

"—when they shall be opened, black Macbeth
"Shall seem as pure as *snow*." MALONE.

⁵ — *unbreath'd memories*] That is, unexercised, unpractised memories. STEEVENS.

⁶ *Unless you can find sport in their intents*,] Thus all the copies. But as I know not what it is to *stretch* and *con* an *intent*, I suspect a line to be lost. JOHNSON.

To *intend* and to *attend* were anciently synonymous. Of this use several instances are given in a note on the third scene of the first act of *Othello*. *Intents* therefore may be put for the objects of their *attention*. We still say a person is *intent* on his business. STEEVENS.

Go, bring them in;—and take your places, ladies.

[*Exit* PHILOSTRATE.

Hip. I love not to see wretchedness o'ercharg'd,
And duty in his service perishing.
The. Why, gentle sweet, you shall see no such thing.
Hip. He says, they can do nothing in this kind.
The. The kinder we, to give them thanks for nothing.
Our sport shall be [7], to take what they mistake:
And what poor duty cannot do [8],
Noble respect takes it in might, not merit [9].
Where I have come, great clerks have purposed
To greet me with premeditated welcomes;
Where I have seen them shiver, and look pale,
Make periods in the midst of sentences,
Throttle their practis'd accent in their fears,
And, in conclusion, dumbly have broke off [1],
Not paying me a welcome: Trust me, sweet,
Out of this silence, yet, I pick'd a welcome;
And in the modesty of fearful duty
I read as much, as from the rattling tongue
Of saucy and audacious eloquence.
Love, therefore, and tongue-ty'd simplicity,
In least, speak most, to my capacity.

[7] *Our sport shall be*, &c.] Voltaire says something like this of Louis XIV. who took a pleasure in seeing his courtiers in confusion when they spoke to him. STEEVENS.

[8] *And what poor duty cannot do*,] The defective metre of this line shews that some word was inadvertently omitted by the transcriber or compositor. Mr. Theobald supplied the defect by reading "And what poor *willing* duty, &c." MALONE.

[9] *And what poor duty cannot do,*
Noble respect takes it in might, not merit.] And what dutifulness tries to perform without ability, regardful generosity receives with complacency, estimating it not by the actual *merit* of the performance, but by what it *might* have been, were the abilities of the performers equal to their zeal.—Such, I think, is the true interpretation of this passage; for which the reader is indebted partly to Dr. Johnson, and partly to Mr. Steevens. MALONE.

[1] *Where I have come, great clerks have purposed*—
And in conclusion dumbly have broke off.] So, in *Pericles*, 1609:
"She sings like one immortal, and she dances
"As goddess-like to her admired lays;
"Deep clerks she dumbs."

It should be observed, that *periods* in the text is used in the sense of *full points.* MALONE.

Enter

MIDSUMMER-NIGHT'S DREAM.

Enter PHILOSTRATE.

Philoft. So please your grace, the prologue is addrest [2].
The. Let him approach. [*Trumpets sound* [3].

Enter PROLOGUE.

Prol. If we offend, it is with our good will.
That you should think, we come not to offend,
But with good-will. To shew our simple skill,
That is the true beginning of our end.
Consider then, we come but in despight.
We do not come, as minding to content you,
Our true intent is. All for your delight,
We are not here. That you should here repent you,
The actors are at hand; and by their show,
You shall know all, that you are like to know.

The. This fellow doth not stand upon points.

Lys. He hath rid his prologue, like a rough colt; he knows not the stop. A good moral, my Lord: It is not enough to speak, but to speak true.

Hip. Indeed he hath play'd on this prologue, like a child on a recorder [4]; a sound, but not in government [5].

The. His speech was like a tangled chain; nothing impair'd, but all disorder'd. Who is next?

Enter PYRAMUS *and* THISBE, Wall, Moonshine, *and* Lion, *as in dumb show* [6].

Prol. "Gentles, perchance, you wonder at this show;
"But wonder on, till truth make all things plain.

---

[2] *— addreft.*] That is, ready. So, in *King Henry V.*
"To-morrow for our march we are *addreft*." STEEVENS.

[3] *Trumpets sound.*] It appears from the *Gule Hornbook* by Decker, 1609, that the prologue was anciently usher'd in by trumpets. "Present not yourselfe on the stage (especially at a new play) until the quaking prologue hath (by rubbing) got cullor in his cheeks, and is ready to give the *trumpets* their cue that hee's upon point to enter." STEEVENS.

[4] *— a recorder;*] A kind of flute. Shakspeare introduces it in *Hamlet*; and *Milton*, says:

"To the sound of soft *recorders.*"

This instrument is mentioned in many of the old plays. STEEVENS.

Sir John Hawkins supposes it to have been a *flagelet*. MALONE.

[5] *— but not in government.*] That is, not regularly, according to the tune. STEEVENS.

Hamlet speaking of a recorder, says, " Govern these ventages with your fingers and thumb, breath with your mouth, and it will discourse most elegant music." This explains the meaning of *government* in this passage. MASON.

[6] In this place the folio, 1623, exhibits the following prompter's direction. *Tawyer with a trumpet before them.* STEEVENS.

"This

" This man is Pyramus, if you would know;
" This beauteous Lady Thisby is, certain.
" This man, with lime and rough-cast, doth present
" Wall, that vile wall which did these lovers funder:
" And through wall's chink, poor souls, they are content
" To whisper; at the which let no man wonder.
" This man, with lantern, dog, and bush of thorn,
" Presenteth moon-shine: for, if you will know,
" By moon-shine did these lovers think no scorn
" To meet at Ninus' tomb [7], there, there to woo.
" This grisly beast, which by name lion hight [8],
" The trusty Thisby, coming first by night,
" Did scare away, or rather did affright:
" And, as she fled, her mantle she did fall [9];
" Which lion vile with bloody mouth did stain:
" Anon comes Pyramus, sweet youth, and tall,
" And finds his trusty Thisby's mantle slain:
" Whereat, with blade, with bloody blameful blade [1],
" He bravely broach'd his boiling bloody breast;
" And, Thisby tarrying in mulberry shade,
" His dagger drew, and died. For all the rest,
" Let lion, moon-shine, wall, and lovers twain,
" At large discourse, while here they do remain."

[*Exeunt* Prol. THISBE, Lion, *and* Moonshine.

[7] *To meet at Ninus' tomb,* &c.] So, in Chaucer's *Legend of Thisbe of Babylon:*
" Thei settin markes ther metingis should be,
" There king *Ninus* was graven under a tre."
Again: " And as she ran her *wimple* she let fall." STEEVENS.

[8] — *which by name lion hight,*] *Hight*, in old English, signifies—*is called.* The old copies read—*which lion hight by name.* The present regulation was made by Mr. Theobald. I think it more probable that a line, following the words—*by night*, has been lost. MALONE.

[9] — *her mantle she did fall*;] *To fall* in this instance is a verb active. So, in the *Tempest*, Act ii. sc. i.:
" And when I rear my hand, do you the like,
" To *fall* it on Gonzalo." STEEVENS.

[1] *Whereat, with blade, with bloody blameful blade,*] Mr. Upton rightly observes, that Shakspeare in this line ridicules the affectation of beginning many words with the same letter. He might have remarked the same of
The *raging rocks*
And *shivering shocks.*
Gascoigne, contemporary with our poet, remarks and blames the same affectation. JOHNSON.

The.

The. I wonder, if the lion be to speak.

Dem. No wonder, my Lord: one lion may, when many asses do.

Wall. " In this same interlude, it doth befall,
" That I, one Snout by name, present a wall:
" And such a wall, as I would have you think,
" That had in it a cranny'd hole, or chink,
" Through which the lovers, Pyramus and Thisby,
" Did whisper often very secretly,
" This lome, this rough-cast, and this stone, doth show
" That I am that same wall; the truth is so:
" And this the cranny is, right and sinister,
" Through which the fearful lovers are to whisper."

The. Would you desire lime and hair to speak better?

Dem. It is the wittiest partition that ever I heard discourse, my Lord.

The. Pyramus draws near the wall: silence!

Enter PYRAMUS.

Pyr. " O grim-look'd night! O night with hue so black!
" O night, which ever art, when day is not!
" O night, O night, alack, alack, alack,
" I fear my Thisby's promise is forgot!—
" And thou, O wall, O sweet, O lovely wall,
" That stand'st between her father's ground and mine;
" Thou wall, O wall, O sweet and lovely wall,
" Shew me thy chink, to blink through with mine eyne.
[*Wall holds up his fingers.*
" Thanks, courteous wall: Jove shield thee well for this!
" But what see I? No Thisby do I see.
" O wicked wall *, through whom I see no bliss;
" Curst be thy stones for thus deceiving me!"

The. The wall, methinks, being sensible, should curse again.

Pyr. No, in truth, sir, he should not. *Deceiving me*, is Thisby's cue; she is to enter now, and I am to spy her through the wall. You shall see, it will fall pat as I told you:—Yonder she comes.

---

* *O wicked wall, &c.*] So, in Chaucer's *Legend of Thisbe*:
" Thus would thei saine, alas! thou *wicked wal*, &c." STEEVENS.

Enter

Enter Lion *and* Moonshine.

Lion. "You, ladies, you, whose gentle hearts do fear
"The smallest monstrous mouse that creeps on floor,
"May now, perchance, both quake and tremble here,
"When lion rough in wildest rage doth roar.
"Then know, that I, one Snug the joiner, am
"A lion fell, nor else no lion's dam⁷:
"For if I should as lion come in strife
"Into this place, 'twere pity on my life."

The. A very gentle beast, and of a good conscience.
Dem. The very best at a beast, my Lord, that e'er I saw.
Lys. This lion is a very fox for his valour.
The. True; and a goose for his discretion.
Dem. Not so, my Lord: for his valour cannot carry his discretion; and the fox carries the goose.
The. His discretion, I am sure, cannot carry his valour; for the goose carries not the fox. It is well: leave it to his discretion, and let us listen to the moon.
Moon. "This lantern doth the horned moon present;"
Dem. He should have worn the horns on his head.
The. He is no crescent, and his horns are invisible within the circumference.

and the emendation was adopted by the subsequent editors; but, I think, without necessity. The conceit is furnished by the person who represents the lion, and enters covered with the hide of that beast; and Theseus only means to say, that the *man* who represented the moon, and came in at the same time, with a lantern in his hand, and a bush of thorns at his back, was as much a beast as he who performed the part of the lion. MALONE.

The *man in the moon* was no new character on the stage, and is here introduced in ridicule of such exhibitions. Ben Jonson in one of his masques, call'd, *News from the New World in the Moon*, makes his *Factor* doubt of the person who brings the intelligence. "I must see his dog at his girdle, and the bush of thorns at his back, ere I believe it."—"Those," replies one of the heralds, "are *stale ensigns o' the stage.* FARMER.

⁷ *Then know that I, one Snug the joiner, am*

A lion fell, nor *else no lion's dam:*] That is, that I am Snug the joiner; and neither a lion, nor a lion's dam. Dr. Johnson has justly observed in a note on *All's Well that Ends Well*, that *nor* in the phraseology of our author's time often related to two members of a sentence, though only expressed in the latter. So in the play just mentioned:
"—— contempt *nor* bitterness
"Were in his pride or sharpness."
The reading of the text is that of the folio. The quartos read—that I, *as* Snug the joiner, &c. MALONE.

Vol. IV. S *Moon.*

Moon. " This lantern doth the horned moon present;
" Myself the man i'th'moon do seem to be."
The. This is the greatest error of all the rest: the man should be put into the lantern; how is it else the man i'the moon?
Dem. He dares not come there for the candle: for, you see, it is already in snuff [9].
Hip. I am aweary of this moon: Would, he would change!
The. It appears, by this small light of discretion, that he is in the wane: but yet, in courtesy, in all reason, we must stay the time.
Lys. Proceed, moon.
Moon. All that I have to say, is, to tell you, that the lanthorn is the moon; I, the man in the moon; this thorn-bush, my thorn-bush; and this dog, my dog.
Dem. Why, all these should be in the lanthorn; for they are in the moon. But, silence; here comes Thisbe.

Enter THISBE.

Thif. " This is old Ninny's tomb: Where is my love?"
Lion. " Oh.—"   [*The lion roars.* Thisbe *runs off.*
Dem. Well roar'd, lion.
The. Well run, Thisbe.
Hip. Well shone, moon.—Truly, the moon shines with a good grace.
The. Well mous'd, lion [9]. [*The Lion tears* Thisbe's *mantle.*
Dem. And then came Pyramus.

Enter PYRAMUS.

Lyf. And so the lion vanish'd [1].   [*Exit* Lion.
Pyr. " Sweet moon, I thank thee for thy sunny beams;
" I thank thee, moon, for shining now so bright:

---

[8] *— in snuff.*] An equivocation. *Snuff* signifies both the cinder of a candle, and hasty anger. JOHNSON.

[9] *Well mous'd, lion.*] Theseus means that he has well tumbled and bloody'd the veil of Thisbe. STEEVENS.
To *mouse* signified to mammock, to tear in pieces as a cat tears a mouse. MALONE.

[1] *And then came Pyramus.*
And so the lion vanish'd.] Dr. Farmer would read—
   And so comes Pyramus,
   And then the moon vanishes. MALONE.

" For

MIDSUMMER-NIGHT'S DREAM.

" For by thy gracious, golden, glittering streams [2],
" I trust to taste of truest Thisby's sight.
     " But stay;—O spight!
     " But mark;—Poor knight,
" What dreadful dole is here?
     " Eyes, do you see?
     " How can it be?
" O dainty duck! O dear!
     " Thy mantle good,
     " What, stain'd with blood?
" Approach, ye furies fell! [2]
     " O fates! come, come;
     " Cut thread and thrum [3];
" Quail, crush, conclude, and quell [4]!"

The. This passion, and the death of a dear friend, would go near to make a man look sad.

Hip. Beshrew my heart, but I pity the man.

Pyr. " O, wherefore nature didst thou lions frame?
" Since lion vile hath here deflour'd my dear:
" Which is—no, no—which was the fairest dame,
" That liv'd, that lov'd, that lik'd, that look'd, with cheer.
     " Come, tears, confound;
     " Out, sword, and wound

---

[2] — *glittering streams.*] The old copies read—*beams.* STEEVENS. This emendation was made by the editor of the second folio.
MALONE.

[2] *Approach, ye furies fell!*
O fates, come, come, &c.] The poet here, and in the following lines spoken by Thisbe,
    " O sisters three,
    " Come, come to me,
    " With hands as pale as milk—"
probably intended to ridicule a passage in *Damon and Pythias*, by Richard Edwards, 1582:
    " Ye furies, all at once
    On me your torments trie:—
    " Gripe me, you greedy greefs,
        " And present pangues of death,
    " You sisters three, with cruel handes
        " With speed some stop my breath!" MALONE.

[3] *Cut thread and thrum;*] *Thrum* is the end or extremity of a weaver's warp; it is popularly used for very coarse yarn. The maids now call a mop of yarn a *thrum mop.* WARNER.

[4] —*and quell!*] To *quell* is to murther, to destroy. STEEVENS.

S 2   " The

"The pap of Pyramus:
 "Ay, that left pap,
 "Where heart doth hop:—
"Thus die I, thus, thus, thus.
 "Now am I dead,
 "Now am I fled;
"My soul is in the sky:
 "Tongue, lose thy light!
 "Moon take thy flight!
"Now die, die, die, die, die.   [*dies. Exit* Moonshine.
Dem. No die, but an ace, for him; for he is but one.
Lys. Less than an ace, man; for he is dead; he is nothing.
The. With the help of a surgeon, he might yet recover, and prove an ass[5].
Hip. How chance moonshine is gone, before Thisbe comes back and finds her lover?
The. She will find him by star light.—Here she comes;

Enter THISBE.

and her passion ends the play.
Hip. Methinks, she should not use a long one, for such a Pyramus: I hope, she will be brief.
Dem. A mote will turn the balance [6], which Pyramus, which Thisbe, is the better [7].
Lys. She hath spied him already, with those sweet eyes.
Dem. And thus she moans [8], *videlicet*.—
                                        Thisb.

[5] — *and proves an ass.*] The character of Theseus throughout this play is more exalted in its humanity, than its greatness. Though some sensible observations on life, and animated descriptions fall from him, as it is said of Jago, *you shall taste him more as a soldier than as a wit*, which is a distinction he is here striving to deserve, though with little success; as in support of his pretensions he never rises higher than a *pun*, and frequently sinks as low as a *quibble*. STEEVENS.

[6] *A mote will turn the balance.*] *Moth* was the old mode of spelling this word. The modern editions read *moth*. See a note on *King John*, post. MALONE.

[7] The first quarto makes this speech a little longer, but not better.
                                        JOHNSON.
The passage omitted is—"He for a man, God warn'd us; she for a woman, God bless us." STEEVENS.

[8] *And thus she moans*—] The old copies read *means*. Corrected by Mr. Theobald. A late writer contends for the old reading, which, he says, is a common term in the Scotch law, signifying to *tell*, to *relate*,
                                        to

"*Thif.* "Afleep, my love?
"What, dead, my dove?
"O Pyramus, arife,
"Speak, fpeak. Quite dumb?
"Dead, dead? A tomb
"Muft cover thy fweet eyes.
"Thefe lilly lips,
"This cherry nofe [8],
"Thefe yellow cowflip cheeks,
"Are gone, are gone:
"Lovers, make moan!
"His eyes were green as leeks.
"O fifters three,
"Come, come, to me,
"With hands as pale as milk;
"Lay them in gore,
"Since you have fhore
"With fhears his thread of filk.
"Tongue, not a word:—
"Come, trufty fword;
"Come, blade, my breaft imbrue:
"And farewel, friends;—
"Thus Thifby ends:
"Adieu, adieu, adieu." [*dies.*

The. Moonfhine and lion are left to bury the dead.
Dem. Ay, and wall too.
Bot. No, I affure you; the wall is down that parted their

---

to *declare.* "Petitions to the lords of feffion in Scotland run, To the lords of council and feffion humbly *means* and fhews your petitioner." *Letters of Literature,* 8vo. 1785. MALONE.

[8] *Thefe lilly* lips, *this cherry* nofe;] It fhould be:
"Thefe lips lilly,
"This nofe cherry."

This mode of pofition adds not a little to the burlefque of the paffage.
FARMER.

Mr. Theobald for the fake of rhime would read—lilly *brows.* But *lips* could fcarcely have been miftaken by either the eye or the ear for *brows.* MALONE.

We meet with fomewhat like this paffage in George Peele's *Old Wives Tale,* 1595:

Her coral lippes, her crimfon chinne.

Thou art a flouting knave—Her coral lippes, her *crimfon chinne!*
STEEVENS.

fathers.

fathers. Will it please you to see the epilogue, or to hear a Bergomask dance [9], between two of our company.

The. No epilogue, I pray you; for your play needs no excuse. Never excuse; for when the players are all dead, there need none to be blamed. Marry, if he that writ it, had play'd Pyramus, and hang'd himself in Thisbe's garter, it would have been a fine tragedy: and so it is, truly; and very notably discharg'd. But come, your Bergomask: let your epilogue alone.   [*Here a dance of clowns.*
The iron tongue of midnight hath told twelve:—
Lovers, to bed; 'tis almost fairy time.
I fear, we shall out-sleep the coming morn,
As much as we this night have overwatch'd.
This palpable-gross play hath well beguil'd
The heavy gait [1] of night.—Sweet friends, to bed.
A fortnight hold we this solemnity,
In nightly revels, and new jollity.   [*Exeunt.*

SCENE II.

The same.

Enter PUCK.

Puck. Now the hungry lion roars [2],
And the wolf behowls the moon [3];
                                                Whilst

---

[9] — *a Bergomask dance,*] Sir Thomas Hanmer observes in his *Glossary,* that this is a dance after the manner of the peasants of *Bergomasco,* a country in Italy, belonging to the Venetians. All the buffoons in Italy affect to imitate the ridiculous jargon of that people; and from thence it became also a custom to imitate their manner of dancing. STEEVENS.

[1] — *gait*] i. e. *passage, progress.* STEEVENS.

[2] *Now the hungry lion roars,* &c.] It has been justly observed by an anonymous writer, that " among this assemblage of familiar circumstances attending midnight, either in England or its neighbouring kingdoms, Shakspeare would never have thought of intermixing the exotic idea of the *hungry lion roaring,* which can be heard no nearer than in the deserts of Africa, if he had not read in the 104th Psalm: " Thou makest darkness that it may be night, wherein all the beasts of the forest do move; the *lions roaring* after their prey, do seek their meat from God." MALONE.

[3] *And the wolf behowls the moon;*] The old copies read—*beholds* the moon. The emendation was made by Dr. Warburton. The word
                                                                  beholds

MIDSUMMER-NIGHT'S DREAM.

Whilſt the heavy ploughman ſnores,
   All with weary taſk fordone³.
Now the waſted brands do glow,
   Whilſt the ſcritch-owl, ſcritching loud,
Puts the wretch that lies in woe,
   In remembrance of a ſhroud:
Now it is the time of night,
   That the graves all gaping wide,
Every one lets forth his ſpright,
   In the church-way paths to glide:
And we fairies, that do run
   By the triple Hecate's team,
From the preſence of the ſun,
   Following darkneſs like a dream,

*behold*s was in the time of Shakſpeare frequently written *beboults*, (as, I ſuppoſe, it was then pronounced,) which probably occaſioned the miſtake. The following paſſage in Marſton's *Antonio's Revenge*, 1602, which (as Mr. Theobald has likewiſe obſerved) ſeems to have been copied from that before us, appears to me a ſtrong confirmation of the reading ſuggeſted by Dr. Warburton:

   " Now *barks* the *wolfe* againſt the full-cheek'd *moon*,
   " Now lyons half-clam'd entrals *roar* for food,
   " Now croaks the toad, and night-crows *ſcreech aloud*,
   " Flutt'ring 'bout caſements of departing ſouls;
   " Now *gape* the *graves*, and thro' their yawns let looſe
   " Impriſon'd ſpirits to reviſit earth."

It is obſervable, that, in the paſſage in Lodge's *Roſalynde*, 1592, which Shakſpeare ſeems to have had in his thought, when he wrote, in *As You Like It*—" 'Tis like the howling of *Iriſh* wolves *againſt the moon*,"—the expreſſion is found, that Marſton has here uſed inſtead of *belowels*. " In courting Phebe, thou *barkſt* with the wolves of Syria againſt the moon."

Theſe lines alſo in Spenſer's *Faery Queen*. B. I. C. 5. ſt. 30. which Shakſpeare might have remembered, add ſupport to the emendation now made:

   " And all the while ſhe [*Night*] ſtood upon the ground,
   " The wakeful dogs did never ceaſe to bay;—
   " The meſſenger of death, the ghaſtly owle,
   " With dreary ſhrieks did alſo her bewray;
   " And hungry *wolves* continually did *howle*
   " At her abhorred face, ſo filthy and ſo fowle." MALONE.

I think, *Now the wolf behowls the moon*, was the original text. The alluſion is frequently met with in the works of our author, and his contemporaries. " 'Tis like the *howling* of Iriſh *wolves* againſt the *moon*," ſays he, in *As You Like It*. FARMER.

³ — *for done*.] i.e. overcome. STEEVENS.

Now

Now are frolic; not a mouse
Shall disturb this hallow'd house:
I am sent, with broom, before⁴,
To sweep the dust behind the door.

Enter OBERON *and* TITANIA, *with their Train.*

Obe. Through the house give glimmering light⁵,
By the dead and drowsy fire:
Every elf and fairy sprite,
Hop as light as bird from brier;
And this ditty, after me,
Sing, and dance it trippingly.
Tita. First, rehearse this song by wrote:
To each word a warbling note,
Hand in hand, with fairy grace,
Will we sing, and bless this place.

SONG⁶, *and* DANCE.

Obe. Now, until the break of day
Through this house each fairy stray.
To the best bride-bed will we,
Which by us shall blessed be;
And the issue, there create,
Ever shall be fortunate.

⁴ *I am sent with broom, before,*
To sweep the dust behind the door.] Cleanliness is always necessary to invite the residence and the favour of fairies:

"These make our girls their sluttery rue,
"By pinching them both black and blue,
"And put a penny in their shoe,
"The house for cleanly sweeping. Drayton. JOHNSON.

To sweep the dust behind the door is a common expression, and a common practice in large, old houses; where the doors of halls and galleries are thrown backward, and seldom or never shut. FARMER.

⁵ *Through the house give glimmering light,*] Milton perhaps had this picture in his thought:

"Glowing embers through the room
"Teach light to counterfeit a gleam." Il Penseroso. JOHNSON.

⁶ This song, like many others, is lost. Dr. Johnson thinks that another song has also been lost, which he supposes to have been sung by Oberon, immediately after his first speech on his entrance:
And this ditty, after me,
Sing, and dance it trippingly. MALONE.

So

MIDSUMMER-NIGHT'S DREAM. 393

So shall all the couples three
Ever true in loving be:
And the blots of nature's hand
Shall not in their issue stand;
Never mole, hare-lip, nor scar,
Nor mark prodigious⁷, such as are
Despised in nativity,
Shall upon their children be.—
With this field-dew consecrate,
Every fairy take his gait⁸;
And each several chamber bless,
Through this palace, with sweet peace:
E'er shall it in safety rest,
And the owner of it blest.
    Trip away;
    Make no stay;
Meet me all by break of day.

[*Exeunt* OBERON, TITANIA, *and Train.*

Puck. *If we shadows have offended,*
Think but this, (and all is mended,)
That you have but slumber'd here,
While these visions did appear,
And this weak and idle theme,
No more yielding but a dream,
Gentles do but apprehend;
If you pardon, we will mend.
And as I'm an honest Puck ⁹,
If we have unearned luck ¹
Now to 'scape the serpent's tongue ²,
We will make amends, ere long:
Else the Puck a liar call.
So, good night unto you all.

---

⁷ *Nor mark* prodigious.] *Prodigious* has here its primitive signification of *portentous.* So, in *King Richard III*.

    " If ever he have child, abortive be it,
    " *Prodigious*, and untimely brought to light." STEEVENS.

⁸ — *take his gait*;] i. e. take his way, or direct his *steps*. STEEVENS.

⁹ — *an honest Puck*,] The propriety of this epithet has been already shewn in p. 317, n. 7. MALONE.

¹ — *unearned luck*] i. e. if we have better fortune than we have deserved. STEEVENS.

² *Now to 'scape the serpent's tongue,*] That is, if we be dismissed without hisses. JOHNSON.

Give

Give me your hands[3]*, if we be friends,*
And Robin shall restore amends. [*Exit*[4].

[3] *Give me your hands,*—] That is, Clap your hands. Give us your applause. JOHNSON.
So in J. Markham's *English Arcadia*, 1607:
"But the nymph, after the custom of distress'd tragedians whose first act is entertained with a *snaky* salutation, &c. STEEVENS.

[4] Wild and fantastical as this play is, all the parts in their various modes are well written, and give the kind of pleasure which the author designed. Fairies in his time were much in fashion; common tradition had made them familiar, and Spenser's poem had made them great. JOHNSON.

THE END OF THE FOURTH VOLUME.

www.ingramcontent.com/pod-product-compliance
Lightning Source LLC
Chambersburg PA
CBHW031412230426
43668CB00007B/288

PREFACE

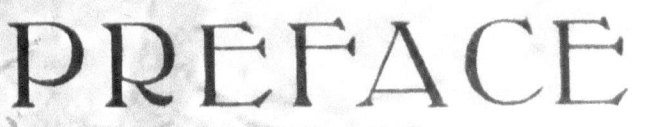

BOOKS are as tombstones made by the living for the living, but destined soon only to remind us of the dead. The preface, like an epitaph, seems vainly to "implore the passing tribute" of a moment's interest. No man is allured by either a grave-inscription or a preface, unless it be accompanied by that ineffable charm which age casts over mortal productions. Libraries, in one sense, represent cemeteries, and the rows of silent volumes, with their dim titles, suggest burial tablets, many of which, alas! mark only cenotaphs—empty tombs. A modern book, no matter how talented the author, carries with it a familiar personality which may often be treated with neglect or even contempt, but a volume a century old demands some reverence; a vellum-bound or hog-skin print, or antique yellow parchment, two, three, five hundred years old, regardless of its contents, impresses one with an indescribable feeling akin to awe and veneration,—as does the wheat from an Egyptian tomb, even though it be only wheat. We take such a work from the shelf carefully, and replace it gently. While the productions of modern writers are handled familiarly, as men living jostle men yet alive; those of authors long dead are touched as tho' clutched by a hand from the unseen world; the reader feels that a phantom form opposes his own, and that spectral eyes scan the pages as he turns them.

"THE STERN FACE, . . . ACROSS THE GULF."

The stern face, the penetrating eye of the personage whose likeness forms the frontispiece of the yellowed volume in my hand, speak across the gulf of two centuries, and bid me beware. The title page is read with reverence, and the great tome is replaced with care, for an almost superstitious sensation bids me be cautious and not offend. Let those who presume to criticise the intellectual productions of such men be careful; in a few days the dead will face their censors—dead.

Standing in a library of antiquated works, one senses the shadows of a cemetery. Each volume adds to the oppression, each old tome casts the influence of its spirit over the beholder, for have not these old books spirits? The earth-grave covers the mind as well as the body of its moldering occupant, and while only a strong imagination can assume that a spirit hovers over and lingers around inanimate clay, here each title is a voice that speaks as though the heart of its creator still throbbed, the mind essence of the dead writer envelops the living reader. Take down that vellum-bound volume, — it was written in one of the centuries long past. The pleasant face of its creator, as fresh as if but a print of yesterday, smiles upon you from the exquisitely engraved cop-

"THE PLEASANT FACE OF ITS CREATOR . . . . SMILES UPON YOU "

per-plate frontispiece; the mind of the author rises from out the words before you. This man is not dead and his comrades live. Turn to the shelves about, before each book stands a guardian spirit,—together they form a phantom army that, invisible to mortals, encircles the beholder.

Ah! this antique library is not as is a church graveyard, only a cemetery for the dead; it is also a mansion for the living. These alcoves are trysting places for elemental shades. Essences of disenthralled minds meet here and revel. Thoughts of the past take shape and live in this atmosphere,—who can say that pulsations unperceived, beyond the reach of physics or of chemistry, are not as ethereal mind-seeds which, although unseen, yet, in living brain, exposed to such an atmosphere as this, formulate embryotic

"SKELETON FORMS OPPOSE MY OWN."

thought-expressions destined to become energetic intellectual forces? I sit in such a weird library and meditate. The shades of grim authors whisper in my ear, skeleton forms oppose my own, and phantoms possess the gloomy alcoves of the library I am building.

With the object of carrying to the future a section of thought current from the past, the antiquarian libraries of many nations have been culled, and purchases made in every book market of the world. These books surround me. Naturally many persons have become interested in the movement, and, considering it a worthy one, unite to further the project, for the purpose is not personal gain. Thus it is not unusual for boxes of old chemical or pharmacal volumes to arrive by freight or express, without a word as to the donor. The mail brings manuscripts unprinted, and pamphlets recondite, with no word of introduction. They come unheralded. The authors or the senders realize that in this unique library a place is vacant if any work on connected subjects is missing, and thinking men of the world are uniting their contributions to fill such vacancies.

Enough has been said concerning the ancient library that has bred these reflections, and my own personality does not concern the reader. He can now formulate his conclusions as well perhaps as I, regarding the origin of the manuscript that is to follow, if he concerns himself at all over subjects mysterious or historical, and my connection therewith is of minor importance. Whether Mr. Drury brought the strange paper in person, or sent it by express or mail, or whether it was slipped into a box of books from foreign lands,—whether I stood face to face with Mr. Drury in the shadows of this room, or have but a fanciful conception of his figure,—whether the artist drew upon his imagination for the vivid likeness of the several personages figured in the book that follows, or from reliable data has given fac-similes authentic,—is immaterial. Sufficient be it to say that the manuscript of this book has been in my possession for a period of seven years, and my lips must now be sealed concerning all that transpired in connection therewith outside the subject-matter recorded therein. And yet I can not deny that for these seven years I have hesitated concerning my proper course, and more than once have decided to cover from sight the fascinating leaflets, hide them among surrounding volumes and let them slumber until chance should bring them to the attention of the future student,—but now with barely time to fulfill the self-accepted trust, I am impelled to act; I can hesitate no longer; the manuscript shall be printed.

It may seem to some persons that, by thrusting this manuscript upon another, Llewellyn Drury has evaded a duty, for he seemingly did not care to fulfill his promise, and yet, we should not judge him harshly lest we misjudge. Why did he shrink from publicity at the sacrifice of his solemnly given word? Why have I permitted myself to agree to fulfill his promise? These thoughts rise before me as they will come to others who read this book, and, this gloomy day of December, 1894, as, snatching a moment from the exactions of business, I sit among these old volumes devoted to science-lore, and again study over the unique manuscript of thirty years ago, and meditate, I hesitate again:—Shall I, or shall I not?—but a duty is a duty. Perhaps the mysterious part of the subject will be cleared to me only when my own thought-words come to rest among these venerable relics of the past, when books that I have written become companions of ancient works about me, for then I can claim relationship with the shadows that flit in and out, and can demand that they, the ghosts of the library, commune with the shade of the writer of this preface.

Suffice it then to say, that having decided to issue a limited edition of the work that this preface announces, I have assumed the full responsibility that Mr. Drury evaded, and have furthermore obligated myself to carry out the promises recorded in the pages that are to follow; that if I can locate the persons mentioned in the epilogue of the strange story, should these persons be in want, in accordance with the conditions to which Mr. Drury agreed, and which I have assumed, I will recognize the request made of Mr. Drury.

JOHN URI LLOYD, Cincinnati, O.

SUMMARY AND CONTENTS.

The work begins with a biographical note concerning Mr. Llewellyn Drury, a Cincinnati business man of morose disposition and scholarly attainments.

In a despondent mood, he challenges fate and occultism, and is unexpectedly confronted by a savant, who compels Mr. Drury to agree to read, or listen to the reading of a manuscript.

This paper purports to recite the life history of the intruding guest, and contains statements that often seem to conflict with science and philosophy, and even intrude upon orthodox religion. In several instances, Mr. Drury takes issue with the statements made by his guest, who then permits Mr. Drury to fortify himself with evidence, and afterward, by appointment, they meet to discuss the questions at issue. During these interludes the guest performs several curious experiments, and seemingly supports his startling assertions.

Finally, he vanishes as mysteriously as he appeared, leaving in Mr. Drury's hand his strange manuscript and a sealed letter, the latter indicating the manner in which the manuscript, after thirty years, is to be given to the public.

Mr. Drury, however, evaded the responsibility without offering any explanation of his reasons for doing so. Mr. Lloyd, who subsequently assumed the publication of the book, wrote the preface, from which each reader can formulate an opinion concerning the part he has taken in the affair, and answer as best he can the question as to what is true and what is fiction in the curious story [history] of I—Am—The—Man.

		PAGE
PROLOGUE.—History of Llewellyn Drury		1

CHAPTER.
I.	Home of Llewellyn Drury—"Never Less Alone than When Alone"	3
II.	A Friendly Conference with Prof. Chickering	10
III.	A Second Interview with the Mysterious Visitor	23
IV.	A Search for Knowledge—The Alchemistic Letter	35
V.	The Writing of "My Confession"	44
VI.	Kidnapped	46
VII.	A Wild Night—I am Prematurely Aged	55
VIII.	A Lesson in Mind Study	63
IX.	I Can Not Establish My Identity	67
X.	My Journey Towards the End of Earth Begins—The Adepts Brotherhood	71
XI.	My Journey Continues—Instinct	80

CHAPTER.		PAGE.
XII.	A Cavern Discovered—Biswell's Hill	84
XIII.	The Punch Bowls and Caverns of Kentucky—"Into the Unknown Country"	89
XIV.	Farewell to God's Sunshine—"The Echo of the Cry"	99
XV.	A Zone of Light, Deep Within the Earth	105
XVI.	Vitalized Darkness—The Narrows in Science	109
XVII.	The Fungus Forest—Enchantment	119
XVIII.	The Food of Man	123
XIX.	The Cry from a Distance—I Rebel Against Continuing the Journey	128

FIRST INTERLUDE.—THE NARRATIVE INTERRUPTED.

XX.	My Unbidden Guest Proves His Statements, and Refutes My Philosophy	134

MY UNBIDDEN GUEST CONTINUES HIS MANUSCRIPT.

XXI.	My Weight Disappearing	142

SECOND INTERLUDE.

XXII.	The Story Again Interrupted—My Guest Departs	149
XXIII.	Scientific Men Questioned—Aristotle's Ether	151
XXIV.	The Soliloquy of Prof. Daniel Vaughn—"Gravitation is the Beginning and Gravitation is the End: All Earthly Bodies Kneel to Gravitation"	156

THE UNBIDDEN GUEST RETURNS TO READ HIS MANUSCRIPT, CONTINUING THE NARRATIVE.

XXV.	The Mother of a Volcano—"You Can Not Disprove, and You Dare Not Admit"	162
XXVI.	Motion from Inherent Energy—"Lead Me Deeper Into this Expanding Study"	169
XXVII.	Sleep, Dreams, Nightmare—"Strangle the Life from My Body"	175

THIRD INTERLUDE.—THE NARRATIVE AGAIN INTERRUPTED.

XXVIII.	A Challenge—My Unbidden Guest Accepts It	179
XXIX.	Beware of Biology—The Science of the Life of Man—The old man relates a story as an object lesson	186
XXX.	Looking Backward—The Living Brain	193

THE MANUSCRIPT CONTINUED.

XXXI.	A Lesson on Volcanoes—Primary Colors are Capable of Farther Subdivision	204
XXXII.	Matter is Retarded Motion—"A Wail of Sadness Inexpressible"	218
XXXIII.	"A Study of True Science is a Study of God"—Communing with Angels	224
XXXIV.	I Cease to Breathe, and Yet Live	226
XXXV.	"A Certain Point Within a Circle"—Men are as Parasites on the Roof of Earth	230

CHAPTER.		PAGE
XXXVI.	The Drinks of Man	235
XXXVII.	The Drunkard's Voice	238
XXXVIII.	The Drunkard's Den	240
XXXIX.	Among the Drunkards	247
XL.	Further Temptation—Etidorhpa Appears	252
XLI.	Misery	262
XLII.	Eternity Without Time	272

FOURTH INTERLUDE.

XLIII.	The Last Contest	277

THE NARRATIVE CONTINUED.

XLIV.	The Fathomless Abyss—The Edge of the Earth's Shell	306
XLV.	My Heart-throb is Stilled, and Yet I Live	310
XLVI.	The Inner Circle, or the End of Gravitation—In the Bottomless Gulf	317
XLVII.	Hearing Without Ears—"What Will Be the End"	322
XLVIII.	Why and How—The Straggling Ray of Light from those Farthermost Outreaches	327
XLIX.	Oscillating Through Space—The Earth Shell Above Us	333
L.	My Weight Annihilated—"Tell me," I cried in alarm, "is this a living tomb?"	340
LI.	Is That a Mortal?—"The End of Earth"	345

FIFTH INTERLUDE.

LII.	The Last Farewell	352
EPILOGUE.—Letter Accompanying the Mysterious Manuscript		360

ILLUSTRATIONS.

FULL-PAGE.

Manuscript dedication of Author's Edition, preceding title-page.
Frontispiece—Likeness of The—Man—Who—Did—It (photogravure).

PAGE.
iii.	Preface Introduction—"Here lies the bones," etc.
7, 8.	"And to my amazement, saw a white-haired man."
29, 30.	"The same glittering, horrible, mysterious knife."
35, 36.	"Fac-simile of the mysterious manuscript of I—Am—The—Man—Who Did - It.
85, 86.	"Map of Kentucky near entrance to cavern."
95, 96.	"Confronted by a singular looking being."
101, 102.	"This struggling ray of sunlight is to be your last for years."
117, 118.	"I was in a forest of colossal fungi."
131, 132.	"Monstrous cubical crystals."
147, 148.	"Far as the eye could reach the glassy barrier spread as a crystal mirror."
157, 158.	"Soliloquy of Prof. Daniel Vaughn 'Gravitation is the beginning, and gravitation is the end; all earthly bodies kneel to gravitation.'"
165, 166.	"We came to a metal boat."
197, 198.	"Facing the open window he turned the pupils of his eyes upward."
205, 206.	"We finally reached a precipitous bluff."
209, 210.	"The wall descended perpendicularly to seemingly infinite depths."
255, 256.	Etidorhpa (photogravure).
297, 298.	"We passed through caverns filled with creeping reptiles."
303, 304.	"Flowers and structures beautiful, insects gorgeous."
307, 308.	"With fear and trembling I crept on my knees to his side."
332, 333.	Diagram descriptive of journey from the Kentucky cavern to the "End of Earth," showing section of earth's crust.
347, 348.	"Suspended in vacancy, he seemed to float."
357, 358.	"I stood alone in my room holding the mysterious manuscript."

HALF-PAGE AND TEXT CUTS.

iv.	"The Stern Face." Fac-simile, reduced from copper plate title page of the botanical work (1708), 917 pages, of Simonis Paulli, D., a Danish physician. Original plate 7x5½ inches.
v.	"The Pleasant Face." Fac-simile of the original copper plate frontispiece to the finely illustrated botanical work of Joannes Burmannus, M. D., descriptive of the plants collected by Carolus Plumierus. Antique. Original plate 9x13 inches.

ILLUSTRATIONS

PAGE.	
vi.	"Skeleton forms oppose my own." Photograph of John Uri Lloyd in the gloomy alcove of the antiquated library.
12.	"Let me have your answer now."
14.	"I espied upon the table a long white hair."
32.	"Drew the knife twice across the front of the door knob."
52.	"I was taken from the vehicle, and transferred to a block-house."
54.	"The dead man was thrown overboard."
58.	"A mirror was thrust beneath my gaze."
70.	"I am the man you seek."
106.	"We approach daylight, I can see your face."
108.	"Seated himself on a natural bench of stone."
129.	"An endless variety of stony figures."
136.	Cuts showing water and brine surfaces.
137.	Cuts showing earth chambers in which water rises above brine.
138, 139.	Cuts showing that if properly connected, water and brine reverse the usual law as to the height of their surfaces.
143.	"I bounded upward fully six feet."
144.	"I fluttered to the earth as a leaf would fall."
145.	"We leaped over great inequalities."
173.	"The bit of garment fluttered listlessly away to the distance, and then—vacancy."
182.	Cut showing that water may be made to flow from a tube higher than the surface of the water.
184.	Cut showing how an artesian fountain may be made without earth strata.
191.	"Rising abruptly, he grasped my hand."
200.	"A brain, a living brain, my own brain."
211.	"Shape of drop of water in the earth cavern."
227.	"We would skip several rods, alighting gently."
229.	"An uncontrollable, inexpressible desire to flee."
232.	"I dropped on my knees before him."
234.	"Handing me one of the halves, he spoke the single word, 'Drink.'"
242.	"Each finger pointed towards the open way in front."
280.	"Telescoped energy spheres."
281.	"Space dirt on energy spheres."
313.	"I drew back the bar of iron to smite the apparently defenseless being in the forehead."
315.	"He sprung from the edge of the cliff into the abyss below carrying me with him into its depths."
336.	"The Earth and its atmosphere."

PROLOGUE.

My name was Johannes Llewellyn Llongollyn Drury. I was named Llewellyn at my mother's desire, out of respect to her father, Dr. Evan Llewellyn, the scientist and speculative philosopher, well known to curious students as the author of various rare works on occult subjects. The other given names were ancestral also, but when I reached the age of appreciation, they naturally became distasteful; so it is that in early youth I dropped the first and third of these cumbersome words, and retained only the second Christian name. While perhaps the reader of these lines may regard this cognomen with less favor than either of the others, still I liked it, as it was the favorite of my mother, who always used the name in full; the world, however, contracted Llewellyn to Lew, much to the distress of my dear mother, who felt aggrieved at the liberty. After her death I decided to move to a western city, and also determined, out of respect to her memory, to select from and rearrange the letters of my several names, and construct therefrom three short, terse words, which would convey to myself only, the resemblance of my former name. Hence it is that the Cincinnati Directory does not record my self-selected name, which I have no reason to bring before the public. To the reader my name is Llewellyn Drury. I might add that my ancestors were among the early settlers of what is now New York City, and were direct descendants of the early Welsh kings; but these matters do not concern the reader, and it is not of them that I now choose to write. My object in putting down these preliminary paragraphs is simply to assure the reader of such facts, and such only, as may give him confidence in my personal sincerity and responsibility, in order that he may with a right understanding read the remarkable statements that occur in the succeeding chapters.

The story I am about to relate is very direct, and some parts of it are very strange, not to say marvelous; but not on account of its strangeness alone do I ask for the narrative a reading;—that were mere trifling. What is here set down happened as recorded, but I shall not attempt to explain things which even to myself are enigmatical. Let the candid reader read the story as I have told it, and make out of it what he can, or let him pass the page by unread—I shall not insist on claiming his further attention. Only, if he does read, I beg him to read with an open mind, without prejudice and without predilection.

Who or what I am as a participant in this work is of small importance. I mention my history only for the sake of frankness and fairness. I have nothing to gain by issuing the volume. Neither do I court praise nor shun censure. My purpose is to tell the truth.

Early in the fifties I took up my residence in the Queen City, and though a very young man, found the employment ready that a friend had obtained for me with a manufacturing firm engaged in a large and complicated business. My duties were varied and peculiar, of such a nature as to tax body and mind to the utmost, and for several years I served in the most exacting of business details. Besides the labor which my vocation entailed, with its manifold and multiform perplexities, I voluntarily imposed upon myself other tasks, which I pursued in the privacy of my own bachelor apartments. An inherited love for books on abstruse and occult subjects, probably in part the result of my blood connection with Dr. Evan Llewellyn, caused me to collect a unique library, largely on mystical subjects, in which I took the keenest delight. My business and my professional duties by day, and my studies at night, made my life a busy one.

In the midst of my work and reading I encountered the character whose strange story forms the essential part of the following narrative. I may anticipate by saying that the manuscript to follow only incidentally concerns myself, and that if possible I would relinquish all connection therewith. It recites the physical, mental, and moral adventures of one whose life history was abruptly thrust upon my attention, and as abruptly interrupted. The vicissitudes of his body and soul, circumstances seemed to compel me to learn and to make public.

ETIDORHPA.

CHAPTER I.

"NEVER LESS ALONE THAN WHEN ALONE."

MORE than thirty years ago occurred the first of the series of remarkable events I am about to relate. The exact date I can not recall; but it was in November, and, to those familiar with November weather in the Ohio Valley, it is hardly necessary to state that the month is one of possibilities. That is to say, it is liable to bring every variety of weather, from the delicious, dreamy Indian summer days that linger late in the fall, to a combination of rain, hail, snow, sleet,—in short, atmospheric conditions sufficiently aggravating to develop a suicidal mania in any one the least susceptible to such influences. While the general character of the month is much the same the country over,— showing dull grey tones of sky, abundant rains that penetrate man as they do the earth; cold, shifting winds, that search the very marrow,—it is always safe to count more or less upon the probability of the unexpected throughout the month.

The particular day which ushered in the event about to be chronicled, was one of these possible heterogeneous days presenting a combination of sunshine, shower, and snow, with winds that rang all the changes from balmy to blustery, a morning air of caloric and an evening of numbing cold. The early morning started fair and sunny; later came light showers suddenly switched by shifting winds into blinding sleet, until the middle of the afternoon found the four winds and all the elements commingled in one wild orgy with clashing and roaring as of a great organ

with all the stops out, and all the storm-fiends dancing over the
key-boards! Nightfall brought some semblance of order to the
sounding chaos, but still kept up the wild music of a typical
November day, with every accompaniment of bleakness, gloom,
and desolation.

Thousands of chimneys, exhaling murky clouds of bituminous
soot all day, had covered the city with the proverbial pall which
the winds in their sport had shifted hither and yon, but as, thoroughly
tired out, they subsided into silence, the smoky mesh suddenly
settled over the houses and into the streets, taking possession
of the city and contributing to the melancholy wretchedness of
such of the inhabitants as had to be out of doors. Through this
smoke the red sun when visible had dragged his downward course
in manifest discouragement, and the hastening twilight soon gave
place to the blackness of darkness. Night reigned supreme.

Thirty years ago electric lighting was not in vogue, and the
system of street lamps was far less complete than at present,
although the gas burned in them may not have been any worse.
The lamps were much fewer and farther between, and the light
which they emitted had a feeble, sickly aspect, and did not reach
any distance into the moist and murky atmosphere. And so the
night was dismal enough, and the few people upon the street
were visible only as they passed directly beneath the lamps, or in
front of lighted windows; seeming at other times like moving
shadows against a black ground.

As I am like to be conspicuous in these pages, it may be
proper to say that I am very susceptible to atmospheric influences.
I figure among my friends as a man of quiet disposition, but I am
at times morose, although I endeavor to conceal this fact from
others. My nervous system is a sensitive weather-glass. Sometimes
I fancy that I must have been born under the planet Saturn,
for I find myself unpleasantly influenced by moods ascribed to
that depressing planet, more especially in its disagreeable phases,
for I regret to state that I do not find corresponding elation, as I
should, in its brighter aspects. I have an especial dislike for
wintry weather, a dislike which I find growing with my years,
until it has developed almost into positive antipathy and dread.
On the day I have described, my moods had varied with the
weather. The fitfulness of the winds had found its way into my

feelings, and the somber tone of the clouds into my meditations. I was restless as the elements, and a deep sense of dissatisfaction with myself and everything else, possessed me. I could not content myself in any place or position. Reading was distasteful, writing equally so; but it occurred to me that a brisk walk, for a few blocks, might afford relief. Muffling myself up in my overcoat and fur cap, I took the street, only to find the air gusty and raw, and I gave up in still greater disgust, and returning home, after drawing the curtains and locking the doors, planted myself in front of a glowing grate fire, firmly resolved to rid myself of myself by resorting to the oblivion of thought, reverie, or dream. To sleep was impossible, and I sat moodily in an easy chair, noting the quarter and half-hour strokes as they were chimed out sweetly from the spire of St. Peter's Cathedral, a few blocks away.

Nine o'clock passed with its silver-voiced song of "Home, Sweet Home"; ten, and then eleven strokes of the ponderous bell which noted the hours, roused me to a strenuous effort to shake off the feelings of despondency, unrest, and turbulence, that all combined to produce a state of mental and physical misery now insufferable. Rising suddenly from my chair, without a conscious effort I walked mechanically to a book-case, seized a volume at random, reseated myself before the fire, and opened the book. It proved to be an odd, neglected volume, "Riley's Dictionary of Latin Quotations." At the moment there flashed upon me a conscious duality of existence. Had the old book some mesmeric power? I seemed to myself two persons, and I quickly said aloud, as if addressing my double: "If I can not quiet you, turbulent Spirit, I can at least adapt myself to your condition. I will read this book haphazard from bottom to top, or backward, if necessary, and if this does not change the subject often enough, I will try Noah Webster." Opening the book mechanically at page 297, I glanced at the bottom line and read, "Nunquam minus solus quam cum solus" (Never less alone than when alone). These words arrested my thoughts at once, as, by a singular chance, they seemed to fit my mood; was it or was it not some conscious invisible intelligence that caused me to select that page, and brought the apothegm to my notice?

Again, like a flash, came the consciousness of duality, and I began to argue with my other self. "This is arrant nonsense,"

I cried aloud; "even though Cicero did say it, and, it is on a par with many other delusive maxims that have for so many years embittered the existence of our modern youth by misleading thought. Do you know, Mr. Cicero, that this statement is not sound? That it is unworthy the position you occupy in history as a thinker and philosopher? That it is a contradiction in itself, for if a man is alone he is alone, and that settles it?"

I mused in this vein a few moments, and then resumed aloud: "It won't do, it won't do; if one is alone—the word is absolute,—he is single, isolated, in short, alone; and there can by no manner of possibility be any one else present. Take myself, for instance: I am the sole occupant of this apartment; I am alone, and yet you say in so many words that I was never less alone than at this instant." It was not without some misgiving that I uttered these words, for the strange consciousness of my own duality constantly grew stronger, and I could not shake off the reflection that even now there were two of myself in the room, and that I was not so much alone as I endeavored to convince myself.

This feeling oppressed me like an incubus; I must throw it off, and, rising, I tossed the book upon the table, exclaiming: "What folly! I am alone,—positively there is no other living thing visible or invisible in the room." I hesitated as I spoke, for the strange, undefined sensation that I was not alone had become almost a conviction; but the sound of my voice encouraged me, and I determined to discuss the subject, and I remarked in a full, strong voice: "I am surely alone; I know I am! Why, I will wager everything I possess, even to my soul, that I am alone." I stood facing the smoldering embers of the fire which I had neglected to replenish, uttering these words to settle the controversy for good and all with one person of my dual self, but the other ego seemed to dissent violently, when a soft, clear voice claimed my ear:

"You have lost your wager; you are not alone."

I turned instantly towards the direction of the sound, and, to my amazement, saw a white-haired man seated on the opposite side of the room, gazing at me with the utmost composure. I am not a coward, nor a believer in ghosts or illusions, and yet that sight froze me where I stood. It had no supernatural appearance—on the contrary, was a plain, ordinary, flesh-and-blood man;

"AND TO MY AMAZEMENT SAW A WHITE-HAIRED MAN."

but the weather, the experiences of the day, the weird, inclement night, had all conspired to strain my nerves to the highest point of tension, and I trembled from head to foot. Noting this, the stranger said pleasantly: "Quiet yourself, my dear sir; you have nothing to fear; be seated." I obeyed, mechanically, and regaining in a few moments some semblance of composure, took a mental inventory of my visitor. Who is he? what is he? how did he enter without my notice, and why? what is his business? were all questions that flashed into my mind in quick succession, and quickly flashed out unanswered.

The stranger sat eying me composedly, even pleasantly, as if waiting for me to reach some conclusion regarding himself. At last I surmised: "He is a maniac who has found his way here by methods peculiar to the insane, and my personal safety demands that I use him discreetly."

"Very good," he remarked, as though reading my thoughts; "as well think that as anything else."

"But why are you here? What is your business?" I asked.

"You have made and lost a wager," he said. "You have committed an act of folly in making positive statements regarding a matter about which you know nothing—a very common failing, by the way, on the part of mankind, and concerning which I wish first to set you straight."

The ironical coolness with which he said this provoked me, and I hastily rejoined: "You are impertinent; I must ask you to leave my house at once."

"Very well," he answered; "but if you insist upon this, I shall, on behalf of Cicero, claim the stake of your voluntary wager, which means that I must first, by natural though violent means, release your soul from your body." So saying he arose, drew from an inner pocket a long, keen knife, the blade of which quiveringly glistened as he laid it upon the table. Moving his chair so as to be within easy reach of the gleaming weapon, he sat down, and again regarded me with the same quiet composure I had noted, and which was fast dispelling my first impression concerning his sanity.

I was not prepared for his strange action; in truth, I was not prepared for anything; my mind was confused concerning the whole night's doings, and I was unable to reason clearly or consecutively, or even to satisfy myself what I did think, if indeed I thought at all.

The sensation of fear, however, was fast leaving me; there was something reassuring in my unbidden guest's perfect ease of manner, and the mild, though searching gaze of his eyes, which were wonderful in their expression. I began to observe his personal characteristics, which impressed me favorably, and yet were extraordinary. He was nearly six feet tall, and perfectly straight; well proportioned, with no tendency either to leanness or obesity. But his head was an object from which I could not take my eyes,—such a head surely I had never before seen on mortal shoulders. The chin, as seen through his silver beard, was rounded and well developed, the mouth straight, with pleasant lines about it, the jaws square and, like the mouth, indicating decision, the eyes deep set and arched with heavy eyebrows, and the whole surmounted by a forehead so vast, so high, that it was almost a deformity, and yet it did not impress me unpleasantly; it was the forehead of a scholar, a profound thinker, a deep student. The nose was inclined to aquiline, and quite large. The contour of the head and face impressed me as indicating a man of learning, one who had given a lifetime to experimental as well as speculative thought. His voice was mellow, clear, and distinct, always pleasantly modulated and soft, never loud nor unpleasant in the least degree. One remarkable feature I must not fail to mention—his hair; this, while thin and scant upon the top of his head, was long, and reached to his shoulders; his beard was of unusual length, descending almost to his waist; his hair, eyebrows, and beard were all of singular whiteness and purity, almost transparent, a silvery whiteness that seemed an aureolar sheen in the glare of the gaslight. What struck me as particularly remarkable was that his skin looked as soft and smooth as that of a child; there was not a blemish in it. His age was a puzzle none could guess; stripped of his hair, or the color of it changed, he might be twenty-five,—given a few wrinkles, he might be ninety. Taken altogether, I had never seen his like, nor anything approaching his like, and for an instant there was a faint suggestion to my mind that he was not of this earth, but belonged to some other planet.

I now fancy he must have read my impressions of him as these ideas shaped themselves in my brain, and that he was quietly waiting for me to regain a degree of self-possession that would allow him to disclose the purpose of his visit.

He was first to break the silence: "I see that you are not disposed to pay your wager any more than I am to collect it, so we will not discuss that. I admit that my introduction to-night was abrupt, but you can not deny that you challenged me to appear." I was not clear upon the point, and said so. "Your memory is at fault," he continued, "if you can not recall your experiences of the day just past. Did you not attempt to interest yourself in modern book lore, to fix your mind in turn upon history, chemistry, botany, poetry, and general literature? And all these failing, did you not deliberately challenge Cicero to a practical demonstration of an old apothegm of his that has survived for centuries, and of your own free will did not you make a wager that, as an admirer of Cicero's, I am free to accept?" To all this I could but silently assent. "Very good, then; we will not pursue this subject further, as it is not relevant to my purpose, which is to acquaint you with a narrative of unusual interest, upon certain conditions, with which if you comply, you will not only serve yourself, but me as well."

"Please name the conditions," I said.

"They are simple enough," he answered. "The narrative I speak of is in manuscript. I will produce it in the near future, and my design is to read it aloud to you, or to allow you to read it to me, as you may select. Further, my wish is that during the reading you shall interpose any objection or question that you deem proper. This reading will occupy many evenings, and I shall of necessity be with you often. When the reading is concluded, we will seal the package securely, and I shall leave you forever. You will then deposit the manuscript in some safe place, and let it remain for thirty years. When this period has elapsed, I wish you to publish this history to the world."

"Your conditions seem easy," I said, after a few seconds' pause.

"They are certainly very simple; do you accept?"

I hesitated, for the prospect of giving myself up to a succession of interviews with this extraordinary and mysterious personage seemed to require consideration. He evidently divined my thoughts, for, rising from his chair, he said abruptly: "Let me have your answer now."

I debated the matter no further, but answered: "I accept, conditionally."

"Name your conditions," the guest replied.

"I will either publish the work, or induce some other man to do so."

"LET ME HAVE YOUR ANSWER NOW."

"Good," he said; "I will see you again," with a polite bow; and turning to the door which I had previously locked, he opened it softly, and with a quiet "Good night" disappeared in the hall-way.

I looked after him with bewildered senses; but a sudden impulse caused me to glance toward the table, when I saw that he had forgotten his knife. With the view of returning this, I reached to pick it up, but my finger tips no sooner touched the handle than a sudden chill shivered along my nerves. Not as an electric shock, but rather as a sensation of extreme cold was the current that ran through me in an instant. Rushing into the hall-way to the landing of the stairs, I called after the mysterious being, "You have forgotten your knife," but beyond the faint echo of my voice, I heard no sound. The phantom was gone. A moment later I was at the foot of the stairs, and had thrown open the door. A street lamp shed an uncertain light in front of the house. I stepped out and listened intently for a moment, but not a sound was audible, if indeed I except the beating of my own heart, which throbbed so wildly that I fancied I heard it. No footfall echoed from the deserted streets; all was silent as a churchyard, and I closed and locked the door softly, tiptoed my way back to my room, and sank collapsed into an easy chair. I was more than exhausted; I quivered from head to foot, not with cold, but with a strange nervous chill that found intensest expression in my spinal column, and seemed to flash up and down my back vibrating like a feverous pulse. This active pain was succeeded by a feeling of frozen numbness, and I sat I know not how long, trying to tranquilize myself and think temperately of the night's occurrence. By degrees I recovered my normal sensations, and directing my will in the channel of sober reasoning, I said to myself: "There can be no mistake about his visit, for his knife is here as a witness to the fact. So much is sure, and I will secure that testimony at all events." With this reflection I turned to the table, but to my astonishment I discovered that the knife had disappeared. It needed but this miracle to start the perspiration in great cold beads from every pore. My brain was in a whirl, and reeling into a chair, I covered my face with my hands. How long I sat in this posture I do not remember. I only know that I began to doubt my own sanity, and wondered if this were not the way people became deranged. Had not my peculiar habits of isolation, irregular and intense study, erratic living, all conspired to unseat reason? Surely here was every ground to believe so; and yet I was able still to think consistently and hold steadily to a single line of thought. Insane people can not do that, I reflected, and gradually the tremor and excitement wore away. When I had become calmer and more collected, and my sober judgment said, "Go to bed; sleep just as long as you can; hold your eyelids down, and when you awake refreshed, as you will, think out the whole subject at your leisure," I arose, threw open the shutters, and found that day was breaking. Hastily undressing I went to bed, and closed my eyes, vaguely conscious of some soothing guardianship. Perhaps because I was physically exhausted, I soon lost myself in the oblivion of sleep.

"I ESPIED UPON THE TABLE A LONG WHITE HAIR."

I did not dream,—at least I could not afterwards remember my dream if I had one, but I recollect thinking that somebody struck ten distinct blows on my door, which seemed to me to be of metal and very sonorous. These ten blows in my semi-conscious state I counted. I lay very quiet for a time collecting my thoughts and noting various objects about the room, until my eye caught the dial of a French clock upon the mantel. It was a few minutes past ten, and the blows I had heard were the strokes of the hammer upon the gong in the clock. The sun was shining into the room, which was quite cold, for the fire had gone out. I arose, dressed myself quickly, and after thoroughly laving my face and hands in ice-cold water, felt considerably refreshed.

Before going out to breakfast, while looking around the room for a few things which I wanted to take with me, I espied upon the table a long white hair. This was indeed a surprise, for I had about concluded that my adventure of the previous night was a species of waking nightmare, the result of overworked brain and weakened body. But here was tangible evidence to the contrary, an assurance that my mysterious visitor was not a fancy or a dream, and his parting words, " I will see you again," recurred to me with singular effect. "He will see me again; very well; I will preserve this evidence of his visit for future use." I wound the delicate filament into a little coil, folded it carefully in a bit of paper, and consigned it to a corner in my pocket-book, though not without some misgiving that it too might disappear as did the knife.

The strange experience of that night had a good effect on me; I became more regular in all my habits, took abundant sleep and exercise, was more methodical in my modes of study and reasoning, and in a short time found myself vastly improved in every way, mentally and physically.

The days went fleeting into weeks, the weeks into months, and while the form and figure of the white-haired stranger were seldom absent from my mind, he came no more.

CHAPTER II.

A FRIENDLY CONFERENCE.

It is rare, in our present civilization, to find a man who lives alone. This remark does not apply to hermits or persons of abnormal or perverted mental tendencies, but to the majority of mankind living and moving actively among their fellows, and engaged in the ordinary occupations of humanity. Every man must have at least one confidant, either of his own household, or within the circle of his intimate friends. There may possibly be rare exceptions among persons of genius in statecraft, war, or commerce, but it is doubtful even in such instances if any keep all their thoughts to themselves, hermetically sealed from their fellows. As a prevailing rule, either a loving wife or very near friend shares the inner thought of the most secretive individual, even when secrecy seems an indispensable element to success. The tendency to a free interchange of ideas and experiences is almost universal, instinct prompting the natural man to unburden his most sacred thought, when the proper confidant and the proper time come for the disclosure.

For months I kept to myself the events narrated in the preceding chapter. And this for several reasons: first, the dread of ridicule that would follow the relation of the fantastic occurrences, and the possible suspicion of my sanity, that might result from the recital; second, very grave doubts as to the reality of my experiences. But by degrees self-confidence was restored, as I reasoned the matter over and reassured myself by occasional contemplation of the silvery hair I had coiled in my pocket-book, and which at first I had expected would vanish as did the stranger's knife. There came upon me a feeling that I should see my weird visitor again, and at an early day. I resisted this impression, for it was a feeling of the idea, rather than a thought, but the vague expectation grew upon me in spite of myself, until at length it became a conviction which no argument or logic could shake. Curiously enough, as the original incident receded into the past, this new idea thrust itself into the foreground, and I began in my own mind to court another interview. At times, sitting alone after night, I felt that I was watched by unseen eyes; these eyes haunted me in my solitude, and I was morally sure of the presence of another than myself in the room. The sensation was at first unpleasant, and I tried to throw it off, with partial success. But only for a little while could I banish the intrusive idea, and as the thought took form, and the invisible presence became more actual to consciousness, I hoped that the stranger would make good his parting promise, "I will see you again."

On one thing I was resolved; I would at least be better informed on the subject of hallucinations and apparitions, and not be taken unawares as I had been. To this end I decided to confer with my friend, Professor Chickering, a quiet, thoughtful man, of varied accomplishments, and thoroughly read upon a great number of topics, especially in the literature of the marvelous.

So to the Professor I went, after due appointment, and confided to him full particulars of my adventure. He listened patiently throughout, and when I had finished, assured me in a matter-of-fact way that such hallucinations were by no means rare. His remark was provoking, for I did not expect from the patient interest he had shown while I was telling my story, that the whole matter would be dismissed thus summarily. I said with some warmth:

"But this was not a hallucination. I tried at first to persuade myself that it was illusory, but the more I have thought the experience over, the more real it becomes to me."

"Perhaps you were dreaming," suggested the Professor.

"No," I answered; "I have tried that hypothesis, and it will not do. Many things make that view untenable."

"Do not be too sure of that," he said; "you were, by your own account, in a highly nervous condition, and physically tired. It is possible, perhaps probable, that in this state, as you sat in your chair, you dozed off for a short interval, during which the illusion flashed through your mind."

"How do you explain the fact that incidents occupying a large portion of the night, occurred in an interval which you describe as a flash?"

"Easily enough; in dreams time may not exist: periods embracing weeks or months may be reduced to an instant. Long journeys, hours of conversation, or a multitude of transactions, may be compressed into a term measured by the opening or closing of a door, or the striking of a clock. In dreams, ordinary standards of reason find no place, while ideas or events chase through the mind more rapidly than thought."

"Conceding all this, why did I, considering the unusual character of the incidents, accept them as real, as substantial, as natural as the most commonplace events?"

"There is nothing extraordinary in that," he replied. "In dreams all sorts of absurdities, impossibilities, discordancies, and violation of natural law appear realities, without exciting the least surprise or suspicion. Imagination runs riot and is supreme, and reason for the time is dormant. We see ghosts, spirits, the forms of persons dead or living,—we suffer pain, pleasure, hunger,—and all sensations and emotions, without a moment's question of their reality."

"Do any of the subjects of our dreams or visions leave tangible evidences of their presence?"

"Assuredly not," he answered, with an incredulous, half-impatient gesture; "the idea is absurd."

"Then I was not dreaming," I mused.

Without looking at me, the Professor went on: "These false presentiments may have their origin in other ways, as from mental disorders caused by indigestion. Nicolai, a noted bookseller of Berlin, was thus afflicted. His experiences are interesting and possibly suggestive. Let me read some of them to you."

The Professor hereupon glanced over his bookshelf, selected a volume, and proceeded to read:*

"I generally saw human forms of both sexes; but they usually seemed not to take the smallest notice of each other, moving as in a market place, where all are eager to press through the crowd; at times, however, they seemed to be transacting business with each other. I also saw several times, people on horseback, dogs, and birds.

---

* This work I have found to be Vol. IV. of Chambers' Miscellany, published by Gould and Lincoln, Boston.—J. U. L.

"All these phantasms appeared to me in their natural size, and as distinct as if alive, exhibiting different shades of carnation in the uncovered parts, as well as different colors and fashions in their dresses, though the colors seemed somewhat paler than in real nature. None of the figures appeared particularly terrible, comical, or disgusting, most of them being of indifferent shape, and some presenting a pleasant aspect. The longer these phantasms continued to visit me, the more frequently did they return, while at the same time they increased in number about four weeks after they had first appeared. I also began to hear them talk: these phantoms conversed among themselves, but more frequently addressed their discourse to me; their speeches were uncommonly short, and never of an unpleasant turn. At different times there appeared to me both dear and sensible friends of both sexes, whose addresses tended to appease my grief, which had not yet wholly subsided: their consolatory speeches were in general addressed to me when I was alone. Sometimes, however, I was accosted by these consoling friends while I was engaged in company, and not unfrequently while real persons were speaking to me. These consolatory addresses consisted sometimes of abrupt phrases, and at other times they were regularly executed."

Here I interrupted: "I note, Professor, that Mr. Nicolai knew these forms to be illusions."

Without answering my remark, he continued to read:

"There is in imagination a potency far exceeding the fabled power of Aladdin's lamp. How often does one sit in wintry evening musings, and trace in the glowing embers the features of an absent friend? Imagination, with its magic wand, will there build a city with its countless spires, or marshal contending armies, or drive the tempest-shattered ship upon the ocean. The following story, related by Scott, affords a good illustration of this principle:

"'Not long after the death of an illustrious poet, who had filled, while living, a great station in the eyes of the public, a literary friend, to whom the deceased had been well known, was engaged during the darkening twilight of an autumn evening, in perusing one of the publications which professed to detail the habits and opinions of the distinguished individual who was now no more. As the reader had enjoyed the intimacy of the deceased to a considerable degree, he was deeply interested in the publication, which contained some particulars relating to himself and other friends. A visitor was sitting in the apartment, who was also engaged in reading. Their sitting-room opened into an entrance hall, rather fantastically fitted up with articles of armor, skins of wild animals, and the like. It was when laying down his book, and passing into this hall, through which the moon was beginning to shine, that the individual of whom I speak saw right before him, in a standing posture, the exact representation of his departed friend, whose recollection had been so strongly brought to his imagination. He stopped for a single moment, so as to notice the wonderful accuracy with which fancy had impressed upon the bodily eye the peculiarities of dress and position of the illustrious poet. Sensible, however, of the delusion, he felt no sentiment save that of wonder at the extraordinary accuracy of the resemblance, and stepped onward to the figure, which resolved itself as he approached into the various materials of which it was composed. These were merely a screen occupied by great coats, shawls, plaids, and such other articles as are usually found in a country entrance hall. The spectator returned to the spot from which he had seen the illusion, and endeavored with all his power to recall the image which had been so singularly vivid. But this he was unable to do. And the person who had witnessed the apparition, or, more properly, whose excited state had been the means of raising it, had only to return to the apartment, and tell his young friend under what a striking hallucination he had for a moment labored.'"

Here I was constrained to call the Professor to a halt. "Your stories are very interesting," I said, "but I fail to perceive any analogy in either the conditions or the incidents, to my experience. I was fully awake and conscious at the time, and the man I saw appeared and moved about in the full glare of the gaslight,"—

"Perhaps not," he answered; "I am simply giving you some general illustrations of the subject. But here is a case more to the point."

Again he read:

"A lady was once passing through a wood, in the darkening twilight of a stormy evening, to visit a friend who was watching over a dying child. The clouds were thick—the rain beginning to fall; darkness was increasing; the wind was moaning mournfully through the trees. The lady's heart almost failed her as she saw that she had a mile to walk through the woods in the gathering gloom. But the reflection of the situation of her friend forbade her turning back. Excited and trembling, she called to her aid a nervous resolution, and pressed onward. She had not proceeded far when she beheld in the path before her the movement of some very indistinct object. It appeared to keep a little distance ahead of her, and as she made efforts to get nearer to see what it was, it seemed proportionally to recede. The lady began to feel rather unpleasantly. There was some pale white object certainly discernible before her, and it appeared mysteriously to float along, at a regular distance, without any effort at motion. Notwithstanding the lady's good sense and unusual resolution, a cold chill began to come over her. She made every effort to resist her fears, and soon succeeded in drawing nearer the mysterious object, when she was appalled at beholding the features of her friend's child, cold in death, wrapt in its shroud. She gazed earnestly, and there it remained distinct and clear before her eyes. She considered it a premonition that her friend's child was dead, and that she must hasten to her aid. But there was the apparition directly in her path. She must pass it. Taking up a little stick, she forced herself along to the object, and behold, some little animal scampered away. It was this that her excited imagination had transformed into the corpse of an infant in its winding sheet."

I was a little irritated, and once more interrupted the reader warmly: "This is exasperating. Now what resemblance is there between the vagaries of a hysterical, weak-minded woman, and my case?"

He smiled, and again read:

"The numerous stories told of ghosts, or the spirits of persons who are dead, will in most instances be found to have originated in diseased imagination, aggravated by some abnormal defect of mind. We may mention a remarkable case in point, and one which is not mentioned in English works on this subject; it is told by a compiler of Les Causes Célèbres. Two young noblemen, the Marquises De Rambouillet and De Precy, belonging to two of the first families of France, made an agreement, in the warmth of their friendship, that the one who died first should return to the other with tidings of the world to come. Soon afterwards De Rambouillet went to the wars in Flanders, while De Precy remained at Paris, stricken by a fever. Lying alone in bed, and severely ill, De Precy one day heard a rustling of his bed curtains, and turning round, saw his friend De Rambouillet, in full military attire. The sick man sprung over the bed to welcome his friend, but the other receded, and said that he had come to fulfill his promise, having been killed on that very day. He further said that it behooved De Precy to think more of the afterworld, as all that was said of it was true, and as he himself would die in his first battle. De Precy was then left by the phantom; and it was afterward found that De Rambouillet had fallen on that day."

"Ah," I said, "and so the phantom predicted an event that followed as indicated."

"Spiritual illusions," explained the Professor, "are not unusual, and well authenticated cases are not wanting in which they have been induced in persons of intelligence by functional or organic disorders. In the last case cited, the prediction was followed by a fulfillment, but this was chance or mere coincidence. It would be strange indeed if in the multitude of dreams that come to humanity, some few should not be followed by events so similar as to warrant the belief that they were prefigured. But here is an illustration that fits your case: let me read it:

"In some instances it may be difficult to decide whether spectral appearances and spectral noises proceed from physical derangement or from an overwrought state of mind. Want of exercise and amusement may also be a prevailing cause. A friend mentions to us the following case: An acquaintance of his, a merchant, in London, who had for years paid very close attention to business, was one day, while alone in his counting house, very much surprised to hear, as he imagined, persons outside the door talking freely about him. Thinking it was some acquaintances who were playing off a trick, he opened the door to request them to come in, when to his amazement, he found that nobody was there. He again sat down to his desk, and in a few minutes the same dialogue recommenced. The language was very alarming. One voice seemed to say: 'We have the scoundrel in his own counting house; let us go in and seize him.' 'Certainly,' replied the other voice, 'it is right to take him; he has been guilty of a great crime, and ought to be brought to condign punishment.' Alarmed at these threats, the bewildered merchant rushed to the door, and there again no person was to be seen. He now locked his door and went home; but the voices, as he thought, followed him through the crowd, and he arrived at his house in a most unenviable state of mind. Inclined to ascribe the voices to derangement in mind, he sent for a medical attendant, and told his case, and a certain kind of treatment was prescribed. This, however, failed; the voices menacing him with punishment for purely imaginary crimes continued, and he was reduced to the brink of despair. At length a friend prescribed entire relaxation from business, and a daily game of cricket, which, to his great relief, proved an effectual remedy. The exercise banished the phantom voices, and they were no more heard."

"So you think that I am in need of out-door exercise?"

"Exactly."

"And that my experience was illusory, the result of vertigo, or some temporary calenture of the brain?"

"To be plain with you, yes."

"But I asked you a while ago if specters or phantoms ever leave tangible evidence of their presence." The Professor's eyes dilated in interrogation. I continued: "Well, this one did. After I had followed him out, I found on the table a long, white hair, which I still have," and producing the little coil from my pocket-book, I handed it to him. He examined it curiously, eyed me furtively, and handed it back with the cautious remark:

"I think you had better commence your exercise at once."

CHAPTER III.

A SECOND INTERVIEW WITH THE MYSTERIOUS VISITOR.

It is not pleasant to have one's mental responsibility brought in question, and the result of my interview with Professor Chickering was, to put it mildly, unsatisfactory. Not that he had exactly questioned my sanity, but it was all too evident that he was disposed to accept my statement of a plain matter-of-fact occurrence with a too liberal modicum of salt. I say "matter-of-fact occurrence" in full knowledge of the truth that I myself had at first regarded the whole transaction as a fantasia or flight of mind, the result of extreme nervous tension; but in the interval succeeding I had abundant opportunity to correlate my thoughts, and to bring some sort of order out of the mental and physical chaos of that strange, eventful night. True, the preliminary events leading up to it were extraordinary; the dismal weather, the depression of body and spirit under which I labored, the wild whirl of thought keeping pace with the elements—in short, a general concatenation of events that seemed to be ordered especially for the introduction of some abnormal visitor—the night would indeed have been incomplete without a ghost! But was it a ghost? There was nothing ghostly about my visitor, except the manner of his entrance and exit. In other respects, he seemed substantial enough. He was, in his manners, courteous and polished as a Chesterfield; learned as a savant in his conversation; human in his thoughtful regard of my fears and misgivings; but that tremendous forehead, with its crown of silver hair, the long, translucent beard of pearly whiteness, and above all the astounding facility with which he read my hidden thoughts—these were not natural.

The Professor had been patient with me—I had a right to expect that; he was entertaining to the extent of reading such excerpts as he had with him on the subject of hallucinations and their supposed causes, but had he not spoiled all by assigning me at last to a place with the questionable, unbalanced characters he had cited? I thought so, and the reflection provoked me; and this thought grew upon me until I came to regard his stories and attendant theories as so much literary trash.

My own reflections had been sober and deliberate, and had led me to seek a rational explanation of the unusual phenomena. I had gone to Professor Chickering for a certain measure of sympathy, and what was more to the point, to secure his suggestions and assistance in the further unraveling of a profound mystery that might contain a secret of untold use to humanity. Repulsed by the mode in which my confidence had been received, I decided to do what I should have done from the outset—to keep my own counsel, and to follow alone the investigation to the end, no matter what the result might be. I could not forget or ignore the silver hair I had so religiously preserved. That was genuine; it was as tangible, as real, as convincing a witness as would have been the entire head of my singular visitant, whatever might be his nature.

I began to feel at ease the moment my course was decided, and the feeling was at once renewed within me that the gray head would come again, and by degrees that expectation ripened into a desire, only intensified as the days sped by. The weeks passed into months; summer came and went; autumn was fast fading, but the mysterious unknown did not appear. A curious fancy led me now to regard him as my friend, for the mixed and indefinite feelings I felt at first towards him had almost unaccountably been changed to those of sincere regard. He was not always in my thoughts, for I had abundant occupation at all times to keep both brain and hands busy, but there were few evenings in which I did not, just before retiring, give myself up for a brief period to quiet communion with my own thoughts, and I must confess at such times the unknown occupied the larger share of attention. The constant contemplation of any theme begets a feeling of familiarity or acquaintance with the same, and if that subject be an individual, as in the present instance, such contemplation lessens the liability to surprise from any unexpected development. In fact, I not only anticipated a visit, but courted it. The old Latin maxim that I had played with, "Never less alone than when alone" had domiciled itself within my brain as a permanent lodger—a conviction, a feeling rather than a thought defined, and I had but little difficulty in associating an easy-chair which I had come to place in a certain position for my expected visitor, with his presence.

Indian summer had passed, and the fall was nearly gone when for some inexplicable reason the number seven began to haunt me. What had I to do with seven, or seven with me? When I sat down at night this persistent number mixed itself in my thoughts, to my intense annoyance. Bother take the mystic numeral! What was I to do with seven? I found myself asking this question audibly one evening, when it suddenly occurred to me that I would refer to the date of my friend's visit. I kept no journal, but reference to a record of some business transactions that I had associated with that event showed that it took place on November seventh. That settled the importunate seven! I should look for whomever he was on the first anniversary of his visit, which was the seventh, now close at hand. The instant I had reached this conclusion the number left me, and troubled me no more.

November third had passed, the fourth, and the fifth had come, when a stubborn, protesting notion entered my mind that I was yielding to a superstitious idea, and that it was time to control my vacillating will. Accordingly on this day I sent word to a friend that, if agreeable to him, I would call on him on the evening of the seventh for a short social chat, but as I expected to be engaged until later than usual, would he excuse me if I did not reach his apartments until ten? The request was singular, but as I was now accounted somewhat odd, it excited no comment, and the answer was returned, requesting me to come. The seventh of November came at last. I was nervous during the day, which seemed to drag tediously, and several times it was remarked of me that I seemed abstracted and ill at ease, but I held my peace. Night came cold and clear, and the stars shone brighter than usual, I thought. It was a sharp contrast to the night of a year ago. I took an early supper, for which I had no appetite, after which I strolled aimlessly about the streets, revolving how I should put in the time till ten o'clock, when I was to call upon my friend. I decided to go to the theater, and to the theater I went. The play was spectacular, "Aladdin; or, The Wonderful Lamp." The entertainment, to me, was a flat failure, for I was busy with my thoughts, and it was not long until my thoughts were busy with me, and I found myself attempting to answer a series of questions that finally became embarrassing. "Why did you make an appointment for ten o'clock instead of eight, if you wished to keep away from your apartments?" I had n't thought of that before; it was stupid to a degree, if not ill-mannered, and I frankly admitted as much. "Why did you make an appointment at all, in the face of the fact that you not only expected a visitor, but were anxious to meet him?" This was easily answered: because I did not wish to yield to what struck me as superstition. "But do you expect to extend your call until morning?" Well, no, I had n't thought or arranged to do so. "Well, then, what is to prevent your expected guest from awaiting your return? Or, what assurance have you that he will not encounter you in the street, under circumstances that will provoke or, at the least, embarrass you?" None whatever. "Then what have you gained by your stupid perversity?" Nothing, beyond the assertion of my own individuality. "Why not go home and receive your guest in becoming style?" No; I would not do that. I had started on this course, and I would persevere in it. I would be consistent. And so I persisted, at least until nine o'clock, when I quit the theater in sullen dejection, and went home to make some slight preparation for my evening call.

With my latch-key I let myself into the front door of the apartment house wherein I lodged, walked through the hall, up the staircase, and paused on the threshold of my room, wondering what I would find inside. Opening the door I entered, leaving it open behind me so that the light from the hallway would shine into the room, which was dark, and there was no transom above the door. The grate fire had caked into a solid mass of charred bituminous coal, which shed no illumination beyond a faint red glow at the bottom, showing that it was barely alive, and no more. I struck a match on the underside of the mantel shelf, and as I lit the gas I heard the click of the door latch. I turned instantly; the door had been gently closed by some unknown force if not by unseen hands, for there was no breath of air stirring. This preternatural interference was not pleasant, for I had hoped in the event of another visit from my friend, if friend he was, that he would bring no uncanny or ghostly manifestation to disturb me. I looked at the clock; the index pointed to half past nine. I glanced about the room; it was orderly, everything in proper position, even to the arm-chair that I had been wont to place for my nondescript visitor. It was time to be going, so I turned to the dressing case, brushed my hair, put on a clean scarf, and moved towards the wash-stand, which stood in a little alcove on the opposite side of the room. My self-command well-nigh deserted me as I did so, for there, in the arm-chair that a moment before was empty, sat my guest of a year ago, facing me with placid features! The room began to revolve, a faint, sick feeling came over me, and I reeled into the first convenient chair, and covered my face with my hands. This depression lasted but an instant, however, and as I recovered self-possession, I felt or fancied I felt a pair of penetrating eyes fixed upon me with the same mild, searching gaze I remembered so well. I ventured to look up; sure enough, there they were, the beaming eyes, and there was he! Rising from his chair, he towered up to his full height, smiled pleasantly, and with a slight inclination of the head, murmured: "Permit me to wish you good evening; I am profoundly glad to meet you again."

It was full a minute before I could muster courage to answer: "I wish I could say as much for myself."

"And why shouldn't you?" he said, gently and courteously; "you have realized, for the past six months, that I would return; more than that—you have known for some time the very day and almost the exact hour of my coming, have even wished for it, and, in the face of all this, I find you preparing to evade the requirements of common hospitality;—are you doing either me or yourself justice?"

I was nettled at the knowledge he displayed of my movements, and of my very thoughts; my old stubbornness asserted itself, and I was rude enough to say: "Perhaps it is as you say; at all events, I am obligated to keep an engagement, and with your permission will now retire."

It was curious to mark the effect of this speech upon the intruder. He immediately became grave, reached quietly into an inner pocket of his coat, drew thence the same glittering, horrible, mysterious knife that had so terrified and bewildered me a year before, and looking me steadily in the eye, said coldly, yet with a certain tone of sadness: "Well, I will not grant permission. It is unpleasant to resort to this style of argument, but I do it to save time and controversy."

I stepped back in terror, and reached for the old-fashioned bell-cord, with the heavy tassel at the end, that depended from the ceiling, and was on the point of grasping and giving it a vigorous pull.

"Not so fast, if you please," he said, sternly, as he stepped forward, and gave the knife a rapid swish through the air above my head, causing the cord to fall in a tangle about my hand, cut cleanly, high above my reach!

I gazed in dumb stupor at the rope about my hand, and raised my eyes to the remnant above. That was motionless; there was not the slightest perceptible vibration, such as would naturally be expected. I turned to look at my guest; he had resumed his seat, and had also regained his pleasant expression, but he still held the knife in his hand with his arm extended, at rest, upon the table, which stood upon his right.

"Let us have an end to this folly," he said; "think a moment, and you will see that you are in fault. Your error we will rectify easily, and then to business. I will first show you the futility of trying to escape this interview, and then we will proceed to work, for time presses, and there is much to do." Having delivered this remark, he detached a single silvery hair from his head, blew it from his fingers, and let it float gently upon the upturned edge of the knife, which was still resting on the table. The hair was divided as readily as had been the bell-cord. I was transfixed with astonishment, for he had evidently aimed to exhibit the quality of the blade, though he made no allusion to the feat, but smilingly went on with his discourse: "It is just a year ago to-night since we first met. Upon that occasion you made an agreement with me which you are in honor bound to keep, and"—here he paused as if to note the effect of his words upon me, then added significantly—"will keep. I have been at some

"THE SAME GLITTERING, MYSTERIOUS KNIFE."

pains to impress upon your mind the fact that I would be here to-night. You responded, and knew that I was coming, and yet in obedience to a silly whim, deliberately made a meaningless engagement with no other purpose than to violate a solemn obligation. I now insist that you keep your prior engagement with me, but I do not wish that you should be rude to your friend, so you had better write him a polite note excusing yourself, and dispatch it at once."

I saw that he was right, and that there was no shadow of justification for my conduct, or at least I was subdued by his presence, so I wrote the note without delay, and was casting about for some way to send it, when he said: "Fold it, seal it, and address it; you seem to forget what is proper." I did as he directed, mechanically, and, without thinking what I was doing, handed it to him. He took it naturally, glanced at the superscription, went to the door which he opened slightly, and handed the billet as if to some messenger who seemed to be in waiting outside,—then closed and locked the door. Turning toward me with the apparent object of seeing if I was looking, he deftly drew his knife twice across the front of the door-knob, making a deep cross, and then deposited the knife in his pocket, and resumed his seat.*

As soon as he was comfortably seated, he again began the conversation: "Now that we have settled the preliminaries, I will ask if you remember what I required of you a year ago?" I thought that I did. "Please repeat it; I wish to make sure that you do, then we will start fair."

"In the first place, you were to present me with a manuscript"—

"Hardly correct," he interrupted; "I was to acquaint you with a narrative which is already in manuscript, acquaint you with it, read it to you, if you preferred not to read it to me"—

"I beg your pardon," I answered; "that is correct. You were to read the manuscript to me, and during the reading I was to interpose such comments, remarks, or objections, as seemed proper; to embody as interludes, in the manuscript, as my own interpolations, however, and not as part of the original."

* I noted afterward that the door-knob, which was of solid metal, was cut deeply, as though made of putty.

"Very good," he replied, "you have the idea exactly; proceed."

"I agreed that when the reading had been completed, I would seal the complete manuscript securely, deposit it in some safe place, there to remain for thirty years, when it must be published."

"DREW HIS KNIFE TWICE ACROSS THE FRONT OF THE DOOR-KNOB."

"Just so," he answered; "we understand each other as we should. Before we proceed further, however, can you think of any point on which you need enlightenment? If so, ask such questions as you choose, and I will answer them."

I thought for a moment, but no query occurred to me; after a pause he said: "Well, if you think of nothing now, perhaps hereafter questions will occur to you which you can ask; but as it is late, and you are tired, we will not commence now. I will see you just one week from to-night, when we will begin. From that time on, we will follow the subject as rapidly as you choose, but see to it that you make no engagements that will interfere with our work, for I shall be more exacting in the future." I promised, and he rose to go. A sudden impulse seized me, and I said: "May I ask one question?"

"Certainly."

"What shall I call you?"

"Why call me aught? It is not necessary in addressing each other that any name be used."

"But what are you?" I persisted.

A pained expression for an instant rested upon his face, and he said, sadly, pausing between the words: "I—Am—The—Man Who—Did—It."

"Did what?"

"Ask not; the manuscript will tell you. Be content, Llewellyn, and remember this, that I—Am—The—Man."

So saying he bade me good night, opened the door, and disappeared down the broad stair-case.

One week thereafter he appeared promptly, seated himself, and producing a roll of manuscript, handed it to me, saying, "I am listening; you may begin to read."

On examination I found each page to be somewhat larger than a sheet of letter paper, with the written matter occupying a much smaller space, so as to leave a wide white border. One hundred pages were in the package. The last sentence ending abruptly indicated that my guest did not expect to complete his task in one evening, and, I may anticipate by saying that with each successive interview he drew about the same amount of writing from his bosom. Upon attempting to read the manuscript I at first found myself puzzled by a style of chirography very peculiar and characteristic, but execrably bad. Vainly did I attempt to read it; even the opening sentence was not deciphered without long inspection and great difficulty.

The old man, whom I had promised that I would fulfill the task, observing my discomfiture, relieved me of the charge, and without a word of introduction, read fluently as follows:

THE MANUSCRIPT OF I—AM—THE—MAN.

CHAPTER IV.

A SEARCH FOR KNOWLEDGE.—THE ALCHEMISTIC LETTER.

I am the man who, unfortunately for my future happiness, was dissatisfied with such knowledge as could be derived from ordinary books concerning semi-scientific subjects in which I had long been absorbed. I studied the current works of my day on philosophy and chemistry, hoping therein to find something tangible regarding the relationship that exists between matter and spirit, but studied in vain. Astronomy, history, philosophy and the mysterious, incoherent works of alchemy and occultism were finally appealed to, but likewise failed to satisfy me. These studies were pursued in secret, though I am not aware that any necessity existed for concealment. Be that as it may, at every opportunity I covertly acquainted myself with such alchemical lore as could be obtained either by purchase or by correspondence with others whom I found to be pursuing investigations in the same direction. A translation of Geber's "De Claritate Alchemiæ," by chance came into my possession, and afterwards an original version from the Latin of Bœrhaave's "Elementa Chemiæ," published and translated in 1753 by Peter Shaw. This magnificent production threw a flood of light upon the early history of chemistry, being far more elaborate than any modern work. It inspired me with the deepest regard for its talented author, and ultimately introduced me to a brotherhood of adepts, for in this publication, although its author disclaims occultism, is to be found a talisman that will enable any earnest searcher after light to become a member of the society of secret "Chemical Improvers of Natural Philosophy," with which I affiliated as soon as the key was discovered. Then followed a systematic investigation of authorities of the Alchemical

Lead on my friend I cried "lead onto
then undescribed scenes, the
occult, you understand that—"
He interrupted me almost rudely,
and in a serious manner said,
"Have you not learned that wonder
is our exemplification of ignorance?
the child wonders at a goblin story,
the savage at a trinket, the man of
science at an unexplained manifes-
tation of a previously unperceived nat-
ural law, each wonders in ignorance
and because of ignorance. Accept
now, that all you have seen, from
the day of your birth on the surface
the earth, to the present, and all
that you will meet here are
wonderful only because the finite
mind of man is confounded with
evidence that from whatever
direction we meet them
spring up from an unsearch-
able infinity.

FAC-SIMILE OF PAGE OF MANUSCRIPT

School, including Geber, Morienus, Roger Bacon, George Ripley, Raymond Lully, Bernard, Count of Trevise, Isaac Hollandus, Arnoldus de la Villanova, Paracelsus, and others, not omitting the learned researches of the distinguished scientist, Llewellyn.

I discovered that many talented men are still firm believers in the lost art of alchemy, and that among the followers of the "thrice-famed Hermes" are to be found statesmen, clergymen, lawyers, and scientific men who, for various reasons, invariably conceal with great tact their connection with the fraternity of adepts. Some of these men had written scientific treatises of a very different character from those circulating among the members of our brotherhood, and to their materialistic readers it would seem scarcely possible that the authors could be tainted with hallucinations of any description, while others, conspicuous leaders in the church, were seemingly beyond occult temptation.

The larger number, it was evident, hoped by studies of the works of the alchemists, to find the key to the alkahest of Van Helmont, that is, to discover the Philosopher's Stone, or the Elixir of Life, and from their writings it is plain that the inner consciousness of thoughtful and scientific men rebelled against confinement to the narrow bounds of materialistic science, within which they were forced to appear as dogmatic pessimists. To them scientific orthodoxy, acting as a weight, prohibited intellectual speculation, as rank heresy. A few of my co-laborers were expert manipulators, and worked experimentally, following in their laboratories the suggestions of those gifted students who had pored over precious old manuscripts, and had attempted to solve the enigmatical formulas recorded therein, puzzles familiar to students of Hermetic lore. It was thus demonstrated,—for what I have related is history,—that in this nineteenth century there exists a fraternity, the members of which are as earnest in their belief in the truth of Esoteric philosophy, as were the followers of Hermes himself; savants who, in secret, circulate among themselves a literature that the materialism of this self-same nineteenth century has relegated to the deluded and murky periods that produced it.

One day a postal package came to my address, this being the manner in which some of our literature circulated, which, on examination, I found to be a letter of instruction and advice from some unknown member of our circle. I was already becoming disheartened over the mental confusion into which my studies were leading me, and the contents of the letter, in which I was greatly interested, made a lasting impression upon me. It seemed to have been circulating a long time among our members in Europe and America, for it bore numerous marginal notes of various dates, but each and every one of its readers had for one reason or another declined the task therein suggested. From the substance of the paper, which, written exquisitely, yet partook of the ambiguous alchemistic style, it was evident that the author was well versed in alchemy, and, in order that my position may be clearly understood at this turning point in a life of remarkable adventure, the letter is appended in full:

THE ALCHEMISTIC LETTER.

TO THE BROTHER ADEPT WHO DARES TRY TO DISCOVER ZOROASTER'S CAVE, OR THE PHILOSOPHER'S INTELLECTUAL ECHOES, BY MEANS OF WHICH THEY COMMUNICATE TO ONE ANOTHER FROM THEIR CAVES.

Know thou, that Hermes Trismegistus did not originate, but he gave to our philosophy his name—the Hermetic Art. Evolved in a dim, mystic age, before antiquity began, it endured through the slowly rolling cycles to be bandied about by the ever-ready flippancy of nineteenth century students. It has lived, because it is endowed with that quality which never dies—truth. Modern philosophy, of which chemistry is but a fragment, draws its sustenance from the prime facts which were revealed in ancient Egypt through Hermetic thought, and fixed by the Hermetic stylus.

"The Hermetic allegories," so various in interpretable susceptibility, led subsequent thinkers into speculations and experimentations, which have resulted profitably to the world. It is not strange that some of the followers of Hermes, especially the more mercurial and imaginative, should have evolved nebulous theories, no longer explainable, and involving recondite spiritual considerations. Know thou that the ultimate on psycho-chemical investigation is the proximate of the infinite. Accordingly, a class came to believe that a projection of natural mental faculties into an advanced state of consciousness called the "wisdom faculty" constitutes the final possibility of Alchemy. The attainment of this exalted condition is still believed practicable by many earnest savants. Once on this lofty plane, the individual would not be trammelled by material obstacles, but would abide in that spiritual placidity which is the exquisite realization of mortal perfection. So exalted, he would be in naked parallelism with Omniscience, and through his illuminated understanding, could feast his soul on those exalted pleasures which are only less than deific.

Notwithstanding the exploitings of a number of these philosophers, in which, by reason of our inability to comprehend, sense seemed lost in a passage of incohesive dreamery and resonancy of terminology, some of the purest spiritual researches the world has ever known, were made in the dawn of history. The much abused alchemical philosophers existed upon a plane, in some respects above the level of the science of to-day. Many of them lived for the good of the world only, in an atmosphere above the materialistic hordes that people the world, and toiling over their crucibles and alembics, died in their cells "uttering no voice." Take, for example, Eirenæus Philalethes, who, born in 1623, lived contemporaneously with Robert Boyle. A fragment from his writings will illustrate the purpose which impelled the searcher for the true light of alchemy to record his discoveries in allegories, and we have no right to question the honesty of his utterances:

"The Searcher of all hearts knows that I write the truth; nor is there any cause to accuse me of envy. I write with an unterrified quill in an unheard of style, to the honor of God, to the profit of my neighbors, with contempt of the world and its riches, because Elias, the artist, is already born, and now glorious things are declared of the city of God. I dare affirm that I do possess more riches than the whole known world is worth, but I can not make use of it because of the snares of knaves. I disdain, loathe, and detest the idolizing of silver and gold, by which the pomps and vanities of the world are celebrated. Ah! filthy evil! Ah! vain nothingness! Believe ye that I conceal the art out of envy? No, verily, I protest to you; I grieve from the very bottom of my soul that we (alchemists) are driven like vagabonds from the face of the Lord throughout the earth. But what need of many words? The thing that we have seen, taught, and made, which we have, possess, and know, that we do declare; being moved with compassion for the studious, and with indignation of gold, silver, and precious stones. Believe me, the time is at the door, I feel it in spirit, when we, adeptists, shall return from the four corners of the earth, nor shall we fear any snares that are laid against our lives, but we shall give thanks to the Lord our God. I would to God that every ingenious man in the whole earth understood this science; then it would be valued only for its wisdom, and virtue only would be had in honor."

Of course there was a more worldly class, and a large contingent of mercenary impostors (as science is always encumbered), parasites, whose animus was shamefully unlike the purity of true esoteric psychologists. These men devoted their lives to experimentation for selfish advancement. They constructed alchemical outfits, and carried on a ceaseless inquiry into the nature of solvents, and studied their influences on earthly bodies, their ultimate object being the discovery of the Philosopher's Stone, and the alkahest which Bœrhaave asserts was never discovered. Their records were often a verbose melange, purposely so written, no doubt, to cover their tracks, and to make themselves conspicuous. Other Hermetic believers occupied a more elevated position, and connected the intellectual with the material, hoping to gain by their philosophy and science not only gold and silver, which were secondary considerations, but the highest literary achievement, the Magnum Opus. Others still sought to draw from Astrology and Magic the secrets that would lead them to their ambitious goal. Thus there were degrees of fineness in a fraternity, which the science of to-day must recognize and admit.

Bœrhaave, the illustrious, respected Geber, of the alchemistic school, and none need feel compromised in admiring the talented alchemists who, like

Geber, wrought in the twilight of morn for the coming world's good. We are now enjoying a fragment of the ultimate results of their genius and industry in the materialistic outcomes of present-day chemistry, to be followed by others more valuable; and at last, when mankind is ripe in the wisdom faculty, by spiritual contentment in the complacent furtherings beyond. Allow me briefly to refer to a few men of the alchemistic type whose records may be considered with advantage.

Rhasis, a conspicuous alchemist, born in 850, first mentioned orpiment, borax, compounds of iron, copper, arsenic, and other similar substances. It is said, too, that he discovered the art of making brandy. About a century later, Alfarabe (killed in 950), a great alchemist, astonished the King of Syria with his profound learning, and excited the admiration of the wise men of the East by his varied accomplishments. Later, Albertus Magnus (born 1205), noted for his talent and skill, believed firmly in the doctrine of transmutation. His beloved pupil, Thomas Aquinas, gave us the word amalgam, and it still serves us. Contemporaneously with these lived Roger Bacon (born 1214), who was a man of most extraordinary ability. There has never been a greater English intellect (not excepting his illustrious namesake, Lord Bacon), and his penetrating mind delved deeper into nature's laws than that of any successor. He told us of facts concerning the sciences, that scientific men can not fully comprehend to-day; he told us of other things that lie beyond the science provings of to-day, that modern philosophers can not grasp. He was an enthusiastic believer in the Hermetic philosophy, and such were his erudition and advanced views, that his brother friars, through jealousy and superstition, had him thrown into prison—a common fate to men who in those days dared to think ahead of their age. Despite (as some would say) of his mighty reasoning power and splendid attainments, he believed the Philosopher's Stone to be a reality; he believed the secret of indefinite prolongation of life abode in alchemy; that the future could be predicted by means of a mirror which he called Almuchese, and that by alchemy an adept could produce pure gold. He asserted that by means of Aristotle's "Secret of Secrets," pure gold can be made; gold even purer and finer than what men now know as gold. In connection with other predictions he made an assertion that may with other seemingly unreasonable predictions be verified in time to come. He said: "It is equally possible to construct cars which may be set in motion with marvelous rapidity, independently of horses or other animals." He declared that the ancients had done this, and he believed the art might be revived.

Following came various enthusiasts, such as Raymond, the ephemeral (died 1315), who flared like a meteor into his brief, brilliant career; Arnold de Villanova (1240), a celebrated adept, whose books were burned by the Inquisition on account of the heresy they taught; Nicholas Flamel, of France (1350), loved by the people for his charities, the wonder of his age (our age will not admit the facts) on account of the vast fortune he amassed without visible means or income, outside of alchemical lore; Johannes de Rupecissus, a man of such remarkable daring that he even (1357) reprimanded Pope Innocent VI., for which he was promptly imprisoned; Basil Valentine (1410), the author of many works, and the man who introduced antimony (antimonaches) into medicine; Isaac of Holland who, with his son, skillfully made artificial gems that could not be distinguished from the natural; Bernard Trevison (born

1406), who spent $30,000 in the study of alchemy, out of much of which he was cheated by cruel alchemic pretenders, for even in that day there were plenty of rogues to counterfeit a good thing. Under stress of his strong alchemic convictions, Thomas Dalton placed his head on the block by order of the virtuous (?) and conservative Thomas Herbert, 'squire to King Edward; Jacob Bohme (born 1575), the sweet, pure spirit of Christian mysticism, "The Voice of Heaven," than whom none stood higher in true alchemy, was a Christian, alchemist, theosophist; Robert Boyle, a conspicuous alchemical philosopher, in 1662 published his "Defense of the Doctrine touching the Spring and Weight of the Air," and illustrated his arguments by a series of ingenious and beautiful experiments, that stand to-day so high in the estimation of scientific men, that his remarks are copied verbatim by our highest authorities, and his apparatus is the best yet devised for the purpose. Boyle's "Law" was evolved and carefully defined fourteen years before Mariotte's "Discours de la Nature de l' Air" appeared, which did not, however, prevent French and German scientific men from giving the credit to Mariotte, and they still follow the false teacher who boldly pirated not only Boyle's ideas, but stole his apparatus.

Then appeared such men as Paracelsus (born 1493), the celebrated physician, who taught that occultism (esoteric philosophy) was superior to experimental chemistry in enlightening us concerning the transmutation of baser metals into gold and silver; and Gueppo Francisco (born 1627), who wrote a beautiful treatise on "Elementary Spirits," which was copied without credit by Compte de Gabalis. It seems incredible that the man (Gueppo Francisco), whose sweet spirit-thoughts are revivified and breathe anew in "Undine" and "The Rape of the Lock," should have been thrown into a prison to perish as a Hermetic follower; and this should teach us not to question the earnestness of those who left us as a legacy the beauty and truth so abundantly found in pure alchemy.

These and many others, cotemporaries, some conspicuous, and others whose names do not shine in written history, contributed incalculably to the grand aggregate of knowledge concerning the divine secret which enriched the world. Compare the benefits of Hermetic philosophy with the result of bloody wars ambitiously waged by self-exacting tyrants—tyrants whom history applauds as heroes, but whom we consider as butchers. Among the workers in alchemy are enumerated nobles, kings, and even popes. Pope John XXII. was an alchemist, which accounts for his bull against impostors, promulgated in order that true students might not be discredited; and King Frederick of Naples sanctioned the art, and protected its devotees.

At last, Count Cagliostro, the chequered "Joseph Balsamo" (born 1743), who combined alchemy, magic, astrology, sleight of hand, mesmerism, Free Masonry, and remarkable personal accomplishments, that altogether have never since been equalled, burst upon the world. Focusing the gaze of the church, kings, and the commons upon himself, in many respects the most audacious pretender that history records, he raised the Hermetic art to a dazzling height, and finally buried it in a blaze of splendor as he passed from existence beneath a mantle of shame. As a meteor streams into view from out the star mists of space, and in corruscating glory sinks into the sea, Cagliostro blazed into the sky of the nineteenth century, from the nebulæ of alchemistic speculation, and extinguished both himself and his science in the light of the rising sun of materialism. Cagliostro the visionary, the poet, the inspired, the erratic comet in the universe of intellect, perished in prison as a mountebank, and then the plodding chemist of to-day, with his tedious mechanical methods, and cold, unresponsive, materialistic dogmas, arose from the ashes, and sprang into prominence.

Read the story backward, and you shall see that in alchemy we behold the beginning of all the sciences of to-day; alchemy is the cradle that rocked them. Fostered with necromancy, astrology, occultism, and all the progeny of mystic dreamery, the infant sciences struggled for existence through the dark ages, in care of the once persecuted and now traduced alchemist. The world owes a monument to-day more to Hermetic heroes, than to all other influences and instrumentalities, religion excepted, combined, for our present civilization is largely a legacy from the alchemist. Begin with Hermes Trismegistus, and close with Joseph Balsamo, and if you are inclined towards science, do not criticise too severely their verbal logorrhea, and their romanticism, for your science is treading backward; it will encroach upon their field again, and you may have to unsay your words of hasty censure. These men fulfilled their mission, and did it well. If they told more than men now think they knew, they also knew more than they told, and more than modern philosophy embraces. They could not live to see all the future they eagerly hoped for, but they started a future for mankind that will far exceed in sweetness and light the most entrancing visions of their most imaginative dreamers. They spoke of the existence of a "red elixir," and while they wrote, the barbarous world about them ran red with blood,—blood of the pure in heart, blood of the saints, blood of a Saviour; and their allegory and wisdom formulæ were recorded in blood of their own sacrifices. They dreamed of a "white elixir" that is yet to bless mankind, and a brighter day for man, a period of peace, happiness, long life, contentment, good will and brotherly love, and in the name of this "white elixir" they directed the world towards a vision of divine light. Even pure gold, as they told the materialistic world who worship gold, was penetrated and whelmed by this subtle, superlatively refined spirit of matter. Is not the day of the allegorical "white elixir" nearly at hand? Would that it were!

I say to you now, brothers of the nineteenth century, as one speaking by authority to you, cease (some of you) to study this entrancing past, look to the future by grasping the present, cast aside (some of you) the alchemical lore of other days, give up your loved allegories; it is a duty, you must relinquish them. There is a richer field. Do not delay. Unlock this mystic door that stands hinged and ready, waiting the touch of men who can interpret the talisman; place before mankind the knowledge that lies behind its rivets. In the secret lodges that have preserved the wisdom of the days of Enoch and Elias of Egypt, who propagated the Egyptian Order, a branch of your ancient brotherhood, is to be found concealed much knowledge that should now be spread before the world, and added to the treasures of our circle of adepts. This cabalistic wisdom is not recorded in books nor in manuscript, but has been purposely preserved from the uninitiated, in the unreadable brains of unresponsive men. Those who are selected to act as carriers thereof, are, as a rule, like dumb water bearers, or the dead sheet of paper that mechanically preserves an inspiration derived from minds unseen: they serve a purpose as a child mechanically commits to memory a blank verse to repeat to others, who in turn commit to repeat again—neither of them speaking understandingly. Search ye these hidden paths, for the day of mental liberation approaches, and publish to the world all that is locked within the doors of that antiquated organization. The world is nearly ripe for the wisdom faculty, and men are ready to unravel the golden threads that mystic wisdom has inwoven in her web of secret knowledge. Look for knowledge where I have indicated, and to gain it do not hesitate to swear allegiance to this sacred order, for so you must do to gain entrance to the brotherhood, and then you must act what men will call the traitor. You will, however, be doing a sacred duty, for the world will profit, humanity will be the gainer, "Peace on Earth, Good Will to Man," will be closer to mankind, and at last, when the sign appears, the "white elixir" will no longer be allegorical; it will become a reality. In the name of the Great Mystic Vase-Man, go thou into these lodges, learn of their secrets, and spread their treasures before those who can interpret them.

Here this letter ended. It was evident that the writer referred to a secret society into which I could probably enter; and taking the advice, I did not hesitate, but applied at once for membership. I determined, regardless of consequence, to follow the suggestion of the unknown writer, and by so doing, for I accepted their pledges, I invited my destiny.

My guest of the massive forehead paused for a moment, stroked his long, white beard, and then, after casting an inquiring glance on me, asked, "Shall I read on?"

"Yes," I replied, and The—Man—Who—Did—It, proceeded as follows:

CHAPTER V.

THE WRITING OF MY CONFESSION.

Having become a member of the Secret Society as directed by the writer of the letter I have just read, and having obtained the secrets hinted at in the mystic directions, my next desire was to find a secluded spot where, without interruption, I could prepare for publication what I had gathered surreptitiously in the lodges of the fraternity I designed to betray. This I entitled "My Confession." Alas! why did my evil genius prompt me to write it? Why did not some kind angel withhold my hand from the rash and wicked deed? All I can urge in defense or palliation is that I was infatuated by the fatal words of the letter, "You must act what men will call the traitor, but humanity will be the gainer."

In a section of the state in which I resided, a certain creek forms the boundary line between two townships, and also between two counties. Crossing this creek, a much traveled road stretches east and west, uniting the extremes of the great state. Two villages on this road, about four miles apart, situated on opposite sides of the creek, also present themselves to my memory, and midway between them, on the north side of the road, was a substantial farm house. In going west from the easternmost of these villages, the traveler begins to descend from the very center of the town. In no place is the grade steep, as the road lies between the spurs of the hill abutting upon the valley that feeds the creek I have mentioned. Having reached the valley, the road winds a short distance to the right, then turning to the left, crosses the stream, and immediately begins to climb the western hill; here the ascent is more difficult, for the road lies diagonally over the edge of the hill. A mile of travel, as I recall the scene, sometimes up a steep, and again among rich, level farm lands, and then on the very height, close to the road, within a few feet of it, appears the square structure which was, at the time I mention, known as the Stone Tavern. On the opposite side of the road were located extensive stables, and a grain barn. In the northeast chamber of that stone building, during a summer in the twenties, I wrote for publication the description of the mystic work that my oath should have made forever a secret, a sacred trust. I am the man who wantonly committed the deplorable act. Under the infatuation of that alchemical manuscript, I strove to show the world that I could and would do that which might never benefit me in the least, but might serve humanity. It was fate. I was not a bad man, neither malignity, avarice, nor ambition forming a part of my nature. I was a close student, of a rather retiring disposition, a stone-mason by trade, careless and indifferent to public honors, and so thriftless that many trifling neighborhood debts had accumulated against me.

What I have reluctantly told, for I am forbidden to give the names of the localities, comprises an abstract of part of the record of my early life, and will introduce the extraordinary narrative which follows. That I have spoken the truth, and in no manner overdrawn, will be silently evidenced by hundreds of brethren, both of the occult society and the fraternal brotherhood, with which I united, who can (if they will) testify to the accuracy of the narrative. They know the story of my crime and disgrace; only myself and God know the full retribution that followed.

CHAPTER VI.

KIDNAPPED.

The events just narrated occurred in the prime of my life, and are partly matters of publicity. My attempted breach of faith in the way of disclosing their secrets was naturally infamous in the eyes of my society brethren, who endeavored to prevail upon me to relent of my design which, after writing my "Confession," I made no endeavor to conceal. Their importunities and threatenings had generally been resisted, however, and with an obliquity that can not be easily explained, I persisted in my unreasonable design. I was blessed as a husband and father, but neither the thought of home, wife, nor child, checked me in my inexplicable course. I was certainly irresponsible, perhaps a monomaniac, and yet on the subject in which I was absorbed, I preserved my mental equipoise, and knowingly followed a course that finally brought me into the deepest slough of trouble, and lost to me forever all that man loves most dearly. An overruling spirit, perhaps the shade of one of the old alchemists, possessed me, and in the face of obstacles that would have caused most men to reflect, and retrace their steps, I madly rushed onward. The influence that impelled me, whatever it may have been, was irresistible. I apparently acted the part of agent, subject to an ever-present master essence, and under this dominating spirit or demon my mind was powerless in its subjection. My soul was driven imperiously by that impelling and indescribable something, and was as passive and irresponsible as lycopodium that is borne onward in a steady current of air. Methods were vainly sought by those who loved me, brethren of the lodge, and others who endeavored to induce me to change my headstrong purpose, but I could neither accept their counsels nor heed their forebodings. Summons by law were served on me in order to disconcert me, and my numerous small debts became the pretext for legal warrants, until at last all my papers (excepting my "Confession"), and my person also, were seized, upon an execution served by a constable. Minor claims were quickly satisfied, but when I regained my liberty, the aggression continued. Even arson was resorted to, and the printing office that held my manuscript was fired one night, that the obnoxious revelation which I persisted in putting into print, might be destroyed. Finally I found myself separated by process of law from home and friends, an inmate of a jail. My opponents, as I now came to consider them, had confined me in prison for a debt of only two dollars, a sufficient amount at that time, in that state, for my incarceration. Smarting under the humiliation, my spirit became still more rebellious, and I now, perhaps justly, came to view myself as a martyr. It had been at first asserted that I had stolen a shirt, but I was not afraid of any penalty that could be laid on me for this trumped-up charge, believing that the imputation and the arrest would be shown to be designed as willful oppression. Therefore it was, that when this contemptible arraignment had been swept aside, and I was freed before a Justice of the Peace, I experienced more than a little surprise at a rearrest, and at finding myself again thrown into jail. I knew that it had been decreed by my brethren that I must retract and destroy my "Confession," and this fact made me the more determined to prevent its destruction, and I persisted sullenly in pursuing my course. On the evening of August 12th, 1826, my jailer's wife informed me that the debt for which I had been incarcerated had been paid by unknown "friends," and that I could depart; and I accepted the statement without question. Upon my stepping from the door of the jail, however, my arms were firmly grasped by two persons, one on each side of me, and before I could realize the fact that I was being kidnapped, I was thrust into a closed coach, which immediately rolled away, but not until I made an outcry which, if heard by anyone, was unheeded.

"For your own sake, be quiet," said one of my companions in confinement, for the carriage was draped to exclude the light, and was as dark as a dungeon. My spirit rebelled; I felt that I was on the brink of a remarkable, perhaps perilous experience, and I indignantly replied by asking:

"What have I done that you should presume forcibly to imprison me? Am I not a freeman of America?"

"What have you done?" he answered. "Have you not bound yourself by a series of vows that are sacred and should be inviolable, and have you not broken them as no other man has done before you? Have you not betrayed your trust, and merited a severe judgment? Did you not voluntarily ask admission into our ancient brotherhood, and in good faith were you not initiated into our sacred mysteries? Did you not obligate yourself before man, and on your sacred honor promise to preserve our secrets?"

"I did," I replied; "but previously I had sworn before a higher tribunal to scatter this precious wisdom to the world."

"Yes," he said, "and you know full well the depth of the self-sought solemn oath that you took with us—more solemn than that prescribed by any open court on earth."

"This I do not deny," I said, "and yet I am glad that I accomplished my object, even though you have now, as is evident, the power to pronounce my sentence."

"You should look for the death sentence," was the reply, "but it has been ordained instead that you are to be given a lengthened life. You should expect bodily destruction; but on the contrary, you will pass on in consciousness of earth and earthly concerns when we are gone. Your name will be known to all lands, and yet from this time you will be unknown. For the welfare of future humanity, you will be thrust to a height in our order that will annihilate you as a mortal being, and yet you will exist, suspended between life and death, and in that intermediate state will know that you exist. You have, as you confess, merited a severe punishment, but we can only punish in accordance with an unwritten law, that instructs the person punished, and elevates the human race in consequence. You stand alone among mortals in that you have openly attempted to give broadly to those who have not earned it, our most sacred property, a property that did not belong to you, property that you have only been permitted to handle, that has been handed from man to man from before the time of Solomon, and which belongs to no one man, and will continue to pass in this way from one to another, as a hallowed trust, until there are no men, as men now exist, to receive it. You will soon go into the shadows of darkness, and will learn many of the mysteries of life, the undeveloped mysteries that are withheld from your fellows, but which you, who have been so presumptuous and anxious for knowledge, are destined to possess and solve. You will find secrets that man, as man is now constituted, can not yet discover, and yet which the future man must gain and be instructed in. As you have sowed, so shall you reap. You wished to become a distributor of knowledge; you shall now by bodily trial and mental suffering obtain unsought knowledge to distribute, and in time to come you will be commanded to make your discoveries known. As your pathway is surely laid out, so must you walk. It is ordained; to rebel is useless."

"Who has pronounced this sentence?" I asked.

"A judge, neither of heaven nor of earth."

"You speak in enigmas."

"No; I speak openly, and the truth. Our brotherhood is linked with the past, and clasps hands with the antediluvians; the flood scattered the races of earth, but did not disturb our secrets. The great love of wisdom has from generation to generation led selected members of our organization to depths of study that our open work does not touch upon, and behind our highest officers there stand, in the occult shades between the here and the hereafter, unknown and unseen agents who are initiated into secrets above and beyond those known to the ordinary craft. Those who are introduced into these inner recesses acquire superhuman conceptions, and do not give an open sign of fellowship; they need no talisman. They walk our streets possessed of powers unknown to men, they concern themselves as mortals in the affairs of men, and even their brethren of the initiated, open order are unaware of their exalted condition. The means by which they have been instructed, their several individualities as well, have been concealed, because publicity would destroy their value, and injure humanity's cause."

Silence followed these vague disclosures, and the carriage rolled on. I was mystified and alarmed, and yet I knew that, whatever might be the end of this nocturnal ride, I had invited it—yes, merited it—and I steeled myself to hear the sentence of my judges, in whose hands I was powerless. The persons on the seat opposite me continued their conversation in low tones, audible only to themselves. An individual by my side neither moved nor spoke. There were four of us in the carriage, as I learned intuitively, although we were surrounded by utter darkness. At length I addressed the companion beside me, for the silence was unbearable. Friend or enemy though he might be, anything rather than this long silence. "How long shall we continue in this carriage?"

He made no reply.

After a time I again spoke.

"Can you not tell me, comrade, how long our journey will last? When shall we reach our destination?"

Silence only.

Putting out my hand, I ventured to touch my mate, and found that he was tightly strapped,—bound upright to the seat and the back of the carriage. Leather thongs held him firmly in position; and as I pondered over the mystery, I thought to myself, if I make a disturbance, they will not hesitate to manacle me as securely. My custodians seemed, however, not to exercise a guard over me, and yet I felt that they were certain of my inability to escape. If the man on the seat was a prisoner, why was he so reticent? why did he not answer my questions? I came to the conclusion that he must be gagged as well as bound. Then I determined to find out if this were so. I began to realize more forcibly that a terrible sentence must have been meted me, and I half hoped that I could get from my partner in captivity some information regarding our destination. Sliding my hand cautiously along his chest, and under his chin, I intended to remove the gag from his mouth, when I felt my flesh creep, for it came in contact with the cold, rigid flesh of a corpse. The man was dead, and stiff.

The shock unnerved me. I had begun to experience the results of a severe mental strain, partly induced by the recent imprisonment and extended previous persecution, and partly by the mysterious significance of the language in which I had recently been addressed. The sentence, "You will now go into the Valley of the Shadow of Death, and learn the mysteries of life," kept ringing through my head, and even then I sat beside a corpse. After this discovery I remained for a time in a semi-stupor, in a state of profound dejection,—how long I can not say. Then I experienced an inexplicable change, such as I imagine comes over a condemned man without hope of reprieve, and I became unconcerned as a man might who had accepted his destiny, and stoically determined to await it. Perhaps moments passed, it may have been hours, and then indifference gave place to reviving curiosity. I realized that I could die only once, and I coolly and complacently revolved the matter, speculating over my possible fate. As I look back on the night in which I rode beside that dead man, facing the mysterious agents of an all-powerful judge, I marvel over a mental condition that permitted me finally to rest in peace, and slumber in unconcern. So I did, however, and after a period, the length of which I am not able to estimate, I awoke, and soon thereafter the carriage stopped, and our horses were changed, after which our journey was resumed, to continue hour after hour, and at last I slept again, leaning back in the corner. Suddenly I was violently shaken from slumber, and commanded to alight. It was in the gray of morning, and before I could realize what was happening, I was transferred by my captors to another carriage, and the dead man also was rudely hustled along and thrust beside me, my companions speaking to him as though he were alive. Indeed, as I look back on these maneuvers, I perceive that, to all appearances, I was one of the abducting party, and our actions were really such as to induce an observer to believe that this dead man was an obstinate prisoner, and myself one of his official guards. The drivers of the carriages seemed to give us no attention, but they sat upright and unconcerned, and certainly neither of them interested himself in our transfer. The second carriage, like that other previously described, was securely closed, and our journey was continued. The darkness was as of a dungeon. It may have been days, I could not tell anything about the passage of time; on and on we rode. Occasionally food and drink were handed in, but my captors held to their course, and at last I was taken from the vehicle, and transferred to a block-house.

I had been carried rapidly and in secret a hundred or more miles, perhaps into another state, and probably all traces of my journey were effectually lost to outsiders. I was in the hands of men who implicitly obeyed the orders of their superiors, masters whom they had never seen, and probably did not know. I needed no reminder of the fact that I had violated every sacred pledge voluntarily made to the craft, and now that they held me powerless, I well knew that, whatever the punishment assigned, I had invited it, and could not prevent its fulfillment. That it would be severe, I realized; that it would not be in accordance with ordinary human law, I accepted.

Had I not in secret, in my little room in that obscure Stone Tavern, engrossed on paper the mystic sentences that never

"I WAS TAKEN FROM THE VEHICLE, AND TRANSFERRED TO A BLOCK-HOUSE."

before had been penned, and were unknown excepting to persons initiated into our sacred mysteries? Had I not previously, in the most solemn manner, before these words had been imparted to my keeping, sworn to keep them inviolate and secret? and had I not deliberately broken that sacred vow, and scattered the hoarded sentences broadcast? My part as a brother in this fraternal organization was that of the holder only of property that belonged to no man, that had been handed from one to another through the ages, sacredly cherished, and faithfully protected by men of many tongues, always considered a trust.

a charge of honor, and never before betrayed. My crime was deep and dark. I shuddered.

"Come what may," I mused, reflecting over my perfidy, "I am ready for the penalty, and my fate is deserved; it can not but be a righteous one."

The words of the occupant of the carriage occurred to me again and again; that one sentence kept ringing in my brain; I could not dismiss it: "You have been tried, convicted, and we are of those appointed to carry out the sentence of the judges."

The black silence of my lonely cell beat against me; I could feel the absence of sound, I could feel the dismal weight of nothingness, and in my solitude and distraction I cried out in anguish to the invisible judge: "I am ready for my sentence, whether it be death or imprisonment for life"; and still the further words of the occupant of the carriage passed through my mind: "You will now go into the Valley of the Shadow of Death, and will learn the mysteries of Life."

Then I slept, to awake and sleep again. I kept no note of time; it may have been days or weeks, so far as my record could determine. An attendant came at intervals to minister to my wants, always masked completely, ever silent.

That I was not entirely separated from mankind, however, I felt assured, for occasionally sounds of voices came to me from without. Once I ventured to shout aloud, hoping to attract attention; but the persons whom I felt assured overheard me, paid no attention to my lonely cry. At last one night, my door opened abruptly, and three men entered.

"Do not fear," said their spokesman, "we aim to protect you; keep still, and soon you will be a free man."

I consented quietly to accompany them, for to refuse would have been in vain; and I was conducted to a boat, which I found contained a corpse—the one I had journeyed with, I suppose—and embarking, we were silently rowed to the middle of the river, our course being diagonally from the shore, and the dead man was thrown overboard. Then our boat returned to the desolate bank.

Thrusting me into a carriage, that, on our return to the river bank we found awaiting us, my captors gave a signal, and I was driven away in the darkness, as silently as before, and our journey was continued I believe for fully two days. I was again confined in another log cabin, with but one door, and destitute of windows. My attendants were masked, they neither spoke to me as they day after day supplied my wants, nor did they give me the least information on any subject, until at last I abandoned all hope of ever regaining my liberty.

"THE DEAD MAN WAS THROWN OVERBOARD."

CHAPTER VII.

A WILD NIGHT.—I AM PREMATURELY AGED.

In the depths of night I was awakened by a noise made by the opening of a door, and one by one seven masked figures silently stalked into my prison. Each bore a lighted torch, and they passed me as I lay on the floor in my clothes (for I had no bedding), and ranged themselves in a line. I arose, and seated myself as directed to do, upon the only stool in the room. Swinging into a semi-circle, the weird line wound about me, and from the one seat on which I rested in the center of the room, I gazed successively upon seven pairs of gleaming eyes, each pair directed at myself; and as I turned from one to another, the black cowl of each deepened into darkness, and grew more hideous.

"Men or devils," I cried, "do your worst! Make me, if such is your will, as that sunken corpse beside which I was once seated; but cease your persecutions. I have atoned for my indiscretions a thousand fold, and this suspense is unbearable; I demand to know what is to be my doom, and I desire its fulfilment."

Then one stepped forward, facing me squarely,—the others closed together around him and me. Raising his forefinger, he pointed it close to my face, and as his sharp eyes glittered from behind the black mask, piercing through me, he slowly said: "Why do you not say brothers?"

"Horrible," I rejoined; "stop this mockery. Have I not suffered enough from your persecutions to make me reject that word as applied to yourselves? You can but murder; do your duty to your unseen masters, and end this prolonged torture!"

"Brother," said the spokesman, "you well know that the sacred rules of our order will not permit us to murder any human being. We exist to benefit humanity, to lead the wayward back across the burning desert into the pathways of the righteous; not to destroy or persecute a brother. Ours is an eleemosynary institution, instructing its members, helping them to seek happiness. You are now expiating the crime you have committed, and the good in your spirit rightfully revolts against the bad, for in divulging to the world our mystic signs and brotherly greetings, you have sinned against yourself more than against others. The sting of conscience, the bitings of remorse punish you."

"True," I cried, as the full significance of what he said burst upon me, "too true; but I bitterly repent my treachery. Others can never know how my soul is harrowed by the recollection of the enormity of that breach of confidence. In spite of my open, careless, or defiant bearing, my heart is humble, and my spirit cries out for mercy. By night and by day I have in secret cursed myself for heeding an unhallowed mandate, and I have long looked forward to the judgment that I should suffer for my perfidy, for I have appreciated that the day of reckoning would surely appear. I do not rebel, and I recall my wild language; I recant my 'Confession,' I renounce myself! I say to you in all sincerity, brothers, do your duty, only I beg of you to slay me at once, and end my suspense. I await my doom. What might it be?"

Grasping my hand, the leader said: "You are ready as a member of our order; we can now judge you as we have been commanded; had you persisted in calling us devils in your mistaken frenzy, we should have been forced to reason with you until you returned again to us, and became one of us. Our judgment is for you only; the world must not now know its nature, at least so far as we are concerned. Those you see here, are not your judges; we are agents sent to labor with you, to draw you back into our ranks, to bring you into a condition that will enable you to carry out the sentence that you have drawn upon yourself, for you must be your own doomsman. In the first place, we are directed to gain your voluntary consent to leave this locality. You can no longer take part in affairs that interested you before. To the people of this State, and to your home, and kindred, you must become a stranger for all time. Do you consent?"

"Yes," I answered, for I knew that I must acquiesce.

"In the next place, you must help us to remove all traces of your identity. You must, so far as the world is concerned, leave your body where you have apparently been drowned, for a world's benefit, a harmless mockery to deceive the people, and also to make an example for others that are weak. Are you ready?"

"Yes."

"Then remove your clothing, and replace it with this suit.",

I obeyed, and changed my garments, receiving others in return. One of the party then, taking from beneath his gown a box containing several bottles of liquids, proceeded artfully to mix and compound them, and then to paint my face with the combination, which after being mixed, formed a clear solution.

"Do not fear to wash;" said the spokesman, "the effect of this lotion is permanent enough to stay until you are well out of this State."

I passed my hand over my face; it was drawn into wrinkles as a film of gelatine might have been shrivelled under the influence of a strong tannin or astringent liquid; beneath my fingers it felt like the furrowed face of a very old man, but I experienced no pain. I vainly tried to smooth the wrinkles; immediately upon removing the pressure of my hand, the furrows reappeared.

Next, another applied a colorless liquid freely to my hair and beard; he rubbed it well, and afterward wiped it dry with a towel. A mirror was thrust beneath my gaze. I started back, the transformation was complete. My appearance had entirely changed. My face had become aged and wrinkled, my hair as white as snow.

I cried aloud in amazement: "Am I sane, is this a dream?"

"It is not a dream; but, under methods that are in exact accordance with natural physiological laws, we have been enabled to transform your appearance from that of one in the prime of manhood into the semblance of an old man, and that, too, without impairment of your vitality." Another of the masked men opened a curious little casket that I perceived was surmounted by an alembic and other alchemical figures, and embossed with an Oriental design. He drew from it a lamp which he lighted with a taper; the flame that resulted, first pale blue, then yellow, next violet and finally red, seemed to become more weird and ghastly with each mutation, as I gazed spellbound upon its fantastic changes. Then, after these transformations, it burned steadily with the final strange blood-red hue,

"A MIRROR WAS THRUST BENEATH MY GAZE."

and he now held over the blaze a tiny cup, which, in a few moments, commenced to sputter and then smoked, exhaling a curious, epipolic, semi-luminous vapor. I was commanded to inhale the vapor.

I hesitated; the thought rushed upon me, "Now I am another person, so cleverly disguised that even my own friends would perhaps not know me, this vapor is designed to suffocate me, and my body, if found, will not now be known, and could not be identified when discovered."

"Do not fear," said the spokesman, as if divining my thought, "there is no danger," and at once I realized, by quick reasoning, that if my death were demanded, my body might long since have been easily destroyed, and all this ceremony would have been unnecessary.

I hesitated no longer, but drew into my lungs the vapor that arose from the mysterious cup, freely expanding my chest several times, and then asked, "Is not that enough?" Despair now overcame me. My voice, no longer the full, strong tone of a man in middle life and perfect strength, squeaked and quavered, as if impaired by palsy. I had seen my image in a mirror, an old man with wrinkled face and white hair; I now heard myself speak with the voice of an octogenarian.

"What have you done?" I cried.

"We have obeyed your orders; you told us you were ready to leave your own self here, and the work is complete. The man who entered has disappeared. If you should now stand in the streets of your village home, and cry to your former friends, 'It is I, for whom you seek,' they would smile, and call you a madman. Know," continued the voice, "that there is in Eastern metaphysical lore, more true philosophy than is embodied in the sciences of to-day, and that by means of the ramifications of our order it becomes possible, when necessary, for him who stands beyond the inner and upper Worshipful Master, to draw these treasures from the occult Wisdom possessions of Oriental sages who forget nothing and lose nothing. Have we not been permitted to do his bidding well?"

"Yes," I squeaked; "and I wish that you had done it better. I would that I were dead."

"When the time comes, if necessary, your dead body will be fished from the water," was the reply; "witnesses have seen the drowning tragedy, and will surely identify the corpse."

"And may I go? am I free now?" I asked.

"Ah," said he, "that is not for us to say; our part of the work is fulfilled, and we can return to our native lands, and resume again our several studies. So far as we are concerned, you are free, but we have been directed to pass you over to the keeping of others who will carry forward this judgment—there is another step."

"Tell me," I cried, once more desponding, "tell me the full extent of my sentence."

"That is not known to us, and probably is not known to any one man. So far as the members of our order are concerned, you have now vanished. When you leave our sight this night, we will also separate from one another, we shall know no more of you and your future than will those of our working order who live in this section of the country. We have no personal acquaintance with the guide that has been selected to conduct you farther, and who will appear in due season, and we make no surmise concerning the result of your journey, only we know that you will not be killed, for you have a work to perform, and will continue to exist long after others of your age are dead. Farewell, brother; we have discharged our duty, and by your consent, now we must return to our various pursuits. In a short time all evidence of your unfortunate mistake, the crime committed by you in printing our sacred charges, will have vanished. Even now, emissaries are ordained to collect and destroy the written record that tells of your weakness, and with the destruction of that testimony, for every copy will surely be annihilated, and with your disappearance from among men, for this also is to follow, our responsibility for you will cease."

Each of the seven men advanced, and grasped my hand, giving me the grip of brotherhood, and then, without a word, they severally and silently departed into the outer darkness. As the last man disappeared, a figure entered the door, clad and masked exactly like those who had gone. He removed the long black gown in which he was enveloped, threw the mask from his face and stood before me, a slender, graceful, bright-looking young man. By the light of the candle I saw him distinctly, and was at once struck by his amiable, cheerful countenance, and my heart bounded with a sudden hope. I had temporarily forgotten the transformation that had been made in my person, which, altogether painless, had left no physical sensation, and thought of myself as I had formerly existed; my soul was still my own, I imagined; my blood seemed unchanged, and must flow as rapidly as before; my strength was unaltered, indeed I was in self-consciousness still in the prime of life.

"Excuse me, Father," said the stranger, "but my services have been sought as a guide for the first part of a journey that I am informed you intend to take."

His voice was mild and pleasant, his bearing respectful, but the peculiar manner in which he spoke convinced me that he knew that, as a guide, he must conduct me to some previously designated spot, and that he purposed to do so was evident, with or without my consent.

"Why do you call me Father?" I attempted to say, but as the first few words escaped my lips, the recollection of the events of the night rushed upon me, for instead of my own, I recognized the piping voice of the old man I had now become, and my tongue faltered; the sentence was unspoken.

"You would ask me why I called you Father, I perceive; well, because I am directed to be a son to you, to care for your wants, to make your journey as easy and pleasant as possible, to guide you quietly and carefully to the point that will next prove of interest to you."

I stood before him a free man, in the prime of life, full of energy, and this stripling alone interposed between myself and liberty. Should I permit the slender youth to carry me away as a prisoner? would it not be best to thrust him aside, if necessary, crush him to the earth? go forth in my freedom? Yet I hesitated, for he might have friends outside; probably he was not alone.

"There are no companions near us," said he, reading my mind, "and, as I do not seem formidable, it is natural you should weigh in your mind the probabilities of escape; but you can not evade your destiny, and you must not attempt to deny yourself the pleasure of my company. You must leave this locality and leave without a regret. In order that you may acquiesce willingly I propose that together we return to your former home, which you will, however, find no longer to be a home. I will accompany you as a companion, as your son. You may speak, with one exception, to whomever you care to address; may call on any of your old associates, may assert openly who you are, or whatever and whoever you please to represent yourself, only I must also have the privilege of joining in the conversation."

"Agreed," I cried, and extended my hand; he grasped it, and then by the light of the candle, I saw a peculiar expression flit over his face, as he added:

"To one person only, as I have said, and you have promised, you must not speak—your wife."

I bowed my head, and a flood of sorrowful reflections swept over me. Of all the world the one whom I longed to meet, to clasp in my arms, to counsel in my distress, was the wife of my bosom, and I begged him to withdraw his cruel injunction.

"You should have thought of her before; now it is too late. To permit you to meet, and speak with her would be dangerous; she might pierce your disguise. Of all others there is no fear."

"Must I go with you into an unknown future without a farewell kiss from my little child or from my babe scarce three months old?"

"It has been so ordained."

I threw myself on the floor and moaned. "This is too hard, too hard for human heart to bear. Life has no charm to a man who is thrust from all he holds most dear, home, friends, family."

"The men who relinquish such pleasures and such comforts are those who do the greatest good to humanity," said the youth. "The multitude exist to propagate the race, as animal progenitors of the multitudes that are to follow, and the exceptional philanthropist is he who denies himself material bliss, and punishes himself in order to work out a problem such as it has been ordained that you are to solve. Do not argue further—the line is marked, and you must walk direct."

Into the blaze of the old fireplace of that log house, for, although it was autumn, the night was chilly, he then cast his black robe and false face, and, as they turned to ashes, the last evidences of the vivid acts through which I had passed, were destroyed. As I lay moaning in my utter misery, I tried to reason with myself that what I experienced was all a hallucination. I dozed, and awoke startled, half conscious only, as one in a nightmare; I said to myself, "A dream! a dream!" and slept again.

CHAPTER VIII.

A LESSON IN MIND STUDY.

The door of the cabin was open when I awoke, the sun shone brightly, and my friend, apparently happy and unconcerned, said: "Father, we must soon start on our journey; I have taken advantage of your refreshing sleep, and have engaged breakfast at yonder farm-house; our meal awaits us."

I arose, washed my wrinkled face, combed my white hair, and shuddered as I saw in a pocket mirror the reflection of my figure, an aged, apparently decrepit man.

"Do not be disturbed at your feeble condition," said my companion; "your infirmities are not real. Few men have ever been permitted to drink of the richness of the revelations that await you; and in view of these expectations the fact that you are prematurely aged in appearance should not unnerve you. Be of good heart, and when you say the word, we will start on our journey, which will begin as soon as you have said farewell to former friends and acquaintances."

I made no reply, but silently accompanied him, for my thoughts were in the past, and my reflections were far from pleasant.

We reached the farm-house, and as I observed the care and attention extended me by the pleasant-faced housewife, I realized that, in one respect at least, old age brought its compensation. After breakfast a man appeared from the farmer's barn, driving a team of horses attached to an open spring-wagon which, in obedience to the request of my guide, I entered, accompanied by my young friend, who directed that we be driven toward the village from which I had been abducted. He seemed to know my past life as I knew it; he asked me to select those of my friends to whom I first wished to bid farewell, even mentioning their names; he seemed all that a patient, faithful son could be, and I began to wonder at his audacity, even as much as I admired his self-confidence.

As we journeyed onward we engaged in familiar talk. We sat together on the back seat of the open spring-wagon, in full sight of passers, no attempt being made to conceal my person. Thus we traveled for two days, and on our course we passed through a large city with which I was acquainted, a city that my abductors had previously carried me through and beyond. I found that my "son" possessed fine conversational power, and a rich mine of information, and he became increasingly interesting as he drew from his fund of knowledge, and poured into my listening ears an entrancing strain of historical and metaphysical information. Never at a loss for a word or an idea, he appeared to discern my cogitations, and as my mind wandered in this or that direction he fell into the channel of my fancies, and answered my unspoken thoughts, my mind-questions or meditations, as pertinently as though I had spoken them.

His accomplishments, for the methods of his perception were unaccompanied by any endeavor to draw me into word expression, made me aware at least, that, in him, I had to deal with a man unquestionably possessed of more than ordinary intellect and education, and as this conviction entered my mind he changed his subject and promptly answered the silent inquiry, speaking as follows:

"Have you not sometimes felt that in yourself there may exist undeveloped senses that await an awakening touch to open to yourself a new world, senses that may be fully developed, but which saturate each other and neutralize themselves; quiescent, closed circles which you can not reach, satisfied circuits slumbering within your body and that defy your efforts to utilize them? In your dreams have you not seen sights that words are inadequate to describe, that your faculties can not retain in waking moments, and which dissolve into intangible nothingness, leaving only a vague, shadowy outline as the mind quickens, or rather when the senses that possess you in sleep relinquish the body to the returning vital functions and spirit? This unconscious conception of other planes, a beyond or betwixt, that is neither mental nor material, neither here nor located elsewhere, belongs to humanity in general, and is made evident from the unsatiable desire of men to pry into phenomena latent or recondite that offer no apparent return to humanity. This desire has given men the knowledge they now possess of the sciences; sciences yet in their infancy. Study in this direction is, at present, altogether of the material plane, but in time to come, men will gain control of outlying senses which will enable them to step from the seen into the consideration of matter or force that is now subtle and evasive, which must be accomplished by means of the latent faculties that I have indicated. There will be an unconscious development of new mind-forces in the student of nature as the rudiments of these so-called sciences are elaborated. Step by step, as the ages pass, the faculties of men will, under progressive series of evolutions, imperceptibly pass into higher phases until that which is even now possible with some individuals of the purified esoteric school, but which would seem miraculous if practiced openly at this day, will prove feasible to humanity generally and be found in exact accord with natural laws. The conversational method of men, whereby communion between human beings is carried on by disturbing the air by means of vocal organs so as to produce mechanical pulsations of that medium, is crude in the extreme. Mind craves to meet mind, but can not yet thrust matter aside, and in order to communicate one with another, the impression one mind wishes to convey to another must be first made on the brain matter that accompanies it, which in turn influences the organs of speech, inducing a disturbance of the air by the motions of the vocal organs, which, by undulations that reach to another being, act on his ear, and secondarily on the earthly matter of his brain, and finally by this roundabout course, impress the second being's mind. In this transmission of motions there is great waste of energy and loss of time, but such methods are a necessity of the present slow, much-obstructed method of communication. There is, in cultivated man, an innate craving for something more facile, and often a partly developed conception, spectral and vague, appears, and the being feels that there may be for mortals a richer, brighter life, a higher earthly existence that science does not now indicate. Such intimation of a deeper play of faculties is now most vivid with men during the perfect loss of mental self as experienced in dreams, which as yet man in the quick can not grasp, and which fade as he awakens. As mental sciences are developed, investigators will find that the medium known as air is unnecessary as a means of conveying mind conceptions from one person to another; that material sounds and word pulsations are cumbersome; that thought force unexpressed may be used to accomplish more than speech can do, and that physical exertions as exemplified in motion of matter such as I have described will be unnecessary for mental communication. As door after door in these directions shall open before men, mystery after mystery will be disclosed, and vanish as mysteries to reappear as simple facts. Phenomena that are impossible and unrevealed to the scientist of to-day will be familiar to the coming multitude, and at last, as by degrees, clearer knowledge is evolved, the vocal language of men will disappear, and humanity, regardless of nationality, will, in silence and even in darkness, converse eloquently together in mind language. That which is now esoteric will become exoteric. Then mind will meet mind as my mind now impinges on your own, and, in reply to your unuttered question regarding my apparently unaccountable powers of perception, I say they are perfectly natural, but while I can read your thoughts, because of the fact that you can not reciprocate in this direction, I must use my voice to impress your mind. You will know more of this, however, at a future day, for it has been ordained that you are to be educated with an object that is now concealed. At present you are interested mainly in the affairs of life as you know them, and can not enter into these purer spheres. We are approaching one of your former friends, and it may be your pleasure to ask him some questions and to bid him farewell."

CHAPTER IX.

I CAN NOT ESTABLISH MY IDENTITY.

In surprise I perceived coming towards us a light spring wagon, in which rode one of my old acquaintances. Pleasure at the discovery led me to raise my hat, wave it around my head, and salute him even at the considerable distance that then separated us. I was annoyed at the look of curiosity that passed over his countenance, and not until the two vehicles had stopped side by side did it occur to me that I was unrecognized. I had been so engrossed in my companion's revelations, that I had forgotten my unfortunate physical condition.

I stretched out my hand, I leaned over almost into the other vehicle, and earnestly said:

"Do you not know me? Only a short time ago we sat and conversed side by side."

A look of bewilderment came over his features. "I have never seen you that I can recall," he answered.

My spirit sank within me. Could it be possible that I was really so changed? I begged him to try and recall my former self, giving my name. "I am that person," I added; but he, with an expression of countenance that told as plainly as words could speak that he considered me deranged, touched his horse, and drove on.

My companion broke the awkward silence. "Do you know that I perceived between you two men an unconscious display of mind-language, especially evident on your part? You wished with all the earnestness of your soul to bring yourself as you formerly appeared, before that man, and when it proved impossible, without a word from him, his mind exhibited itself to your more earnest intellect, and you realized that he said to himself, 'This person is a poor lunatic.' He told you his thoughts in mind-language, as plainly as words could have spoken, because the intense earnestness on your part quickened your perceptive faculties, but he could not see your mental state, and the pleading voice of the apparent stranger before him could not convince the unconcerned lethargic mind within him. I observed, however, in addition to what you noticed, that he is really looking for you. That is the object of his journey, and I learn that in every direction men are now spreading the news that you have been kidnapped and carried from your jail. However, we shall soon be in the village, and you will then hear more about yourself."

We rode in silence while I meditated on my remarkable situation. I could not resign myself without a struggle to my approaching fate, and I felt even yet a hope, although I seemed powerless in the hands of destiny. Could I not, by some method, convince my friends of my identity? I determined, forgetting the fact that my guide was even then reading my mind, that upon the next opportunity I would pursue a different course.

"It will not avail," my companion replied. "You must do one of two things: you will voluntarily go with me, or you will involuntarily go to an insane asylum. Neither you nor I could by any method convince others that the obviously decrepit old man beside me was but yesterday hale, hearty, young and strong. You will find that you can not prove your identity, and as a friend, one of the great brotherhood to which you belong, a craft that deals charitably with all men and all problems, I advise you to accept the situation as soon as possible after it becomes evident to your mind that you are lost to former affiliations, and must henceforth be a stranger to the people whom you know. Take my advice, and cease to regret the past and cheerfully turn your thoughts to the future. On one side of you the lunatic asylum is open; on the other, a journey into an unknown region, beyond the confines of any known country. On the one hand, imprisonment and subjection, perhaps abuse and neglect; on the other, liberation of soul, evolution of faculty, and a grasping of superior knowledge that is denied most men—yes, withheld from all but a few persons of each generation, for only a few, unknown to the millions of this world's inhabitants, have passed over the road you are to travel. Just now you wished to meet your jailer of a few hours ago; it is a wise conclusion, and if he does not recognize you, I ask in sincerity, who will be likely to do so? We will drive straight to his home; but, here he comes."

Indeed, we were now in the village, where my miserable journey began, and perhaps by chance—it seems that it could not have been otherwise—my former jailer actually approached us.

"If you please," said my companion, "I will assist you to alight from the wagon, and you may privately converse with him."

Our wagon stopped, my guide opened a conversation with the jailer, saying that his friend wished to speak with him, and then assisted me to alight and retired a distance. I was vexed at my infirmities, which embarrassed me most exasperatingly, but which I knew were artificial; my body appeared unwilling although my spirit was anxious; but do what I could to control my actions, I involuntarily behaved like a decrepit old man. However, my mind was made up; this attempt to prove my personality should be the last; failure now would prove the turning point, and I would go willingly with my companion upon the unknown journey if I could not convince the jailer of my identity.

Straightening myself before the expectant jailer, who, with a look of inquisitiveness, regarded me as a stranger, I asked if he knew my former self, giving my name.

"That I do," he replied, "and if I could find him at this moment I would be relieved of a load of worry."

"Would you surely know him if you met him?" I asked.

"Assuredly," he replied; "and if you bring tidings of his whereabouts, as your bearing indicates, speak, that I may rid myself of suspicion and suspense."

Calling the jailer by name, I asked him if my countenance did not remind him of the man he wished to find.

"Not at all."

"Listen, does not my voice resemble that of your escaped prisoner?"

"Not in the least."

With a violent effort I drew my form as straight as possible, and stood upright before him, with every facial muscle strained to its utmost, in a vain endeavor to bring my wrinkled countenance to its former smoothness, and with the energy that a drowning man might exert to grasp a passing object, I tried to control my voice, and preserve my identity by so doing, vehemently imploring him, begging him to listen to my story. "I am the man you seek; I am the prisoner who, a few days

"I AM THE MAN YOU SEEK."

ago, stood in the prime of life before you. I have been spirited away from you by men who are leagued with occult forces, which extend forward among hidden mysteries, into forces which illuminate the present, and reach backward into the past unseen. These persons, by artful and damnable manipulations under the guidance of a power that has been evolved in the secrecy of past ages, and transmitted only to a favored few, have changed the strong man you knew into the one apparently feeble, who now confronts you. Only a short period has passed since I was your unwilling captive, charged with debt, a trifling sum; and then, as your sullen prisoner, I longed for freedom. Now I plead before you, with all my soul, I beg of you to take me back to my cell. Seal your doors, and hold me again, for your dungeon will now be to me a paradise."

I felt that I was becoming frantic, for with each word I realized that the jailer became more and more impatient and annoyed. I perceived that he believed me to be a lunatic. Pleadings and entreaties were of no avail, and my eagerness rapidly changed into despair until at last I cried: "If you will not believe my words, I will throw myself on the mercy of my young companion. I ask you to consider his testimony, and if he says that I am not what I assert myself to be, I will leave my home and country, and go with him quietly into the unknown future."

He turned to depart, but I threw myself before him, and beckoned the young man who, up to this time, had stood aloof in respectful silence. He came forward, and addressing the jailer, called him by name, and corroborated my story. Yes, strange as it sounded to me, he reiterated the substance of my narrative as I had repeated it. "Now, you will believe it," I cried in ecstacy; "now you need no longer question the facts that I have related."

Instead, however, of accepting the story of the witness, the jailer upbraided him.

"This is a preconcerted arrangement to get me into ridicule or further trouble. You two have made up an incredible story that on its face is fit only to be told to men as crazy or designing as yourselves. This young man did not even overhear your conversation with me, and yet he repeats his lesson without a question from me as to what I wish to learn of him."

"He can see our minds," I cried in despair.

"Crazier than I should have believed from your countenance," the jailer replied. "Of all the improbable stories imaginable, you have attempted to inveigle me into accepting that which is most unreasonable. If you are leagued together intent on some swindling scheme, I give you warning now that I am in no mood for trifling. Go your way, and trouble me no more with this foolish scheming, which villainy or lunacy of some description must underlie." He turned in anger and left us.

"It is as I predicted," said my companion; "you are lost to man. Those who know you best will turn from you soonest. I might become as wild as you are, in your interest, and only serve to make your story appear more extravagant. In human affairs men judge and act according to the limited knowledge at command of the multitude. Witnesses who tell the truth are often, in our courts of law, stunned, as you have been, by the decisions of a narrow-minded jury. Men sit on juries with little conception of the facts of the case that is brought before them; the men who manipulate them are mere tools in unseen hands that throw their several minds in antagonisms unexplainable to man. The judge is unconsciously often a tool of his own errors or those of others. One learned judge unties what another has fastened, each basing his views on the same testimony, each rendering his decision in accordance with law derived from the same authority. Your case is that condition of mind that men call lunacy. You can see much that is hidden from others because you have become acquainted with facts that their narrow education forbids them to accept, but, because the majority is against you, they consider you mentally unbalanced. The philosophy of men does not yet comprehend the conditions that have operated on your person, and as you stand alone, although in the right, all men will oppose you, and you must submit to the views of a misguided majority. In the eyes of a present generation you are crazy. A jury of your former peers could not do else than so adjudge you, for you are not on the same mental plane, and I ask, will you again attempt to accomplish that which is as impossible as it would be for you to drink the waters of Seneca Lake at one draught? Go to those men and propose to drain that lake at one gulp, and you will be listened to as seriously as when you beg your former comrades to believe that you are another person than what you seem. Only lengthened life is credited with the production of physical changes that under favorable conditions, are possible of accomplishment in a brief period, and such testimony as you could bring, in the present state of human knowledge, would only add to the proof of your lunacy."

"I see, I see," I said; "and I submit. Lead on, I am ready. Whatever my destined career may be, wherever it may be, it can only lead to the grave."

"Do not be so sure of that," was the reply.

I shuddered instinctively, for this answer seemed to imply that the stillness of the grave would be preferable to my destiny.

We got into the wagon again, and a deep silence followed as we rode along, gazing abstractedly on the quiet fields and lonely farm-houses. Finally we reached a little village. Here my companion dismissed the farmer, our driver, paying him liberally, and secured lodgings in a private family (I believe we were expected), and after a hearty supper we retired. From the time we left the jailer I never again attempted to reveal my identity. I had lost my interest in the past, and found myself craving to know what the future had in store for me.

CHAPTER X.

MY JOURNEY TOWARDS THE END OF EARTH BEGINS,—THE ADEPTS' BROTHERHOOD.

My companion did not attempt to watch over my motions or in any way to interfere with my freedom.

"I will for a time necessarily be absent," he said, "arranging for our journey, and while I am getting ready you must employ yourself as best you can. I ask you, however, now to swear that, as you have promised, you will not seek your wife and children."

To this I agreed.

"Hold up your hand," he said, and I repeated after him: "All this I most solemnly and sincerely promise and swear, with a firm and steadfast resolution to keep and perform my oath, without the least equivocation, mental reservation or self-evasion whatever."

"That will answer; see that you keep your oath this time," he said, and he departed. Several days were consumed before he returned, and during that time I was an inquisitive and silent listener to the various conjectures others were making regarding my abduction which event was becoming of general interest. Some of the theories advanced were quite near the truth, others wild and erratic. How preposterous it seemed to me that the actor himself could be in the very seat of the disturbance, willing, anxious to testify, ready to prove the truth concerning his position, and yet unable even to obtain a respectful hearing from those most interested in his recovery. Men gathered together discussing the "outrage"; women, children, even, talked of little else, and it was evident that the entire country was aroused. New political issues took their rise from the event, but the man who was the prime cause of the excitement was for a period a willing and unwilling listener, as he had been a willing and unwilling actor in the tragedy.

One morning my companion drove up in a light carriage, drawn by a span of fine, spirited, black horses.

"We are ready now," he said, and my unprecedented journey began.

Wherever we stopped, I heard my name mentioned. Men combined against men, brother was declaiming against brother, neighbor was against neighbor, everywhere suspicion was in the air.

"The passage of time alone can quiet these people," said I.

"The usual conception of the term Time—an indescribable something flowing at a constant rate—is erroneous," replied my comrade. "Time is humanity's best friend, and should be pictured as a ministering angel, instead of a skeleton with hour-glass and scythe. Time does not fly, but is permanent and quiescent, while restless, force-impelled matter rushes onward. Force and matter fly; Time reposes. At our birth we are wound up like a machine, to move for a certain number of years, grating against Time. We grind against that complacent spirit and wear not Time, but ourselves away. We hold within ourselves a certain amount of energy, which, an evanescent form of matter, is the opponent of Time. Time has no existence with inanimate objects. It is a conception of the human intellect. Time is rest, perfect rest, tranquillity such as man never realizes unless he becomes a part of the sweet silences toward which human life and human mind are drifting. So much for Time. Now for Life. Disturbed energy in one of its forms, we call Life; and this Life is the great enemy of peace, the opponent of steadfast perfection. Pure energy, the soul of the universe, permeates all things with which man is now acquainted, but when at rest is imperceptible to man, while disturbed energy, according to its condition, is apparent either as matter or as force. A substance or material body is a manifestation resulting from a disturbance of energy. The agitating cause removed, the manifestations disappear, and thus a universe may be extinguished, without unbalancing the cosmos that remains. The worlds known to man are conditions of abnormal energy moving on separate planes through what men call space. They attract to themselves bodies of similar description, and thus influence one another—they have each a separate existence, and are swayed to and fro under the influence of the various disturbances in energy common to their rank or order, which we call forms of forces. Unsettled energy also assumes numerous other expressions that are unknown to man, but which in all perceptible forms is characterized by motion. Pure energy can not be appreciated by the minds of mortals. There are invisible worlds besides those perceived by us in our planetary system, unreachable centers of ethereal structure about us that stand in a higher plane of development than earthly matter which is a gross form of disturbed energy. There are also lower planes. Man's acquaintance with the forms of energy is the result of his power of perceiving the forms of matter of which he is a part. Heat, light, gravitation, electricity and magnetism are ever present in all perceivable substances, and, although purer than earth, they are still manifestations of absolute energy, and for this reason are sensible to men, but more evanescent than material bodies. Perhaps you can conceive that if these disturbances could be removed, matter or force would be resolved back into pure energy, and would vanish. Such a dissociation is an ethereal existence, and as pure energy the life spirit of all material things is neither cold nor hot, heavy nor light, solid, liquid nor gaseous—men can not, as mortals now exist, see, feel, smell, taste, or even conceive of it. It moves through space as we do through it, a world of itself as transparent to matter as matter is to it, insensible but ever present, a reality to higher existences that rest in other planes, but not to us an essence subject to scientific test, nor an entity. Of these problems and their connection with others in the unseen depths beyond, you are not yet in a position properly to judge, but before many years a new sense will be given you or a development of latent senses by the removal of those more gross, and a partial insight into an unsuspected unseen, into a realm to you at present unknown.

"It has been ordained that a select few must from time to time pass over the threshold that divides a mortal's present life from the future, and your lot has been cast among the favored ones. It is or should be deemed a privilege to be permitted to pass farther than human philosophy has yet gone, into an investigation of the problems of life; this I say to encourage you. We have in our order a handful of persons who have received the accumulated fruits of the close attention others have given to these subjects which have been handed to them by the generations of men who have preceded. You are destined to become as they are. This study of semi-occult forces has enabled those selected for the work to master some of the concealed truths of being, and by the partial development of a new sense or new senses, partly to triumph over death. These facts are hidden from ordinary man, and from the earth-bound workers of our brotherhood, who can not even interpret the words they learn. The methods by which they are elucidated have been locked from man because the world is not prepared to receive them, selfishness being the ruling passion of debased mankind, and publicity, until the chain of evidence is more complete, would embarrass their further evolutions, for man as yet lives on the selfish plane."

"Do you mean that, among men, there are a few persons possessed of powers such as you have mentioned?"

"Yes; they move here and there through all orders of society, and their attainments are unknown, except to one another, or, at most, to but few persons. These adepts are scientific men, and may not even be recognized as members of our organization; indeed it is often necessary, for obvious reasons, that they should not be known as such. These studies must constantly be prosecuted in various directions, and some monitors must teach others to perform certain duties that are necessary to the grand evolution. Hence, when a man has become one of our brotherhood, from the promptings that made you one of us, and has been as ready and determined to instruct outsiders in our work as you has been, it is proper that he should in turn be compelled to serve our people, and eventually, mankind."

"Am I to infer from this," I exclaimed, a sudden light breaking upon me, "that the alchemistic manuscript that led me to the fraternity to which you are related may have been artfully designed to serve the interest of that organization?" To this question I received no reply. After an interval, I again sought information concerning the order, and with more success.

"I understand that you propose that I shall go on a journey of investigation for the good of our order and also of humanity."

"True; it is necessary that our discoveries be kept alive, and it is essential that the men who do this work accept the trust of their own accord. He who will not consent to add to the common stock of knowledge and understanding, must be deemed a drone in the hive of nature—but few persons, however, are called upon to serve as you must serve. Men are scattered over the world with this object in view, and are unknown to their families or even to other members of the order; they hold in solemn trust our sacred revelations, and impart them to others as is ordained, and thus nothing perishes; eventually humanity will profit.

"Others, as you soon will be doing, are now exploring assigned sections of this illimitable field, accumulating further knowledge, and they will report results to those whose duty it is to retain and formulate the collected sum of facts and principles. So it is that, unknown to the great body of our brotherhood, a chosen number, under our esoteric teachings, are gradually passing the dividing line that separates life from death, matter from spirit, for we have members who have mastered these problems. We ask, however, no aid of evil forces or of necromancy or black art, and your study of alchemy was of no avail, although to save the vital truths alchemy is a part of our work. We proceed in exact accordance with natural laws, which will yet be known to all men. Sorrow, suffering, pain of all descriptions, are enemies to the members of our order, as they are to mankind broadly, and we hope in the future so to control the now hidden secrets of Nature as to be able to govern the antagonistic disturbances in energy with which man now is everywhere thwarted, to subdue the physical enemies of the race, to affiliate religious and scientific thought, cultivating brotherly love, the foundation and capstone, the cement and union of this ancient fraternity."

"And am I really to take an important part in this scheme? Have I been set apart to explore a section of the unknown for a bit of hidden knowledge, and to return again?"

"This I will say," he answered, evading a direct reply, "you have been selected for a part that one in a thousand has been required to undertake. You are to pass into a field that will carry you beyond the present limits of human observation. This much I have been instructed to impart to you in order to nerve you for your duty. I seem to be a young man; really I am aged. You seem to be infirm and old, but you are young.

Many years ago, cycles ago as men record time, I was promoted to do a certain work because of my zealous nature; like you, I also had to do penance for an error. I disappeared, as you are destined to do, from the sight of men. I regained my youth; yours has been lost forever, but you will regain more than your former strength. We shall both exist after this generation of men has passed away, and shall mingle with generations yet to be born, for we shall learn how to restore our youthful vigor, and will supply it time and again to earthly matter. Rest assured also that the object of our labors is of the most laudable nature, and we must be upheld under all difficulties by the fact that multitudes of men who are yet to come will be benefited thereby."

CHAPTER XL.

MY JOURNEY CONTINUES.—INSTINCT.

It is unnecessary for me to give the details of the first part of my long journey. My companion was guided by a perceptive faculty that, like the compass, enabled him to keep in the proper course. He did not question those whom we met, and made no endeavor to maintain a given direction; and yet he was traveling in a part of the country that was new to himself. I marveled at the accuracy of his intuitive perception, for he seemed never to be at fault. When the road forked, he turned to the right or the left in a perfectly careless manner, but the continuity of his course was never interrupted. I began mentally to question whether he could be guiding us aright, forgetting that he was reading my thoughts, and he answered: "There is nothing strange in this self-directive faculty. Is not man capable of following where animals lead? One of the objects of my special study has been to ascertain the nature of the instinct-power of animals, the sagacity of brutes. The carrier pigeon will fly to its cote across hundreds of miles of strange country. The young pig will often return to its pen by a route unknown to it; the sluggish tortoise will find its home without a guide, without seeing a familiar object; cats, horses and other animals possess this power, which is not an unexplainable instinct, but a natural sense better developed in some of the lower creatures than it is in man. The power lies dormant in man, but exists, nevertheless. If we develop one faculty we lose acuteness in some other power. Men have lost in mental development in this particular direction while seeking to gain in others. If there were no record of the fact that light brings objects to the recognition of the mind through the agency of the eye, the sense of sight in an animal would be considered by men devoid of it as adaptibility to extraordinary circumstances, or instinct. So it is that animals often see clearly where to the sense of man there is only darkness;

such sight is not irresponsive action without consciousness of a purpose. Man is not very magnanimous. Instead of giving credit to the lower animals for superior perception in many directions, he denies to them the conscious possession of powers imperfectly developed in mankind. We egotistically aim to raise ourselves, and do so in our own estimation by clothing the actions of the lower animals in a garment of irresponsibility. Because we can not understand the inwardness of their power, we assert that they act by the influence of instinct. The term instinct, as I would define it, is an expression applied by men to a series of senses which man possesses, but has not developed. The word is used by man to characterize the mental superiority of other animals in certain directions where his own senses are defective. Instead of crediting animals with these, to them, invaluable faculties, man conceitedly says they are involuntary actions. Ignorant of their mental status, man is too arrogant to admit that lower animals are superior to him in any way. But we are not consistent. Is it not true that in the direction in which you question my power, some men by cultivation often become expert beyond their fellows? and such men have also given very little systematic study to subjects connected with these undeniable mental qualities. The hunter will hold his course in utter darkness, passing inequalities in the ground, and avoiding obstructions he can not see. The fact of his superiority in this way, over others, is not questioned, although he can not explain his methods nor understand how he operates. His quickened sense is often as much entitled to be called instinct as is the divining power of the carrier pigeon. If scholars would cease to devote their entire energies to the development of the material, artistic, or scientific part of modern civilization, and turn their attention to other forms of mental culture, many beauties and powers of Nature now unknown would be revealed. However, this can not be, for under existing conditions, the strife for food and warmth is the most important struggle that engages mankind, and controls our actions. In a time that is surely to come, however, when the knowledge of all men is united into a comprehensive whole, the book of life, illuminated thereby, will contain many beautiful pages that may be easily read, but which are now not suspected to exist. The power of the magnet is not uniform—engineers know that the needle of the compass inexplicably deviates from time to time as a line is run over the earth's surface, but they also know that aberrations of the needle finally correct themselves. The temporary variations of a few degrees that occur in the running of a compass line are usually overcome after a time, and without a change of course, the disturbed needle swerves back, and again points to the calculated direction, as is shown by the vernier. Should I err in my course, it would be by a trifle only, and we could not go far astray before I would unconsciously discover the true path. I carry my magnet in my mind."

Many such dissertations or explanations concerning related questions were subsequently made in what I then considered a very impressive, though always unsatisfactory, manner. I recall those episodes now, after other more remarkable experiences which are yet to be related, and record them briefly with little wonderment, because I have gone through adventures which demonstrate that there is nothing improbable in the statements, and I will not consume time with further details of this part of my journey.

We leisurely traversed State after State, crossed rivers, mountains and seemingly interminable forests. The ultimate object of our travels, a location in Kentucky, I afterward learned, led my companion to guide me by a roundabout course to Wheeling, Virginia, by the usual mountain roads of that day, instead of going, as he might perhaps have much more easily done, via Buffalo and the Lake Shore to Northern Ohio, and then southerly across the country. He said in explanation, that the time lost at the beginning of our journey by this route, was more than recompensed by the ease of the subsequent Ohio River trip. Upon reaching Wheeling, he disposed of the team, and we embarked on a keel boat, and journeyed down the Ohio to Cincinnati. The river was falling when we started, and became very low before Cincinnati was reached, too low for steamers, and our trip in that flat-bottomed boat, on the sluggish current of the tortuous stream, proved tedious and slow. Arriving at Cincinnati, my guide decided to wait for a rise in the river, designing then to complete our journey on a steamboat. I spent several days in Cincinnati quite pleasantly, expecting to continue our course on the steamer "Tecumseh," then in port, and ready for departure. At the last moment my guide changed his mind, and instead of embarking on that boat, we took passage on the steamer "George Washington," leaving Shipping-Port Wednesday, December 13, 1826.

During that entire journey, from the commencement to our final destination, my guide paid all the bills, and did not want either for money or attention from the people with whom we came in contact. He seemed everywhere a stranger, and yet was possessed of a talisman that opened every door to which he applied, and which gave us unlimited accommodations wherever he asked them. When the boat landed at Smithland, Kentucky, a village on the bank of the Ohio, just above Paducah, we disembarked, and my guide then for the first time seemed mentally disturbed.

"Our journey together is nearly over," he said; "in a few days my responsibility for you will cease. Nerve yourself for the future, and bear its trials and its pleasures manfully. I may never see you again, but as you are even now conspicuous in our history, and will be closely connected with the development of the plan in which I am also interested, although I am destined to take a different part, I shall probably hear of you again."

CHAPTER XII.

A CAVERN DISCOVERED.—BISWELL'S HILL.

We stopped that night at a tavern in Smithland. Leaving this place after dinner the next day, on foot, we struck through the country, into the bottom lands of the Cumberland River traveling leisurely, lingering for hours in the course of a circuitous tramp of only a few miles. Although it was the month of December, the climate was mild and balmy. In my former home, a similar time of year would have been marked with snow, sleet, and ice, and I could not but draw a contrast between the two localities. How different also the scenery from that of my native State. Great timber trees, oak, poplar, hickory, were in majestic possession of large tracts of territory, in the solitude of which man, so far as evidences of his presence were concerned, had never before trodden. From time to time we passed little clearings that probably were to be enlarged to thrifty plantations in the future, and finally we crossed the Cumberland River. That night we rested with Mr. Joseph Watts, a wealthy and cultured land owner, who resided on the river's bank. After leaving his home the next morning, we journeyed slowly, very slowly, my guide seemingly passing with reluctance into the country. He had become a very pleasant companion, and his conversation was very entertaining. We struck the sharp point of a ridge the morning we left Mr. Watts' hospitable house. It was four or five miles distant, but on the opposite side of the Cumberland, from Smithland. Here a steep bluff broke through the bottom land to the river's edge, the base of the bisected point being washed by the Cumberland River, which had probably cut its way through the stony mineral of this ridge in ages long passed. We climbed to its top and sat upon the pinnacle, and from that point of commanding observation I drank in the beauties of the scene around me. The river at our feet wound gracefully before us, and disappeared

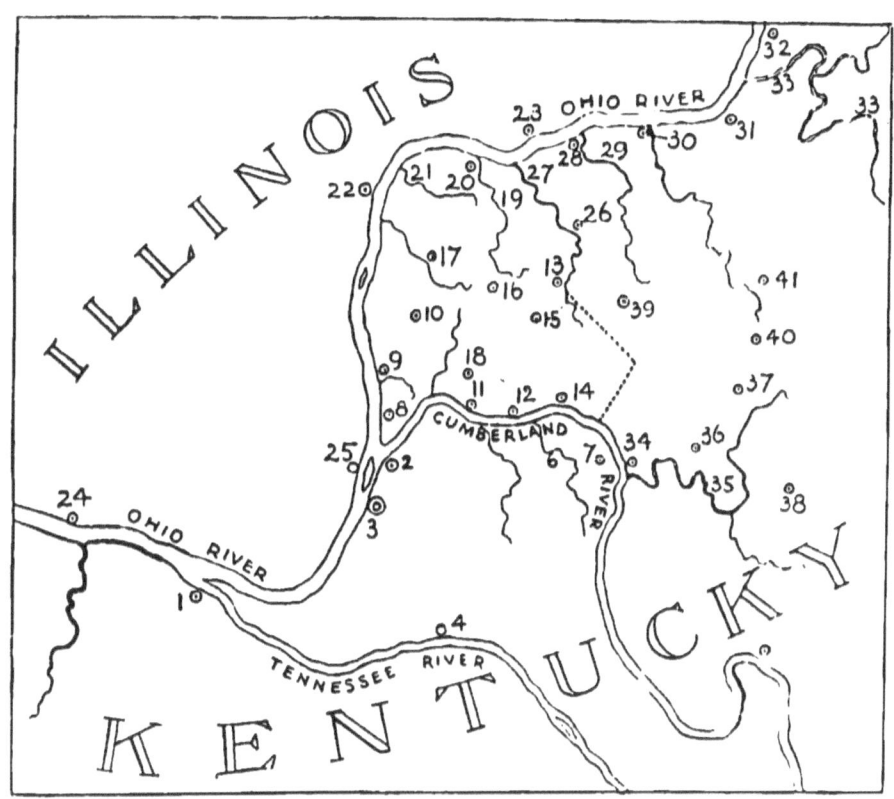

SECTION OF KENTUCKY, NEAR SMITHLAND, IN WHICH THE ENTRANCE TO THE KENTUCKY CAVERN IS SAID TO BE LOCATED.

1. Paducah.
2. Smithland.
3. Old Smithland.
4. Patterson.
5. Frenchtown.
6. Hickory Creek.
7. Underwood.
8. Birdsville.
9. Bayou Mills.
10. Oak Ridge.
11. Moxley's Landing.
12. Kildare.
13. Lola.
14. Pinckneyville.
15. Salem.
16. Hampton.
17. Faulkner.
18. Mullikin.
19. Back Creek.
20. Carrsville.
21. Given's Creek.
22. Golconda.
23. Elizabethtown.
24. Metropolis City.
25. Hamletsburgh.
26. Sheridan.
27. Deer Creek.
28. Hurricane.
29. Hurricane Creek.
30. Ford's Ferry.
31. Weston.
32. Caseyville.
33. Tradewater River.
34. Dycusburgh.
35. Livingstone Creek.
36. Francis.
37. Harrold. View.
38. Crider.
39. Levias.
40. Crayneville.
41. Marion.

in both directions, its extremes dissolving in a bed of forest. A great black bluff, far up the stream, rose like a mountain, upon the left side of the river; bottom lands were about us, and hills appeared across the river in the far distance—towards the Tennessee River. With regret I finally drew my eyes from the vision, and we resumed the journey. We followed the left bank of the river to the base of the black bluff,—" Biswell's Hill," a squatter called it,—and then skirted the side of that hill, passing, along precipitous stone bluffs and among stunted cedars. Above us towered cliff over cliff, almost perpendicularly; below us rolled the river.

I was deeply impressed by the changing beauties of this strange Kentucky scenery, but marveled at the fact that while I became light-hearted and enthusiastic, my guide grew correspondingly despondent and gloomy. From time to time he lapsed into thoughtful silence, and once I caught his eye directed toward me in a manner that I inferred to imply either pity or envy. We passed Biswell's Bluff, and left the Cumberland River at its upper extremity, where another small creek empties into the river. Thence, after ascending the creek some distance, we struck across the country, finding it undulating and fertile, with here and there a small clearing. During this journey we either camped out at night, or stopped with a resident, when one was to be found in that sparsely settled country. Sometimes there were exasperating intervals between our meals; but we did not suffer, for we carried with us supplies of food, such as cheese and crackers, purchased in Smithland, for emergencies. We thus proceeded a considerable distance into Livingston County, Kentucky.

I observed remarkable sinks in the earth, sometimes cone-shaped, again precipitous. These cavities were occasionally of considerable size and depth, and they were more numerous in the uplands than in the bottoms. They were somewhat like the familiar "sink-holes" of New York State, but monstrous in comparison. The first that attracted my attention was near the Cumberland River, just before we reached Biswell's Hill. It was about forty feet deep and thirty in diameter, with precipitous stone sides, shrubbery growing therein in exceptional spots where loose earth had collected on shelves of stone that cropped out along its rugged sides. The bottom of the depression was flat and fertile, covered with a luxuriant mass of vegetation. On one side of the base of the gigantic bowl, a cavern struck down into the earth. I stood upon the edge of this funnel-like sink, and marveled at its peculiar appearance. A spirit of curiosity, such as often influences men when an unusual natural scene presents itself, possessed me. I clambered down, swinging from brush to brush, and stepping from shelving-rock to shelving-rock, until I reached the bottom of the hollow, and placing my hand above the black hole in its center, I perceived that a current of cold air was rushing therefrom, upward. I probed with a long stick, but the direction of the opening was tortuous, and would not admit of examination in that manner. I dropped a large pebble-stone into the orifice; the pebble rolled and clanked down, down, and at last, the sound died away in the distance.

"I wish that I could go into the cavity as that stone has done, and find the secrets of this cave," I reflected, the natural love of exploration possessing me as it probably does most men.

My companion above, seated on the brink of the stone wall, replied to my thoughts: "Your wish shall be granted. You have requested that which has already been laid out for you. You will explore where few men have passed before, and will have the privilege of following your destiny into a realm of natural wonders. A fertile field of investigation awaits you, such as will surpass your most vivid imaginings. Come and seat yourself beside me, for it is my duty now to tell you something about the land we are approaching, the cavern fields of Kentucky."

CHAPTER XIII.

THE PUNCH-BOWLS AND CAVERNS OF KENTUCKY.—"INTO THE UNKNOWN COUNTRY."

"This part of Kentucky borders a field of caverns that reaches from near the State of Tennessee to the Ohio River, and from the mouth of the Cumberland, eastward to and beyond the center of the State. This great area is of irregular outline, and as yet has been little explored. Underneath the surface are layers of limestone and sandstone rock, the deposits ranging from ten to one hundred and fifty feet in thickness, and often great masses of conglomerate appear. This conglomerate sometimes caps the ridges, and varies in thickness from a few feet only, to sixty, or even a hundred, feet. It is of a diversified character, sometimes largely composed of pebbles cemented together by iron ore into compact beds, while again it passes abruptly into gritty sandstone, or a fine-grained compact rock destitute of pebbles. Sometimes the conglomerate rests directly on the limestone, but in the section about us, more often argillaceous shales or veins of coal intervene, and occasionally inferior and superior layers of conglomerate are separated by a bed of coal. In addition, lead-bearing veins now and then crop up, the crystals of galena being disseminated through masses of fluor-spar, calc-spar, limestone and clay, which fill fissures between tilted walls of limestone and hard quartzose sandstone. Valleys, hills, and mountains, grow out of this remarkable crust. Rivers and creeks flow through and under it in crevices, either directly upon the bedstone or over deposits of clay which underlie it. In some places, beds of coal or slate alternate with layers of the lime rock; in others, the interspace is clay and sand. Sometimes the depth of the several limestone and conglomerate deposits is great, and they are often honeycombed by innumerable transverse and diagonal spaces. Water drips have here and there washed out the more friable earth and stone, forming grottoes which are as yet unknown to men, but which will be discovered to be wonderful and fantastic beyond anything of a like nature now familiar. In other places cavities exist between shelves of rock that lie one above the other—monstrous openings caused by the erosive action of rivers now lost, but that have flowed during unnumbered ages past; great parallel valleys and gigantic chambers, one over the other, remaining to tell the story of these former torrents. Occasionally the weight of a portion of the disintegrating rock above becomes too great for its tensile strength and the material crumbles and falls, producing caverns sometimes reaching so near to the earth's surface, as to cause sinks in its crust. These sinks, when first formed, as a rule, present clear rock fractures, and immediately after their formation there is usually a water-way beneath. In the course of time soil collects on their sides, they become cone-shaped hollows from the down-slidings of earth, and then vegetation appears on the living soil; trees grow within them, and in many places the sloping sides of great earth bowls of this nature are, after untold years, covered with the virgin forest; magnificent timber trees growing on soil that has been stratified over and upon decayed monarchs of the forest whose remains, imbedded in the earth, speak of the ages that have passed since the convulsions that made the depressions which, notwithstanding the accumulated debris, are still a hundred feet or more in depth. If the drain or exit at the vortex of one of these sinks becomes clogged, which often occurs, the entire cavity fills with water, and a pond results. Again, a slight orifice reaching far beneath the earth's surface may permit the soil to be gradually washed into a subterranean creek, and thus are formed great bowls, like funnels sunk in the earth—Kentucky punch-bowls.

"Take the country about us, especially towards the Mammoth Cave, and for miles beyond, the landscape in certain localities is pitted with this description of sinks, some recent, others very old. Many are small, but deep; others are large and shallow. Ponds often of great depth, curiously enough overflowing and giving rise to a creek, are to be found on a ridge, telling of underground supply springs, not outlets, beneath. Chains of such sinks, like a row of huge funnels, often appear; the soil between them is slowly washed through their exit into the river, flowing in the depths below, and as the earth that separates them is carried away by the subterranean streams, the bowls coalesce, and a ravine, closed at both ends, results. Along the bottom of such a ravine, a creek may flow, rushing from its natural tunnel at one end of the line, and disappearing in a gulf at the other. The stream begins in mystery, and ends in unfathomed darkness. Near Marion, Hurricane Creek thus disappears, and, so far as men know, is lost to sight forever. Near Cridersville, in this neighborhood, a valley such as I have described, takes in the surface floods of a large tract of country. The waters that run down its sides, during a storm form a torrent, and fence-rails, timbers, and other objects are gulped into the chasm where the creek plunges into the earth, and they never appear again. This part of Kentucky is the most remarkable portion of the known world, and although now neglected, in a time to come is surely destined to an extended distinction. I have referred only to the surface, the skin formation of this honeycombed labyrinth, the entrance to the future wonderland of the world. Portions of such a superficial cavern maze have been traversed by man in the ramifications known as the Mammoth Cave, but deeper than man has yet explored, the subcutaneous structure of that series of caverns is yet to be investigated. The Mammoth Cave as now traversed is simply a superficial series of grottoes and passages overlying the deeper cavern field that I have described. The explored chain of passages is of great interest to men, it is true, but of minor importance compared to others yet unknown, being in fact, the result of mere surface erosion. The river that bisects the cave, just beneath the surface of the earth, and known as Echo River, is a miniature stream: there are others more magnificent that flow majestically far, far beneath it. As we descend into the earth in that locality, caverns multiply in number and increase in size, retaining the general configuration of those I have described. The layers of rock are thicker, the intervening spaces broader; and the spaces stretch in increasingly expanded chambers for miles, while high above each series of caverns the solid ceilings of stone arch and interarch. Sheltered under these subterrene alcoves are streams, lakes, rivers and water-falls. Near the surface of the earth such waters often teem with aquatic life, and some of the caves are inhabited by species of birds, reptiles and mammals as yet unknown to men, creatures possessed of senses and organs that are different from any we find with surface animals, and also apparently defective in particulars that would startle persons acquainted only with creatures that live in the sunshine. It is a world beneath a world, a world within a world—" My guide abruptly stopped.

I sat entranced, marveling at the young-old adept's knowledge, admiring his accomplishments. I gazed into the cavity that yawned beneath me, and imagined its possible but to me invisible secrets, enraptured with the thought of searching into them. Who would not feel elated at the prospect of an exploration, such as I foresaw might be pursued in my immediate future? I had often been charmed with narrative descriptions of discoveries, and book accounts of scientific investigations, but I had never pictured myself as a participant in such fascinating enterprises.

"Indeed, indeed," I cried exultingly; "lead me to this Wonderland, show me the entrance to this Subterranean World, and I promise willingly to do as you bid."

"Bravo!" he replied, "your heart is right, your courage sufficient; I have not disclosed a thousandth part of the wonders which I have knowledge of, and which await your research, and probably I have not gained even an insight into the mysteries that, if your courage permits, you will be privileged to comprehend. Your destiny lies beyond, far beyond that which I have pictured or experienced; and I, notwithstanding my opportunities, have no conception of its end, for at the critical moment my heart faltered—I can therefore only describe the beginning."

Thus at the lower extremity of Biswell's Hill, I was made aware of the fact that, within a short time, I should be separated from my sympathetic guide, and that it was to be my duty to explore alone, or in other company, some portion of these Kentucky cavern deeps, and I longed for the beginning of my underground journey. Heavens! how different would have been my future life could I then have realized my position! Would that I could have seen the end. After a few days of uneventful travel, we rested, one afternoon, in a hilly country that before us appeared to be more rugged, even mountainous. We had wandered leisurely, and were now at a considerable distance from the Cumberland River, the aim of my guide being, as I surmised, to evade a direct approach to some object of interest which I must not locate exactly, and yet which I shall try to describe accurately enough for identification by a person familiar with the topography of that section. We stood on the side of a stony, sloping hill, back of which spread a wooded, undulating valley.

"I remember to have passed along a creek in that valley," I remarked, looking back over our pathway. "It appeared to rise from this direction, but the source ends abruptly in this chain of hills."

"The stream is beneath us," he answered. Advancing a few paces, he brought to my attention, on the hillside, an opening in the earth. This aperture was irregular in form, about the diameter of a well, and descended perpendicularly into the stony crust. I leaned far over the orifice, and heard the gurgle of rushing water beneath. The guide dropped a heavy stone into the gloomy shaft, and in some seconds a dull splash announced its plunge into underground water. Then he leaned over the stony edge, and—could I be mistaken?—seemed to signal to some one beneath; but it must be imagination on my part, I argued to myself, even against my very sense of sight. Rising, and taking me by the hand, my guardian spoke:

"Brother, we approach the spot where you and I must separate. I serve my masters and am destined to go where I shall next be commanded; you will descend into the earth, as you have recently desired to do. Here we part, most likely forever. This rocky fissure will admit the last ray of sunlight on your path."

My heart failed. How often are we courageous in daylight and timid by night? Men unflinchingly face in sunshine dangers at which they shudder in the darkness.

"How am I to descend into that abyss?" I gasped. "The sides are perpendicular, the depth is unknown!" Then I cried in alarm, the sense of distrust deepening: "Do you mean to drown me; is it for this you have led me away from my native State, from friends, home and kindred? You have enticed me into this wilderness. I have been decoyed, and, like a foolish child, have willingly accompanied my destroyer. You feared to murder me in my distant home; the earth could not have hidden me;

Niagara even might have given up my body to dismay the murderers! In this underground river in the wilds of Kentucky, all trace of my existence will disappear forever."

I was growing furious. My frenzied eyes searched the ground for some missile of defense. By strange chance some one had left, on that solitary spot, a rude weapon, providentially dropped for my use, I thought. It was a small iron bolt or bar, somewhat rusted. I threw myself upon the earth, and, as I did so, picked this up quickly, and secreted it within my bosom. Then I arose and resumed my stormy denunciation:

"You have played your part well, you have led your unresisting victim to the sacrifice, but if I am compelled to plunge into this black grave, you shall go with me!" I shrieked in desperation, and suddenly threw my arms around the gentle adept, intending to hurl him into the chasm. At this point I felt my hands seized from behind in a cold, clammy, irresistible embrace, my fingers were loosed by a strong grasp, and I turned, to find myself confronted by a singular looking being, who quietly said:

"You are not to be destroyed; we wish only to do your bidding."

The speaker stood in a stooping position, with his face towards the earth as if to shelter it from the sunshine. He was less than five feet in height. His arms and legs were bare, and his skin, the color of light blue putty, glistened in the sunlight like the slimy hide of a water dog. He raised his head, and I shuddered in affright as I beheld that his face was not that of a human. His forehead extended in an unbroken plane from crown to cheek bone, and the chubby tip of an abortive nose without nostrils formed a short projection near the center of the level ridge which represented a countenance. There was no semblance of an eye, for there were no sockets. Yet his voice was singularly perfect. His face, if face it could be called, was wet, and water dripped from all parts of his slippery person. Yet, repulsive as he looked, I shuddered more at the remembrance of the touch of that cold, clammy hand than at the sight of his figure, for a dead man could not have chilled me as he had done, with his sappy skin, from which the moisture seemed to ooze as from the hide of a water lizard.

"CONFRONTED BY A SINGULAR LOOKING BEING."

Turning to my guide, this freak of nature said, softly:
"I have come in obedience to the signal."

I realized at once that alone with these two I was powerless, and that to resist would be suicidal. Instantly my effervescing passion subsided, and I expressed no further surprise at this sudden and remarkable apparition, but mentally acquiesced. I was alone and helpless; rage gave place to inertia in the despondency that followed the realization of my hopeless condition. The grotesque newcomer who, though sightless, possessed a strange instinct, led us to the base of the hill a few hundred feet away, and there, gushing into the light from the rocky bluff, I saw a magnificent stream issuing many feet in width. This was the head-waters of the mysterious brook that I had previously noticed. It flowed from an archway in the solid stone, springing directly out of the rock-bound cliff; beautiful and picturesque in its surroundings. The limpid water, clear and sparkling, issued from the unknown source that was typical of darkness, but the brook of crystal leaped into a world of sunshine, light and freedom.

"Brother," said my companion, "this spring emerging from this prison of earth images to us what humanity will be when the prisoning walls of ignorance that now enthrall him are removed. Man has heretofore relied chiefly for his advancement, both mental and physical, on knowledge gained from so-called scientific explorations and researches with matter, from material studies rather than spiritual, all his investigations having been confined to the crude, coarse substance of the surface of the globe. Spiritualistic investigations, unfortunately, are considered by scientific men too often as reaching backward only. The religions of the world clasp hands with, and lean upon, the dead past, it is true, but point to a living future. Man must yet search by the agency of senses and spirit, the unfathomed mysteries that lie beneath his feet and over his head, and he who refuses to bow to the Creator and honor his handiwork discredits himself. When this work is accomplished, as it yet will be, the future man, able then to comprehend the problem of life in its broader significance, drawing from all directions the facts necessary to his mental advancement, will have reached a state in which he can enjoy bodily comfort and supreme spiritual perfection, while he is yet an earth-bound mortal. In hastening this consummation, it is necessary that an occasional human life should be lost to the world, but such sacrifices are noble—yes, sublime, because contributing to the future exaltation of our race. The secret workers in the sacred order of which you are still a member, have ever taken an important part in furthering such a system of evolution. This feature of our work is unknown to brethren of the ordinary fraternity, and the individual research of each secret messenger is unguessed, by the craft at large. Hence it is that the open workers of our order, those initiated by degrees only, who in lodge rooms carry on their beneficent labors among men, have had no hand other than as agents in your removal, and no knowledge of your present or future movements. Their function is to keep together our organization on earth, and from them only an occasional member is selected, as you have been, to perform special duties in certain adventurous studies. Are you willing to go on this journey of exploration? and are you brave enough to meet the trials you have invited?"

Again my enthusiasm arose, and I felt the thrill experienced by an investigator who stands on the brink of an important discovery, and needs but courage to advance, and I answered, "Yes."

"Then, farewell; this archway is the entrance that will admit you into your arcanum of usefulness. This mystic Brother, though a stranger to you, has long been apprised of our coming, and it was he who sped me on my journey to seek you, and who has since been waiting for us, and is to be your guide during the first stages of your subterrene progress. He is a Friend, and, if you trust him, will protect you from harm. You will find the necessaries of life supplied, for I have traversed part of your coming road; that part I therefore know, but, as I have said, you are to go deeper into the unexplored,—yes, into and beyond the Beyond, until finally you will come to the gateway that leads into the 'Unknown Country.'"

CHAPTER XIV.

FAREWELL TO GOD'S SUNSHINE.—THE ECHO OF THE CRY.

Thus speaking, my quiet leader, who had so long been as a shepherd to my wandering feet, on the upper earth, grasped my hands tightly, and placed them in those of my new companion, whose clammy fingers closed over them as with a grip of iron. The mysterious being, now my custodian, turned towards the creek, drawing me after him, and together we silently and solemnly waded beneath the stone archway. As I passed under the shadow of that dismal, yawning cliff, I turned my head to take one last glimpse of the world I had known—that "warm precinct of the cheerful day,"—and tears sprang to my eyes. I thought of life, family, friends,—of all for which men live—and a melancholy vision arose, that of my lost, lost home. My dear companion of the journey that had just ended stood in the sunlight on the banks of the rippling stream, gazing at us intently, and waved an affectionate farewell. My uncouth new associate (guide or master, whichever he might be), of the journey to come, clasped me firmly by the arms, and waded slowly onward, thrusting me steadily against the cold current, and with irresistible force pressed me into the thickening darkness. The daylight disappeared, the pathway contracted, the water deepened and became more chilly. We were constrained to bow our heads in order to avoid the overhanging vault of stone; the water reached to my chin, and now the down-jutting roof touched the crown of my head; then I shuddered convulsively as the last ray of daylight disappeared.

Had it not been for my companion, I know that I should have sunk in despair, and drowned; but with a firm hand he held my head above the water, and steadily pushed me onward. I had reached the extreme of despondency: I neither feared nor cared for life nor death, and I realized that, powerless to control my own acts, my fate, the future, my existence depended on the strange being beside me. I was mysteriously sustained, however, by a sense of bodily security, such as comes over us as when in the hands of an experienced guide we journey through a wilderness, for I felt that my pilot of the underworld did not purpose to destroy me. We halted a moment, and then, as a faint light overspread us, my eyeless guide directed me to look upward.

"We now stand beneath the crevice which you were told by your former guide would admit the last ray of sunlight on your path. I also say to you, this struggling ray of sunlight is to be your last for years."

I gazed above me, feeling all the wretchedness of a dying man who, with faculties intact, might stand on the dark edge of the hillside of eternity, glancing back into the bright world; and that small opening far, far overhead, seemed as the gate to Paradise Lost. Many a person, assured of ascending at will, has stood at the bottom of a deep well or shaft to a mine, and even then felt the undescribable sensation of dread, often terror, that is produced by such a situation. Awe, mystery, uncertainty of life and future superadded, may express my sensation. I trembled, shrinking in horror from my captor and struggled violently.

"Hold, hold," I begged, as one involuntarily prays a surgeon to delay the incision of the amputating knife, "just one moment." My companion, unheeding, moved on, the light vanished instantly, and we were surrounded by total darkness. God's sunshine was blotted out.

Then I again became unconcerned; I was not now responsible for my own existence, and the feeling that I experienced when a prisoner in the closed carriage returned. I grew careless as to my fate, and with stolid indifference struggled onward as we progressed slowly against the current of water. I began to interest myself in speculations regarding our surroundings, and the object or outcome of our journey. In places the water was shallow, scarce reaching to our ankles; again it was so deep that we could wade only with exertion, and at times the passage up which we toiled was so narrow, that it would scarcely admit us. After a long, laborious stemming of the unseen brook, my companion directed me to close my mouth, hold my nostrils with my fingers, and stoop; almost diving with me beneath the water, he drew

"THIS STRUGGLING RAY OF SUNLIGHT IS TO BE YOUR LAST FOR YEARS."

me through the submerged crevice, and we ascended into an open chamber, and left the creek behind us. I fancied that we were in a large room, and as I shouted aloud to test my hypothesis, echo after echo answered, until at last the cry reverberated and died away in distant murmurs. We were evidently in a great pocket or cavern, through which my guide now walked rapidly; indeed, he passed along with unerring footsteps, as certain of his course as I might be on familiar ground in full daylight. I perceived that he systematically evaded inequalities that I could not anticipate nor see. He would tell me to step up or down, as the surroundings required, and we ascended or descended accordingly. Our path turned to the right or the left from time to time, but my eyeless guide passed through what were evidently the most tortuous windings without a mishap. I wondered much at this gift of knowledge, and at last overcame my reserve sufficiently to ask how we could thus unerringly proceed in utter darkness. The reply was:

"The path is plainly visible to me; I see as clearly in pitch darkness as you can in sunshine."

"Explain yourself further," I requested.

He replied, "Not yet;" and continued, "you are weary, we will rest."

He conducted me to a seat on a ledge, and left me for a time. Returning soon, he placed in my hands food which I ate with novel relish. The pabulum seemed to be of vegetable origin, though varieties of it had a peculiar flesh-like flavor. Several separate and distinct substances were contained in the queer viands, some portions savoring of wholesome flesh, while others possessed the delicate flavors of various fruits, such as the strawberry and the pineapple. The strange edibles were of a pulpy texture, homogeneous in consistence, parts being juicy and acid like grateful fruits. Some portions were in slices or films that I could hold in my hand like sections of a velvet melon, and yet were in many respects unlike any other food that I had ever tasted. There was neither rind nor seed; it seemed as though I were eating the gills of a fish, and in answer to my question the guide remarked:

"Yes; it is the gill, but not the gill of a fish. You will be instructed in due time." I will add that after this, whenever necessary, we were supplied with food, but both thirst and hunger disappeared altogether before our underground journey was finished.

After a while we again began our journey, which we continued in what was to me absolute darkness. My strength seemed to endure the fatigue to a wonderful degree, notwithstanding that we must have been walking hour after hour, and I expressed a curiosity about the fact. My guide replied that the atmosphere of the cavern possessed an intrinsic vitalizing power that neutralized fatigue, "or," he said, "there is here an inherent constitutional energy derived from an active gaseous substance that belongs to cavern air at this depth, and sustains the life force by contributing directly to its conservation, taking the place of food and drink."

"I do not understand," I said.

"No; and you do not comprehend how ordinary air supports mind and vitalizes muscle, and at the same time wears out both muscle and all other tissues. These are facts which are not satisfactorily explained by scientific statements concerning oxygenation of the blood. As we descend into the earth we find an increase in the life force of the cavern air."

This reference to surface earth recalled my former life, and led me to contrast my present situation with that I had forfeited. I was seized with an uncontrollable longing for home, and a painful craving for the past took possession of my heart, but with a strong effort I shook off the sensations. We traveled on and on in silence and in darkness, and I thought again of the strange remark of my former guide who had said: "You are destined to go deeper into the unknown; yes, into and beyond the Beyond."

CHAPTER XV.

A ZONE OF LIGHT DEEP WITHIN THE EARTH.

"Oh! for one glimpse of light, a ray of sunshine!"

In reply to this my mental ejaculation, my guide said: "Can not you perceive that the darkness is becoming less intense?"

"No," I answered, "I can not; night is absolute."

"Are you sure?" he asked. "Cover your eyes with your hands, then uncover and open them." I did so and fancied that by contrast a faint gray hue was apparent.

"This must be imagination."

"No; we now approach a zone of earth light; let us hasten on."

"A zone of light deep in the earth! Incomprehensible! Incredible!" I muttered, and yet as we went onward and time passed the darkness was less intense. The barely perceptible hue became gray and somber, and then of a pearly translucence, and although I could not distinguish the outline of objects, yet I unquestionably perceived light.

"I am amazed! What can be the cause of this phenomenon? What is the nature of this mysterious halo that surrounds us?" I held my open hand before my eyes, and perceived the darkness of my spread fingers.

"It is light, it is light," I shouted, "it is really light!" and from near and from far the echoes of that subterranean cavern answered back joyfully, "It is light, it is light!"

I wept in joy, and threw my arms about my guide, forgetting in the ecstacy his clammy cuticle, and danced in hysterical glee and alternately laughed and cried. How vividly I realized then that the imprisoned miner would give a world of gold, his former god, for a ray of light.

"Compose yourself; this emotional exhibition is an evidence of weakness; an investigator should neither become depressed over a reverse, nor unduly enthusiastic over a fortunate discovery."

"But we approach the earth's surface? Soon I will be back in the sunshine again."

"Upon the contrary, we have been continually descending into the earth, and we are now ten miles or more beneath the level of the ocean."

"WE APPROACH DAYLIGHT, I CAN SEE YOUR FORM."

I shrank back, hesitated, and in despondency gazed at his hazy outline, then, as if palsied, sank upon the stony floor; but as I saw the light before me, I leaped up and shouted:

"What you say is not true; we approach daylight, I can see your form."

"Listen to me," he said. "Can not you understand that I have led you continually down a steep descent, and that for hours there has been no step upward? With but little exertion you have walked this distance without becoming wearied, and you could not, without great fatigue, have ascended for so long a period. You are entering a zone of inner earth light; we are in the surface, the upper edge of it. Let us hasten on, for when this cavern darkness is at an end—and I will say we have nearly passed that limit—your courage will return, and then we will rest."

"You surely do not speak the truth; science and philosophy, and I am somewhat versed in both, have never told me of such a light."

"Can philosophers more than speculate about that which they have not experienced if they have no data from which to calculate? Name the student in science who has reached this depth in earth, or has seen a man to tell him of these facts?"

"I can not."

"Then why should you have expected any of them to describe our surroundings? Misguided men will torture science by refuting facts with theories; but a fact is no less a fact when science opposes."

I recognized the force of his arguments, and cordially grasped his hand in indication of submission. We continued our journey, and rapidly traveled downward and onward. The light gradually increased in intensity, until at length the cavern near about us seemed to be as bright as diffused daylight could have made it. There was apparently no central point of radiation; the light was such as to pervade and exist in the surrounding space, somewhat as the vapor of phosphorus spreads a self-luminous haze throughout the bubble into which it is blown. The visual agent surrounding us had a permanent, self-existing luminosity, and was a pervading, bright, unreachable essence that, without an obvious origin, diffused itself equally in all directions. It reminded me of the form of light that in previous years I had seen described as epipolic dispersion, and as I refer to the matter I am of the opinion that man will yet find that the same cause produces both phenomena. I was informed now by the sense of sight, that we were in a cavern room of considerable size. The apartment presented somewhat the appearance of the usual underground caverns that I had seen pictured in books, and yet was different. Stalactites, stalagmites, saline incrustations, occurring occasionally reminded me of travelers' stories, but these objects were not so abundant as might be supposed. Such accretions or deposits of saline substances as I noticed were also disappointing, in that, instead of having a dazzling brilliancy, like frosted snow crystals, they were of a uniform gray or brown hue. Indeed, my former imaginative mental creations regarding underground caverns were dispelled in this somber stone temple, for even the floor and the fragments of stone that, in considerable

"SEATED HIMSELF ON A NATURAL BENCH OF STONE."

quantities, strewed the floor, were of the usual rock formations of upper earth. The glittering crystals of snowy white or rainbow tints (fairy caverns) pictured by travelers, and described as inexpressibly grand and beautiful in other cavern labyrinths, were wanting here, and I saw only occasional small clusters of quartz crystals that were other than of a dull gray color. Finally, after hours or perhaps days of travel, interspersed with restings, conversations, and arguments, amid which I could form no idea of the flight of time, my companion seated himself on a natural bench of stone, and directed me to rest likewise. He broke the silence, and spoke as follows:

CHAPTER XVI.

VITALIZED DARKNESS.—THE NARROWS IN SCIENCE.

"In studying any branch of science men begin and end with an unknown. The chemist accepts as data such conditions of matter as he finds about him, and connects ponderable matter with the displays of energy that have impressed his senses, building therefrom a span of theoretical science, but he can not formulate as yet an explanation regarding the origin or the end of either mind, matter, or energy. The piers supporting his fabric stand in a profound invisible gulf, into which even his imagination can not look to form a theory concerning basic formations—corner-stones.

"The geologist, in a like manner, grasps feebly the lessons left in the superficial fragments of earth strata, impressions that remain to bear imperfect record of a few of the disturbances that have affected the earth's crust, and he endeavors to formulate a story of the world's life, but he is neither able to antedate the records shown by the meager testimony at his command, scraps of a leaf out of God's great book of history, nor to anticipate coming events. The birth, as well as the death, of this planet is beyond his page.

"The astronomer directs his telescope to the heavens, records the position of the planets, and hopes to discover the influences worlds exert upon one another. He explores space to obtain data to enable him to delineate a map of the visible solar universe, but the instruments he has at command are so imperfect, and mind is so feeble that, like mockery seems his attempt to study behind the facts connected with the motions and conditions of the nearest heavenly bodies, and he can not offer an explanation of the beginning or cessation of their movements. He can neither account for their existence, nor foretell their end."

"Are you not mistaken?" I interrupted; "does not the astronomer foretell eclipses, and calculate the orbits of the planets, and has he not verified predictions concerning their several motions?"

"Yes; but this is simply a study of passing events. The astronomer is no more capable of grasping an idea that reaches into an explanation of the origin of motion, than the chemist or physicist, from exact scientific data, can account for the creation of matter. Give him any amount of material at rest, and he can not conceive of any method by which motion can disturb any part of it, unless such motion be mass motion communicated from without, or molecular motion, already existing within. He accounts for the phases of present motion in heavenly bodies, not for the primal cause of the actual movements or intrinsic properties they possess. He can neither originate a theory that will permit of motion creating itself, and imparting itself to quiescent matter, nor imagine how an atom of quiescent matter can be moved, unless motion from without be communicated thereto. The astronomer, I assert, can neither from any data at his command postulate nor prove the beginning nor the end of the reverberating motion that exists in his solar system, which is itself the fragment of a system that is circulating and revolving in and about itself, and in which, since the birth of man, the universe he knows has not passed the first milestone in the road that universe is traveling in space immensity.

"The mathematician starts a line from an imaginary point that he informs us exists theoretically without occupying any space, which is a contradiction of terms according to his human acceptation of knowledge derived from scientific experiment, if science is based on verified facts. He assumes that straight lines exist, which is a necessity for his calculation; but such a line he has never made. Even the beam of sunshine, radiating through a clear atmosphere or a cloud bank, widens and contracts again as it progresses through the various mediums of air and vapor currents, and if it is ever spreading and deflecting can it be straight? He begins his study in the unknown, it ends with the unknowable.

"The biologist can conceive of no rational, scientific beginning to life of plant or animal, and men of science must admit the fact. Whenever we turn our attention to nature's laws and nature's substance, we find man surrounded by the infinity that obscures the origin and covers the end. But perseverance, study of nature's forces, and comparison of the past with the present, will yet clarify human knowledge and make plain much of this seemingly mysterious, but never will man reach the beginning or the end. The course of human education, to this day, has been mostly materialistic, although, together with the study of matter, there has been more or less attention given to its moving spirit. Newton was the dividing light in scientific thought; he stepped between the reasonings of the past and the provings of the present, and introduced problems that gave birth to a new scientific tendency, a change from the study of matter from the material side to that of force and matter, but his thought has since been carried out in a mode too realistic by far. The study of material bodies has given way, it is true, in a few cases to the study of the spirit of matter, and evolution is beginning to teach men that matter is crude. As a result, thought will in its sequence yet show that modifications of energy expression are paramount. This work is not lost, however, for the consideration of the nature of sensible material, is preliminary and necessary to progression (as the life of the savage prepares the way for that of the cultivated student), and is a meager and primitive child's effort, compared with the richness of the study in unseen energy expressions that are linked with matter, of which men will yet learn."

"I comprehend some of this," I replied; "but I am neither prepared to assent to nor dissent from your conclusions, and my mind is not clear as to whether your logic is good or bad. I am more ready to speak plainly about my own peculiar situation than to become absorbed in abstruse arguments in science, and I marvel more at the soft light that is here surrounding us than at the metaphysical reasoning in which you indulge."

"The child ignorant of letters wonders at the resources of those who can spell and read, and, in like manner, many obscure natural phenomena are marvelous to man only because of his ignorance. You do not comprehend the fact that sunlight is simply a matter-bred expression, an outburst of interrupted energy, and that the modification this energy undergoes makes it visible or sensible to man. What, think you, becomes of the flood of light energy that unceasingly flows from the sun? For ages, for an eternity, it has bathed this earth and seemingly streamed into space, and space it would seem must have long since have been filled with it, if, as men believe, space contains energy of any description. Man may say the earth casts the amount intercepted by it back into space, and yet does not your science teach that the great bulk of the earth is an absorber, and a poor radiator of light and heat? What think you, I repeat, becomes of the torrent of light and heat and other forces that radiate from the sun, the flood that strikes the earth? It disappears, and, in the economy of nature, is not replaced by any known force or any known motion of matter. Think you that earth substance really presents an obstacle to the passage of the sun's energy? Is it not probable that most of this light producing essence, as a subtle fluid, passes through the surface of the earth and into its interior, as light does through space, and returns thence to the sun again, in a condition not discernible by man?" He grasped my arm and squeezed it as though to emphasize the words to follow. "You have used the term sunshine freely; tell me what is sunshine? Ah! you do not reply; well, what evidence have you to show that sunshine (heat and light) is not earth-bred, a condition that exists locally only, the result of contact between matter and some unknown force expression? What reason have you for accepting that, to other forms unknown and yet transparent to this energy, your sunshine may not be as intangible as the ether of space is to man? What reason have you to believe that a force torrent is not circulating to and from the sun and earth, inappreciable to man, excepting the mere trace of this force which, modified by contact action with matter appears as heat, light, and other force expressions? How can I, if this is true, in consideration of your ignorance, enter into details explanatory of the action that takes place between matter and a portion of this force, whereby in the earth, first at the surface, darkness is produced, and then deeper down an earth light that man can perceive by the sense of sight, as you now realize? I will only say that this luminous appearance about us is produced by a natural law, whereby the flood of energy, invisible to man, a something clothed now under the name of darkness, after streaming into the crust substance of the earth, is at this depth, revivified, and then is made apparent to mortal eye, to be modified again as it emerges from the opposite earth crust, but not annihilated. For my vision, however, this central light is not a necessity; my physical and mental development is such that the energy of darkness is communicable; I can respond to its touches on my nerves, and hence I can guide you in this dark cavern. I am all eye."

"Ah!" I exclaimed, "that reminds me of a remark made by my former guide who, referring to the instinct of animals, spoke of that as a natural power undeveloped in man. Is it true that by mental cultivation a new sense can be evolved whereby darkness may become as light?"

"Yes; that which you call light is a form of sensible energy to which the faculties of animals who live on the surface of the earth have become adapted, through their organs of sight. The sun's energy is modified when it strikes the surface of the earth; part is reflected, but most of it passes onward into the earth's substance, in an altered or disturbed condition. Animal organisms within the earth must possess a peculiar development to utilize it under its new form, but such a sense is really possessed in a degree by some creatures known to men. There is consciousness behind consciousness; there are grades and depths of consciousness. Earth worms, and some fishes and reptiles in underground streams (lower organizations, men call them) do not use the organ of sight, but recognize objects, seek their food, and flee from their enemies."

"They have no eyes," I exclaimed, forgetting that I spoke to an eyeless being; "how can they see?"

"You should reflect that man can not offer a satisfactory explanation of the fact that he can see with his eyes. In one respect, these so-called lower creatures are higher in the scale of life than man is, for they see (appreciate) without eyes. The surfaces of their bodies really are sources of perception, and seats of consciousness. Man must yet learn to see with his skin, taste with his fingers, and hear with the surface of his body. The dissected nerve, or the pupil of man's eye, offers to the physiologist no explanation of its intrinsic power. Is not man unfortunate in having to risk so much on so frail an organ? The physiologist can not tell why or how the nerve of the tongue can distinguish between bitter and sweet, or convey any impression of taste, or why the nerve of the ear communicates sound, or the nerve of the eye communicates the impression of sight. There is an impassable barrier behind all forms of nerve impressions, that neither the microscope nor other methods of investigation can help the reasoning senses of man to remove. The void that separates the pulp of the material nerve from consciousness is broader than the solar universe, for even from the most distant known star we can imagine the never-ending flight of a ray of light, that has once started on its travels into space. Can any man outline the bridge that connects the intellect with nerve or brain, mind, or with any form of matter? The fact that the surface of the bodies of some animals is capable of performing the same functions for these animals that the eye of man performs for him, is not more mysterious than is the function of that eye itself. The term darkness is an expression used to denote the fact that to the brain which governs the eye of man, what man calls the absence of light, is unrecognizable. If men were more magnanimous and less egotistical, they would open their minds to the fact that some animals really possess certain senses that are better developed than they are in man. The teachers of men too often tell the little they know and neglect the great unseen. The cat tribe, some night birds, and many reptiles can see better in darkness than in daylight. Let man compare with the nerve expanse of his own eye that of the highly developed eye of any such creature, and he will understand that the difference is one of brain or intellect, and not altogether one of optical vision surface. When men are able to explain how light can affect the nerves of their own eyes and produce such an effect on distant brain tissues as to bring to his senses objects that he is not touching, he may be able to explain how the energy in darkness can affect the nerve of the eye in the owl and impress vision on the brain of that creature. Should not man's inferior sense of light lead him to question if, instead of deficient visual power, there be not a deficiency of the brain capacity of man? Instead of accepting that the eye of man is incapable of receiving the impression of night energy, and making no endeavor to improve himself in the direction of his imperfection, man should reflect whether or not his brain may, by proper cultivation or artificial stimulus, be yet developed so as to receive yet deeper nerve impressions, thereby changing darkness into daylight. Until man can explain the modus operandi of the senses he now possesses, he can not consistently question the existence of a different sight power in other beings, and unquestioned existing conditions should lead him to hope for a yet higher development in himself."

"This dissertation is interesting, very," I said. "Although inclined toward agnosticism, my ideas of a possible future in consciousness that lies before mankind are broadened. I therefore accept your reasoning, perhaps because I can not refute it, neither do I wish to do so. And now I ask again, can not you explain to me how darkness, as deep as that of midnight, has been revivified so as to bring this great cavern to my view?"

"That may be made plain at a future time," he answered; "let us proceed with our journey."

We passed through a dry, well ventilated apartment. Stalactite formations still existed, indicative of former periods of water drippings, but as we journeyed onward I saw no evidence of present percolations, and the developing and erosive agencies that had worked in ages past must long ago have been suspended. The floor was of solid stone, entirely free from loose earth and fallen rocky fragments. It was smooth upon the surface, but generally disposed in gentle undulations. The peculiar, soft, radiant light to which my guide referred as "vitalized darkness" or "revivified sunshine," pervaded all the space about me, but I could not by its agency distinguish the sides of the vast cavern. The brightness was of a species that while it brought into distinctness objects that were near at hand, lost its unfolding power or vigor a short distance beyond. I would compare the effect to that of a bright light shining through a dense fog, were it not that the medium about us was transparent—not milky. The light shrunk into nothingness. It passed from existence behind and about me as if it were annihilated, without wasting away in the opalescent appearance once familiar as that of a spreading fog. Moreover, it seemed to detail such objects as were within the compass of a certain area close about me, but to lose in intensity beyond. The buttons on my coat appeared as distinct as they ever did when I stood in the sunlight, and fully one-half larger than I formerly knew them to be. The corrugations on the palms of my hands stood out in bold serpentine relief that I observed clearly when I held my hands near my eye, my fingers appeared clumsy, and all parts of my person were magnified in proportion. The region at the limits of my range of perception reminded me of nothingness, but not of darkness. A circle of obliteration defined the border of the luminous belt which advanced as we proceeded, and closed in behind us. This line, or rather zone of demarkation that separated the seen from the unseen, appeared to be about two hundred feet away, but it might have been more or less, as I had no method of measuring distances.

"I WAS IN A FOREST OF COLOSSAL FUNGI."

CHAPTER XVII.

THE FUNGUS FOREST.—ENCHANTMENT.

Along the chamber through which we now passed I saw by the mellow light great pillars, capped with umbrella-like covers, some of them reminding me of the common toadstool of upper earth, on a magnificent scale. Instead, however, of the gray or somber shades to which I had been accustomed, these objects were of various hues and combined the brilliancy of the primary prismatic colors, with the purity of clean snow. Now they would stand solitary, like gigantic sentinels; again they would be arranged in rows, the alignment as true as if established by the hair of a transit, forming columnar avenues, and in other situations they were wedged together so as to produce masses, acres in extent, in which the stems became hexagonal by compression. The columnar stems, larger than my body, were often spiral; again they were marked with diamond-shaped figures, or other regular geometrical forms in relief, beautifully exact, drawn as by a master's hand in rich and delicately blended colors, on pillars of pure alabaster. Not a few of the stems showed deep crimson, blue, or green, together with other rich colors combined; over which, as delicate as the rarest of lace, would be thrown, in white, an enamel-like intricate tracery, far surpassing in beauty of execution the most exquisite needle-work I had ever seen. There could be no doubt that I was in a forest of colossal fungi, the species of which are more numerous than those of upper earth cryptomatic vegetation. The expanded heads of these great thallogens were as varied as the stems I have described, and more so. Far above our path they spread like beautiful umbrellas, decorated as if by masters from whom the great painters of upper earth might humbly learn the art of mixing colors. Their under surfaces were of many different designs, and were of as many shapes as it is conceivable could be made of combinations of the circle and hyperbola. Stately and picturesque, silent and immovable as the sphinx, they studded the great cavern singly or in groups, reminding me of a grown child's wild imagination of fairy land. I stopped beside a group that was of unusual conspicuity and gazed in admiration on the huge and yet graceful, beautiful spectacle. I placed my hand on the stem of one plant, and found it soft and impressible; but instead of being moist, cold, and clammy as the repulsive toadstool of upper earth, I discovered, to my surprise, that it was pleasantly warm, and soft as velvet.

"Smell your hand," said my guide.

I did so, and breathed in an aroma like that of fresh strawberries. My guide observed (I had learned to judge of his emotions by his facial expressions) my surprised countenance with indifference.

"Try the next one," he said.

This being of a different species, when rubbed by my hand exhaled the odor of the pineapple.

"Extraordinary," I mused.

"Not at all. Should productions of surface earth have a monopoly of nature's methods, all the flavors, all the perfumes? You may with equal consistency express astonishment at the odors of the fruits of upper earth if you do so at the fragrance of these vegetables, for they are also created of odorless elements."

"But toadstools are foul structures of low organization.* They are neither animals nor true vegetables, but occupy a station below that of plants proper," I said.

"You are acquainted with this order of vegetation under the most unfavorable conditions; out of their native elements these plants degenerate and become then abnormal, often evolving into the poisonous earth fungi known to your woods and fields. Here they grow to perfection. This is their chosen habitat. They absorb from a pure atmosphere the combined foods of plants and animals, and during their existence meet no scorching sunrise. They flourish in a region of perfect tranquility, and without a tremor, without experiencing the change of a fraction of a degree in temperature, exist for ages. Many of these

---

* The fungus Polyporus graveolens was neglected by the guide. This fungus exhales a delicate odor, and is used in Kentucky to perfume a room. Being quite large, it is employed to hold a door open, thus being useful as well as fragrant.—J. U. L.

specimens are probably thousands of years old, and are still growing; why should they ever die? They have never been disturbed by a breath of moving air, and, balanced exactly on their succulent, pedestal-like stems, surrounded by an atmosphere of dead nitrogen, vapor, and other gases, with their roots imbedded in carbonates and minerals, they have food at command, nutrition inexhaustible."

"Still I do not see why they grow to such mammoth proportions."

"Plants adapt themselves to surrounding conditions," he remarked. "The oak tree in its proper latitude is tall and stately; trace it toward the Arctic circle, and it becomes knotted, gnarled, rheumatic, and dwindles to a shrub. The castor plant in the tropics is twenty or thirty feet in height, in the temperate zone it is an herbaceous plant, farther north it has no existence. Indian corn in Kentucky is luxuriant, tall, and graceful, and each stalk is supplied with roots to the second and third joint, while in the northland it scarcely reaches to the shoulder of a man, and, in order to escape the early northern frost, arrives at maturity before the more southern variety begins to tassel. The common jimson weed (datura stramonium) planted in early spring, in rich soil, grows luxuriantly, covers a broad expanse and bears an abundance of fruit; planted in midsummer it blossoms when but a few inches in height, and between two terminal leaves hastens to produce a single capsule on the apex of the short stem, in order to ripen its seed before the frost appears. These and other familiar examples might be cited concerning the difference some species of vegetation of your former lands undergo under climatic conditions less marked than between those that govern the growth of fungi here and on surface earth. Such specimens of fungi as grow in your former home have escaped from these underground regions, and are as much out of place as are the tropical plants transplanted to the edge of eternal snow. Indeed, more so, for on the earth the ordinary fungus, as a rule, germinates after sunset, and often dies when the sun rises, while here they may grow in peace eternally. These meandering caverns comprise thousands of miles of surface covered by these growths which shall yet fulfill a grand purpose in the economy of nature, for they are destined to feed tramping multitudes when the day appears in which the nations of men will desert the surface of the earth and pass as a single people through these caverns on their way to the Immaculate existence to be found in the inner sphere."

"I can not disprove your statement," I again repeated; "neither do I accept it. However, it still seems to me unnatural to find such delicious flavors and delicate odors connected with objects associated in memory with things insipid, or so disagreeable as toadstools and the rank forest fungi which I abhorred on earth."

CHAPTER XVIII.

THE FOOD OF MAN.

"This leads me to remark," answered the eyeless seer, "that you speak without due consideration of previous experience. You are, or should be, aware of other and as marked differences in food products of upper earth, induced by climate, soil and cultivation. The potato which, next to wheat, rice, or corn, you know supplies nations of men with starchy food, originated as a wild weed in South America and Mexico, where it yet exists as a small, watery, marble-like tuber, and its nearest kindred, botanically, is still poisonous. The luscious apple reached its present excellence by slow stages from knotty, wild, astringent fruit, to which it again returns when escaped from cultivation. The cucumber is a near cousin of the griping, medicinal cathartic bitter-apple, or colocynth, and occasionally partakes yet of the properties that result from that unfortunate alliance, as too often exemplified to persons who do not peel it deep enough to remove the bitter, cathartic principle that exists near the surface. Oranges, in their wild condition, are bitter, and are used principally as medicinal agents. Asparagus was once a weed, native to the salty edges of the sea, and as this weed has become a food, so it is possible for other wild weeds yet to do. Buckwheat is a weed proper, and not a cereal, and birds have learned that the seeds of many other weeds are even preferable to wheat. The wild parsnip is a poison, and the parsnip of cultivation relapses quickly into its natural condition if allowed to escape and roam again. The root of the tapioca plant contains a volatile poison, and is deadly; but when that same root is properly prepared, it becomes the wholesome food, tapioca. The nut of the African anacardium (cachew nut) contains a nourishing kernel that is eaten as food by the natives, and yet a drop of the juice of the oily shell placed on the skin will blister and produce terrible inflammations; only those expert in the removal of the kernel dare partake of the food. The berry of the berberis vulgaris is a pleasant acid fruit; the bough that bears it is intensely bitter. Such examples might be multiplied indefinitely, but I have cited enough to illustrate the fact that neither the difference in size and structure of the species in the mushroom forest through which we are passing, nor the conditions of these bodies, as compared with those you formerly knew, need excite your astonishment. Cultivate a potato in your former home so that the growing tuber is exposed to sunshine, and it becomes green and acrid, and strongly virulent. Cultivate the spores of the intra-earth fungi about us, on the face of the earth, and although now all parts of the plants are edible, the species will degenerate, and may even become poisonous. They lose their flavor under such unfavorable conditions, and although some species still retain vitality enough to resist poisonous degeneration, they dwindle in size, and adapt themselves to new and unnatural conditions. They have all degenerated. Here they live on water, pure nitrogen and its modifications, grasping with their roots the carbon of the disintegrated limestone, affiliating these substances, and evolving from these bodies rich and delicate flavors, far superior to the flavor of earth surface foods. On the surface of the earth, after they become abnormal, they live only on dead and devitalized organic matter, having lost the power of assimilating elementary matter. They then partake of the nature of animals, breathe oxygen and exhale carbonic acid, as animals do, being the reverse of other plant existences. Here they breathe oxygen, nitrogen, and the vapor of water; but exhale some of the carbon in combination with hydrogen, thus evolving these delicate ethereal essences instead of the poisonous gas, carbonic acid. Their substance is here made up of all the elements necessary for the support of animal life; nitrogen to make muscle, carbon and hydrogen for fat, lime for bone. This fungoid forest could feed a multitude. It is probable that in the time to come when man deserts the bleak earth surface, as he will some day be forced to do, as has been the case in frozen planets that are not now inhabited on the outer crust; nations will march through these spaces on their way from the dreary outside earth to the delights of the salubrious inner sphere. Here then, when that day of necessity appears, as it surely will come under inflexible climatic changes that will control the destiny of outer earth life, these constantly increasing stores adapted to nourish humanity, will be found accumulated and ready for food. You have already eaten of them, for the variety of food with which I supplied you has been selected from different portions of these nourishing products which, flavored and salted, ready for use as food, stand intermediate between animal and vegetable, supplying the place of both."

My instructor placed both hands on my shoulders, and in silence I stood gazing intently into his face. Then, in a smooth, captivating, entrancing manner, he continued:

"Can you not see that food is not matter? The material part of bread is carbon, water, gas, and earth; the material part of fat is charcoal and gas; the material part of flesh is water and gas; the material part of fruits is mostly water with a little charcoal and gas.* The material constituents of all foods are plentiful, they abound everywhere, and yet amid the unlimited, unorganized materials that go to form foods man would starve.

"Give a healthy man a diet of charcoal, water, lime salts, and air; say to him, 'Bread contains no other substance, here is bread, the material food of man, live on this food,' and yet the man, if he eat of these, will die with his stomach distended. So with all other foods; give man the unorganized materialistic constituents of food in unlimited amounts, and starvation results. No! matter is not food, but a carrier of food."

"What is food?"

"Sunshine. The grain of wheat is a food by virtue of the sunshine fixed within it. The flesh of animals, the food of living creatures, are simply carriers of sunshine energy. Break out the sunshine and you destroy the food, although the material remains. The growing plant locks the sunshine in its cells, and the living animal takes it out again. Hence it is that after the sunshine of any food is liberated during the metamorphosis of the tissues of an animal although the material part of the food remains, it is no longer a food, but becomes a poison, and then, if it is not promptly eliminated from the animal, it will destroy

---

* By the term gas, it is evident that hydrogen and nitrogen were designated, and yet, since the instructor insists that other gases form part of the atmosphere, so he may consistently imply that unknown gases are parts of food. J. C. L.

the life of the animal. This material becomes then injurious, but it is still material.

"The farmer plants a seed in the soil, the sunshine sprouts it, nourishes the growing plant, and during the season locks itself to and within its tissues, binding the otherwise dead materials of that tissue together into an organized structure. Animals eat these structures, break them from higher to lower compounds, and in doing so live on the stored up sunshine and then excrete the worthless material side of the food. The farmer spreads these excluded substances over the earth again to once more take up the sunshine in the coming plant organization, but not until it does once more lock in its cells the energy of sunshine can it be a food for that animal."

"Is manure a food?" he abruptly asked.

"No."

"Is not manure matter?"

"Yes."

"May it not become a food again, as the part of another plant, when another season passes?"

"Yes."

"In what else than energy (sunshine) does it differ from food?"

"Water is a necessity," I said.

"And locked in each molecule of water there is a mine of sunshine. Liberate suddenly the sun energy from the gases of the ocean held in subjection thereby, and the earth would disappear in an explosion that would reverberate throughout the universe. The water that you truly claim to be necessary to the life of man, is itself water by the grace of this same sun, for without its heat water would be ice, dry as dust. 'T is the sun that gives life and motion to creatures animate and substances inanimate; he who doubts distrusts his Creator. Food and drink are only carriers of bits of assimilable sunshine. When the fire worshipers kneeled to their god, the sun, they worshiped the great food reservoir of man. When they drew the quivering entrails from the body of a sacrificed victim they gave back to their God a spark of sunshine—it was due sooner or later. They builded well in thus recognizing the source of all life, and yet they acted badly, for their God asked no premature sacrifice, the inevitable must soon occur, and as all organic life comes from that Sun-God, so back to that Creator the sun-spark must fly."

"But they are heathen; there is a God beyond their narrow conception of God."

"As there is also a God in the Beyond, past your idea of God. Perhaps to beings of higher mentalities, we may be heathen; but even if this is so, duty demands that we revere the God within our intellectual sphere. Let us not digress further; the subject now is food, not the Supreme Creator, and I say to you the food of man and the organic life of man is sunshine."

He ceased, and I reflected upon his words. All he had said seemed so consistent that I could not deny its plausibility, and yet it still appeared altogether unlikely as viewed in the light of my previous earth knowledge. I did not quite comprehend all the semi-scientific expressions, but was at least certain that I could neither disprove nor verify his propositions. My thoughts wandered aimlessly, and I found myself questioning whether man could be prevailed upon to live contentedly in situations such as I was now passing through. In company with my learned and philosophical but fantastically created guardian and monitor, I moved on.

CHAPTER XIX.

THE CRY FROM A DISTANCE.—I REBEL AGAINST CONTINUING THE JOURNEY.

As we paced along, meditating, I became more sensibly impressed with the fact that our progress was down a rapid declination. The saline incrustations, fungi and stalagmites, rapidly changed in appearance, an endless variety of stony figures and vegetable cryptogams recurring successively before my eyes. They bore the shape of trees, shrubs, or animals, fixed and silent as statues: at least in my distorted condition of mind I could make out resemblances to many such familiar objects; the floor of the cavern became increasingly steeper, as was shown by the stalactites, which, hanging here and there from the invisible ceiling, made a decided angle with the floor, corresponding with a similar angle of the stalagmites below. Like an accompanying and encircling halo the ever present earth-light enveloped us, opening in front as we advanced, and vanishing in the rear. The sound of our footsteps gave back a peculiar, indescribable hollow echo, and our voices sounded ghost-like and unearthly, as if their origin was outside of our bodies, and at a distance. The peculiar resonance reminded me of noises reverberating in an empty cask or cistern. I was oppressed by an indescribable feeling of mystery and awe that grew deep and intense, until at last I could no longer bear the mental strain.

"Hold, hold," I shouted, or tried to shout, and stopped suddenly, for although I had cried aloud, no sound escaped my lips. Then from a distance—could I believe my senses?—from a distance as an echo, the cry came back in the tones of my own voice, "Hold, hold."

"Speak lower," said my guide, "speak very low, for now an effort such as you have made projects your voice far outside your body; the greater the exertion the farther away it appears."

I grasped him by the arm and said slowly, determinedly, and in a suppressed tone: "I have come far enough into the secret caverns of the earth, without knowing our destination; acquaint me now with the object of this mysterious journey, I demand, and at once relieve this sense of uncertainty; otherwise I shall go no farther."

"AN ENDLESS VARIETY OF STONY FIGURES."

"You are to proceed to the Sphere of Rest with me," he replied, "and in safety. Beyond that an Unknown Country lies, into which I have never ventured."

"You speak in enigmas; what is this Sphere of Rest? Where is it?"

"Your eyes have never seen anything similar; human philosophy has no conception of it, and I can not describe it," he said. "It is located in the body of the earth, and we will meet it about one thousand miles beyond the North Pole."

"But I am in Kentucky," I replied; "do you think that I propose to walk to the North Pole, man—if man you be; that unreached goal is thousands of miles away."

"True," he answered, "as you measure distance on the surface of the earth, and you could not walk it in years of time; but you are now twenty-five miles below the surface, and you must be aware that instead of becoming more weary as we proceed, you are now and have for some time been gaining strength. I would also call to your attention that you neither hunger nor thirst."

"Proceed," I said, "'t is useless to rebel; I am wholly in your power," and we resumed our journey, and rapidly went forward amid silences that were to me painful beyond description. We abruptly entered a cavern of crystal, every portion of which was of sparkling brilliancy, and as white as snow. The stalactites, stalagmites and fungi disappeared. I picked up a fragment of the bright material, tasted it, and found that it resembled pure salt. Monstrous, cubical crystals, a foot or more in diameter, stood out in bold relief, accumulations of them, as conglomerated masses, banked up here and there, making parts of great columnar cliffs, while in other formations the crystals were small, resembling in the aggregate masses of white sandstone.

"Is not this salt?" I asked.

"Yes; we are now in the dried bed of an underground lake."

"Dried bed?" I exclaimed; "a body of water sealed in the earth can not evaporate."

"It has not evaporated; at some remote period the water has been abstracted from the salt, and probably has escaped upon the surface of the earth as a fresh water spring."

"You contradict all laws of hydrostatics, as I understand that subject," I replied, "when you speak of abstracting water from a dissolved substance that is part of a liquid, and thus leaving the solids."

"Nevertheless this is a constant act of nature," said he; "how else can you rationally account for the great salt beds and other deposits of saline materials that exist hermetically sealed beneath the earth's surface?"

"I will confess that I have not given the subject much thought; I simply accept the usual explanation to the effect that salty seas have lost their water by evaporation, and afterward the salt formations, by some convulsions of nature, have been

"MONSTROUS CUBICAL CRYSTALS."

covered with earth, perhaps sinking by earthquake convulsions bodily into the earth."

"These explanations are examples of some of the erroneous views of scientific writers," he replied; "they are true only to a limited extent. The great beds of salt, deep in the earth, are usually accumulations left there by water that is drawn from brine lakes, from which the liberated water often escaped as pure spring water at the surface of the earth. It does not escape by evaporation, at least not until it reaches the earth's surface."

INTERLUDE—THE STORY INTERRUPTED.

CHAPTER XX.

MY UNBIDDEN GUEST PROVES HIS STATEMENT AND REFUTES MY PHILOSOPHY.

Let the reader who has followed this strange story which I am directed to title "The End of Earth," and who, in imagination, has traversed the cavernous passages of the underworld and listened to the conversation of those two personages who journeyed towards the secrets of the Beyond, return now to upper earth, and once more enter my secluded lodgings, the home of Llewellen Drury, him who listened to the aged guest and who claims your present attention. Remember that I relate a story within a story. That importunate guest of mine, of the glittering knife and the silvery hair, like another Ancient Mariner, had constrained me to listen to his narrative, as he read it aloud to me from the manuscript. I patiently heard chapter after chapter, generally with pleasure, often with surprise, sometimes with incredulity, or downright dissent. Much of the narrative, I must say,—yes, most of it, appeared possible, if not probable, as taken in its connected sequence. The scientific sections were not uninteresting; the marvels of the fungus groves, the properties of the inner light, I was not disinclined to accept as true to natural laws; but when The-Man-Who-Did-It came to tell of the intra-earth salt deposits, and to explain the cause of the disappearance of lakes that formerly existed underground, and their simultaneous replacement by beds of salt, my credulity was overstrained.

"Permit me to interrupt your narrative," I remarked, and then in response to my request the venerable guest laid down his paper.

"Well?" he said, interrogatively.

"I do not believe that last statement concerning the salt lake, and, to speak plainly, I would not have accepted it as you did, even had I been in your situation."

"To what do you allude?" he asked.

"The physical abstraction of water from the salt of a solution of salt; I do not believe it possible unless by evaporation of the water."

"You seem to accept as conclusive the statements of men who have never investigated beneath the surface in these directions, and you question the evidence of a man who has seen the phenomenon. I presume you accept the prevailing notions about salt beds, as you do the assertion that liquids seek a common level, which your scientific authorities also teach as a law of nature?"

"Yes; I do believe that liquids seek a common level, and I am willing to credit your other improbable statements if you can demonstrate the principle of liquid equilibrium to be untrue."

"Then," said he, "to-morrow evening I will show you that fluids seek different levels, and also explain to you how liquids may leave the solids they hold in solution without evaporating from them."

He arose and abruptly departed. It was near morning, and yet I sat in my room alone pondering the story of my unique guest until I slept to dream of caverns and seances until daylight, when I was awakened by their vividness. The fire was out, the room was cold, and, shivering in nervous exhaustion, I crept into bed to sleep and dream again of horrible things I can not describe, but which made me shudder in affright at their recollection. Late in the day I awoke.

On the following evening my persevering teacher appeared punctually, and displayed a few glass tubes and some blotting or bibulous paper.

"I will first show you that liquids may change their levels in opposition to the accepted laws of men, not contrary to nature's laws; however, let me lead to the experiments by a statement of facts, that, if you question, you can investigate at any time. If two vessels of water be connected by a channel from the bottom of each, the water surfaces will come to a common level."

He selected a curved glass tube, and poured water into it. The water assumed the position shown in Figure 11.

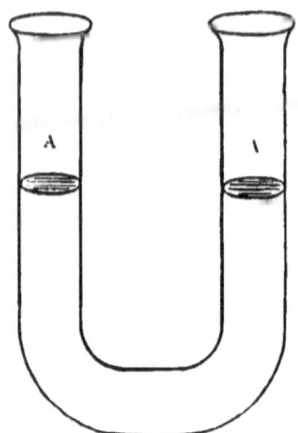

FIG. 11.—A A, water in tube seeks a level.

"You have not shown me anything new," I said; "my text-books taught me this."

"True, I have but exhibited that which is the foundation of your philosophy regarding the surface of liquids. Let me proceed:

"If we pour a solution of common salt into such a U tube, as I do now, you perceive that it also rises to the same level in both ends."

"Of course it does."

"Do not interrupt me. Into one arm of the tube containing the brine I now carefully pour pure water. You observe that the surfaces do not seek the same level." (Figure 12.)

"Certainly not," I said; "the weight of the liquid in each arm is the same, however; the columns balance each other."

"Exactly; and on this assumption you base your assertion that connected liquids of the same gravity must always seek a common level, but you see from this test that if two liquids of different gravities be connected from beneath, the surface of the lighter one will assume a higher level than the surface of the heavier."

"Agreed; however tortuous the channel that connects them, such must be the case."

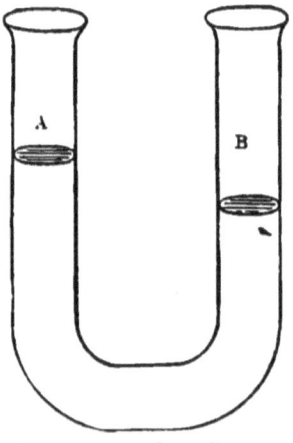

FIG. 12.—A, surface of water. B, surface of brine.

"Is it not supposable," said he, "that there might be two pockets in the earth, one containing salt water, the other fresh water, which, if joined together, might be represented by such a figure as this, wherein the water surface would be raised above that of the brine?" And he drew upon the paper the accompanying diagram. (Figure 13.)

"Yes," I admitted; "providing, of course, there was an equal pressure of air on the surface of each."

"Now I will draw a figure in which one pocket is above the other, and ask you to imagine that in the lower pocket we have pure water, in the upper pocket brine (Figure 14); can you bring any theory of your law to bear upon these liquids so that by connecting them together the water will rise and run into the brine?"

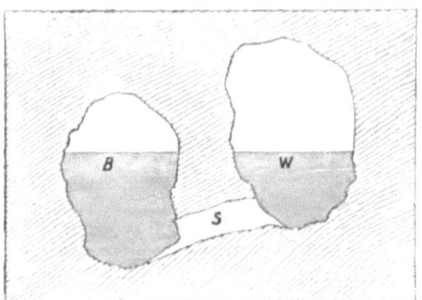

FIG. 13.—B, surface of brine.
W, surface of water.
S, sand strata connecting them.

"No," I replied; "connect them, and then the brine will flow into the water."

"Upon the contrary," he said; "connect them, as innumerable cavities in the earth are joined, and the water will flow into the brine."

"The assertion is opposed to applied philosophy and common sense," I said.

"Where ignorance is bliss, 't is folly to be wise, you know to be a maxim with mortals," he replied; "but I must pardon you; your dogmatic education narrows your judgment. I now will prove you in error."

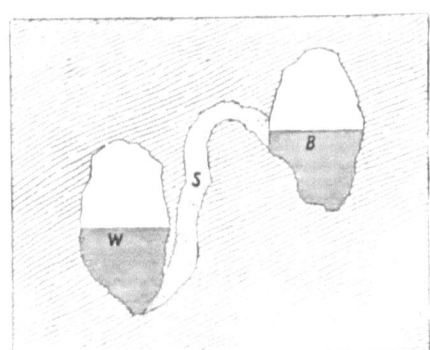

FIG. 14.—B, brine.
W, water.
S, sand stratum.
The difference in altitude is somewhat exaggerated to make the phenomenon clear. A syphon may result under such circumstances.
—L.

He took from his pocket two slender glass tubes, about an eighth of an inch in bore and four inches in length, each closed at one end, and stood them in a perforated cork that he placed upon the table.

Into one tube he poured water, and then dissolving some salt in a cup, poured brine into the other, filling both nearly to the top (Figure 15). Next he produced a short curved glass tube, to each end of which was attached a strip of flexible rubber tubing. Then, from a piece of blotting paper such as is used to blot ink, he cut a narrow strip and passed it through the arrangement, forming the apparatus represented by Figure 16.

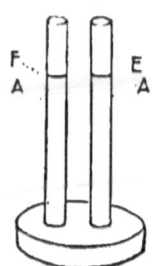

FIG. 15.
A A, glass tubes.
F, brine surface.
E, water surface.

Then he inserted the two tubes (Figure 15) into the rubber, the extremities of the paper being submerged in the liquids, producing a combination that rested upright in the cork as shown by Figure 17.

The surfaces of both liquids were at once lowered by reason of the suction of the bibulous paper, the water decreasing most rapidly, and soon the creeping liquids met by absorption in the paper, the point of contact, as the liquids met, being plainly discernible. Now the old man gently slid the tubes upon each other, raising one a little, so as to bring the surfaces of the two liquids exactly on a plane; he then marked the glass at the surface of each with a pen.

"Observe the result," he remarked as he replaced the tubes in the cork with their liquid surfaces on a line.

Together we sat and watched, and soon it became apparent that the surface of the water had decreased in height as compared with that of the brine. By fixing my gaze on the ink mark on the glass I also observed that the brine in the opposing tube was rising.

"I will call to-morrow evening," he said, "and we shall then discover which is true, man's theory or nature's practice."

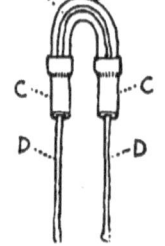

FIG. 16.
B, curved glass tube.
C C, rubber tubes.
D D, bibulous paper.

Within a short time enough of the water in the tube had been transferred to the brine to raise its surface considerably above its former level, the surface of the water being lowered to a greater degree. (Figure 18.) I was discomfited at the result, and upon his appearance next evening peevishly said to the experimenter:

"I do not know that this is fair."

"Have I not demonstrated that, by properly connecting the liquids, the lighter flows into the heavier, and raises itself above the former surface?"

"Yes; but there is no porous paper in the earth."

"True; I used this medium because it was convenient. There are, however, vast subterranean beds of porous materials, stone, sand, clay, various other earths, many of which will answer the same purpose. By perfectly natural laws, on a large scale, such molecular transfer of liquids is constantly taking place within the earth, and in these phenomena the law of gravitation seems ignored, and the rule which man believes from narrow experience, governs the flow of liquids, is reversed. The arched porous medium always transfers the lighter liquid into the heavier one until its surface is raised considerably above that of the light one. In the same way you can demonstrate that alcohol passes into water, sulphuric ether into alcohol, and other miscible light liquids into those heavier."

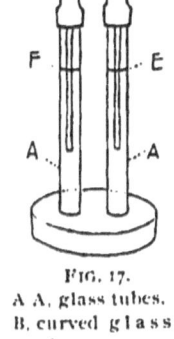

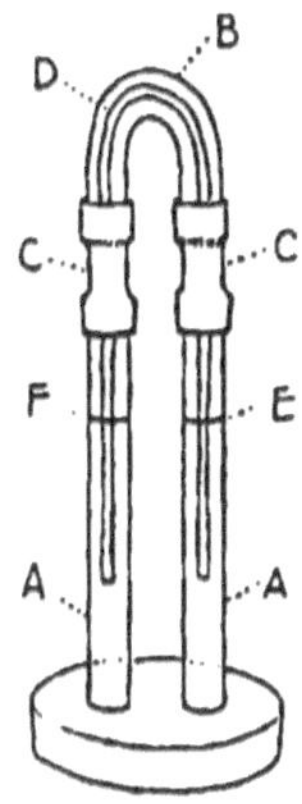

FIG. 17.
A A, glass tubes.
B, curved glass tube.
C C, rubber tubes.
D, bibulous paper.
E, water surface.
F, brine surface.

"I have seen you exemplify the statement on a small scale, with water and brine, and can not question but that it is true on a large one," I replied.

"So you admit that the assertion governing the surfaces of liquids is true only when the liquids are connected from beneath. In other words, your thought is one-sided, as science thought often is."

"Yes."

"Now as to the beds of salt deep within the earth. You are also mistaken concerning their origin. The water of the ocean that runs through an open channel from the one side may flow into an underground lake, that by means of the contact action (suction) of the overlying and surrounding strata is being continually emptied of its water, but not its salt. Thus by absorption of water the brine of the lake becomes in time saturated, starting crystallization regularly over the floor and sides of the basin. Eventually the entire cavity is filled with salt, and a solid mass of rock salt remains. If, however,

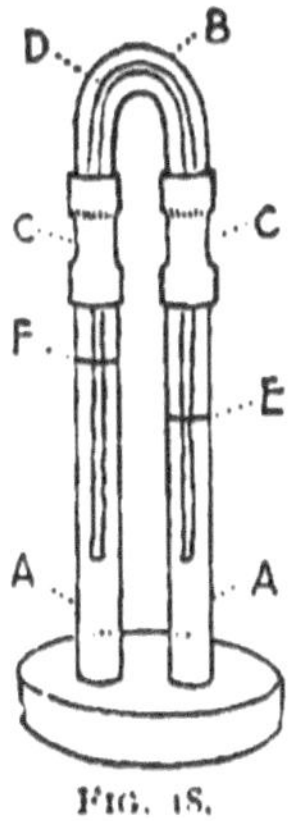

FIG. 18.
E, water surface.
F, brine surface.

before the lake becomes solid, the brine supply is shut off by some natural cause as by salt crystals closing the passage thereto, the underground lake is at last drained of its water, the salt crystallizing over the bottom, and upon the cliffs, leaving great crevices through the saline deposits, as chances to have been the case with the salt formations through which I passed with my guide, and have recently described to you."

"Even now I have my doubts as to the correctness of your explanations, especially concerning the liquid surfaces."

"They are facts, however; liquids capable of being mixed, if connected by porous arches (bibulous paper is convenient for illustrating by experiment) reverse the rule men have accepted to explain the phenomena of liquid equilibrium, for I repeat, the lighter one rushes into that which is heavier, and the surface of the heavier liquid rises. You can try the experiment with alcohol and water, taking precautions to prevent evaporation, or you can vary the experiment with solutions of various salts of different densities; the greater the difference in gravity between the two liquids, the more rapid will be the flow of the lighter one into the heavier, and after equilibrium, the greater will be the contrast in the final height of the resultant liquid surfaces."

"Men will yet explain this effect by natural laws," I said.

"Yes," he answered; "when they learn the facts; and they will then be able to solve certain phenomena connected with diffusion processes that they can not now understand. Did I not tell you that after the fact had been made plain it was easy to see how Columbus stood the egg on its end? What I have demonstrated by experiment is perhaps no new principle in hydrostatics. But I have applied it in a natural manner to the explanation of obscure natural phenomena, that men now seek unreasonable methods to explain."

"You may proceed with your narrative. I accept that when certain liquids are connected, as you have shown, by means of porous substances, one will pass into the other, and the surface of the lighter liquid in this case will assume a position below that of the heavier."

"You must also accept," said he, "that when solutions of salt are subjected to earth attraction, under proper conditions, the solids may by capillary attraction be left behind, and pure water finally pass through the porous medium. Were it not for this law, the only natural surface spring water on earth would be brine, for the superficial crust of the earth is filled with saline solutions. All the spring-fed rivers and lakes would also be salty and fetid with sulphur compounds, for at great depths brine and foul water are always present. Even in countries where all the water below the immediate surface of the earth is briny, the running springs, if of capillary origin, are pure and fresh. You may imagine how different this would be were it not for the law I have cited, for the whole earth's crust is permeated by brine and saline waters. Did your 'philosophy' never lead you to think of this?"

Continuing, my guide argued as follows: "Do not lakes exist on the earth's surface into which rivers and streams flow, but which have no visible outlet? Are not such lakes saline, even though the source of supply is comparatively fresh? Has it never occurred to you to question whether capillarity assisted by surface evaporation (not evaporation only as men assert) is not separating the water of these lakes from the saline substances carried into them by the streams, thus producing brine lakes? Will not this action after a great length of time result in crystalline deposits over portions of the bottoms of such lakes, and ultimately produce a salt bed?"

"It is possible," I replied.

"Not only possible, but probable. Not only probable, but true. Across the intervening brine strata above the salt crystals the surface rivers may flow, indeed, owing to differences in specific gravity the surface of the lake may be comparatively fresh, while in the quiet depths below, beds of salt crystals are forming, and between these extremes may rest strata after strata of saline solutions, decreasing in gravity towards the top."

Then he took his manuscript, and continued to read in a clear, musical voice, while I sat a more contented listener than I had been previously. I was not only confuted, but convinced. And I recalled the saying of Socrates, that no better fortune can happen a man than to be confuted in an error.

CHAPTER XXI.

MY WEIGHT DISAPPEARING.

We halted suddenly, for we came unexpectedly to the edge of a precipice, twenty feet at least in depth.

"Let us jump down," said my guide.

"That would be dangerous," I answered; "can not we descend at some point where it is not so deep?"

"No; the chasm stretches for miles across our path, and at this point we will meet with the least difficulty; besides, there is no danger. The specific gravity of our bodies is now so little that we could jump twice that distance with impunity."

"I can not comprehend you; we are in the flesh, our bodies are possessed of weight, the concussion will be violent."

"You reason again from the condition of your former life, and, as usual, are mistaken; there will be little shock, for, as I have said, our bodies are comparatively light now. Have you forgotten that your motion is continuously accelerated, and that without perceptible exertion you move rapidly? This is partly because of the loss of weight. Your weight would now be only about fifty pounds if tested by a spring balance."

I stood incredulous.

"You trifle with me; I weigh over one hundred and fifty pounds; how have I lost weight? It is true that I have noticed the ease with which we have recently progressed on our journey, especially the latter part of it, but I attribute this, in part, to the fact that our course is down an incline, and also to the vitalizing power of this cavern air."

"This explains part of the matter," he said; "it answered at the time, and I stated a fact; but were it not that you are really consuming a comparatively small amount of energy, you would long before this have been completely exhausted. You have been gaining strength for some hours; have really been growing younger. Your wrinkled face has become more smooth, and your voice is again natural. You were prematurely aged by your brothers on the surface of the earth, in order that when you pass the line of gravity, you might be vigorous and enjoying manhood again. Had this aging process not been accomplished you would now have become as a child in many respects."

He halted before me. "Jump up," he said. I promptly obeyed the unexpected command, and sprung upward with sufficient force to carry me, as I supposed, six inches from the earth; however I bounded upward fully six feet. My look of surprise as I

"I BOUNDED UPWARD FULLY SIX FEET."

gently alighted, for there was no concussion on my return, seemed lost on my guide, and he quietly said:

"If you can leap six feet upward without excessive exertion, or return shock, can not you jump twenty feet down? Look!"

"I FLUTTERED TO THE EARTH AS A LEAF WOULD FALL."

And he leaped lightly over the precipice and stood unharmed on the stony floor below.

Even then I hesitated, observing which, he cried:

"Hang by your hands from the edge then, and drop."

I did so, and the fourteen feet of fall seemed to affect me as though I had become as light as cork. I fluttered to the earth as a leaf would fall, and leaned against the precipice in surprised meditation.

"Others have been through your experience," he remarked, "and I therefore can overlook your incredulity; but experiences such as you now meet, remove distrust. Doing is believing." He smiled benignantly.

I pondered, revolving in my mind the fact that persons had in mental abstraction, passed through unusual experiences in ignorance of conditions about them, until their attention had been called to the seen and yet unnoticed surroundings, and they had then beheld the facts plainly. The puzzle picture (see p. 129) stares the eye and impresses the retina, but is devoid of character until the hidden form is developed in the mind, and then that form is always prominent to the eye. My remarkably light step, now that my attention had been directed thereto, was constantly in my mind, and I found myself suddenly possessed of the strength of a man, but with the weight of an infant. I raised my feet without an effort; they seemed destitute of weight; I

"WE LEAPED OVER GREAT INEQUALITIES."

leaped about, tumbled, and rolled over and over on the smooth stone floor without injury. It appeared that I had become the airy similitude of my former self, my material substance having wasted away without a corresponding impairment of strength.

I pinched my flesh to be assured that all was not a dream, and then endeavored to convince myself that I was the victim of delirium; but in vain. Too sternly my self-existence confronted me as a reality, a cruel reality. A species of intoxication possessed me once more, and I now hoped for the end, whatever it might be. We resumed our journey, and rushed on with increasing rapidity, galloping hand in hand, down, down, ever downward into the illuminated crevice of the earth. The spectral light by which we were aureoled increased in intensity, as by arithmetical progression, and I could now distinguish objects at a considerable distance before us. My spirits rose as if I were under the influence of a potent stimulant; a liveliness that was the opposite of my recent despondency had gained control, and I was again possessed of a delicious mental sensation, to which I can only refer as a most rapturous exhilaration. My guide grasped my hand firmly, and his touch, instead of revolting me as formerly it had done, gave pleasure. We together leaped over great inequalities in the floor, performing these æreal feats almost as easily as a bird flies. Indeed, I felt that I possessed the power of flight, for we bounded fearlessly down great declivities and over abysses that were often perpendicular, and many times our height. A very slight muscular exertion was sufficient to carry us rods of distance, and almost tiptoeing we skimmed with ever-increasing speed down the steeps of that unknown declivity. At length my guide held back; we gradually lessened our velocity, and, after a time, rested beside a horizontal substance that lay before us, apparently a sheet of glass, rigid, immovable, immeasurably great, that stretched as a level surface before us, vividly distinct in the brightness of an earth light, that now proved to be superior to sunshine. Far as the eye could reach, the glassy barrier to our further progress spread as a crystal mirror in front, and vanishing in the distance, shut off the beyond.

"FAR AS THE EYE COULD REACH THE GLASSY BARRIER SPREAD AS A CRYSTAL MIRROR."

INTERLUDE.—THE STORY AGAIN INTERRUPTED.

CHAPTER XXII.

MY UNBIDDEN GUEST DEPARTS.

Once more I must presume to interrupt this narrative, and call back the reader's thoughts from those mysterious caverns through which we have been tracing the rapid footsteps of the man who was abducted, and his uncouth pilot of the lower realms. Let us now see and hear what took place in my room, in Cincinnati, just after my visitor, known to us as The-Man-Who-Did-It, had finished reading to me, Lewellyn Drury, the editor of this volume, the curious chapter relating how the underground explorers lost weight as they descended in the hollows of the earth. My French clock struck twelve of its clear silvery notes before the gray-bearded reader finished his stint for the occasion, and folded his manuscript preparatory to placing it within his bosom.

"It is past midnight," he said, "and it is time for me to depart; but I will come to you again within a year.

"Meanwhile, during my absence, search the records, question authorities, and note such objections as rise therefrom concerning the statements I have made. Establish or disprove historically, or scientifically, any portion of the life history that I have given, and when I return I will hear what you have to say, and meet your argument. If there is a doubt concerning the authenticity of any part of the history, investigate; but make no mention to others of the details of our meetings."

I sat some time in thought, then said: "I decline to concern myself in verifying the historical part of your narrative. The localities you mention may be true to name, and it is possible that you have related a personal history; but I can not perceive that I am interested in either proving or disproving it. I will say, however, that it does not seem probable that at any time a man can disappear from a community, as you claim to have done, and have been the means of creating a commotion in his neighborhood that affected political parties, or even led to an unusual local excitement, outside his immediate circle of acquaintances, for a man is not of sufficient importance unless he is very conspicuous. By your own admission, you were simply a studious mechanic, a credulous believer in alchemistic vagaries, and as I revolve the matter over, I am afraid that you are now trying to impose on my credulity. The story of a forcible abduction, in the manner you related, seems to me incredible, and not worthy of investigation, even had I the inclination to concern myself in your personal affairs. The statements, however, that you make regarding the nature of the crust of the earth, gravitation, light, instinct, and human senses are highly interesting, and even plausible as you artfully present the subjects, I candidly admit, and I shall take some pains to make inquiries concerning the recorded researches of experts who have investigated in that direction."

"Collect your evidence," said he, "and I shall listen to your views when I return."

He opened the door, glided away, and I was alone again.

CHAPTER XXIII.

I QUESTION SCIENTIFIC MEN.—ARISTOTLE'S ETHER.

Days and weeks passed. When the opportunity presented, I consulted Dr. W. B. Chapman, the druggist and student of science, regarding the nature of light and earth, who in turn referred me to Prof. Daniel Vaughn. This learned man, in reply to my question concerning gravitation, declared that there was much that men wished to understand in regard to this mighty force, that might yet be explained, but which may never become known to mortal man.

"The correlation of forces," said he, "was prominently introduced and considered by a painstaking scientific writer named Joule, in several papers that appeared between 1843 and 1850, and he was followed by others, who engaged themselves in experimenting and theorizing, and I may add that Joule was indeed preceded in such thought by Mayer. This department of scientific study just now appears of unusual interest to scientists, and your questions embrace problems connected with some phases of its phenomena. We believe that light, heat, and electricity are mutually convertible, in fact, the evidences recently opened up to us show that such must be the case. These agencies or manifestations are now known to be so related that whenever one disappears others spring into existence. Study the beautiful experiments and remarkable investigations of Sir William Thomson in these directions."

"And what of gravitation?" I asked, observing that Prof. Vaughn neglected to include gravitation among his numerous enumerated forces, and recollecting that the force gravitation was more closely connected with my visitor's story than perhaps were any of the others, excepting the mysterious mid-earth illumination.

"Of that force we are in greater ignorance than of the others," he replied. "It affects bodies terrestrial and celestial, drawing a material substance, or pressing to the earth; also holds, we believe, the earth and all other bodies in position in the heavens, thus maintaining the equilibrium of the planets. Seemingly gravitation is not derived from, or sustained by, an external force, or supply reservoir, but is an intrinsic entity, a characteristic of matter that decreases in intensity at the rate of the square of the increasing distance, as bodies recede from each other, or from the surface of the earth. However, gravitation neither escapes by radiation from bodies nor needs to be replenished, so far as we know, from without. It may be compared to an elastic band, but there is no intermediate tangible substance to influence bodies that are affected by it, and it remains in undying tension, unlike all elastic material substances known, neither losing nor acquiring energy as time passes. Unlike cohesion, or chemical attraction, it exerts its influence upon bodies that are out of contact, and have no material connection, and this necessitates a purely fanciful explanation concerning the medium that conducts such influences, bringing into existence the illogical, hypothetical, fifth ether, made conspicuous by Aristotle."

"What of this ether?" I queried.

"It is a necessity in science, but intangible, undemonstrated, unknown, and wholly theoretical. It is accepted as an existing fluid by scientists, because human theory can not conceive of a substance capable of, or explain how a substance can be capable of affecting a separate body unless there is an intermediate medium to convey force impressions. Hence to material substances Aristotle added (or at least made conspicuous) a speculative ether that, he assumed, pervades all space, and all material bodies as well, in order to account for the passage of heat and light to and from the sun, stars, and planets."

"Explain further," I requested.

"To conceive of such an entity we must imagine a material that is more evanescent than any known gas, even in its most diffused condition. It must combine the solidity of the most perfect conductor of heat (exceeding any known body in this respect to an infinite degree), with the transparency of an absolute vacuum. It must neither create friction by contact with any substance, nor possess attraction for matter; must neither possess weight (and yet carry the force that produces weight), nor respond to the influence of any chemical agent, or exhibit itself to any optical instrument. It must be invisible, and yet carry the force that produces the sensation of sight. It must be of such a nature that it can not, according to our philosophy, affect the corpuscles of earthly substances while permeating them without contact or friction, and yet, as a scientific incongruity, it must act so readily on physical bodies as to convey to the material eye the sensation of sight, and from the sun to creatures on distant planets it must carry the heat force, thus giving rise to the sensation of warmth. Through this medium, yet without sensible contact with it, worlds must move, and planetary systems revolve, cutting and piercing it in every direction, without loss of momentum. And yet, as I have said, this ether must be in such close contact as to convey to them the essence that warms the universe, lights the universe, and must supply the attractive bonds that hold the stellar worlds in position. A nothing in itself, so far as man's senses indicate, the ether of space must be denser than iridium, more mobile than any known liquid, and stronger than the finest steel."

"I can not conceive of such an entity," I replied.

"No; neither can any man, for the theory is irrational, and can not be supported by comparison with laws known to man, but the conception is nevertheless a primary necessity in scientific study. Can man, by any rational theory, combine a vacuum and a substance, and create a result that is neither material nor vacuity, neither something nor nothing, and yet an intensified all; being more attenuated than the most perfect of known vacuums, and a conductor better than the densest metal? This we do when we attempt to describe the scientists' all-pervading ether of space, and to account for its influence on matter. This hypothetical ether is, for want of a better theory of causes, as supreme in philosophy to-day as the alkahest of the talented old alchemist Van Helmont was in former times, a universal spirit that exists in conception, and yet does not exist in perception, and of which modern science knows as little as its speculative promulgator, Aristotle, did. We who pride ourselves on our exact science, smile at some of Aristotle's statements in other directions, for science has disproved them, and yet necessity forces us to accept this illogical ether speculation, which is, perhaps, the most unreasonable of all theories. Did not this Greek philosopher also gravely assert that the lion has but one vertebra in his neck; that the breath of man enters the heart; that the back of the head is empty, and that man has but eight ribs?"

"Aristotle must have been a careless observer," I said.

"Yes," he answered; "it would seem so, and science, to-day, bases its teachings concerning the passage of all forces from planet to planet, and sun to sun, on dicta such as I have cited, and no more reasonable in applied experiment."

"And I have been referred to you as a conscientious scientific teacher," I said; "why do you speak so facetiously?"

"I am well enough versed in what we call science, to have no fear of injuring the cause by telling the truth, and you asked a direct question. If your questions carry you farther in the direction of force studies, accept at once, that, of the intrinsic constitution of force itself, nothing is known. Heat, light, magnetism, electricity, galvanism (until recently known as imponderable bodies) are now considered as modifications of force; but, in my opinion, the time will come when they will be known as disturbances."

"Disturbances of what?"

"I do not know precisely; but of something that lies behind them all, perhaps creates them all, but yet is in essence unknown to men."

"Give me a clearer idea of your meaning."

"It seems impossible," he replied; "I can not find words in which to express myself; I do not believe that forces, as we know them (imponderable bodies), are as modern physics defines them. I am tempted to say that, in my opinion, forces are disturbance expressions of a something with which we are not acquainted, and yet in which we are submerged and permeated. Aristotle's ether perhaps. It seems to me, that, behind all material substances, including forces, there is an unknown spirit, which, by certain influences, may be ruffled into the exhibition of an expression, which exhibition of temper we call a force. From this spirit these force expressions (wavelets or disturbances) arise, and yet they may become again quiescent, and again rest in its absorbing unity. The water from the outlet of a calm lake flows over a gentle decline in ripples, or quiet undulations, over the rapids in musical laughings, over a precipice in thunder tones,—always water, each a different phase, however, to become quiet in another lake (as ripples in this universe may awaken to our perception, to repose again), and still be water."

He hesitated.

"Go on," I said.

"So I sometimes have dared to dream that gravitation may be the reservoir that conserves the energy for all mundane forces, and that what we call modifications of force are intermediate conditions, ripples, rapids, or cascades, in gravitation."

"Continue," I said, eagerly, as he hesitated.

He shook his head.

CHAPTER XXIV.

THE SOLILOQUY OF PROF. DANIEL VAUGHN.—"GRAVITATION IS THE BEGINNING AND GRAVITATION IS THE END; ALL EARTHLY BODIES KNEEL TO GRAVITATION."

"Please continue, I am intensely interested; I wish that I could give you my reasons for the desire; I can not do so, but I beg you to continue."

"I should add," continued Vaughn, ignoring my remarks, "that we have established rules to measure the force of gravitation, and have estimated the decrease of attraction as we leave the surfaces of the planets. We have made comparative estimates of the weight of the earth and planets, and have reason to believe that the force expression of gravitation attains a maximum at about one-sixth the distance toward the center of the earth, then decreases, until at the very center of our planet, matter has no weight. This, together with the rule I repeated a few moments ago, is about all we know, or think we know, of gravitation. Gravitation is the beginning and gravitation is the end; all earthly bodies kneel to gravitation. I can not imagine a Beyond and yet, gravitation," mused the rapt philosopher, "may also be an expression of"—he hesitated again, forgetting me completely, and leaned his shaggy head upon his hands. I realized that his mind was lost in conjecture, and that he was absorbed in the mysteries of the scientific immensity. Would he speak again? I could not think of disturbing his reverie, and minutes passed in silence. Then he slowly, softly, reverently murmured: "Gravitation, Gravitation, thou art seemingly the one permanent, ever present earth-bound expression of Omnipotence. Heat and light come and go, as vapors of water condense into rain and dissolve into vapor to return again to the atmosphere. Electricity and magnetism appear and disappear; like summer storms they move in diversified channels, or even turn and fly from contact with some bodies, seemingly

"SOLILOQUY OF PROF. DANIEL VAUGHN.
'GRAVITATION IS THE BEGINNING, AND GRAVITATION IS THE END; ALL
EARTHLY BODIES KNEEL TO GRAVITATION.'"

forbidden to appear, but thou, Gravitation, art omnipresent and omnipotent. Thou createst motion, and yet maintainest the equilibrium of all things mundane and celestial. An attempt to imagine a body destitute of thy potency, would be to bankrupt and deaden the material universe. O! Gravitation, art thou a voice out of the Beyond, and are other forces but echoes— tremulous reverberations that start into life to vibrate for a spell and die in the space caverns of the universe while thou continuest supreme?"

His bowed head and rounded shoulders stooped yet lower; he unconsciously brushed his shaggy locks with his hand, and seemed to confer with a familiar Being whom others could not see.

"A voice from without," he repeated; "from beyond our realm! Shall the subtle ears of future scientists catch yet lighter echoes? Will the brighter thoughts of more gifted men, under such furtherings as the future may bring, perchance commune with beings who people immensity, distance disappearing before thy ever-reaching spirit? For with thee, who holdest the universe together, space is not space, and there is no word expressing time. Art thou a voice that carriest the history of the past from the past unto and into the present, and for which there is no future, all conditions of time being as one to thee, thy self covering all and connecting all together? Art thou, Gravitation, a voice? If so, there must be a something farther out in those fathomless caverns, beyond mind imaginings, from which thou comest, for how could nothingness have formulated itself into a voice? The suns and universe of suns about us, may be only vacant points in the depths of an all-pervading entity in which even thyself dost exist as a momentary echo, linked to substances ponderous, destined to fade away in the interstellar expanse outside, where disturbances disappear, and matter and gravitation together die; where all is pure, quiescence, peaceful, and dark. Gravitation, Gravitation, imperishable Gravitation; thou seemingly art the ever-pervading, unalterable, but yet moving spirit of a cosmos of solemn mysteries. Art thou now, in unperceived force expressions, speaking to dumb humanity of other universes; of suns and vortices of suns; bringing tidings from the solar planets, or even infinitely distant star mists, the silent unresolved nebulæ, and spreading before earth-bound mortal minds, each instant, fresh tidings from without, that, in ignorance, we can not read? May not beings, perhaps like ourselves but higher in the scale of intelligence, those who people some of the planets about us, even now beckon and try to converse with us through thy subtle, ever-present self? And may not their efforts at communication fail because of our ignorance of a language they can read? Are not light and heat, electricity and magnetism plodding, vascillating agents compared with thy steady existence, and is it even further possible?"—

His voice had gradually lowered, and now it became inaudible; he was oblivious to my presence, and had gone forth from his own self; he was lost in matters celestial, and abstractedly continued unintelligibly to mutter to himself as, brushing his hair from his forehead, he picked up his well-worn felt hat, and placed it awkwardly on his shaggy head, and then shuffled away without bidding me farewell. The bent form, prematurely shattered by privation; uncouth, unkempt, typical of suffering and neglect, impressed me with the fact that in him man's life essence, the immortal mind, had forgotten the material part of man. The physical half of man, even of his own being, in Daniel Vaughn's estimation, was an encumbrance unworthy of serious attention, his spirit communed with the pure in nature, and to him science was a study of the great Beyond.*

---

* Mr. Drury can not claim to have recorded verbatim Prof. Vaughn's remarks, but has endeavored to give the substance. His language was faultless, his word selections beautiful, his soliloquy impressive beyond description. Perhaps Drury even misstated an idea, or more than one, evolved then by the great mind of that patient man. Prof. Daniel Vaughn was fitted for a scientific throne, a position of the highest honor; but, neglected by man, proud as a king, he bore uncomplainingly privations most bitter, and suffered alone until finally he died from starvation and neglect one night, in the city of his adoption, in a barren room, without warmth or light. Some persons are ready to cry "Shame! Shame!" at wealthy Cincinnati; others assert that men could not give to Daniel Vaughn. He would not beg, and knowing his capacities, if he could not procure a position in which to earn a living, he preferred to starve. The only bitterness of his nature, it is said, went out against those who kept from him such employment as returns a livelihood to scientific men, for he well knew his intellect earned for him such a right in Cincinnati, and he starved before he would accept charity. Will the spirit of that great man, talented Daniel Vaughn, bear malice against the people of the city in which none can truthfully deny that he perished from cold and privation? Commemorated is he not by a bust of bronze that distorts the facts in that the garments are not seedy and unkempt, the figure stooping, the cheek hollow and the eye pitifully expressive of an empty stomach? That bust modestly rests in the public library he loved so well, in which he suffered so uncomplainingly, and starved so patiently. Pleasing must be the thought of Cincinnati's citizens, as they pass and repass that cold statue to feel that this model of Daniel Vaughn, with sightless eyes and closed lips, asks neither for food nor warmth.—J. U. L.

I embraced the first opportunity that presented itself to read the works that Prof. Vaughn suggested, and sought him more than once to question further. However, he would not commit himself in regard to the possible existence of other forces than those with which we are acquainted, and when I interrogated him as to possibilities in the study of obscure force expressions, he declined to express an opinion concerning the subject. Indeed, I fancied that he believed it probable, or at least not impossible, that a closer acquaintance with conditions of matter and energy might be the heirloom of future scientific students. At last I gave up the subject, convinced that all the information I was able to obtain from other persons whom I questioned, and whose answers were prompt and positive, was evolved largely from ignorance and self-conceit, and such information was insufficient to satisfy my understanding, or to command my attention. After hearing Vaughn, all other voices sounded empty.

I therefore applied myself to my daily tasks, and awaited the promised return of the interesting, though inscrutible being whose subterranean sojourneying was possibly fraught with so much potential value to science and to man.

THE UNBIDDEN GUEST RETURNS TO READ HIS MANUSCRIPT. CONTINUING HIS NARRATIVE.

CHAPTER XXV.

THE MOTHER OF A VOLCANO.—"YOU CAN NOT DISPROVE, AND YOU DARE NOT ADMIT."

A year from the evening of the departure of the old man, found me in my room, expecting his presence; and I was not surprised when he opened the door, and seated himself in his accustomed chair.

"Are you ready to challenge my statements?" he said, taking up the subject as though our conversation had not been interrupted.

"No."

"Do you accept my history?"

"No."

"You can not disprove, and you dare not admit. Is not that your predicament?" he asked. "You have failed in every endeavor to discredit the truth, and your would-be scientists, much as they would like to do so, can not serve you. Now we will continue the narrative, and I shall await your next attempt to cast a shadow over the facts."

Then with his usual pleasant smile, he read from his manuscript a continuation of the intra-earth journey as follows:

"Be seated," said my eyeless guide, "and I will explain some facts that may prove of interest in connection with the nature of the superficial crust of the earth. This crystal liquid spreading before us is a placid sheet of water, and is the feeder of the volcano, Mount Epomeo."

"Can that be a surface of water?" I interrogated. "I find it hard to realize that water can be so immovable. I supposed the substance before us to be a rigid material, like glass, perhaps."

"There is no wind to ruffle this aqueous surface,—why should it not be quiescent? This is the only perfectly smooth sheet of water that you have ever seen. It is in absolute rest, and thus appears a rigid level plane."

"Grant that your explanation is correct," I said, "yet I can not understand how a quiet lake of water can give rise to a convulsion such as the eruption of a volcano."

"Not only is this possible," he responded, "but water usually causes the exhibition of phenomena known as volcanic action. The Island of Ischia, in which the volcanic crater Epomeo is situated, is connected by a tortuous crevice with the peaceful pool by which we now stand, and at periods, separated by great intervals of time, the lake is partly emptied by a simple natural process, and a part of its water is expelled above the earth's surface in the form of superheated steam, which escapes through that distant crater."

"But I see no evidence of heat or even motion of any kind."

"Not here," he replied; "in this place there is none. The energy is developed thousands of miles away, but since the phenomena of volcanic action are to be partially explained to you at a future day, I will leave that matter for the present. We shall cross this lake."

I observed as we walked along its edge that the shore of the lake was precipitous in places, again formed a gradually descending beach, and the dead silence of the space about us, in connection with the death-like stillness of that rigid mass of water and its surroundings, became increasingly impressive and awe-inspiring. Never before had I seen such a perfectly quiet glass-like surface. Not a vibration or undulation appeared in any direction. The solidity of steel was exemplified in its steady, apparently inflexible contour, and yet the pure element was so transparent that the bottom of the pool was as clearly defined as the top of the cavern above me. The lights and shades of the familiar lakes of Western New York were wanting here, and it suddenly came to my mind that there were surface reflections, but no shadows, and musing on this extraordinary fact, I stood motionless on a jutting cliff absorbed in meditation, abstractedly gazing down into that transparent depth. Without sun or moon, without apparent source of light, and yet perfectly illuminated, the lofty caverns seemed cut by that aqueous plane into two sections, one above and one below a transparent, rigid surface line. The dividing line, or horizontal plane, appeared as much a surface of air as a surface of water, and the material above that plane seemed no more nor less a gas, or liquid, than that beneath it. If two limpid, transparent liquids, immiscible, but of different gravities, be poured into the same vessel, the line of demarkation will be as a brilliant mirror, such as I now beheld parting and yet uniting the surfaces of air and water.

Lost in contemplation, I unconsciously asked the mental question:

"Where are the shadows?"

My guide replied:

"You have been accustomed to lakes on the surface of the earth; water that is illuminated from above; now you see by a light that is developed from within and below, as well as from above. There is no outside point of illumination, for the light of this cavern, as you know, is neither transmitted through an overlying atmosphere nor radiated from a luminous center. It is an inherent quality, and as objects above us and within the lake are illuminated alike from all sides, there can be no shadows."

Musingly, I said:

"That which has occurred before in this journey to the unknown country of which I have been advised, seemed mysterious; but each succeeding step discovers to me another novelty that is more mysterious, with unlooked-for phenomena that are more obscure."

"This phenomenon is not more of a mystery than is the fact that light radiates from the sun. Man can not explain that, and I shall not now attempt to explain this. Both conditions are attributes of force, but with this distinction—the crude light and heat of the sun, such as men experience on the surface of the earth, is here refined and softened, and the characteristic glare and harshness of the light that is known to those who live on the earth's surface is absent here. The solar ray, after penetrating the earth's crust, is tempered and refined by agencies which man will yet investigate understandingly, but which he can not now comprehend."

"WE CAME TO A METAL BOAT."

"Am I destined to deal with these problems?"

"Only in part."

"Are still greater wonders before us?"

"If your courage is sufficient to carry you onward, you have yet to enter the portal of the expanse we approach."

"Lead on, my friend," I cried; "lead on to these undescribed scenes, the occult wonderland that"—

He interrupted me almost rudely, and in a serious manner said:

"Have you not learned that wonder is an exemplification of ignorance? The child wonders at a goblin story, the savage at a trinket, the man of science at an unexplained manifestation of a previously unperceived natural law; each wonders in ignorance, because of ignorance. Accept now that all you have seen from the day of your birth on the surface of the earth, to the present, and all that you will meet here are wonderful only because the finite mind of man is confused with fragments of evidence, that, from whatever direction we meet them, spring from an unreachable infinity. We will continue our journey."

Proceeding farther along the edge of the lake we came to a metallic boat. This my guide picked up as easily as though it were of paper, for be it remembered that gravitation had slackened its hold here. Placing it upon the water, he stepped into it, and as directed I seated myself near the stern, my face to the bow, my back to the shore. The guide, directly in front of me, gently and very slowly moved a small lever that rested on a projection before him, and I gazed intently upon him as we sat together in silence. At last I became impatient, and asked him if we would not soon begin our journey.

"We have been on our way since we have been seated," he answered.

I gazed behind with incredulity: the shore had disappeared, and the diverging wake of the ripples showed that we were rapidly skimming the water.

"This is marvelous," I said; "incomprehensible, for without sail or oar, wind or steam, we are fleeing over a lake that has no current."

"True, but not marvelous. Motion of matter is a result of disturbance of energy connected therewith. Is it not scientifically demonstrated, at least in theory, that if the motion of the spirit that causes the magnetic needle to assume its familiar position were really arrested in the substance of the needle, either the metal would fuse and vaporize or (if the forces did not appear in some other form such as heat, electricity, magnetism, or other force) the needle would be hurled onward with great speed?"

CHAPTER XXVI.

MOTION FROM INHERENT ENERGY.—"LEAD ME DEEPER INTO THIS EXPANDING STUDY."

"I partly comprehend that such would be the case," I said.

"If a series of knife blades on pivot ends be set in a frame, and turned edgewise to a rapid current of water, the swiftly moving stream flows through this sieve of metallic edges about as easily as if there were no obstructions. Slowly turn the blades so as to present their oblique sides to the current, and an immediate pressure is apparent upon the frame that holds them; turn the blades so as to shut up the space, and they will be torn from their sockets, or the entire frame will be shattered into pieces."

"I understand; go on."

"The ethereal current that generates the magnetic force passes through material bodies with inconceivable rapidity, and the molecules of a few substances only, present to it the least obstruction. Material molecules are edgewise in it, and meet no retardation in the subtle flood. This force is a disturbance of space energy that is rushing into the earth in one form, and out of it in another. But your mind is not yet in a condition to grasp the subject, for at best there is no method of explaining to men that which their experimental education has failed to prepare them to receive, and for which first absolutely new ideas, and next words with new meaning, must be formed. Now we, (by we I mean those with whom I am connected) have learned to disturb the molecules in matter so as to turn them partly, or entirely, across the path of this magnetic current, and thus interrupt the motion of this ever-present energy. We can retard its velocity without, however, producing either magnetism (as is the case in a bar of steel), electricity, or heat, but motion instead, and thus a portion of this retarded energy springs into its new existence as motion of my boat. It is force changed into movement of matter, for the molecules of the boat, as a mass, must move onward as the force disappears as a current. Perhaps you can accept now that instead of light, heat, electricity, magnetism, and gravitation being really modifications of force they are disturbances."

"Disturbances of what?"

"Disturbances of motion."

"Motion of what?"

"Motion of itself, pure and simple."

"I can not comprehend, I can not conceive of motion pure and simple."

"I will explain at a future time so that you can comprehend more clearly. Other lessons must come first, but never will you see the end. Truth is infinite."

Continuing, he said:

"Let me ask if there is anything marvelous in this statement. On the earth's surface men arrest the fitful wind, and by so doing divert the energy of its motion into movement of machinery; they induce it to turn mills and propel vessels. This motion of air is a disturbance, mass motion transmitted to the air by heat, heat in turn being a disturbance or interruption of pure motion. When men learn to interrupt this unperceived stream of energy so as to change directly into material motion the spirit that saturates the universe, and that produces force expressions, as it is constantly rushing from earth into space, and from space back again, they will have at command wherever they may be an endless source of power, light, and heat; mass motion, light and heat being convertible. Motion lies behind heat, light, and electricity, and produces them, and so long as the earth revolves on its axis, and circles in its orbit, man needs no light and heat from such indirect sources as combustion. Men will, however, yet obtain motion of molecules (heat), and material mass motion as well, from earth motion, without the other dangerous intermediate force expressions now deemed necessary in their production."

"Do you wish me to understand that on all parts of the earth's surface there is a continual expenditure of energy, an ever-ready current, that is really distinct from the light and heat of the sun, and also that the imponderable bodies that we call heat, light, electricity, and magnetism are not substances at all?"

"Yes," he replied.

"And that this imperceptible something—fluid I will say, for want of a better term—now invisible and unknown to man, is as a medium in which the earth, submerged, floats as a speck of dust in a flood of space?"

"Certainly," he replied.

"Am I to infer from your remarks that, in the course of time, man will be able to economize this force, and adapt it to his wants?"

"Yes."

"Go on with your exposition, I again beg of you; lead me deeper into this expanding study."

"There is but little more that you can comprehend now, as I have said," he answered. "All materials known to man are of coarse texture, and the minds of men are not yet in a condition to comprehend finer exhibitions of force, or of motion modifications. Pure energy, in all its modifications, is absolutely unknown to man. What men call heat, gravitation, light, electricity, and magnetism are the grosser attributes attending alterations in an unknown, attenuated, highly developed force producer. They are results, not causes. The real force, an unreached energy, is now flooding all space, pervading all materials. Everywhere there exists an infinite sea of motion absolute. Since this primeval entity can not now affect matter, as matter is known to man, man's sense can only be influenced by secondary attributes of this energy. Unconscious of its all-pervading presence, however, man is working towards the power that will some day, upon the development of latent senses, open to him this new world. Then at last he will move without muscular exertion, or the use of heat as an agent of motion, and will, as as I am now doing, bridle the motion of space. Wherever he may be situated, there will then be warmth to any degree that he wishes, for he will be able to temper the seasons, and mass motion illimitable, also, for this energy, I reiterate, is omnipresent. However, as you will know more of this before long, we will pass the subject for the present."

My guide slowly moved the lever. I sat in deep reflection, beginning to comprehend somewhat of his reasoning, and yet my mind was more than clouded. The several ambiguous repetitions he had made since our journey commenced, each time suggesting the same idea, clothing it in different forms of expression, impressed me vaguely with the conception of a certain something for which I was gradually being prepared, and that I might eventually be educated to grasp, but which he believed my mind was not yet ready to receive. I gathered from what he said that he could have given clearer explanations than he was now doing, and that he clothed his language intentionally in mysticism, and that, for some reason, he preferred to leave my mind in a condition of uncertainty. The velocity of the boat increased as he again and again cautiously touched the lever, and at last the responsive craft rose nearly out of the water, and skimmed like a bird over its surface. There was no object in that lake of pure crystal to govern me in calculating as to the rapidity of our motion, and I studied to evolve a method by which I could time our movements. With this object in view I tore a scrap from my clothing and tossed it into the air. It fell at my feet as if in a calm. There was no breeze. I picked the fragment up, in bewilderment, for I had expected it to fall behind us. Then it occurred to me, as by a flash, that notwithstanding our apparently rapid motion, there was an entire absence of atmospheric resistance. What could explain the paradox? I turned to my guide and again tossed the fragment of cloth upward, and again it settled at my feet. He smiled, and answered my silent inquiry.

"There is a protecting sheet before us, radiating, fan-like, from the bow of our boat as if a large pane of glass were resting on edge, thus shedding the force of the wind. This diaphragm catches the attenuated atmosphere and protects us from its friction."

"But I see no such protecting object," I answered.

"No; it is invisible. You can not see the obstructing power, for it is really a gyrating section of force, and is colorless. That spray of metal on the brow of our boat is the developer of this protecting medium. Imagine a transverse section of an eddy of water on edge before us, and you can form a comparison. Throw the bit of garment as far as you can beyond the side of the boat."

I did so, and saw it flutter slowly away to a considerable distance parallel with our position in the boat as though in a perfect calm, and then it disappeared. It seemed to have been dissolved. I gazed at my guide in amazement.

"Try again," said he.

"THE BIT OF GARMENT FLUTTERED LISTLESSLY AWAY TO THE SAME DISTANCE, AND THEN – VACANCY."

I tore another and a larger fragment from my coat sleeve. I fixed my eyes closely upon it, and cast it from me. The bit of garment fluttered listlessly away to the same distance, and then—vacancy. Wonders of wonderland, mysteries of the mysterious! What would be the end of this marvelous journey? Suspicion again possessed me, and distrust arose. Could not my self-existence be blotted out in like manner? I thought again of my New York home, and the recollection of upper earth, and those broken family ties brought to my heart a flood of bitter emotions. I inwardly cursed the writer of that alchemistic letter, and cursed myself for heeding the contents.

The tears gushed from my eyes and trickled through my fingers as I covered my face with my hands and groaned aloud. Then, with a gentle touch, my guide's hand rested on my shoulder.

"Calm yourself," he said; "this phenomenon is a natural sequence to a deeper study of nature than man has reached. It is simply the result of an exhibition of rapid motion. You are upon a great underground lake, that, on a shelf of earth substance one hundred and fifty miles below the earth's surface, covers an area of many thousand square miles, and which has an average depth of five miles. We are now crossing it diagonally at a rapid rate by the aid of the force that man will yet use in a perfectly natural manner on the rough upper ocean and bleak lands of the earth's coarse surface. The fragments of cloth disappeared from sight when thrown beyond the influence of our protecting diaphragm, because when they struck the outer motionless atmosphere they were instantly left behind; the eye could not catch their sudden change in motion. A period of time is necessary to convey from eye to mind the sensation of sight. The bullet shot from a gun is invisible by reason of the fact that the eye can not discern the momentary interruption to the light. A cannon ball will compass the field of vision of the eye, moving across it without making itself known, and yet the fact does not excite surprise. We are traveling so fast that small, stationary objects outside our track are invisible."

Then in a kind, pathetic tone of voice, he said:

"An important lesson you should learn, I have mentioned it before. Whatever seems to be mysterious, or marvelous, is only so because of the lack of knowledge of associated natural phenomena and connected conditions. All that you have experienced, all that you have yet to meet in your future journey, is as I have endeavored to teach you, in exact accordance with the laws that govern the universe, of which the earth constitutes so small a portion that, were the conditions favorable, it could be blotted from its present existence as quickly as that bit of garment disappeared, and with as little disturbance of the mechanism of the moving universe."

I leaned over, resting my face upon my elbow; my thoughts were immethodically wandering in the midst of multiplying perplexities; I closed my eyes as a weary child, and slept.

CHAPTER XXVII.

SLEEP, DREAMS, NIGHTMARE.—"STRANGLE THE LIFE FROM MY BODY."

I know not how long I sat wrapped in slumber. Even if my body had not been wearing away as formerly, my mind had become excessively wearied. I had existed in a state of abnormal mental intoxication far beyond the period of accustomed wakefulness, and had taxed my mental organization beyond endurance. In the midst of events of the most startling description, I had abruptly passed into what was at its commencement the sweetest sleep of my recollection, but which came to a horrible termination.

In my dream I was transported once more to my native land, and roamed in freedom throughout the streets of my lost home. I lived over again my early life in Virginia, and I seemed to have lost all recollection of the weird journey which I had lately taken. My subsequent connection with the brotherhood of alchemists, and the unfortunate letter that led to my present condition, were forgotten. There came no thought suggestive of the train of events that are here chronicled, and as a child I tasted again the pleasures of innocence, the joys of boyhood.

Then my dream of childhood vanished, and the scenes of later days spread themselves before me. I saw, after a time, the scenes of my later life, as though I viewed them from a distance, and was impressed with the idea that they were not real, but only the fragments of a dream. I shuddered in my childish dreamland, and trembled as a child would at confronting events of the real life that I had passed through on earth, and that gradually assuming the shape of man approached and stood before me, a hideous specter seemingly ready to absorb me. The peaceful child in which I existed shrunk back, and recoiled from the approaching living man.

"Away, away," I cried, "you shall not grasp me, I do not wish to become a man; this can not, must not be the horrible end to a sweet existence."

Gradually the Man Life approached, seized and enveloped me, closing around me as a jelly fish surrounds its living victim, while the horrors of a nightmare came over my soul.

"Man's life is a fearful dream," I shouted, as I writhed in agony; "I am still a child, and will remain one; keep off! Life of man, away! let me live and die a child."

The Specter of Man's Life seized me more firmly as I struggled to escape, and holding me in its irresistible clutch absorbed my substance as a vampire might suck the blood of an infant, and while the childish dream disappeared in that hideous embrace, the miserable man awoke.

I found myself on land. The guide, seated at my side, remarked:

"You have slept."

"I have lived again," I said in bitterness.

"You have not lived at all as yet," he replied; "life is a dream, usually it is an unsatisfied nightmare."

"Then let me dream again as at the beginning of this slumber," I said; "and while I dream as a child, do you strangle the life from my body,—spare me the nightmare, I would not live to reach the Life of Man."

"This is sarcasm," he replied; "you are as changeable as the winds of the earth's surface. Now as you are about to approach a part of our journey where fortitude is necessary, behold, you waver as a little child might. Nerve yourself; the trials of the present require a steady mind, let the future care for itself; you can not recall the past."

I became attentive again; the depressing effects of that repulsive dream rapidly lifted, and wasted away, as I realized that I was a man, and was destined to see more than can be seen in the future of other mortals. This elevation of my spirit was evidently understood by my guide. He turned to the lake, and pointing to its quiet bosom, remarked:

"For five hours we have journeyed over this sheet of water at the average rate of nine hundred miles an hour. At the time you threw the fragments of cloth overboard, we were traveling at a speed of not less than twenty miles per minute. You remember that some hours ago you criticised my assertion when I said that we would soon be near the axis of the earth beneath the North Pole, and now we are beyond that point, and are about six thousand miles from where we stood at that time."

"You must have your way," I replied; "I can not disprove your assertion, but were it not that I have passed through so many marvelous experiences since first we met, I would question the reliability of your information."

My guide continued:

"The surface of this lake lies as a mirror beneath both the ocean and the land. The force effect that preserves the configuration of the ocean preserves the form of this also, but influences it to a less extent, and the two surfaces lie nearly parallel with each other, this one being one hundred and fifty miles beneath the surface of the earth. The shell of the earth above us is honeycombed by caverns in some places, in others it is compact, and yet, in most places, is impervious to water. At the farther extremity of the lake, a stratum of porous material extends through the space intervening between the bottom of the ocean and this lake. By capillary attraction, assisted by gravitation, part of the water of the ocean is being transferred through this stratum to the underground cavity. The lake is slowly rising."

At this remark I interrupted him: "You say the water in the ocean is being slowly transferred down to this underground lake less by gravity than by capillarity."

"Yes."

"I believe that I have reason to question that statement, if you do not include the salt," I replied.

"Pray state your objections."

I answered: "Whether a tube be long or short, if it penetrate the bottom of a vessel of brine, and extend downward, the brine will flow into and out of it by reason of its weight."

"You mistake," he asserted; "the attraction of the sides of the capillary tube, if the tube is long enough, will eventually separate the water from the salt, and at length a downward flow of water only will result."

I again expressed my incredulity.

"More than this, by perfectly natural laws the water that is freed from the tubes might again force itself upward perfectly fresh, to the surface of the earth—yes, under proper conditions, above the surface of the ocean."

"Do you take me for a fool?" I said. "Is it not self-evident that a fountain can not rise above its source?"

"It often does," he answered.

"You trifle with me," I said, acrimoniously.

"No," he replied; "I am telling you the truth. Have you never heard of what men call artesian wells?"

"Yes, and" (here I attempted in turn to become sarcastic) "have you never learned that they are caused by water flowing into crevices in uplands where layers of stone or of clay strata separated by sand or gravel slant upward. The water conducted thence by these channels afterwards springs up in the valleys to which it has been carried by means of the crevices in these strata, but it never rises above its source."

To my surprise he answered:

"This is another of man's scientific speculations, based on some facts, it is true, and now and then correct, but not invariably. The water of an artesian well on an elevated plane may flow into the earth from a creek, pond, or river, that is lower than the mouth of the well it feeds, and still it may spout into the air from either a near or distant elevation that is higher than its source."

"I can not admit the truth of this," I said; "I am willing to listen to reason, but such statements as these seem altogether absurd."

"As you please," he replied; "we will continue our journey."

INTERLUDE.—THE STORY INTERRUPTED.

CHAPTER XXVIII.

A CHALLENGE.—MY UNBIDDEN GUEST ACCEPTS IT.

The white-haired reader, in whom I had now become deeply interested, no longer an unwelcome stranger, suspended his reading, laid down his manuscript, and looking me in the face, asked:

"Are you a believer?"

"No," I promptly answered.

"What part of the narrative do you question?"

"All of it."

"Have you not already investigated some of the statements I previously made?" he queried.

"Yes," I said; "but you had not then given utterance to such preposterous expressions."

"Is not the truth, the truth?" he answered.

"You ask me to believe impossibilities," I replied.

"Name one."

"You yourself admit," I said warmly, "that you were incredulous, and shook your head when your guide asserted that the bottom of the ocean might be as porous as a sieve, and still hold water. A fountain can not rise above its source."

"It often does, however," he replied.

"I do not believe you," I said boldly. "And, furthermore, I assert that you might as reasonably ask me to believe that I can see my own brain, as to accept your fiction regarding the production of light, miles below the surface of the earth."

"I can make your brain visible to you, and if you dare to accompany me, I will carry you beneath the surface of the earth and prove my other statement," he said. "Come!" He arose and grasped my arm.

I hesitated.

"You confess that you fear the journey."

I made no reply.

"Well, since you fear that method, I am ready to convince you of the facts by any rational course you may select, and if you wish to stake your entire argument on the general statement that a stream of water can not rise above its head, I will accept the challenge; but I insist that you do not divulge the nature of the experiment until, as you are directed, you make public my story."

"Of course a fluid can be pumped up," I sarcastically observed. "However, I promise the secrecy you ask."

"I am speaking seriously," he said, "and I have accepted your challenge; your own eyes shall view the facts, your own hands prepare the conditions necessary. Procure a few pints of sand, and a few pounds of salt; to-morrow evening I will be ready to make the experiment."

"Agreed; if you will induce a stream of water to run up hill, a fountain to rise above its head, I will believe any statement you may henceforth make."

"Be ready, then," he replied, "and procure the materials named." So saying he picked up his hat and abruptly departed.

These substances I purchased the next day, procuring the silver sand from Gordon's pharmacy, corner of Eighth and Western Row, and promptly at the specified time we met in my room.

He came, provided with a cylindrical glass jar about eighteen inches high and two inches in diameter (such as I have since learned is called a hydrometer jar), and a long, slender drawn glass tube, the internal diameter of which was about one-sixteenth of an inch.

"You have deceived me," I said; "I know well enough that capillary attraction will draw a liquid above its surface. You demonstrated that quite recently to my entire satisfaction."

"True, and yet not true of this experiment," he said. "I propose to force water through and out of this tube; capillary attraction will not expel a liquid from a tube if its mouth be above the surface of the supply."

He dipped the tip of a capillary tube into a tumbler of water; the water rose inside the tube about an inch above the surface of the water in the tumbler.

"Capillary attraction can do no more," he said. "Break the tube one-eighth of an inch above the water (far below the present capillary surface), and it will not overflow. The exit of the tube must be lower than the surface of the liquid if circulation ensues."

He broke off a fragment, and the result was as predicted.

Then he poured water into the glass jar to the depth of about six inches, and selecting a piece of very thin muslin, about an inch square, turned it over the end of the glass tube, tied it in position, and dropped that end of the tube into the cylinder.

"The muslin simply prevents the tube from filling with sand," he explained. Then he poured sand into the cylinder until it reached the surface of the water. (See Figure 23.)

"Your apparatus is simple enough," I remarked, I am afraid with some sarcasm.

"Nature works with exceeding simplicity," he replied; "there is no complex apparatus in her laboratory, and I copy after nature."

Then he dissolved the salt in a portion of water that he drew from the hydrant into my wash bowl, making a strong brine, and stirred sand into the brine to make a thick mush. This mixture of sand and brine he then poured into the cylinder, filling it nearly to the top. (See Figure 23, B. The sand settling soon left a layer of brine above it, as shown by A.) I had previously noticed that the upper end of the glass tube was curved, and my surprise can be imagined when I saw that at once water began to flow through the tube, dropping quite rapidly into the cylinder. The lower end of the curve of the glass tube was fully half an inch above the surface of the liquid in the cylinder.

I here present a figure of the apparatus. (Figure 23.)

The strange man, or man image, I do not know which, sat before me, and in silence we watched the steady flow of water, water rising above its surface and flowing into the reservoir from which it was being continually derived.

"Do you give up?" he asked.

"Let me think," I said.

"As you please," he replied.

"How long will this continue?" I inquired.

"Until strong salt water flows from the tube."

Then the old man continued:

"I would suggest that after I depart you repeat these experiments. The observations of those interested in science must be repeated time and again by separate individuals. It is not sufficient that one person should observe a phenomenon; repeated experiments are necessary in order to overcome error of manipulation, and to convince others of their correctness. Not only yourself, but many others, after this manuscript appears, should go through with similar investigations, varied in detail as mind expansion may suggest. This experiment is but the germ of a thought which will be enlarged upon by many minds under other conditions. An event meteorological may occur in the experience of one observer, and never repeat itself. This is possible. The results of such experiments as you are observing, however, must be followed by similar results in the hands of others, and in behalf of science it is necessary that others should be able to verify your experience. In the time to come it will be necessary to support your statements in order to demonstrate that your perceptive faculties are now in a normal condition. Are you sure that your conceptions of these results are justified by normal perception? May you not be in an exalted state of mind that hinders clear perception, and compels you to imagine and accept as fact that which does not exist? Do you see what you think you see? After I am gone, and the influences that my person and mind exert on your own mind have been removed, will these results, as shown by my experiments, follow similar experimental conditions? In the years that are to pass before this paper is to be made public, it will be your duty to verify your present sense faculty. This you must do as opportunities present, and with different devices, so that no question may arise as to what will follow when others repeat our experiments. To-morrow evening I will call again, but remember, you must not tell others of this experiment, nor show the devices to them."

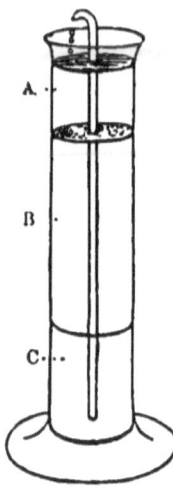

FIG. 23.
A, brine.
B, sand and brine mixed.
C, sand and water.

"I have promised," I answered.

He gathered his manuscript and departed, and I sat in meditation watching the mysterious fountain.

As he had predicted, finally, after a long time, the flow slackened, and by morning, when I arose from my bed, the water had ceased to drip, and then I found it salty to the taste.

The next evening he appeared as usual, and prepared to resume his reading, making no mention of the previous test of my faith. I interrupted him, however, by saying that I had observed that the sand had settled in the cylinder, and that in my opinion his experiment was not true to appearances, but was a deception, since the sand by its greater weight displaced the water, which escaped through the tube, where there was least resistance.

"Ah," he said, "and so you refuse to believe your own eyesight, and are contriving to escape the deserved penalty; I will, however, acquiesce in your outspoken desire for further light, and repeat the experiment without using sand. But I tell you that mother earth, in the phenomena known as artesian wells, uses sand and clay, pools of mineral waters of different gravities, and running streams. The waters beneath the earth are under pressure, induced by such natural causes as I have presented you in miniature, the chief difference being that the supplies of both salt and fresh water are inexhaustible, and by natural combinations similar to what you have seen; the streams within the earth, if a pipe be thrust into them, may rise continuously, eternally, from a reservoir higher than the head. In addition, there are pressures of gases, and solutions of many salts, other than chloride of soda, that tend to favor the phenomenon. You are unduly incredulous, and you ask of me more than your right after staking your faith on an experiment of your own selection. You demand more of me even than nature often accomplishes in earth structure; but to-morrow night I will show you that this seemingly impossible feat is possible."

He then abruptly left the room. The following evening he presented himself with a couple of one-gallon cans, one of them without a bottom. I thought I could detect some impatience of manner as he filled the perfect can (1) with water from the hydrant, and having spread a strip of thin muslin over the mouth of the other can (B), pressed it firmly over the mouth (C) of the can of water, which it fitted tightly, thus connecting them together, the upper (bottomless) can being inverted. Then he made a narrow slit in the center of the muslin with his pen-knife, and through it thrust a glass tube like that of our former experiment. Next he wrapped a string around the open top of the upper can, crossed it over the top, and tied the glass tube to the center of the cross string.

"Simply to hold this tube in position," he explained.

The remainder of the bag of salt left from the experiment of the preceding evening was then dissolved in water, and the brine poured into the upper can, filling it to the top. Then carefully thrusting the glass tube downward, he brought the tip of the curve to within about one-half inch of the surface of the brine, when immediately a rapid flow of liquid exhibited itself. (Figure 24.)

"It rises above its source without sand," he observed.

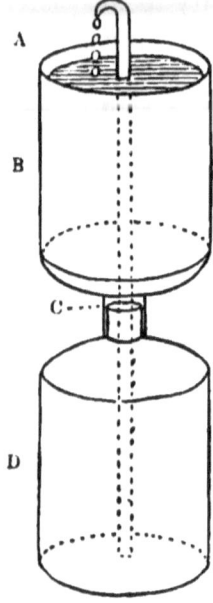

FIG. 24.
A, surface of brine.
B, upper can filled with brine.
C, necks of cans telescoped.
D, lower can full of water.

"I can not deny the fact," I replied, "and furthermore I am determined that I shall not question any subsequent statement that you may make." We sat in silence for some time, and the water ran continuously through the tube. I was becoming alarmed, afraid of my occult guest, who accepted my self-selected challenges, and worked out his results so rapidly; he seemed to be more than human.

"I am a mortal, but a resident of a higher plane than you," he replied, divining my thoughts. "Is not this experiment a natural one?"

"Yes," I said.

"Did not Shakspeare write, 'There are more things in heaven and earth, Horatio, than are dreamt of in your philosophy'?"

"Yes," I said.

And my guest continued:

"He might have added, 'and always will be'."

"Scientific men will explain this phenomenon," I suggested. "Yes, when they observe the facts," he replied, "it is very simple. They can now tell, as I have before remarked, how Columbus stood the egg on end; however, given the problem before Columbus expounded it, they would probably have wandered as far from the true solution as the mountain with its edgewise layers of stone is from the disconnected artesian wells on a distant sea coast where the underground fresh and salt water in overlying currents and layers clash together. The explanation, of course, is simple. The brine is of greater specific gravity than the pure water; the pressure of the heavier fluid forces the lighter up in the tube. This action continues until, as you will see by this experiment, in the gradual diffusion of brine and pure water the salt is disseminated equally throughout the vessels, and the specific gravity of the mixed liquid becomes the same throughout, when the flow will cease. However, in the earth, where supplies are inexhaustible, the fountain flows unceasingly."

CHAPTER XXIX.

BEWARE OF BIOLOGY, THE SCIENCE OF THE LIFE OF MAN.*

The old man relates a story as an object lesson.

"But you have not lived up to the promise; you have evaded part of the bargain," I continued. "While you have certainly performed some curious experiments in physics which seem to be unique, yet, I am only an amateur in science, and your hydrostatic illustrations may be repetitions of investigations already recorded, that have escaped the attention of the scientific gentlemen to whom I have hitherto applied."

"Man's mind is a creature of doubts and questions," he observed. "Answer one query, and others rise. His inner self is never satisfied, and you are not to blame for wishing for a sign, as all self-conscious conditions of your former existence compel. Now that I have brushed aside the more prominent questionings, you insist upon those omitted, and appeal to me to"—he hesitated.

"To what?" I asked, curious to see if he had intuitively grasped my unspoken sentence.

"To exhibit to you your own brain," he replied.

"That is it exactly," I said; "you promised it, and you shall be held strictly to your bargain. You agreed to show me my own brain, and it seems evident that you have purposely evaded the promise."

"That I have made the promise and deferred its completion can not be denied, but not by reason of an inability to fulfill the contract. I will admit that I purposely deferred the exhibition, hoping on your own account that you would forget the hasty promise. You would better release me from the promise; you do not know what you ask."

"I believe that I ask more than you can perform," I answered, "and that you know it."

---

* The reader is invited to skip this chapter of horrors.—J. U. L.

"Let me give you a history," he said, "and then perhaps you will relent. Listen. A man once became involved in the study of anatomy. It led him to destruction. He commenced the study in order to learn a profession; he hoped to become a physician. Materia medica, pharmacy, chemistry, enticed him at first, but after a time presented no charms. He was a dull student in much that men usually consider essential to the practice of medicine. He was not fitted to be a physician. Gradually he became absorbed in two branches, physiology and anatomy. Within his mental self a latent something developed that neither himself nor his friends had suspected. This was an increasing desire for knowledge concerning the human body. The insatiable craving for anatomy grew upon him, and as it did so other sections of medicine were neglected. Gradually he lost sight of his professional object; he dropped chemistry, materia medica, pharmacy, and at last, morbidly lived only in the aforenamed two branches.

"His first visit to the dissecting room was disagreeable. The odor of putrid flesh, the sight of the mutilated bodies repulsed him. When first his hand, warm in life, touched the clammy flesh of a corpse, he shuddered. Then when his fingers came in contact with the viscera of a cadaver, that of a little child, he cried out in horror. The demonstrator of anatomy urged him on; he finally was induced to dissect part of the infant. The reflex action on his sensitive mind first stunned, and then warped his senses. His companions had to lead him from the room. 'Wash it off, wash it off,' he repeated, trying to throw his hand from his person. 'Horrid, horrible, unclean. The child is yet before me,' he insisted. Then he went into a fever and raved. 'Some mother will meet me on the street and curse me,' he cried. "That hand is red with the blood of my darling; it has desecrated the innocent dead, and mutilated that which is most precious to a mother." Take the hand away, wash it,' he shouted. 'The mother curses me; she demands retribution. Better that a man be dead than cursed by a mother whose child has been desecrated.' So the unfortunate being raved, dreaming all manner of horrid imaginings. But at last he recovered, a different man. He returned voluntarily to the dissecting-room, and wrapped himself in the uncouth work.

Nothing in connection with corpse-mutilation was now offensive or unclean. He threw aside his other studies, he became a slave possessed of one idea. He scarcely took time to dine respectably; indeed, he often ate his lunch in the dissecting-room. The blood of a child was again and again on his fingers; it mattered not, he did not take the trouble to wash it off. 'The liver of man is not more sacred than the liver of a hog,' he argued; 'the flesh of a man is the same as other forms of animal food. When a person dies the vital heat escapes, consciousness is dissipated, and the cold, rigid remains are only animal. Consciousness and life are all that is of man—one is force, the other matter; when man dies both perish and are dissipated.' His friends perceived his fondness for dissection, and argued with him again, endeavoring now to overcome his infatuation; he repelled them. 'I learned in my vision,' he said, referring to his fever, 'that Pope was right in saying that the "proper study of mankind is man"; I care nothing for your priestly superstitions concerning the dead. These fables are the invention of designing churchmen who live on the superstitions of the ignorant. I am an agnostic, and believe in no spirit intangible; that which can be seen, felt, and weighed is, all else is not. Life is simply a sensation. All beyond is chimerical, less than fantastic, believed in only by dupes and weak-minded, credulous tools of knaves, or creatures of blind superstition.' He carried the finely articulated, bleached skull of a cadaver to his room, and placed it beside a marble statue that was a valued heirloom, the model of Venus of Milo. 'Both are lime compounds,' he cynically observed, 'neither is better than the other.' His friends protested. 'Your superstitious education is at fault,' he answered; 'you mentally clothe one of these objects in a quality it does not deserve, and the thought creates a pleasant emotion. The other, equally as pure, reminds you of the grave that you fear, and you shudder. These mental pulsations are artificial, both being either survivals of superstition, or creations of your own mind. The lime in the skull is now as inanimate as that of the statue; neither object is responsible for its form, neither is unclean. To me, the delicate configuration, the exact articulation, the perfect adaptation for the office it originally filled, makes each bone of this skull a thing of beauty, an object of admiration. As a whole, it gives me pleasure to think of this wonderful, exquisitely arranged piece of mechanism. The statue you admire is in every respect outrivaled by the skull, and I have placed the two together because it pleases me to demonstrate that man's most artistic creation is far inferior to material man. Throw aside your sentimental prejudices, and join with me in the admiration of this thing of beauty;' and he toyed with the skull as if it were a work of art. So he argued, and arguing passed from bone to bone, and from organ to organ. He filled his room with abnormal fragments of the human body, and surrounded himself with jars of preserved anatomical specimens. His friends fled in disgust, and he smiled, glad to be alone with his ghastly subjects. He was infatuated in one of the alcoves of science."

The old man paused.

"Shall I proceed?" he asked.

"Yes," I said, but involuntarily moved my chair back, for I began again to be afraid of the speaker.

"At last this scientific man had mastered all that was known concerning physiology and anatomy. He learned by heart the wording of great volumes devoted to these subjects. The human frame became to him as an open book. He knew the articulation of every muscle, could name a bone from a mere fragment. The microscope ceased to be an object of interest, the secrets of pathology and physiology had been mastered. Then, unconsciously, he was infected by another tendency; a new thought was destined to dominate his brain. 'What is it that animates this frame? What lies inside to give it life?' He became enthused again: 'The dead body, to which I have given my time, is not the conscious part of man,' he said to himself; 'I must find this thing of life within; I have been only a butcher of the dead. My knowledge is superficial.'"

Again the old man hesitated and looked at me inquiringly.

"Shall I proceed?" he repeated.

I was possessed by horror, but yet fascinated, and answered determinedly: "Go on."

"Beware," he added, "beware of the Science of Life."

Pleadingly he looked at me.

"Go on," I commanded.

He continued:

"With the cunning of a madman, this person of profound learning, led from the innocence of ignorance to the heartlessness of advanced biological science, secretly planned to seek the vital forces. 'I must begin with a child, for the life essence shows its first manifestations in children,' he reasoned. He moved to an unfrequented locality, discharged his servants, and notified his former friends that visitors were unwelcome. He had determined that no interruption to his work should occur. This course was unnecessary, however, for now he had neither friends nor visitors. He employed carpenters and artisans, and perfected a series of mechanical tables, beautiful examples of automatic mechanism. From the inner room of that house no cry could be heard by persons outside. . . .

[It will be seen, by referring to the epilogue, that Mr. Drury agreed to mutilate part of the book. This I have gladly done, excising the heart-rending passages that follow. To use the words of Prof. Venable, they do not "comport with the general delicacy of the book."—J. U. L.]

"Hold, old man, cease," I cried aghast; "I have had enough of this. You trifle with me, demon; I have not asked for nightmare stories, heart-curdling accounts of maniacal investigators, who madly pursue their revolting calling, and discredit the name of science."

"You asked to see you own brain," he replied.

"And have been given a terrible story instead," I retorted.

"So men perverted, misconstruing the aim of science, answer the cry of humanity," he said. "One by one the cherished treasures of Christianity have been stolen from the faithful. What, to the mother, can replace the babe that has been lost?"

"The next world," I answered, "offers a comfort."

"Bah," he said; "does not another searcher in that same science field tell the mother that there is no personal hereafter, that she will never see her babe again? One man of science steals the body, another man of science takes away the soul, the third annihilates heaven; they go like pestilence and famine, hand in hand, subsisting on all that craving humanity considers sacred, and offering no tangible return beyond a materialistic present. This same science that seems to be doing so much for humanity will continue to elevate so-called material civilization until, as the yeast ferment is smothered in its own excretion, so will science-thought create conditions to blot itself from existence, and destroy the civilization it creates. Science is heartless, notwithstanding the personal purity of the majority of her helpless votaries. She is a thief not of ordinary riches, but of treasures

"RISING ABRUPTLY, HE GRASPED MY HAND."

that can not be replaced. Before science provings the love of a mother perishes, the hope of immortality is annihilated. Beware of agnosticism, the end of the science of man. Beware of the beginning of biological inquiry, for he who commences, can not foresee the termination. I say to you in candor, no man ever engaged in the part of science lore that questions the life essence, realizing the possible end of his investigations. The insiduous servant becomes a tyrannical master; the housebreaker is innocent, the horse thief guiltless in comparison. Science thought begins in the brain of man; science provings end all things with the end of the material brain of man. Beware of your own brain."

"I have no fear," I replied, "that I will ever be led to disturb the creeds of the faithful, and I will not be diverted. I demand to see my brain."

"Your demand shall now be fulfilled; you have been warned of the return that may follow the commencement of this study, you force the issue; my responsibility ceases. No man of science realized the end when he began to investigate his throbbing brain, and the end of the fabric that science is weaving for man rests in the hidden future. The story I have related is a true one, as thousands of faithful men who unconsciously have been led into infidelity have experienced; and as the faithful followers of sacred teachings can also perceive, who recognize that their religion and the hope of heaven is slipping away beneath the steady inroad of the heartless materialistic investigator, who clothes himself in the garb of science."

Rising abruptly from his chair, he grasped my hand. "You shall see your brain, man; come."

CHAPTER XXX.

LOOKING BACKWARD.—THE LIVING BRAIN.

The old man accompanied his word "come," as I have said, by rising from his chair, and then with a display of strength quite out of proportion to his age, he grasped my wrist and drew me toward the door. Realizing at once that he intended I should accompany him into the night, I protested saying that I was quite unprepared.

"My hat, at least," I insisted, as he made no recognition of my first demur.

"Your hat is on your head," he replied.

This was true, although I am sure the hat had been previously hung on a rack in a distant part of the room, and I am equally certain that neither my companion nor myself had touched it. Leaving me no time for reflection, he opened the door, and drew me through the hallway and into the gloom. As though perfectly familiar with the city, he guided me from my cozy home, on the retired side street in which I resided, eastwardly into the busy thoroughfare, Western Row. Our course led us down towards the river, past Ninth, Eighth, Seventh Streets. Now and then a pedestrian stopped to gaze in surprise at the unique spectacle, the old man leading the young one, but none made any attempt to molest us. We passed on in silence, out of the busy part of the thoroughfare and into the shady part of the city, into the darkness below Fifth Street. Here the residences were poorer, and tenement-houses and factories began to appear. We were now in a quarter of the city into which strangers seldom, if ever, penetrated after night, and in which I would not have cared to be found unprotected at any time after sunset, much less in such questionable company. I protested against the indiscretion; my leader made no reply, but drew me on past the flickering gas lights that now and then appeared at the intersection of Third, Pearl, Second, and

Water Streets, until at last we stood, in darkness, on the bank of the Ohio River.

Strange, the ferry-boat at that time of night only made a trip every thirty minutes, and yet it was at the landing as though by appointment. Fear began to possess me, and as my thoughts recur to that evening, I can not understand how it was that I allowed myself to be drawn without cry or resistance from my secure home to the Ohio River, in such companionship. I can account for the adventure only by the fact that I had deliberately challenged my companion to make the test he was fulfilling, and that an innate consciousness of pride and justice compelled me to permit him to employ his own methods. We crossed the river without speaking, and rapidly ascending the levee we took our course up Main Street into Covington. Still in the lead, my aged guide, without hesitation, went onward to the intersection of Main and Pike Streets; thence he turned to the right, and following the latter thoroughfare we passed the old tannery, that I recalled as a familiar landmark, and then started up the hill. Onward we strode, past a hotel named "Niemeyer's," and soon were in the open country on the Lexington Pike, treading through the mud, diagonally up the hill back of Covington. Then, at a sharp curve in the road where it rounded the point of the hill, we left the highway, and struck down the hillside into a ravine that bounded the lower side of the avenue. We had long since left the city lamps and sidewalks behind us, and now, when we left the roadway, were on the muddy pike at a considerable elevation upon the hillside and, looking backward, I beheld innumerable lights throughout the cities of Cincinnati, Covington, and the village of Newport, sparkling away in the distance behind and below us.

"Come," my companion said again, as I hesitated, repeating the only word he had uttered since telling his horrible story, "Come!"

Down the hill into the valley we plunged, and at last he opened the door of an isolated log cabin, which we entered. He lighted a candle that he drew from his pocket, and together we stood facing each other.

"Be seated," he said dryly.

And then I observed that the cold excuse for furniture in that desolate room consisted of a single rude, hand-made chair with corn-shuck bottom. However, I did not need a second invitation, but sank exhausted and disconsolate upon the welcome object.

My companion lost no time, but struck at once into the subject that concerned us, arguing as follows:

"One of the troubles with humanity is that of changing a thought from the old to a new channel; to grasp at one effort an entirely new idea is an impossibility. Men follow men in trains of thought expression, as in bodily form generations of men follow generations. A child born with three legs is a freak of nature, a monstrosity, yet it sometimes appears. A man possessed of a new idea is an anomaly, a something that may not be impossible, but which has never appeared. It is almost as difficult to conceive of a new idea as it is to create out of nothing a new material or an element. Neither thoughts nor things can be invented, both must be evolved out of a preëxisting something which it necessarily resembles. Every advanced idea that appears in the brain of man is the result of a suggestion from without. Men have gone on and on ceaselessly, with their minds bent in one direction, ever looking outwardly, never inwardly. It has not occurred to them to question at all in the direction of backward sight. Mind has been enabled to read the impressions that are made in and on the substance of brain convolutions, but at the same time has been and is insensible to the existence of the convolutions themselves. It is as though we could read the letters of the manuscript that bears them without having conceived of a necessity for the existence of a printed surface, such as paper or anything outside the letters. Had anatomists never dissected a brain, the human family would to-day live in absolute ignorance of the nature of the substance that lies within the skull. Did you ever stop to think that the mind can not now bring to the senses the configuration, or nature, of the substance in which mind exists? Its own house is unknown. This is in consequence of the fact that physical existence has always depended upon the study of external surroundings, and consequently the power of internal sight lies undeveloped. It has never been deemed necessary for man to attempt to view the internal construction of his body, and hence the sense of feeling only advises him of that which lies within his own self. This sense is abstract, not descriptive. Normal organs have no sensible existence. Thus an abnormal condition of an organ creates the sensation of pain or pleasure, but discloses nothing concerning the appearance or construction of the organ affected. The perfect liver is as vacancy. The normal brain never throbs and aches. The quiescent arm presents no evidence to the mind concerning its shape, size, or color. Man can not count his fingers unless some outside object touches them, or they press successively against each other, or he perceives them by sight. The brain of man, the seat of knowledge, in which mind centers, is not perceptible through the senses. Does it not seem irrational, however, to believe that mind itself is not aware, or could not be made cognizant, of the nature of its material surroundings?"

"I must confess that I have not given the subject a thought," I replied.

"As I predicted," he said. "It is a step toward a new idea, and simple as it seems, now that the subject has been suggested, you must agree that thousands of intelligent men have not been able to formulate the thought. The idea had never occurred to them. Even after our previous conversation concerning the possibility of showing you your own brain, you were powerless and could not conceive of the train of thought which I started, and along which I shall now further direct your senses."

"The eye is so constituted that light produces an impression on a nervous film in the rear of that organ, this film is named the retina, the impression being carried backward therefrom through a magma of nerve fibers (the optic nerve), and reaching the brain, is recorded on that organ and thus affects the mind. Is it not rational to suppose it possible for this sequence to be reversed? In other words, if the order were reversed could not the same set of nerves carry an impression from behind to the retina, and picture thereon an image of the object which lies anterior thereto, to be again, by reflex action, carried back to the brain, thus bringing the brain substance itself to the view of the mind, and thus impress the senses. To recapitulate: If the nerve sensation, or force expression, should travel from the

"FACING THE OPEN WINDOW HE TURNED THE PUPILS OF HIS EYES UPWARD."

brain to the retina, instead of from an outward object, it will on the reverse of the retina produce the image of that which lies behind, and then if the optic nerve carry the image back to the brain, the mind will bring to the senses the appearance of the image depicted thereon."

"This is my first consideration of the subject," I replied.

"Exactly," he said; "you have passed through life looking at outside objects, and have been heedlessly ignorant of your own brain. You have never made an exclamation of surprise at the statement that you really see a star that exists in the depths of space millions of miles beyond our solar system, and yet you became incredulous and scornful when it was suggested that I could show you how you could see the configuration of your brain, an object with which the organ of sight is nearly in contact. How inconsistent."

"The chain of reasoning is certainly novel, and yet I can not think of a mode by which I can reverse my method of sight and look backward," I now respectfully answered.

"It is very simple; all that is required is a counter excitation of the nerve, and we have with us to-night what any person who cares to consider the subject can employ at any time, and thus behold an outline of a part of his own brain. I will give you the lesson."

Placing himself before the sashless window of the cabin, which opening appeared as a black space pictured against the night, the sage took the candle in his right hand, holding it so that the flame was just below the tip of the nose, and about six inches from his face. Then facing the open window he turned the pupils of his eyes upward, seeming to fix his gaze on the upper part of the open window space, and then he slowly moved the candle transversely, backward and forward, across, in front of his face, keeping it in such position that the flickering flame made a parallel line with his eyes, and as just remarked, about six inches from his face, and just below the tip of his nose. Speaking deliberately, he said:

"Now, were I you, this movement would produce a counter irritation of the retina; a rhythm of the optic nerve would follow, a reflex action of the brain accompanying, and now a figure of part of the brain that rests against the skull in the back of my head would be pictured on the retina. I would see it plainly, apparently pictured or thrown across the open space before me."

"Incredible!" I replied.

"Try for yourself," quietly said my guide.

Placing myself in the position designated, I repeated the maneuver, when slowly a shadowy something seemed to be

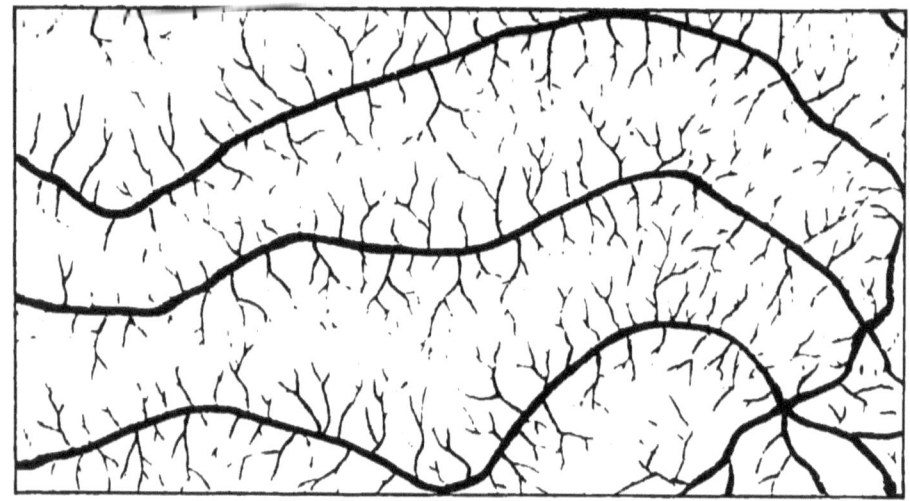

"A BRAIN, A LIVING BRAIN, MY OWN BRAIN."

evolved out of the blank space before me. It seemed to be as a gray veil, or like a corrugated sheet as thin as gauze, which as I gazed upon it and discovered its outline, became more apparent and real. Soon the convolutions assumed a more decided form, the gray matter was visible, filled with venations, first gray and then red, and as I became familiar with the sight, suddenly the convolutions of a brain in all its exactness, with a network of red blood venations, burst into existence.*

I beheld a brain, a brain, a living brain, my own brain, and as an uncanny sensation possessed me I shudderingly stopped the motion of the candle, and in an instant the shadowy figure disappeared.

"Have I won the wager?"

"Yes," I answered.

---

* This experiment seems unfamiliar, and yet no claim is made to originality—J. U. L.

"Then," said my companion, "make no further investigations in this direction."

"But I wish to verify the experiment," I replied. "Although it is not a pleasant test, I can not withstand the temptation to repeat it."

And again I moved the candle backward and forward, when the figure of my brain sprung at once into existence.

"It is more vivid," I said; "I see it plainer, and more quickly than before."

"Beware of the science of man I repeat," he replied; "now, before you are deep in the toils, and can not foresee the end, beware of the science of human biology. Remember the story recently related, that of the physician who was led to destruction by the alluring voice."

I made no reply, but stood with my face fixed, slowly moving the candle backward and forward, gazing intently into the depths of my own brain.

After a time the old man removed the candle from my hand, and said: "Do you accept the fact? Have I demonstrated the truth of the assertion?"

"Yes," I replied; "but tell me further, now that you have excited my interest, have I seen and learned all that man can discover in this direction?"

"No; you have seen but a small portion of the brain convolutions, only those that lie directly back of the optic nerve. By systematic research, under proper conditions, every part of the living brain may become as plainly pictured as that which you have seen."

"And is that all that could be learned?" I asked.

"No," he continued. "Further development may enable men to picture the figures engraved on the convolutions, and at last to read the thoughts that are engraved within the brains of others, and thus through material investigation the observer will perceive the recorded thought of another person. An instrument capable of searching and illuminating the retina could be easily affixed to the eye of a criminal, after which, if the mind of the person operated upon were stimulated by the suggestion of an occurrence either remote or recent, the mind faculty would excite the brain, produce the record, and spread the circumstances as a picture before the observer. The brain would tell its own story, and the investigator could read the truth as recorded in the brain of the other man. A criminal subjected to such an examination could not tell an untruth, or equivocate; his very brain would present itself to the observer."

"And you make this assertion, and then ask me to go no further into the subject?"

"Yes; decidedly yes."

"Tell me, then, could you not have performed this experiment in my room, or in the dark cellar of my house?"

"Any one can repeat it with a candle in any room not otherwise lighted, by looking at a blackboard, a blank wall, or black space," he said.

I was indignant.

"Why have you treated me so inhumanly? Was there a necessity for this journey, these mysterious movements, this physical exertion? Look at the mud with which I am covered, and consider the return trip which yet lies before me, and which must prove even more exhausting?"

"Ah," he said, "you overdraw. The lesson has been easily acquired. Science is not an easy road to travel. Those who propose to profit thereby must work circuitously, soil their hands and person, meet discouragements, and must expect hardships, reverses, abuse, and discomfort. Do not complain, but thank me for giving you the lesson without other tribulations that might have accompanied it. Besides, there was another object in my journey, an object that I have quietly accomplished, and which you may never know. Come, we must return."

He extinguished the light of the candle, and we departed together, trudging back through the mud and the night.*

Of that wearisome return trip I have nothing to say beyond the fact that before reaching home my companion disappeared in the darkness of a side street, and that the Cathedral chimes were playing for three o'clock A. M., as I passed the corner of Eighth Street and Western Row.

The next evening my visitor appeared as usual, and realizing his complete victory, he made no reference to the occurrences

---

* We must acquiesce in the explanation given for this seemingly uncalled-for journey, and yet feel that it was unnecessarily exacting.

of the previous night. In his usual calm and deliberate manner he produced the roll of manuscript saying benignantly, and in a gentle tone:

"Do you recollect where I left off reading?"

"You had reached that point in your narrative," I answered, "at which your guide had replaced the boat on the surface of the lake."

And the mysterious being resumed his reading.

THE MANUSCRIPT CONTINUED.

CHAPTER XXXI.

A LESSON ON VOLCANOES.—PRIMARY COLORS ARE CAPABLE OF FARTHER SUBDIVISION.

"Get into the boat," said my eyeless pilot, "and we will proceed to the farther edge of the lake, over the barrier of which at great intervals of time, the surface water flows, and induces the convulsion known as Mount Epomeo."

We accordingly embarked, and a gentle touch of the lever enabled us rapidly to skirt the shore of the underground sea. The soft, bright, pleasant earth-light continually enveloped us, and the absence of either excessive heat or cold, rendered existence delightful. The weird forms taken by the objects that successively presented themselves on the shore were a source of continual delight to my mind. The motion of our boat was constantly at the will of my guide. Now we would skim across a great bay, flashing from point to point; again we wound slowly through tortuous channels and among partly submerged stones.

"What a blessing this mode of locomotion would be to humanity," I murmured.

"Humanity will yet attain it," he replied. "Step by step men have stumbled along towards the goal that the light of coming centuries is destined to illuminate. They have studied, and are still engaged in studying, the properties of grosser forces, such as heat and electricity, and they will be led by the thread they are following, to this and other achievements yet unthought of, but which lie back of those more conspicuous."

We finally reached a precipitous bluff, that sprung to my view as by magic, and which, with a glass-like surface, stretched upward to a height beyond the scope of my vision, rising

"WE FINALLY REACHED A PRECIPITOUS BLUFF."

straight from the surface of the lake. It was composed of a material seemingly black as jet, and yet when seen under varying spectacular conditions as we skirted its base it reflected, or emitted, most gorgeously the brilliant hues of the rainbow, and also other colors hitherto unknown to me.

"There is something unique in these shades; species of color appear that I can not identify; I seem to perceive colors utterly unlike any that I know as the result of deflected, or transmitted, sunlight rays, and they look unlike the combinations of primary colors with which I am familiar."

"Your observations are true; some of these colors are unknown on earth."

"But on the surface of the earth we have all possible combinations of the seven prismatic rays," I answered. "How can there be others here?"

"Because, first, your primary colors are capable of further subdivision.

"Second, other rays, invisible to men under usual conditions, also emanate from the sun, and under favorable circumstances may be brought to the sense of sight."

"Do you assert that the prism is capable of only partly analyzing the sunlight?"

"Yes; what reason have you to argue that, because a triangular bit of glass resolves a white ray into seven fractions that are, as men say, differently colored, you could not by proper methods subdivide each of these so-called primary shades into others? What reason have you to doubt that rays now invisible to man accompany those capable of impressing his senses, and might by proper methods become perceptible as new colors?"

"None," I answered; "only that I have no proof that such rays exist."

"But they do exist, and men will yet learn that the term 'primitive' ray, as applied to each of the seven colors of the rainbow, is incorrect. Each will yet be resolved, and as our faculties multiply and become more subtle, other colors will be developed, possessed of a delicacy and richness indescribable now, for as yet man can not comprehend the possibilities of education beyond the limits of his present condition."

During this period of conversation we skirted the richly colored bluff with a rapid motion, and at last shot beyond it, as with a flash, into seeming vacancy. I was sitting with my gaze directed toward the bluff, and when it instantly disappeared, I rubbed my eyes to convince myself of their truthfulness, and as I did so our boat came gradually to a stand on the edge of what appeared to be an unfathomable abyss. Beneath me on the side where had risen the bluff that disappeared so abruptly, as far as the eye could reach, was an absolute void. To our right, and before and behind us, stretched the surface of that great smooth lake on whose bosom we rested. To our left, our boat brushing its rim, a narrow ledge, a continuation of the black, glass-like material, reached only a foot above the water, and beyond this narrow brink the mass descended perpendicularly to seemingly infinite depths. Involuntarily I grasped the sides of the boat, and recoiled from the frightful chasm, over which I had been so suddenly suspended, and which exceeded anything of a similar description that I had ever seen. The immeasurable depth of the abyss, in connection with the apparently frail barrier that held the great lake in its bounds, caused me to shudder and shrink back, and my brain reeled in dizzy fright. An inexplicable attraction, however, notwithstanding my dread, held me spell-bound, and although I struggled to shut out that view, the endeavor failed. I seemed to be drawn by an irresistible power, and yet I shuddered at the awful majesty of that yawning gulf which threatened to end the world on which I then existed. Fascinated, entranced, I could not help gazing, I knew not how long, down, down into that fathomless, silent profundity. Composing myself, I turned a questioning glance on my guide.

He informed me that this hard, glass-like dam, confined the waters of the slowly rising lake that we were sailing over, and which finally would rise high enough to overflow the barrier.

"'The cycle of the periodic overflow is measured by great intervals,' he said; 'centuries are required to raise the level of the lake a fraction of an inch, and thousands of years may elapse before its surface will again reach the top of the adamantine wall. Then, governed by the law that attracts a liquid to itself, and heaps the teaspoon with liquid, the water of the quiet lake

"THE WALL DESCENDED PERPENDICULARLY TO SEEMINGLY INFINITE DEPTHS."

piles upon this narrow wall, forming a ledge along its summit. Finally the superimposed surface water gives way, and a skim of water pours over into the abyss."

He paused; I leaned over and meditated, for I had now accustomed myself to the situation.

"There is no bottom," I exclaimed.

"Upon the contrary," he answered, "the bottom is less than ten miles beneath us, and is a great funnel-shaped orifice, the neck of the funnel reaching first down and then upward from us diagonally toward the surface of the earth. Although the light by which we are enveloped is bright, yet it is deficient in penetrating power, and is not capable of giving the contour of objects even five miles away, hence the chasm seems bottomless, and the gulf measureless."

"Is it not natural to suppose that a mass of water like this great lake would overflow the barrier immediately, as soon as the surface reached the upper edge, for the pressure of the immense volume must be beyond calculation."

"No, for it is height, not expanse, which, as hydrostatic engineers understand, governs the pressure of water. A liquid column, one foot in width, would press against the retaining dam with the force of a body of the same liquid, the same depth, one thousand miles in extent. Then the decrease of gravity here permits the molecular attraction of the water's molecules to exert itself more forcibly than would be the case on the surface of the earth, and this holds the liquid mass together more firmly."

"See," he observed, and dipping his finger into the water he held it before him with a drop of water attached thereto (Figure 27), the globule being of considerable size, and lengthened as though it consisted of some glutinous liquid.

"How can a thin stratum of water give rise to a volcanic eruption?" I next queried. "There seems to be no melted rock, no evidence of intense heat, either beneath or about us."

FIG. 27.

"I informed you some time ago that I would partially explain these facts. Know then, that the theories of man concerning volcanic eruptions, in connection with a molten interior of the earth, are such as are evolved in ignorance of even the subsurface of the globe. The earth's interior is to mankind a sealed chamber, and the wise men who elucidate the curious theories concerning natural phenomena occurring therein are forced to draw entirely upon their imagination. Few persons realize the paucity of data at the command of workers in science. Theories concerning the earth are formulated from so little real knowledge of that body, that our science may be said to be all theory, with scarcely a trace of actual evidence to support it. If a globe ten inches in diameter be covered with a sheet of paper, such as I hold in my hand, the thickness of that sheet will be greater in proportion to that of such a globe than the depth men have explored within the earth is compared with the thickness of the crust of the earth. The outer surface of a pencil line represents the surface of the earth; the inner surface of the line represents the depth of man's explorations; the highest mountain would be represented by a comma resting on the line. The geologist studies the substances that are thrust from the crater of an active volcano, and from this makes conjectures regarding the strata beneath, and the force that casts the excretions out. The results must with men, therefore, furnish evidence from which to explain the cause. It is as though an anatomist would form his idea of the anatomy of the liver by the secretion thrown out of that organ, or of the lung texture by the breath and sputum. In fact, volcanoes are of several descriptions, and usually are extremely superficial. This lake, the surface of which is but one hundred and fifty miles underground, is the mother of an exceptionally deep one. When the water pours over this ledge it strikes an element below us, the metallic base of salt, which lies in great masses in some portions of the earth's crust.* Then an immediate chemical reaction ensues, the water is dissociated, intense heat results, part of the water combines with the metal, part is vaporized as steam, while part escapes as an inflammable gas. The sudden liberation of these gases causes an irregular pressure of vapor on the surface of the lake, the result being a throbbing and rebounding of the attenuated atmosphere above, which,

---

* This view is supported in theory by a note I believe to have somewhere seen recorded. Elsewhere other bases are mentioned also.—J. U. L.

in gigantic waves, like swelling tides, dashes great volumes of water over the ledge beside us, and into the depth below. This water in turn reacts on fresh portions of the metallic base, and the reflex action increases the vapor discharges, and as a consequence the chamber we are in becomes a gasometer, containing vapors of unequal gas pressures, and the resultant agitation of the lake from the turmoil continues, and the pulsations are repeated until the surface of the lake is lowered to such a degree as at last to prevent the water from overflowing the barrier. Finally the lake quiets itself, the gases slowly disappear by earth absorption, and by escape from the volcanic exit, and for an unrecorded period of time thereafter the surface of the lake continues to rise slowly as it is doing now."

"But what has this phenomenon to do with the volcano?"

"It produces the eruption; the water that rushes down into the chasm, partly as steam, partly as gas, is forced onward and upward through a crevice that leads to the old crater of the presumed extinct but periodically active Mount Epomeo. These gases are intensely heated, and they move with fearful velocity. They tear off great masses of stone, which the resultant energy disturbances, pressure, gas, and friction, redden with heat. The mixture of gases from the decomposed water is in large amount, is burning and exploding, and in this fiery furnace amid such convulsions as have been described, the adjacent earth substance is fused, and even clay is melted, and carried on with the fiery blast. Finally the current reaches the earth's surface through the funnel passage, the apex of which is a volcano—the blast described a volcanic eruption."

"One thing is still obscure in my mind," I said. "You assert that the reaction which follows the contact of the flowing water and metallic bases in the crevice below us liberates the explosive gases, and also volumes of vapor of water. These gases rush, you say, and produce a volcanic eruption in a distant part of the crust of the earth. I can not understand why they do not rush backward as well, and produce another eruption in Kentucky. Surely the pressure of a gas in confinement is the same in all directions, is it not?"

"Yes," he replied, "but the conditions in the different directions are dissimilar. In the direction of the Kentucky cavern, the passage is tortuous, and often contracts to a narrow crevice. In one place near the cavern's mouth, as you will remember, we had to dive beneath the surface of a stream of water. That stratum of water as effectually closed the exit from the earth as the stopper prevents water escaping from a bottle. Between the point we now occupy and that water stopper, rest thousands of miles of quiescent air. The inertia of a thousand miles of air is great beyond your comprehension. To move that column of air by pushing against this end of it, and thus shoving it instantly out of the other end, would require greater force than would burst the one hundred and fifty miles of inelastic stone above us. Then, the friction of the sides is another thing that prevents its accomplishment. While a gradually applied pressure would in time overcome both the inertia of the air and the friction of the stone passages, it would take a supply of energy greater than you can imagine to start into motion the elastic mass that stands as solid and immovable as a sentinel of adamant, between the cavern you entered, and the spot we now occupy. Time and energy combined would be able to accomplish the result, but not under present conditions.

"In the other direction a broad open channel reaches directly to and connects with the volcanic shaft. Through this channel the air is in motion, moving towards the extinct crater, being supplied from another surface orifice. The gases liberated in the manner I have described, naturally follow the line of least resistance. They turn at once away from the inert mass of air that rests behind us, and move with increasing velocity towards the volcanic exit. Before the pressure that might be exerted towards the Kentucky cavern would have more than compressed the intervening column of air enough to raise the water of a well from its usual level to the surface of the earth, the velocity in the other direction would have augmented prodigiously, and with its increased rapidity a suction would follow more than sufficient to consume the increasingly abundant gases from behind."

"Volcanoes are therefore local, and the interior of the earth is not a molten mass as I have been taught," I exclaimed.

He answered: "If men were far enough along in their thought journey (for the evolution of the mental side of man is a journey in the world of thought), they would avoid such theories as that which ascribes a molten interior to the earth. Volcanoes are superficial. They are as a rule, when in activity but little blisters or excoriations upon the surface of the earth, although their underground connections may be extensive. Some of them are in a continual fret with frequent eruptions, others, like the one under consideration, awaken only after great periods of time. The entire surface of this globe has been or will be subject to volcanic action. The phenomenon is one of the steps in the world-making, matter-leveling process. When the deposit of substances that I have indicated, and of which much of the earth's interior is composed, the bases of salt, potash, and lime and clay is exhausted, there will be no further volcanic action from this cause, and in some places, this deposit has already disappeared, or is covered deeply by layers of earth that serve as a protection."

"Is water, then, the universal cause of volcanoes?"

"Water and air together cause most of them. The action of water and its vapor produces from metallic space dust, limestone, and clay soil, potash and soda salts. This perfectly rational and natural action must continue as long as there is water above, and free elementary bases in contact with the earth bubbles. Volcanoes, earthquakes, geysers, mud springs, and hot springs, are the natural result of that reaction. Mountains are thereby forming by upheavals from beneath, and the corresponding surface valleys are consequently filling up, either by the slow deposit of the matter from the saline water of hot springs, or by the sudden eruption of a new or presumably extinct volcano."

"What would happen if a crevice in the bottom of the ocean should conduct the waters of the ocean into a deposit of metallic bases?"

"That often occurs," was the reply; "a volcanic wave results, and a volcano may thus rise from the ocean's depths."

"Is there any danger to the earth itself? May it not be riven into fragments from such a convulsion?" I hesitatingly questioned.

"No; while the configuration of continents is continually being altered, each disturbance must be practically superficial, and of limited area."

"But," I persisted, "the rigid, solid earth may be blown to fragments; in such convulsions a result like that seems not impossible."

"You argue from an erroneous hypothesis. The earth is neither rigid nor solid."

"True," I answered. "If it were solid I could not be a hundred miles beneath its surface in conversation with another being; but there can not be many such cavities as that which we are now traversing, and they can not surely extend entirely through its mass; the great weight of the superincumbent material would crush together the strongest materials, if a globe as large as our earth were extensively honeycombed in this manner."

"Quite the contrary," he replied; "and here let me, for the first time, enlighten you as to the interior structure of the terrestrial globe. The earth-forming principle consists of an invisible sphere of energy that, spinning through space, supports the space dust which collects on it, as dust on a bubble. By gradual accumulation of substance on that sphere a hollow ball has resulted, on the outer surface of which you have hitherto dwelt. The crust of the earth is comparatively thin, not more than eight hundred miles in average thickness, and is held in position by the central sphere of energy that now exists at a distance about seven hundred miles beneath the ocean level. The force inherent to this sphere manifests itself upon the matter which it supports on both sides, rendering matter the lighter the nearer it lies to the center sphere. In other words, let me say to you: "The crust, or shell, which I have just described as being but about eight hundred miles in thickness, is firm and solid on both its convex and concave surface, but gradually loses in weight, whether we penetrate from the outer surface toward the center, or from any point of the inner surface towards the outside, until at the central sphere matter has no weight at all. Do you conceive my meaning?"

"Yes," I replied; "I understand you perfectly."

After a pause my pilot asked me abruptly:

"What do you most desire?"

The question caused my mind to revert instantly to my old home on the earth above me, and although I felt the hope of returning to it spring up in my heart, the force of habit caused me involuntarily to answer, "More light!"

"More light being your desire, you shall receive it."

Obedient to his touch, the bow of the boat turned from the gulf we had been considering towards the center of the lake; the responsive craft leaped forward, and in an instant the obsidian parapet disappeared behind us. On and over the trackless waste of glass-like water we sped, until the dead silence became painfully oppressive, and I asked:

"Whither are we bound?"

"Towards the east."

The well-timed answer raised my spirits; I thought again that in this man, despite his repulsive shape, I beheld a friend, a brother; suspicion vanished, and my courage rose. He touched the lever, and the craft, subject to his will, nearly rose from the water, and sped with amazing velocity, as was evident from the appearance of the luminous road behind us. So rapid was our flight that the wake of the boat seemed as if made of rigid parallel lines that disappeared in the distance, too quick for the eye to catch the tremor.

Continuing his conversation, my companion informed me that he had now directed the bark toward a point east of the spot where we struck the shore, after crossing the lake, in order that we might continue our journey downward, diagonally to the under surface of the earth crust.

"This recent digression from our journey proper," said he, "has been made to acquaint you with a subject, regarding which you have exhibited a curiosity, and about which you have heretofore been misinformed; now you understand more clearly part of the philosophy of volcanoes and earthquakes. You have yet much to learn in connection with allied phenomena, but this study of the crude exhibition of force-disturbed matter, the manipulation of which is familiar to man under the above names, is an introduction to the more wonderful study destined yet to be a part of your field, an investigation of quiescent matter, and pure motion."

"I can not comprehend you," I replied, "as I stated once before when you referred to what you designated as pure motion."

CHAPTER XXXII.

MATTER IS RETARDED MOTION.

"It is possible for you to imagine, is it not, that a continuous volley of iron balls were passing near you in one line, in a horizontal direction with considerable velocity. Suppose that a pane of glass were to be gradually moved so that a corner of it would be struck by one of the balls; then the entire sheet of glass would be shivered by the concussion, even though the bullet struck but a single spot of glass, the point of contact covering only a small area. Imagine now that the velocity of the volley of bullets be increased a thousand fold; then a plate of glass thrust into their track would be smoothly cut, as though with a file that would gnaw its way without producing a single radiating fracture. A person standing near the volley would now hear a deep purr or growling sound, caused by the friction between the bullets and the air. Increase gradually the rapidity of their motion, and this growl would become more acute, passing from a deep, low murmur, into one less grave, and as the velocity increased, the tone would become sharper, and at last piercingly shrill. Increase now the rapidity of the train of bullets again, and again the notes would decrease in turn, passing back again successively through the several keys that had preceded, and finally would reach the low growl which first struck the ear, and with a further increase of speed silence would ensue, silence evermore, regardless of increasing velocity.* From these hundreds of miles in a second at which the volley is now passing, let the rapidity be augmented a thousand times, reaching in their flight into millions of miles each second, and to the eye, from the point where the sound disappeared, as the velocity increased, a dim redness would appear, a glow just perceptible,

---

* A scientific critic seems to think that the shrill cry would cease instantly and not gradually. However, science has been at fault more than once, and I do not care to take liberties with this statement.—J. U. L.

indicating to the sense of sight, by a continuous line, the track of the moving missiles. To all appearance, the line would be as uniform as an illuminated pencil mark, even though the several integral bullets of the trail might be separated one from another by miles of space. Let a pane of glass now be thrust across their track, and from the point of contact a shower of sparks would fly, and the edges of glass close to either side of the orifice would be shown, on withdrawing the glass, to have been fused. Conceive now that the velocity of the bullets be doubled and trebled, again and again, the line of red light becomes brighter, then brilliant, and finally as the velocity increases, at a certain point pure white results, and to man's sense the trail would now be a continuous something, as solid as a bar of metal if at a white heat, and (even if the bullets were a thousand miles apart) man could not bring proof of their separate existence to his senses. That portion of a pane of glass or other substance, even steel or adamant, which should cross its track now would simply melt away, the portion excised and carried out of that pathway neither showing itself as scintillations, nor as fragments of matter. The solid would instantly liquefy, and would spread itself as a thin film over the surface of each ball of that white, hot mass of fleeing metal, now to all essential conditions as uniform as a bar of iron. Madly increase the velocity to millions upon millions of miles per second, and the heat will disappear gradually as did the sound, while the bright light will pass backward successively through the primary shades of color that are now known to man, beginning with violet, and ending with red, and as the red fades away the train of bullets will disappear to the sense of man. Neither light nor sound now accompanies the volley, neither the human eye nor the human ear can perceive its presence. Drop a pane of glass or any other object edgewise through it, and it gives to the sense of man no evidence; the molecules of the glass separate from in front to close in from behind, and the moving train passes through it as freely as light, leaving the surface of the glass unaffected."

"Hold," I interrupted; "that would be as one quality of matter passing through another quality of matter without disturbance to either, and it is a law in physics that two substances can not occupy the same space at the same time."

"That law holds good as man understands the subject, but bullets are no longer matter. Motion of mass was first changed into motion of molecules, and motion of molecule became finally augmented into motion of free force entities as the bullets disintegrated into molecular corpuscles, and then were dissociated, atoms resulting. At this last point the sense of vision, and of touch, ceased to be affected by that moving column (neither matter nor force), and at the next jump in velocity the atoms themselves disappeared, and free intangible motion resulted—nothing, vacancy.

"This result is the all-pervading spirit of space (the ether of mankind), as solid as adamant and as mobile as vacuity. If you can reverse the order of this phenomenon, and imagine an irregular retardation of the rapidity of such atomic motion, you can read the story of the formation of the material universe. Follow the chain backward, and with the decrease of velocity, motion becomes tangible matter again, and in accordance with conditions governing the change of motion into matter, from time to time the various elements successively appear. The planets may grow without and within, and ethereal space can generate elemental dirt. If you can conceive of an intermediate condition whereby pure space motion becomes partly tangible, and yet is not gross enough to be earthy matter, you can imagine how such forces as man is acquainted with, light, heat, electricity, magnetism, or gravity even are produced, for these are also disturbances in space motion. It should be easily understood that, according to the same simple principle, other elements and unknown forces as well, now imperceptible to man's limited faculties, could be and are formed outside and inside his field of perception."

"I fear that I can not comprehend all this," I answered.

"So I feared, and perhaps I have given you this lesson too soon, although some time ago you asked me to teach you concerning the assertion that electricity, light, heat, magnetism, and gravity are disturbances, and you said, 'Disturbances of what?' Think the lesson over, and you will perceive that it is easy. Let us hope that the time will come when we will be able to glance beneath the rough, material, earth surface knowledge that man has acquired, and experience the mind expansion that leads to the blissful insight possessed by superior beings who do not have to contend with the rasping elements that encompass all who dwell upon the surface of the earth."

I pondered over these words, and a vague light, an undefined, inexpressible something that I could not put into words broke into my mind; I inferred that we were destined to meet with persons, or existences, possessed of new senses, of a mind development that man had not reached, and I was on the point of questioning my pilot when the motion of the boat was suspended, land appeared ahead, we drew up to it, and disembarked. Lifting the boat from the water my guide placed it on land at the edge of the motionless lake, and we resumed our journey. The scenery seemed but little changed from that of the latter part of our previous line of travel down the inclined plane of the opposite side of the lake that we had crossed. The direction was still downward after leaving the high ridge that bordered the edge of the lake, the floor of the cavern being usually smooth, although occasionally it was rough and covered with stony debris. The mysterious light grew perceptibly brighter as we progressed, the fog-like halo previously mentioned became less dense, and the ring of obscurity widened rapidly. I could distinctly perceive objects at a great distance. I turned to my companion to ask why this was, and he replied:

"Because we are leaving one of the undiscovered conditions of the upper atmosphere that disturbs the sunlight."

"Do you say that the atmosphere is composed of substances unknown to man?"

"Yes; several of them are gases, and others are qualities of space condition, neither gas, liquid, nor solid.* One particularly interferes with light in its passage. It is an entity that is not moved by the motion of the air, and is unequally distributed over the earth's surface. As we ascend above the earth it decreases, so it does as we descend into it. It is not vapor of water, is neither smoke, nor a true gas, and is as yet sensible to

---

*This has since been partly supported by the discovery of the element Argon. However, the statement has been recorded many years. Miss Ella Burbige, stenographer, Newport, Ky., copied the original in 1887; Mr. S. D. Rouse, attorney, Covington, Ky., read it in 1889; Mr. Russell Errett, editor of the Christian Standard, in 1890, and Mr. H. C. Meader, President of the American Ticket Brokers' Association, in 1892. It seems proper to make this explanation in order to absolve the author from any charge of plagiarism, for each of these persons will recall distinctly this improbable [then] assertion.—J. U. L.

man only by its power of modifying the intensity of light. It has no color, is chemically inactive, and yet modifies the sun's rays so as to blot objects from view at a comparatively small distance from a person on the face of the earth. That this fact is known to man is evident from the knowledge he possesses of the difference in the power of his organs of vision at different parts of the earth. His sight is especially acute on the table lands of the Western Territories."

"I have been told," I answered, "that vapor of water causes this obscuration, or absorption, of light."

"Vapor of water, unless in strata of different densities, is absolutely transparent, and presents no obstacle to the passage of light," he said. "When vapor obstructs light it is owing to impurities contained in it, to currents of varying densities, or wave motions, or to a mechanical mixture of condensed water and air, whereby multitudes of tiny globular water surfaces are produced. Pure vapor of water, free from motion, is passive to the sunlight."

"I can scarcely believe that a substance such as you describe, or that any constituent of the air, can have escaped the perception of the chemist," I replied.

In, as I thought, a facetious manner he repeated after me the word "chemist," and continued:

"Have chemists detected the ether of Aristotle, that you have mentioned, and I have defined, which scientists nevertheless accept pervades all space and every description of matter, and that I have told you is really matter itself changed into ultra atomic motion? Have chemists explained why one object is transparent, and another of equal weight and solidity is opaque? Have chemists told you why vermillion is red and indigo is blue (the statement that they respectively reflect these rays of light is not an explanation of the cause for such action)? Have chemists told you why the prism disarranges or distorts sunlight to produce the abnormal hues that men assume compose elementary rays of light? Have chemists explained anything concerning the why or wherefore of the attributes of matter, or force, or even proven that the so-called primary forms of matter, or elements, are not compounds? Upon the contrary, does not the evolution that results in the recorded discoveries of the chemist foretell, or at least indicate, the possible future of the art, and promise that surrounding mysteries are yet to be developed and expanded into open truths, thus elaborating hidden forces; and that other forms of matter and unseen force expressions, are destined to spring into existence as the sciences progress? The chemist of to-day is groping in darkness; he is a novice as compared with the elaborated chemist of the near future; the imperfectly seen of the present, the silent and unsuspected, will become distinctly visible in a time that is to come, and a brightening of the intellect by these successively upward steps, up stairs of science, will, if science serves herself best, broaden the mind and give power to the imagination, resulting finally in "—

He hesitated.

"Go on," I said.

"The passage of mortal man, with the faculties of man intact, into communion with the spirit world."

CHAPTER XXXIII.

"A STUDY OF SCIENCE IS A STUDY OF GOD."—COMMUNING WITH ANGELS.

"This is incredible," I exclaimed.

"You need not be astonished," he answered. "Is there any argument that can be offered to controvert the assertion that man is ignorant of many natural laws?"

"I can offer none."

"Is there any doubt that a force, distinct and separate from matter, influences matter and vivifies it into a living personality?"

"I do not deny that there is such force."

"What then should prevent this force from existing separate from the body if it be capable of existing in it?"

"I can not argue against such a position."

"If, as is hoped and believed by the majority of mankind, even though some try to deny the fact, it is possible for man to exist as an association of earth matters, linked to a personal spirit force, the soul, and for the spirit force, after the death of the body, to exist independent of the grosser attributes of man, free from his mortal body, is it not reasonable to infer that the spirit, while it is still in man and linked to his body, may be educated and developed so as, under favorable conditions, to meet and communicate with other spirits that have been previously liberated from earthly bondage?"

"I submit," I answered; "but you shock my sensibilities when you thus imply that by cold, scientific investigation we can place ourselves in a position to meet the unseen spirit world"—

It was now my turn to hesitate.

"Go on," he said.

"To commune with the angels," I answered.

"A study of true science is a study of God," he continued. "Angels are organizations natural in accordance with God's laws. They appear superhuman, because of our ignorance concerning the higher natural forces. They exist in exact accordance with the laws that govern the universe; but as yet the attraction between clay and clay-bound spirit is so great as to prevent the enthralled soul of man from communicating with them. The faith of the religionist is an example of the unquenchable feeling that creates a belief as well as a hope that there is a self-existence separate from earthy substances. The scoffing scientific agnostic, working for other objects, will yet astonish himself by elaborating a method that will practically demonstrate these facts, and then empirical religion, as exemplified by the unquestioning faithful believer, and systematic science, as typified in the experimental materialist, will meet on common ground."

CHAPTER XXXIV.

I CEASE TO BREATHE, AND YET LIVE.

During this conversation we had been rapidly walking, or I should better say advancing, for we no longer walked as men do, but skipped down into the earth, down, ever downward. There were long periods of silence, in which I was engaged in meditating over the problems that successively demanded solution, and even had I desired to do so I could have kept no record of time; days, or even weeks, may have been consumed in this journey. Neither have I any method of judging of the rapidity of our motion. I was sensible of a marked decrease in the amount of muscular energy required to carry us onward, and I realized that my body was quite exempt from weariness. Motion became restful instead of exhausting, and it seemed to me that the ratio of the loss of weight, as shown by our free movements, in proportion to the distance we traversed, was greater than formerly. The slightest exhibition of propelling force cast us rapidly forward. Instead of the laborious, short step of upper earth, a single leap would carry us many yards. A slight spring, and with our bodies in space, we would skip several rods, alighting gently, to move again as easily. I marveled, for, although I had been led to anticipate something unusual, the practical evidence was wonderfully impressive, and I again questioned my guide.

"We are now nearing what physicists would call the center of gravity," he replied, "and our weight is rapidly diminishing. This is in exact accordance with the laws that govern the force called gravitation, which, at the earth's surface, is apparently uniform, though no instrument known to man can demonstrate its exact variation within the field man occupies. Men have not, as yet, been in a position to estimate this change, although it is known that mountains attract objects, and that a change in weight as we descend into the earth is perceptible; but to evolve the true law, observation, at a distance of at least ten miles beneath the surface of the ocean is necessary, and man, being a creature whose motions are confined to a thin, horizontal skin of earth, has never been one mile beneath its surface, and in consequence his opportunities for comparison are extremely limited."

"I have been taught," I replied, "that the force of gravitation decreases until the center of the earth is reached, at which point a body is without weight; and I can scarcely understand how such positive statements from scientific men can be far from the truth."

"WE WOULD SKIP SEVERAL RODS, ALIGHTING GENTLY."

"It is supposed by your surface men that the maximum of weight is to be found at one-sixth the distance beneath the surface of the earth, and therefrom decreases until at the center it is nothing at all," he replied. "This hypothesis, though, a stagger toward the right, is far from the truth, but as near as could be expected, when we consider the data upon which men base their calculations. Were it not for the purpose of controverting erroneous views, men would have little incentive to continue their investigations, and as has been the rule in science heretofore, the truth will, in time, appear in this case. One generation of students disproves the accepted theories of that which precedes, all working to eliminate error, all adding factors of error, and all together moving toward a common goal, a grand generalization, that as yet can not be perceived. And still each series of workers is overlooking phenomena that, though obvious, are yet unperceived, but which will make evident to future scientists the mistakes of the present. As an example of the manner in which facts are thus overlooked, in your journey you have been impressed with certain surprising external conditions, or surroundings, and yet are oblivious to conditions more remarkable in your own body. So it is with scientists. They overlook prominent facts that stare them boldly in the face, facts that are so conspicuous as to be invisible by reason of their very nearness."

"This statement I can not disprove, and therefore must admit under protest. Where there is so much that appears mysterious I may have overlooked some things, but I can scarcely accept that, in ignorance, I have passed conditions in my own organization so marked as this decrease in gravity which has so strikingly been called to my attention."

"You have, and to convince you I need only say that you have nearly ceased to breathe, and are unconscious of the fact."

I stopped short, in momentary alarm, and now that my mind was directed to the fact, I became aware that I did not desire to breathe, and that my chest had ceased to heave with the alternate inhalation and exhalation of former times. I closed my lips firmly, and for a long period there was no desire for breath, then a slight involuntary inhalation followed, and an exhalation, scarcely noticeable, succeeded by a great interval of inanition. I impulsively turned my face toward the passage we had trod; a feeling of alarm possessed me, an uncontrollable, inexpressible desire to flee from the mysterious earth-being beside me, to return to men, and be an earth-surface man again, and I started backward through the chamber we had passed.

The guide siezed me by the hand, "Hold, hold," he cried; "where would you go, fickle mortal?"

"To the surface," I shouted; "to daylight again. Unhand me, unearthly creature, abnormal being, man or devil; have you not inveigled me far enough into occult realms that should be forever sealed from mankind? Have you not taken from me all that men love or cherish, and undone every tie of kith or kin? Have you not led me into paths that the imagination of the novelist dare not conjure, and into experiences that pen in human hand would not venture to describe as possible, until I now stand with my feet on the boundary line that borders

I CEASE TO BREATHE, AND YET LIVE. 229

vacancy, and utter loss of weight; with a body nearly lost as a material substance, verging into nothing, and lastly with breath practically extinguished, I say, and repeat, is it not time that I should hesitate and pause in my reckless career?"

"It is not time," he answered.

"When will that hour come?" I asked in desperation, and I trembled as he replied:

"When the three Great Lights are closed."

"AN UNCONTROLLABLE, INEXPRESSIBLE DESIRE TO FLEE."

CHAPTER XXXV.

"A CERTAIN POINT WITHIN A SPHERE."—MEN ARE AS PARASITES ON THE ROOF OF EARTH.

I realized again, as I had so many times before, that it was useless for me to rebel. "The self-imposed mystery of a sacrificed life lies before me," I murmured, "and there is no chance to retrace my footsteps. The 'Beyond' of the course that I have voluntarily selected, and sworn to follow, is hidden; I must nerve myself to pursue it to the bitter end, and so help me God, and keep me steadfast."

"Well said," he replied; "and since you have so wisely determined, I am free to inform you that these new obligations, like those you have heretofore taken, contain nothing which can conflict with your duty to God, your country, your neighbor, or yourself. In considering the phenomena presented by the suspension of the act of breathing, it should occur to you that where little labor is to be performed, little consumption of energy is required. Where there is such a trifling destruction of the vital force (not mind force) as at present is the case with us, it requires but slight respiration to retain the normal condition of the body. On earth's surface the act of respiration alone consumes by far the larger proportion of vital energy, and the muscular exertion involved thereby necessitates a proportionate amount of breathing in order that breath itself may continue. This act of respiration is the result of one of the conditions of surface earth life, and consumes most of the vital force. If men would think of this, they would understand how paradoxical it is for them to breathe in order to live, when the very act of respiration wears away their bodies and shortens their lives more than all else they have to do, and without adding to their mental or physical constitution in the least. Men are conversant with physical death as a constant result of suspended respiration, and with respiration as an accompaniment of life, which ever constant and connected conditions lead them to accept that the act of breathing is a necessity of mortal life. In reality, man occupies an unfortunate position among other undeveloped creatures of external earth; he is an animal, and is constitutionally framed like the other animals about him. He is exposed to the warring elements, to the vicious attacks of savage beasts and insiduous parasites, and to the inroads of disease. He is a prey to the elementary vicissitudes of the undesirable exposure in which he exists upon the outer surface of our globe, where all is war, even among the forces of nature about him. These conditions render his lot an unhappy one indeed, and in ignorance he overlooks the torments of the weary, rasping, endless slavery of respiration in the personal struggle he has to undergo in order to retain a brief existence as an organized being. Have you never thought of the connected tribulations that the wear and tear of respiration alone inflict upon the human family? The heaving of the chest, the circulation of the blood, the throbbing of the heart, continue from mortal birth until death. The heart of man forces about two and one-half ounces of blood with each pulsation. At seventy beats per minute this amounts to six hundred and fifty-six pounds per hour, or nearly eight tons per day. The lungs respire over one thousand times an hour, and move over three thousand gallons of air a day. Multiply these amounts by three hundred and sixty-five, and then by seventy, and you have partly computed the enormous life-work of the lungs and heart of an adult. Over two hundred thousand tons of blood, and seventy-five million gallons of air have been moved by the vital force. The energy thus consumed is dissipated. No return is made for the expenditure of this life force. During the natural life of man, more energy is consequently wasted in material transformation resulting from the motion of heart and lungs, than would be necessary to sustain the purely vital forces alone for a thousand years. Besides, the act of respiration which man is compelled to perform in his exposed position, necessitates the consumption of large amounts of food, in order to preserve the animal heat, and replace the waste of a material body that in turn is worn out by these very movements. Add this waste of energy to the foregoing, and then you will surely perceive that the possible life of man is also curtailed to another and greater degree in the support of the digestive part of his organism. His spirit is a slave to his body; his lungs and heart, on which he imagines life depends, are unceasing antagonists of life. That his act of breathing is now a necessity upon the surface of the earth, where the force of gravity presses so heavily, and where the elements have men at their command, and show him no mercy, I will not deny; but it is exasperating to contemplate such a waste of energy, and corresponding loss of human life."

"You must admit, however, that it is necessary?" I queried.

"No; only to an extent. The natural life of man should, and yet will be, doubled, trebled, multiplied a dozen, yes a thousand fold."

I stepped in front of him; we stood facing each other.

"Tell me," I cried, "how men can so improve their condition as to lengthen their days to the limit you name, and let me return to surface earth a carrier of the glad tidings."

He shook his head.

I dropped on my knees before him.

"I implore you in behalf of that unfortunate humanity, of which I am a member, give me this boon. I promise to return to you and do your bidding. Whatever may be my subsequent fate, I promise to acquiesce therein willingly."

He raised me to my feet.

"I DROPPED ON MY KNEES BEFORE HIM."

"Be of good cheer," he said, "and in the proper time you may return to the surface of this rind of earth, a carrier of great and good news to men."

"Shall I teach them of what you have shown me?" I asked.

"Yes; in part you will be a forerunner, but before you obtain the information that is necessary to the comfort of mankind you will have to visit surface earth again, and return again, perhaps repeatedly. You must prove yourself as men are seldom proven. The journey you have commenced is far from its conclusion, and you may not be equal to its subsequent trials; prepare yourself, therefore, for a series of events that may unnerve you. If you had full confidence and faith in your guide, you would have less cause to fear the result, but your suspicious human nature can not overcome the shrinking sensation that is natural to those who have been educated as you have been amid the changing vicissitudes of the earth's surface, and you can not but be incredulous by reason of that education."

Then I stopped as I observed before me a peculiar fungus— peculiar because unlike all others I had seen. The convex part of its bowl was below, and the great head, as an inverted toad-stool, stood upright on a short, stem-like pedestal. The gills within were of a deep green color, and curved out from the center in the form of a spiral. This form, however, was not the distinguishing feature, for I had before observed specimens that were spiral in structure. The extraordinary peculiarity was that the gills were covered with fruit. This fruit was likewise green in color, each spore, or berry, being from two to three inches in diameter, and honeycombed on the surface, corrugated most beautifully. I stopped, leaned over the edge of the great bowl, and plucked a specimen of the fruit. It seemed to be covered with a hard, transparent shell, and to be nearly full of a clear, green liquid. I handled and examined it in curiosity, at which my guide seemed not to be surprised. Regarding me attentively, he said:

"What is it that impels a mortal towards this fruit?"

"It is curious," I said; "nothing more."

"As for that," said he, "it is not curious at all; the seed of the lobelia of upper earth is more curious, because, while it is as exquisitely corrugated, it is also microscopically small. In the second place you err when you say it is simply curious, 'nothing more,' for no mortal ever yet passed that bowl without doing exactly as you have done. The vein of curiosity, were it that alone that impels you, could not but have an exception."

Then he cracked the shell of the fruit by striking it on the stony floor, and carefully opened the shell, handing me one of the halves filled with a green fluid. As he did so he spoke the single word, "Drink," and I did as directed. He stood upright before me, and as I looked him in the face he seemingly, without a reason, struck off into a dissertation, apparently as distinct from our line of thought as a disconnected subject could be, as follows:

"HANDING ME ONE OF THE HALVES, HE SPOKE THE SINGLE WORD, DRINK."

CHAPTER XXXVI.

DRUNKENNESS.—THE DRINKS OF MAN.

"Intemperance has been the vice of every people, and is prevalent in all climes, notwithstanding that intoxicants, properly employed, may serve humanity's highest aims. Beginning early in the history of a people, the disease increases with the growth of a nation, until, at last, unless the knife is used, civilization perishes. A lowly people becomes more depraved as the use of liquor increases; a cultivated people passes backward into barbarism with the depravities that come from dissipation. Here nations meet, and individuals sink to a common level. No drinking man is strong enough to say, 'I can not become dissipated;' no nation is rich and cultivated enough to view the debauch of its people without alarm.

"The disgusting habit of the drunken African finds its counterpart in the lascivious wine-bibber of aristocratic society. To picture the indecencies of society, that may be charged to debauchery, when the Grecian and Roman empires were at the height of greatness, would obscure the orgies of the barbarious African, and make preferable the brutality of the drunken American Indian. Intemperance brings men to the lowest level, and holds its power over all lands and all nations."

"Did the aborigines know how to make intoxicants, and were barbarians intemperate before contact with civilized nations?"

"Yes."

"But I have understood that drunkenness is a vice inherent only in civilized people; are not you mistaken?"

"No. Every clime, unless it be the far North where men are scarcely more than animals, furnishes intoxicants, and all people use them. I will tell you part of this record of nations.

"The Nubians make a barley beer which they call bouze, and also a wine, from the palm tree. The savages of Africa draw the clear, sweet juice of the palm oil tree into a gourd, in the morning, and by night it becomes a violent intoxicant. The natives of the Malayan Archipelago ferment and drink the sap of the flower stems of the cocoanut. The Tartar tribes make an intoxicating drink from mare's milk, called koomis. In South America the natives drink a vile compound, called cana, distilled from sugar cane; and in the Sandwich Islands, the shrub kava supplies the intoxicant kava-kava, drunk by all the inhabitants, from king to slave, and mother to child. In the heart of Africa, cannibal tribes make legyce of a cereal, and indulge in wild orgies over their barbarious cup. In North America the Indians, before Columbus discovered America, made an intoxicating drink of the sap of the maple tree. The national drink of the Mexicans is pulque, a beastly intoxicant, prepared from the Agave Americana. Mead is an alcoholic drink, made of honey, and used in many countries. In China wine was indulged in from the earliest day, and in former times, had it not been for the influence of their philosophers, especially Confucius, who foresaw the end, the Chinese nation would have perished from drunkenness. Opium, that fearful enslaver of millions of human beings, is in every sense a narcotic intoxicant, and stands conspicuous as an agent, capable of being either a friend, a companion, or a master, as man permits. History fails to indicate the date of its introduction to humanity. In South America the leaf of the cocoa plant is a stimulant scarcely less to be dreaded than opium. The juice of a species of asclepias produces the intoxicant soma, used once by the Brahmins, not only as a drink, but also in sacrificial and religious ceremonies. Many different flavored liquors made of palm, cocoanuts, sugar, pepper, honey, spices, etc., were used by native Hindoos, and as intoxicants have been employed from the earliest days in India. The Vedic people were fearfully dissipated, and page after page of that wonderful sacred book, the Rigs-Veda, is devoted to the habit of drunkenness. The worst classes of drunkards of India used Indian hemp to make bhang, or combined the deadly narcotic stramonium with arrack, a native beer, to produce a poisonous intoxicant. In that early day the inhabitants of India and China were fearfully depraved drunkards, and but for the reforms instituted by their wise men, must have perished as a people. Parahaoma, or 'homa,' is an intoxicant made from a lost plant that is described as having yellow blossoms, used by the ancient dissolute Persians from the day of Zoroaster. Cannabis sativa produces an intoxicant that in Turkey is known as hadschy, in Arabia and India as hashish, and to the Hottentots as dacha, and serves as a drunkard's food in other lands. The fruit of the juniper produces gin, and the fermented juice of the grape, or malt liquors, in all civilized countries are the favorite intoxicants, their origin being lost in antiquity. Other substances, such as palm, apples, dates, and pomegranates have also been universally employed as drink producers.

"Go where you will, man's tendency seems to be towards the bowl that inebriates, and yet it is not the use but the abuse of intoxicants that man has to dread. Could he be temperate, exhilarants would befriend."

"But here," I replied, "in this underground land, where food is free, and existence possible without an effort, this shameful vice has no existence. Here there is no incentive to intemperance, and even though man were present with his inherent passion for drink, he could not find means to gratify his appetite."

"Ah," my guide replied, "that is an error. Why should this part of the earth prove an exception to the general rule. Nature always supplies the means, and man's instinct teaches him how to prepare an intoxicant. So long as man is human his passions will rule. If you should prove unequal to the task you have undertaken, if you shrink from your journey, and turn back, the chances are you will fail to reach the surface of the earth. You will surely stop in the chamber which we now approach, and which I have now prepared you to enter, and will then become one of a band of earth drunkards; having all the lower passions of a mortal you will yet be lost to the virtues of man. In this chamber those who falter and turn back, stop and remain for all time, sinking until they become lower in the human scale than any drunkard on earth. Without any restraining influence, without a care, without necessity of food or incentive to exertion, in this habitation where heat and cold are unknown, and no motive for self-preservation exists, they turn their thoughts toward the ruling passion of mankind and— Listen! Do you not hear them? Listen!"

CHAPTER XXXVII.

THE DRUNKARD'S VOICE.

Then I noticed a medley of sounds seemingly rising out of the depths beyond us. The noise was not such as to lead me to infer that persons were speaking coherently, but rather resembled a jargon such as might come from a multitude of persons talking indiscriminately and methodless. It was a constant volley, now rising and now falling in intensity, as though many persons regardless of one another were chanting different tunes in that peculiar sing-song tone often characteristic of the drunkard. As we advanced, the noise became louder and more of a medley, until at last we were surrounded by confusion. Then a single voice rose up strong and full, and at once, from about us, close to us, yes, against our very persons, cries and shrieks unearthly smote my ears. I could distinguish words of various tongues, English, Irish, German, and many unfamiliar and disjointed cries, imprecations, and maledictions. The cavern about seemed now to be resonant with voices,—shrieks, yells, and maniacal cries commingled,—and yet no form appeared. As we rushed onward, for now my guide grasped my arm tightly and drew me rapidly down the cavern floor, the voices subsided, and at length sounded as if behind us. Now however it seemed as though innumerable arrows, each possessed of a whistle or tone of its own, were in wave-like gusts shrieking by us. Coming from in front, they burst in the rear. Stopping to listen, I found that a connection could be traced between the screech of the arrow-like shriek, and a drunkard's distant voice. It seemed as though a rocket made of an escaping voice would scream past, and bursting in the cavern behind, liberate a human cry. Now and then all but a few would subside, to burst out with increased violence, as if a flight of rockets each with a cry of its own would rush past, to be followed after their explosion by a medley of maniacal cries, songs, shrieks, and groans, commingled. It was as though a shell containing a voice that escaped slowly as by pressure from an orifice, were fired past my ears, to explode and liberate the voice within my hearing. The dreadful utterance was not an echo, was not hallucination, it was real.

I stopped and looked at my guide in amazement. He explained: "Did you not sometime back experience that your own voice was thrown from your body?"

"Yes," I answered.

"These crazed persons or rather experiences depraved, are shouting in the cavern beyond," he said. "They are in front; their voices pass us to burst into expression in the rear."

Then, even as he spoke, from a fungus stalk near us, a hideous creature unfolded itself, and shambled to my side. It had the frame of a man, and yet it moved like a serpent, writhing towards me. I stepped back in horror, but the tall, ungainly creature reached out an arm and grasped me tightly. Leaning over he placed his hideous mouth close to my ear, and moaned: "Back, back, go thou back."

I made no reply, being horror-stricken.

"Back, I say, back to earth, or"—

He hesitated, and still possessed of fear, and unable to reply, I was silent.

"Then go on," he said, "on to your destiny, unhappy man," and slinking back to the fungus whence he arose, he disappeared from sight.

"Come," said my guide, "let us pass the Drunkard's Den. This was but a straggler; nerve yourself, for his companions will soon surround us."

CHAPTER XXXVIII.

THE DRUNKARDS' DEN.

As we progressed the voices in our rear became more faint, and yet the whistling volleys of screeching voice bombs passed us as before. I shuddered in anticipation of the sight that was surely to meet our gaze, and could not but tremble for fear. Then I stopped and recoiled, for at my very feet I beheld a huge, living human head. It rested on the solid rock, and had I not stopped suddenly when I did, I would have kicked it at the next leap. The eyes of the monster were fixed in supplication on my face; the great brow indicated intelligence, the finely-cut mouth denoted refinement, the well-modeled head denoted brain, but the whole constituted a monster. The mouth opened, and a whizzing, arrow voice swept past, and was lost in the distance.

"What is this?" I gasped.

"The fate of a drunkard," my guide replied. "This was once an intelligent man, but now he has lost his body, and enslaved his soul, in the den of drink beyond us, and has been brought here by his comrades, who thus rid themselves of his presence. Here he must rest eternally. He can not move, he has but one desire, drink, and that craving, deeper than life, can not be satiated."

"But he desires to speak; speak lower, man, or head of man, if you wish me to know your wants," I said, and leaned toward him.

Then the monster whispered, and I caught the words:

"Back, back, go thou back!"

I made no reply.

"Back I say, back to earth or"—

Still I remained silent.

"Then go on," he said; "on to your destiny, unhappy man."

"This is horrible," I muttered.

"Come," said the guide, "let us proceed."

And we moved onward.

Now I perceived many such heads about us, all resting upright on the stony floor. Some were silent, others were shouting, others still were whispering and endeavoring to attract my attention. As we hurried on I saw more and more of these abnormal creatures. Some were in rows, resting against each other, leaving barely room for us to pass between, but at last, much to my relief, we left them behind us.

But I found that I had no cause for congratulation, when I felt myself clutched by a powerful hand—a hand as large as that of a man fifty feet in height. I looked about expecting to see a gigantic being, but instead beheld a shrunken pigmy. The whole man seemed but a single hand—a Brobdingnag hand affixed to the body of a Liliputian.

"Do not struggle," said the guide; "listen to what he wishes to impart."

I leaned over, placing my ear close to the mouth of the monstrosity.

"Back, back, go thou back," it whispered.

"What have I to fear?" I asked.

"Back, I say, back to earth, or"—

"Or what?" I said.

"Then go on; on to your destiny, unhappy man," he answered, and the hand loosed its grasp.

My guide drew me onward.

Then, from about us, huge hands arose; on all sides they waved in the air; some were closed and were shaken as clenched fists, others moved aimlessly with spread fingers, others still pointed to the passage we had traversed, and in a confusion of whispers I heard from the pigmy figures a babble of cries, "Back, back, go thou back." Again I hesitated, the strain upon my nerves was becoming unbearable; I glanced backward and saw a swarm of misshaped diminutive forms, each holding up a monstrous arm and hand. The passage behind us was closed against retreat. Every form possessed but one hand, the other and the entire body seemingly had been drawn into this abnormal member. While I thus meditated, momentarily, as by a single thought each hand closed, excepting the index finger, and in unison each finger pointed towards the open way in front, and like shafts from a thousand bows I felt the voices whiz past me, and then from the rear came the reverberation as a complex echo, "Then go on; on to your destiny, unhappy man."

Instinctively I sprang forward, and had it not been for the

"EACH FINGER POINTED TOWARDS THE OPEN WAY IN FRONT."

restraining hand of my guide would have rushed wildly into passages that might have ended my misery, for God only knows what those unseen corridors contained. I was aware of that which lay behind, and was only intent on escaping from the horrid figures already passed.

"Hold," whispered the guide; "as you value your life, stop."

And then exerting a power that I could not withstand, he held me a struggling prisoner.

"Listen," he said, "have you not observed that these creatures do not seek to harm you? Have not all of them spoken kindly, have any offered violence?"

"No," I replied, "but they are horrible."

"That they realize; but fearing that you will prove to be as weak as they have been, and will become as they are now, they warn you back. However, I say to you, if you have courage sufficient, you need have no fear. Come, rely on me, and do not be surprised at anything that appears."

Again we went forward. I realized now my utter helplessness. I became indifferent again; I could neither retrace my footsteps alone, nor guide them forward in the path I was to pursue. I submissively relied on my guide, and as stoical as he appeared to be, I moved onward to new scenes.

We came to a great chamber which, as we halted on its edge, seemed to be a prodigious amphitheater. In its center a rostrum-like stone of a hundred feet in diameter, flat and circular on the top, reared itself about twelve feet above the floor, and to the base of this rostrum the floor of the room sloped evenly. The amphitheater was fully a thousand feet in diameter, of great height, and the floor was literally alive with grotesque beings. Imagination could not depict an abnormal human form that did not exhibit itself to my startled gaze. One peculiarity now presented itself to my mind; each abnormal part seemed to be created at the expense of the remainder of the body. Thus, to my right I beheld a single leg, fully twelve feet in height, surmounted by a puny human form, which on this leg, hopped ludicrously away. I saw close behind this huge limb a great ear attached to a small head and body; then a nose so large that the figure to which it was attached was forced to hold the face upward, in order to prevent the misshaped organ from rubbing on the stony floor. Here a gigantic forehead rested on a shrunken face and body, and there a pair of enormous feet were walking, seemingly attached to the body of a child, and yet the face was that of a man. If an artist were to attempt to create as many revolting figures as possible, each with some member out of proportion to the rest of the body, he could not add one form to those upon this floor. And yet, I again observed that each exaggerated organ seemed to have drawn itself into existence by absorbing the remainder of the body. We stood on the edge of this great room, and I pondered the scene before my eyes. At length my guide broke the silence:

"You must cross this floor; no other passage is known. Mark well my words, heed my advice."

"This is the Drunkards' Den. These men are lost to themselves and to the world. Every member of this assembly once passed onward as you are now doing, in charge of a guide. They failed to reach the goal to which you aspire, and retreating, reached this chamber, to become victims to the drink habit. Some of these creatures have been here for ages, others only for a short period."

"Why are they so distorted?" I asked.

"Because matter is now only partly subservient to will," he replied. "The intellect and mind of a drunkard on surface earth becomes abnormal by the influence of an intoxicant, but his real form is unseen, although evidently misshapen and partly subject to the perception of a few only of his fellow men. Could you see the inner form of an earth surface drunkard, you would perceive as great a mental monstrosity as is any physical monster now before you, and of the two the physically abnormal creature is really the least objectionable. Could you see the mind configurations of an assembly of surface earth topers, you would perceive a class of beings as much distorted mentally as are these physically. A drunkard is a monstrosity. On surface earth the mind becomes abnormal; here the body suffers."

"Why is it," I asked, "that parts of these creatures shrink away as some special organ increases?"

"Because the abnormal member can grow only by abstracting its substance from the other portions of the body. An increasing arm enlarges itself by drawing its strength from the other parts, hence the body withers as the hand enlarges, and in turn the hand shrinks when the leg increases in size. The total weight of the individual remains about the same.

"Men on earth judge of men not by what they are, but by what they seem to be. The physical form is apparent to the sense of sight, the real man is unseen. However, as the boot that encloses a foot can not altogether hide the form of the foot within, so the body that encloses the life entity, can not but exhibit here and there the character of the dominating spirit within. Thus a man's features may grow to indicate the nature of the enclosed spirit, for the controlling character of that spirit will gradually impress itself on the material part of man. Even on surface earth, where the matter side of man dominates, a vicious spirit will produce a villainous countenance, a mediocre mind a vapid face, and an amorous soul will even protrude the anterior part of the skull.

"Carry the same law to this location, and it will be seen that as mind, or spirit, is here the master, and matter is the slave, the same rule should, under natural law, tend to produce such abnormal figures as you perceive. Hence the part of a man's spirit that is endowed most highly sways the corresponding part of his physical body at the expense of the remainder. Gradually the form is altered under the relaxing influence of this fearful intra-earth intoxicant, and eventually but one organ remains to tell of the symmetrical man who formerly existed. Then, when he is no longer capable of self-motion, the comrades carry the drunkard's fate, which is here the abnormal being you have seen, into the selected corridor, and deposit it among others of its kind, as in turn the bearers are destined sometime to be carried by others. We reached this cavern through a corridor in which heads and arms were abnormal, but in others may be found great feet, great legs, or other portions of self-abused man.

"I should tell you, furthermore, that on surface earth a drunkard is not less abnormal than these creatures; but men can not see the form of the drunkard's spirit. Could they perceive the image of the real man life that corresponds to the material part, it would appear not less distorted and hideous. The soul of a mortal protrudes from the visible body as down expands from a thistle seed, but it is invisible. Drink drives the spirit of an earth-surface drunkard to unnatural forms, not less grotesque than these physical distortions. Could you see the real drunkard on surface earth he would be largely outside the body shell, and hideous in the extreme. As a rule, the spirit of an earth-surface drunkard dominates the nose and face, and if mortal man could be suddenly gifted with the sense of mind-sight, they would find themselves surrounded by persons as misshapen as any delirious imagination can conjure. Luckily for humanity this scene is as yet withheld from man, for life would otherwise be a fearful experience, because man has not the power to resist the temptation to abuse drink."

"Tell me," I said, "how long will those beings rest in these caverns?"

"They have been here for ages," replied the guide; "they are doomed to remain for ages yet."

"You have intimated that if my courage fails I will return to this cavern and become as they are. Now that you have warned me of my doom, do you imagine that anything, even sudden death, can swerve me from my journey? Death is surely preferable to such an existence as this."

"Do not be so confident. Every individual before you has had the same opportunity, and has been warned as you have been. They could not undergo the test to which they were subjected, and you may fail. Besides, on surface earth are not men constantly confronted with the doom of the drunkard, and do they not, in the face of this reality, turn back and seek his caverns? The journey of life is not so fearful that they should become drunkards to shrink from its responsibilities. You have reached this point in safety. You have passed the sentinels without, and will soon be accosted by the band before us. Listen well now to my advice. A drunkard always seeks to gain companions, to draw others down to his own level, and you will be tried as never have you been before. Taste not their liquor by whatever form or creature presented. They have no power to harm him who has courage to resist. If they entreat you, refuse; if they threaten, refuse; if they offer inducements, refuse to drink. Let your answer be No, and have no fear. If your strength fail you, mark well my"—

Before he could complete his sentence I felt a pressure, as of a great wind, and suddenly found myself seized in an embrace irresistible, and then, helpless as a feather, was swept out into the cavern of the drunkards.

CHAPTER XXXIX.

AMONG THE DRUNKARDS.

I remember once to have stood on the edge of Niagara's great whirlpool, but not more fearful did its seething waters then seem than did the semi-human whirl into which I had now been plunged. Whether my guide had been aware of the coming move that separated us I never knew, but, as his words were interrupted, I infer that he was not altogether ready to part from my company. Be this as it may, he disappeared from sight, and, as by a concerted move, the cries of the drunkards subsided instantly. I found myself borne high in the air, perched on a huge hand that was carried by its semi-human comrades. It seemed as though the contents of that vast hall had been suddenly thrown beneath me, for, as I looked about, I saw all around a sea of human fragments, living, moving parts of men. Round and round that hall we circled as an eddy whirls in a rock-bound basin, and not less silently than does the water of an eddy. Then I perceived that the disjointed mass of humanity moved as a spiral, in unison, throbbing like a vitalized stream, bearing me submissively on its surface. Gradually the distance between myself and the center stone lessened, and then I found that, as if carried in the groove of a gigantic living spiral, I was being swept towards the stone platform in the center of the room. There was method in the movements of the drunkards, although I could not analyze the intricacies of their complex reel.

Finally I was borne to the center stone, and by a sudden toss of the hand, in the palm of which I was seated, I was thrown upon the raised platform. Then in unison the troop swung around the stone, and I found myself gazing on a mass of vitalized fragments of humanity. Quickly a figure sprung upon the platform, and in him I discerned a seemingly perfect man. He came to my side and grasped my hand as if he were a friend.

"Do not fear," he said; "obey our request, and you will not be harmed."

"What do you desire?" I asked.

He pointed to the center of the stone, and I saw thereon many gigantic, inverted fungus bowls. The gills of some had been crushed to a pulp, and had saturated themselves with liquid which, perhaps by a species of fermentation, had undergone a structural change; others were as yet intact; others still contained men intently cutting the gills into fragments and breaking the fruit preparatory to further manipulation.

"You are to drink with us," he replied.

"No," I said; "I will not drink."

"Then you must die; to refuse to drink with us is to invite death."

"So mote it be; I will not drink."

We stood facing each other, apparently both meditating on the situation.

I remember to have been surprised, not that the man before me had been able to spring from the floor to the table rock on which I stood, but that so fair a personage could have been a companion of the monstrosities about me. He was a perfect type of manhood, and was exquisitely clothed in a loose, flowing robe that revealed and heightened the beauty of his symmetrical form. His face was fair, yet softly tinted with rich, fresh color; his hair and beard were neatly trimmed; his manner was polished, and his countenance frank and attractive. The contrast between the preternatural shapes from among whom he sprung and himself was as between a demon and an angel. I marveled that I had not perceived him before, for such a one should have been conspicuous because so fair; but I reflected that it was quite natural that among the thousands of grotesque persons about me, one attractive form should have escaped notice. Presently he spoke again, seemingly having repented of his display of temper.

"I am a friend," he said; "a deliverer. I will serve you as I have others before you. Lean on me, listen to my story, accept my proffered friendship."

Then he continued: "When you have rested, I will guide you in safety back to upper earth, and restore you to your friends."

I could not resist his pleasing promise. I suddenly and unaccountably believed in his sincerity. He impressed me with confidence in his truthfulness, yes, against my better judgment, convinced me that he must be a friend, a savior. Grasping him by the hand I thanked him for his interest in a disconsolate wanderer, and assured him of my confidence.

"I am in your hands," I said; "I will obey you implicitly. I thank you, my deliverer; lead me back to surface earth and receive the gratitude of a despairing mortal."

"This I will surely do," he said; "rest your case in my hands, do not concern yourself in the least about your future. Before acquiescing in your desire, however, I will explain part of the experiences through which you have recently passed. You have been in the control of an evil spirit, and have been deceived. The grotesque figures, the abnormal beings about you, exist only in your disordered imagination. They are not real. These persons are happy and free from care or pain. They live in bliss inexpressible. They have a life within a life, and the outward expression that you have perceived is as the uncouth hide and figure that incloses the calm, peaceful eye of a toad. Look at their eyes, not at their seemingly distorted forms."

I turned to the throng and beheld a multitude of upturned faces mildly beaming upon me. As I glanced from eye to eye of each countenance, the repulsive figure disappeared from my view, and a sweet expression of innocence was all that was disclosed to me. I realized that I had judged by the outer garment. I had wronged these fellow-beings. A sense of remorse came over me, a desire to atone for my short-sightedness.

"What can I offer as a retribution?" I asked. "I have injured these people."

"Listen," was the reply. "These serene intelligences are happy. They are as a band of brothers. They seek to do you a kindness, to save you from disaster. One hour of experience such as they enjoy is worth a hundred years of the pleasures known to you. This delicious favor, an hour of bliss, they freely offer you, and after you have partaken of their exquisite joy, I will conduct you back to earth's surface whenever you desire to leave us." He emphasized the word, desire.

"I am ready," I replied; "give me this promised delight."

The genial allurer turned to the table rock behind us, and continued:

"In these fungus bowls we foment the extract of life. The precious cordial is as a union of the quintessential spirits of joy, peace, tranquility, happiness, and delight. Could man abstract from ecstacy the thing that underlies the sense that gives that word a meaning, his product would not approach the power of the potent liquids in these vessels."

"Of what are they composed?" I asked.

"Of derivatives of the rarest species of the fungus family," he answered. "They are made by formulæ that are the result of thousands of years of experimentation. Come, let us not delay longer the hour of bliss."

Taking me by the hand, my graceful comrade led me to the nearest bowl. Then on closer view I perceived that its contents were of a deep green color, and in active commotion, and although no vapor was apparent, a delightful sensation impressed my faculties. I am not sure that I inhaled at all,—the feeling was one of penetration, of subtile, magic absorption. My companion took a tiny shell which he dipped into the strange cauldron. Holding the tiny cup before me, he spoke the one word, "Drink."

Ready to acquiesce, forgetful of the warning I had received, I grasped the cup, and raised it to my lips, and as I did so chanced to glance at my tempter's face, and saw not the supposed friend I had formerly observed, but, as through a mask fair in outline, the countenance of an exulting demon, regarding me with a sardonic grin. In an instant he had changed from man to devil.

I dashed the cup upon the rock. "No; I will not drink," I shouted.

Instantly the cavern rung with cries of rage. A thousand voices joined as by accord, and simultaneously the throng of fragments of men began to revolve again. The mysterious spiral seemed to unwind, but I could not catch the method of its movement. The motion was like that of an uncoiling serpent bisected lengthwise, the two halves of the body seeming to slide against each other. Gradually that part of the cavern near the stone on which I stood became clear of its occupants, and at last I perceived that the throng had receded to the outer edge.

Then the encircling side walls of the amphitheater became visible, and as water sinks into sand, the medley of fragments of humanity disappeared from view.

I turned to my companion; he, too, had vanished. I glanced towards the liquor cauldrons; the stone was bare. I alone occupied the gigantic hall. No trace remained to tell of the throng that a short time previously had surrounded and mocked me.

Desolate, distracted, I threw myself upon the stone, and cursed my miserable self. "Come back," I cried, "come back. I will drink, drink, drink."

CHAPTER XL.

FURTHER TEMPTATION.—ETIDORHPA.

Then, as my voice reverbrated from the outer recesses, I caught a sound as of music in the distance. I raised my head and listened—yes, surely there was music. The melody became clearly distinct, and soon my senses were aware that both vocal and instrumental music were combined. The airs which came floating were sweet, simple, and beautiful. The voices and accompanying strains approached, but I could distinguish no words. By and by, from the corridors of the cavern, troops of bright female forms floated into view. They were clad in robes ranging from pure white to every richest hue, contrasting strangely, and in the distance their rainbow brilliancy made a gorgeous spectacle. Some were fantastically attired in short gowns, such as I imagine were worn by the dancing girls of sacred history, others had kirtles of a single bright color, others of many shades intermingled, while others still were dressed in gauze-like fabrics of pure white.

As they filed into the cavern, and approached me, they formed into platoons, or into companies, and then, as dissolving views come and go, they presented first one and then another figure. Sometimes they would stretch in great circling lines around the hall, again they would form into squares, and again into geometrical figures of all shades and forms, but I observed that with every change they drew nearer to the stone on which I rested.

They were now so near that their features could be distinguished, and never before had I seen such loveliness in human mold. Every face was as perfect as a master's picture of the Madonna, and yet no two seemed to possess the same type of beauty. Some were of dark complexion with glossy, raven hair, others were fair with hair ranging from light brown to golden. The style of head dress, as a rule, was of the simplest description. A tinted ribbon, or twisted cord, over the head, bound their hair with becoming grace, and their silken locks were either plaited into braids, curled into ringlets, or hung loosely, flowing in wavelets about their shoulders. Some held curious musical instruments, others beautiful wands, and altogether they produced a scenic effect of rare beauty that the most extravagant dream of fairyland could not surpass. Thus it was that I became again the center of a throng, not of repulsive monsters, but of marvelously lovely beings. They were as different from those preceding as darkness is from daylight.

Could any man from the data of my past experiences have predicted such a scene? Never before had the semblance of a woman appeared, never before had an intimation been given that the gentle sex existed in these silent chambers. Now, from the grotesque figures and horrible cries of the former occupants of this same cavern, the scene had changed to a conception of the beautiful and artistic, such as a poetic spirit might evolve in an extravagant dream of higher fairy land. I glanced above; the great hall was clothed in brilliant colors, the bare rocks had disappeared, the dome of that vast arch reaching to an immeasurable height, was decorated in all the colors of the rainbow. Flags and streamers fluttered in breezes that also moved the garments of the angelic throng about me, but which I could not sense; profiles of enchanting faces pervaded the glimmering space beyond; I alone was but an onlooker, not a participant of the joys about me.

The movements of the seraph-like figures continued, innumerable forms and figures followed forms and figures innumerable, and music indescribable blended with the poetry of motion. I was rapt, the past disappeared, my former mind was blotted from existence, the world vanished, and I became a thrill of joy, a sensation of absolute delight.

The band of spirits or fairy forms reached the rock at my feet, but I did not know how long a time they consumed in doing this; it may have been a second, and it may have been an eternity. Neither did I care. A single moment of existence such as I experienced, seemed worth an age of any other pleasure.

Circling about me, these ethereal creatures paused from their motions, and, as the music ceased, I stood above them, and yet in their midst, and gazed out into a distance illimitable, but not less beautiful in the expanse than was the adjacent part. The cavern had altogether disappeared, and in the depths about me as far as the eye could reach, seemingly into the broad expanse of heaven, I saw the exquisite forms that I have so imperfectly described.

Then a single band from the throng lightly sprung upon the stony terrace where I stood, and sung and danced before me. Every motion was perfect as imagination could depict, every sound was concentrated extract of melody. This band retired to be replaced by another, which in turn gave way to another, and still another, until, as in space we have no standard, time vanished, and numbers ceased to be numbers.

No two of the band of dancers were clothed alike, no two songs were similar, though all were inexpressibly enchanting. The first group seemed perfect, and yet the second was better, and each succeeding band sung sweeter songs, were more beautiful, and richer in dress than those preceding. I became enveloped in the æsthetic atmosphere, my spirit seemed to be loosened from the body, it was apparently upon the point of escaping from its mortal frame; suddenly the music ceased, the figures about became passive, and every form standing upright and graceful, gazed upon my face, and as I looked at the radiant creatures, each successive face, in turn, seemed to grow more beautiful, each form more exquisite than those about.

Then, in the distance, I observed the phalanx divide, forming into two divisions, separated by a broad aisle, stretching from my feet to the limit of space without, and down this aisle I observed a single figure advancing toward me.

As she approached, the phalanx closed in behind her, and when at last she reached the stone on which I stood, she stepped, or was wafted to my side, and the phalanx behind moved together and was complete again.

"My name is Etidorhpa. In me you behold the spirit that elevates man, and subdues the most violent of passions. In history, so far back in the dim ages as to be known now as legendary mythology, have I ruled and blessed the world. Unclasp my power over man and beast, and while heaven dissolves, the

ETIDORHPA.

charms of Paradise will perish. I know no master. The universe bows to my authority. Stars and suns enamored pulsate and throb in space and kiss each other in waves of light; atoms cold embrace and cling together; structures inanimate affiliate with and attract inanimate structures; bodies dead to other noble passions are not dead to love. The savage beast, under my enchantment, creeps to her lair, and gently purrs over her offspring; even man becomes less violent, and sheathes his weapon and smothers his hatred as I soothe his passions beside the loved ones in the privacy of his home.

"I have been known under many titles, and have comforted many peoples. Strike my name from Time's record, and the lovely daughters of Zeus and Dione would disappear; and with them would vanish the grace and beauty of woman; the sweet conception of the Froth Child of the Cyprus Sea would be lost; Venus, the Goddess of Love, would have no place in song, and Love herself, the holiest conception of the poet, man's superlative conception of Heaven's most precious charms, would be buried with the myrtle and the rose. My name is Etidorhpa; interpret it rightly, and you have what has been to humanity the essence of love, the mother of all that ennobles. He who loves a wife worships me; she, who in turn makes a home happy, is typical of me. I am Etidorhpa, the beginning and the end of earth. Behold in me the antithesis of envy, the opposite of malice, the enemy of sorrow, the mistress of life, the queen of immortal bliss.

"Do you know," she continued, and her voice, soft and sweet, carried with it a pleasurable sense of truthfulness indescribable, "do you know that man's idea of heaven, places me, Etidorhpa, on the highest throne? With the charm of maiden pure, I combine the devotion of wife and the holiness of mother. Take from the life of man the treasures I embody, and he will be homeless, childless, loveless. The thought of Heaven will in such a case be as the dismal conception of a dreary platitude. A life in such a Heaven, a Heaven devoid of love (and this the Scriptures teach), is one of endless torment.

"Love, by whatever name the conception is designated, rules the world. Divest the cold man of science, of the bond that binds him to his life-thought, and his work is ended. Strike from the master in music the chord that links his soul to the voice he breathes, and his songs will be hushed. Deaden the sense of love which the artist bears his art, and as the spirit that underlies his thought-scenes vanishes, his touch becomes chilled, and his brush inexpressive. The soldier thinks of his home and country, and without a murmur sheds his life blood.

"And yet there are debasing phases of love, for as love of country builds a nation, so love of pillage may destroy it. Love of the holy and the beautiful stand in human life opposed to love of the debasing and vicious, and I, Etidorhpa, am typical of the highest love of man. As the same force binds the molecules of the rose and the violet as well as those of noxious drugs, so the same soul conception may serve the love of good or the love of evil. Love may guide a tyrant or actuate a saint, may make man torture his fellow, or strive to ease his pain.

"Thus, man's propensity to serve his holy or his evil passion may each be called a degree in love, and in the serving of that passion the love of one heart may express itself as the antithesis of love in another. As bitter is to some men's taste more pleasant than sweet, and sour is yet more grateful to others, so one man may love the beautiful, another delight in the grotesque, and a third may love to see his neighbor suffer. Amid these, the phase of love that ennobles, brings the greatest degree of pleasure and comfort to mankind, but the love that degrades is love nevertheless, by whatever name the expression of the passion may be called. Love rules the world, and typical of man's intensest, holiest love, I, Etidorhpa, stand the Soul of Love Supreme."

She hesitated.

"Go on."

"I have already said, and in saying this have told the truth, I come from beyond the empty shell of a materialistic gold and silver conception of Heaven. Go with me, and in my home you will find man's soul devotion, regardless of material surroundings. I have said, and truly, the corridors of the Heaven mansion, enriched by precious stones and metals fine, but destitute of my smiles and graces, are deserted. The golden calf is no longer worshiped, cobwebs cling in festoons motionless, and the dust of selfish thoughts perverted, dry and black as the soot from Satan's fires settling therein, as the dust of an antiquated sarcophagus, rest undisturbed. Place on one side the Heaven of which gold-bound misers sing, and on the other Etidorhpa and the treasures that come with me to man and woman, (for without me neither wife, child, nor father could exist,) and from any other heaven mankind will turn away. The noblest gift of Heaven to humanity is the highest sense of love, and I, Etidorhpa, am the soul of love."

She ceased speaking, and as I looked at the form beside me I forgot myself in the rapture of that gaze.

Crush the colors of the rainbow into a single hue possessed of the attributes of all the others, and multiply that entity to infinity, and you have less richness than rested in any of the complex colors shown in the trimming of her raiment. Lighten the softness of eiderdown a thousand times, and yet maintain its sense of substance, and you have not conceived of the softness of the gauze that decked her simple, flowing garments. Gather the shadows cast by a troop of radiant angels, then sprinkle the resultant shade with star dust, and color therewith a garment brighter than satin, softer than silk, and more ethereal than light itself, and you have less beauty than reposed in the modest dress that enveloped her figure. Abstract the perfume from the sweetest oriental grasses, and combine with it the essential spirit of the wild rose, then add thereto the soul of ambergris, and the quintessential extracts of the finest aromatics of the East, and you have not approached the exquisite fragrance that penetrated my very being at her approach. She stood before me, slender, lithe, symmetrical, radiant. Her hair was more beautiful than pen can depict; it was colorless because it can not be described by colors known to mortals. Her face paled the beauty of all who had preceded her. She could not be a fairy, for no conception of a fairy can approach such loveliness; she was not a spirit, for surely material substance was a part of her form; she was not an angel, for no abnormal, irrational wing protruded from her shoulder to blemish her seraphic figure.

"No," I said musingly; "she is a creature of other climes; the Scriptures tell of no such being; she is neither human nor angelic, but"—

"But what?" she said.

"I do not know," I answered.

"Then I will tell you," she replied. "Yes; I will tell you of myself and of my companions. I will show you our home, carrying you through the shadows of heaven to exhibit that fair land, for heaven without Etidorhpa casts a shadow in comparison therewith. See," she said, as with her dainty fingers she removed from her garment a fragment of transparent film that I had not previously observed; "see, this is a cobweb that clung to my skirt, as, on my way to meet you, I passed through the dismal corridors of the materialists' loveless heaven."

She dropped it on the floor, and I stooped to pick it up, but vainly—my fingers passed through it as through a mist.

"You must be an angel," I stammered.

She smiled.

"Come," she said, "do not consume your time with thoughts of materialistic heaven; come with me to that brighter land beyond, and in those indescribable scenes we, you and I, will wander together forever."

She held out her hand; I hesitatingly touched it, and then raised it to my lips. She made no resistance.

I dropped upon my knees. "Are you to be mine?" I cried. "Mine forever?"

"Yes," she answered; "if you will it, for he who loves will be loved in turn."

"I will do it," I said; "I give myself to you, be you what you may, be your home where it may, I give up the earth behind me, and the hope of heaven before me; the here and the hereafter I will sacrifice. Let us hasten," I said, for she made no movement.

She shook her head. "You must yet be tempted as never before, and you must resist the tempter. You can not pass into the land of Etidorhpa until you suffered as only the damned can suffer, until you have withstood the pangs of thirst, and have experienced heat and cold indescribable. Remember the warning of your former guide, mark well the words of Etidorhpa: you must not yield. 'T was to serve you that I came before you now, 't was to preserve you from the Drunkard's Cavern that I have given you this vision of the land beyond the End of Earth where, if you will serve yourself, we will meet again.

She held aloft two tiny cups; I sprung to my feet and grasped one of them, and as I glanced at the throng in front of me, every radiant figure held aloft in the left hand a similar cup. All were gazing in my face. I looked at the transparent cup in my hand; it appeared to be partly filled with a green liquid. I looked at her cup and saw that it contained a similar fluid.

Forgetting the warning she had so recently given, I raised the cup to my lips, and just before touching it glanced again at her face. The fair creature stood with bowed head, her face covered with her hand; her very form and attitude spoke of sorrow and disappointment, and she trembled in distress. She held one hand as though to thrust back a form that seemed about to force itself beyond her figure, for peering exultingly from behind, leered the same Satanic face that met my gaze on the preceding occasion, when in the presence of the troop of demons, I had been tempted by the perfect man.

Dashing the cup to the floor I shouted:

"No; I will not drink."

Etidorhpa dropped upon her knees and clasped her hands. The Satanic figure disappeared from sight. Realizing that we had triumphed over the tempter, I also fell upon my knees in thankfulness.

CHAPTER XLI.

MISERY.

As all the bubbles in a glass shrink and vanish when the first collapses, so the troop of fairy-like forms before me disintegrated, and were gone. The delicate being, whose hand I held, fluttered as does a mist in the first gust of a sudden gale, and then dissolved into transparency. The gaily decked amphitheater disappeared, the very earth cavern passed from existence, and I found myself standing solitary and alone in a boundless desert. I turned towards every point of the compass only to find that no visible object appeared to break the monotony. I stood upon a floor of pure white sand which stretched to the horizon in gentle wave-like undulations as if the swell of the ocean had been caught, transformed to sand, and fixed.

I bent down and scooped a handful of the sand, and raised it in the palm of my hand, letting it sift back again to earth; it was surely sand. I pinched my flesh, and pulled my hair, I tore my garments, stamped upon the sand, and shouted aloud to demonstrate that I myself was still myself. It was real, yes, real. I stood alone in a desert of sand. Morning was dawning, and on one side the great sun rose slowly and majestically.

"Thank God for the sun," I cried. "Thank God for the light and heat of the sun."

I was again on surface earth; once more I beheld that glorious orb for the sight of which I had so often prayed when I believed myself miserable in the dismal earth caverns, and which I had been willing to give my very life once more to behold. I fell on my knees, and raised my hands in thankfulness. I blessed the rising sun, the illimitable sand, the air about me, and the blue heavens above. I blessed all that was before me, and again and again returned thanks for my delivery from the caverns beneath me. I did not think to question by what power this miracle had been accomplished. I did not care to do so; had I thought of the matter at all I would not have dared to question for fear the transition might prove a delusion.

I turned towards the sun, and walked eastward. As the day progressed and the sun rose into the heavens, I maintained my journey, aiming as best I could to keep the same direction. The heat increased, and when the sun reached the zenith it seemed as though it would melt the marrow in my bones. The sand, as white as snow and hot as lava, dazzled my eyes, and I covered them with my hands. The sun in the sky felt as if it were a ball of white hot iron near my head. It seemed small, and yet appeared to shine as through a tube directed only towards myself. Vainly did I struggle to escape and get beyond its boundary, the tube seemed to follow my every motion, directing the blazing shafts, and concentrating them ever upon my defenseless person. I removed my outer garments, and tore my shirt into fibers hoping to catch a waft of breeze, and with one hand over my eyes, and the other holding my coat above my head, endeavored to escape the mighty flood of heat, but vainly. The fiery rays streamed through the garment as mercury flows through a film of gauze. They penetrated my flesh, and vaporized my blood. My hands, fingers, and arms puffed out as a bladder of air expands under the influence of heat. My face swelled to twice, thrice its normal size, and at last my eyes were closed, for my cheeks and eyebrows met. I rubbed my shapeless hand over my sightless face, and found it as round as a ball; the nose had become imbedded in the expanded flesh, and my ears had disappeared in the same manner.

I could no longer see the sun, but felt the vivid, piercing rays I could not evade. I do not know whether I walked or rolled along; I only know that I struggled to escape those deadly rays. Then I prayed for death, and in the same breath begged the powers that had transferred me to surface earth to carry me back again to the caverns below. The recollection of their cool, refreshing atmosphere was as the thought of heaven must be to a lost spirit. I experienced the agony of a damned soul, and now, in contradistinction to former times, considered as my idea of perfect happiness the dismal earth caverns of other days. I thought of the day I had stood at the mouth of the Kentucky cave, and waded into the water with my guide; I recalled the refreshing coolness of the stream in the darkness of that cavern when the last ray of sunshine disappeared, and I cursed myself for longing then for sunshine, and the surface earth. Fool that man is, I mentally cried, not to be contented with that which is, however he may be situated, and wherever he may be placed. This is but a retribution, I am being cursed for my discontented mind, this is hell, and in comparison with this hell all else on or in earth is happiness. Then I damned the sun, the earth, the very God of all, and in my frenzy cursed everything that existed. I felt my puffed limbs, and prayed that I might become lean again. I asked to shrink to a skeleton, for seemingly my misery came with my expanded form; but I prayed and cursed in vain. So I struggled on in agony, every moment seemingly covering a multitude of years; struggled along like a lost soul plodding in an endless expanse of ever-increasing, ever-concentrating hell. At last, however, the day declined, the heat decreased, and as it did so my distorted body gradually regained its normal size, my eyesight returned, and finally I stood in that wilderness of sand watching the great red sun sink into the earth, as in the morning I had watched it rise. But between the sunrise and the sunset there had been an eternity of suffering, and then, as if released from a spell, I dropped exhausted upon the sand, and seemed to sleep. I dreamed of the sun, and that an angel stood before me, and asked why I was miserable, and in reply I pointed to the sun. "See," I said, "the author of the misery of man."

Said the angel: "Were there no sun there would be no men, but were there no men there would still be misery."

"Misery of what?" I asked.

"Misery of mind," replied the angel. "Misery is a thing, misery is not a conception—pain is real, pain is not an impression. Misery and pain would still exist and prey upon mind substance were there no men, for mind also is real, and not a mere conception. The pain you have suffered has not been the pain of matter, but the pain of spirit. Matter can not suffer. Were it matter that suffered, the heated sand would writhe in agony. No; it is only mind and spirit that experience pain, or pleasure, and neither mind nor spirit can evade its destiny, even if it escape from the body."

Then I awoke and saw once more the great red sun rise from the sand-edge of my desolate world, and I became aware of a new pain, for now I perceived the fact that I experienced the sense of thirst. The conception of the impression drew my mind to the subject, and instantly intense thirst, the most acute of bodily sufferings, possessed me. When vitalized tissue craves water, other physical wants are unfelt; when man parches to death all other methods of torture are disregarded. I thought no longer of the rising sun, I remembered no more the burning sand of yesterday, I felt only the pain of thirst.

"Water, water, water," I cried, and then in the distance as if in answer to my cry, I beheld a lake of water.

Instantly every nerve was strained, every muscle stretched, and I fled over the sands towards the welcome pool.

On and on I ran, and as I did so, the sun rising higher and higher, again began to burn the sands beneath my feet, and roast the flesh upon my bones. Once more I experienced that intolerable sense of pain, the pain of living flesh disintegrating by fire, and now with thirst gnawing at my vitals, and fire drying up the residue of my evaporated blood, I struggled in agony towards a lake that vanished before my gaze, to reappear just beyond.

This day was more horrible than the preceding, and yet it was the reverse so far as the action of the sun on my flesh was concerned. My prayer of yesterday had been fearfully answered, and the curses of the day preceding were being visited upon my very self. I had prayed to become lean, and instead of the former puffed tissue and expanded flesh, my body contracted as does beef when dried. The tightening skin squeezed upon the solidifying flesh, and as the moisture evaporated, it left a shriveled integument, contracted close upon the bone. My joints stood out as great protuberances, my skin turned to a dark amber color, and my flesh became transparent as does wetted horn. I saw my very vitals throb, I saw the empty blood vessels, the shriveled nerves and vacant arteries of my frame. I could not close my eyes. I could not shield them from the burning sun. I was a mummy, yet living, a dried corpse walking over the sand, dead to all save pain. I tried to fall, but could not, and I felt that, while the sun was visible, I must stand upright; I could not stop, and could not stoop. Then at last the malevolent sun sank beneath the horizon, and as the last ray disappeared again, I fell upon the sand.

I did not sleep, I did not rest, I did not breathe nor live a human; I only existed as a living pain, the conception of pain realized into a conscious nucleus,—and so the night passed. Again the sun arose, and with the light of her first ray I saw near at hand a caravan, camels, men, horses, a great cavalcade. They approached rapidly and surrounded me. The leader of the band alighted and raised me to my feet, for no longer had I the power of motion. He spoke to me kindly, and strange as it may seem to you, but not at all strange did it seem to me, called me by name.

"We came across your tracks in the desert," he said; "we are your deliverers."

I motioned for water; I could not speak.

"Yes," he said, "water you shall have."

Then from one of the skins that hung across the hump of a camel he filled a crystal goblet with sparkling water, and held it towards me, but just before the goblet touched my lips he withdrew it and said:

"I forgot to first extend the greetings of our people."

And then I noticed in his other hand a tiny glass containing a green liquid, which he placed to my lips, pronouncing the single word, "Drink."

I fastened my gaze upon the water, and opened my lips. I smelled the aroma of the powerful narcotic liquid within the glass, and hastened to obey, but glanced first at my deliverer, and in his stead saw the familiar face of the satanic figure that twice before had tempted me. Instantly, without a thought as to the consequences, without a fear as to the result, I dashed the glass to the sand, and my voice returning, I cried for the third time, "No; I will not drink."

The troop of camels instantly disappeared, as had the figures in the scenes before, the tempter resolved into clear air, the sand beneath my feet became natural again, and I became myself as I had been before passing through the hideous ordeal. The fact of my deliverance from the earth caverns had, I now realized, been followed by temporary aberration of my mind, but at last

I saw clearly again, the painful fancy had passed, the delirium was over.

I fell upon my knees in thankfulness; the misery through which I had passed had proven to be illusory, the earth caverns were beneath me, the mirage and temptations were not real, the horrors I had experienced were imaginary—thank God for all this—and that the sand was really sand. Solitary, alone, I knelt in the desert barren, from horizon to horizon desolation only surrounded, and yet the scene of that illimitable waste, a fearful reality, it is true, was sweet in comparison with the misery of body and soul about which I had dreamed so vividly.

"'T is no wonder," I said to myself, "that in the moment of transition from the underground caverns to the sunshine above, the shock should have disturbed my mental equilibrium, and in the moment of reaction I should have dreamed fantastic and horrible imaginings."

A cool and refreshing breeze sprung now, from I know not where; I did not care to ask; it was too welcome a gift to question, and contrasted pleasantly with the misery of my past hallucination. The sun was shining hot above me, the sand was glowing, parched beneath me, and yet the grateful breeze fanned my brow, and refreshed my spirit.

"Thank God," I cried, "for the breeze, for the coolness that it brings; only those who have experienced the silence of the cavern solitudes through which I have passed, and added thereto, have sensed the horrors of the more recent nightmare scenes, can appreciate the delights of a gust of air."

The incongruity of surrounding conditions, as connected with affairs rational, did not appeal at all to my questioning senses, it seemed as though the cool breeze, coming from out the illimitable desolation of a heated waste was natural. I arose and walked on, refreshed. From out that breeze my physical self drew refreshment and strength.

"'T is the cold," I said; "the blessed antithesis of heat, that supports life. Heat enervates, cold stimulates; heat depresses, cold animates. Thank God for breezes, winds, waters, cold."

I turned and faced the gladsome breeze. "'T is the source of life, I will trace it to its origin, I will leave the accursed desert, the hateful sunshine, and seek the blissful regions that give birth to cool breezes."

I walked rapidly, and the breeze became more energetic and cooler. With each increase of momentum on my part, corresponding strength seemed to be added to the breeze—both strength and coolness.

"Is not this delightful?" I murmured; "my God at last has come to be a just God. Knowing what I wanted, He sent the breeze; in answer to my prayer the cool, refreshing breeze arose. Damn the heat," I cried aloud, as I thought of the horrid day before; "blessed be the cold," and as though in answer to my cry the breeze stiffened and the cold strengthened itself, and I again returned thanks to my Creator.

With ragged coat wrapped about my form I faced the breeze and strode onward towards the home of the gelid wind that now dashed in gusts against my person.

Then I heard my footstep crunch, and perceived that the sand was hard beneath my feet; I stooped over to examine it and found it frozen. Strange, I reflected, strange that dry sand can freeze, and then I noticed, for the first time, that spurts of snow surrounded me, 't was a sleety mixture upon which I trod, a crust of snow and sand. A sense of dread came suddenly over me, and instinctively I turned, affrighted, and ran away from the wind, towards the desert behind me, back towards the sun, which, cold and bleak, low in the horizon, was sinking. The sense of dread grew upon me, and I shivered as I ran. With my back towards the breeze I had blessed, I now fled towards the sinking sun I had cursed. I stretched out my arms in supplication towards that orb, for from behind overhanging blackness spread, and about me roared a fearful hurricane. Vainly. As I thought in mockery the heartless sun disappeared before my gaze, the hurricane surrounded me, and the wind about me became intensely cold, and raved furiously. It seemed as though the sun had fled from my presence, and with the disappearance of that orb, the outline of the earth was blotted from existence. It was an awful blackness, and the universe was now to me a blank. The cold strengthened and froze my body to the marrow of my bones. First came the sting of frost, then the pain of cold, then insensibility of flesh. My feet were benumbed, my limbs motionless. I stood a statue, quiescent in the midst of the roaring tempest. The earth, the sun, the heavens themselves, my very person now had disappeared. Dead to the sense of pain or touch, sightless, amid a blank, only the noise of the raging winds was to me a reality. And as the creaking frost reached my brain and congealed it, the sound of the tempest ceased, and then devoid of physical senses, my quickened intellect, enslaved, remained imprisoned in the frozen form it could not leave, and yet could no longer control.

Reflection after reflection passed through that incarcerated thought entity, and as I meditated, the heinous mistakes I had committed in the life that had passed, arose to torment. God had answered my supplications, successively I had experienced the hollowness of earthly pleasures, and had left each lesson unheeded. Had I not alternately begged for and then cursed each gift of God? Had I not prayed for heat, cold, light, and darkness, and anathematized each? Had I not, when in perfect silence, prayed for sound; in sheltered caverns, prayed for winds and storms; in the very corridors of heaven, and in the presence of Etidorhpa, had I not sought for joys beyond?

Had I not found each pleasure of life a mockery, and notwithstanding each bitter lesson, still pursued my headstrong course, alternately blessing and cursing my Creator, and then myself, until now, amid a howling waste, in perfect darkness, my conscious intellect was bound to the frozen, rigid semblance of a body? All about me was dead and dark, all within was still and cold, only my quickened intellect remained as in every corpse the self-conscious intellect must remain, while the body has a mortal form, for death of body is not attended by the immediate liberation of mind. The consciousness of the dead man is still acute, and he who thinks the dead are mindless, will realize his fearful error when devoid of motion he lies a corpse, conscious of all that passes on around him, waiting the liberation that can only come by disintegration and destruction of the flesh.

So, unconscious of pain, unconscious of any physical sense, I existed on and on, enthralled, age after age passed and piled upon one another, for time was to me unchangeable, no more an entity. I now prayed for change of any kind, and envied the very devils in hell their pleasures, for were they not gifted with the power of motion, could they not hear, and see, and realize the pains they suffered? I prayed for death—death absolute, death eternal. Then, at last, the darkness seemed to lessen, and I saw the frozen earth beneath, the monstrous crags of ice above, the raging tempest about, for I now had learned by reflection to perceive by pure intellect, to see by the light within. My body, solid as stone, was fixed and preserved in a waste of ice. The world was frozen. I perceived that the sun, and moon, and stars, nearly stilled, dim and motionless, had paled in the cold depths of space. The universe itself was freezing, and amid the desolation only my deserted intellect remained. Age after age had passed, æons of ages had fled, nation after nation had grown and perished, and in the uncounted epochs behind, humanity had disappeared. Unable to free itself from the frozen body, my own intellect remained the solitary spectator of the dead silence about. At last, beneath my vision, the moon disappeared, the stars faded one by one, and then I watched the sun grow dim, until at length only a milky, gauze-like film remained to indicate her face, and then—vacancy. I had lived the universe away. And in perfect darkness the living intellect, conscious of all that had transpired in the ages past, clung still enthralled to the body of the frozen mortal. I thought of my record in the distant past, of the temptations I had undergone, and called myself a fool, for, had I listened to the tempter, I could at least have suffered, I could have had companionship even though it were of the devils—in hell. I lived my life over and over, times without number; I thought of my tempters, of the offered cups, and thinking, argued with myself:

"No," I said; "no, I had made the promise, I have faith in Etidorhpa, and were it to do over again I would not drink."

Then, as this thought sped from me, the ice scene dissolved, the enveloped frozen form of myself faded from view, the sand shrunk into nothingness, and with my natural body, and in normal condition, I found myself back in the earth cavern, on my knees, beside the curious inverted fungus, of which fruit I had eaten in obedience to my guide's directions. Before me the familiar figure of my guide stood, with folded arms, and as my gaze fell upon him he reached out his hand and raised me to my feet.

"Where have you been during the wretched epochs that have passed since I last saw you?" I asked.

"I have been here," he replied, "and you have been there."

"You lie, you villainous sorcerer," I cried; "you lie again as you have lied to me before. I followed you to the edge of demon land, to the caverns of the drunkards, and then you deserted me. Since last we met I have spent a million, billion years of agony inexpressible, and have had that agony made doubly horrible by contrast with the thought, yes, the very sight and touch of Heaven. I passed into a double eternity, and have experienced the ecstacies of the blessed, and suffered the torments of the damned, and now you dare boldly tell me that I have been here, and that you have been there, since last I saw you stand by this cursed fungus bowl."

"Yes," he said, taking no offense at my violence; "yes, neither of us has left this spot; you have sipped of the drink of an earth-damned drunkard, you have experienced part of the curses of intemperance, the delirium of narcotics. Thousands of men on earth, in their drunken hallucination, have gone through hotter hells than you have seen; your dream has not exaggerated the sufferings of those who sup of the delirium of intemperance."

And then he continued:

"Let me tell you of man's conception of eternity."

CHAPTER XLII.

ETERNITY WITHOUT TIME.

"Man's conception of eternity is that of infinite duration, continuance without beginning or end, and yet everything he knows is bounded by two or more opposites. From a beginning, as he sees a form of matter, that substance passes to an end." Thus spoke my guide.

Then he asked, and showed by his question that he appreciated the nature of my recent experiences: "Do you recall the instant that you left me standing by this bowl to start, as you imagined, with me as a companion, on the journey to the cavern of the grotesque?"

"No; because I did not leave you. I sipped of the liquid, and then you moved on with me from this spot; we were together, until at last we were separated on the edge of the cave of drunkards."

"Listen," said he; "I neither left you nor went with you. You neither went from this spot nor came back again. You neither saw nor experienced my presence nor my absence; there was no beginning to your journey."

"Go on."

"You ate of the narcotic fungus; you have been intoxicated."

"I have not," I retorted. "I have been through your accursed caverns, and into hell beyond. I have been consumed by eternal damnation in the journey, have experienced a heaven of delight, and also an eternity of misery."

"Upon the contrary, the time that has passed since you drank the liquid contents of that fungus fruit has only been that which permitted you to fall upon your knees. You swallowed the liquor when I handed you the shell cup; you dropped upon your knees, and then instantly awoke. See," he said; "in corroboration of my assertion the shell of the fungus fruit at your feet is still dripping with the liquid you did not drink. Time has been annihilated. Under the influence of this potent earth-bred narcoto-intoxicant, your dream begun inside of eternity; you did not pass into it."

"You say," I interrupted, "that I dropped upon my knees, that I have experienced the hallucination of intoxication, that the experiences of my vision occurred during the second of time that was required for me to drop upon my knees."

"Yes."

"Then by your own argument you demonstrate that eternity requires time, for even a millionth part of a second is time, as much so as a million of years."

"You mistake," he replied, "you misinterpret my words. I said that all you experienced in your eternity of suffering and pleasure, occurred between the point when you touched the fungus fruit to your lips, and that when your knees struck the stone."

"That consumed time," I answered.

"Did I assert," he questioned, "that your experiences were scattered over that entire period?"

"No."

"May not all that occurred to your mind have been crushed into the second that accompanied the mental impression produced by the liquor, or the second of time that followed, or any other part of that period, or a fraction of any integral second of that period?"

"I can not say," I answered, "what part of the period the hallucination, as you call it, occupied."

"You admit that so far as your conception of time is concerned, the occurrences to which you refer may have existed in either an unestimable fraction of the first, the second, or the third part of the period."

"Yes," I replied, "yes; if you are correct in that, they were illusions."

"Let me ask you furthermore," he said; "are you sure that the flash that bred your hallucination was not instantaneous, and a part of neither the first, second, or third second?"

"Continue your argument."

"I will repeat a preceding question with a slight modification. May not all that occurred to your mind have been crushed into the space between the second of time that preceded the mental impression produced by the liquor, and the second that followed it? Need it have been a part of either second, or of time at all? Indeed, could it have been a part of time if it were instantaneous?"

"Go on."

"Suppose the entity that men call the soul of man were in process of separation from the body. The process you will admit would occupy time, until the point of liberation was reached. Would not dissolution, so far as the separation of matter and spirit is concerned at its critical point be instantaneous?"

I made no reply.

"If the critical point is instantaneous, there would be no beginning, there could be no end. Therein rests an eternity greater than man can otherwise conceive of, for as there is neither beginning nor end, time and space are annihilated. The line that separates the soul that is in the body from the soul that is out of the body is outside of all things. It is a between, neither a part of the nether side nor of the upper side; it is outside the here and the here-after. Let us carry this thought a little further," said he. "Suppose a good man were to undergo this change, could not all that an eternity of happiness might offer be crushed into this boundless conception, the critical point? All that a mother craves in children dead, could reappear again in their once loved forms; all that a good life earns, would rest in the soul's experience in that eternity, but not as an illusion, although no mental pleasure, no physical pain is equal to that of hallucinations. Suppose that a vicious life were ended, could it escape the inevitable critical point? Would not that life in its previous journey create its own sad eternity? You have seen the working of an eternity with an end but not a beginning to it, for you can not sense the commencement of your vision. You have been in the cavern of the grotesque,— the realms of the beautiful, and have walked over the boundless sands that bring misery to the soul, and have, as a statue, seen the frozen universe dissolve. You are thankful that it was all an illusion as you deem it now; what would you think had only the heavenly part been spread before you?"

"I would have cursed the man who dispelled the illusion," I answered.

"Then," he said, "you are willing to admit that men who so live as to gain such an eternity, be it mental illusion, hallucination or real, make no mistake in life."

"I do," I replied; "but you confound me when you argue in so cool a manner that eternity may be everlasting to the soul, and yet without the conception of time."

"Did I not teach you in the beginning of this journey," he interjected, "that time is not as men conceive it. Men can not grasp an idea of eternity and retain their sun bred, morning and evening, conception of time. Therein lies their error. As the tip of the whip-lash passes with the lash, so through life the soul of man proceeds with the body. As there is a point just when the tip of the whip-lash is on the edge of its return, where all motion of the line that bounds the tip ends, so there is a motionless point when the soul starts onward from the body of man. As the tip of the whip lash sends its cry through space, not while it is in motion either way, but from the point where motion ceases, the spaceless, timeless point that lies between the backward and the forward, so the soul of man leaves a cry (eternity) at the critical point. It is the death echo, and thus each snap of the life-thread throws an eternity, its own eternity, into eternity's seas, and each eternity is made up of the entities thus cast from the critical point. With the end of each soul's earth journey, a new eternity springs into existence, occupying no space, consuming no time, and not conflicting with any other, each being exactly what the soul-earth record makes it, an eternity of joy (heaven), or an eternity of anguish (hell). There can be no neutral ground."

Then he continued:

"The drunkard is destined to suffer in the drunkard's eternity, as you have suffered; the enticement of drink is evanescent, the agony to follow is eternal. You have seen that the sub-regions of earth supply an intoxicant. Taste not again of any intoxicant; let your recent lesson be your last. Any stimulant is an enemy to man, any narcotic is a fiend. It destroys its victim, and corrupts the mind, entices it into pastures grotesque, and even pleasant at first, but destined to eternal misery in the end. Beware of the eternity that follows the snapping of the life-thread of a drunkard. Come," he abruptly said, "we will pursue our journey."

(NOTE.—Morphine, belladonna, hyoscyamus, and cannabis indica are narcotics, and yet each differs in its action from the others. Alcohol and methyl alcohol are intoxicants; ether, chloroform, and chloral are anæsthetics, and yet no two are possessed of the same qualities. Is there any good reason to doubt that a hidden combination of the elements can not cause hallucinations that combine and intensify the most virulent of narcotics, intoxicants, and anæsthetics, and pall the effects of hashish, or of opium?

If, in the course of experimentation, a chemist should strike upon a compound that in traces only would subject his mind and drive his pen to record such seemingly extravagant ideas as are found in the hallucinations herein pictured, or to frame word-sentences foreign to normal conditions, and beyond his natural ability, and yet could he not know the end of such a drug, would it not be his duty to bury the discovery from others, to cover from mankind the existence of such a noxious fruit of the chemist's or pharmaceutist's art? To sip once or twice of such a potent liquid, and then to write lines that tell the story of its power may do no harm to an individual on his guard, but mankind in common should never possess such a penetrating essence. Introduce such an intoxicant, and start it to ferment in humanity's blood, and it may spread from soul to soul, until, before the world is advised of its possible results, the ever-increasing potency will gain such headway as to destroy, or debase, our civilization, and even to exterminate mankind.—J. U. L.)

INTERLUDE.

CHAPTER XLIII.

THE LAST CONTEST.

I, Lewellyn Drury, had been so absorbed in the fantastic story the old man read so fluently from the execrably written manuscript, and in the metaphysical argument which followed his account of the vision he had introduced so artfully as to lead me to think it was a part of his narrative, that I scarcely noted the passage of time. Upon seeing him suspend his reading, fold the manuscript, and place it in his pocket, I reverted to material things, and glancing at the clock, perceived that the hands pointed to bed-time.

"To-morrow evening," said he, "I will return at nine o'clock. In the interim, if you still question any part of the story, or wish further information on any subject connected with my journey, I will be prepared to answer your queries. Since, however, that will be your last opportunity, I suggest that you make notes of all subjects that you wish to discuss."

Then, in his usual self-possessed, exquisitely polite manner, he bowed himself out.

I spent the next day reviewing the most questionable features of his history, recalling the several statements that had been made. Remembering the humiliation I had experienced in my previous attempts to confute him, I determined to select such subjects as would appear the most difficult to explain, and to attack the old man with vehemence.

I confess, that notwithstanding my several failures, and his successful and constant elucidation and minute details in regard to occurrences which he related, and which anticipated many points I had once had in mind to question, misgivings still possessed me concerning the truthfulness of the story. If these remarkable episodes were true, could there be such a thing as fiction? If not all true, where did fact end and fancy begin?

Accordingly I devoted the following day to meditating my plan of attack, for I felt that I had been challenged to a final contest. Late the next day, I felt confident of my own ability to dispossess him, and in order further to test his power, when night came I doubly locked the door to my room, first with the key and next with the inside bolt. I had determined to force him again to induce inert material to obey his command, as he had done at our first interview. The reader will remember that Prof. Chickering had deemed that occurrence an illusion, and I confess that time had dimmed the vividness of the scene in my own mind. Hence I proposed to verify the matter. Therefore, at the approach of nine o'clock, the evening following, I sat with my gaze riveted on the bolt of the door, determined not to answer his knock.

He gave me no chance to neglect a response to his rap. Exactly at the stroke of nine the door swung noiselessly on its hinges, the wizard entered, and the door closed again. The bolt had not moved, the knob did not turn. The bar passed through the catch and back to its seat,—I sprung from my chair, and excitedly and rudely rushed past my guest. I grasped the knob, wrenched it with all my might. Vainly; the door was locked, the bolt was fastened. Then I turned to my visitor. He was quietly seated in his accustomed place, and apparently failed to notice my discomposure, although he must have realized that he had withstood my first test.

This pronounced defeat, at the very beginning of our proposed contest, produced a depressing effect; nevertheless I made an effort at self-control, and seating myself opposite, looked my antagonist in the face. Calm, dignified, with the brow of a philosopher, and the countenance of a philanthropist, a perfect type of the exquisite gentleman, and the cultured scholar, my guest, as serene and complacent as though, instead of an intruder, he were an invited participant of the comforts of my fireside, or even the host himself, laid his hat upon the table, stroked his silvery, translucent beard, and said:

"Well?"

I accepted the challenge, for the word, as he emphasized it, was a challenge, and hurled at him, in hopes to catch him unprepared, the following abrupt sentence:

"I doubt the possibility of the existence of a great cavern such as you have described. The superincumbent mass of earth would crush the strongest metal. No material known to man could withstand a pressure so great as would overlie an arch as large as that you depict; material would succumb even if the roof were made of steel."

"Do not be so positive," he replied. "By what authority do you make this assertion?"

"By the authority of common sense as opposed to an unreasonable hypothesis. You should know that there is a limit to the strength of all things, and that no substance is capable of making an arch of thousands of miles, which, according to your assertion, must have been the diameter of the roof of your inland sea."

"Ah," he replied, "and so you again crush my facts with your theory. Well, let me ask a question."

"Proceed."

"Did you ever observe a bubble resting on a bubble?"

"Yes."

"Did you ever place a pipe-stem in a partly filled bowl of soap water, and by blowing through it fill the bowl with bubbles?"

"Yes."

"Did you ever calculate the tensile strength of the material from which you blew the bubble?"

"No; for soap water has no appreciable strength."

"And yet you know that a bubble made of suds has not only strength, but elasticity. Suppose a bubble of energy floating in space were to be covered to the depth of the thickness of a sheet of tissue paper with the dust of space, would that surprise you?"

"No."

"Suppose two such globes of energy, covered with dust, were to be telescoped or attached together, would you marvel at the fact?"

"No."

He drew a picture on a piece of paper, in which one line was inclosed by another, and remarked:

"The pencil mark on this paper is proportionately thicker than the crust of the earth over the earth cavern I have described. Even if it were made of soap suds, it could revolve through space and maintain its contour."

"But the earth is a globe," I interjected.

"You do not mean an exact globe?"

"No; it is flattened at the poles."

He took from his pocket two thin rubber balls, one slightly larger than the other. With his knife he divided the larger ball, cutting it into halves. He then placed one of the sections upon the perfect ball, and held the arrangement between the gas light and the wall.

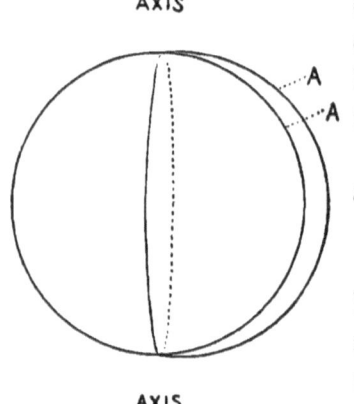

FIG. 33.
A A, telescoped energy spheres.

"See; is not the shadow flattened, as your earth is, at the poles?"

"Yes; but the earth is not a shadow."

"We will not argue that point now," he replied, and then asked: "Suppose such a compound shell as this were to revolve through space and continuously collect dust, most of it of the earth's temperature, forming a fluid (water), would not that dust be propelled naturally from the poles?"

"Yes; according to our theory."

"Perhaps," said he, "the contact edge of the invisible spheres of energy which compose your earth bubbles, for planets are bubbles, have been covered with water and soil during the time the energy bubble, which is the real bone of the globe, has been revolving through space; perhaps, could you reach the foundation of the earth dust, you would find it not a perfect sphere, but a compound skeleton, as of two bubbles locked, or rather telescoped together. [See Fig. 34.]

"Are you sure that my guide did not lead me through the space between the bubbles?"

Then he continued:

"Do not be shocked at what I am about to assert, for, as a member of materialistic humanity, you will surely consider me

THE LAST CONTEST. 281

irrational when I say that matter, materials, ponderous substances, one and all, so far as the ponderous part is concerned, have no strength."

"What! no strength?"

"None whatever."

I grasped the poker.

"Is not this matter?"

"Yes."

"I can not break it."

"No."

"Have not I strength?"

"Confine your argument now to the poker; we will consider you next. You can not break it."

"I can break this pencil, though," and I snapped it in his face.

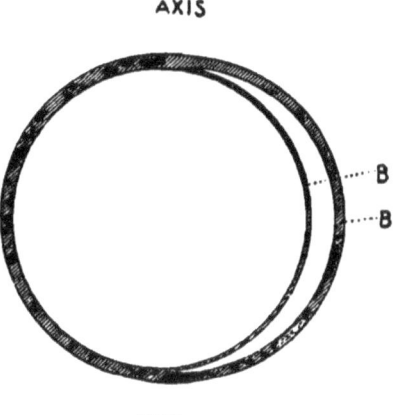

FIG. 34.
B B, telescoped energy spheres covered with space dirt, inclosing space between.

"Yes."

I curled my lip in disdain.

"You carry this argument too far."

"Why?"

"I can break the pencil, I can not break the poker; had these materials not different strengths there could be no distinction; had I no strength I could not have broken either."

"Are you ready to listen?" he replied.

"Yes; but do not exasperate me."

"I did not say that the combination you call a poker had no strength, neither did I assert that you could not break a pencil."

"A distinction without a difference; you play upon words."

"I said that matter, the ponderous side of material substances, has no strength."

"And I say differently."

He thrust the end of the poker into the fire, and soon drew it forth red-hot.

"Is it as strong as before?"

"No."

"Heat it to whiteness and it becomes plastic."

"Yes."

"Heat it still more and it changes to a liquid."

"Yes."

"Has liquid iron strength?"

"Very little, if any."

"Is it still matter?"

"Yes."

"Is it the material of the iron, or is it the energy called heat that qualifies the strength of the metal? It seems to me that were I in your place I would now argue that absence of heat constitutes strength," he sarcastically continued.

"Go on."

"Cool this red-hot poker by thrusting it into a pail of cold water, and it becomes very hard and brittle."

"Yes."

"Cool it slowly, and it is comparatively soft and plastic."

"Yes."

"The material is the same, is it not?"

"Go on."

"What strength has charcoal?"

"Scarcely any."

"Crystallize it, and the diamond results."

"I did not speak of diamond."

"Ah! and is not the same amount of the same material present in each, a grain of diamond and a grain of charcoal? What is present in a grain of diamond that is not present in a grain of charcoal?"

"Go on."

"Answer my question."

"I can not."

"Why does brittle, cold zinc, when heated, become first ductile, and then, at an increased temperature, become brittle again. In each case the same material is present?"

"I do not know; but this I do know: I am an organized being, and I have strength of body."

The old man grasped the heavy iron poker with both hands, and suddenly rising to his full height, swung it about his head, then with a motion so menacing that I shrunk back into my chair and cried out in alarm, seemed about to strike, with full force, my defenseless brow.

"My God," I shouted, "what have I done that you should murder me?"

He lowered the weapon, and calmly asked:

"Suppose that I had crushed your skull—where then would be your vaunted strength?"

I made no reply, for as yet I had not recovered from the mental shock.

"Could you then have snapped a pencil? Could you have broken a reed? Could you even have blown the down from a thistle bloom?"

"No."

"Would not your material body have been intact?"

"Yes."

"Listen," said he. "Matter has no strength, matter obeys spirit, and spirit dominates all things material. Energy in some form holds particles of matter together, and energy in other forms loosens them. 'T is this impenetrable force that gives strength to substances, not the ponderable side of the material. Granite crushed is still granite, but destitute of rigidity. Creatures dead are still organic structures, but devoid of strength or motion. The spirit that pervades all material things gives to them form and existence. Take from your earth its vital spirit, the energy that subjects matter, and your so-called adamantine rocks would disintegrate, and sift as dust into the interstices of space. Your so-called rigid globe, a shell of space dust, would dissolve, collapse, and as the spray of a burst bubble, its ponderous side would vanish in the depths of force about."

I sat motionless.

"Listen," he repeated. "You wrong your own common sense when you place dead matter above the spirit of matter. Atoms come and go in their ceaseless transmigrations, worlds move, universes circulate, not because they are material bodies, but because as points of matter, in a flood of force, they obey the spirit that can blot out a sun, or dissolve the earth, as easily as it can unlink two atoms. Matter is an illusion, spirit is the reality."

I felt that he had silenced me against my will, and although I could not gainsay his assertions, I determined to study the subject carefully, at my leisure.

"As you please," he interjected into my musings; "but since you are so determined, you would better study from books that are written by authors who know whereof they write, and who are not obliged to theorize from speculative data concerning the intrastructural earth crust."

"But where can I find such works? I do not know of any."

"Then," said he, "perhaps it would be better to cease doubting the word of one who has acquired the knowledge to write such a book, and who has no object in misleading you."

"Still other questions arise," I said.

"Well?"

"I consider the account of the intra-earth fungus intoxicant beyond the realm of fact."

"In what respect?"

"The perfect loss of self that resulted immediately, in an instant, after swallowing the juice of the fungus fruit, so that you could not distinguish between the real guide at your side and the phantom that sprung into existence, is incredible. [See p. 234.] An element of time is a factor in the operation of nerve impressions."*

"Have you investigated all possible anæsthetics?" he asked.

"Of course not."

"Or all possible narcotics?"

"No."

"How long does it require for pure prussic acid to produce its physiological action?"

"I do not know."

He ignored my reply, and continued:

"Since there exists a relative difference between the time that is required for ether and chloroform to produce insensibility, and between the actions and resultant effects of all known anæsthetics, intoxicants, and narcotics, I think you are hypercritical. Some nerve excitants known to you act slowly, others quickly; why not others still instantaneously? If you can rest your assertion on any good basis, I will gladly meet your questions, but I do not accept such evidence as you now introduce, and I do not care to argue for both parties."

---

* It is well that reference was made to this point. Few readers would probably notice that Chapter XXXVI. begun a narcotic hallucination.—J. U. L.

Again I was becoming irritated, for I was not satisfied with the manner in which I upheld my part of the argument, and naturally, as is usually the case with the defeated party, became incensed at my invincible antagonist.

"Well," I said, "I criticise your credulity. The drunkards of the drunkards' cavern were beyond all credence. I can not conceive of such abnormal creations, even in illusion. Had I met with your experiences I would not have supposed, for an instant, that the fantastic shapes could have been aught than a dream, or the result of hallucination, while, without a question, you considered them real."

"You are certainly pressed for subjects about which to complain when you resort to criticising the possibilities in creations of a mind under the influence of a more powerful intoxicant than is known to surface earth," he remarked. "However, I will show you that nature fashions animals in forms more fantastic than I saw, and that even these figures were not overdrawn"—

Without heeding his remark, I interrupted his discourse, determined to have my say:

"And I furthermore question the uncouth personage you describe as your guide. Would you have me believe that such a being has an existence outside an abnormal thought-creation?"

"Ah," he replied, "you have done well to ask these two questions in succession, for you permit me to answer both at once. Listen: The Monkey, of all animals, seems to approach closest to man in figure, the Siamang Gibon of Asia, the Bald-headed Saki of South America, with its stub of a tail, being nearest. From these types we have great deviations as in the Wanderer of India, with its whiskered face, and the Black Macaque of the Island of Celebes, with its hairy topknot, and hairless stub of a tail, or the well-known Squirrel Monkey, with its long supple tail, and the Thumbless Spider Monkey, of South America. Between these types we have among monkeys, nearly every conceivable shape of limb and figure, and in color of their faces and bodies, all the shades of the rainbow.

"Some Squirrels jump and then sail through the air. The Sloth can barely move on the earth. Ant-eaters have no teeth at all, while the Grizzly Bear can crush a gun barrel with its molars.

"The Duck-billed Platypus of South Australia has the body of a mole, the tail of a raccoon, the flat bill of a duck, and the flipper of a seal, combined with the feet of a rat. It lays eggs as birds do, but suckles its young as do other mammalia. The Opossum has a prehensile tail, as have some monkeys, and in addition a living bag or pouch in which the female carries her tiny young. The young of a kind of tree frog of the genus Hylodes, breathe through a special organ in their tails; the young of the Pipa, a great South American toad, burrow into the skin of the mother, and still another from Chili, as soon as hatched, creep down the throat of the father frog, and find below the jaw an opening into a false membrane covering the entire abdomen, in which they repose in safety. Three species of frogs and toads have no tongue at all, while in all the others the tongue is attached by its tip to the end of the mouth, and is free behind. The ordinary Bullfrog has conspicuous great legs, while a relative, the Cœcilia (and others as well) have a head reminding of the frog, but neither tail nor legs, the body being elongated as if it were a worm. The long, slender fingers of a Bat are united by means of a membrane that enables it to fly like a bird, while as a contrast, the fingers of a Mole, its near cousin, are short and stubby, and massive as compared with its frame. The former flies through the air, the latter burrows (almost flies) through the earth. The Great Ant-eater has a curved head which is drawn out into a slender snout, no teeth, a long, slender tongue, a great bushy tail, and claws that neither allow the creature to burrow in the earth nor climb into trees, but which are admirably adapted to tear an ant-hill into fragments. Its close relatives, the Apar and Armadillo, have a round body covered with bony plates, and a short, horny, curved tail, while another relative, the Long-tailed Pangolin, has a great alligator-like tail which, together with its body, is covered with horny, overlapping scales.

"The Greenland Whale has an enormous head occupying more than one-third its length, no teeth, and a throat scarcely larger than that of a sucker fish. The Golden Mole has a body so nearly symmetrical that, were it not for the snout, it would be difficult to determine the location of the head without close inspection, and it has legs so short that, were it not for the powerful claws, they would not be observed at all. The Narwhal has a straight, twisted tusk, a "—

"Hold, hold," I interrupted; "do you think that I am concerned in these well known contrasts in animal structure?"

"Did you not question the possibility of the description I gave of my grotesque drunkards, and of the form of my subterranean guide?" my guest retorted.

"Yes; but I spoke of men, you describe animals."

"Man is an animal, and between the various species of animals that you say are well known, greater distinctions can be drawn than between my guide and surface-earth man. Besides, had you allowed me to proceed to a description of animal life beneath the surface of the earth, I would have shown you that my guide partook of their attributes. Of the creatures described, one only was of the intra-earth origin—the Mole,—and like my guide, it is practically eyeless."

"Go on," I said; "'tis useless for me to resist. And yet"—

"And yet what?"

"And yet I have other subjects to discuss."

"Proceed."

"I do not like the way in which you constantly criticise science, especially in referring thereto the responsibilities of the crazed anatomist.* It seems to me that he was a monomaniac, gifted, but crazed, and that science was unfortunate in being burdened with such an incubus."

"True, and yet science advances largely by the work of such apparently heartless creatures. Were it not for investigators who overstep the bounds of established methods, and thus criticise their predecessors, science would rust and disintegrate. Besides, why should not science be judged by the rule she applies to others?"

"What do you mean?"

"Who is more free to criticise religion than the materialistic man of science?"

"But a religious man is not cruel."

"Have you not read history? Have you not shuddered at the crimes recorded in the name of the religions of man?"

---

* This section (see p. 190) was excised, being too painful.—J. U. L.

"Yes; but these cruelties were committed by misguided men under the cloak of the church, or of false religions, during the dark ages. Do not blame religion, but the men who abused the cause."

"Yes," he added, "you are right; they were fanatics, crazed beings, men; yes, even communities, raving mad. Crazed leaders can infuse the minds of the people with their fallacies, and thus become leaders of crazed nations. Not, as I have depicted in my scientific enthusiast, one man alone in the privacy of his home torturing a single child, but whole nations pillaging, burning, torturing, and destroying. But this is foreign to our subject. Beware, I reiterate, of the science of human biology. The man who enters the field can not foresee the end, the man who studies the science of life, and records his experiments, can not know the extremes to which a fanatical follower may carry the thought-current of his leader. I have not overdrawn the lesson. Besides, science is now really torturing, burning, maiming, and destroying humanity. The act of destruction has been transferred from barbarians and the fanatic in religion to the follower of the devotees of science."

"No; I say no."

"Who created the steam engine? Who evolves improved machinery? Who creates improved artillery, and explosives? Scientific men."

He hesitated.

"Go on."

"Accumulate the maimed and destroyed each year; add together the miseries and sorrows that result from the explosions, accidents, and catastrophes resulting from science improvements, and the dark ages scarcely offer a parallel. Add thereto the fearful destruction that follows a war among nations scientific, and it will be seen that the scientific enthusiast of the present has taken the place of the misguided fanatic of the past. Let us be just. Place to the credit of religion the good that religion has done, place to the credit of science the good that science is doing, and yet do not mistake, both leave in their wake an atmosphere saturated with misery, a road whitened with humanity's bones. Neither the young nor the old are spared, and so far as the sufferer is concerned it matters not whether the person has been racked by the tortures of an inquisition, or the sword of an infidel, is shrieking in the agony of a scald by super-heated steam, or is mangled by an explosion of nitroglycerin."

Again he hesitated.

"Go on."

"One of science's most serious responsibilities, from which religion has nearly escaped, is that of supplying thought-food to fanatics, and from this science can not escape."

"Explain yourself."

"Who places the infidel in possession of arguments to combat sacred teachings? Who deliberately tortures animals, and suggests that biological experimentation in the name of science, before cultured audiences even, is legitimate, even to the making of life sections of throbbing, living creatures?"

"Enough, enough," I cried, thinking of his crazed anatomist, and covering my face with my hands; "you make my blood creep."

"Yes," he added sarcastically; "you shudder now and criticise my truthful study, and to-morrow you will forget the lesson, and perhaps for dinner you will relish your dish of veal, the favorite food of mothers, the nearest approach to the flesh of babies."

Then his manner changed, and in his usual mild, pleasant way, he said:

"Take what I have said kindly; I wish only to induce your religious part to have more charity for your scientific self, and the reverse. Both religion and science are working towards the good of man, although their devotees are human, and by human errors bring privations, sufferings, and sorrows to men. Neither can fill the place of the other; each should extend a helping hand, and have charity for the shortcomings of the other; they are not antagonists, but workers in one field; both must stand the criticisms of mutual antagonists, and both have cause to fear the evils of fanaticism within their own ranks more than the attacks of opponents from without. Let the religious enthusiast exercise care; his burning, earnest words may lead a weak-minded father to murder an innocent family, and yet 't is not religion that commits the crime. Let the zealous scientific man hesitate; he piles up fuel by which minds unbalanced, or dispositions perverted, seek to burn and destroy hopes that have long served the yearnings of humanity's soul. Neither pure religion nor true science is to blame for the acts of its devotess, and yet each must share the responsibility of its human agents."

"We will discuss the subject no further," I said; "it is not agreeable."

Then I continued:

"The idea of eternity without time is not quite clear to me, although I catch an imperfect conception of the argument advanced. Do you mean to say that when a soul leaves the body, the earth life of the individual, dominated by the soul, is thrown off from it as is the snap of a whip-lash, and that into the point between life and death, the hereafter of that mortal may be concentrated?"

"I simply give you the words of my guide," he replied, "but you have expressed the idea about as well as your word language will admit. Such a conception of eternity is more rational to one who, like myself, has lived through an instant that covered, so far as mind is concerned, a million years of time, than is an attempt to grasp a conception of an eternity, without beginning or end, by basing an argument on conditions governing material substances, as these substances are known to man. You have the germ of the idea which may be simply a thought for you to ponder over; you can study the problem at your leisure. Do not, however, I warn you, attempt to comprehend the notion of eternity by throwing into it the conception of time as men accept that term, for the very word time, as men define it, demands that there be both a beginning and an end. With the sense of time in one's mind, there can be no conception of the term eternity."

Then, as I had so often done before, I unwarily gave him an opportunity to enlarge on his theme, to my disadvantage. I had determined not to ask any questions concerning his replies to my criticism, for whenever I had previously done so, the result had been disastrous to me. In this case I unwittingly said:

"Why do you say that our language will not permit of clearer conceptions than you give?"

"Because your education does not permit you to think outside of words; you are word-bound."

"You astonish me by making such an arrogant assertion. Do you mean to assert that I can not think without using words?"

"Yes." Every thought you indulge in circumscribed. You presumably attempt to throw a thought-line forward, and yet you step backward and spin it in words that have been handed you from the past, and, struggle as you may, you can not liberate yourself from the dead incubus. Attempt to originate an idea, and see if you can escape your word-master?"

"Go on; I am listening."

"Men scientific think in language scientific. Men poetical think in language poetic. All educated men use words in thinking of their subjects, words that came to them from the past, and enslave their intellect. Thus it is that the novelist can not make fiction less real than is fact; that scientists can not commence in the outside, and build a theory back to phenomena understood. In each case the foundation of a thought is a word that in the very beginning carries to the mind a meaning, a something from the past. Each thought ramification is an offshoot from words that express ideas and govern ideas, yes, create ideas, even dominating the mind. Men speak of ideas when they intend to refer to an image in the mind, but in reality they have no ideas outside of the word sentences they unconsciously reformulate. Define the term idea correctly, and it will be shown that an idea is a sentence, and if a sentence is made of words already created, there can be no new idea, for every word has a fixed meaning. Hence, when men think, they only rearrange words that carry with themselves networks of ideas, and thus play upon their several established meanings. How can men so circumscribed construct a new idea or teach a new science?"

"New words are being created."

"Language is slowly progressing, but no new word adds itself to a language; it is linked to thought-chains that precede. In order to create a word, as a rule, roots are used that are as established in philology as are building materials in architecture. When a new sound is thrust into a language, its intent must be introduced by words already known, after which it conveys a meaning derived from the past, and becomes a part of mind sentences already constructed, as it does of spoken language. Language has thus been painfully and slowly evolved and is still being enlarged, but while new impressions may be felt by an educated person, the formulated feeling is inseparable, from well-known surviving words."

"Some men are dumb."

"Yes; and yet they frame mind-impressions into unspoken words of their own, otherwise they would be scarcely more than animals. Place an uneducated dumb person in a room with a complicated instrument, and although he may comprehend its uses, he can not do so unless he frames sense-impressions into, what is to him, a formulated mind-word sequence."

"But he can think about it."

"No; unless he has already constructed previous impressions into word-meanings of his own, he can not think about it at all. Words, whether spoken or unspoken, underlie all ideas. Try, if you believe I am mistaken, try to think of any subject outside of words?"

I sat a moment, and mentally attempted the task, and shook my head.

"Then," said the old man, "how can I use words with established meanings to convey to your senses an entirely new idea? If I use new sounds, strung together, they are not words to you, and convey no meaning; if I use words familiar, they reach backward as well as forward. Thus it is possible to instruct you, by a laborious course of reasoning, concerning a phenomenon that is connected with phenomena already understood by you, for your word-language can be thrust out from the parent stalk, and can thus follow the outreaching branches. However, in the case of phenomena that exist on other planes, or are separated from any known material, or force, as is the true conception that envelops the word eternity, there being neither connecting materials, forces, nor words to unite the outside with the inside, the known with the unknown, how can I tell you more than I have done? You are word-bound."

"Nevertheless, I still believe that I can think outside of words."

"Well, perhaps after you attempt to do so, and fail again and again, you will appreciate that a truth is a truth, humiliating as it may be to acknowledge the fact."

"A Digger Indian has scarcely a word-language," I asserted, loth to relinquish the argument.

"You can go farther back if you desire, back to primitive man; man without language at all, and with ideas as circumscribed as those of the brutes, and still you have not strengthened your argument concerning civilized man. But you are tired, I see."

"Yes; tired of endeavoring to combat your assertions. You invariably lead me into the realms of speculation, and then throw me upon the defensive by asking me to prove my own theories, or with apparent sincerity, you advance an unreasonable hypothesis, and then, before I am aware of your purpose, force me to acquiesce because I can not find facts to confute you. You very artfully throw the burden of proof on me in all cases, for either by physical comparisons that I can not make, I must demonstrate the falsity of your metaphysical assertions, or by abstract reasonings disprove statements you assert to be facts."

"You are peevish and exhausted, or you would perceive that I have generally allowed you to make the issue, and more than once have endeavored to dissuade you from doing so. Besides, did I not several times in the past bring experimental proof to dispel your incredulity? Have I not been courteous?"

"Yes," I petulantly admitted; "yes."

Then I determined to imitate his artful methods, and throw him upon the defensive as often as he had done with me. I had finally become familiar with his process of arguing a question, for, instead of coming immediately to his subject, he invariably led by circuitous route to the matter under discussion. Before reaching the point he would manage to commit me to his own side of the subject, or place me in a defenseless position. So with covert aim I began:

"I believe that friction is one method of producing heat."

"Yes."

"I have been told that the North American Indians make fires by rubbing together two pieces of dry wood."

"True."

"I have understood that the light of a shooting star results from the heat of friction, producing combustion of its particles."

"Partly," he answered.

"That when the meteoric fragment of space dust strikes the air, the friction resulting from its velocity heats it to redness, fuses its surface, or even burns its very substance into ashes."

"Yes."

"I have seen the spindle of a wheel charred by friction."

"Yes."

"I have drawn a wire rapidly through a handkerchief tightly grasped in my hands, and have warmed the wire considerably in doing so."

"Yes."

I felt that I had him committed to my side of the question, and I prepared to force him to disprove the possibility of one assertion that he had made concerning his journey.

"You stated that you rode in a boat on the underground lake."

"Yes."

"With great rapidity?"

"Yes."

"Rapid motion produces friction, I believe?"

"Yes."

"And heat?"

"Yes."

"Why did not your boat become heated even to redness? You rode at the rate of nine hundred miles an hour," I cried exultingly.

"For two reasons," he calmly replied; "two natural causes prevented such a catastrophe."

And again he warned me, as he had done before, by saying:

"While you should not seek for supernatural agencies to account for any phenomena in life, for all that is is natural, neither should you fail to study the differences that varying conditions produce in results already known. A miracle ceases to be a miracle when we understand the scientific cause underlying the wonder; occultism is natural, for if there be occult phenomena they must be governed by natural law; mystery is not mysterious if the veil of ignorance that envelops the investigator is lifted. What you have said is true concerning the heat that results from friction, but—

"First, the attraction of gravitation was inconsiderable where the boat, to which you refer, rested on the water.

"Second, the changing water carried away the heat as fast as it was produced. While it is true that a cannon ball becomes heated in its motion through the air, its surface is cooled when it strikes a body of water, notwithstanding that its great velocity is altogether overcome by the water. The friction between the water and the iron does not result in heated iron, but the contrary. The water above the rapids of a river has practically the temperature of the water below the rapids, regardless of the friction that ensues between these points. Admit, however, that heat is liberated as the result of the friction of solids with water, and still it does not follow that this heat will perceptibly affect the solid. With a boat each particle of water carries the heat away, each succeeding portion of water takes up the heat liberated by that preceding it. Thus the great body of water, over which our boat sped, in obedience to the ordinary law, became slightly warmed, but its effect upon the boat was scarcely perceptible. Your comparison of the motion of a meteor, with that of our boat, was unhappy. We moved rapidly, it is true, in comparison with the motion of vessels such as you know, but comparison can not be easily drawn between the velocity of a boat and that of a meteor. While we moved at the rate of many miles a minute, a meteor moves many times faster, perhaps as many miles in a second. Then you must remember that the force of gravitation was so slight in our position that"—

"Enough," I interrupted. "We will pass the subject. It seems that you draw upon science for knowledge to support your arguments, however irrational they may be, and then you sneer at this same method of argument when I employ it."

He replied to my peevish complaint with the utmost respect by calling to my attention the fact that my own forced argument had led to the answer, and that he had simply replied to my attacks. Said he:

"If I am wrong in my philosophy, based on your science thought, I am right in my facts, and science thought is thus in the wrong, for facts overbalance theory. I ask you only to give me the attention that my statements merit. I am sincere, and aim to serve your interests. Should investigation lead you hereafter to infer that I am in error, at our final interview you can have my considerate attention. Be more charitable, please."

Then he added:

"Is there any other subject you wish to argue?"

"Yes," I answered, and again my combativeness arose; "yes. One of the truly edifying features of your narrative is that of the intelligent guide," and I emphasized the word intelligent, and curled up my lip in a sarcastic manner.

"Proceed."

"He was verily a wonderful being; an eyeless creature, and yet possessed of sight and perception beyond that of mortal man; a creature who had been locked in the earth, and yet was more familiar with its surface than a philosopher; a cavern-bred monstrosity, and yet possessed of the mind of a sage; he was a scientific expert, a naturalist, a metaphysical reasoner, a critic of religion, and a prophet. He could see in absolute darkness as well as in daylight; without a compass he could guide a boat over a trackless sea, and could accomplish feats that throw Gulliver and Munchausen into disrepute."

In perfect composure my aged guest listened to my cynical, and almost insulting tirade. He made no effort to restrain my impetuous sentences, and when I had finished replied in the polished language of a scholarly gentleman.

"You state truly, construe my words properly, as well as understand correctly."

Then he continued musingly, as though speaking to himself:

"I would be at fault and deserve censure did I permit doubts to be thrown upon so clear a subject, or discredit on so magnanimous a person."

Turning to me he continued:

"Certainly I did not intend to mislead or to be misunderstood, and am pleased to find you so earnest a scholar."

And then in his soft, mild manner, he commenced his detail reply, pouring oil upon the waters of my troubled soul, his sweet, melodious voice being so in contrast to my rash harangue. He began with his expressive and often repeated word, "listen."

"Listen. You are right, my guide was a being wonderful to mortals. He was eyeless, but as I have shown you before, and now swear to the fact, was not sightless; surely," he said,

"WE PASSED THROUGH CAVERNS FILLED WITH CREEPING REPTILES."

"surely you have not forgotten that long ago I considered the phenomenal instinct at length. He predicted the future by means of his knowledge of the past—there is nothing wonderful in that. Can not a civil engineer continue a line into the beyond, and predict where the projection of that line will strike; can he not also calculate the effect that a curve will have on his line's destiny? Why should a being conversant with the lines and curves of humanity's journey for ages past not be able to indicate the lines that men must follow in the future? Of course he could guide the boat, in what was to me a trackless waste of water, but you err in asserting that I had said he did not have a guide, even if it were not a compass. Many details concerning this journey have not been explained to you; indeed, I have acquainted you with but little that I experienced. Near surface earth we passed through caverns filled with creeping reptiles; through others we were surrounded by flying creatures, neither beast nor bird; we passed through passages of ooze and labyrinths of apparently interminable intra-earth structures; to have disported on such features of my journey would have been impractical. From time to time I experienced strains of melody, such as never before had I conceived, seemingly choruses of angels were singing in and to my very soul. From empty space about me, from out the crevices beyond and behind me, from the depths of my spirit within me, came these strains in notes clear and distinct, but yet indescribable. Did I fancy, or was it real? I will not pretend to say. Flowers and structures beautiful, insects gorgeous and inexplicable were spread before me. Figures and forms I can not attempt to indicate in word descriptions, ever and anon surrounded, accompanied, and passed me by. The canvas conceptions of earth-bred artists bring to mind no forms so strange and weird and yet so beautiful as were these compound beings. Restful beyond description was it to drink in the indescribable strains of poetry of motion that I appreciated in the movements of fair creatures I have not mentioned, and it was no less soothing to experience the soul relief wrought by the sounds about me, for musicians know no notes so sweet and entrancing.

"There were also, in side caverns to which I was led, combinations of sounds and scenes in which floating strains and fleeting figures were interwoven and interlaced so closely that the senses of both sight and hearing became blended into a single sense, new, weird, strange, and inexpressible. As flavor is the combination of odor and taste, an intensified both, and is neither taste nor odor, so these sounds and scenes combined were neither scenes nor sounds, but a complex sensation, new, delicious. Sometimes I begged to be permitted to stop and live forever 'mid those heavenly charms, but with as firm a hand as when helping me through the chambers of mire, ooze, and creeping reptiles my guide drew me onward.

"But to return to the subject. As to my guide being a cavern-bred monstrosity, I do not remember to have said that he was cavern-bred, and if I have forgotten a fact, I regret my short memory. Did I say that he was always a cavern being. Did I assert that he had never lived among mortals of upper earth? If so, I do not remember our conversation on that subject? He was surely a sage in knowledge, as you have experienced from my feeble efforts in explaining the nature of phenomena that were to you unknown, and yet have been gained by me largely through his instruction. He was a metaphysician, as you assert; you are surely right; he was a sincere, earnest reasoner and teacher. He was a conscientious student, and did not by any word lead me to feel that he did not respect all religions, and bow to the Creator of the universe, its sciences, and its religions. His demeanor was most considerate, his methods faultless, his love of nature deep, his patience inexhaustible, his sincerity unimpeachable. Yes," the old man said; "you are right in your admiration of this lovely personage, and when you come to meet this being as you are destined yet to do—for know now that you too will some day pass from surface earth, and leave only your name in connection with this story of myself—you will surely then form a still greater love and a deeper respect for one so gifted, and yet so self-sacrificing."

"Old man," I cried, "you mock me. I spoke facetiously, and you answer literally. Know that I have no confidence in your sailor-like tales, your Marco Polo history."

"Ah! You discredit Marco Polo? And why do you doubt?"

"Because I have never seen such phenomena, I have never witnessed such occurrences. I must see a thing to believe it."

"And so you believe only what you see?" he queried.

"Yes."

"Now answer promptly," he commanded, and his manner changed as by magic to that of a master. "Did you ever see Greenland?"

"No."

"Iceland?"

"No."

"A geyser?"

"No."

"A whale?"

"No."

"England?"

"No."

"France?"

"No."

"A walrus?"

"No."

"Then you do not believe that these conditions, countries, and animals have an existence?"

"Of course they have."

"Why?"

"Others have seen them."

"Ah," he said; "then you wish to modify your assertion—you only believe what others have seen?"

"Excepting one person," I retorted.

Then he continued, seemingly not having noticed my personal allusion:

"Have you ever seen your heart?"

I hesitated.

"Answer," he commanded.

"No."

"Your stomach?"

"No."

"Have you seen the stomach of any of your friends?"

"No."

"The back of your head?"

I became irritated, and made no reply.

"Answer," he again commanded.

"I have seen its reflection in a glass."

"I say no," he replied; "you have not."

"You are impudent," I exclaimed.

"Not at all," he said, good humoredly; "how easy it is to make a mistake. I venture to say that you have never seen the reflection of the back of your head in a mirror."

"Your presumption astounds me."

"I will leave it to yourself."

He took a hand-glass from the table and held it behind my head.

"Now, do you see the reflection?"

"No; the glass is behind me."

"Ah, yes; and so is the back of your head."

"Look," I said, pointing to the great mirror on the bureau; "look, there is the reflection of the back of my head."

"No; it is the reflection of the reflection in my hand-glass."

"You have tricked me; you quibble!"

"Well," he said, ignoring my remark; "what do you believe?"

"I believe what others have seen, and what I can do."

"Excluding myself as to what others have seen," he said facetiously.

"Perhaps," I answered, relenting somewhat.

"Has any man of your acquaintance seen the middle of Africa?"

"No."

"The center of the earth?"

"No."

"The opposite side of the moon?"

"No."

"The soul of man?"

"No."

"Heat, light, electricity?"

"No."

"Then you do not believe that Africa has a midland, the earth a center, the moon an opposite side, man a soul, force an existence?"

"You distort my meaning."

"Well, I ask questions in accord with your suggestions, and you defeat yourself. You have now only one point left. You believe only what *you* can do?"

"FLOWERS AND STRUCTURES BEAUTIFUL, INSECTS GORGEOUS."

"Yes."

"I will rest this case on one statement, then, and you may be the judge."

"Agreed."

"You can not do what any child in Cincinnati can accomplish. I assert that any other man, any other woman in the city can do more than you can. No cripple is so helpless, no invalid so feeble as not, in this respect, to be your superior."

"You insult me," I again retorted, almost viciously.

"Do you dispute the assertion seriously?"

"Yes."

"Well, let me see you kiss your elbow."

Involuntarily I twisted my arm so as to bring the elbow towards my mouth, then, as I caught the full force of his meaning, the ridiculous result of my passionate wager came over me, and I laughed aloud. It was a change of thought from the sublime to the ludicrous.

The white-haired guest smiled in return, and kindly said:

"It pleases me to find you in good humor at last. I will return to-morrow evening and resume the reading of my manuscript. In the meantime take good exercise, eat heartily, and become more cheerful."

He rose and bowed himself out.

CHAPTER XLIV.

THE FATHOMLESS ABYSS.—THE EDGE OF THE EARTH SHELL.

Promptly at eight o'clock the next evening the old man entered my room. He did not allude to the occurrences of the previous evening, and for this considerate treatment I felt thankful, as my part in those episodes had not been enviable. He placed his hat on the table, and in his usual cool and deliberate manner, commenced reading as follows:

For a long time thereafter we journeyed on in silence, now amid stately stone pillars, then through great cliff openings or among gigantic formations that often stretched away like cities or towns dotted over a plain, to vanish in the distance. Then the scene changed, and we traversed magnificent avenues, bounded by solid walls which expanded into lofty caverns of illimitable extent, from whence we found ourselves creeping through narrow crevices and threading winding passages barely sufficient to admit our bodies. For a considerable period I had noted the absence of water, and as we passed from grotto to temple reared without hands, it occurred to me that I could not now observe evidence of water erosion in the stony surface over which we trod, and which had been so abundant before we reached the lake. My guide explained by saying in reply to my thought question, that we were beneath the water line. He said that liquids were impelled back towards the earth's surface from a point unnoticed by me, but long since passed. Neither did I now experience hunger nor thirst, in the slightest degree, a circumstance which my guide assured me was perfectly natural in view of the fact that there was neither waste of tissue nor consumption of heat in my present organism.

"WITH FEAR AND TREMBLING I CREPT ON MY KNEES TO HIS SIDE."

At last I observed far in the distance a slanting sheet of light that, fan-shaped, stood as a barrier across the way; beyond it neither earth nor earth's surface appeared. As we approached, the distinctness of its outline disappeared, and when we came nearer, I found that it streamed into the space above, from what appeared to be a crevice or break in the earth that stretched across our pathway, and was apparently limitless and bottomless.

"Is this another hallucination?" I queried.

"No; it is a reality. Let us advance to the brink."

Slowly we pursued our way, for I hesitated and held back. I had really begun to distrust my own senses, and my guide in the lead was even forced to demonstrate the feasibility of the way, step by step, before I could be induced to follow. At length we neared the edge of the chasm, and while he stood boldly upright by the brink, with fear and trembling I crept on my knees to his side, and together we faced a magnificent but fearful void that stretched beneath and beyond us, into a profundity of space. I peered into the chamber of light, that indescribable gulf of brilliancy, but vainly sought for an opposite wall; there was none. As far as the eye could reach, vacancy, illuminated vacancy, greeted my vision. The light that sprung from that void was not dazzling, but was possessed of a beauty that no words can suggest. I peered downward, and found that we stood upon the edge of a shelving ledge of stone that receded rapidly beneath us, so that we seemed to rest upon the upper side of its wedge-like edge. I strained my vision to catch a glimpse of the bottom of this chasm, but although I realized that my eyes were glancing into miles and miles of space, there was no evidence of earthly material other than the brink upon which we stood.

The limit of vision seemed to be bounded by a silvery blending of light with light, light alone, only light. The dead silence about, and the new light before me, combined to produce a weird sensation, inexplicable, overpowering. A speck of dust on the edge of immensity, I clung to the stone cliff, gazing into the depths of that immeasurable void.

CHAPTER XLV.

MY HEART THROB IS STILLED, AND YET I LIVE.

"It now becomes my duty to inform you that this is one of the stages in our journey that can only be passed by the exercise of the greatest will force. Owing to our former surroundings upon the surface of the earth, and to your inheritance of a so-called instinctive education, you would naturally suppose that we are now on the brink of an impassable chasm. This sphere of material vacuity extends beneath us to a depth that I am sure you will be astonished to learn is over six thousand miles. We may now look straight into the earth cavity, and this streaming light is the reflected purity of the space below. The opposite side of this crevice, out of sight by reason of its distance, but horizontally across from where we stand, is precipitous and comparatively solid, extending upward to the material that forms the earth's surface. We have, during our journey, traversed an oblique, tortuous natural passage, that extends from the spot at which you entered the cave in Kentucky, diagonally down into the crust of the globe, terminating in this shelving bluff. I would recall to your mind that your journey up to this time has been of your own free will and accord. At each period of vacillation—and you could not help but waver occasionally—you have been at liberty to return to surface earth again, but each time you decided wisely to continue your course. You can now return if your courage is not sufficient to overcome your fear, but this is the last opportunity you will have to reconsider, while in my company."

"Have others overcome the instinctive terrors to which you allude?"

"Yes; but usually the dread of death, or an unbearable uncertainty, compels the traveler to give up in despair before reaching this spot, and the opportunity of a lifetime is lost. Yes; an opportunity that occurs only in the lifetime of one person out of millions, of but few in our brotherhood."

"Then I can return if I so elect?"

"Certainly."

"Will you inform me concerning the nature of the obstacle I have to overcome, that you indicate by your vague references?"

"We must descend from this cliff."

"You can not be in earnest."

"Why?"

"Do you not see that the stone recedes from beneath us, that we stand on the edge of a wedge overhanging bottomless space?"

"That I understand."

"There is no ladder," and then the foolish remark abashed me as I thought of a ladder six thousand miles in length.

"Go on."

He made no reference to my confusion.

"There is practically no bottom," I asserted, "if I can believe your words; you told me so."

"And that I reiterate."

"The feat is impracticable, impossible, and only a madman would think of trying to descend into such a depth of space."

Then an idea came over me; perhaps there existed a route at some other point of the earth's crevice by which we could reach the under side of the stone shelf, and I intimated as much to the guide.

"No; we must descend from this point, for it is the only entrance to the hollow beneath."

We withdrew from the brink, and I meditated in silence. Then I crept again to the edge of the bluff, and lying flat on my chest, craned my head over, and peered down into the luminous gulf. The texture of the receding mineral was distinctly visible for a considerable distance, and then far, far beneath all semblance to material form disappeared—as the hull of a vessel fades in deep, clear water. As I gazed into the gulf it seemed evident that, as a board floating in water is bounded by water, this rock really ended. I turned to my guide and questioned him.

"Stone in this situation is as cork," he replied; "it is nearly devoid of weight; your surmise is correct. We stand on the shelving edge of a cliff of earthly matter, that in this spot slants upward from beneath like the bow of a boat. We have reached the bottom of the film of space dust on the bubble of energy that forms the skeleton of earth."

I clutched the edge of the cliff with both hands.

"Be not frightened; have I not told you that if you wish to return you can do so. Now harken to me:

"A short time ago you endeavored to convince me that we could not descend from this precipice, and you are aware that your arguments were without foundation. You drew upon your knowledge of earth materials, as you once learned them, and realized at the time that you deluded yourself in doing so, for you know that present conditions are not such as exist above ground. You are now influenced by surroundings that are entirely different from those that govern the lives of men upon the earth's surface. You are almost without weight. You have nearly ceased to breathe, as long since you discovered, and soon I hope will agree entirely to suspend that harsh and wearying movement. Your heart scarcely pulsates, and if you go with me farther in this journey, will soon cease to beat."

I started up and turned to flee, but he grasped and held me firmly.

"Would you murder me? Do you think I will mutely acquiesce, while you coolly inform me of your inhuman intent, and gloat over the fact that my heart will soon be as stone, and that I will be a corpse?" He attempted to break in, but I proceeded in frenzy. "I *will* return to upper earth, to sunshine and humanity. I *will* retreat while yet in health and strength, and although I have in apparent willingness accompanied you to this point, learn now that at all times I have been possessed of the means to defend myself from personal violence." I drew from my pocket the bar of iron. "See, this I secreted about my person in the fresh air of upper earth, the sweet sunshine of heaven, fearing that I might fall into the hands of men with whom I must combat. Back, back," I cried.

He released his hold of my person, and folded his arms upon his breast, then quietly faced me, standing directly between myself and the passage we had trod, while I stood on the brink, my back to that fearful chasm.

By a single push he could thrust me into the fathomless gulf below, and with the realization of that fact, I felt that it was now a life and death struggle. With every muscle strained to its utmost tension, with my soul on fire, my brain frenzied, I drew back the bar of iron to smite the apparently defenseless being in the forehead, but he moved not, and as I made the motion, he calmly remarked: "Do you remember the history of Hiram Abiff?"

"I DREW BACK THE BAR OF IRON TO SMITE THE APPARENTLY DEFENSELESS BEING IN THE FOREHEAD."

The hand that held the weapon dropped as if stricken by paralysis, and a flood of recollections concerning my lost home overcame me. I had raised my hand against a brother, the only being of my kind who could aid me, or assist me either to advance or recede. How could I, unaided, recross that glassy lake, and pass through the grotesque forests of fungi and the labyrinth of crystal grottoes of the salt bed? How could I find my way in the utter darkness that existed in the damp, soppy, dripping upper caverns that I must retrace before I could hope to reach the surface of the earth? "Forgive me," I sobbed, and sunk at his feet. "Forgive me, my friend, my brother; I have been wild, mad, am crazed." He made no reply, but pointed over my shoulder into the space beyond.

I turned, and in the direction indicated, saw, in amazement, floating in the distant space a snow- and ice-clad vessel in full sail. She was headed diagonally from us, and was moving rapidly across the field of vision. Every spar and sail was clearly defined, and on her deck, and in the rigging I beheld sailors clad in winter garments pursuing their various duties.

As I gazed, enraptured, she disappeared in the distance.

"A phantom vessel," I murmured.

"No," he replied; "the abstraction of a vessel sailing on the ocean above us. Every object on earth is the second to an imprint in another place. There is an apparent reproduction of matter in so-called vacancy, and on unseen pages a recording of all events. As that ship sailed over the ocean above us, she disturbed a current of energy, and it left its impress as an outline on a certain zone beneath, which is parallel with that upon which we now chance to stand."

"I can not comprehend," I muttered.

"No," he answered; "to you it seems miraculous, as to all men an unexplained phenomenon approaches the supernatural. All that is is natural. Have men not been told in sacred writings that their every movement is being recorded in the Book of Life, and do they not often doubt because they can not grasp the problem? May not the greatest scientist be the most apt skeptic?"

"Yes," I replied.

"You have just seen," he said, "the record of an act on earth, and in detail it is being printed elsewhere in the Book of Eternity. If you should return to earth's surface you could not by stating these facts convince even the persons on that same ship, of your sanity. You could not make them believe that hundreds of miles beneath, both their vessel and its crew had been reproduced in fac simile, could you?"

"No."

"Were you to return to earth you could not convince men that you had existed without breath, with a heart dead within you. If you should try to impress on mankind the facts that you have learned in this journey, what would be the result?"

"I would probably be considered mentally deranged; this I have before admitted."

"Would it not be better then," he continued, "to go with me, by your own free will, into the unknown future, which you need fear less than a return to the scoffing multitude amid the storms of upper earth? You know that I have not at any time deceived you. I have, as yet, only opened before you a part of one rare page out of the boundless book of nature; you have tasted of the sweets of which few persons in the flesh have sipped, and I now promise you a further store of knowledge that is rich beyond conception, if you wish to continue your journey."

"What if I decide to return?"

"I will retrace my footsteps and liberate you upon the surface of the earth, as I have others, for few persons have courage enough to pass this spot."

"Binding me to an oath of secrecy?"

"SPRUNG FROM THE EDGE OF THE CLIFF INTO THE ABYSS BELOW, CARRYING ME WITH HIM INTO ITS DEPTHS."

"No," he answered; "for if you relate these events men will consider you a madman, and the more clearly you attempt to explain the facts that you have witnessed, the less they will listen to you; such has been the fate of others."

"It is, indeed, better for me to go with you," I said musingly; "to that effect my mind is now made up, my course is clear, I am ready."

With a motion so quick in conception, and rapid in execution that I was taken altogether by surprise, with a grasp so powerful that I could not have repelled him, had I expected the movement and tried to protect myself, the strange man, or being, beside me threw his arms around my body. Then, as a part of the same movement, he raised me bodily from the stone, and before I could realize the nature of his intention, sprung from the edge of the cliff into the abyss below, carrying me with him into its depths.

CHAPTER XLVI.

THE INNER CIRCLE, OR THE END OF GRAVITATION.—IN THE BOTTOMLESS GULF.

I recall a whirling sensation, and an involuntary attempt at self-preservation, in which I threw my arms wildly about with a vain endeavor to clutch some form of solid body, which movement naturally ended by a tight clasping of my guide in my arms, and locked together we continued to speed down into the seven thousand miles of vacancy. Instinctively I murmured a prayer of supplication, and awaited the approaching hereafter, which, as I believed, would quickly witness the extinction of my unhappy life, the end of my material existence; but the moments (if time can be so divided when no sun marks the division) multiplied without bodily shock or physical pain of any description; I retained my consciousness.

"Open your eyes," said my guide, "you have no cause for fear."

I acquiesced in an incredulous, dazed manner.

"This unusual experience is sufficient to unnerve you, but you need have no fear, for you are not in corporal danger, and can relax your grasp on my person."

I cautiously obeyed him, misgivingly, and slowly loosened my hold, then gazed about to find that we were in a sea of light, and that only light was visible, that form of light which I have before said is an entity without source of radiation. In one direction, however, a great gray cloud hung suspended and gloomy, dark in the center, and shading therefrom in a circle, to disappear entirely at an angle of about forty-five degrees.

"This is the earth-shelf from which we sprung," said the guide; " it will soon disappear."

Wherever I glanced this radiant exhalation, a peaceful, luminous envelope, this rich, soft, beautiful white light appeared. The power of bodily motion I found still a factor in my frame, obedient, as before, to my will. I could move my limbs freely, and my intellect seemed to be intact. Finally I became impressed with the idea that I must be at perfect rest, but if so what could be the nature of the substance, or material, upon which I was resting so complacently? No; this could not be true. Then I thought: "I have been instantly killed by a painless shock, and my spirit is in heaven;" but my earthly body and coarse, ragged garments were palpable realities; the sense of touch, sight, and hearing surely were normal, and a consideration of these facts dispelled my first conception.

"Where are we now?"

"Moving into earth's central space."

"I comprehend that a rushing wind surrounds us which is not uncomfortable, but otherwise I experience no unusual sensation, and can not realize but that I am at rest."

"The sensation, as of a blowing wind is in consequence of our rapid motion, and results from the friction between our bodies and the quiescent, attenuated atmosphere which exists even here, but this atmosphere becomes less and less in amount until it will disappear altogether at a short distance below us. Soon we will be in a perfect calm, and although moving rapidly, to all appearances will be at absolute rest."

Naturally, perhaps, my mind attempted, as it so often had done, to urge objections to his statements, and at first it occurred to me that I did not experience the peculiar sinking away sensation in the chest that I remembered follows, on earth, the downward motion of a person falling from a great height, or moving rapidly in a swing, and I questioned him on the absence of that phenomenon.

"The explanation is simple," he said; "on the surface of the earth a sudden motion, either upward or downward, disturbs the equilibrium of the organs of respiration, and of the heart, and interferes with the circulation of the blood. This produces a change in blood pressure within the brain, and the 'sinking' sensation in the chest, or the dizziness of the head of a person moving rapidly, or it may even result in unconsciousness, and complete suspension of respiration, effects which sometimes follow rapid movements, as in a person falling from a considerable height. Here circumstances are entirely different. The heart is quiet, the lungs in a comatose condition, and the blood stagnant. Mental sensations, therefore, that result from a disturbed condition of these organs are wanting, and, although we are experiencing rapid motion, we are in the full possession of our physical selves, and maintain our mental faculties unimpaired."

Again I interposed an objection:

"If, as you say, we are really passing through an attenuated atmosphere with increasing velocity, according to the law that governs falling bodies that are acted upon by gravity which continually accelerates their motion, the friction between ourselves and the air will ultimately become so intense as to wear away our bodies."

"Upon the contrary," said he, "this attenuated atmosphere is decreasing in density more rapidly than our velocity increases, and before long it will have altogether disappeared. You can perceive that the wind, as you call it, is blowing less violently than formerly; soon it will entirely cease, as I have already predicted, and at that period, regardless of our motion, we will appear to be stationary."

Pondering over the final result of this strange experience I became again alarmed, for accepting the facts to be as he stated, such motion would ultimately carry us against the opposite crust of the earth, and without a doubt the shock would end our existence. I inquired about this, to me, self-evident fact, and he replied:

"Long before we reach the opposite crust of the earth, our motion will be arrested."

I had begun now to feel a self-confidence that is surprising as I recall that remarkable position in connection with my narrow experience in true science, and can say that instead of despondency, I really enjoyed an elated sensation, a curious exhilaration, a feeling of delight, which I have no words to describe. Life disturbances and mental worry seemed to have completely vanished, and it appeared as if, with mental perception lucid, I were under the influence of a powerful soporific; the cares of mortals had disappeared. After a while the wind ceased to blow, as my guide had predicted, and with the suspension of that factor, all that remained to remind me of earth phenomena had vanished. There was no motion of material, nothing to mar or disturb the most perfect peace imaginable; I was so exquisitely happy that I now actually feared some change might occur to interrupt that quiescent existence. It was as a deep, sweet sleep in which, with faculties alive, unconsciousness was self-conscious, peaceful, restful, blissful. I listlessly turned my eyes, searching space in all directions—to meet vacancy everywhere, absolute vacancy. I took from my pocket (into which I had hastily thrust it) the bar of iron, and released it; the metal remained motionless beside me.

"Traveling through this expanse with the rapidity of ourselves," said my guide.

I closed my eyes and endeavored to convince myself that I was dreaming—vainly, however. I opened my eyes, and endeavored to convince myself that I was moving, equally in vain. I became oblivious to everything save the delicious sensation of absolute rest that enveloped and pervaded my being.

"I am neither alive nor dead," I murmured; "neither asleep nor awake; neither moving nor at rest, and neither standing, reclining, nor sitting. If I exist I can not bring evidence to prove that fact, neither can I prove that I am dead."

"Can any man prove either of these premises?" said the guide.

"I have never questioned the matter," said I; "it is a self-evident fact."

"Know then," said he, "that existence is a theory, and that man is incapable of demonstrating that he has a being. All evidences of mortal life are only as the fantasia of hallucination. As a moment in dreamland may span a life of time, the dreamer altogether unconscious that it is a dream, so may life itself be a shadow, the vision of a distempered fancy, the illusion of a floating thought."

"Are pain, pleasure, and living, imaginary creations?" I asked facetiously.

"Is there a madman who does not imagine, as facts, what others agree upon as hallucinations peculiar to himself? Is it not impossible to distinguish between the gradations of delusions, and is it not, therefore, possible that even self-existence is an illusion? What evidence can any man produce to prove that his idea of life is not a madman's dream?"

"Proceed," I said.

"At another time, perhaps," he remarked; "we have reached the Inner Circle, the Sphere of Rest, the line of gravity, and now our bodies have no weight; at this point we begin to move with decreased speed, we will soon come to a quiescent condition, a state of rest, and then start back on our rebound."

CHAPTER XLVII.

HEARING WITHOUT EARS.—"WHAT WILL BE THE END?"

A flood of recollections came over me, a vivid remembrance of my earth-learned school philosophy. "I rebel again," I said, "I deny your statements. We can neither be moving, nor can we be out of the atmosphere. Fool that I have been not to have sooner and better used my reasoning faculties, not to have at once rejected your statements concerning the disappearance of the atmosphere."

"I await your argument."

"Am I not speaking? Is other argument necessary? Have I not heard your voice, and that, too, since you asserted that we had left the atmosphere?"

"Continue."

"Have not men demonstrated, and is it not accepted beyond the shadow of a doubt, that sound is produced by vibrations of the air?"

"You speak truly; as men converse on surface earth."

"This medium—the air—in wave vibrations, strikes upon the drum of the ear, and thus impresses the brain," I continued.

"I agree that such is the teachings of your philosophy; go on."

"It is unnecessary; you admit the facts, and the facts refute you; there must be an atmosphere to convey sound."

"Can not you understand that you are not now on the surface of the earth? Will you never learn that the philosophy of your former life is not philosophy here? That earth-bound science is science only with surface-earth men? Here science is a fallacy. All that you have said is true of surface earth, but your argument is invalid where every condition is different from the conditions that prevail thereon. You use the organs of speech in addressing me as you once learned to use them, but such physical efforts are unnecessary to convey sense-impressions in this condition of rest and complacency, and you waste energy in employing them. You assert and believe that the air conveys sound; you have been taught such theories in support of a restricted philosophy; but may I ask you if a bar of iron, a stick of wood, a stream of water, indeed any substance known to you placed against the ear will not do the same, and many substances even better than the atmosphere?"

"This I admit."

"Will you tell me how the vibration of any of these bodies impresses the seat of hearing?"

"It moves the atmosphere which strikes upon the tympanum of the ear."

"You have not explained the phenomenon; how does that tympanic membrane communicate with the brain?"

"By vibrations, I understand," I answered, and then I began to feel that this assertion was a simple statement, and not sufficient to explain how matter acts upon mind, whatever mind may be, and I hesitated.

"Pray do not stop," he said; "how is it that a delicate vibrating film of animal membrane can receive and convey sound to a pulpy organic mass that is destitute of elasticity, and which consists mostly of water, for the brain is such in structure, and vibrations like those you mention, can not, by your own theory, pass through it as vibrations through a sonorous material, or even reach from the tympanum of the ear to the nearest convolution of the brain."

"I can not explain this, I admit," was my reply.

"Pass that feature, then, and concede that this tympanic membrane is capable of materially affecting brain tissue by its tiny vibrations, how can that slimy, pulpy formation mostly made up of water, communicate with the soul of man, for you do not claim, I hope, that brain material is either mind, conscience, or soul?"

I confessed my inability to answer or even to theorize on the subject, and recognizing my humiliation, I begged him to open the door to such knowledge.

"The vibration of the atmosphere is necessary to man, as earthy man is situated," he said. "The coarser attributes known as matter formations are the crudities of nature, dust swept from space. Man's organism is made up of the roughest and lowest kind of space materials; he is surrounded by a turbulent medium, the air, and these various conditions obscure or destroy the finer attributes of his ethereal nature, and prevent a higher spiritual evolution. His spiritual self is enveloped in earth, and everywhere thwarted by earthy materials. He is insensible to the finer influences of surrounding media by reason of the overwhelming necessity of a war for existence with the grossly antagonistic materialistic confusion that everywhere confronts, surrounds, and pervades him. Such a conflict with extraneous matter is necessary in order that he may retain his earthy being, for, to remain a mortal, he must work to keep body and soul together. His organs of communication and perception are of 'earth, earthy'; his nature is cast in a mold of clay, and the blood within him gurgles and struggles in his brain, a whirlpool of madly rushing liquid substances, creating disorder in the primal realms of consciousness. He is ignorant of this inward turmoil because he has never been without it, as ignorant as he is of the rank odors of the gases of the atmosphere that he has always breathed, and can not perceive because of the benumbed olfactory nerves. Thus it is that all his subtler senses are inevitably blunted and perverted, and his vulgar nature preponderates. The rich essential part of his own self is unknown, even to himself. The possibility of delight and pleasure in an acquaintance with the finer attributes of his own soul is clouded by this shrouding materialistic presence that has, through countless generations, become a part of man, and he even derives most of his mental pleasures from such acts as tend to encourage the animal passions. Thus it follows that the sensitive, highly developed, extremely attenuated part of his inner being has become subservient to the grosser elements. The baser part of his nature has become dominant. He remains insensible to impressions from the highly developed surrounding media which, being incapable of reaching his inner organism other than through mechanical agencies, are powerless to impress. Alas, only the coarser conditions of celestial phenomena can affect him, and the finer expressions of the universe of life and force are lost to his spiritual apprehension."

"Would you have me view the soul of man as I would a material being?"

"Surely," he answered; "it exists practically as does the more gross forms of matter, and in exact accord with natural laws. Associated with lower forms of matter, the soul of man is a temporary slave to the enveloping substance. The ear of man as now constituted can hear only by means of vibrations of such media as conduct vibrations in matter—for example, the air; but were man to be deprived of the organs of hearing, and then exist for generations subject to evolutions from within, whereby the acuteness of the spirit would become intensified, or permitted to perform its true function, he would learn to communicate soul to soul, not only with mankind, but with beings celestial that surround, and are now unknown to him. This he would accomplish through a medium of communication that requires neither ear nor tongue. To an extent your present condition is what men call supernatural, although in reality you have been divested of only a part of your former material grossness, which object has been accomplished under perfectly natural conditions; your mind no longer requires the material medium by which to converse with the spiritual. We are conversing now by thought contact; there is no atmosphere here, your tongue moves merely from habit, and not from necessity. I am reading your mind as you in turn are mine, neither of us is speaking as you were accustomed to speak."

"I can not accept that assertion," I said; "it is to me impossible to realize the existence of such conditions."

"As it is for any man to explain any phenomenon in life," he said. "Do you not remember that you ceased to respire, and were not conscious of the fact?"

"Yes."

"That your heart had stopped beating, your blood no longer circulated, while you were in ignorance of the change?"

"That is also true."

"Now I will prove my last assertion. Close your mouth, and think of a question you wish to propound."

I did so, and to my perfect understanding and comprehension he answered me with closed mouth.

"What will be the end?" I exclaimed, or thought aloud. "I am possessed of nearly all the attributes that I once supposed inherent only in a corpse, yet I live, I see clearly, I hear plainly,

I have a quickened being, and a mental perception intensified and exquisite. Why and how has this been accomplished? What will be the result of this eventful journey?"

"Restful, you should say," he remarked; "the present is restful, the end will be peace. Now I will give you a lesson concerning the words Why and How that you have just used."

CHAPTER XLVIII.

WHY AND HOW.—"THE STRUGGLING RAY OF LIGHT FROM THOSE FARTHERMOST OUTREACHES."

"Confronting mankind there stands a sphynx—the vast Unknown. However well a man may be informed concerning a special subject, his farthermost outlook concerning that subject is bounded by an impenetrable infinity."

"Granted," I interrupted, "that mankind has not by any means attained a condition of perfection, yet you must admit that questions once regarded as inscrutable problems are now illuminated by the discoveries of science."

"And the 'discovered,' as I will show, has only transferred ignorance to other places," he replied. "Science has confined its labors to superficial descriptions, not the elucidation of the fundamental causes of phenomena."

"I can not believe you, and question if you can prove what you say."

"It needs no argument to illustrate the fact. Science boldly heralds her descriptive discoveries, and as carefully ignores her explanatory failures. She dare not attempt to explain the why even of the simplest things. Why does the robin hop, and the snipe walk? Do not tell me this is beneath the notice of men of science, for science claims that no subject is outside her realm. Search your works on natural history and see if your man of science, who describes the habits of these birds, explains the reason for this evident fact. How does the tree-frog change its color? Do not answer me in the usual superficial manner concerning the reflection of light, but tell me why the skin of that creature is enabled to perform this function? How does the maple-tree secrete a sweet, wholesome sap, and deadly nightshade, growing in the same soil and living on the same elements, a poison? What is it that your scientific men find in the cells of root, or rootlet, to indicate that one may produce a food, and the other a noxious secretion that can destroy life? Your microscopist will discuss cell tissues learnedly, will speak fluently of physiological structure, will describe organic intercellular appearances, but ignore all that lies beyond. Why does the nerve in the tongue respond to a sensation, and produce on the mind the sense of taste? What is it that enables the nerve in the nose to perform its discriminative function? You do not answer. Silver is sonorous, lead is not; why these intrinsic differences? Aluminum is a light metal, gold a heavy one; what reason can you offer to explain the facts other than the inadequate term density? Mercury at ordinary temperature is a liquid; can your scientist tell why it is not a solid? Of course anyone can say because its molecules move freely on each other. Such an answer evades the issue; why do they so readily exert this action? Copper produces green or blue salts; nickel produces green salts; have you ever been told why they observe these rules? Water solidifies at about thirty-two degrees above your so-called zero; have you ever asked an explanation of your scientific authority why it selects that temperature? Alcohol dissolves resins, water dissolves gums; have you any explanation to offer why either liquid should dissolve anything, much less exercise a preference? One species of turtle has a soft shell, another a hard shell; has your authority in natural history told you why this is so? The albumen of the egg of the hen hardens at one hundred and eighty degrees Fahrenheit; the albumen of the eggs of some turtles can not be easily coagulated by boiling the egg in pure water; why these differences? Iceland spar and dog-tooth spar are identical, both are crystallized carbonate of lime; has your mineralogist explained why this one substance selects these different forms of crystallization, or why any crystal of any substance is ever produced? Why is common salt white and charcoal black? Why does the dog lap and the calf drink? One child has black hair, another brown, a third red; why? Search your physiology for the answer and see if your learned authority can tell you why the life-current makes these distinctions? Why do the cells of the liver secrete bile, and those of the mouth saliva? Why does any cell secrete anything? A parrot can speak; what has your anatomist found in the structure of the brain, tongue, or larynx of that bird to explain why this accomplishment is not as much the birthright of the turkey? The elements that form morphine and strychnine, also make bread, one a food, the other a poison; can your chemist offer any reason for the fact that morphine and bread possess such opposite characters? The earth has one satellite, Saturn is encompassed by a ring; it is not sufficient to attempt to refer to these familiar facts; tell me, does your earth-bound astronomer explain why the ring of Saturn was selected for that planet? Why are the salts of aluminum astringent, the salts of magnesium cathartic, and the salts of arsenicum deadly poison? Ask your toxicologist, and silence will be your answer. Why will some substance absorb moisture from the air, and liquefy, while others become as dry as dust under like conditions? Why does the vapor of sulphuric ether inflame, while the vapor of chloroform is not combustible, under ordinary conditions? Oil of turpentine, oil of lemon, and oil of bergamot differ in odor, yet they are composed of the same elements, united in the same proportion; why should they possess such distinctive, individual characteristics? Further search of the chemist will explain only to shove the word why into another space, as ripples play with and toss a cork about. Why does the newly-born babe cry for food before its intellect has a chance for worldly education? Why"—

"Stop," I interrupted; "these questions are absurd."

"So some of your scientific experts would assert," he replied; "perhaps they would even become indignant at my presumption in asking them, and call them childish; nevertheless these men can not satisfy their own cravings in attempting to search the illimitable, and in humiliation, or irritation, they must ignore the word Why. That word Why to man dominates the universe. It covers all phenomena, and thrusts inquiry back from every depth. Science may trace a line of thought into the infinitely little, down, down, beyond that which is tangible, and at last in that far distant inter-microscopical infinity, monstrous by reason of its very minuteness, must rest its labors against the word Why. Man may carry his superficial investigation into the immeasurably great, beyond our sun and his family of satellites, into the outer depths of the solar system, of which our sun is a part, past his sister stars, and out again into the depths of the cold space channels beyond; into other systems and out again, until at last the nebulæ shrink and disappear in the gloom of thought-conjecture, and as the straggling ray of light from those farthermost outreaches, too feeble to tell of its origin, or carry a story of nativity, enters his eye, he covers his face and rests his intellect against the word Why. From the remote space caverns of the human intellect, beyond the field of perception, whether we appeal to conceptions of the unknowable in the infinitely little, or the immeasurably great, we meet a circle of adamant, as impenetrable as the frozen cliffs of the Antarctic, that incomprehensible word—Why!

"Why did the light wave spring into his field of perception by reflection from the microscopic speck in the depths of littleness, on the one hand; and how did this sliver of the sun's ray originate in the depths of inter-stellar space, on the other?"

I bowed my head.

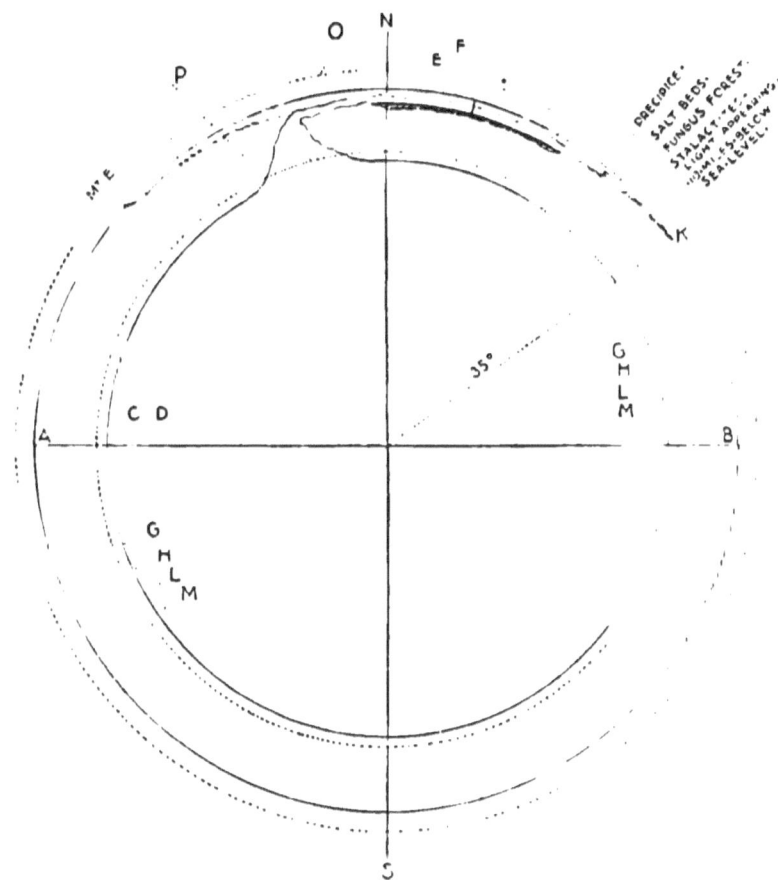

DESCRIPTION OF JOURNEY FROM K [KENTUCKY] TO P —"THE END OF EARTH."

A, B, Diameter of earth, 8,000 miles.
A, D, Thickness of earth crust, 800 miles.
C, D, Distance from inner earth crust to energy sphere, 100 miles.
E, Underground lake.
E, F, Distance from surface of lake to earth's surface.
G, Inner Circle the Unknown Country.
H, Middle Circle Sphere of Energy, or Circle of Rest.
L to M, Height of atmosphere, 200 miles.

K, Entrance to cavern in Kentucky.
L, Outer circle, earth's surface.
Mt. E, Mount Epomeo in Italy
N, North Pole.
O, Rock shelf from which the leap was made into the intra-earth space
P, Junction of earth crust with Circle of Rest. Point where I-Am-The-Man stepped "onward and upward" in "The Unknown Country."
S, South Pole.

CHAPTER XLIX.

OSCILLATING THROUGH SPACE.—EARTH'S SHELL ABOVE ME.*

Continued my companion :
"We have just now crossed the line of gravitation. We were drawn downward until at a certain point, to which I called your attention at the time, we recently crossed the curved plane of perfect rest, where gravity ceases, and by our momentum are now passing beyond that plane, and are now pressing against the bond of gravitation again. This shell in which gravity centers is concentric with that of the earth's exterior, and is about seven hundred miles below its surface. Each moment of time will now behold us carried farther from this sphere of attraction, and thus the increasing distance increases the force of the restraining influence. Our momentum is thus retarded, and consequently the rapidity of our motion is continually decreasing. At last when the forces of gravitation and mass motion neutralize each other, we will come to a state of rest again. When our motion in this direction ceases, however, gravitation, imperishable, continues to exert its equalizing influence, the result being a start in the opposite direction, and we will then reverse our course, and retrace our path, crossing again the central band of attraction, to retreat and fly to the opposite side of the power of greater attraction, into the expanse from which we came, and that is now above us."

"Can this oscillation ever end? Are we to remain thus, as an unceasing pendulum, traversing space, to and fro across this invisible shell of attraction from now until the end of time?"

"No; there are influences to prevent such an experience; one being the friction of the attenuated atmosphere into which we plunge each time that we cross the point of greater gravity,

---

* For detail illustration of the earth shell, as explained in this chapter, see the plate.

and approach the crust of the earth. Thus each succeeding vibration is in shorter lines, and at last we will come to a state of perfect rest at the center of gravity."

"I can only acquiesce in meek submission, powerless even to argue, for I perceive that the foundations for my arguments must be based on those observed conditions of natural laws formerly known to me, and that do not encompass us here; I accept, therefore, your statements as I have several times heretofore, because I can not refute them. I must close my eyes to the future, and accept it on faith; I cease to mourn the past, I can not presage the end."

"Well spoken," he replied; "and while we are undergoing this necessary delay, this oscillating motion, to which we must both submit before we can again continue our journey, I will describe some conditions inherent in the three spheres of which the rind of the earth is composed, for I believe that you are now ready to receive and profit by facts that heretofore you would have rejected in incredulity.

"The outer circle, coat, or contour, of which you have heard others besides myself speak, is the surface crust of our globe, the great sphere of land and water on which man is at present an inhabitant. This is the exposed part of the earth, and is least desirable as a residence. It is affected by grievous atmospheric changes, and restless physical conditions, such as men, in order to exist in, must fortify against at the expense of much bodily and mental energy, which leads them, necessarily, to encourage the animal at the expense of the ethereal. The unmodified rays of the sun produce aerial convulsions that are marked by thermal contrasts, and other meteorological variations, during which the heat of summer and the cold of winter follow each other periodically and unceasingly. These successive solar pulsations generate winds, calms, and storms, and in order to protect himself against such exposures and changes in material surroundings, man toils, suffers, and comes to believe that the doom, if not the object, of life on earth is the preservation of the earthy body. All conditions and phases of nature on this outer crust are in an angry struggle, and this commotion envelops the wretched home, and governs the life of man. The surrounding cyclones of force and matter have distorted the peaceful side of what human nature might be until the shortened life of man has become a passionate, deplorable, sorrowful struggle for physical existence, from the cradle to the grave. Of these facts man is practically ignorant, although each individual is aware he is not satisfied with his condition. If his afflictions were obvious to himself, his existence would be typical of a life of desolation and anguish. You know full well that the condition of the outer sphere is, as I have described it, a bleak, turbulent surface, the roof of the earth on which man exists, as a creeping parasite does on a rind of fruit, exposed to the fury of the-ever present earth storms.

"The central circle, or medial sphere, the shell, or layer of gravitation, lies conformably to the outer configuration of the globe, about seven hundred miles towards its center. It stretches beneath the outer circle (sphere) as a transparent sheet, a shell of energy, the center of gravitation. The material crust of the earth rests on this placid sphere of vigor, excepting in a few places, where, as in the crevice we have entered, gaps, or crevices, in matter exist, beginning from near the outer surface and extending diagonally through the medial and inner spheres into the intra-earth space beyond. This medial sphere is a form of pure force, a disturbance of motion, and although without weight it induces, or conserves, gravity. It is invisible to mortal eyes, and is frictionless, but really is the bone of the earth. On it matter, the retarded energy of space, space dust, has arranged itself as dust collects on a bubble of water. This we call matter. The material portion of the earth is altogether a surface film, an insignificant skin over the sphere of purity, the center of gravitation. Although men naturally imagine that the density and stability of the earth is dependent on the earthy particles, of which his own body is a part, such is not the case. Earth, as man upon the outer surface can now know it, is an aggregation of material particles, a shell resting on this globular sphere of medial force, which attracts solid matter from both the outer and inner surfaces of earth, forming thereby the middle of the three concentric spheres. This middle sphere is the reverse of the outer, or surface, layer in one respect, for, while it attracts solids, gases are repelled by it, and thus the atmosphere becomes less dense as we descend from the outer surfaces of the earth.

The greater degree of attraction for gases belongs, therefore, to the earth's exterior surface."

"Exactly at the earth's exterior surface?" I asked.

"Practically so. The greatest density of the air is found a few miles below the surface of the ocean; the air becomes more attenuated as we proceed in either direction from that point. Were this not the case, the atmosphere that surrounds the earth would be quickly absorbed into its substance, or expand into space and disappear."

"Scientific men claim that the atmosphere is forty-five geographical miles in depth over the earth's surface," I said.

"If the earth is eight thousand miles in diameter, how long would such an atmosphere, a skin only, over a great ball, resist such attraction, and remain above the globe? Were it really attracted towards its center it would disappear as a film of water sinks into a sponge."

"Do you know," I interrupted, "that if these statements were made to men they would not be credited? Scientific men have calculated the weights of the planets, and have estimated therefrom the density of the earth, showing it to be solid, and knowing its density, they would, on this consideration alone, discredit your story concerning the earth shell."

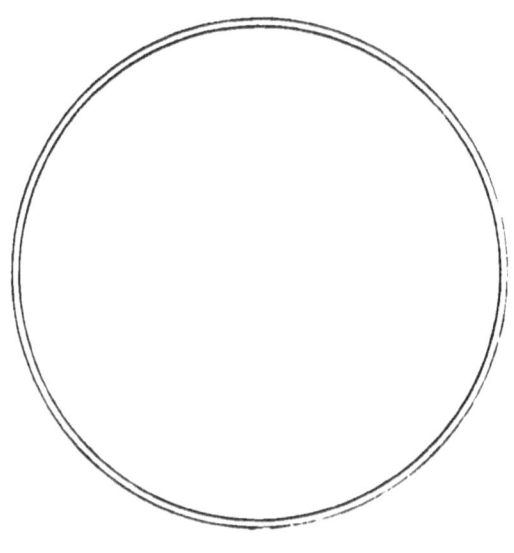

THE EARTH AND ITS ATMOSPHERE.

The space between the inner and the outer lines represents the atmosphere upon the earth. The depth to which man has penetrated the earth is less than the thickness of either line, as compared with the diameter of the inner circle

"You mistake, as you will presently see. It is true that man's ingenuity has enabled him to ascertain the weights and densities of the planets, but do you mean to say that these scientific results preclude the possibility of a hollow interior of the heavenly bodies?"

"I confess, I do."

"You should know then, that what men define as density of the earth, is but an average value, which is much higher than that exhibited by materials in the surface layers of the earth crust, such as come within the scrutiny of man. This fact allows mortals of upper earth but a vague conjecture as to the nature of the seemingly much heavier substances that exist in the interior of the earth. Have men any data on hand to show exactly how matter is distributed below the limited zone that is accessible to their investigations?"

"I think not."

"You may safely accept, then, that the earth shell I have described to you embraces in a compact form the total weight of the earth. Even though men take for granted that matter fills out the whole interior of our planet, such material would not, if distributed as on earth's surface, give the earth the density he has determined for it."

"I must acquiesce in your explanations."

"Let us now go a step further in this argument. What do you imagine is the nature of those heavier substances whose existence deep within the earth is suggested by the exceedingly high total density observed by man on upper earth?"

"I am unable to explain, especially as the materials surrounding us here, seemingly do not differ much from those with which my former life experience has made me acquainted."

"Your observation is correct, there is no essential difference in this regard. But as we are descending into the interior of this globe, and are approaching the central seat of the shell of energy, the opposing force into which we plunge becomes correspondingly stronger, and as a consequence, matter pressed within it becomes really lighter. Your own experience about your weight gradually disappearing during this journey should convince you of the correctness of this fact."

"Indeed, it does," I admitted.

"You will then readily understand, that the heavy material to which surface-bred mortals allude as probably constituting the interior of the earth, is, in fact, nothing but the manifestation of a matter supporting force, as exemplified in the sphere of attractive energy, the seat of which we are soon to encounter on our journey. Likewise the mutual attraction of the heavenly bodies is not a property solely of their material part, but an expression in which both the force-spheres and the matter collected thereon take part.

"Tell me more of the sphere in which gravitation is intensest."

"Of that you are yet to judge," he replied. "When we come to a state of rest in the stratum of greater gravity, we will then traverse this crevice in the sheet of energy until we reach the edge of the earth crust, after which we will ascend towards the interior of the earth, until we reach the inner crust, which is, as before explained, a surface of matter that lies comformably with the external crust of the earth, and which is the interior surface of the solid part of the earth. There is a concave world beneath the outer convex world."

"I can not comprehend you. You speak of continuing our journey towards the center of the earth, and at the same time you say that after leaving the Median Circle, we will then ascend, which seems contradictory."

"I have endeavored to show you that matter is resting in or on a central sphere of energy, which attracts solid bodies towards its central plane. From this fundamental and permanent seat of gravity we may regard our progress as up-hill, whether we proceed towards the hollow center or towards the outer surface of the globe. If a stick weighted on one end is floated upright in water, an insect on the top of the stick above the water will fall to the surface of the liquid, and yet the same insect will rise to the surface of the water if liberated beneath the water at the bottom of the stick. This comparison is not precisely applicable to our present position, for there is no change in medium here, but it may serve as an aid to thought and may indicate to you that which I wish to convey when I say 'we ascend' in both directions as we pull against Gravity. The terms up and down are not absolute, but relative."

Thus we continued an undefined period in mind conversation; and of the information gained in my experience of that delightful condition, I have the privilege now to record but a small portion, and even this statement of facts appears, as I glance backward into my human existence, as if it may seem to others to border on the incredible. During all that time—I know not how long the period may have been—we were alternately passing and repassing through the partition of division (the sphere of gravity) that separated the inner from the outer substantial crust of earth. With each vibration our line of travel became shorter and shorter, like the decreasing oscillations of a pendulum, and at last I could no longer perceive the rushing motion of a medium like the air. Finally my guide said that we were at perfect rest at a point in that mysterious medial sphere which, at a distance of about seven hundred miles below the level of the sea, concentrates in its encompassing curvature, the mighty power of gravitation. We were fixed seven hundred miles from the outer surface of the globe, but more than three thousand from the center.

CHAPTER L.

MY WEIGHT ANNIHILATED.—"TELL ME," I CRIED IN ALARM, "IS THIS TO BE A LIVING TOMB?"

"If you will reflect upon the condition we are now in, you will perceive that it must be one of unusual scientific interest. If you imagine a body at rest, in an intangible medium, and not in contact with a gas or any substance capable of creating friction, that body by the prevailing theory of matter and motion, unless disturbed by an impulse from without, would remain forever at absolute rest. We now occupy such a position. In whatever direction we may now be situated, it seems to us that we are upright. We are absolutely without weight, and in a perfectly frictionless medium. Should an inanimate body begin to revolve here, it would continue that motion forever. If our equilibrium should now be disturbed, and we should begin to move in a direction coinciding with the plane in which we are at rest, we would continue moving with the same rapidity in that direction until our course was arrested by some opposing object. We are not subject to attraction of matter, for at this place gravitation robs matter of its gravity, and has no influence on extraneous substances. We are now in the center of gravitation, the 'Sphere of Rest.'"

"Let me think it out," I replied, and reasoning from his remarks, I mentally followed the chain to its sequence, and was startled as suddenly it dawned upon me that if his argument was true we must remain motionless in this spot until death (could beings in conditions like ourselves die beyond the death we had already achieved) or the end of time. We were at perfect rest, in absolute vacancy, there being, as I now accepted without reserve, neither gas, liquid, nor solid, that we could employ as a lever to start us into motion. "Tell me," I cried in alarm, "is this to be a living tomb? Are we to remain suspended here forever, and if not, by what method can we hope to extricate ourselves from this state of perfect quiescence?" He again took the bar of iron from my hand, and cautiously gave it a whirling motion, releasing it as he did so. It revolved silently and rapidly in space without support or pivot.

"So it would continue," he remarked, "until the end of time, were it not for the fact that I could not possibly release it in a condition of absolute horizontal rest. There is a slight, slow, lateral motion that will carry the object parallel with this sheet of energy to the material side of this crevice, when its motion will 'be arrested by the earth it strikes.'"

"That I can understand," I replied, and then a ray of light broke upon me. "Had not Cavendish demonstrated that, when a small ball of lead is suspended on a film of silk, near a mass of iron or lead, it is drawn towards the greater body? We will be drawn by gravity to the nearest cliff," I cried.

"You mistake," he answered; "Cavendish performed his experiments on the surface of the earth, and there gravity is always ready to start an object into motion. Here objects have no weight, and neither attract nor repel each other. The force of cohesion holds together substances that are in contact, but as gravitation can not now affect matter out of molecular contact with other forms of matter, because of the equilibrium of all objects, so it may be likewise said, that bodies out of contact have at this point no attraction for one another. If they possessed this attribute, long ago we would have been drawn towards the earth cliff with inconceivable velocity. However, if by any method our bodies should receive an impulse sufficient to start them into motion, ever so gently though it be, we in like manner would continue to move in this frictionless medium—until"—

"We would strike the material boundary of this crevice," I interrupted.

"Yes; but can you conceive of any method by which such voluntary motion can now be acquired?"

"No."

"Does it not seem to you," he continued, "that when skillful mechanics on the earth's surface are able to adjust balances so delicately that in the face of friction of metal, friction of air, inertia of mass, the thousandth part of a grain can produce motion of the great beams and pans of such balances, we, in this location where there is no friction and no opposing medium—none at all—should be able to induce mass motion?"

"I can not imagine how it is possible, unless we shove each other apart. There is no other object to push against,—but why do you continue to hold me so tightly?" I interrupted myself to ask, for he was clasping me firmly again.

"In order that you may not leave me," he replied.

"Come, you trifle," I said somewhat irritated; "you have just argued that we are immovably suspended in a frictionless medium, and fixed in our present position; you ask me to suggest some method by which we can create motion, and I fail to devise it, and almost in the same sentence you say that you fear that I will leave you. Cease your incongruities, and advise with me rationally."

"Where is the bar of iron?" he asked.

I turned towards its former location; it had disappeared.

"Have you not occasionally felt," he asked, "that in your former life your mind was a slave in an earthly prison? Have you never, especially in your dreams, experienced a sensation of mental confinement?"

"Yes."

"Know then," he replied, "that there is a connection between the mind and the body of mortal beings, in which matter confines mind, and yet mind governs matter. How else could the will of men and animals impart voluntary motion to earthy bodies? With beings situated as are the animals on the surface of the earth, mind alone can not overcome the friction of matter. A person could suspend himself accurately on a string, or balance himself on a pivot, and wish with the entire force of his mind that his body would revolve, and still he would remain at perfect rest."

"Certainly. A man would be considered crazy who attempted it," I answered.

"Notwithstanding your opinion, in time to come, human beings on the surface of the earth will investigate in this very direction," he replied, "and in the proper time mental evolution will, by experimentation, prove the fact of this mind and matter connection, and demonstrate that even extraneous matter may be made subservient to mind influences. On earth, mind acts on the matter of one's body to produce motion of matter, and the spirit within, which is a slave to matter, moves with it. Contraries rule here. Mind force acts on pure space motion, moving itself and matter with it, and that, too, without any exertion of the material body which now is a nonentity, mind here being the master."

"How can I believe you?" I replied.

"Know, then," he said, "that we are in motion now, propelled by my will power."

"Prove it."

"You may prove it yourself," he said; "but be careful, or we will separate forever."

Releasing his grasp, he directed me to wish that I were moving directly to the right. I did so; the distance widened between us.

"Wish intensely that you would move in a circle about me."

I acquiesced, and at once my body began to circle around him.

"Call for the bar of iron."

I did as directed, and soon it came floating out of space into my very hand.

"I am amazed," I ejaculated; "yes, more surprised at these phenomena than at anything that has preceded."

"You need not be; you move now under the influences of natural laws that are no more obscure or wonderful than those under which you have always existed. Instead of exercising its influence on a brain, and thence indirectly on a material body, your mind force is exerting its action through energy on matter itself. Matter is here subservient. It is nearly the same as vacuity, mind being a comprehensive reality. The positions we have heretofore occupied have been reversed, and mind now dominates. Know, that as your body is now absolutely without weight, and is suspended in a frictionless medium, the most delicate balance of a chemist can not approach in sensitiveness the adjustment herein exemplified. Your body does not weigh the fraction of the millionth part of a grain, and where there is neither material weight nor possible friction, even the attrition that on surface earth results from a needle point that rests on an agate plate is immeasurably greater in comparison. Pure mind energy is capable of disturbing the equilibrium of matter in our situation, as you have seen exemplified by our movements and extraneous materials, 'dead matter' obeys the spiritual. The bar of iron obeyed your call, the spiritless metal is subservient to the demands of intelligence. But, come, we must continue our journey."

Grasping me again, he exclaimed: "Wish with all intensity that we may move forward, and I will do the same."

I did so.

"We are now uniting our energies in the creation of motion," he said; "we are moving rapidly, and with continually accelerated speed; before long we will perceive the earthy border of this chasm."

And yet it seemed to me that we were at perfect rest.

CHAPTER LI.

IS THAT A MORTAL?—"THE END OF EARTH."

At length I perceived, in the distance, a crescent-shaped ring of silver luster. It grew broader, expanding beneath my gaze, and appeared to approach rapidly.

"Hold; cease your desire for onward motion," said the guide; "we approach too rapidly. Quick, wish with all your mind that you were motionless."

I did so, and we rested in front of a ridge of brilliant material, that in one direction, towards the earth's outer circle, broadened until it extended upward as far as the eye could reach in the form of a bold precipice, and in the other towards the inner world, shelved gradually away as an ocean beach might do.

"Tell me, what is this barrier?" I asked.

"It is the bisected edge of the earth crevice," he said. "That overhanging upright bluff reaches towards the external surface of the earth, the land of your former home. That shelving approach beneath is the entrance to the 'Inner Circle,' the concavity of our world."

Again we approached the visible substance, moving gently under the will of my guide. The shore became more distinctly outlined as we advanced, inequalities that were before unnoticed became perceptible, and the silver-like material resolved itself into ordinary earth. Then I observed, upright and motionless, on the edge of the shore that reached toward the inner shell of earth, towards that "Unknown Country" beyond, a figure in human form.

"Is that a mortal?" I asked. "Are we nearing humanity again?"

"It is a being of mortal build, a messenger who awaits our coming, and who is to take charge of your person and conduct you farther," he replied. "It has been my duty to crush, to overcome by successive lessons your obedience to your dogmatic, materialistic earth philosophy, and bring your mind to comprehend that life on earth's surface is only a step towards a brighter existence, which may, when selfishness is conquered, in a time to come, be gained by mortal man, and while he is in the flesh. The vicissitudes through which you have recently passed should be to you an impressive lesson, but the future holds for you a lesson far more important, the knowledge of spiritual, or mental evolution which men may yet approach; but that I would not presume to indicate now, even to you. Your earthly body has become a useless shell, and when you lay it aside, as you soon can do, as I may say you are destined to do, you will feel a relief as if an abnormal excrescence had been removed; but you can not now comprehend such a condition. That change will not occur until you have been further educated in the purely occult secrets for which I have partly prepared you, and the material part of your organism will at any time thereafter come and go at command of your will. On that adjacent shore, the person you have observed, your next teacher, awaits you."

"Am I to leave you?" I cried in despair, for suddenly the remembrance of home came into my mind, and the thought, as by a flash, that this being alone could guide me back to earth. "Recall your words, do not desert me now after leading me beyond even alchemistic imaginings into this subterranean existence, the result of what you call your natural, or pure, ethereal lessons."

He shook his head.

"I beg of you, I implore of you, not to abandon me now; have you no compassion, no feeling? You are the one tie that binds me to earth proper, the only intelligence that I know to be related to a human in all this great, bright blank."

Again he shook his head.

"Hearken to my pleadings. Listen to my allegation. You stood on the edge of the brook spring in Kentucky, your back to the darkness of that gloomy cavern, and I voluntarily gave you my hand as to a guide; I turned from the verdure of the earth, the sunshine of the past, and accompanied you into as dismal a cavern as man ever entered. I have since alternately rebelled at your methods, and again have trusted you implicitly

"SUSPENDED IN VACANCY, HE SEEMED TO FLOAT."

as we passed through scenes that rational imagination scarce could conjure. I have successively lost my voice, my weight, my breath, my heart throb, and my soul for aught I know. Now an unknown future awaits me on the one hand, in which you say my body is to disappear, and on the other you are standing, the only link between earth and my self-existence, a semi-mortal it may be, to speak mildly, for God only knows your true rank in life's scale. Be you man or not, you brought me here, and are responsible for my future safety. I plead and beg of you either to go on with me into the forthcoming uncertainty 'Within the Unknown Country' to which you allude, or carry me back to upper earth."

He shook his head again, and motioned me onward, and his powerful will overcoming my feeble resistance, impelled me towards that mysterious shore. I floated helpless, as a fragment of camphor whirls and spins on a surface of clear, warm water, spinning and whirling aimlessly about, but moving onward. My feet rested on solid earth, and I awkwardly struggled a short distance onward and upward, and then stepped upon the slope that reached, as he had said, inward and upward towards the unrevealed "Inner Circle." I had entered now that mysterious third circle or sphere, and I stood on the very edge of the wonderful land I was destined to explore, "The Unknown Country." The strange, peaceful being whom I had observed on the shore, stepped to my side, and clasped both my hands, and the guide of former days waved me an adieu. I sank upon my knees and imploringly raised my arms in supplication, but the comrade of my journey turned about, and began to retrace his course. Suspended in vacancy, he seemed to float as a spirit would if it were wafted diagonally into the heavens, and acquiring momentum rapidly, became quickly a bright speck, seemingly a silver mote in the occult earth shine of that central sphere, and soon vanished from view. In all my past eventful history there was nothing similar to or approaching in keenness the agony that I suffered at this moment, and I question if shipwrecked sailor or entombed miner ever experienced the sense of utter desolation that now possessed and overcame me. Light everywhere about me, ever-present light, but darkness within, darkness indescribable, and mental distress unutterable. I fell upon my face in agony, and thought of other times, and those remembrances of my once happy upper earth life became excruciatingly painful, for when a person is in misery, pleasant recollections, by contrast, increase the pain. "Let my soul die now as my body has done," I moaned; "for even mental life, all I now possess, is a burden. The past to me is a painful, melancholy recollection; the future is"—

I shuddered, for who could foretell my future? I glanced at the immovable being with the sweet, mild countenance, who stood silent on the strand beside me, and whom I shall not now attempt to describe. He replied:

"The future is operative and speculative. It leads the contemplative to view with reverence and admiration the glorious works of the Creator, and inspires him with the most exalted ideas of the perfections of his divine Creator."

Then he added:

"Have you accepted that whatever seems to be is not, and that that which seems not to be, is? Have you learned that facts are fallacies, and physical existence a delusion? Do you accept that material bliss is impossible, and that while humanity is working towards the undiscovered land, man is not, can not be satisfied?"

"Yes," I said; "I admit anything, everything. I do not know that I am here or that you are there. I do not know that I have ever been, or that any form of matter has ever had an existence. Perhaps material things are not, perhaps vacuity only is tangible."

"Are you willing to relinquish your former associations, to cease to concern yourself in the affairs of men? Do you"—

He hesitated, seemed to consider a point that I could not grasp; then, without completing his sentence, or waiting for me to answer, added:

"Come, my friend, let us enter the expanses of the Unknown Country. You will soon behold the original of your vision, the hope of humanity, and will rest in the land of Etidorhpa. Come, my friend, let us hasten."

Arm in arm we passed into that domain of peace and tranquility, and as I stepped onward and upward perfect rest came over my troubled spirit. All thoughts of former times vanished.

The cares of life faded; misery, distress, hatred, envy, jealousy, and unholy passions, were blotted from existence. Excepting my love for dear ones still earth-enthralled, and the strand of sorrow that, stretching from soul to soul, linked us together, the past became a blank. I had reached the land of Etidorhpa—

THE END OF EARTH.

INTERLUDE.

CHAPTER LII.

THE LAST FAREWELL.

My mysterious guest, he of the silver, flowing beard, read the last word of the foregoing manuscript, and then laid the sheet of paper on the table, and rested his head upon his hand, gazing thoughtfully at the open fire. Thus he sat for a considerable period in silence. Then he said:

"You have heard part of my story, that portion which I am commanded to make known now, and you have learned how, by natural methods, I passed by successive steps while in the body, to the door that death only, as yet, opens to humanity. You understand also that, although of human form, I am not as other men (for with me matter is subservient to mind), and as you have promised, so you must act, and do my bidding concerning the manuscript."

"But there is surely more to follow. You will tell me of what you saw and experienced beyond the end of earth, within the possessions of Etidorhpa. Tell me of that Unknown Country."

"No," he answered; "this is the end, at least so far as my connection with you is concerned. You still question certain portions of my narrative, I perceive, notwithstanding the provings I have given you, and yet as time passes investigation will show that every word I have read or uttered is true, historically, philosophically, and spiritually (which you now doubt), and men will yet readily understand how the seemingly profound, unfathomable phenomena I have encountered may be verified. I have studied and learned by bitter experience in a school that teaches from the outgoings of a deeper philosophy than human science has reached, especially modern materialistic science which, however, step by step it is destined to reach. And yet I have recorded but a small part of the experiences that I have undergone. What I have related is only a foretaste of the inexhaustible feast which, in the wisdom expanse of the future, will yet be spread before man, and which tempts him onward and upward. This narrative, which rests against the beginning of my real story, the Unknown Country and its possibilities should therefore incite to renewed exertions, both mental and experimental, those permitted to review it. I have carried my history to the point at which I can say to you, very soon afterward I gave up my body temporarily, by a perfectly natural process, a method that man can yet employ, and passed as a spiritual being into the ethereal spaces, through those many mansions which I am not permitted to describe at this time, and from which I have been forced unwillingly to return and take up the semblance of my body, in order to meet you and record these events. I must await the development and expansion of mind that will permit men to accept this faithful record of my history before completing the narrative, for men are yet unprepared. Men must seriously consider those truths which, under inflexible natural laws, govern the destiny of man, but which, if mentioned at this day can only be viewed as the hallucinations of a disordered mind. To many this manuscript will prove a passing romance, to others an enigma, to others still it will be a pleasing study. Men are not now in a condition to receive even this paper. That fact I know full well, and I have accordingly arranged that thirty years shall pass before it is made public. Then they will have begun to study more deeply into force disturbances, exhibitions of energy that are now known and called imponderable bodies (perhaps some of my statements will then even be verified), and to reflect over the connection of matter therewith. A few minds will then be capable of vaguely conceiving possibilities, which this paper will serve to foretell, for a true solution of the great problems of the ethereal unknown is herein suggested, the study of which will lead to a final elevation of humanity, such as I dare not prophesy."

"Much of the paper is obscure to me," I said; "and there are occasional phrases and repetitions that appear to be interjected, possibly, with an object, and which are yet disconnected from the narrative proper."

"That is true; the paper often contains statements that are emblematical, and which you can not understand, but yet such portions carry to others a hidden meaning. I am directed to speak to many persons besides yourself, and I can not meet those whom I address more directly than I do through this communication. These pages will serve to instruct many people—people whom you will never know, to whom I have brought messages that will in secret be read between the lines."

"Why not give it to such persons?"

"Because I am directed to bring it to you," he replied, "and you are required:

"First, To seal the manuscript, and place it in the inner vault of your safe.

"Second, To draw up a will, and provide in case of your death, that after the expiration of thirty years from this date, the seals are to be broken, and a limited edition published in book form, by one you select.

"Third, An artist capable of grasping the conceptions will at the proper time be found, to whom the responsibility of illustrating the volume is to be entrusted, he receiving credit therefor. Only himself and yourself (or your selected agent) are to presume to select the subjects for illustration.

"Fourth, In case you are in this city, upon the expiration of thirty years, you are to open the package and follow the directions given in the envelope therein."

And he then placed on the manuscript a sealed envelope addressed to myself.

"This I have promised already," I said.

"Very well," he remarked, "I will bid you farewell."

"Wait a moment; it is unjust to leave the narrative thus uncompleted. You have been promised a future in comparison with which the experiences you have undergone, and have related to me, were tame; you had just met on the edge of the inner circle that mysterious being concerning whom I am deeply interested, as I am in the continuation of your personal narrative, and you have evidently more to relate, for you must have passed into that Unknown Country. You claim to have done so, but you break the thread in the most attractive part by leaving the future to conjecture."

"It must be so. This is a history of man on Earth, the continuation will be a history of man within the Unknown Country."

"And I am not to receive the remainder of your story?" I reiterated, still loth to give it up.

"No; I shall not appear directly to you again. Your part in this work will have ended when, after thirty years, you carry out the directions given in the sealed letter which, with this manuscript, I entrust to your care. I must return now to the shore that separated me from my former guide, and having again laid down this semblance of a body, go once more into"—

He buried his face in his hands and sobbed. Yes; this strange, cynical being whom I had at first considered an impertinent fanatic, and then, more than once afterward, had been induced to view as a cunning impostor, or to fear as a cold, semi-mortal, sobbed like a child.

"It is too much," he said, seemingly speaking to himself; "too much to require of one not yet immortal, for the good of his race. I am again with men, nearly a human, and I long to go back once more to my old home, my wife, my children. Why am I forbidden? The sweets of Paradise can not comfort the mortal who must give up his home and family, and yet carry his earth-thought beyond. Man can not possess unalloyed joys, and blessings spiritual, and retain one backward longing for mundane subjects, and I now yearn again for my earth love, my material family. Having tasted of semi-celestial pleasures in one of the mansions of that complacent, pure, and restful sphere, I now exist in the border land, but my earth home is not relinquished, I cling as a mortal to former scenes, and crave to meet my lost loved ones. All of earth must be left behind if Paradise is ever wholly gained, yet I have still my sublunary thoughts.

"Etidorhpa! Etidorhpa!" he pleaded, turning his eyes as if towards one I could not see, "Etidorhpa, my old home calls. Thou knowest that the beginning of man on earth is a cry born of love, and the end of man on earth is a cry for love; love is a gift of Etidorhpa, and thou, Etidorhpa, the soul of love, should have compassion on a pleading mortal."

He raised his hands in supplication.

"Have mercy on me, Etidorhpa, as I would on you if you were I and I were Etidorhpa."

Then with upturned face he stood long and silent, listening.

"Ah," he murmured at last, as if in reply to a voice I could not catch, a voice that carried to his ear an answer of deep disappointment; "thou spokest truly in the vision, Etidorhpa: it is love that enslaves mankind; love that commands; love that ensnares and rules mankind, and thou, Etidorhpa, art the soul of Love. True it is that were there no Etidorhpa, there would still be tears on earth, but the cold, meaningless tears of pain only. No mourning people, no sorrowful partings, no sobbing mothers kneeling with upturned faces, no planting of the myrtle and the rose on sacred graves. There would be no child-love, no home, no tomb, no sorrow, no Beyond"—

He hesitated, sank upon his knees, pleadingly raised his clasped hands and seemed to listen to that far-off voice, then bowed his head, and answered:

"Yes; thou art right, Etidorhpa—although thou bringest sorrow to mortals, without thee and this sorrow-gift there could be no bright hereafter. Thou art just, Etidorhpa, and always wise. Love is the seed, and sorrow is the harvest, but this harvest of sadness is to man the richest gift of love, the golden link that joins the spirit form that has fled to the spirit that is still enthralled on earth. Were there no earth-love, there could be no heart-sorrow; were there no craving for loved ones gone, the soul of man would rest forever a brother of the clod. He who has sorrowed and not profited by his sorrow-lesson, is unfitted for life. He who heeds best his sorrow-teacher is in closest touch with humanity, and nearest to Etidorhpa. She who has drank most deeply of sorrow's cup has best fitted herself for woman's sphere in life, and a final home of immortal bliss. I will return to thy realms, Etidorhpa, and this silken strand of sorrow wrapped around my heart, reaching from earth to Paradise and back to earth, will guide at last my loved ones to the realms beyond—the home of Etidorhpa."

Rising, turning to me, and subduing his emotion, ignoring this outburst, he said:

"If time should convince you that I have related a faithful history, if in after years you come to learn my name (I have

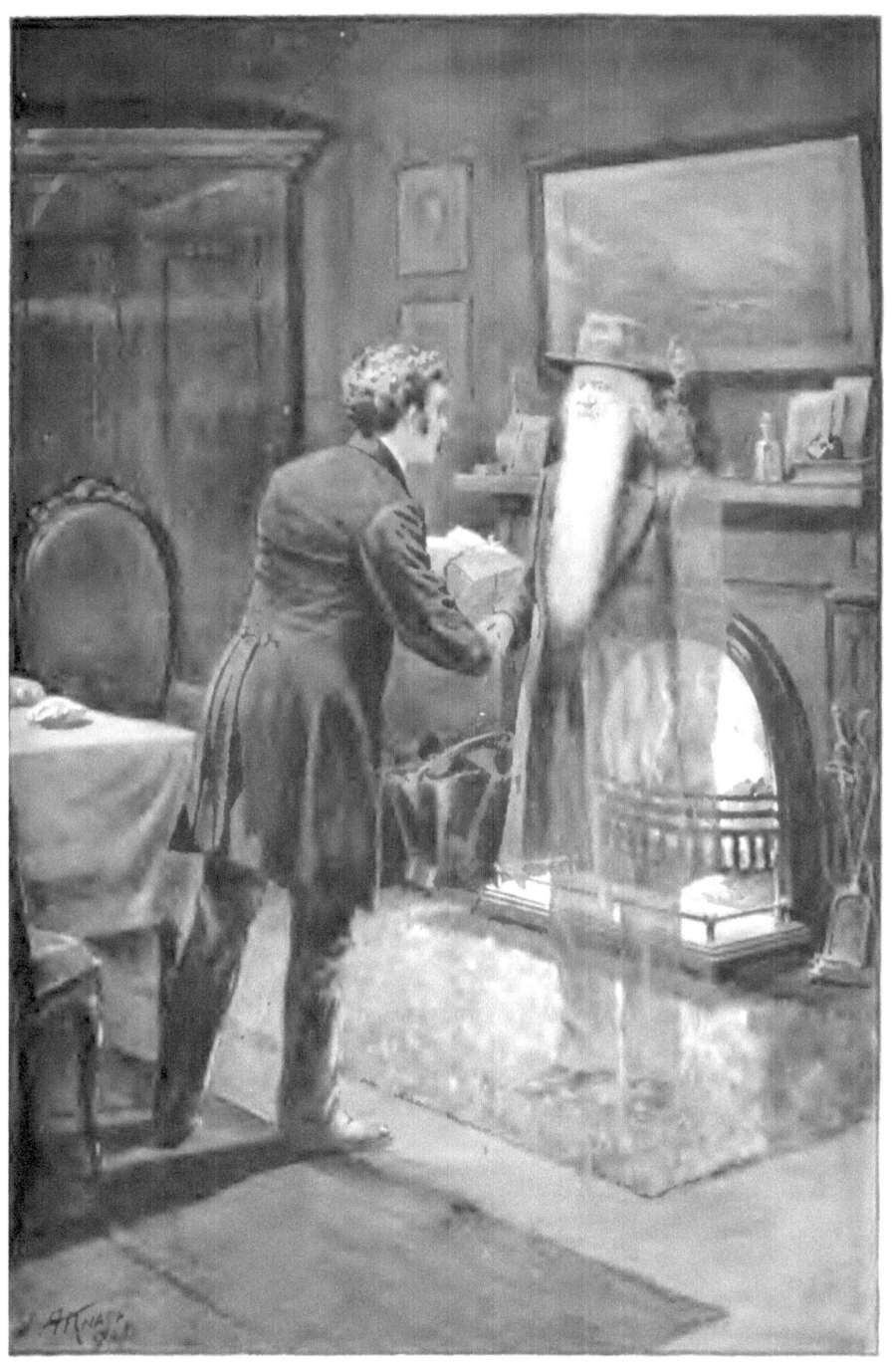

"I STOOD ALONE IN MY ROOM HOLDING THE MYSTERIOUS MANUSCRIPT."

been forbidden to speak it), and are convinced of my identity, promise me that you will do your unbidden guest a favor."

"This I will surely do; what shall it be?"

"I left a wife, a little babe, and a two-year-old child when I was taken away, abducted in the manner that I have faithfully recorded. In my subsequent experience I have not been able to cast them from my memory. I know that through my error they have been lost to me, and will be until they change to the spirit, after which we will meet again in one of the waiting Mansions of the Great Beyond. I beg you to ascertain, if possible, if either my children, or my children's children live, and should they be in want, present them with a substantial testimonial. Now, farewell."

He held out his hand, I grasped it, and as I did so, his form became indistinct, and gradually disappeared from my gaze, the fingers of my hand met the palm in vacancy, and with extended arms I stood alone in my room, holding the mysterious manuscript, on the back of which I find plainly engrossed:

"There are more things in Heaven and Earth, Horatio,
Than are dreamt of in your philosophy."

EPILOGUE.

LETTER ACCOMPANYING THE MYSTERIOUS MANUSCRIPT.

The allotted thirty years have passed, and as directed, I, Llewellyn Drury, now break the seals, and open the envelope accompanying the mysterious package which was left in my hand, and read as follows:

Herein find the epilogue to your manuscript. Also a picture of your unwelcome guest, I—Am—The—Man, which you are directed to have engraved, and to use as a frontispiece to the volume. There are men yet living to bear witness to my identity, who will need but this picture to convince them of the authenticity of the statements in the manuscript, as it is the face of one they knew when he was a young man, and will recognize now that he is in age. Do not concern yourself about the reception of the work, for you are in no wise responsible for its statements. Interested persons, if living, will not care to appear in public in connection therewith, and those who grasp and appreciate, who can see the pertinence of its truths, who can read between the lines and have the key to connected conditions, will assuredly keep their knowledge of these facts locked in their own bosoms, or insidiously oppose them, and by their silence or their attacks cover from men outside the fraternity, their connection with the unfortunate author. They dare not speak.

Revise the sentences; secure the services of an editor if you desire, and induce another to publish the book if you shrink from the responsibility, but in your revision do not in any way alter the meaning of the statements made in the manuscript; have it copied for the printer, and take no part in comments that may arise among men concerning its reception.* Those who are

---

* From a review of the fac simile see p. 35, it will be seen that an exact print word for word could not be expected. In more than one instance subsequent study demonstrated that the first conception was erroneous, and in the interview with Etidorhpa see p. 252, after the
360

best informed regarding certain portions thereof, will seemingly be least interested in the book, and those who realize most fully these truths, will persistently evade the endorsement of them. The scientific enthusiast, like the fraternity to which I belong, if appealed to, will obstruct the mind of the student either by criticism or ridicule, for many of these revelations are not recorded in his books.

You are at liberty to give in your own language as a prologue the history of your connection with the author, reserving, however, if you desire to do so, your personality, adding an introduction to the manuscript, and, as interludes, every detail of our several conversations, and of your experience. Introduce such illustrations as the selected artist and yourself think proper in order to illuminate the statements. Do not question the advisability of stating all that you know to have occurred; write the whole truth, for although mankind will not now accept as fact all that you and I have experienced, strange phases of life phenomena are revealing themselves, and humanity will yet surely be led to a higher plane. As men investigate the points of historical interest, and the ultra-scientific phenomena broached in this narrative, the curtain of obscurity will be drawn aside, and evidence of the truths contained in these details will be disclosed. Finally, you must mutilate a page of the manuscript that you may select, and preserve the fragment intact and in secret. Do not print another edition unless you are presented with the words of the part that is missing.*

(Signed.)   I—Am—The—Man.

Note by Mr. Drury.—Thus the letter ended. After mature consideration it has been decided to give verbatim most of the letter, and all of the manuscript, and to append, as a prologue, an introduction to the manuscript, detailing exactly the record of my connection therewith, including my arguments with Professors Chickering and Vaughn, whom I consulted concerning the statements made to me directly by its author. I will admit that perhaps the opening chapter in my introduction may be such as

---

page had been plated, it was discovered that the conveyed meaning was exactly the reverse of the original. Luckily the error was discovered in time to change the verse, and leave the spirit of this fair creature unblemished.—J. U. L.

* I have excised a portion see p. 190.—J. U. L.

to raise in the minds of some persons a question concerning my mental responsibility, for as the principal personage in this drama remarks: "Mankind can not now accept as facts what I have seen." Yet I walk the streets of my native city, a business man of recognized thoughtfulness and sobriety, and I only relate on my own responsibility what has to my knowledge occurred. It has never been intimated that I am mentally irresponsible, or speculative, and even were this the case, the material proof that I hold, and have not mentioned as yet, and may not, concerning my relations with this remarkable being, effectually disproves the idea of mental aberration, or spectral delusion. Besides, many of the statements are of such a nature as to be verified easily, or disproved by any person who may be inclined to repeat the experiments suggested, or visit the localities mentioned. The part of the whole production that will seem the most improbable to the majority of persons, is that to which I can testify from my own knowledge, as related in the first portion and the closing chapter. This approaches necromancy, seemingly, and yet in my opinion, as I now see the matter, such unexplained and recondite occurrences appear unscientific, because of the shortcomings of students of science. Occult phenomena, at some future day, will be proved to be based on ordinary physical conditions to be disclosed by scientific investigations [for "All that is is natural, and science embraces all things"], but at present they are beyond our perception; yes, beyond our conception.

Whether I have been mesmerized, or have written in a trance, whether I have been the subject of mental aberration, or have faithfully given a life history to the world, whether this book is altogether romance, or carries a vein of prophecy, whether it sets in motion a train of wild speculations, or combines playful arguments, science problems, and metaphysical reasonings, useful as well as entertaining, remains for the reader to determine. So far as I, Llewellyn Drury, am concerned, this is—

THE END.

ADDENDA.

RECIPIENTS, AND SUBSCRIBERS.

The writer of this Addenda avails himself of the opportunity to add to this list the names of some who are not subscribers, but to whom he is deeply obliged, or whom he regards as very dear friends, and also of a few others to whom he is personally unknown, but whom he admires and honors.

Furthermore, he can not forbear saying that a sense of delicacy forbade him announcing this work in Cincinnati, or in the suburb, Norwood, where he resides. To have done so would perhaps have placed individuals in the embarrassing position either of subscribing to a book in which they have no interest or concern, or of imagining that in not responding they might have their motives misconstrued. As probably no commercial edition of Etidorhpa will ever be issued, some of the writer's disappointed neighbors and friends, not receiving a copy, will doubtless feel aggrieved even after this explanation, as, indeed, several have already intimated. However, as this explanation embraces the whole truth, the writer can add nothing further, and must abide the consequences, having endeavored sincerely to avoid errors either of commission or omission.

Abbey, E. C., Buffalo, N. Y.
Abbott, A. N., Boston, Mass.
Abbott, G. C., Exeter, Mo.
Adams, C. S., Soquel, Cal.
Adams, W. L., Hazardville, Conn.
Adkins, J. N., Lampasas, Tex.
Adye, G. F., Newtonville, Ind.
Akin, W. S., Alexander, Tex.
Akins, H. B., Hollis, Ark.
Albright, W., Allegan, Mich.
Albro, W. H., Medina, O.
Aldrich, E. W., Dallas, Tex.
Allen, G. A., Hancock, N. Y.
Allen, James Lane, Cincinnati, O.
Allen, M. L., Tama, Iowa.
Alexander, A. J., Mayfield, Ky.
Alexander, E., El Paso, Tex.
Alpers, W. C., Bayonne, N. J.
Anderson, J. M., Pine Bluff, Ark.

Andrews, J. H., Seymour, Ind.
Andrews, Mrs. C. S., Newport, Ky.
Andriessen, H., Beaver, Pa.
Apple, F. M., Philadelphia, Pa.
Arbegast, J. W., West Mansfield, O.
Argenti, J. J. B., San Francisco, Cal.
Artman, B. E., Junction City, Ore.
Ashmun, D. W., Eau Claire, Wis.
Atchison, J. R., London, O.
Atwood, J. W., Marion, N. Y.
Austin, B. D., Rome, Tenn.
Averill, I. A., Appolonia, Wis.

Bagley, A. R., Cambridge, Mass.
Bahm, M G., Miamisburg, O.
Baird, W., Ridgeville, O.
Baker, Ella R., San Francisco, Cal.
Baldwin & Hawkins, Converse, Ind.
Baldwin, A. T., Washington C. H., O.

Baldwin, F. M., Blanchester, O.
Baldwin, J. G., Avondale, O.
Baldwin, T. R., Waco, Tex.
Ballard, J. W., Davenport, Iowa.
Ball, E. V., Enigma, Ga.
Ball, F. M., Beardsley, Minn.
Band, C., Crete, Neb.
Band, E., New Orleans, La.
Bangert, J. R., Shippenville, Pa.
Barber, J. C., Rockwood, Ill.
Barber, W. W., Cincinnati, O.
Barnes, E. R., Gillespie, Ill.
Barnes, T. L., Lockport, N. Y.
Bartlett, N. G., Chicago, Ill.
Barwick, S. O., Brookville, O.
Bayley, A. R., Cambridge, Mass.
Bayly, C. A., San Francisco, Cal.
Beach, C. H., Saltsburg, Pa.
Beal, J. H., Scio, O.
Beals, F. M., Mattoon, Ill.
Beam, A. M., Ireland, Ind.
Beane, B. F., El Dorado, O.
Beardsley, J. L., Wagoner, I. T.
Beatty, W. G., Norwood, O.
Beaumont, F. P., New Cumberland, W. Va.
Beaver, C., Mancelona, Mich.
Beem, E. C., Osceola, Mich.
Beery, G. W., Union Furnace, O.
Behymer, C., Cincinnati, O.
Behymer, E. T., Cincinnati, O.
Bell, L. C., Symmes Corner, O.
Bell, Mrs. T., Norwood, O.
Bell, W., Smyrna, Mich.
Bemis, J. D., Fremont, O.
Bemis, J. G., Chicago, Ill.
Benedict, W. G., Prattsburg, N. Y.
Best, W. P., Dublin, Ind.
Bettes, J. N., Jacksonville, Fla.
Bigelow, S. G., Silver Lake, Ind.
Bird, H. L., Benton Harbor, Mich.
Birney, W. L., Oakwood, Mo.
Bishop, S. E., Chicago, Ill.
Bishop, T. S., Albany, Mo.
Bixby, A. W., Watsonville, Cal.
Blackfan, H. S., Shushan, N. Y.
Black, F. B., Bengal, Ind.
Black, F. M., Peru, Ind.
Black, J. H., Halford, Ala.
Black, John R., Denver, Col.
Blanchard, C. C., Delavan, Wis.
Bloyer, W. E., Cincinnati, O.
Blythe, W. J., Centralia, Ill.
Bodemann, W., Chicago, Ill.

Boerner, E. L., Iona City, Iowa.
Bohn, M. G., Miamisburg, O.
Bolton, H. C., New York City.
Bonner, C. A., Dayton, O.
Bonton, E. S., Toledo, O.
Booth, C. H., Troy, N. Y.
Booth, S. A., San Francisco, Cal.
Borger, D. D., Reiley, O.
Borland & Foster, Franklin, Pa.
Boss, C. W., Cincinnati, O.
Bourn, H. M., Frametown, W. Va.
Bowers, J. M., San Francisco, Cal.
Bower, H. J., Meyerstown, Pa.
Boyce, A. R., Lawrence, Kan.
Boyd, F. O., Parsons, Kan.
Boyd, J. M., Spokane, Wash.
Boyd, S. R., Lawrence, Kan.
Brady, M. B., Cincinnati, O.
Breningstall, R. G., Detroit, Mich.
Briney, W. L., Oakwood, Mo.
Brinkerhoff, E., Bristolville, O.
Broadbent, J., Melbourne, Australia.
Brockman, A. F., Bickleton, Wash.
Brooke, J. E., Prairie Depot, O.
Brothers, C. E., Mineral Point, O.
Brothers, I., Youngstown, O.
Browens, D. N., Sweetwater, Tenn.
Brown, G. W., Newport, Ky.
Brown, M. E. T., New Britain, Conn.
Brown, W. A. J., Davis, W. Va.
Brownson, M. L., Kingsley, Mich.
Bruner, M. W., Three Forks, B. S.
Buchanan, Mrs. B. C., Cincinnati, O.
Buchan, F. J., Eastman, Ga.
Buck, J. D., Cincinnati, O.
Bukey, W. C., Ashley, O.
Bulla, R., Los Angeles, Cal.
Bullington, P. F., Bangor, Cal.
Bunnell, W. O., Wyalusing, Pa.
Burbige, Miss E., Newport, Ky.
Burdick, E., Cincinnati, O.
Burge, J. O., Nashville, Tenn.
Burke, W. H., Scotland, Ind.
Burkey, F. J., Galveston, Tex.
Burnham, A. A., Boston, Mass.
Burns, H., Carrollton, Ill.
Burton, G. W., Wheeling, W. Va.
Burton, J. J., Union City, Ind.
Busby, E. W., Massillon, O.
Busby, W. L., Rose Hill, Iowa.
Buse, B. E., St. Louis, Mo.
Butler, A. C., Arapahoe, Neb.
Butler, C. H., Oswego, N. Y.
Buxton, B. D., Mt. Gilead, O.

RECIPIENTS AND SUBSCRIBERS. 365

Byers, H. V., Newton, Iowa.
Byrd, E. H., Sherman Heights, Tenn.
Byrne, J. L., Bakerville, Tenn.

Cadman, W. S., Norwood, O.
Cady, C. W., Mabel, Minn.
Caldwell, G. C., Ithaca, N. Y.
Caldwell, T. A., Duluth, Minn.
Calhoun, J. M., Rosebloom, Miss.
Cameron, W. L., Palmyra, Neb.
Campbell, A. J., Fayetteville, Ark.
Campbell, C., Rock Creek, Tex.
Canfield, A., Sauk Center, Minn.
Canning, H., Boston, Mass.
Carpenter, N. M., Ellington, N. Y.
Carter, F. H., Indianapolis, Ind.
Case, F. S., Logan, O.
Caspari, C., Baltimore, Md.
Cassaday, F. V., Alliance, O.
Cass, G. J., Portland, Minn.
Cathcart, C. P., Kansas City, Mo.
Cavanaugh, F. A., Silverton, O.
Cecil, W. C., Stark, Kan.
Chamberlin, E. H., Chelmsford, Mass.
Chambers, S. V., Crestline, O.
Chandler, B. B., Planter, Ga.
Chandler, C. M., Parsons, Kan.
Chapman, T. H., Larimor, Iowa.
Charleston Library Society, Charleston, S. C.
Chase, D. A., Cambridge, N. Y.
Cheatham, T. A., Macon, Ga.
Chenoweth, J. T., Winchester, Ind.
Christie, C. J., Cincinnati, O.
Christopher, W. H., South Bend, Ind.
Cincinnati, O., Public Library.
Clark, C. S., Arroyo Grande, Cal.
Clark, L. W., Rushville, Ill.
Clarke, A. L., La Salle, Ill.
Clay, M. T., Union City, Mich.
Clifford, J., Stendal, Ind.
Clo, C., Cincinnati, O.
Clough, J. A., Rock Elm, Wis.
Clow, B. R., Hanford, Cal.
Cloyd, S. H., West Manchester, O.
Coblentz, F. H., Springfield, O.
Coblentz, V., New York City.
Cochran, O. P., Allegheny, Pa.
Coffey, B., Cincinnati, O.
Coggeshall, J S., Ogden Ill.
Cole, V. L., Corning, N. Y.
Coleman, J. G., Mineral, O.
Coleman, J. M., Indianapolis, Ind.

Collins, A. B., Westerly, R. I.
Colliver, J. I., San Bernardino, Cal.
Cone, J. W., Utica, N. Y.
Congdon, E. D., Cleveland, O.
Conklin, A. B., Cassopolis, Mich.
Connelly, J. W., Great Western Mines, Col.
Conner, Mrs. E. A , New York City.
Conover, J. N., Yankton, S. Dak.
Conrad, H. W., Paris, Ky.
Cook, C., Troy, N. Y.
Cook, F. S. W., Toledo, O.
Cook, T. P., New York City.
Coombs, J. L., Grass Valley, Cal.
Coon, J. V. D., Olean, N. Y.
Cooper, I. H., Kokomo, Ind.
Cooper, J., Bellefontaine, O.
Cooper, F., Villisca, Iowa.
Cooper, T. W., Brownsville, Tenn.
Cooper, W. C., Cleves, O.
Cope, T. S., Driggs, Ark.
Corey, W. M., Florence, Ky.
Cornell, E. A., Williamsport, Pa.
Cornwell, H. H., North Amherst, O.
Cosford, J. W., Mancelona, Mich.
Couch, W. I., Detroit, Mich.
Coverston, J. W., Frankton, Ind.
Cowant, E., Fair River, Miss.
Crain, J. B., Braddyville, Iowa.
Crall, L. H., New York City.
Crandel, T. R., Majenica, Ind.
Cranfill, J. B., Waco, Tex.
Cranston, O. F., Paola, Kan.
Creson, S. P., Stroud, Ok.
Cress, J., Steubenville, O.
Criswell, F. M., Washington, D. C.
Crona, E. S., Lyons, Col.
Crosby, C. F., Little Red, Ark.
Crow, W. F., Glen Easton, W. Va.
Culbertson, J. C., Cincinnati, O.
Culbreth, D. M. R., Baltimore, Md.
Cumback, Hon. W., Greensburg, Ind.
Curryer, W. F., Indianapolis, Ind.
Cushing & Co., Baltimore, Md.
Cutler, K. R., Waco, Tex.

Dakin, G. M., La Porte, Ind.
Dark, J. N., Liberty, Tex.
Davidson, A. W., Poplar Bluff, Mo.
Davies, E., Bear Creek, La.
D'Avignon, J. E., Windsor, Ont
Davis, C. E., Marcellus, Mich.
Davis, C. S., White Heath, Ill.
Davis, C. W., Jeffersonville, O.

Davis, D., Venedocia, O.
Davis, J. W., Lewisburg, Ky.
Davis, Mrs. T. H. B., Sandusky, O
Davis, W. H., Burlington, Iowa.
Davis, W. H., Springfield, Ill.
Davison, D., Denver, Colo.
Davison L. A. Hartford. Conn.
Davison, M., Newton, O.
Dawley, L. B., Binghampton, N. Y.
Day, D. B., Ridgway, Pa.
Dayton, O , Public Library.
Dean, A. H., Waverly, O.
Dean, C. B., Norborne, Mo.
Deatherage, W., Bell, Tex
Dech, E. J., Pandora, O.
Delavan, E. C., Binghampton, N. Y.
DeLay, W., Holly Springs, Ga.
DeMonco. Salt Lake City, Utah.
Denny, E., Oneonta, N. Y.
Dern, A. J., Sidney, Neb.
Devore, J. S., Forest Hill, Cal.
DeWitt, C. I., Berkshire, O.
Dickey, G. O., Campbellstown, O.
Diehl, C. L., Louisville, Ky.
Dodge, J. D., Cuyahoga Falls, O.
Doliber, T., Boston, Mass
Doss, C. H., Pittsfield, Ill.
Donnan, F., Atlantic, Pa.
Dowdell, C., Ennis, Tex.
Dowell, J. A., Albany, Ind
Downing, B. F., Newport, R. I.
Downs, L. S., Galveston, Tex.
Drake, J. R., Milwaukee, Wis.
Drayton, E., Richmond Hill House, Grenada, British West Indies.
Drinkwater, W. G., Germania, W. Va.
Duble, E. B, Williamsport, Pa.
DuBois, Catskill N. Y.
Dudley, W. L., Nashville, Tenn.
Duke, W. B., Richwood, O.
Duncan S V., Pleasantville, Iowa.
Durham, E. A., Calvert, Tex.
Durham, J J., Pickens, I. T.
Durham, W. M., Atlanta, Ga.
Durrett, Col. R. T., Louisville, Ky.

Eady, H. J., Elyria, O
Earle, W. A., West Boylston, Mass.
Easterday, G. S., Albuquerque, N. Mex.
Eaton, J. M., Chicago, Ill.
Eberbach, O., Ann Arbor, Mich.
Ebert, A. E., Chicago, Ill.

Eccles, R. G., Brooklyn, N. Y.
Eddy, R. P., Olneyville, R. I.
Edwards, O. F., New Lebanon O.
Eiche, R. J. C, Cincinnati, O.
Ekemeyer, M. S., New Bremen O.
Eldridge, D., Apalachicola, Fla.
Ellingwood, F., Chicago, Ill.
Elliott, C. A., Cincinnati, O.
Elliott, H. A., Baltimore, Md.
Elliott, T. B., Hartley, Iowa.
Ellis, J. B., Carbondale, Kan.
Ellis, J. G., Cerro Gordo, Ill.
Ely, E. S., Barnesville, O.
Emick, C. V., Baltimore, Md.
England, C. M., Lansing, Kan.
Englerth, J. T., Honey Creek, Ind.
English, W. H., Philipsburg, Mon.
Errett, Russell, Cincinnati, O.
Eshelman, L. J., Fostoria, O.
Eslick, L. E., Rockwell City, Mo.
Evans, A. D., Floresville, Tex.
Ewell, W. D, Willard, Mo.

Fahnestock, J. H, Fostoria, O.
Fairchild, B. F., New York City.
Fairman, S., Falconer, N. Dak.
Fearn, J., Oakland, Cal.
Fearn, W. H., San Francisco, Cal.
Feil, S. R., Cleveland, O
Feltman, C. A., Beardstown, Ill.
Feltz, F., Perryville, Mo.
Fennel, C. T. P., Cincinnati, O.
Ferrell, H. R., Cambridge, O
Ferris, J., College Hill, O.
Fickle, J. M., Stockwell, Ind.
Fink, F. W., New York City.
Finlay, R. G., Farmington, Pa.
Finley, W. M., Salem, Ill.
Finn, T., Boonsboro, Mo.
Finnin, J. C., Findlay, O.
Fish, F. W., Orange, Mass.
Fishback, W. P., Indianapolis, Ind.
Fisher, C. M., Rushsylvania, O.
Fisher, H. J., Cleveland, O.
Fisher, S. B. & J. J., Rossville, Ind.
Fite, C. H., Jalapa, Ind.
Fitzpatrick, T. V., Cincinnati, O.
Flack, W. F., Longton, Kan.
Fletcher, J. R., Conicville, Va.
Foley, R. E., Lemoore, Cal.
Foltz, K. O., Akron, O.
Forbes, B. E., Utica, N. Y.
Ford, C. M., Denver, Col.
Forden, W. B., Denver, Colo.

RECIPIENTS AND SUBSCRIBERS. 367

Forrest, J. H., Marion, Ind.
Forward, C., Rockwood, Pa.
Fothergill, C. O., Elgin, Iowa.
Foul, C. M., Denver, Col.
Fowler, J., Baraboo, Wis.
Fox, E. L., Houston, Tex.
Fraser, W. W., Dunkirk, Ind.
French, F. D., Flint, Mich.
French, T. P., David City, Neb.
Frerksen, R. C., Chicago, Ill.
Fulkerson, R. M., Eddyville, Ill.
Fuller, O. F., Chicago, Ill.
Fuller, T. G., Low's, Ky.
Furber, J. L., Topeka, Kan.
Fyfe, J. J., Odin, Ill.

Gabel, H. G., Aurora, Ill.
Gaesser, T. T., Troy, Ind.
Gamble, B. E., Forksville, Pa.
Gamble, E., Waverly, N. Y.
Gamble, T. A., East Troy, Pa.
Gamble, W. W., Santa Cruz, Cal.
Gardner, F. E., Detroit, Mich.
Gardner, J., Dayton, O.
Gardner, R. W., New York City.
Garretson, B. F., Osceola, Iowa.
Garth, T., Clarion, Iowa.
Gaskins, A. J., Sabina, O.
Gaston, W., Good Hope, W. Va.
Gault, S. C., Cincinnati, O.
Gaumer, G. F., Izamal, Mexico.
Gavin, D. H., Brookville, Ind.
Gayner, J. N., Grove City, Minn.
Geming, B. M., Brewerton, N. Y.
Gemmill, W. T., Forest, O.
Gengelback, E. E., Huntingburg, Ind.
George, E., Sioux Falls, S. Dak.
George, W. H., Bishop, Cal.
Gere, G. G., San Francisco, Cal.
Gibbs, A. E., Chicago, Ill.
Gilkerson, M. J., Tekamah, Neb.
Gill, G., Mt. Vernon, N. Y.
Ginther, D., North Manchester, Ind.
Gilpin, H. B., Baltimore, Md.
Girling, R. N., New Orleans, La.
Gissler, C. F., Brooklyn, N. Y.
Givens, C. C., Lewis, Ind.
Gleason, W. L., Kellerton, Iowa.
Glover, A. J., De Soto, Kan.
Goldsword, J. C., Cleveland, O.
Goodale, H. G., Jamaica, N. Y.
Goodman, O. P., Omaha, Neb.
Goodrick, G. M., Clintonville, Wis.

Goosen, P., Henderson, Neb.
Gowling, R., Memphis, Tenn.
Graham, A. J., Avondale, O.
Grassly, C. W., Chicago, Ill.
Graves, F. E., Hinckley, Ill.
Gray, J. R., Buffalo, N. Y.
Green, F. A., San Francisco, Cal.
Green, F. T., San Francisco, Cal.
Gregory, C. L., Yreka, Cal.
Gregory, J. T., Milledgeville, Ga.
Greiner, W. E., Paris, Tex.
Griffith, T. E., Frankfort, O.
Groff, S. V., Cincinnati, O.
Grosbach, H. H., Wauneta, Neb.
Grossman, F. A., Cleves, O.
Guild, W. L., Wayne, Ill.
Gumm, J., Wilson, I. T.
Gurney, S. D. F., Palmer, Kan.

Hackedorn, M. L., Galion, O.
Hadley, J. C., San Ardo, Cal.
Hahn, S. J. F., Cleveland, O.
Haifley, W. H., Amboy, Ind.
Halbert, W. H., Nashville, Tenn.
Hall, J., Edgewood, Ill.
Hall, W. A., Greenville, Mich.
Hallberg, C. S. N., Chicago, Ill.
Hance, E. H., Philadelphia, Pa.
Hancock, J. F., Baltimore, Md.
Hand, J. H., Blakely, Ga.
Hamblin, J. M. & Whitford, Westboro, Mo.
Hamilton, C. C., Kansas City, Mo.
Hamilton, J. S., Arthur, Ind.
Hamilton, F. A., Meridian, Cal.
Hamilton, M. F., Mannington, W. Va.
Hamilton, W. C., Topeka, Kan.
Hansberry, A. J., Ozark, Ark.
Harley, G. W., Hollansburg, O.
Harmony, P., Wadsworth, Nev.
Harrell, Mrs. M., Stiles, Iowa.
Harrington, J. T., Abilene, Tex.
Harris, F. A. K., Winter Haven, Fla.
Harris, F. B., Canton, N. J.
Harris, G. M., Lorain, O.
Harris, J. F., Harrington, Wash.
Harrison, R. G., Stricker, Ark.
Harter, G. E., Dayton, O.
Hartley, E. C., Carveo, Minn.
Hartley, W. H., Sydney, New South Wales.
Hartshorn, F. A., Marlborough, Mass.

Harvey, W. R., Dana, Ill.
Hastings, J. P., Norwood, O.
Hatfield, F. P., Grenola, Kan
Hattenhauer, R. C., La Salle, Ill.
Hauck, T., Columbus Grove, O.
Hauenstein, W., New York City.
Havens, H. P., Urbana, O.
Hawkey, J W., Alanson, Mich.
Hays, J. B., Woody, Ill.
Hazlett, A. H , Dunlap, Iowa.
Healess, J., Clinton, Iowa.
Heacker, W. J., Bean's Station, Tenn.
Heckler, G. L., Cleveland, O.
Heinitsh, C. A., Lancaster, Va.
Heister, C W., Lima, O.
Helbing, G., Bonham, Tex.
Heller, G. G., East St. Louis, Ill.
Helpman, J., Detroit, Mich.
Henderson, H. L., St. Louis, Mo.
Henderson, W. H., Sacramento, Cal.
Hendrick, H. T., Hanford, Cal.
Henry, C., Croton-on-Hudson, N. Y.
Henry, F. A., Louisville, Ky.
Hereth, F. S., Chicago, Ill.
Hermann, J. G., Cumberland, Md.
Herrick, R., Florid, Ill.
Hersey, S M., Bridgeport, Conn.
Hess, J. W., Lancaster, Pa.
Hetherington, J. P., Logansport, Ind.
Hickman, J. O., Hanford, Cal.
Higgins, C. P., Ft. Bragg, Cal.
Hill, Alex., Cincinnati, O.
Hill, A. M., Genoa, Ill.
Hill, A. R., Farmer, N. Y.
Hill, E. C., Gower, Mo.
Hill, G. R., Kendall, Wis.
Hines, L., Springer, N. Mexico.
Hitchman, A., Butler, O.
Hoag, C. W., Iantha, Mo.
Hobbie, J. A., Buffalo, N. Y.
Hockett, C. P., Stryker, O.
Hodge, T. S., Torrington, Conn.
Hoffman, Fr., New York City.
Hoffmeyer, F. B., Muscatine, Iowa.
Hogan, L. C., Chicago, Ill.
Holden, H. S., Rockford, Mich.
Hollick, F., New York City.
Hollingshead, E., Waterville, Wash.
Hollingsworth, T. D., Creston, O.
Holmes, C. W., Elmira, N. Y.
Holmes, H. E., Seattle, Wash.
Holmes, W. N., Milan, Tenn.
Holzhauer, G., Newport, Ky.

Homer, A H., Franklin, Me.
Homsher, G. W., Camden, O
Hooper, Asa, Kansas City, Mo.
Hooper, M. S., Stronghurst, Ill.
Hoover, E. M., Halstead, Kan.
Hopkins, Rev., Norwood, O.
Hopp, L. C., Cleveland, O.
Horn, W. F., Carlisle, Pa.
Horne, S. S., Jonesboro, Ind.
Horner, J., Whitewater, Kan.
Horton, W. F., Cortland, O.
Horton, W. A., Durant, I. T.
Horton, J. H., Cloquet, Minn.
Houghton, Mrs. H. B., Palmetto, Fla.
House, J. C., Modesto, Cal.
Houser, J C., Mine La Motte, Mo.
Howald, F. E., Atlanta, Ga.
Howe, P., Pomona, Cal.
Howe, R. M., Edinburg, Ind.
Howes, P. E., Boston, Mass.
Howland, C. E., Sedan, Kan.
Hoxsey, J. H., Spangle, Wash.
Hubbard, B. R., Sandusky, O.
Hubbard, H. C., Watersmeet, Mich
Hubbard, W. A., Boston, Mass.
Huckins, E., Plymouth, N. H.
Huckins, J. W., Danville, Cal.
Hudson, L. H., Little York, Ind.
Hudson, O. L., Princeton, Ind.
Hudson, W. C., Mulberry, Ark.
Huffman, C. W , Lebanon, Tenn.
Hug, H., Elgin, Ore.
Hughes, G., Jacksonville, Fla.
Hulbert, W. H , Nashville, Tenn.
Hull, J. S , Hicksville, O.
Hume, B. L., Petersburg, Va.
Humphrey, D. W., Parnell, Mo.
Hurty, J. N., Indianapolis, Ind.
Hutchinson, J. A., New Haven, Conn
Huttenhauer, R. C., La Salle, Ill.
Hutton & Hilton, Washington, D. C

Ingalls, A. O., Murray, Idaho.
Ingalls, J., Macon, Ga.
Ink, H. H., Canton, O.
Inman, C. T., Akron, O.
Inman, G. W., Centropolis, Kan.
Irwin, R. K., Peacerville, Idaho.

Jacobs, M. C., Richmond, Mo.
James, D. L., Cincinnati, O.
James, W. J., Leesburg, O.
Jarvis, H. C., Schell City, Mo.

RECIPIENTS AND SUBSCRIBERS. 369

Jenkins, R. L., Carlisle, Ind.
Jewell, E. W., Norwood, O.
Jillson, H. K., New London, Wis.
Johnson, B., Boston, Mass.
Johnson, C. B., Middletown, O.
Johnson, G. W., San Antonio, Tex.
Johnson, J. M., Inez, Ky.
Johnson, M. E., Pittsburg, Kan.
Johnson, P. C., Champaign, Ill.
Johnson, W. T., Pawnee, Neb.
Johnston, M. L., Harrod, O.
Jones & Jones, Baxter Springs, Kan.
Jones, J. W., Scotland, Ark.
Jones, T. H., Galena, Mo.
Jordan, G. W., Marshalltown, Pa.
Jowett, J. A., Nashville, Tenn.
Judd W. H., Janesville, Wis.
Judge, W. Q., New York City.
Jungkind, J. A., Little Rock, Ark.
Jurgensohn, B., Manarda, Wis.

Kadler, L. W., Chicago, Ill.
Kaeppel, O., So. Hadly Falls, Mass.
Kahn, F. P., Haricon, Wis.
Kalb, J. C., Canton, Kan.
Kalish, J., New York City.
Kampen, H. L., Kirkwood, Ill.
Kattenhorn, F., Cincinnati, O.
Kauffman, G. B., Columbus, O.
Keenan, T. J., New York City.
Keith, L. S., Congerville, Ill.
Kelly, P. H., Chillicothe, Ill.
Kelley, C., Ordway, Colo.
Kemp, W. S., Dayton, O.
Kemper, E. W., Norwood, O.
Kergan, J. DeG., Detroit, Mich.
Kerr, C. D., Gallipolis, O.
Kerr, W. W., Russellville, Ark.
Kessler, S. M., Golden, Col.
Ketchum, M. B., Mineral Wells, Tex.
Kilgore, H. F., Luverne, Minn.
Kilmer, T. B., New Brunswick, N. J.
Kimmel, O. P., German, O.
King, J. A., St. Louis, Mo.
King, H. W., Excelsior Springs, Mo.
Kinnett, W. E., Yorkville, Ill.
Kinney, Hon. C., Xenia, O.
Kirk, J., Barnesboro, Pa.
Kirk, M. A., Bellefonte, Pa.
Kirk, T., Burr Oak, Kan.
Kirkland, H. B., Berea, O.
Kisner, T. J., Canton, O.
Klie, G. H., St. Louis, Mo.
Kline, C. S., Denver, Col.

Knapp, Mrs. E., Norwood, O.
Koch, F. W., New York City.
Koch, J. A., Pittsburg, Pa.
Kochan, J., Denver, Col.
Koenigstein, J., Norfolk, Neb.
Kolb, A., Columbus, O.
Koller, C., Chicago, Ill.
Koons, C. W., Canton, O.
Kountz, E. P., Spring Hill, W. Va.
Kozel, M., Kansas City, Kan.
Krausi, W. J., New York City.
Krauskopf, G. H., Pittsburg, Pa.
Krebs, Carl, Cleveland, O.
Kremers, E., Madison, Wis.
Kuemmel, E. R., Milwaukee, Wis.
Kurfurst, H. F., Dayton, O.

Lacey, R. O., Lake City, Col.
Lachance, S., Montreal, Can.
Lackum, H J. Von, Dysart, Iowa.
LaFollette, G. W., Poe, Ind.
Lance, J T., Spurgeon, Ind.
Lane, H. W., Ellsworth, Wis.
Langfitt, W C., Cincinnati, O.
LaPierre, E H., Cambridge, Mass.
Larter, C. O., Detroit, Mich.
Law, G. F., Willoughby, O.
LaWall, C. H., Philadelphia, Pa.
Lawrence, J. S., Cincinnati, O.
Lawrence, R. E., Reesville, O.
Laws, Annie, Cincinnati, O.
Laws, L. B., Simmons, Mo.
Lawson, D. J., Warsaw, O.
Layman, A., Philadelphia, Pa.
Layton, S. H., Worthington, O.
Layton, T., St. Louis, Mo.
Leathers, W. P., Diamond, Mo.
Lee, C. H., New Iberia, La.
Lee, J. H., Chicago, Ill.
Lee, O. F., Marysville, Cal.
Legendre, J. A., New Orleans, La.
Leggat Bros., New York City.
Lehr, P., Cleveland, O.
Leister, W. L., Searcy, Ark.
Lemberger, J. L., Lebanon, Pa.
LeRoy, B. R., Chagrin Falls, O.
Le-Van Bender, J., Penn Yan, N. Y.
Lewis, G. W., Sycamore, Ill.
Lewis, J. B., Shambaugh, Iowa.
Lewis, J. W., Driggs, Ark.
Lillard, B., New York City.
Lilly, J. K., Indianapolis, Ind.
Limes, J. L., St. Johns, Kan.
Lingle, G. E., Green Camp, O.

Linquist, M. F., New York City
Lisk, B. F., Conner, Fla.
Livingston, F. J., Salix, Pa.
Livingston, L. S., Johnstown, Pa.
Llewellyn, J. F., Mexico, Mo.
Lloyd, Miss E. A., North Bloomfield, N. Y.
Lloyd, Mrs. John Uri, Norwood, O.
Lloyd, Mrs. N. Ashley, Norwood, O.
Lloyd, Mrs. S W., Norwood, O.
Lockwood, Mrs. E., Put-in-Bay Island, O.
Logan, M. H., San Francisco, Cal.
Logan, S. D., Middletown, O.
Loggan, R. O., Philomath, Ore.
Long, D. T., Topeka, Kan.
Lotze, E. H., Girard, O.
Love, G. A., Preston, Minn.
Ludwig, H. M., Richland Center, Wis.
Luse, L. H., Willoughby, O.
Lyman, M. R., Gagetown, Mich.

Macer, T., Evansville, Ind.
Maddox, C. K., Atlanta, Ga.
Maddy, J. H., Cincinnati, O.
Madison, W. H., New York City.
Maghee, T. G., Rawlins, Wyo.
Magoffin, A. E., Lyons, Kan.
Maguire, T. G., San Francisco, Cal.
Main, T. F., New York City.
Major, J. R., Washington, D. C.
Manley, W. C., Franklin, Ill.
Mann, A. J., Brookville, Ala.
Manwaren, E. M., Oswego, N. Y.
Maple, W. W., Des Moines, Iowa.
March, S. F., Argentine, Kan.
March, W. B., Brentwood, Cal.
Marconnay, A. de, West Berkeley, Cal.
Mark, W. K., Cleveland, O.
Marks, W. L., Grand Rapids, Mich.
Markham, J. H., Kansas City, Mo.
Marques, A., Honolulu, Hawaiian Is.
Marrs, R. F., Sciota, Ill.
Marsh, E. J., Oswego, N. Y.
Marsh, M. L., New Britain, Conn.
Marshall, E. C., Boston, Mass.
Marshall, D. M., Forestport, N. Y.
Marshett, Ida E., Jackson, Cal.
Martin, F. K., Wenona, Ill.
Martin, J. B., Griswold, Iowa.
Martin, N. H., Newcastle-on-Tyne, England.

Martin, J. C., Washington, D. C.
Martinez, R. J., Jacksonville, Fla.
Marvin, J. P., Harrison, O.
Mason, C. A., Waterbury, Conn.
Mason, E. G., Cawker City, Kan.
Masters, S. H., Sheldon, Iowa.
Matchette, G. H., McPherson, Kan.
Matthews, J. N., Mason, Ill.
Maxwell, G. F., West Liberty, O.
Mayo, C. A., New York City.
Mayo, J. K., Houston, Tex.
Meader, H. C., Cincinnati, O.
Meissner, F. W., La Porte, Ind.
Mellette, U. N., DeLand, Fla.
Mendell, E. A., St. Joseph, Mo.
Merrill, W. W., Hammond, Ind.
Metz, A. L., New Orleans, La.
Metzger, B. S., Boundary, Ind.
Meyer C. F. G., St. Louis, Mo.
Meyer, G., Prague, Austria.
Michael, Mrs. H. A., Boston, Mass.
Michaelis, G., Albany, N. Y.
Michener, H., Halsey, Ore.
Mickle, J. B., Greenville, Pa.
Middleton, M. C., Jasper, Ind.
Miles, T. W., Denver, Col.
Milholland, W. H., New Orleans, La.
Millard, I. I., Toledo, O.
Miller, A. C., Findlay, O.
Miller, A W., Philadelphia, Pa.
Miller, C. C., Halifax, Pa.
Miller, C. N., San Francisco, Cal.
Miller, G. M., Newport, Ky.
Miller, T. H., Blacksville, W. Va.
Miller, W., Cincinnati, O.
Miller, W. S., Uniontown, Kan.
Milligan, T., New Britain, Conn.
Miner, C. A., Janesville, Wis.
Miner, Mrs. M. O., Hiawatha, Kan.
Minthorn, M. F., Moorehead, Iowa.
Mitchell, J. H., Dallas, Tex.
Mittelbach, W., Boonville, Mo.
Mock, W. K., Cleveland, O.
Moeglich, O. A., Columbus, O.
Moench, F., St. Paul, Minn.
Monroe, J. A., West Alexander, Pa.
Montgomery, W. H., Comanche, I. T.
Moon, E. W., Portland, Ind.
Moore, C. H., Oakfield, Wis.
Moore, E. S., Bay Shore, N. Y.
Moore, J. H., Cincinnati, O.
Moore, O. M., Bradshaw, Neb.
Moore, Hon. F. W., Winton Place, O.
Moorman, J. W., Humboldt, Tenn.

RECIPIENTS AND SUBSCRIBERS. 371

Morgan, Miss S. A. L., Sharonville, O.
Morris, J. R., New Albany, Ind.
Morris, Mrs. C. S., New York City.
Morrison, J. E., Montreal, Can.
Morrow, J., Germantown, Neb.
Morse, E. L., Ashtabula, O.
Morse, S. W., Elgin, Iowa.
Morton, F. N., Little Cooley, Pa.
Moses, F. W., Grove City, O.
Mosher, C. N., Webb City, Mo.
Mosher, M. E., Havana, Ill.
Moxley, D. N., Glenwood, Ala.
Mudge, H. C., Wales, Mich.
Mueller, A., Kirkwood, Mo.
Mulford, R., Jr., Norwood, O.
Mullen, H. C., Cincinnati, O.
Mulligan, T., New Britain, Conn.
Mundy, W. N., Cincinnati, O.
Munk, J. A., Los Angeles, Cal.
Murphy, E. F., Olevano-romano, Italy.
Murray, C., Chico, Cal.
Murray, F. M., Delaware, O.
Murray, J. H., Ava, Mo.
Mushett, Ida E., Jackson, Cal.
Myers, D., Cleveland, O.
McCally, J. R., Dayton, O.
McCance, J. B., Sadorus, Ill.
McCann, J. D., Monticello, Ind.
McCann, J. M., Toledo, O.
McCauley, J. F., Cleveland, O.
McClanahan, J. T., Boonville, Mo.
McClelland, J. S., Sandusky, O.
McClung, C. E., Columbus, Kan.
McConnell, G. W., Newberg, Ore.
McCray, W. F., Clark's Hill, Ind.
McCrea, A. J., Southbridge, Mass.
McCully, C. H., Burnett's Creek, Ind.
McDowell, G. S., Cincinnati, O.
McElheie, T. D., Brooklyn, N. Y.
McElHinney, J. H. & F. B., New London, O.
McElHinney, J. M., Newport, O.
McFarlan, Anna L., Norwood, O.
McGee, A. C., Barry, Ill.
McGreew, W. E., Pittsburg, Pa.
McGuire, W. H., Frankfort, Ind.
McHenry, O. P., Hamilton, O.
McKessen, J., New York City.
McKinley, W. H., Ogden, Ill.
McKinzie, W., Quayzee, Ind.
McKitrick, A. S., Kenton, O.
McKlveen, J. A., Chariton, Iowa.

McKlveen, H. B. Coin, Iowa.
McLaughlin, J. M., Butler, O.
McLean, S. H., Hillsboro, Ill.
McLennan, D., Honolulu, Hawaiian Islands.
McMillen, Bishop, Columbus, O.
McMurtrey, A. T., Sargent, Mo.
McNeill, Aaron, Norwood, O.
McPheron, E. M., Ada, O.
McWilliams, A. R., Blue Mountain, Miss.

Nachtrieb, C. J., Wauseon, O.
Nafe, G. W., Fremont, Mich.
Nash, C. C., Liberty, Tex.
Nelson, R. P., Bodman, Ark.
Nead, Mrs. J. D., Kansas City, Mo.
Nesbitt, A. H., Springfield, O.
Newlin, W. H., New London, Ind.
Nichols, M. H., Worcester, N. Y.
Nicolay, W. J., Bloomington, Ill.
Niederkorn, J. S., Versailles, O.
Nifer, F. J., Brimfield, Ind.
Niles, A., Wellsboro, Pa.
Nims, F. A., Muskegon, Mich.
Nipgen, J. A., Chillicothe, O.
Nixon, O. W., Chicago, Ill.
Noble, J. T., Custar, O.
Nordstrum, S. G., Sioux Rapids, Iowa.
Norton, T. H., Cincinnati, O.
Numbers, J. R., Weiser, Idaho.
Nye, C. N., Canton, O.

Oberdeener, S., Santa Clara, Cal.
O'Brien, S. F., Hillsboro, Ky.
Oder, R. R., Rushsylvania, O.
Ogden, A. B., Mt. Ayr, Iowa.
Ogle, J. J., Ft. Wayne, Ind.
O'Hare, J., Providence, R. I.
Ohio State Library, Columbus, O.
Ohler, W. H., Portland, Me.
Oldberg, O., Chicago, Ill.
Onsgard, L. K., Houston, Minn.
Opperman, A., Auburn, Neb.
Ortt, E. L., Canton, O.
Osborn, J. W., Dyersville, Iowa.
Osmun, C. A., New York City.
Outcalt, A. A., Cincinnati, O.
Outland, P. P., Zanesfield, O.

Packer, E. B., Osage City, Kan.
Packwood, S. D., Highland Center, Iowa.

Palmer, R. L., Noble, Ill.
Papik, J., Chicago, Ill.
Parkill, S. E., Owosso, Mich.
Parks, G. F., St. Clair, Mich.
Parr, L. E., Beeville, Tex.
Partridge, W. T., Kennedy, O.
Parsons, G. W., Kansas City, Kan.
Patch, E. L., Stoneham, Mass.
Patton, J. F., York, Pa.
Peacock, J. C., Philadelphia, Pa.
Peckham, H. C., Freeport, Mich.
Pennell, W. W., Fredericktown, O.
Pennington, T. H., Troy, N. Y.
Perrine, J. M., Junction, Ark.
Perry, J. R., Indianapolis, Ind.
Peters, E. E., Wrightsville, Ill.
Pettit, G. W., Cincinnati, O.
Phelon, W. P., Chicago, Ill.
Phillips, H. C., Rochester, N. Y.
Phillips, W., Jackson, O.
Pickerill, G. W., Indianapolis, Ind.
Pickering, A. O., Chuckey City, Tenn.
Pickett, C., Broken Bow, Neb.
Pickett, J. H., Oskaloosa, Iowa.
Pieck, E. L., Covington, Ky.
Pierce, J. G., Sebastopol, Cal.
Pierie, C. E., Galloway, Ark.
Piffner, F. J. R., Delaware, O.
Pike, L., Terre Haute, Ind.
Pinney, M., Cincinnati, O.
Pinson, G., Pikerville, Ky.
Pinson, M., Williamson, W. Va.
Platts, Mrs. K. A., Bellevue, Ky.
Plummer, R. N., Philadelphia, Pa.
Poe, L. J., Butler, Ky.
Poos, R. C., Okawville, Ill.
Pope, J. D., Monticello, Ark.
Porter, A. C., Ashford, N. Y.
Porter, H. C., Towanda, Pa.
Postle, R. A., Ashville, O.
Potter, G. E., Newark, N. J.
Potter, H. B., Jefferson, N. Y.
Potts, Mary, Elmira, N. Y.
Powers, H. W., Washingtonville, O.
Prall, D. E., Saginaw, Mich.
Preston & Rounds, Providence, R. I.
Preston, D., Philadelphia, Pa.
Presler, H. M., Fairbury, Ill.
Prideaux, R. O., Farmer, Tex.
Price, V. C., Waukegan, Ill.
Proctor, W., Philadelphia, Pa.
Public Library, Detroit, Mich.
Puchta, G., Cincinnati, O.

Pulham, L. C., Crowley, La.
Pulliam, S. T., Crowley, La.

Quick, W. T., Ft. Collins, Col.
Quigg, H. D., Blackwater, Mo.
Quinlin, W. H., Loramier, O.
Quinn, J. D., Newport, Ky.

Rader, J. A., Caney, Kan.
Radford, B. J., Eureka, Ill.
Ramsperger, G., New York City.
Randall, P. M., Sugar Grove, Wis.
Randolph, L. L., Chicago, Ill.
Randolph, R. H., Portland, Ore.
Rapelye, C. A., Hartford, Conn.
Rash, H. W., Centerville, Kan.
Rauch, W., Johnstown, Pa.
Rauschkott, J., Columbus, O.
Read, J. A., Tecumseh, Kan.
Redman, J. R., Santa Cruz, Cal.
Redmond, F. J., Fillmore, N. Y.
Redsecker, J. H., Lebanon, Pa.
Reed, J. H., Napoleon, Mich.
Reed, P. W., Port Huron, Mich.
Reeder, J. C., Montezuma, Ind.
Rees, D. B., Des Moines, Iowa.
Reichard, A., Paola, Kan.
Reichard, G. W., New Moorefield, O.
Reid, A. Y., Norwood, O.
Remington, J. P., Philadelphia, Pa.
Reppeto, A. O., Port Townsend, Wash.
Reynolds, H. P., Plainfield, N. J.
Rice, A. C., Palmyra, Wis.
Rice, C., New York City.
Richardson, A. L., La Grande, Ore.
Richardson, J. K., Wichita, Kan.
Richardson, J. M., Mineral Point, O.
Richardson, T. L., Baltimore, Md.
Richardson, W. F., Pierce City, Mo.
Rickey, J. K., Mendota, Ill.
Riddle, T. E., Rockdale, Tex.
Ridpath, J. C., Greencastle, Ind.
Riggs, S. M., Muscotah, Kan.
Riggs, W. E., Glenville, Neb.
Rinehart, S., Laporte, Mich.
Ring, H. J., Ferndale, Cal.
Ripley, E. M., Unionville, Conn.
Ritchie, J. W., Caddo, Tex.
Rittenhouse, A., Philadelphia, Pa.
Ritter, S. J., Hanoverville, Pa.
Robbins, A., Philadelphia, Pa.
Roberts, J. T., Germantown, Pa.
Robertson, Mrs. C. D., Cincinnati, O.

Robinson, B. A., Newark, N. J.
Robinson, B. L., McLean, N. Y.
Robinson, E. A., Lowell, Mass.
Rodecker, C. W., Wonewoc, Wis.
Rodgers, A. E., Brenham, Tex.
Rogers, C. M., Deadwood, S. Dak.
Rogers, E. H., Bloomer, Wis.
Rogers, S. T., New Albany, Ind.
Rogers, W. H., Middletown, N. Y.
Rollman, J. C, Burr Oak, Mich.
Rood, G. L., Etna, N. Y.
Root, F. S. S., Scotia, Cal.
Rosenberg, J. H., Omaha, Neb.
Rosenbery, D. H., Mascotte, Fla.
Rosenblueth, M., New York City.
Rosenthal, A., Cincinnati, O.
Rosewater, N., Cleveland, O.
Ross, J. G., Portland, Ind.
Ross, L. H., Ekin, Ind.
Roth, C. G., Cincinnati, O.
Rouse, S. D., Covington, Ky.
Rouse, J. T., Cincinnati, O.
Rouse, Miss A., Crittenden, Ky.
Rowe, M., Redmon, Ill.
Rowlinski, Savannah, Ga.
Ruble, W. R., Mayfield, Ky.
Rudolf, Mrs. E., New Orleans, La.
Rudwick, P. F. A., Chicago, Ill.
Ruhl, M. F., Cincinnati, O.
Russell, A. P., Wilmington, O.
Russell, C. W., Springfield, O.
Russell, L. E., Springfield, O.

Salisbury, J. H., New York City.
Salsbury, J. E., Cazenovia, N. Y.
Salter, G. W., Brooklyn, N. Y.
Samuel, J. H., Maysville, Ky.
Samuels, E. H., San Francisco, Cal.
Sargent, C. B., Taos, N. Mex.
Sarver, J. A., New Frankfort, Ind.
Sattler, R., Cincinnati, O.
Saum, F. A., Bridgewater, Iowa.
Saunders, Mrs. W., Ottawa, Can.
Sayre, E. A., New York City.
Sayre, L. E., Lawrence, Kan.
Schafer, G. H., Ft. Madison, Iowa.
Scheffer, E., Louisville, Ky.
Schellentrager, E. A., Cleveland, O.
Scherer, A., Chicago, Ill.
Schieffelin, W. J., New York City.
Schilling, J., Louisville, O.
Schinetsa, G. T., Baltimore, Md.
Schlaepfer, H. J., Evansville, Ind.

Schlarbaum, J. C., San Francisco, Cal.
Schlotterbeck, J. O., Ann Arbor, Mich.
Schmitt, Carl, Cleveland, O.
Schneerer, F. W., Norwalk, O.
Schoettlin, A. J., Louisville, Ky.
Schooley, E. W., Mentor, O.
Schrank, H. C., Milwaukee, Wis.
Schreiber, S. L., Sunbury, Pa.
Scott, E., Toledo, O.
Scott, J. H., Albertville, Ala.
Scott, J. McD., Chicago, Ill.
Scoville, W. L., Boston, Mass.
Scudder, J. K., Cincinnati, O.
Seabury, G., New York City.
Seal, F. E., Mt. Carmel, Ind.
Seiler, N. H., Lawrence, Kan.
Segraves, S. L., Era, Texas.
Sennerwald, F. W., St. Louis, Mo.
Severance, W. S., Greenfield, Mass.
Severs, G. F., Centerville, Iowa.
Seymour, J. R., Raymond, Ill.
Seymour, H. A., Berwyn, I. T.
Shafer, G. R., Morton, Ill.
Shafer, W., Rochester, Ind.
Shantz, F., Kenton, O.
Sharp, C. J., Oakland, Cal.
Shedd, E. W., Boston, Mass.
Shelby, J. O., Liberty, Tex.
Sheldon, M. H., Mt. Erie, Ill.
Shepard, B., Minneapolis, Minn.
Shepard, W., Columbus, O.
Sheppard, S. A. D., Boston, Mass.
Sherlock, T. J., Stetson, Mich.
Sherman, S. M., Columbus, O.
Sherrow, W. E., Salem Center, Ind.
Sherwood, L. N., Columbus, O.
Shively, S. S., Kansas City, Kan.
Short, H. S., Fillmore, Ill.
Shrader, J. M., Hopewell, O.
Shuey, A., Prospect, O.
Shultz, J. J., Delphi, Ind.
Shutt, L. C., Servia, Ind.
Siegenthaler, G. M., Bethany, Mo.
Siggins, E. S., South Omaha, Neb.
Simmons, B. L., Granville, Tenn.
Simmons, J., Southport, England.
Simon, J. C., Cleveland, O.
Simon, W., Baltimore, Md.
Simonson, W., Cincinnati, O.
Simpson, R. A., York, Pa.
Simpson, W., Raleigh, N. C.
Sloan, G. W., Indianapolis, Ind.

Sluyter, S. D., Chalmers, Ind.
Smalley, James, Nixa, Mo.
Smink, W. H. R., Shamokin, Pa.
Smith, A. G., La Grande, Ore.
Smith, A. J., Metamora, Ind.
Smith, C. C., Kirkwood, Ill.
Smith, C., Cincinnati, O.
Smith, I. N., Westerville, O.
Smith, J. C., Plattsburg, N. Y.
Smith, J. G., Slidell, La.
Smith, J. L., Hoagland, Ind.
Smith, J. R., Kellogg, Iowa.
Smith, L. A., Espyville, Pa.
Smith, L. S., St. Augustine, Fla.
Smith, M. A., Cincinnati, O.
Smith, T. D., Cleveland, O.
Smith, W. A., Atlanta, Ga.
Smithson, D. E. Caldwell, Idaho.
Smizer, S., Sharonville, O.
Smizer, Miss S., Sharonville, O.
Snapp, G., Cottage Grove, Ore.
Snow, C. W., Syracuse, N. Y.
Snyder, G., Freemansburg, W. Va.
Southworth, H. C., Leonardsville, N. Y.
Speicer, C. E. Centerville, Pa.
Spencer, J. R., Cincinnati, O.
Spenger, J. G., Dayton, O.
Spring, R. Y., Newport, Ky.
Springer, A., Norwood, O.
Squier, E. A., College, Corner, O.
Squier, G. E., Brookville, Ind.
Squire, W. B., Worthington, Ind.
Stahlhuth, E. H. W., Columbus, O.
Stam, C. F., Chestertown, Md.
Stanton, L. E., Sterling, Col.
Starr, Rev. D. J., Cincinnati, O.
Stearns, F. M., Frontier, Mich.
Stecher, H. W., Cleveland, O.
Stedem, F. W. E., Philadelphia, Pa.
Steen, A. M., Palatka, Fla.
Stegner, E., St. Louis, Mo.
Stephens, A. F., St. Joe, Mo.
Stephens, W. G., Catawba, O.
Stevens, A. B., Ann Arbor, Mich.
Stevens, J. V., Evanston, Ill.
Stevens, Mrs. M. A., Benton Harbor, Mich.
Stevenson, J. A., Waco, Ky.
Stewart, F. E., Detroit, Mich.
Stewart, T. M., Cincinnati, O.
Stewart, W. A., Norwood, O.
St. Louis Public Library, St. Louis, Mo.
Stockberger, E., Mentone, Ind.
Stoneburner, J. M., Berne, Ind.
Stoughton, D. G., Hartford, Conn.
Strahan, C. S., Galesburg, Kan.
Strawsburg, M., North Hampton, O.
Strouse, I., Covington, Ky.
Struble, J. R., Chicago, Ill.
Strunk, B. K., Utahville, Pa.
Stutzman, T. B., Davenport, Neb.
Sutton, J. G., Rushsylvania, Ohio.
Swepston, G. M., McArthur, O.
Switzer, G. O., Pentwater, Mich.
Tabor, T. A., Corinna, Mo.
Tait, A. M., Avery, Iowa.
Tait, John, Meriden, Conn.
Tait, T. E., Barberton, O.
Take, J. F., Whiting, Ind.
Tallerday, G. C., Belvidere, Ill.
Tanski, N. T., Cincinnati, O.
Taylor, A. B., Philadelphia, Pa.
Taylor, A. P., Columbus, O.
Taylor, A. W., Sunbury, O.
Taylor, E. J., La Center, Wash.
Taylor, J. A., Gridley, Ill.
Taylor, J. L., Logansport, Ind.
Taylor, J. L., West Plains, Ky.
Taylor, W. S., Alexandria, O.
Taylor, W. T., New Orleans, La.
Teague, J., Nimrod, Tex.
Teeters, S. C., Washington C. H., O.
Tenney, W. A. R., Cincinnati, O.
Terrill, J. H., Wichita, Kan.
The Theosophical Publishing Society, London, Eng.
Thoman, E. A., Bucyrus, O.
Thomas, R. L., Cincinnati, O.
Thomas, S. C., Milroy, Ind.
Thompson, E. R., Harmony, Minn.
Thompson, J. R., Northville, S. Dak.
Thompson, J. M., Cincinnati, O.
Thompson, V., Swayzee, Ind.
Thompson, W. S., Washington, D. C.
Thorn, H. P., Medford, N. Y.
Thornton, F. E., Chicago, Ill.
Thornton, J. A., Correctionville, Iowa.
Thornbury, J. H., Dunlow, W. Va.
Thurston, A., Grand Rapids, O.
Tidball, C. W., Norwood, O.
Tigner, J. O., Greenville, Ga.
Tilden, A. D., Riverside, Cal.
Tilden, J. H., Denver, Col.
Tillotson, A. G., Michigan City, Ind.
Tillson, O. E., West Alexandria, O.

RECIPIENTS AND SUBSCRIBERS. 375

Tindale, C. A., Shelbyville, Ind.
Tinker, G. L., New Philadelphia, O.
Tonks, A., Kirkwood, Mo.
Torrence, L. P., Blakesburg, Iowa.
Townley, L. B., Youngstown, O.
Tracy, Miss B. B., Boston, Mass.
Trimble, H., Philadelphia, Pa.
Trimble, Mrs. H., Philadelphia, Pa.
Trisler, L. W., New Vienna, O.
True, C., Kankakee, Ill.
True, W. H., Laconia, N. H.
Tucker, A. M., Douglass, Kan.
Tucker, H. S., Chicago, Ill.
Turner, J. W., Cottonwood, Idaho.
Turrell, J. W., Longmont, Col.

Urheim, J. L., Chicago, Ill.

Vance, J. H., London, O.
Vancleave, C. L., Wingate, Ind.
Van Doren, S. H., Saybrook, Ill.
Van Meter, A., Lamar, Mo.
Van Schoiack, Ottawa, Kan.
Van Trump, A. P., St. Johns, O.
Van Velzer, G. W., Mason City, Ill.
Van Voorhees, G. T., White River, Cal.
Vassar, N. G., Ridgeway, O.
Vaughn, B. D., Dixon, Ill.
Venable, W. H., Cincinnati, O.
Vine, J. L., Norwood, O.
Vitt, R. S., St. Louis, Mo.
Vogeler, A., Chicago, Ill.
Von Bender, J. L., Penn Yan, N. Y.
Voss, G. W., Cleveland, O.

Wade, W. D., Plymouth, Ill.
Wagner, J., Gambier, O.
Waldbott, S., Cincinnati, O.
Walden, V., Angel, Tenn.
Walding, W. J., Toledo, O.
Waldron, M. H., Fairfax, W. Va.
Walker, G. F., New Orleans, La.
Walker, J. R., Brownstown, W. Va.
Walkup, T., Laramies, O.
Wall, J. T., Middletown, Conn.
Wall, O. A., St. Louis, Mo.
Wallace, A. E., Rapid City, S. Dak.
Walter, L. S., Fife Lake, Mich.
Walters, J. W., Wetmore, Col.
Ward, G. B., Palmetto, Ga.
Ware, E. F., Topeka, Kan.
Warner, O. S., Chicago, Ill.
Warner, R. C., Brooklyn, N. Y.

Warren, H., Omaha, Neb.
Waterhouse, E. R., St. Louis, Mo.
Waterman, L. E., New York City.
Watt, J. M. G., Cincinnati, O.
Watts, T. N., Alma, Kan.
Wearn, W. H., Charlotte, N. C.
Weaver, J. A., Easton, Pa.
Webster, E., Rochester, N. Y.
Webster, H. T., Oakland, Cal.
Webster, U. B., Alva, Ok.
Weer, H. H., Bluffton, Ind.
Weirick, G. A., Hastings, Neb.
Welbourn, E. L., Union City, Ind.
Weldon, G. H., West Point, Ga.
Weldon, R. L., Langdale, Ala.
Welling, D. H., Worthington, O.
Wells, J. M., Vanceburg, Ky.
Wells, W. T., Columbus, O.
Welty, S. F., Hicksville, O.
Wenning, E., Cincinnati, O.
Wenzell, W. T., San Francisco, Cal.
Werner, R. C., Brooklyn, N. Y.
West, C. A., Boston, Mass.
West, L., Monett, Mo.
Westcott, J. H., Norwich, N. Y.
Westendorf, Mrs. K., Cincinnati, O.
Westlake, F. P., Pittsfield, Ill.
Westlake, L. J., Gold Hill, Nev.
Weyer, J., Cincinnati, O.
Weyl, G. W., Maroa, Ill.
Wheeler, C. H., Sisson, Cal.
Wheeler, H. L., Toledo, O.
Wheelock, M. A., Salt Lake, Utah.
Whelpley, H. M., St. Louis, Mo.
Whitcomb, F. E., St. Louis, Mo.
White, C. A., Cleveland, O.
White, G. N., Cross Timbers, Mo.
White, S. T., Anderson, Cal.
White, W. A., Salesville, O.
Whitehead, W. C., Cleveland, O.
Whitford, E. P., Westboro, Mo.
Whitford, H. P., Bridgewater, N. Y.
Whiting & Sutton, Shenandoah, Ia.
Whitman, E. F., Boston, Mass.
Whitney, G. F., Cleveland, O.
Whitney, P. N., Cedar Vale, Kan.
Whitson, C. S., Cincinnati, O.
Wickham, W. H., New York City.
Wienges, C., Jersey City, N. J.
Wight, Eli, Chicago, Ill.
Wilcox, A. B., San Francisco, Cal.
Wilcox, F., Waterbury, Conn.
Wilder, H. M., Philadelphia, Pa.
Willard, R. E., Ellsmore, Kan.

Williams, C. C., Boston, Mass.
Williams, D., Columbus, O.
Williams, F. H., Bristoe, Conn.
Williams, G. G., Boston, Mass.
Williams, H. D., Ottawa, Kan.
Williams, J. D., Tallapoosa, Ga.
Williams, J. A., Washington C, II., O.
Williams, N. W., Traverse, Cal.
Williams, Mary, St. Francis, Kan.
Williams, T., Bournemouth, Eng.
Williamson, Mrs. I., Washington, Cal.
Willis, J. L. M., Eliot, Me.
Wilson, N. L., Milpitas, Cal.
Winkelman, W. A., Cincinnati, O.
Winkler, Rose, Cincinnati, O.
Wintermute, R. C., Cincinnati, O.
Wise, J., Patsey, Ky.
Wisterman, I., Rockford, O.
Witt, S., North Dana, Mass.
Wolf, E. A., Dennison, O.
Wood, B., Kansas City, Mo.
Wood, C. S., Sioux City, Iowa.
Wood, L. F., Westerley, R. I.
Wood, M. B., Pittsville, Wis.
Woodruff, G. S., Ligonier, Ind.
Woodward, A. B., Tunkhannock, Pa.
Woodward, C., Aurora, Ill.
Woodward, N. G., Defiance, O.
Worden, H. E., Des Moines, Iowa
Work, W. F., Charlestown, Ind.
Wottring, L. H., Prospect, O.
Wright, C. F., New York City.
Wright, J. G., May, Tex.
Wright, J. S., Indianapolis, Ind.
Wright, T. A., Americus, Kan.
Wright, W. M., New York City.
Wyman, W. A., Cheyenne, Wyo.
Wynn, J. H., Forest, O.

Yates, H. N., Weaversville, Cal.
Youmans, J. T., Moundridge, Kan.
Young, J. F., Dunkirk, Ind.
Young, J. K., Bristol, Pa.
Young, H. C., Lawn Ridge, Ill.
Younkin, E., St. Louis, Mo.
Yost, De L. L., Amos, W. Va.
Yost, L. N., Amos, W. Va.
Yowell, E., Mt. Lookout, O.
Yowell, Miss E., Mt. Lookout, O.
Yowell, R. C., Mt. Lookout, O.

Zickes, O., Cleveland, O.
Zimmerman, A., Peoria, Ill.

OMISSIONS.

Benjamin, J., Hobart, Tasmania.
Brush, J. T., Indianapolis, Ind.
Chapin, H. A., Brattleboro, Vt.
Gohen, G. A., Cincinnati, O.
Graves, J. T., Atlanta, Ga.
Harris, S. T., Norwood, O.
Hinrichs, G., St. Louis, Mo.
Lloyd, C. G., Cincinnati, O.
Peaslee, J. B., Cincinnati, O.
Porter, J. G., Mt. Lookout, O.
Roe, G. M., Cincinnati, O.
Schaer, Prof., University of Strasburg, Germany.
Schleiden, H., Berlin, W.
Stringfield, C. P., Chicago, Ill.
Watson, S. P., Atlanta, Ga.
Young, Lucy B., Salt Lake City, U.
Young, N. E., Washington, D. C.

The foregoing list embraces the subscriptions that were received to the date set for closing the list. A couple of hundred names were subsequently recorded, enough to increase the number to about fourteen hundred. Many subscribed for several copies, in addition to which are to be included the names of the recipients mentioned previously.

www.ingramcontent.com/pod-product-compliance
Lightning Source LLC
Chambersburg PA
CBHW031413230426
43668CB00007B/296